F

November 13, 1993

Trey,

Thanks for being in our
Wedding!

Nancy & Mark

Voices of The Game

The Acclaimed Chronicle of Baseball Radio
and Television Broadcasting — from 1921
to the Present

CURT SMITH

A Fireside Book
Published by Simon & Schuster
New York   London   Toronto   Sydney   Tokyo   Singapore

FIRESIDE
Simon & Schuster Building
Rockefeller Center
1230 Avenue of the Americas
New York, New York 10020

First Fireside Edition 1992
Published by arrangement with Diamond Communications,
Inc.
FIRESIDE and colophon are registered trademarks
of Simon & Schuster Inc.
Manufactured in the United States of America

3 5 7 9 10 8 6 4 2

Library of Congress Cataloging in Publication Data is available
ISBN: 0-671-73848-8

Contents

For

Helen E. Smith, 1901–1985;
Howard F. Smith, Sr., 1899–1990;
and Checkers, 1975–1985

"Whoever wants to know the
heart and mind of America
had better learn baseball."

—Jacques Barzun
God's Country and Mine

"It's not just play-by-play that
matters. It's what you say between the pitches that counts."

— Pirates' announcer
Rosey Rowswell

An Acknowledgment

ONE HUNDRED AND THIRTY-ONE YEARS AGO, ABRAHAM LINCOLN LEFT SPRING-field, Illinois, to assume the presidency, never to return again. He addressed his home people at the Great Western Railway Station and bespoke how "all the strange checkered past seems now to crowd upon my mind." To this place, Lincoln said, "and the kindness of these people, I owe all that I have, all that I am."

To many sources, and the kindnesses they have extended, this book too owes all that it has, all that it is. I want to thank these people for their contributions to the work, for they were generous with their time and memories — and I cannot help but be generous in my gratitude toward them.

Voices of The Game could not have been written without the help of broad-casters of uncommon cloth. I am particularly thankful to Nat Allbright, Mel Allen, the late Harold Arlin, Richie Ashburn, Red Barber, Bud Blattner, Lou Boudreau, Jack Brickhouse, Jack Buck, Harry Caray, Ken Coleman, Bob Costas, Dan Daniels, Jimmy Dudley, Leo Egan, Dick Enberg, Lanny Frattare, Earl Gillespie, Curt Gowdy, Milo Hamilton, Merle Harmon, Ernie Harwell, Ernie Johnson, Harry Kalas, Vince Lloyd, Ned Martin, Lindsey Nelson, Ted Patterson, the late Bob Prince, Pee Wee Reese, Byrum Saam, Ray Scott, Vin Scully, Lon Simmons, Chuck Thompson, Al Wester, Bob Wolff, and the late Jim Woods. My first year in college, a song by Carly Simon proclaimed, "That's the Way I've Always Heard It Should Be." Through the creative qualities of this diverse troupe of Voices, baseball be-came the way I'd always hoped it would be.

A number of writers were most helpful. Harold Rosenthal, for many years the baseball writer of the *New York Herald Tribune,* and Bob Broeg of the *St. Louis Post-Dispatch* offered past files and remembrances. John Hutchens, for-mer book critic and radio editor of the *New York Times,* was kind enough to review my manuscript. Jack Craig, the *Boston Globe*'s talented radio/TV critic, made comments and, invariably, sense. So did Phil Mushnick of the *New York Post.* I also wish to thank Gary Deeb, Til Ferdenzi, Jim Murray, Shirley Povich, Bob Raissman, Morris Siegel, Ken Smith, John Steadman, Larry Stewart, Maynard Good Stoddard, and George Vecsey.

There have been few more astute television observers than Scotty Connal, former vice-president, production, ESPN Cable Network; the late Carl Lin-demann, former vice-president, NBC Sports; and Bill MacPhail, CBS's once-director of sports and now vice-president, Cable News Network Sports. I would be remiss too not to acknowledge former NBC director Harry Coyle and Kevin Monaghan of that network's sports publicity; Ken Nigro, formerly of ABC Sports information; Tom Merritt, formerly of NBC; Dick Brescia, former senior vice-president, and Helene Blieberg, director, media relations, of CBS Radio; and WGN-Chicago's Jack Rosenberg and Kay Joyce. Many baseball and broadcast officials, both active in and retired from their field, contributed facts and recollections; I am specially grateful to Tom Gallery, Bowie Kuhn, John Lazarus, Tom Mee, Gabe Paul, Chuck Schriver, Larry Shenk, Stu Smith, and Tom Villante, Bob Wirz, Bryan Burns, Joe Podesta, and the late Joe Reichler of the Commissioner's Office. I am also indebted to Steve Sabol, executive vice-president of NFL Films.

The Baseball Hall of Fame Library in Cooperstown was, in a real sense, a partner in bringing *Voices of The Game* to birth; I am grateful for the assistance of its staff, most notably the guidance of researchers Bill Deane, Jeff Kernan, Matt Reese, and photo collection manager Pat Kelly. Extremely helpful too were *The Sporting News,* where Craig Carter, Lisa Robinson, and the late Stan Isle gave liberally of their publication's resources; the Library of Congress, whose microfilm facilities are unsurpassed; Lou Harris Associates, that treasure lode of polling data; and Jeff James of the A.C. Nielsen Co., who made available the raw numbers of baseball's television history. Together, they supplied hundreds of articles, official records, and broadcast memoranda.

Bruce Fingerhut edited this manuscript with intelligence and care. My literary agent, Bobbe Siegel, provided more help than I can suitably say. Jill and Jim Langford of Diamond Communications skillfully nursed the project toward completion. Finally, I want to thank my parents for the haven of their home — and the example of their lives.

Preface

THE POETESS MARIANNE MOORE ONCE OBSERVED, "BASEBALL IS LIKE WRITING. You can never tell with either how it will go or what you will do."

When the first edition of *Voices of The Game* was published in 1987, *Parade* magazine, reviewing it, noted how "more Americans get their baseball via radio and TV than any other way." Via the wireless and the kinetic webs we see and hear a game whose beauty is embedded in our lives. The late Bart Giamatti referred to baseball played "in the only place it will last — the enclosed, green fields of the mind." That has not changed since the first publication of *Voices* five years ago.

This new edition of *Voices* is updated, which is not to say thoroughly revised. It reports on baseball broadcasting during the seventy-one years since the game's first radiocast in 1921 — including significant new material on baseball broadcasting since 1987.

The first eleven chapters, covering 1921 to 1988, are essentially intact from the first edition. Readers will discover minor discrepancies — for instance, Ken Coleman is now the *former* Voice of the Boston Red Sox; the wondrous Red Barber is now eighty-two, not seventy-eight; Comiskey Park is not "the oldest stadium in the major leagues" — it no longer exists, and baseball is the poorer for it.

The final four chapters, on the other hand, are either fully rewritten or totally new. Here the reader will find the signposts of the past five years — among them, Ralph Kiner's latest malapropisms, Brent Musburger's firing, and three generations of Carays airing a Braves-Cubs' game.

The most dramatic development of this era — and an unforgivable change, in my view — is how baseball has sacrificed its strongest link to its fans by canceling network television's longest-running sports series, the "Game of the Week."

This edition of *Voices* documents baseball's shift from emphasizing national presence and national network TV exposure to dependence on local broadcasts and cable — shrinking the game's presence on the networks.

The change has split America into baseball haves and baseball have-nots and reeks of Social Darwinism — survival of the richest — punishing those without access to cable, or those who can't afford it.

We will also review the other major broadcasting events of the last five years — the Tigers' firing of Ernie Harwell, the retirement of Vince Lloyd, Ernie Johnson, and Joe Garagiola; ESPN's growing (though still unprofitable) cable coverage — and its hits and misses; Tony Kubek's fall from national eminence and Jon Miller's rise — along with the enduring magic of the marvel named Vin Scully.

One can admire sports like football and basketball. Only baseball — pacific and passionate and individual, like the people of the United States — can one truly love.

In a tribute to former prime minister Asquith, Winston Churchill said, "His children are his best memorial." *Voices of The Game* is also a memorial — sketching the broadcasters whose careers remain among the best tributes to America's nonpareil institution.

Curt Smith
December 20, 1991
Washington, D.C.

1
Yesterday Once More

"If youth is a defect, it is one we outgrow
too soon."
— Robert Lowell

WE HAD BEEN HERE, THE RIBBON OF REMINISCENCES REMINDED ME, MANY TIMES before. Listening to the woven quilt of baseball on radio, I retreated to the announcers of my sleepy, sheltered childhood — back to the welcome beckoners of a thousand afternoons. Their voices, more than two decades later, were a part of me; they had settled on my consciousness. They formed as much the web of baseball as did my first fielder's mitt, small and brown and fragile.

In the tender ear of memory, they had gentled and rewarded youth; they told of plots and stories and comedy that rounded out scenes. They also introduced me, in their wise, knowing way, to a world whose dividing line, once crossed, few would double back upon — the surf of sounds of the Los Angeles Coliseum, or the green boxed fortress at Michigan and Trumbull, or the steep-walled rectangle on the South Side of Chicago, or, more exaltedly, the triple-tiered enormity of the Home of Champions — a world unseen yet passionately encountered.

Even now, I often thought of baseball in the late 1950s and early 1960s, when Mays and Mantle dwarfed each summer and Clemente and Musial lent a luster to their game. There were fewer players to learn and emulate (sixteen teams, then twenty), two leagues instead of four divisions, less talk of diluted talent and mercenary personnel. It was not an elegaic age, exactly, but neither was the future unmanageable, and baseball basked amid Ike and his glorious somnolence and Kennedy in the primacy of Camelot. Baseball was simpler then, more of a family affair; sure and certain of its place.

Later, revisionists would speak of the era's discontent and nauseating complacency, embodied by Peggy Lee's standard, "Is That All There Is?" and crystallized in Walt Whitman's "Facing West from California's Shore," his persona asking, "Where is what I started for so long ago? And why is it yet unfound?" At the time, though, life seemed softer and more settled, an idyllic moment for an ideal America where ebullience bound the country's texture, the Mother Lode of television nourished a generation, and where Everyman — James Fenimore Cooper wrote a novel, *Satanstoe*, about such a site — might rule his own terrain, his own vast habitat, and remain, without impingement, free.

1

Ordered and impervious, baseball's aureole fit the nation's, its solitary grace not obscured by a bedlam of bodies, a jarring crash near the backboard, or a madcap scramble near the goal. Was the summer game, even then, slow and often sedentary? Possibly, although inscience tugged at my friends and me; particularly before one's maturity, it is difficult to separate reality from convention. What we *knew*, with a certitude untinged by doubt, was that baseball was *ours*, a social crucible. It endured and lured and consumed the public — the unrivaled National Game; from brief perspective, an heirloom of the heart.

Like the larger "Wagon Train"/New Frontier Society, baseball disdained the finite, for America felt no patina of brooding insecurity; she did not feel diminished. Few ordained, as had Robert Lowell about the Republic, circa 1953, that the "mausoleum [was] in her heart," or that tomorrow might sire tearful welcome to calamity. Except, perhaps, for the Washington Senators, tomorrow lay out ahead of us, like a day right behind the rain. So believed every team ("That there future belongs to us," said Charles Dillon [Casey] Stengel of his hapless fledglings. "The Mets, the Mets. The Youth of America"). So did a product of the tiny village of Caledonia, New York (pop. 2,100), three hundred miles from the nearest major-league ball park, aware (at least mildly) of the era's possibilities, and for whom embracing baseball was as natural as a smile.

By day, in a moss-colored chair, my lap adorned with cookies, chocolate milk, a ballpoint pen, and a battered blue scorebook, I inhaled through my parents' Zenith console (over clear-channel WHAM, "1180 on your dial") the high deeds and holidays of the New York Yankees, the holy minaret of baseball. Later, banished by bedtime to my second-floor room, I lay beneath the blankets, a transistor wedged beside my ear, and with reception multiplied, clasped wistful ventures that might speak of impossible dreams. Traversing the dial, I turned to baseball like a heliotrope turns toward the sun.

There, *there*, on KMOX Radio, 1120 AM, St. Louis, towered the lusty Harry Caray — armed with the fish net he used to corral foul balls — and his "Holy Cow!" a midwestern covenant unleashed invariably (but not exclusively) when the Redbirds stormed from behind. Meandering leftward, one found Curt Gowdy, Voice of the Boston Red Sox, and his colleague, Ned Martin, more married to baseball's rhythm than Bogart and Bacall, or (on the clearest of evenings) Ray Scott of the Minnesota Twins, at once vivid and attentive, or Chuck Thompson and his Baltimore Orioles, erupting over WBAL, or Philadelphia's Byrum Saam, he of the dulcet countenance (and who once began a broadcast by saying, "Hello, Byrum Saam, this is everybody speaking"), or Waite Hoyt of Cincinnati, airing homilies from the bandbox chamber of Crosley Field, or Ernie Harwell of Detroit (formerly Baltimore, New York, Brooklyn, and the Atlanta Crackers), a self-effacing conversationalist, a shy and eclectic man, a star.

While Bob Elson, "the Old Commander," etched the exploits of the "Go-Go" White Sox, and Jack Quinlan, with his screeching extroversion, covered the cross-town Cubs, ninety miles to the north, high atop the emerald turf of County Stadium, Earl Gillespie mimed the half-life longings of the Milwaukee Braves. In Washington, Bob Wolff solemnized each summer's embalmment; at Municipal Stadium, with the once-proud Indians entwined in habitual decay, Jimmy Dudley struck verbal candles in the night; and over KDKA, Pittsburgh, Bob Prince — "the Gunner" — by turns wild and cerebral, became a Tri-State institution. "Give me the Hoover, give me the Hoover!" he would chortle, the Pirates needing a double play (ergo, the bases cleaned). Home runs met the thunderclap of "Kiss it good-bye!" and "How sweet it is!" the latter, Prince said plaintively, stolen by Jackie Gleason and nationally unfurled. At ancient Forbes Field, its oven of an infield was baptized "the alabaster plaster"; a contested call looked "as close as fuzz on a tick's ear"; when the Buccos triumphed, "We had 'em alllll the way!" Amid the age's pillars, many cloaked baseball with a rigorous piety; others grasped the middle ground between reverence and unconcern. The airwaves echoed with a collection of elegant performers and roughhewn troubadours, and their most artful themes blended reverberance, personal expression, and an often riveting beguilement. With no picture to assist them, announcers became the sole link between the happening and their public. If the broadcaster was indelible, so was the event.

On Saturday and Sunday, flushed with providence, one retired to the kitchen or patio or family room, where Lindsey Nelson, a grand stylist of broadcasting, and Joe Garagiola, Caray's ex-sidekick and author of the ghost-written then-bestseller, *Baseball Is a Funny Game,* presided over NBC Television's "Major League Baseball." They were forceful and persuasive; they sermonized the faithful; and from our distance, absent bias, their work exudes distinction. Yet in the summers which bookshelved 1960, dissonance (and frightful ratings) plagued their telecasts, for "weekend baseball" meant *another* network, the Columbia Broadcasting System, and *another* announcer, the Master, the Great One, the nonesuch.

For ten seasons, in the entirety of baseball's pioneering national TV series, the CBS "Game of the Week," Jay Hanna (Dizzy) Dean alternately enriched and enraged America, a sheath of pride and bombast and loyalty — reading telegrams to "good 'ol boys" back home, warbling his cherished anthem, "The Wabash Cannon Ball," telling of batters who "swang" and runners who "slud" and pitchers who "throwed" the ball, saying of critics who decried his syntax, "*Sintax?* Are those jokers up in Washington putting a tax on that too?" For those who loathed his foibles, Ol' Diz reeked of the gloom and mucus of the otherworld; for apostles, he meant delight. He was not simply a network totem; he was a presence, full-framed and uncompromising, who declined to conciliate his enemies and who doubled as philosopher and clown. His brusqueness, friends claimed, was an index of his honesty. He split the baseball politic and touched America and said what was on his mind. "In the hinterlands and, even more than that, in the small towns, it was incredible," Bill MacPhail, then director of CBS Sports, said of Dean's high meridian. "Watching Dizzy Dean was a religion. An absolute religion."

Even so, for all its hale, conclusive assurances, Ol' Diz's revival hour appeared, at best, twice-weekly, and after Sunday's denouement I returned to WHAM (Rochester) or WBEN (930, Buffalo) or then-flagship WCBS, ramparts of a network of more than fifty stations, where, aflight with expectation, one measured the major leagues' parish triumvirate of Phil Rizzuto, Walter Lanier Barber, and Melvin Allen Israel—the Scooter, the Ol' Redhead, and their redoubtable companion, the most resplendently talented announcer in baseball's tide of times.

Judging play-by-play men, like one's taste in cars, musicals, and imported gin, must be (of necessity) arbitrary (which is not to say capricious); what means reverie to me may seem abhorrent to you. Yet in the late fifties and the early sixties, unanimity lay in my favorite broadcaster, an ornament on whom chroniclers might engrave, "A florist must have decorated his voice."

For twenty-five years he owned the most fanatical following of any announcer in America. Zealous and seductive, he discoursed with almost maddening detail, and his exuberant narrative brought joy to provinces located time zones away from the Big Ball Park in the Bronx. Always, one wondered at the voice, deep and vibrant, the voice which spoke for hours and had a sustaining quality few would rival and none eclipse, the voice which lent music to its brogue, and which made an audience listen—even princelings swathed by hostility—in spite of itself. In 1939 Mel Allen was hired as the Voice of the Yankees, an Alabamian in New York. In 1964 he was fired, a stunning dismissal that savaged the Yankees (and made me a Red Sox fan).

Across the landscape, its baseball cult divided into two battalions—those who declaimed that Allen was more compelling than being at the ball park, and those who prayed that an attack of laryngitis would silence him forever. Detractors said he talked too much, a catch phrase that (while, perhaps, true enough) masked their *raison inimitié;* the woods were full of Yankee-haters, and Allen drew the haters' wrath. They disputed his lineage, mocked his neutrality, and upbraided his naiveté. Once upon a game at Yankee Stadium, Mel witnessed two teenagers trading kisses in the center-field bleachers. "That's interesting," he observed. "He's kissing her on the strikes, and she's kissing him on the balls," to which Rizzuto added, "Mel, this is just not your day." Few, however, denied his summitry or doubted the impact he made. Allen described more World Series (twenty) and All-Star Games (twenty-four) than any contemporary, aired the Rose Bowl, East-West Shrine Game, and heavyweight fights, and served as the sports impresario of Movietone Newsreels—a household word; he was the nation's most burnished sportscaster; according to *Variety,* he possessed one of the "twenty-five most recognizable voices" in the world.

To The Voice's critics, idolaters staged a dialogue of the deaf—applauding his intensity, hailing his remembrances, echoing his trademark chants. A batter with a full count prompted, "Three and two, what'll he do?" Home runs were "Ballantine blasts" or "White Owl wallops"; a drive assaulting the bleachers was "Going, going, gone!"; a moment of surpassing drama demanded, "How about that!" When Hank Bauer homered, when Whitey Ford sundered docile batsmen, when Lawrence Peter (Yogi) Berra showed that as a "bad-ball hitter," he could call forth good, "How about that!" punctuated the occasion. Born in 1949 (as Joe DiMaggio, rallying from heel surgery, clubbed four balls into the net above the Wall at Fenway Park), it was inevitable; it defined pronouncements; it would evolve, ultimately, into his signature. Allen was the Yankees' mouthpiece, cutting edge, and of thundering consequence to P. Ballantine & Sons, a rarefied sponsor's dream. No one could huckster a can of beer like M. A. Israel.

In the baseball of my boyhood, Mel Allen was a staple. Before his ouster by the Yankees (and subsequent exile from the airwaves for more than a decade, banished as though a nonperson, his hopes and sensibilities spurned), The Voice inscribed continuity on the transient pulp of life—ephemera even then—which we urgently required, lest change overwhelm us all.

As Harry S. Truman yielded to Mamie's husband, and Dwight Eisenhower to the Irish Mafia, as the Edsel lost and the T-Bird won, as Algeria rebelled and Pope John XXIII died and the Supreme Court ruled "one man, one vote," baseball flaunted constancy. It was The Game of Our Fathers; endorsing it, we upheld ourselves. Shibe Park became Connie Mack Stadium, but its essence lingered; it was no Valhalla. The Giants exchanged the Polo Grounds for the icy, ill-designed bog of Candlestick Park. Small matter; "Say Hey" was a paladin still. The Yankees, of course, grasped acclaim. They commandeered a dynasty. They were rapt and resolute, a team, it seemed, always near the solstice of its prime: five consecutive World Series triumphs, nine pennants in ten seasons, and before Olympus crumbled in early 1965, fourteen championships in sixteen years.

Each season began slowly, irreversibly, and built through climaxes, toward that New Jerusalem when, surely, the Red Sox would seize their first world championship since Woodrow Wilson's presidency, or the Chicago Cubs—those cuddlesome, fondled, and impotent cuties—would elude the second division, or the Senators—they of the "First in War, First in Peace, and Last in the American League" — would march, unevenly, to be certain, but *finally,* from the sackcloth of ruin, or the Phillies, Athletics, or Cleveland's beloved Tribe (choose a season, select a team) would fling aside the veil of terminal benumbment, their lot, *requiescat in pace,* the wretched of the earth. A fascinating mix, even for these luckless tatters. A cheerful ministry. An epoch as winsome as the Roaring Twenties, strange and splendid and ingenuously benign.

It was the best of times.

Enter, the Voices of The Game, before and since.

2
Beginnings
(1921–33)

"They couldn't pick a better time to start
in life. It ain't too early and it ain't too
late."

—Aunt Eller, in the Broadway
musical, *Oklahoma!*

DURING THE 1920S, WITH TELEVISION AN INCEPTIVE VISION, RADIO THRUST
baseball into the social bowels of America, luring millions of apprentice fans.
For decades, print journalism had been the nation's sole gospel of big-league
gossip. Inning-by-inning scores silhouetted windows of daily chronicles and
telegraph offices; newspapers issued "baseball editions" with partial scores on
the back or front page; one read the by-lines of John Kieran, with his loping
clauses, and Damon Runyon, the virtuoso of the short story, and Heywood
Broun, who penned, "The Ruth is mighty and shall prevail," and Grantland
Rice—"Grannie," the courser of the press box—and Ring Lardner, *le pere*
grand of "Alibi Ike" in *The Saturday Evening Post.* Now a new conduit took hold,
and rawly, virginally, broadcasters were off and talking. Did radio, in large
measure, propel baseball from its medieval hollow to a clean, better-lighted
place? Each summer, do the San Francisco Giants fold? (No; if needed, they
could always collapse in May.)

On August 5, 1921, in professional baseball's fifty-third season, over KDKA,
the country's first radio station, from Forbes Field, age twelve, in suburban
Pittsburgh, a twenty-six-year-old Illinoisan aired radio's first baseball game.

His vehicle was known as "wireless telegraphy"; his microphone was a converted telephone; he was a Westinghouse Company foreman by day and a
studio announcer by night, a Brigham Young sighting the Great Salt Lake. In
a contest of seven walks, twenty-one hits, and one hour and fifty-seven minutes
(final score: Pirates 8, Phillies 5), he christened the sculpted pageant of baseball broadcasting—a sacrament, looking back, bathed in consequence, but
on that late-summer afternoon, dwarfed by the age's Gullivers, of almost
Lilliputian concern.

As Harold Arlin filled a ground-level box seat, his equipment flanking a
screen behind home plate, a Free State in Ireland neared conception. Benito
Mussolini, pledging to "make the trains run on time," prepared to "liberate"
Rome. In Baltimore, H. L. Mencken rebuked the "booboisie"; in Indiana, the
Ku Klux Klan boasted nearly five hundred thousand members; in Wash-

6

ington, D.C., the 1920 census read, "Population, United States, 106,466,000." Bookstores headlined *Main Street* by Sinclair Lewis, *Winesburg, Ohio* by Sherwood Anderson, and F. Scott Fitzgerald's *This Side of Paradise*. Already, Sacco and Vanzetti formed a *cause célèbre*. Amid the spires and hovels of the forty-eight states, hope (*exemplum:* the nineteenth amendment — women's suffrage) clashed with Prohibition, and alcohol's "reign of terror [was] over," quoth revivalist preacher Billy Sunday, yielding to the hammerlock of organized crime. One heard of speakeasies and raccoon coats and Clara Bow and Rudolph Valentino, of Bobby Jones and Bill Tilden, who brightened golf and tennis, and of Jack Dempsey, the Manassa Mauler, the Frank Merriwell of boxing.

Caricature, not flesh and bones, washed the age's most panoplied trilogy. Warren Gamaliel Harding, of whom William Gibbs McAdoo jeered, "He left the impression of a man of pompous phrases moving over the landscape in search of an idea; sometimes these meandering words would actually capture a straggling thought and bear it triumphantly, a prisoner in their midst, until it died of servitude and overwork," besieged the White House, his greed, as in a moment, obscured by sanctimony. Variously admired and despised, having occupied the vestibules of legal power, Kenesaw Mountain Landis — a gaunt, white-maned prosecutor/judge — now pre-empted baseball's inner sanctum. Appointed commissioner on November 12, 1920, he "got his job," pricked Will Rogers, not through the *New York Times;* rather, "Somebody said, 'Get that old boy who sits behind first base all the time. He's out there every day anyhow.' So they offered him a season's pass and he jumped at it." Meanwhile, at the Polo Grounds, his temporal abode until, in 1923, "The House That Ruth Built" opened, the Bambino wove magic with his bat. "He was . . . a burst of dazzle and jingle," Jimmy Cannon wrote, "Santa Claus drinking his whiskey straight and groaning with a bellyache caused by gluttony." He deified the home run and fulfilled his appetites and secured for baseball (and, not incidentally, the Yankees) an almost Messianic time.

In an era that bespoke extravagance, Harold Arlin spoke without self-puffery and sham. "I was just a nobody, and our broadcast — back then, at least — wasn't that big a deal," he said two years before his death, on March 14, 1986, at ninety, of a heart attack, in Bakersfield, California. "Our guys at KDKA didn't even think that baseball would last on radio. I did it sort of as a one-shot project, a kind of addendum to the events we'd already done."

For Arlin, baseball play-by-play wreathed history's tree: the first man to broadcast a tennis match (August 6, 1921), to air football via the wireless (Pitt v. West Virginia, sixty-three days later), and to unleash baseball scores from the station's studio. "Since I'd already done these things, or was planning to do them, the Pirates were a natural," he announced. "So I went out to Forbes Field and set up shop."

"Did everything work as it should?" I asked.

Laughing softly, Arlin appraised the recollection. "Hardly," he began. "Sometimes the transmitter worked and sometimes it didn't. Sometimes the crowd noise would drown us out and sometimes it wouldn't. And, quite frankly, we didn't know what the reaction would be — whether we'd be talking into a total vacuum or whether somebody would actually hear us."

"So you had a lot of imponderables."

"That's the understatement of the year," he said. "But I enjoyed it, and I think our listeners did too. Having said that, let me add: No one had the foggiest *idea*, the slightest hint of an *inkling*, that what we'd started would take off like it did."

Westinghouse-built, owned, and programmed, KDKA debuted on November 2, 1920; its venue, the presidential election (Harding an easy victor over James M. Cox, 404 electoral votes to 127). Within six years Arlin fled the medium, turning to corporate relations, having introduced such nabobs (another first) as Marshall Foch, David Lloyd George, Lillian Gish, and Herbert Clark Hoover, then secretary of commerce, and subbing as a pinch-speaker for the Sultan of Swat.

In Pittsburgh for an exhibition game, Ruth deigned to appear with Arlin and, traveling to the William Penn Hotel, found a speech awaiting him. "I'd written the entire text. I was so sure I'd thought of everything," Harold said. "After all, how could the Babe flub it with the words right in front of him? Well, I introduce him and, naturally, all of a sudden this big, talkative, garrulous guy — he can't say a word."

"Babe Ruth froze?" I wondered.

"Oh, Babe was struck mute," he jabbed back, relishing every syllable. "I mean, this radio thing was just so *new*. So I grab the speech and now *I'm* Babe Ruth. I'm reading the script and there's the Babe, trying to compose himself, smoking a cigarette and leaning against the wall. And you know something? We pulled it off. I sign off and Babe Ruth hasn't made a sound." In coming weeks, Arlin's ruse secure, KDKA received letters praising the resonant fullness of the Bambino's voice.

By now, hundreds of miles to the east, two other stations, WJZ in Newark, New Jersey (later, of New York City), and WBZ in Springfield, Massachusetts (later, of Boston), had joined the Westinghouse Network, and on October 5, 1921, in the first all-New York autumn festival, the first World Series "broadcast" occurred: Linked by direct line to KDKA, the fedora-topped columnist of the *New York Herald Tribune*, Grantland Rice, earphones clamped over his head, detailed the outs and stolen bases (by Mike McNally, a theft of home) and extra-base wallops (for Frankie Frisch, a wasted triple) of the Yankees' opening-game victory, 3–0.

Deprived of Rice's banter, Newark and Springfield chose more circuitous narrative: the first baseball "re-creation." Inside the Polo Grounds, a reporter for the *Newark Call* stood beside a telephone, mouthing balls, strikes, hits, and errors. At the other end, the receiver pressed against his ear, sat the man who would later announce, ubiquitously, for the first city-owned radio station (WCNY): Tommy Cowan, then thirty-seven, perched atop the Newark Westinghouse Building in a tin-girded shack. He accepted the signals; he repeated their essentials; he converted them for his audience; blindly, ingeniously, he delivered play-by-play. "I know it's hard to imagine now, but just try and think of it," the Voice of the Boston Red Sox, Ken Coleman, said. "Guys like Cowan — they didn't even have a scrap of paper to work from. No scorecards, no press guides, no spotters, no statistics. *Nothing*. All they had were their ears and, even more than that, their brains. It put such an emphasis on imagination. And broadcasting was their bequest."

The Giants won the 1921 World Series, five games to three (in 1923, the Classic reverted to a best-of-seven affair). That first season, Ruth celebrated the most elephantine single year in baseball history — fifty-nine home runs (his second successive fifty-plus season), 170 runs batted in, a .378 average, and a slugging percentage of .846. Four American League teams batted over .300; the Tigers' .316 has never been matched. The Giants won their second of four consecutive pennants, the Cardinals' Rogers Hornsby seized his third of six straight batting crowns, and Pie Traynor, the stubby and well-muscled Pirates' third baseman, competed so ardently that one rival said, "He'd scoop everything off the field — grass, dust, and gravel — and fling it over to first base with the ball. It was like a sandstorm — only worse." The Lincoln Memorial was dedicated. Eddie Collins of the A's observed his seventeenth season in a twenty-five-year career. *Reader's Digest* was born. The 1922 Yankees won a second pennant. The Red Sox, as they would in eight of the next nine years, finished last. Newspapers revealed, "More than 3 million American homes now possess at least one radio." Brooklyn's Zack Wheat, bashing a ball to the bleachers, circled the first-base bag and swooned to the ground, a cramp pinching his leg. After five minutes, he rose, undirtied his woolies, and completed his crusade around the bases: his feat, the "longest home run" ever hit.

No one lofted a home run (though both clubs whacked a triple) on October 4, 1922, when (after Charles W. Horn, WJZ's chief engineer, convinced Western Union vice-president J. C. Williver to lease its wires, fusing Newark and the Polo Grounds), "For the first time, [radio] carried the opening game of the World Series play-by-play direct from the Polo Grounds to great crowds throughout the eastern section of the country [not simply western Pennsylvania]," chorused the *New York Times*. "Through the broadcasting station WJZ, Grantland Rice [teamed with W. B. McGheehan, another writer, and WJZ engineer Raymond F. Guy] related his story direct to an invisible audience, estimated to be 5 million, while WGY at Schenectady and WBZ at Springfield relayed every play of the contest. In place of the scorecards and megaphones of the past, amplifiers connected to radio instruments gave all the details and sidelights to thousands of enthusiasts unable to get into the Polo Grounds. Not only could the voice of the official radio observer be heard, but the voice of the umpire on the field announcing the batteries for the day mingled with the voice of a boy selling ice cream cones. The clamor of the forty thousand baseball fans inside the Polo Grounds made radio listeners feel as if they were in the grandstand. The cheers which greeted Babe Ruth when he stepped to the plate could be heard throughout the land."

Six decades later, after instant replay, fiberglass antennas, and satellite telegraphy, the mind's eye falters at such vagaries as retail radio stores erecting sidewalk speakers, or streets filled with play-by-play, like shopping malls with Muzak, or burgs from Bridgeport, Connecticut, to Southampton, Long Island, gaping wide-mouthed as Rice erupted from a wooden box, his voice the shrine of dreamstuff. Radio seduced; it imitated dance, not seminar; it was a fly-paper medium.

"You have to understand just how big this novelty was to us. It's all there was — it used to stop traffic," counseled Til Ferdenzi, progressively a reporter for the *New York Journal-American*, director of sports publicity for NBC Television, and now retired and living in Yarmouth Port, Massachusetts. "In the area I grew up in, in Ashland, about twenty-five miles west of Boston, the man who owned a car garage had a radio and he'd amplify it — used to blast it all over town. Literally, cars would stop so they could hear the sound."

"So it was new," I conceded. "But why else was it big?"

"Radio's not like TV. Television lets you sit there — it doesn't make you work or think, it's passive," Ferdenzi said. "But radio is *active* — it makes you a part of the broadcast. It gets you *involved*. And remember, this hit us like something from another planet. It shook things up, it made the world wider." He stopped a long moment. "Everything was different after that."

Ferdenzi was seven when Rice, more facile with portable typewriter than as "the voice . . . that crieth in the wilderness" (fleeing to Isaiah 40:2), announced the 1922 World Series; the Giants won, four sets (with one tie) to two; the last two games, bereft of sponsors, never took to the air.

That very year, for the time's emphatic soloists, expansion split the sky: for Giants' manager John J. McGraw, his sixth championship in the last twelve years; for Westinghouse, a propinquity of acceptance; for David Sarnoff, only thirty-one, the general manager of the infant Radio Corporation of America, a search to find the announcer who would vitalize RCA (his choice, Major J. Andrew White, the editor of *Wireless Age*); for baseball, transition.

In 1923, Harry Heilmann batted .403 and Howard Ehmke won twenty games for last-place Boston. The Yankees, in their new stadium, attracted 1,007,066 curiosos. The Phillies, clothed in old malignity, drew 228,168 to Baker Bowl. Lou Gehrig, at nineteen already a squat, full-framed man, played for Columbia against Rutgers; in the stands, glowing, sat superscout Paul Krichell, who hurried back to Yankee Stadium. "I think," he told general manager Ed Barrow, "I saw another Ruth today." Less triflingly, W. B. Yeats won the Nobel Prize in Literature, Gloria Swanson starred in *Prodigal Daughter*, the Ziegfeld Follies graced the New Amsterdam Theatre, and Warren Harding died. Yet all met diminution, their novas wambling, beside a baritone turned colossus. "The greatest announcer," Red Barber said, "we ever had." Graham McNamee.

Born in Washington, D.C., and raised in the Pacific Northwest, where his father, a lawyer, worked for the Union Pacific Railroad, McNamee arrived in New York City with his mother, a divorcée, who insisted upon piano tutelage; at eighteen, McNamee added voice lessons. By 1921, opting for the stage, he found alliance in the *New York Sun*, which said of his debut as a professional, "He sang with a justness, a care and style," and later, after one of more than

150 programs in his first recital season, the good, gray, contumelious *Times*: "Anyone who sings the air 'O Ruddier than the Cherry Tree' from Handel's *Acis Galatea* with such admirable, flexible command over the 'divisions,' with such finished phrasing and such excellent enunciations as McNamee showed, is doing a difficult thing very well indeed."

Surfeited, he might have become a Pinza among the minions, but McNamee was not content, and one day in May 1923, on lunch recess from jury duty at Federal Court, the singer walked up lower Broadway to station WEAF. Entering its two-room, fourth-floor studio, he asked the program director for a tour of its facilities. He left as an employee, the station's utility infielder; his salary, $30 a week. Three months later, a stranger to boxing, McNamee aired the world middleweight championship blow-by-blow of Harry Greb's conquest of Johnny Wilson. In September, his rise laureled with astonishment, he was announced as Rice's companion for the 1923 World Series: Grantland to do play-by-play; McNamee, "color."

In 1963, Barry Goldwater would suggest cutting the Eastern Seaboard off and floating it out to sea. Now, more propitiously, from WMAF in South Dartmouth, Massachusetts, to WCAP in the nation's capital, its occupants heard a World Series, the *Times* reported, over stations "that will also radiate the contests simultaneously with WEAF, as they will be connected with special land wires to microphones controlled by that station."

As scripted, Rice described balls and strikes in the first two outings, but by the fourth inning of Game Three, miscast, weary of the sameness, he yielded story and analysis to McNamee. Filling a ground-level chair at the Polo Grounds and Yankee Stadium, Graham sat amid the then-largest hordes to watch a Series (its six-game figure, 301,430). He used only a carbon microphone (its shelf, a panel stretched across the box seat), a scorecard, and his throaty, bursting voice. He told of Ruth, who crashed three homers; Bob Meusel, whose eight RBIs set a record; Frankie Frisch, subduing grounders and hitting .400; and Casey Stengel, batting .417 and wafting an immemorial inside-the-park home run that prompted Damon Runyon to scrawl: "This is the way old Casey Stengel ran running his home run home when two were out in the ninth inning and the score was tied, and the ball still bounding inside the Yankee yard. This is the way — His mouth wide open. His warped old legs bending beneath him at every stride. His arms flying back and forth like those of a man swimming with a crawl stroke. His flanks heaving, his breath whistling, his head far back. . . . The warped old legs, twisted and bent by many a year of baseball campaigning, just barely held out under Casey until he reached the plate, running his home run home. Then they collapsed." Afterward, anticlimax, like Mrs. Miller following Cher. The Yankees won, four games to two, their first of twenty-two championships. Twenty-six years later, his legs still warped, old Casey became their manager.

For the Giants, October brought a cortege; for McNamee, a sense of almost manic affection. The Series ended on the fifteenth, a Monday; by Saturday, more than seventeen hundred letters had arrived at WEAF.

"Think about that for a moment," canted Jack Brickhouse, the media embodiment of the Chicago Cubs. "Put it into per capita terms. First of all, there weren't that many radios around then, and for one guy — it hadn't happened before — to be swamped like that, well, to equal that response today, you're talking about many hundreds of thousands of letters, minimum." McNamee, in a skilled and novel way, had touched the country, and off he went — covering football and boxing and tennis (ten sports in all); airing, *live*, foreign coronations and Calvin Coolidge's 1923 address to Congress and both political conventions in 1924 (at Madison Square Garden, announcing almost continuously for fourteen days, he endured all 103 Democratic ballots until, finally, John W. Davis was nominated); maturing, by 1926, the birthyear of the National Broadcasting Company, into a family member without portfolio (each broadcast began with "Good evening, ladies and gentlemen of the radio audience" and closed, "This is Graham McNamee speaking. Good night all"); winging his way into the million memories of America.

Writers (often) disliked and (almost always) envied him. Ring Lardner typed, "I don't know which game to write about — the one I saw today, or the one I heard Graham McNamee announce as I sat next to him at the Polo Grounds"; once, during the 1929 World Series, a reporter objected, so audibly it reverberated on the air, "McNamee, will you please pipe down!?" Yet he was mellifluous and, above all, *human*, and until the mid-1930s, when his starburst plunged, the most controversial man in broadcasting. "You must make each of your listeners," he stated, "though miles away from the spot, feel that he or she too is there with you in the press stand, watching the pop bottles thrown in the air; Gloria Swanson arriving in her new ermine coat; McGraw in his dugout, apparently motionless, but giving signals all the time." In 1925, after his third World Series, McNamee received more than fifty thousand letters and telegrams; he died in May 1942, at fifty-three, of an embolism of the brain. Much earlier, Broun had filed an epitaph: "McNamee justified the whole activity of radio broadcasting," he wrote. "A thing may be a marvelous invention and still dull as ditch water. It will be that unless it allows the play of personality. A machine amounts to nothing unless a man can ride. Graham McNamee has been able to take a new medium of expression and through it transmit himself — to give it vividly a sense of movement and of feeling. Of such is the kingdom of art."

By early 1924, the King's monarchy was full-sized, for his broadcasts had multiplied radio's dominion, impelling baseball into drugstores, diners, and homes. Out in Illinois, families noticed too, and on April 23, twenty-three-year-old Hal Totten, fleeing from the *Chicago Daily News*'s rewrite desk, aired the play-by-play of a wireless original — the first contest (a North Siders' triumph over St. Louis, 12–1) of the first station (WMAQ, 670 frequency, *News*-owned and managed) to carry *every* home game of its major-league team (in Chicago, the White Sox and Cubs). Through McNamee, baseball and radio had blossomed in October. Why, the station gauged, could their accents not amplify the *regular* season? Twinkly, not unpleasant, Totten broadcast for twenty-one years; with Major White, he twice co-anchored CBS's World Series coverage, then announced the 1933–35 Classics for NBC; in the early 1950s, joining the Mutual Broadcasting System, he vocalized its "Game of the Day."

Self-effacement gentled Totten's manner. Subdued, he was not immodest; formal, he was not unreceding; he would not attack a listener. Instead, by fits and starts, he solidified baseball on radio and by late summer, near the end of a first year of broadcasts, made uncompromising their appeal.

"Sometimes we get all caught up in the frenzy of the moment," Brickhouse volunteered. "And that's a mistake. Because if these guys, announcers like Totten, had bombed, if they hadn't turned people on, then broadcasting wouldn't have clung to baseball."

"What would have happened?" I said, nostalgia tugging at my sleeve.

"Oh, they'd have dropped the game like a hot potato," he laughed. "It's possible it might have gone that way, you know. And you can imagine what would have become of *us*. But thank God, it didn't. People listened, and they fell in love," and an institution of generous variety ensued.

While Totten patented his laconic sign-off, "G'bye now," Broun's flagship newspaper, the *New York Tribune*, posted advertisements for Macy's Department Store, where one could buy topcoats from $28.25 to $57.50, a cap for $2.12, a landsdowne hat for $5.22. "Take along plenty of smokers," the May 20, 1924, text advised New York's baseball cognoscenti. "And may we also suggest the following items to contribute to your enjoyment of the National Game: Italian briar pipes (42¢ apiece); Three Castle cigarettes, packed in airtight tins of fifty each (at $2.05); or Tampa blunts ($2.63 for a can of fifty)." Tobacco was elusive in Landsberg Prison, where Adolf Hitler began *Mein Kampf,* and not scarce at all in Detroit, where William Green succeeded Samuel Gompers as head of the American Federation of Labor. Vladimir Ilyich Lenin died and General Billy Smith was court-martialed. Rogers Hornsby batted .424, highest average of the century, and Al Simmons joined the Philadelphia A's: Four times, he would bat over .380; in eleven different seasons, he knocked in 100 runs or more.

From Bangor to San Diego, the Charleston spurned quietude. Tom Mix and William S. Hart staged shoot-'em-up westerns, evolution v. creationism (and their principals in the Scopes Monkey Trial, Clarence Darrow and William Jennings Bryant) polarized the nation (into urban v. rural), and within ten months *Arrowsmith, An American Tragedy, The Great Gatsby,* and *The Sun Also Rises* surfaced. At Yankee Stadium, the Bombers did *not* win the 1924 pennant. Instead, the aging, unwavering Washington Senators of Goose Goslin (.344), Sam Rice (leading the league in hits), Walter Johnson (twenty-three victories), Firpo Marberry (fifteen saves, a then-major-league record), and the "boy wonder," player-manager Bucky Harris, won their first pennant and World Series. Pitching very hard, pitching bravely, Johnson, thirty-six ("That's pretty far gone," he said, "to be walking into the last game of the World Series"), threw four shutout innings in Game Seven. On a cold, dank day, he was the winning pitcher; Washington was now first in baseball, edging the Giants in twelve innings, 4–3.

Improbably, the "Nats" (a favored nomenclature of headline writers) won another pennant in 1925 (though Pittsburgh won the Series). Thereafter, as the Senators stumbled, again becoming conversation piece, not success, the seasons blended in an intense and crowded blur.

NBC took formally to the air on November 15, 1926, and soon split into two networks: its "Red" of music and comedy programming, fed by McNamee's WEAF, and its "Blue" of mostly public-affairs programs, rooted in WJZ, now New York. On September 18, 1927, the Columbia Broadcasting System proclaimed *its* debut; ninety-seven days later, the network signed sportscaster Ted Husing, a frequenter of the restaurant 21, an irregular colleague of Andrew White's, and in the coming years which would enlarge and mock him, imperious before the fall. Charles A. Lindbergh traversed the Atlantic. William S. Paley, twenty-six, heir to the Congress Cigar Company (whose La Palma cigar had profited from advertising on WCAU, Philadelphia), became the president of CBS. In Detroit, Ford replaced the Model T with the Model A. In Washington, the Kellogg-Briand Pact "outlawed war"; few listened. In Southern California, Walt Disney released his first animated film. Six states and two thousand miles away, rival stations, startled by Totten's fortune, declared war on WMAQ.

"What I'm always reminding people is that there wasn't any so-called 'exclusivity' in the 1920s," murmured Jack Rosenberg, his voice round and deep. A reporter for the *Peoria Journal Star*, Rosenberg joined WGN, the *Chicago Tribune* station, in 1954. He was now its sports editor. "A station didn't pay money to a club for the privilege of solely carrying the games. In fact, it didn't pay money at *all*."

If one had equipment and a license to broadcast, one had entree to Wrigley Field. By the mid-to-late 1920s, Cubs' home games were transmitted over *five* stations (the pallid White Sox', on two). Chicagoans heard comedian Joe E. Brown, whose son would become Pirates' general manager, and Quin Ryan, the WGN program manager, and Pat Flanagan, emanating from WBBM (and, ultimately, airing three World Series for CBS), and Truman Bradley, the future host of television's "Science Fiction Theatre," and Johnny O'Hara, John Harrington, horse racing's somnambulant Jack Drees, Russ Hodges, the 1949–70 Voice of the Giants, and the paternal, reassuring Bob Elson, his voice an incubative monotone, who lauded sponsors and recited gin-rummy stories and who broadcast for thirty-eight years.

Stations competed for broadcast *listeners*, not broadcast *rights*, for Cubs' owner William Wrigley *wanted* radio ("the more outlets, the better," he told his players. "That way we'll tie up the entire city"), and he believed, as Red Barber later wrote of Brooklyn President Larry MacPhail, "In its promotional power, in its reaching of the game to women . . . he became sold on it. . . . He grasped immediately that radio turned a game played by two teams into a contest involving personalities who had hopes, fears, families, troubles, blue or brown eyes." Wrigley founded the first Ladies Day. He installed the first glass-partitioned radio booth. What Chicago sowed, baseball reaped, and as Cubs' ratings rose in corundum, other clubs, still earthbound, coveted Wrigley's stone. Bill

Dyer debuted in Philadelphia, presiding over Shibe Park (where the Athletics knew both rule and ruin) and the Phillies' crumbling Baker Bowl. From Sportsman's Park, that playful furnace of a yard, Garnett Marks announced St. Louis' first game in 1927; two years later, leaving station KVOO in Tulsa, phlegmatic France Laux launched an eighteen-year stint with the Cardinals and Browns. In 1925, over the Colonial Network, Fred Hoey, a football official and former sportswriter, began coverage of the Braves and Red Sox. At bandbox League Park, enter Tom Manning, the Indians' megaphone man.

As a child, Manning had been named the newsboy in Cleveland with "the loudest voice," converting doubters in the early 1920s, when, armed only with an amplifier, he stood behind home plate in the Tribe's pre-Municipal Stadium lair and bellowed batteries to the crowd. From 1925, sporadically, and 1928, regularly, he detailed the Indians' orbits and misadventures over station WTAM. Red-haired and Irish, his eyes ice-blue, he was a dandy; his tones rasped; he was jocular, effusive. "For most people, he was their first attachment to baseball," noted Jimmy Dudley, the 1948–67 Voice of the Indians. "What had been cold newsprint, Tom brought alive. And a great part of this town simply took a siesta, with a radio on their cot, when he stepped behind the mike."

While Manning conversed (and the Indians finished, successively, sixth, second, sixth, seventh, third, fourth, and fourth), the Decade of Normalcy faded. Calvin Coolidge pronounced: "I do not choose to run for president in 1928." Herbert Hoover, who did, trounced the governor of New York, Alfred E. Smith. Thomas Wolfe wrote *Look Homeward, Angel*; William Faulkner, *The Sound and the Fury*; Erskine Caldwell, *Tobacco Road*. A disheveled "Bonus Army" marched on Washington. Who was Helen Cane? The Boop-boop-be-doop Girl. "The Rudy Vallee Show" assaulted network radio. Sadly, for Tom Manning, misfortune now assaulted *him*; in November 1931, WHK replaced WTAM as the Tribe's flagship station, and Jack Graney replaced Manning as the franchise's principal Voice. An Indians' left-fielder, Graney became the first ex-athlete to occupy the broadcast booth.

For more than two decades, until, in the mid-fifties, deaf in his right ear, he returned for two seasons of last hurrah, Manning heard Graney, Dudley, and lesser notables tell of Lou Boudreau, Larry Doby, Al Rosen, and the pitching staff of Lemon, Garcia, Feller, and Wynn.

"Later on, after he left radio, he became a Cleveland television announcer, doing shows at six and eleven o'clock," Dudley related. "And, of course, long before then — he took to TV in the late forties — he still did the public-address announcing for all the Indians' home games."

"But no play-by-play?" I asked.

"Well, he came back with me in 1956 and '57," he said. "I needed a partner, and Tom helped out. But by then he was losing his hearing, and the pace — the jet travel, all the night games, so different from when he'd broadcast — was just too much for him."

"Did he enjoy it?"

"Coming back to do the games?" Dudley said. "Oh, I think so, even with his problem. After all, like each of us, Tom had an ego, and despite the fact that he'd been busy with television and the P.A. and the rest, I know he'd missed being part of radio."

For Tom Manning, the years 1932–55 spoke of radio separation and forgotten youth. As a play-by-play announcer, he was ignored, without accommodation. He grew disaffected (which is not to say embittered), an echo of what might have been. Still, NBC selected him for three heavyweight championship fights and nine World Series (a majority with McNamee, several with Totten and Barber), where, as always, he was arresting and sure. He died on September 4, 1969, at sixty-nine, at the mercy of his past, without quite understanding it: to millions of Ohioans, the ex-newsboy who made his age extraordinary and who, locally, as a baseball broadcaster, vanished almost as suddenly as he came.

On April 19, 1927, Manning's Tribe visited Detroit; and it was there that a native of Tyrone, Pennsylvania, leaned forward, nudged the WWJ microphone, surveyed the handsome, double-decked ball park, then fifteen years old, and said, for the first time of many, "Good afternoon, boys and girls, this is Ty Tyson speaking to you from Navin Field."

For the next three hours, Edwin Lloyd Tyson described the first baseball game — an 8–5 Tigers' triumph — broadcast in the state of Michigan. Through 1942 and occasionally afterward, he announced thousands of innings and explained the game's nuances and made umpires of fans (and fans of housewives) and, with his scythelike staccato, gripped a region: the Upper Heartland, the Four Seasons Wonderland, the Habitat of Lions and Tigers and (by train) even Bears.

At heart, a working-class pastime, baseball found affinity in Tyson's working-class city. "Detroit has [always] been one of the great baseball towns in the country," Joe Falls, a remarkable columnist for the *Detroit Free Press* and, later, the *News*, wrote in 1975. "The Boston writers tell you that. The Chicago writers tell you that. Even the New York writers, the most provincial of all, tell you they like watching games in Detroit's ball park." Blue collar and union-oriented, lunch-bucket and hard hat, "This is a town of 3 million managers — all of them right. And a town of beer drinkers — all of them thirsty. This is a town that in seventy-five years has developed a true passion for a boy's game and a love-hate relationship for the men who play it."

In Tyson's second season, the Tigers placed sixth, thirty-three games behind New York; six years later, they won the pennant. They became a pandemic, alternately grand and awful, and proved irresistible to a ballplaying, tobacco-chewing, Bengals-loving son of Richfield Center, sixty miles north of Detroit. "I lived in a four-corners kind of settlement," Maynard Good Stoddard, seventy-four, gray-haired, and senior editor and essayist of *The Saturday Evening Post*, recalled. "It was out in the middle of nowhere, about halfway between Davison, where I went to school, and Otisville, where I met my wife, Lois. We had about two dozen houses, my dad's general store, a gas pump, and hope."

Richfield Center lies one mile from Puptown and seven miles from Henpeck. "We had a ball field there," Stoddard said. "We'd play all the time." On soft-summer afternoons, with the heat too rippling to play, Maynard and friends gathered around Billy Williams' garage — "about a half dozen of us" — where, surrounding an old Capehart radio, they heard Tyson reveal (verily, even to Puptown) a brave, new world.

"I remember it like it was yesterday," whistled Stoddard. "There we were, a goodly portion of the town, our thoughts all on WWJ, Detroit. And we'd listen to Ty."

"What did you think of him?" I said.

Delight invaded Maynard's eyes. "Ty was so vivid, he made games come alive," he said, leaning forward. "It was new, naturally, but it was his voice too — it was graphic. There was an *excitement* about him. Ty talked real slow, but he had an urgency inside him, and he transmitted that to us. Later [in 1934], along came Harry Heilmann after he'd retired as a player, but I didn't like him that much. He was more methodical, not as smooth.

"But Ty!" he said. "He just looked around the ball park and talked about what was going on, and he made you feel like Gehringer, Cochrane, and Goslin were right next door — which, believe me, in our neck of the woods, was quite a trick. 'It's going, it's going, it's a home run!' he'd roar. And we'd all cheer."

"For Ty, the Tigers, or the radio?"

"For all three," he glowed. "We didn't know all about how the game got to us, what technology they used. And we didn't care." Gentle laughter. "Ty could raise the hair on the back of your head. It was as real as Billy's radio. And it was the highlight of our day."

For the first seven years of Tyson's fiefdom, WWJ rebuffed commercial sponsorship; "we were doing," Ty explained, "a public service." By 1934, when the station relented (and the Tigers visited their first World Series in twenty-five years), "Yes, sir," Ty liked to say, "I'd already lived a lifetime." He was not alone. In the ten cities of major league baseball, in the sixteen fields where its vectors merged, for the one team with two ball parks (Cleveland) and the one city whose two teams shared a site (St. Louis), and, more exhaustively, in the farms, burgs, and villages where the royalty of baseball fashion seldom neared, the years 1927–33 put boredom to rout.

The Yankees, of course, were a cynosure; even then, the most successful team in sports. Having clasped the 1926 pennant, they won the 1927 and 1928 World Series. The '28 Bombers outscored the Cardinals, 27–10, and swept the Oktoberfest. The Yankees of 1927 won 110 games, scored 975 runs, and lapped second-place Philadelphia by nineteen lengths. Of their eight men on the field, Ruth lashed sixty home runs (four more than hit by any other American League *team*), Gehrig recorded a .373 average, forty-seven home runs, and (another record) 175 runs batted in, Earle Combs batted .356, and Bob Meusel and Tony Lazzeri teamed for more than two hundred RBIs. In the baseball season it came of age, Murderers Row can be cast forth as the all-time most gifted team.

Beyond the Bronx, Heilmann missed a .400 season by one hit. Jimmie Foxx, at twenty, joined Connie Mack's Philadelphia A's. Cleveland's Joe Sewell, the "fanless shortstop," played in 115 straight games without striking out. The Braves' Rabbit Maranville, dubbed by Tom Meany "a midget with the arms and shoulders of a weight lifter," sought proportion. "There is much less drinking now than there was in 1927," he said. "I know because I quit drinking on May 24, 1927." The Cubs won the 1929 pennant, the first of Joe McCarthy's nine. Oft-denied himself, Mack now denied New York; his club thrashed the Yankees by eighteen games to gain the Series, then ousted Chicago in five. In Game One, Howard Ehmke, the Red Sox' retread, struck out a Classic-record thirteen batters. Three games later, the Mackmen summoned ten runs in the seventh inning to expunge the Cubs' 8–0 lead. For Philadelphia, the twenties ended against a prideful backdrop; for Chicago, with a dark, mewling, wintry squall.

The 1930s began with stumbling. Richard Whitney, the "White Knight of Wall Street," became president of the Wall Street Stock Exchange; in 1938, he entered prison. *The Green Pastures*, a slapstick critique of Negro Bible lore, starred Richard Harrison as "de Lawd." Millions found solace in *Vogue, Vanity Fair, Harper's Bazaar*, and Stoddard's *Post*; even a flat story, judged against the entrails of the Great Depression, rose above the permanent dismemberment of life. Long, winding bread lines dotted city blocks. So did soup kitchens, pleas for one full meal a day, apples for sale ("Just a nickel, mister"), billboards declaring, "I Will Share." Men pounded pavement in futile search for employment; winter nights went unmarked by heat. "Happy Days Are Here Again" denoted dirge, not melody. The nightmare smelt more of "Brother, Can You Spare a Dime?"

In Detroit, Chicago, Cleveland, and St. Louis, Herbert Hoover's legacy was defined forever; urban shantytowns of the jobless down by rivers bore his name — "Hoovervilles." Amid drab, rain-soiled tents, if one could find a *radio* (One could *always* find time), one listened to Tyson and Ryan and Manning and Laux tell of jukebox Ebbets Field, that shooting gallery of an edifice; or Griffith Stadium, with its canyon of an outfield; or Forbes Field, hard by Schenley Park; or Braves Field, by the tracks of the Boston & Maine; or (better still) beguiling (even then) Comiskey Park, the South Side's transpontine jewel. One learned of *sluggers* (an *eagle-eye*) with their *foot in the bucket* who *hit the dirt* and who earned the *horse collar* or shook a *slump* and (after clubbing a *long strike*) *laid it down* or *teed off* in their *groove*, and of batted balls that became a *blooper* or *bleeder* or *banjo hit* or *Baltimore chop* or *clothesline* or *Texas Leaguer*, and of fielders who made a *boner* or *boot* or *circus catch* or *shoestring catch* or were *handcuffed* at the *hot corner* or *far corner* or *keystone bag* or *second sack* or (who, behind the plate) donned the *tools of ignorance* or (whose talent) voided the *squeeze play* or (whose largesse) prompted the cry of *butterfingers*, and of pitchers (a *chucker* or, if left-handed, a *southpaw* or, if inept, a *scatter-arm* or, if adept, a *Houdini*) who *winged* the *apple* or *beanball* or *rabbit ball* or *gopher ball* or *cripple* (if behind the hitter) or *free ticket/Annie Oakley* (if he walked the hitter) or *high, hard one* (brushing back the hitter) to *fan* or *whiff* or *strike out* or, in a *shutout*, *whitewash* the hitters so that, bespectacled (a *Cyclops*) or not, he could avoid a *Mexican standoff* and, not *crabbing*, become a *meal ticket*, not *grandstander*, an *Ace*, not *bush leaguer*. Finally, one heard the nicknames that rang like chimes: *Pie, Black Mike, the Rajah, the Fordham Flash, Big and Little Poison, the Iron Horse, Marse Joe, the Lip, the Mechanical Man, the Wild Horse of the Osage,* and *Old Double X*. Respectively: the Pirates' Harold Traynor, enslaving ground balls like a centurion; Mickey Cochrane, of the A's, Tigers, and five championships, who burned with a fire; Rogers Hornsby, he of the .358 career average; Frankie Frisch, urbane and polished; Paul and Lloyd Waner, Pittsburgh 1927–40, collecting 5,806 base hits; Henry Louis Gehrig, Old Biscuit Pants, the Pride of the Yankees, a quiet man, a hero; Joseph Vincent McCarthy, Philadelphian by birth and Victorian by bearing, who said, "Sometimes, I think I'm in the greatest business in the world. Then you lose four straight and want to change places with a farmer"; Leo Durocher, who stormed, "Show me a good loser and I'll show you an idiot"; Detroit's Charlie Gehringer, of whom Cochrane said, "He'd say hello at the start of spring training and good-bye at the end of the season, and the rest of the time he let his bat and glove do all the talking for him"; Pepper Martin of the St. Louis Cardinals, who pawed the earth and slid head-first and wore no underwear; and Jimmie Foxx, who hit 534 home runs and was ajudged the right-handed Babe Ruth, a batter so intimidating that Vernon (Lefty) Gomez, trying to decide which pitch to hurl homeward, told catcher Bill Dickey: "I'd rather not throw the ball at all."

Gomez threw, Foxx singled, and their sock-happy years unfolded. Except for several monoliths — Lefty Grove won fifty-nine games in 1930–31; the Giants' Carl Hubbell averaged twenty-three victories per year in 1933–37 — pitching ebbed and almost disappeared, lost in the headwaters of home runs. In 1930, a year in which Haile Selassie (who was not a baseball fan) became emperor of Ethiopia and Lowell Thomas (who was) began his news commentary, the cannonading crested. Foxx smashed 37 home runs and 156 runs batted in and, strangely, led the league in putouts. Bill Terry forearmed .401. The Cubs' Hack Wilson, of whom Warren Brown wrote, "He was a high-ball hitter on the field, and off it," smacked a National League-record 56 round trippers and 190 ribbies. Every Cardinals' regular hit more than .300. Chuck Klein of the Phillies, in his second full season, batted .386 with 29 home runs and 170 RBIs and 250 hits; nowhere did he lead the league. In the American League, its collective batting average .288, teams *averaged* more than five runs a game. The Yankees hit .309 and finished third. Ruth and Gehrig combined for 327 runs batted in. At Shibe Park, the A's, with seven future Hall of Famers, won their eighth pennant. At Sportsman's Park, the Redbirds won their third. In the sloping boomerang at Cincinnati's Finley and Western Avenues, once called Palace of the Fans, Harry Hartman waddled into a chair behind the backstop and, over station WFBE, often broadcasting in his undershirt, unleashed verbal arrows marked *socko* and *belto* and *whammo* and *bammo*.

Hartman followed Bob Burdette, who, in 1929, closeted in a booth on the ball park's rooftop, first regularly aired Redlegs' games. In February 1930, already a fixture on Cincinnati radio, Harry convinced Sid Weil, then the franchise's owner, that his team needed a more exciting Voice. Burdette had

meandered over to WLW, Cincinnati; Hartman's WFBE was owned by the
Scripps-Howard papers, and for the next four years (until, arriving from
Florida in 1934, Red Barber's brilliance surpassed even Harry's girth),
Hartman monopolized commercials, mangled language, and dwarfed re-
named Redland Field.

Five-foot-six and 320 pounds, he was short, unschooled, obese, and unforgettable. He assailed the ear. He livened the sport. Like Manning, a switch-
speaker, Hartman doubled as radio- and public-address announcer. Laughing,
sweating, flinging flippancies to the crowd, he sat between two microphones,
breathing into one, then the other, and for a game pronouncement over the
park's loudspeaker system, into both. "Harry was a real character, and for
a lot of people, thousands probably, he 'learned 'em baseball,' as Dizzy Dean
would later say," said Cincinnati native Lee Allen, the Hall of Fame historian.
"He became an extension of the team" — a man whose sponsors included a
cigar known as Black Peter (which Harry smoked) and Frank's Radio Shop
(which Harry frequented) and a patent medicine named Udga (relationship
unknown). "You see," Allen continued, "Harry was sort of rough around the
edges, it's true, and his dictionary wasn't too thick, but he was earthy and
people liked him. Please remember — southern Ohio's a very old-fashioned,
cornball sort of place, 'Little Germany' and all that. Well, Harry was like that
anyway, and he fit in," a vaudevillian timepiece, roguishly cast, who vocalized
his phantasma, and by speaking, made them so.

Harry Hartman was accepted by his community. On a humid, sun-glint
afternoon in 1931, in his Midgard as Voice of the Braves and Red Sox, Fred
Hoey was honored with a day. He had risen (albeit, not his teams) six years
earlier, a brusque, incongruous figure. In 1939 he exited, involuntarily, his
time in broadcasting spent, having (largely) made New England (arguably) the
most rabid baseball region in America.

Born in Saxonville, near Framingham, a suburb of Boston, Hoey was already an athletic layman (and forty years old) when he ascended to the booth.
Between 1909 and 1946 he wrote sports for three of Boston's then-six daily
newspapers: the *Journal*, *Post*, and *American*. He officiated high school and
college football games. He pioneered the broadcasts of ice hockey, college and
professional. Often remote, easily wounded, he ranked among Massachusetts'
most credible wordsmen; his wont was matter-of-fact, objective. Upon the
disclosure of Hoey's 1925 entrance into radio, a colleague wrote: "No one can
tell how this man will sound on the air. But *we* can tell that *this* man knows
his sports."

"Fred began his career in radio with a great advantage," I heard Til Ferdenzi
saying. "Most guys have to *prove* themselves in a new profession. Some poor
saps never do — I guess there's a laundry list we could talk about. Frankie
Frisch, the one who replaced Hoey, is an example of that — he bombed. But
Hoey was different. He'd proved himself. He was a part of Boston's sporting
scene."

A laugh ambled across Ferdenzi's breast. "And you know as well as I do," Til
said, "there ain't nowhere on earth that's as provincial as Boston, and that was

especially true with Hoey. 'Oh, we've got the best restaurants,' they say. 'Best museums, best parks, best this, best that, best announcers.' Jesus! They even think the Red Sox are the greatest."

"Come on," I said. "They haven't won a Series since 1918."

"No," he insisted, "I mean it. You read the *Boston Globe* or listen to the TV stations in the spring when the club's in Florida. They make out like it's the Second Coming."

"I'd settle for the First."

"Yeah," he said. "Then the season starts and eventually everybody finds out — same old Red Sox. Or when the Braves were here — same old Braves. So my point is — this area *wants* to believe the Sox have changed. They beg to be deluded. And then they wake up. There's that love-hate relationship. I've covered sports all around America — and I'm telling you, there's nothing like it anywhere."

"Recently," I said, "hasn't the hate won out?"

"Possibly," he chuckled. "But here's the rub. The fans say, 'I've had it. I'm through. Baseball here will *never* get better. I'm never going to the ball park again.' So what happens? A couple of wins and here's Joe Fan — he's storming Fenway Park."

"Doesn't this prove?" I began.

"I say all of this," Ferdenzi said, "with great affection for New England. After all, it's my home. And to their credit, baseball fans around here — they *care*. But they *are* provincial. Remember what FDR said about a Democratic hack? 'He may be an SOB, but he's *our* SOB.' "

"And that was Hoey?" I said.

"Fred was a home-town boy," he said, "and he became a hero, a regional giant. He helped make fans of thousands of people here — men, housewives, young kids. He was excitable — not trained. He had a dry, biting sort of voice. But very much local. And *very much* applauded," ushered into New England's closer than close-knit heart.

Bursting from WAAB and WNAC, heard over the Colonial and, later, simultaneously, Yankee Networks from Augusta, Maine, to Hartford, Connecticut, Fred Hoey recounted each season's swan song: Boston's two baubles entered April full of hope and found calamity. Not *once* between 1925 and 1938 did the Braves place higher than fourth. Twice they finished last; four times, seventh: In 1935, they won 38, lost 115, trailed the Cubs by 61½ games, and lured 232,754 fans, barely three thousand per date. Braves Field resembled a mortuary; its playing field, a slab. At Fenway Park, enter ignominy. In each of Hoey's first *six* seasons, the Red Sox finished eighth in an eight-team league. The box score: 311 victories, 603 defeats, a cumulative 294½ games behind. After vaulting to sixth place in 1931 ("The city fathers," said Ken Coleman, "were prepared to declare a civic holiday"), the Bosox of 1932 raised impotence to Kafkaesque dimensions. Their winning percentage (to use the term advisedly) was .279. They finished sixty-four games behind New York. Their paid attendance totaled 182,150 (per contest average, 2,365): less than the 1979 edition drew in its first nine games. "There used to be a running joke," Ferdenzi recollected, "that the Red Sox had three teams — the one there, one coming, and one going. Whatever, they *always* had a lot of broken-down players from other clubs. And the park was a joke—this is before [Tom] Yawkey bought it [in 1933]. Lots of chairs didn't have bottom parts. There were bird turds all over the seats. The structure itself was beautiful—it was just pathetically kept up. And if you wanted to catch a long nap—boy, Fenway was the place to go."

Outside the Hub of self-abasement, the contrast was often antipodal. The 1931 Athletics won their third successive pennant. Al Simmons hit .390. Of a chatterbox rookie pitcher, Cardinals' vice-president Branch Rickey mumbled to himself, "I'm a man of some intelligence. I've had some education, passed the bar, practiced law. I've been a teacher, and I deal with men of substance, statesmen, business leaders, the clergy. Then why," he demanded, his hands thrusting upward, "*why* do I spend my time arguing with Dizzy Dean!?" In 1932, Joe McCarthy won his first Yankee pennant. Foxx wafted fifty-eight home runs. The next season, the Washington Senators, starring Goslin, Heinie Manush, and player-manager Joe Cronin, won their *final* pennant. Menaced by anonymity, Chuck Klein won the Triple Crown. John Kieran wrote of pitcher Burleigh Grimes: "He always looked like a man who was about ready to commit assault and battery when he threw the ball."

That same spring, having cried, "The country needs and, unless I mistake its temper, the country *demands* bold, persistent experimentation" (and after trouncing Hoover, who only four years earlier declaimed, without fear of contradiction, "We in America are nearer to the final triumph over poverty than ever before in the history of any land"), Franklin Roosevelt took the oath of office as thirty-second president of the United States—for some, today, the President *still*. On March 4, 1933, the date of his swearing-in, unemployment hovered above 13 million; a banking panic shadowed Roosevelt's inauguration; said the outgoing president, "We are at the end of our string." Leaving training camp in early April, baseball writer Rud Rennie, barreling north with the Yankees, confided, "[We] passed through southern cities which looked as though they had been ravaged by an invisible enemy. People seemed to be in hiding. They even would not come out to see Babe Ruth and Lou Gehrig. Birmingham, a once-thriving, bright metropolis, looked as if it had been swept by a plague."

More than 25 percent of America's work force was out of work. Every state had either closed its banks entirely or reduced their capacity to act. Roosevelt *acted*. Later, Arthur Schlesinger, Jr., wrote, "He was all grin and gusto," the nation's bandmaster, a gaiety, but "terribly hard inside . . . a man without illusions, clearheaded and compassionate, who had been close enough to death to understand the frailty of human striving, but who remained loyal enough to life to do his best in the sight of God." He was jaunty and effervescent, laughing, jousting, always *leading*, and despite the polio that paralyzed his legs, seemingly indestructible: often poet, always politician, Father of the New Deal and scourge of Nazi Germany, the president who created Social Security and canonized "My little dog Fala" and was, moreover, the man Adolf Hitler feared—a man so large in his influence that when he died on April 12,

1945, a part of each American died with him. "One remembers Roosevelt as a kind of smiling bus driver," Samuel Grafton said, "with cigarette holder pointed upward, listening to the uproar from behind as he took the sharp turns. They used to tell him that he had not loaded his vehicle right for all eternity. But he knew he had it stacked well enough to round the next corner and he knew when the yells were false and when they were real, and he loved the passengers." Once, conceding a salary larger than Hoover's, Ruth protested of the then-president, "But I had a better year than he did!" Not so with FDR.

Little of this disturbed Fred Hoey, or much impressed him, either. "Let's face it," a reporter for the old *Boston Traveler* said. "Fred's globe was sports, and its capital, baseball."

In the temple of Hoey's primacy, Boston baseball was its fatted calf. Even so, Fred hoped and vivified, for childless and unmarried, broadcasting meant his life, and even sacrifice demands a spokesman. "I never met him, never heard him, or even read much about him," smiled broadcaster Ned Martin, a native of Philadelphia who joined the Red Sox in 1961. "But I feel like I *know* him, because people still swear *by* him. Of course, he was the first one they'd listened to, and I guess like in love or anything else, the first, you don't forget."

The first, the well-remembered, Hoey knew his players, with their magnet for catastrophe, and his region, with its wandering cobblestones and cathedral-vaulted factories, its small shops and maples and Indian names. He knew how to shill for sponsors ("When you mention Fred's name," said Coleman, "they always talk about Kentucky Club pipe tobacco and Mobil's Flying Red Horse. It's like how Mel Allen was with White Owl cigars and Ballantine beer") and how to imbue his public with Euripidean concern. He did not, sadly, know how to obviate the bottle.

"Yes, he liked the sauce, or so I've heard," offered Coleman, born eight miles from Fenway Park. In Game One of the 1933 World Series, having reached, at last, broadcasting's pinnacle event, Hoey reached the radio booth with evident breath and fumbling. "He was bombed," Ferdenzi acknowledged, his manner turning urgent now. "In the second or third inning, they had to yank him off the air." The explanation: Hoey had a "bad cold."

Once sober, Hoey returned a conqueror. "He came back to Boston, where, of course, people knew about his drinking problem, and all was forgiven," Coleman said. "In fact, there'd been a flood tide of letters—I mean, literally, *thousands*—written in his defense. They swamped the newspapers, saying, 'How dare you do this to our Fred?'"

"What about the fans who disliked him?" I said.

"The amazing thing," he vowed, "is that there *weren't* any. There was, and I mean this authentically, a *total* acceptance. I'm serious. The guy was loved. And I think the reason is because he was looked on as 'the man who does the games.' That was *something* then. And the papers were less judgmental—you didn't have radio and TV critics. I quite genuinely never heard *anybody* say—and I grew up, like we all did, listening to Fred—'Gee, I think he's lousy.'"

Hoey was repetitive.

"A phrase he used all the time was, 'He throws to first and gets his man,' "
Coleman affirmed, his voice rising, vigorous, "and I think I subconsciously
picked that up because I catch myself or listen to past tapes and *I've* used it."
Gravelly.

"He wasn't polished. He wasn't a professional. And he had to put up with
crazy things like on the old Yankee Network, every afternoon they'd break for
news at six o'clock no matter how the game was going. There could be a tie
score, ninth inning, bases loaded, three and two, the crowd going berserk —
and if the clock struck six, the carriage became a pumpkin. Boom! You went
to news. *But*," he paused, theatrically, "there was an electricity to him — not in
how he used the language, particularly, but in the feeling he gave that this
mattered, that baseball counted, that it meant something special in our lives."

And, ultimately, deposed from within.

On one flank, debauched by alcohol, and on another, by the afterglow of a
purge in 1937 (when John Shepard, owner of the Colonial and Yankee Networks, ousted Fred, then bowed to letters, telegrams, telephone threats, and
pickets encircling Fenway Park), Hoey finally yielded on March 18, 1939.

"In '37, public pressure had forced Hoey's reinstatement, and it went to his
head. Fred thought he owned New England," Leo Egan, a Red Sox' broadcaster in the late forties, said. "So two years later, he went to Shepard and said,
'I want more money or I'm leaving.' And Shepard, all he said was, 'Oh, by the
way, I forgot to tell you, Fred. You're fired.' "

"What did Hoey say?" I asked.

"He just couldn't believe it," Egan said, "and when he finally did, he thought
the fans would save him again. And out they came, just like two years before,
the hoots and hollers and threats of a commercial boycott unless Fred was
rehired," but General Mills, the Boston clubs' new primal sponsor, wanted its
own barker, not one sired by Kentucky Club and the Flying Red Horse, and
from St. Louis, fired as Cardinals' manager the previous year, sprang Frankie
Frisch, the Fordham Flash.

"On the air, Fred *was* Boston baseball," Coleman eulogized, "and it was not
the same without him." He died on November 17, 1949, alone, at sixty-four, in
a gas-filled room, of "accidental . . . asphyxiation. Hoey was generally credited with building up baseball broadcasting to the lofty spot it holds in the
American sports scene today," the *Boston Daily Globe* reported. "His body was
found on the kitchen floor by a delivery boy."

Memento mori.

3
Where You Lead
(1934–39)

"One generation plants the trees. Another
gets the shade."
— Chinese Proverb

BASEBALL'S MURMUROUS COMPANIONS FLOWERED DESPITE A LABYRINTH OF
lurches, for even as broadcasting struggled into puberty, many in the major
leagues twitched with fear.

Among its sixteen baronies, some, like William Wrigley and Larry MacPhail,
gloried in radio's cajolery. Others beheld the past as sacrosanct; the wireless
was still infantile, its synthesis uncertain. Radio, they warned, might dim incentive to invade their ball park; if one could hear play-by-play, why trespass
outside the home? "Nobody was neutral about this new medium of communica-
tion," Red Barber, no neutral himself, wrote in 1970. "Some powerful men in
baseball and football were deathly afraid. They said, 'Who will pay for something
they can get for free?' "

Already, by the early 1930s, the bigwigs of baseball had hurled down their
testament: In the two-franchise cities of St. Louis, Philadelphia, Boston, and
Chicago, where of an afternoon one team might play at home and the other,
away, the visiting club would meet silence and disfavor; the homestanders, the
floodlit sunshine of radio.

"If the Cardinals were at Sportsman's Park and the Browns in Philadelphia,"
Jack Brickhouse explained, his vibrato sounding eerily like Glenn Ford's, "then
the Cardinal game was carried but the Browns were not."

If, however, not to become overtly technical, the Redbirds were *not* scheduled — or weather decreed postponement — enter, from eastern Pennsylvania,
the abysmally definable Browns. The stratagem endured until the mid-1940s,
when, after World War II, every team aired its entire schedule: to persuade
fans to fill their neighborhood ball yard ("Hey-Hey," said Brickhouse, "support
your hometown Cardinals") and not sit, beer in hand, by the radio, reproach-
ing the Brownies' deeds, and watch one's indignation (and waistline) swell.

"The rationale was simple, really, and back then, when the impact of radio
was still up in the air, it made a lot of sense," Byrum Saam, the former Voice
of the A's and Phillies, said in a soft, thoughtful way. "See, the owners thought
by now — most of 'em, anyway — that broadcasts of home games *advertised* their
team. It was good P.R., it sold fans on the game."

"But what about the away games?" I said.

"As long as there was no conflict, fine," he said, "but if there was any overlap whatsoever, the team on the road was shut out — they wouldn't be carried. Of course, some stations covered both teams, so they obviously *couldn't* broadcast two games at once. But there were other cases in which a city's National and American League teams were broadcast by two *different* stations."

"And the team on the road was *still* kept off the air?"

"That's right," he said. "Remember, baseball people didn't want to provide *any* excuse for fans to stay home and listen to one team while another might be playing a couple blocks away. They figured, 'Hey, if there's only one club available, maybe the guy'll go to their game.' "

Home broadcasts were *live*, from their actual domicile. But until announcers, like writers, went forth to cover teams on the road — "I came from Minneapolis to Philadelphia in 1938," Saam reminisced, "and my first broadcasting trip, and this was true of most clubs, was more than ten years later" — line charges and transportation costs made live *away* coverage the President Stassen of our time: in theory, possible, but disillusioned, absurd. Instead, meet a brain child worthy of a then-slim Orson Welles: the "re-creation," baseball's theatre of the mind.

Re-created games rose in the dawning days of radio, when, for a fee (and so, monopoly), Western Union linked each major-league park. Its wires became the Pony Express of "running" newspaper stories. "You might have a deadline every inning," said Til Ferdenzi, "and so as a writer, you'd file an updated account of how the game was going and give it to the operator," who converted copy into coded messages and transmitted the brattle to the reporter's office. Western Union also created an ancillary service called "Paragraph One" — a spartan encapsulation of every inning, every game. One operator stood in the press box to send the service; a second traveled to the site (i.e., radio studio) of its delivery. The skeletal outline journeyed by Morse Code to the station, where the receiver translated dots and dashes into balls and strikes and hits, runs, and errors, then thrust the paper to an announcer who, reading, might see: "Combs up . . . B1H [ball one high] . . . S1L [strike one low] . . . B2W [ball two wide] . . . single . . . line drive to right field. Meusel up. S1S [strike one swinging] . . . B1I [ball one inside] . . . DP [double play . . . but how?] . . . Ward to Peckinpaugh to Sheely." Circa, 1927, Murderers Row v. Chicago.

In a re-creation, the lingering sense was fantasy, with mythic obbligato near its cockpit. "It was at the very heart of baseball on radio," said Saam. "Re-creations planted the seeds of our coverage — they were the nectar from which most listeners drank." By the early thirties, with broadcasts swelling — in the home (Americans owned 18 million radios) and automobile (D.O.B., the first car radio, 1923, courtesy the Springfield Body Corporation) and bar (mercifully, Prohibition ended in the New Deal's tenth month) — intoxication leaped from studio to set. "All during this period radio was slowly overcoming the Doubting Thomases — it was turning into *the* new thing in baseball," Brickhouse added. "Sure, there were some franchises who still thumbed their noses [in 1932, New York's three teams barred *all* radio, even visitors' re-creations, from Ebbets Field, the Polo Grounds, and Yankee Stadium. Less balefully, the Cardinals, Browns, and Pirates banned the wireless on Sunday and holidays; its void, they hoped, would boost attendance], but the thing to remember is how, despite all the initial fears, a majority of the era's franchises allowed radio coverage with relatively few restrictions."

In Cleveland, the former outfielder Graney, gripping re-creations more easily than the easiest fly ball, dispersed yarns and anecdotes from the showroom of an auto dealer. "Only a pane of glass separated Jack from customers wandering in and out," was Jimmy Dudley's recollection, "and, you know, he could have been a great used-car salesman. You didn't find many more accurate than Jack. You didn't find *any* more enthusiastic. And that combination — yes, there were others later on who specialized in re-creations, but Jack was one of the first — made him, in my mind, probably also the best."

Over WWJ, brought to you (post-1933) by Mobil's "The Sign of the Flying Red Horse," Ty Tyson called second baseman Gehringer "Mr. Tiger," outfielder Hank Greenberg "Hankus Pancus," pitcher Lynwood (Schoolboy) Rowe "Schoolhouse" or "Schoolie" or "the guy who's playing hooky today." In Chicago, with its maze of on-air baying, baseball re-creations dominated the dial. Meanwhile, to the south and east, at a juncture of the Ohio, a distant relative of writer Sidney Lanier became one of three Voices of the Cincinnati Reds, and for the next thirty-three years, in his graceful and often righteous chords, made of baseball almost existential pleasure.

In 1933, flayed by bankruptcy, Sid Weil had lost the Reds. They tumbled to a bank, which hired Leland Stanford MacPhail to oversee the ball club. The Flamboyant, in turn, sold Powel Crosley (owner of radio stations WSAI and larger, then-500,000-watt WLW) a majority percentage of the team; and in 1934, Barber's first season in Cincinnati, over WSAI (one of three stations to broadcast Reds' games), the Ol' Redhead, twenty-six, ousted lethargy (not a trifling deed; the team finished last) and spawned exhilaration ("He was like nothing they'd ever heard before," barked MacPhail. "Sort of like the Sermon on the Mount") and reduced Harry Hartman to the periphery. That same year MacPhail allowed fewer than twenty broadcasts to bloom from Crosley Field; only later, by now aware that daily coverage helped, not hurt, the gate, would he allow unlimited home coverage. On the road, exposure was continuous, and from the studio, weaned on the hypnotic fabric of Western Union, Barber re-created games with equal parts dexterity and charm.

"I never tried to fool anybody," Barber, seventy-eight, said at his home in Tallahassee, Florida. "I couldn't be — didn't *intend* to be — like most guys. They deceived by omission."

"How so?" I said.

"They didn't tell their listeners that this was a game based on cold type," he began. "They'd jazz it up, they'd pretend. They'd try to convince their audience that it was all real, that they were somehow *at* the ball park." Disdain filled Barber's voice. "If the wire went dead, and the announcer couldn't get the signals, he'd make up some diversion — a guy fouling off fifteen pitches, a sudden storm that hit the field, whatever. And maybe by the time he'd finished playing fairy tale, the wire would come back. And they'd make out like nothing had happened."

"And you?"

"I couldn't go for that dishonesty," he said. "To me, the audience should know the truth. So what I did was intentionally arrange for the sounds of the wire service to be in close proximity to the mike. At home, you heard the dots and dashes — the sounds of the operating receiver typing away. I *wanted* the sounds to be heard — nobody was going to con the fans. I always felt that even with a re-creation, if you were a professional, if you had the talent, the audience would be pleased."

Barber *was* a professional, and his audiences *were* pleased. He attracted with soft, rhythmic accents, and with such contempt for provinciality and grasp of verbal mannerisms that, ultimately — after moving to Brooklyn in 1939, and to Yankee Stadium in 1954, and then, after his harsh dismissal twelve years later (affirming the Yankees' genius for public misrelations), to syndicated radio and the printed page; after airing the Rose, Orange, and Sugar Bowls, the Army-Navy autumn pageant, professional football championships, five All-Star Games, and thirteen World Series; and, even more, after teaching the second third of Henry Luce's American Century the apothegms of baseball — he was the first broadcaster, with Mel Allen, on August 7, 1978, to enter the Hall of Fame.

A writer for the *New York Morning Telegraph*, espying Barber as the Yankees and Dodgers traveled by train, recalled, "God, he was opinionated. And he'd sometimes bug the hell out of you — tough, you know, and there was a conceit to him. *But*," he scowled, removing his glasses and releasing a sigh, "the guy was beautifully restrained as a broadcaster. Allen, he'd wear you out; it was like a volcano. But Barber! He flowed like a quiet stream."

Of his former Dodgers' colleague, Ernie Harwell said: "It was a marriage of a guy and his teams. He did a fantastic job. But what impressed me the most was his absolute bid for perfection — he was a class act, no-nonsense."

"How do you remember him?" I said.

The Hall of Famer (inducted, 1981) came on slowly, his wont dispassionate and calm. "Red was the first to take broadcasting out of the era of getting a scorecard and just being a fan," he said. "He turned it into studying players, supplying information, and taking folks behind the scene. What was also interesting was that he was much different on the air than off — much more so than Mel, who's the same everywhere."

"Different how?"

"People expected Red to be this cornball, relaxed, Arthur Godfrey-type of guy. And yet," Harwell declared, a tone of resolution to his voice, "he wasn't. He was serious, disciplined, very intense. But on the air, he was a star. And I know this: Probably more than any announcer, we learned from him, every one of us."

Barber broadcast with an anxious, concomitant reserve. He did not, however, prize disinterest. "This indifferent age of announcing," Harry Caray, a reveler in broadcasting's high baroque, fairly snorted in 1986. " 'Ball one.

Strike one. Ball two.' And that's it — that's all they give you. Nothing more. People fall asleep, and it probably hurts the game more than anything." Few slept in the early 1930s. Announcers could be (a) blind, (b) biased, (c) inaccurate, (d) loathsome, or (e) all of the above. They could not, though, *must* not, be blasé.

"I think a lot of it had to do with the times, and even more than that, radio's novelty," concluded Ken Smith, from 1927 to 1962 a sportswriter for the *New York Graphic* and *Daily Mirror*, then director of the Hall of Fame, and now eighty-four and living in Connecticut. "Guys broadcasting today, they've been around TV and radio all their lives. And they've been buried by sports — in the paper, on the screen, you name it; they're swamped."

"What's your point?" I asked. "That they become inured, a little cynical?"

"It's all different now," Smith said. "Back then, baseball was the only game in town. You either liked it, or you didn't like sports. And radio was like a shiny toy on Christmas morning — a new sled every day of the year. So broadcasting games, even guys with lousy voices — Jesus, we had a lot — they had to sound excited, because they *were*. It's not that their tonsils were great. It's that their love of the game was great."

"Any other differences?"

"Yeah," he said. "These guys were on their own — like writers. And they didn't have a traveling party of hundreds. They weren't hamstrung. No production trucks, no directors yelling in your ear, nothing. They could be creative, just let 'er rip," which, in the tradition of New Haven tryouts, is what generations of broadcasters did.

A self-styled "uncontemporary," Ken Smith was not unintuitive. Among broadcasters who thought themselves a Thespian, re-creation formed a stage. Props were varied: a hollow block of wood, tapped with stick or pencil to mirror the sound of bat hitting ball; the obligatory "canned" sound track of cheering, blasted multitudes, whose volume one could raise or lower to emulate (dis)passion; and the sound effects of vendor pawning ice cream, umpire flailing, "You're ouuut!" or, more delectably, baseball's incessant, rumbling background noise. From the infield: "Come on, babe, come on, get 'im, get 'im, bear down, down," or the dugout: "Nothin' good to hit, Jake. Don't give in to 'im. Watch 'im on second, atta boy, think, *think*," or, at once ludicrous and entrancing, The Apostles According to Fan: "What are you *doing*? You idiot — what a . . . you bum! . . . Man, you couldn't hit my *house*. You couldn't strike out my *grandmother!*"

Many announcers warmed to the off-Broadway of re-creations, and many stations (WHO in Des Moines, for one) relied on them extensively. In the 1930s, WHO's sportscaster was a promising, unaffected comer. Iowa knew him as Dutch Reagan. Five decades later, he became the fortieth president of the United States.

"In those days a team didn't have its own announcers, and so there were about five or six of us doing the same game. We had to kind of compete for the audience," President Reagan started, his fingers tapping on a podium. "Even worse, some of our competitors were at the ball park. And, of course, I was doing *ours* in Des Moines, hundreds of miles away. I'd get something that said S-I-C. And you can't sell many Wheaties if you just excitedly yell, 'S-I-C.' So, I would say, 'Dean comes out of the windup, here comes the pitch, and . . . it's a called strike breaking over the outside corner to a batter that likes the ball a little higher.'

"I have a story that I've told at times. One day a fellow on the other side of the window of our booth — he had headphones and would get the Morse Code — started, I saw, to type, so I started another ball on the way to the plate. Then I saw that he was shaking his head. It was the ninth inning, and it was the Cubs and the Cardinals. And I didn't know what the trouble was. Well, when I got the slip from him, it read, 'The wire's gone dead.' "

Dutch unlatched a short, knowing smile. "Well, with those other five or six fellows out there broadcasting, I knew that if I said, 'We will pause for a brief interlude of transcribed music until they get the wire fixed,' everybody'd just switch stations, and I wouldn't have any audience left. So, I thought, there's one thing that doesn't get in the scorebook. And I looked at Curly on the other side of the window there, and he was just — he was helpless. And so, I had Dean use the resin bag, and then he shook off a couple signs to take up some time. Then he threw another one.

"Billy Jurges was the batter, and when he hit a foul ball, this time behind third base, I described the two kids that got in a fight over the baseball. And then he fouled one to the left that just missed being a home run by a foot. And about six minutes and forty-five seconds later," and now, he was laughing, "I think I had set a world record for someone standing at the plate. Then suddenly," Reagan said, his eyes widening, "Curly stopped typing. And then when he handed me the slip, I started to giggle, and I could hardly get it out. That wire said Jurges had popped out on the first ball pitched. But maybe I shouldn't tell that story. People are suspicious enough of those in politics."

From our perspective, the Dutchman's cosmos flared; yearning for a microphone at Wrigley Field, Reagan must settle for the Oval Office. Yet even the once and future Huck Finn paled beside the "Rembrandt of the Re-Creation," as one writer scribbled: the oracular Arch McDonald, a.k.a. "The Old Pine Tree."

Debuting, like Barber, in 1934, McDonald reigned for twenty-two years as Voice of the Washington Senators, a florid, gutty presence, a small-town announcer in populist garb.

"He was a very flamboyant guy, a fine broadcaster," observed Shirley Povich, the former sports editor and award-winning columnist of the *Washington Post.* Together, Povich and McDonald played bridge, made news, and bemoaned the Senators. They walked with pitchers, peers, and presidents. Their incandescence brightened the age.

"Arch started here the year after Washington won the pennant," he said, "and he came up from the minor-league team in Chattanooga [the Lookouts, the Senators' Class-A affiliate]. You see, Clark Griffith, the Washington president, had a scouting system, not just for players — for announcers too. So he brought Arch here, and Arch was a sensation. Part of it, I suppose, is because he had so much to talk about." In 1934, Lou Gehrig captured the Triple Crown. Lefty Gomez, winning twenty-six games, revealed his secret of success: "It's simple — clean living and a fast outfield." Detroit seized its first pennant since 1909. Dizzy Dean won thirty games for the Cardinals. Bill Terry asked: "Is Brooklyn still in the league?" A country welcomed the Gas House Gang. "But even more of Arch's appeal had to do with *him*," Povich mused. "He had an informal way about him, and this then was a casual sort of city. Being from Arkansas, he had a southern voice, and this then was very much a southern town."

Before attending to Griffith Stadium, with its yawning pasture (402 feet down the left-field line), tree-dotted neighborhood, and 27,410-seat capacity (save League Park, the smallest in the league), McDonald had worked as delivery boy, crophand, peanut vendor, boxing referee, and patent-medicine salesman. He was a huckster, a hustler, and his broadcasts, a midway. Starting on WJSV (later, WTOP), the station of Godfrey's radio maturation, he regaled Washingtonians with such epigrams as "ducks on the pond" (translated: Senators' runners on base) or "right down Broadway" (a pitch cutting the plate) or, upon a rare Washington home run, "There she goes, Mrs. Murphy," or his Holiness of war whoops, quoting from the hillbilly ballad, "They Cut Down the Old Pine Tree." Whenever a Senators' drive found the Griffith Stadium bleachers, "our boys" banked a 6-4-3, or, even more infrequently, a reliever marched from the center-field bull pen to actually record a *save*, Washington, brace thyself: "Well," Arch would say, slowly, surely, flashing a grin. "They did it again. 'They Cut Down the Old Pine Tree.' "

"So it came from a song," I said to Arch McDonald, Jr., fifty-eight and a former local television executive, now owner of a Hagerstown, Maryland, liquor store. "But where did 'Mrs. Murphy' come from?"

He laughed and left to sell a bottle. "Beats the hell out of me," he said, returning from the cash register. "Out of thin air, I think."

"Was that typical?" I said.

"Of dad?"

"Yes."

"In a way," he said. "Ideas just came to him, phrases, expressions. And he just said what crossed his mind — that's why he was indelible in the *public's* mind." Silence and hesitation. "Today, you have to have those Madison Avenue, pearl-shaped, carefully scripted tones. You're a robot, not an individual."

"Your father was hardly that," I offered.

"Oh, dad was 'individual' with a capital *I*. And I think the game really misses something now because it *lacks* that kind — it's more sterile because of it," he said. "A guy like dad, a colorful blazer, somebody who had style without even trying to, a character like that — he couldn't get a job today."

After five years in Washington, McDonald ambled to New York, becoming Voice of the Yankees in 1939. "Remember who replaced him?" said Harold Rosenthal, long-time writer for the *New York Herald Tribune*. "A guy by the name of Walter Johnson. And remember who Arch teamed with in New York? His assistant was a guy named Mel Allen."

Rosenthal stared at the sunlight. "I knew Arch quite well," he said, "and he wasn't very happy in New York. You'll recall, he lasted only a year before returning home."

"Why the proverbial 'cup of coffee?' " I said.

"Arch was country," he said, "a little bit on the air like Dizzy Dean, and to be honest, he wasn't too well-received. That kind of personality just doesn't cut it here."

Back on the Potomac, constants reassured. Washington still loved him. The ball club still drew poorly. The Senators still swarmed in catatonia and disarray. Through 1956, when a change of beer sponsorship ended his career, Arch chanted and narrated and interminably drawled.

"He was very much on the low-key, very funny. He was a medicine man before he came to Washington, and he never really changed," Morris Siegel, former *Washington Star* sports columnist, explained, and as he spoke I felt that warmth touched him. "His voice was understated, especially when the club was losing, so naturally, because they lost all the time, he got a lot of practice."

When summer's heat, pre-air conditioning, violated the capital, Arch shed habiliments and broadcast in his underwear. After WWDC pilfered the team's games, he still hosted a sports program on WTOP. He performed at dinner theatres, ran for Congress in 1944 from Maryland's then-rural Montgomery County (a Democrat, Arch was blistered by Republican Glen Beall, later a United States Senator), and on the afternoon or evening of a Senators' road encounter, made of re-creations a happening.

"Remember Roy Campanella saying that 'you have to be a man to play this game, but there has to be a lot of little boy in you too'?" Povich said. "Well, when Arch did re-creations, all the little boy came out. I remember at one point, Arch staged them in the window of People's Drugstore up on G Street," three blocks from the White House, "and he'd be up on the second floor, you know, with the crowd noise and the taped bells going off. As he was doing the games, people would crowd around the store on the sidewalk. And as he broadcast, sweating up a storm, they'd roar."

"What did the town as a whole think of it?" I said.

" 'What'll he think of next?' they were saying. People then called it outrageous," Povich answered. "I don't know what we'd call it now. Probably just fun."

In the drugstore's basement, a studio was soon erected, and in its middle stood a glass booth, encircled by rising tiers. "On every side of the booth were bleachers," McDonald, Jr., said, "and dad would stand in the middle, with the Western Union operators sitting next to him, and as the signals came from the away ball park, he'd restage the game. He always stayed about an inning behind — in case the wires went dead, he'd play it safe that way. If anything bad happened, he'd ad-lib until the wire came back on."

Halting, he replayed the uproar. "Dad would be all set to go, and he'd look out at the bleachers, and they'd be *filled*. People would stand in line to come in, have a seat, and watch dad and the Senators roll."

"At least one out of two's not bad," I said.

"That's the amazing thing," McDonald said. His voice was mellow, soft-spoken. "The club was so *awful*, and it was still so *wild*. Dad had a gong in the booth."

"A *gong?*" I interrupted.

"Oh, sure," he said, talking quickly now, "and when, say, Clint Courtney got a single — he loved Clint — dad would smash it once. Or when Cecil Travis tripled, three hits, or, if Roy Sievers parked one over the left-field fence, he'd belt it four times."

"With a gong," I said, making a faint stab at whimsy, "did that make it a 'Chinese home run'?"

Charitably, McDonald humored my humor. "I don't know," he said, "but people used to tell me, 'Man, it's the best show in town.' "

Arch left the Senators four years before the Senators left Washington. "After they let him go," Siegel said, "he never went to another baseball game. And it was a shame, really, because they *needed* him. God, his impact was tremendous." On October 16, 1960, McDonald traveled with the Redskins to Yankee Stadium; their opponent, the football Giants; the final score, twenty-four all. Boarding the train for return to Washington, McDonald joined colleagues for a game of hearts. There, at the table, he died of a heart attack. He was fifty-nine years old.

At Arch's funeral, friends quoted liberally from "The Old Pine Tree." They did not, however, discuss the events which cushioned and shocked the *reality* of his early years in Washington, for memory (and priorities) had withered, and few cared to live again the seasons of the mid-1930s in which America limply, unevenly convalesced.

By McDonald's second year at Griffith Stadium, acronyms lit official Washington: CCC and AAA, TVA and NRA, SEC and FHA, CWA and FDIC. A postage stamp cost 3¢. Black lynchings occurred at the rate of one every twenty days. Scotch sold for $2.50 a quart. In Boston, the Red Sox' new millionaire owner, Thomas Austin Yawkey, paid $250,000 for Joe Cronin. Bourbon was less expensive: $1.50 a pint. Sally Rand, the bareskin fan dancer, exposed all to entertain. George Herman Ruth retired; "I never saw a ball hit so hard," mourned Pittsburgh's Guy Bush, the victim of Babe's last home run. "He was fat and old, but he still had that great swing." Grant Wood's painting, *Daughters of Revolution*, retreated to a placid, more rustic time. James T. Farrell completed his *Studs Lonigan* trilogy. Leo Durocher, his needle practiced, lanced Brooklyn's Van Lingle Mungo: "He talked like Edgar Bergen doing Mortimer Snerd from the bottom of a well. And he drank a bit. A bit of everything." Bill Dickey said of teammate Gehrig: "Every day, any day, he just goes out and does his job." Most Americans gasped when Caldwell's *God's Little Acre* and Joyce's *Ulysses* were freed of obscenity charges. The Catholic League of Decency thundered: "We will begin to rate the moral quality of motion pictures." In the country's heartland, despair pinned morality's arm. Ignored or exploited since the Civil War, its rich land abused for generations, the rural South saw topsoil crumble and hillsides erode away. Further north and west, out beyond the prairies and Great Plains, winds and drought shriveled and buried farms under currents of sand. Tenant farmers, both black and white, endured the wreckage; poverty, one gleaned, could eclipse even the barriers of race. Charlie Gehringer struck out only sixteen times in 610 at-bats. Joe McCarthy said, "Give a boy a bat and a ball and a place to play and he'll be a good citizen." Still writhing from their 1934 World Series loss, the 1935 Tigers growled again.

Until the networks seized control in the mid-1960s, the Commissioner of Baseball's Office (and, for more than two decades, the Gillette Company) chose announcers for the World Series and All-Star Game: In 1934, for instance, barring Ty Tyson from Series coverage ("too excessively partisan," the good Judge sniffed), Kenesaw Mountain Landis named the troikas of France Laux, Ted Husing, and Pat Flanagan (CBS) and NBC's Tom Manning, Ford Bond, and Graham McNamee. Michiganders had appealed the verdict, fashioned a petition with (huzza) more than six hundred thousand signatures, and Landis half-relented; Tyson could broadcast *locally* over WWJ. Now, with the 1935 Bengals streaking toward another pennant, the word erupted: *This* year, for NBC, Tyson would work the Classic.

"Back then, it was a lousy time to find a job," Gehringer, eighty-three, said at his home in Birmingham, Michigan, "but like John McGraw [actually, Larry Doyle, his second baseman] said about the Giants, it was a great time to be young and a Tiger. Ty had a lot to talk about." Gehringer hit .330, Cochrane .319. Greenberg knocked in 170 runs. Tommy Bridges won twenty-one games. The Tigers broke their all-time attendance record.

"Of course, I wasn't here yet," recited Harwell, then seventeen and an Atlantan, "but after I came to Detroit, I talked with a lot of people who were."

"What did they recall?"

"That it was the same in '35 as it was in 1968 [when the Tigers, rallying, downed St. Louis in the Series], that the club," he said, "was a common denominator," evoking not just exciting baseball, but a tinge of sociology too. "They brought the city together in very tough times — in '68, after that terrible year of urban rioting the previous summer, and before that, in the thirties, when the auto plants had practically shut down."

"A bond," I said.

"Yes. They mean that much to Detroit."

So did Tyson. "I got to know him in his later years," Harwell said. "He used to live where I did, in Grosse Point, to the north of the city, and I'll never forget how on Father's Day of '65 — he would have been in his seventies by then [seventy-seven] — we brought Ty out to Tiger Stadium. He came down on the field, we introduced him to the crowd, and then I put him on the air for an inning. I have to say, it was one of the most popular broadcasts we ever had — overwhelming, the public reaction. People *remembered*. And I guess what *I* remember most about him is Ty's good, dry sense of humor."

"Some claimed it was bitter," I said.

"Let's just say it was droll," he announced, "and leave it at that. Whatever he had, it worked. He enjoyed himself in a quiet sort of way. And maybe it worked because there was nobody to compare him with. He didn't have a tough act to follow."

"In fact," I said, "he had *no* act to follow."

"That always makes it easier, and so did the lack of pressure back then," Harwell said. "Ty told me that when his station finally accepted a sponsor for the first time — Mobil — you know all they wanted? For Ty to say at the start of the broadcast, 'This game is brought to you by Mobil Oil,' and then at the end, 'This game has been brought to you by Mobil Oil.' That was it. Let me tell you, things should be that uncomplicated now."

In 1934, Ty Tyson gained a sponsor. He also gained a competitor.

For seventeen seasons (1916–32), Harry Edwin Heilmann was a solid, combative ballplayer, a self-made hitter who averaged .342 and (on July 21, 1952) was inducted into the Hall of Fame. His four batting titles draped odd years: .394 in 1921, .403 in 1923, .395 in 1925, .398 in 1927. "Mr. Navin [Frank, the Tigers' owner] would give me a two-year contract," he said, "and I'd take it easy the second year." Even Heilmann's *easy* riveted: in 1922, .356; in '24, .346; in '26, .367; in 1928, a vigorous .328. Like Al Kaline, a similar, hard-working orb, he practiced and persevered and played with pain; his consistency rivaled the noonday whistle. Beset by arthritis, Heilmann retired in 1932. Two years later, he took a job broadcasting baseball over the Michigan Radio Network, owned by businessman George W. Trendle, the originator of radio's "The Lone Ranger" and "Call of the Yukon."

As an announcer, the early Heilmann resembled a Boy George on the Metropolitan Opera. He favored slang; he painted word-pictures by number; he met the English language and, ambushed, fled behind his Maginot Line. "People said that when he started," Harwell said, "to put it kindly, he wasn't very smooth." But he knew his baseball and he loved his stories, and he took lessons in English and elocution, and slowly, "He got better, working at it as he had his hitting, and he stayed on the air long enough to become popular in his own right" — seventeen years on the field, seventeen years (1934–50) above it.

"During the war, we went to Egypt and got talking to the servicemen there,' Heilmann would say, the Tigers' game unfolding below, Greenberg standing wide-legged at the plate, "and the same question kept coming up again. They asked it wherever we went: 'Who is a better second baseman, Joe Gordon or Bobby Doerr?' A ball outside to big Number Five, Hank almost went for it, one and one. So I kept answering the guys and my answer was always the same: 'Charlie Gehringer.' There's ball two, high and inside."

Unlike most, the Tigers' Network was two-pronged: Tyson broadcast to metropolitan Detroit; Heilmann, over flagship station WXYZ, to out-state Michigan. "It was unique, the way it operated. For years, these two guys broadcast games against each other. They were rivals in a sense," Harwell said. "If you were in the Upper Peninsula or western Michigan, you heard Heilmann. If you lived in Detroit or in some nearby area where you could pick up WWJ [Maynard Good Stoddard, and his torrents of memory], you got Ty. And I have to think that Tyson, being more popular, got the better of it," until, in 1942, Ty retired and the networks merged. Ironically, if not poetically, with Heilmann dying of cancer, Tyson returned in 1951 for the first of two final years of play-by-play. They buried H. Heilmann on July 12, 1951, on the eve of the All-Star Game at Briggs Stadium. In Detroit, even now, some still echo: "You can take your Barbers and Gowdys and McNamees and Cosells. We'll never have another like the Old Slug."

Heilmann never broadcast a World Series; among them, Tyson, Barber, and McNamee covered twenty-nine. Their spheres intersected in October 1935, a clatter of change and improvisation: the Ol' Redhead's first Fall Classic, the King's last, the second sponsored by the Ford Motor Company, and the first under a three-network umbrella.

The instrument of much of this intrigue was the stick-framed figure newspapermen called the Czar, the Boss, the Second-Most Powerful Man in America (none of whose appellations survived his death), the being who bleached baseball white after the Black Sox Scandal and who accepted the commissionership on unconditional terms: "the authority to do anything I consider right in any matter detrimental to baseball." In 1934, negotiating with Henry Ford, Judge Landis had styled a four-year, $400,000 World Series contract; until then, the event lacked radio sponsors. Fifteen months later, he named announcers for the Series' two perennial networks: for CBS, Laux of KMOX, Truman Bradley of WBBM, and WHK's Graney, the first former player to cover the convention; for NBC, pooling its Red and Blue outlets, Hal Totten of WMAQ, Tyson of WWJ, Boake Carter, the Philco Inquiring Reporter, and an aging McNamee. Next, on October 1, the day before the Series opener, Landis midwived its third network.

Five months earlier, the Mutual Broadcasting System had been born a Caesarian; its first sports event was major league baseball's first night game — May 24, 1935, at Crosley Field. The new entablature included only three columns: WOR in New York, WGN in Chicago, and CKLW in Detroit, and when Mutual asked Landis for official blessing as a network (thus enabled, like CBS and NBC, to carry the Series), the Judge, reclaiming Mt. Sinai, bellowed "No!" — except. Except if Mutual could persuade WLW in Cincinnati to join *its* network, deserting NBC. The general manager of WLW, John Clark, sputtered "Yes!" — if. If the network would allow the local broadcaster, Red Barber, to cover Mutual's Oktoberfest. Mutual consented, Barber hurtled a train to Detroit, and on October 2, in a game where the Cubs' Lon Warneke four-hit the Tigers, 3-0, at sepulchral Navin Field, Barber, Quin Ryan, and Bob Elson (of nine network icons, four worked in Chicago) formed Mutual's first World Series trinity.

Landis did *not* engineer one injunction: NBC's removal of McNamee from Fall Classic play-by-play, his first on-air absence since 1922. The *St. Louis Post-Dispatch* wrote, in vivid understatement, "McNamee was dropped at the last minute." He would simply "appear at the Series," the network stated; not to do color, not to grace the microphone, but to glad hand and show the flag, a demeaning, vainglorious end. The Judge, however, *did* issue an even larger credo: Dismissing the importunities of CBS President William Paley, he ordered Ted Husing banned from this (or any) baseball (i.e., World Series). Paley's director of sports, the aureole who owned college football and would make the Orange Bowl a New Year's rite, Husing had broadcast the Classic since 1928. But success, moaned Landis, made him heedless, and in 1934, he defamed Series umpiring as "some of the worst I've ever seen." Presently, on the morning of Game One, Landis bumped against Husing's transgression. "There is one announcer, you gentlemen know him," he declared to Bradley, Barber, and Totten, "who isn't here, and I don't have to go into that."

Because of Landis, other notables also missed the 1935 World Series: Bill Munday of the Southeast's clay and pine, a left-handed pitcher for the University of Georgia, former *Atlanta Journal* sportswriter, 1929–34 NBC commentator, and the first to call football's end zone "the Promised Land"; Bill Slater, a graduate of the U.S. Military Academy, ex-headmaster of Brooklyn's Adelphi Academy, network pigskin mugwump, and moderator of radio's "20 Questions"; Harry Wismer, an extrovert and con man, bullhorn of college and professional football, and in the early 1960s, majority stockholder of the New York Titans; and Bill Stern, a national magnifico — newsreel host, ghosted author and magazine poseur, weekly autocrat of Colgate-Palmolive's network program, NBC broadcaster and director of sports. Vigorous men, yes, and absorbing announcers. But not *baseball* men, and not baseball *announcers*. "The World Series is for people who work and love this game," Landis glowered hours before its opening pitch. "You know baseball," he told Tyson. "You work it all year. And you can express what you know. *That* — and *only* that — is the reason you're here."

Unchallenged, Judge Landis swaggered (does anyone remember how opponents said of Thomas E. Dewey, "He is the only man who can strut sitting down"?). Meanwhile, Congress passed the Neutrality Act, forbidding the sale of arms and other materials to "belligerents" (a polemic opponents often cast at Landis). Italy invaded Ethiopia. Huey P. Long, Jr., "the Kingfish," forty-two, was murdered. Margaret Mitchell's *Gone with the Wind* was published. Hitler remilitarized the Rhineland. FDR won a second term, carrying forty-six states to Alf Landon's two ("As Maine goes," jeered James A. Farley, "so goes Vermont"). In England, renouncing empire for "the woman I love," Edward VIII abdicated; George VI succeeded him. In Spain, enter Civil War; in China, the Japanese; in America, Walt Disney's *Snow White*.

By 1936, the first year in the Tigers' history that Detroit could call out, "defending world champions," thirteen teams in the major leagues regularly broadcast baseball. Only in New York, where the sum of radio's fascination, and the response it lured among many listeners, was a phenomenon not without its mysteries (and where, two years earlier, the Dodgers, Yankees, and Giants had signed a five-year pact shunning the medium through 1938), did the entity of baseball lack its sounds and profiles.

"Colonel Ruppert [Jacob, the Yankees' owner] and Ed Barrow, the team's general manager, were very afraid of radio. At this time, they were totally opposed," recalled Mel Allen.

"What about the Giants?" I asked.

"Same for them," he said. "Charles Stoneham [their owner] was dead set against it, and when he died, his son [Horace] took over [in 1936]. And his reaction was absolutely, adamantly against."

"And the Dodgers?"

"As far as Brooklyn went, this was before they got Larry MacPhail," he said, "they were so fouled up internally — ownership squabbles, money problems, and all — that they pretty much just went along with what the other two did." Softly caustic laughter. "So what you had, it's incredible, really, was baseball taking off on radio all around the country while here in New York — the communications capital of the world — Jiminy Cricket, you couldn't hear a game."

Minus radio, if a New Yorker ignored the newspaper (in 1936, the city had thirteen English-speaking dailies; who could?), one missed little which would disturb him. The 1936–37 Giants won two pennants and left-hander "King Carl" Hubbell won twenty-four straight games. Heywood Broun wrote: "During the reign of Hubbell, first base itself was a marathon route." From 1936 through 1939, the Yankees cascaded across the American League; their nearest rival trailed by 19½, 13, 9½, and 17 games. In 1936, every regular but two batted higher than .300; Gehrig's forty-nine home runs led the league; Charles (Red) Ruffing enacted the first of four consecutive twenty-victory seasons. Two years later, Joe DiMaggio (.381) won his first batting title, the last right-handed hitter to clear .380. All told, the 1936–39 Yankees won sixteen World Series games to opponents' three. Even in Brooklyn, with its hardy band of loyalists, frustration took a nap. The 1936 Dodgers, managed by Casey Stengel, attracted only 490,000 fans and lost eighty-seven games; three years later, under Leo Durocher, they finished 84–69 and nearly drew a million.

Elsewhere, three outsiders knew a commiserating sadness. The Browns and Athletics shared the 1936–39 cellar. On the outfield wall at Baker Bowl, in the center of an advertisement for Lifebuoy soap, a discerning fan wrote, "The Phillies use Lifebuoy and they still stink." Not all exuded misanthropy. The White Sox' Luke Appling hit .388, highest ever for a shortstop. On August 23, 1936, for his major-league debut, Bob Feller fanned fifteen Browns; in September, he struck out seventeen A's to tie the league record. Joe Medwick won the 1937 Triple Crown. Congress stilled Roosevelt's quest to "pack" the Supreme Court. Joe Louis became heavyweight champion of the globe. In 1938, Greenberg wafted fifty-eight home runs; Foxx tagged fifty. Traded by St. Louis, Dizzy Dean (who, in 1947, would lecture about "Radio Announcing I Have Did" and propose this thawing of the Cold War: "I'd get me a bunch of bats and balls and sneak me a couple of empires and learn them kids behind the Iron Curtain how to tote a bat and play baseball. . . . And if Joe Stallion knowed how much money they was in the concessions at a ball park, he'd get outta politics and get in a honest business") helped the Cubs win a pennant. Johnny Vander Meer threw two straight no-hitters. Orson Welles jolted normality with "War of the Worlds." Stubby Ernie Lombardi, his legs clustered furrows of muscle, stole only eight bases in 1,853 games; in 1938, he also became the second catcher to win a batting championship. Striving to be neighborly, new Cubs' owner P. K. Wrigley announced: "In deference to people living around our ball park, we will install lights" — pause; the audience grows eager — "only if the standards can be disguised as trees." Adolf Hitler seized Austria. *Krystal Nacht* rocked Germany. Overseas, the age shook with contention. In Brooklyn, the age shook with Larry MacPhail.

At Crosley Field, MacPhail had rescued a moribund settlement, proving that though volcanic, he could be creative. He was frontal and intractable; deference seldom pierced his outer barrier, but obsessive candor did. He treasured his reputation as a baseball Balboa, severe and tart-tongued and visionary. He was a builder of teams and a user of men. He made history move his way. Now, in 1938, National League officials proposed MacPhail to forestall an impending Dodger bankruptcy; their charge, to resurrect the indebted Brooklyn franchise. Reluctantly, the Dodgers' directors agreed to meet the league's intended. More surprising, they approved his terms: as title, executive vice-president; as authority, "full and complete . . . over the operation of the club"; as salary, to rise with home attendance; as dessert, an unlimited expense account.

"He took over," Red Barber wrote, "in the last year of that five-year radio ban among the three New York clubs." At Ebbets Field, MacPhail installed lights and cleansed the ball park; stocked the Dodgers' farm system, the assembly line of baseball; acquired Hugh Casey and Dolph Camilli, Pete Reiser and Medwick and Pee Wee Reese; named Durocher as Brooklyn's player-manager; and in late 1938, within months of his arrival, violated the inviolate. The Dodgers, MacPhail scalded, would *not* renew the radio abridgement. They would take to the wireless in 1939, home *and* away, their games broadcast exclusively (Brooklyn received $77,000 in rights) over WOR (a 50,000-watt station) and announced by Barber, formerly of WLW, Cincinnati, and, ultimately, *The Sporting News* 1939 Announcer of the Year. What of the Yankees and Giants? They could, cursed MacPhail, do as they preferred. What they preferred, of course, was for MacPhail to sail up the Hudson River, leaving the boycott intact. Failing that, acquiescence; they must broadcast too.

Buoyed by Barber, a firmament of recognizable talent, respected for the quality of his craft, and sponsored by Mobil Oil, Proctor and Gamble's Ivory Soap, and General Mills' new food, Wheaties, the Breakfast of Champions, Dodgers' broadcasts became a Flatbush institution. Away, by re-creation, and from tiny, irregular Ebbets Field, *live*, radio coverage of all regular-season games nurtured the sunlight before Brooklyn's carnage, the *affaire de coeur* before the O'Malley heist.

"There were 3 million people in Brooklyn," Barber said, "and if every one of them wasn't rooting for the Dodgers, every one seemed to be." Many also rooted for the Giants and Yankees, airing home contests from polar sides of the Harlem River. When MacPhail first floated the 154-game balloon, Eddie Brannick, the Giants' road secretary, threatened to "blast me into the [East] River" if the broadcasts arose. They had; he had not. The two Dodgers' rivals shared one station, WABC; they covered no away outings; their principal announcer, McDonald, was no Ol' Redhead; and while The Old Pine Tree's assistant made of baseball a carnival, as the thirties ended, Dodgers' radio loomed first among equals. Raucous, almost magically devoted, the Faithful flocked to Bedford Avenue, and with play-by-play blanketing a borough (on summer evenings, with the car window down, one could drive by front stoops and candy stores and not miss a pitch), Brooklyn baseball stirred a kinship and zealotry — a zany, misplaced sense that "baseball belongs to the fans" — that had not previously impelled The Game, and that has not embraced it since.

For the first time, all sixteen teams broadcast games and cheered the promise of radio. Neville Chamberlain chose appeasement. T. S. Williams joined the Boston Red Sox. The Third Reich swallowed Czechoslovakia. Eight dates into the 1939 season, Lou Gehrig left the Yankees' lineup; his dying cry, 2,130 straight games. In more than fifteen thousand movie houses, one could follow Garbo and Barrymore and Rogers and Astaire. On May 17, NBC Television — using one camera and announcer Bill Stern — offered its first sports event: a baseball game, Columbia v. Princeton at Manhattan's Baker Field. To the *New York Times*, "It was apparent that considerable progress has been made in the technical requirements and apparatus for this sort of outdoor pickup where the action is fast."

John Steinbeck's *Grapes of Wrath* was published, its "Okies" a national flame. Jack Benny and Fred Allen dueled on NBC Radio. Baseball dedicated the Hall of Fame, Judge Landis presiding. The populace gyrated to the King of Swing. Clark Gable said, "Frankly, my dear, I don't give a damn." On July 4, the Iron Horse gave a speech. "I consider myself," he told the crowd at Yankee Stadium, "the luckiest man on the face of the earth." Gillette bought exclusive rights to the World Series and, ending multiple coverage, awarded the pageant to the Mutual Broadcasting System: its announcers, Bob Elson and Walter Barber. The Reds neared their second pennant; the Yankees would sweep the Series.

Each week, "the Songbird of the South," CBS's inescapably popular Kate Smith, opened her program with, "Hello, everybody"; presenting her to the visiting king of England, FDR said, "This *is* America." On August 22, 1939, Hitler and Joseph Stalin — Truman's future "Uncle Joe" — signed the Russo-German Nonaggression Pact. On August 26, in a year where broadcasting totaled only 7 percent of baseball's revenue, NBC Television (this time, with *two* cameras) again bewitched. Over station W2XBS, its cinema viewed in a handful of homes, the network bestowed the first major-league telecast: the Reds and Dodgers at Ebbets Field. "This is Red Barber speaking," the broadcast began. "Let me say hello to you all." Five days later, as German Panzer tanks crossed the Polish frontier, the world said hello to hell.

4
Words

"Language is the archives of poetry.
Language is fossil poetry."
— Ralph Waldo Emerson

THE BABE'S FINEST HOUR

We're in the first half of the fifth inning of the World Series game between the New York Yankees and the Chicago Cubs. The score, 4 to 3, in favor of the Yanks. Charlie Root is in the box for Chicago, and the first man up in this inning will be the mighty Babe Ruth. Babe has already hit a home run with two on — and now, as we look out into the outfield, they're shifting just slightly over into right-center field. And there comes Babe out of the Yankee dugout now, swinging his big club, and the crowd gives him a standing ovation. He seems to be having some kind of an argument with the boys on the Chicago bench. They're been ribbing Babe Ruth all afternoon. They've been warned several times by the umpire to get back there on the bench or he'd chase them to the showers! Now the fans are ribbing Babe as well! Ah, but looking down there at the smiling face of Babe Ruth, he's taking it good naturedly! And now he doffs his cap in acknowledgment for his first plaudits.

Babe Ruth steps into the batter's box. Now Charlie Root gets the sign from his catcher, Gabby Hartnett. Here's the first pitch. And it's a strike — right down the middle! And the fans are certainly giving it to Babe Ruth now. Looking over at the Cubs' bench, the Cubs are all up on the top step. And they're yelling "flatfoot" and throwing liniment and everything else at Babe Ruth! But he steps out of the batter's box. He takes a hitch in his trousers, knocks the dust off his shoes. And now he's back in there again. And Root winds up again and here it comes! And it's outside — and it's evened up on Babe Ruth! Boy, what a powerful figure he is at that plate! And once again, Root gets the signal, winds up, and here it comes . . . and it's called strike two! And the fans are giving it to him from all corners of this Wrigley Field. The Cubs are up on the bench — they're all hoping that Babe Ruth will strike out. Again, Charlie Root winds up. And here's that pitch — and it's high inside, and it drove Babe Ruth out of the batter's box! And the count is ball two and strike two. And, boy, the Cubs are giving it to Babe now!   •

Oh, oh, Babe Ruth has stepped out of the batter's box. And he steps about two feet away from home plate. Now he steps toward the Cubs' dugout! We thought for a moment that he was going over and toss his bat at them or something! No, he's smiling at them! He takes off his hat, he holds up his two fingers with his right hand. Now he drops his bat and he's indicating that the count is ball two and strike two. He gets back into the batter's box. The umpire again warns the Cubs! Charlie Root gets his signal. And Babe Ruth steps out of the batter's box again! He's holding up his two and two. Oh, oh, and now Babe Ruth is pointing out to center field and he's yelling at the Cubs that the next pitch over is going into center field! . . . Someone just tossed a lemon down there. Babe Ruth has picked up the lemon and now he tosses it over to the Cubs' bench. He didn't throw anything, he sort of

41

kicked it over there. After he turns, he points again to center field!
And here's the pitch . . . It's going! Babe Ruth connects and here it goes! The ball is
going, going, going—high into the center-field stands, into the scoreboard! And it's a home
run! It's gone! Whoopee! Listen to that crowd!

—TOM MANNING, October 1, 1932.

Wrigley Field, Chicago, IL. Years later, the debate still bubbles. Did he or
didn't he? Did sport's most full-sized figure truly "call his shot," and with one
arc of his cumbrous bat, make his brazen fantasies real? Among principals, the
recollections still vary; not so for George Herman (Babe) Ruth's steadfast eminence in American mythology and lore.

FINALLY, FOR DETROIT, A ROAR

The crowd has become surprisingly quiet here in Detroit. Mickey Cochrane, the potential
winning run, is at second. Larry French goes into the stretch. The southpaw delivers. Goose
Goslin swings and the ball is hit into right-center! And it's going to drop in—it does!
Cochrane is heading for home. And here comes the throw—but it's too late! And Cochrane
scores. The Tigers are the world champions of baseball! This stadium is absolutely mad!

—JOHN HARRINGTON, October 7, 1935.

Navin Field, Detroit, MI. Four times, the Tigers had won the American League
pennant; four times, October wrought catastrophe. Now, with Detroit ahead,
three games to two, World Series redemption. Entering the ninth inning of Game
Six, Mickey Cochrane singled, took second base on an infield out, and scored
on Goose Goslin's single. Final score: 4 to 3, Tigers. Wrote Grantland Rice:
"The leaning tower can now crumble and find its level with the Pisan plain.
The Hanging Garden can grow up in weeds. After waiting forty-eight years,
the Detroit Tigers at last are champions of the world."

FOUR OF A KIND

Once again Coffman gets a new ball in shape to pitch. Standing out there motionless, now
he glances toward third. Toes the rubber, starts his windup. Here it is. It's a fastball and
Lazzeri flies to right field. It's over in the stands for a home run! A home run in the lower
deck in right field chasing home Gehrig, and now Dickey, and here comes Powell, and
Lazzeri jogs on in and stabs the plate for the fourth run on that hit! This has been quite
an inning for the Yanks.

—FRANCE LAUX, October 2, 1936.

The Polo Grounds, New York, NY. Ten years earlier, enfeebled by Grover
Cleveland Alexander, Tony Lazzeri had fanned in the seventh game of the World

Series, sealing a corpeslike still. Today, in Game Two of the first "Subway Series" since 1923, his grand-slam thunderclap helped lambaste the Giants, 18–4.

A ground ball to Gehrig. Scoops it up, touches the bag for the third out . . . and the 1936 World Series is over. The final score . . . Yankees, 13 runs, 17 hits, 2 errors . . . the Giants, 5 runs, 9 hits, 1 error.

—F. L., 10/6/36.

The Polo Grounds. Of Joe McCarthy's seven world champions, none were more redoubtable than the 1936 Yankees. Buoyed by a latter-day Murderers Row, Marse Joe downed the Giants, four games to two, the first of four straight Series titles. For McCarthy, the dynasty was retributive; critics had termed him a "push-button manager." Others bequeathed a more enduring sobriquet: the greatest field leader of all time.

"LORD GOD ALMIGHTY"

It's official now. There won't be another inning. National League President Ford Frick is in the press box, and the umpires have passed up the word. It's now or never. Gabby swings—he hits it! It's a long, long drive—way, way back into left-center! Lloyd Waner is racing back. It's going, it's going. It might be, it may be! It is! Home run! The Cubs win it, 6 to 5!

—QUIN RYAN, September 28, 1938.

Wrigley Field, Chicago, IL. In a park that had no lights, it was a home run that almost no one saw. Only ten days earlier, Pittsburgh had led second-place Chicago by three-and-one-half games; now, with its edge reduced to one-half game, the two clubs began the final inning, tied, 5–5, on a dank gloaming of an afternoon. The umpires, conferring, unveiled their mandate: If neither team scored in inning nine, the game would be called because of darkness. The Pirates fell meekly, as did Chicago's first two batters. Enter Gabby Hartnett, the Cubs' player-manager, to face relief pitcher Mace Brown. The Bucco threw, the Cubbie swung, and the ball attacked the left-field seats. "A lot of people have told me they didn't know the ball was in the bleachers," Hartnett recalled years later. "Well, I did— maybe I was the only one in the park who did." Wondered Cubs' second baseman Billy Herman: "Lord God Almighty."

OL' DIZ'S LAST HURRAH

There's the pitch. A hard-hit fly ball going far out into left field! Reynolds goes near it and the ball is over the fence for a home run! Over the fence for a home run! Crosetti hitting a home run over the left-center-field fence—driving in Hoag ahead of him and putting the Yankees out in front by a score of 4 to 3. The first home run of the Series is hit by Frankie

Crosetti in the first half of the eighth inning. He drives in two runs and the Yankees are out in front by a score of 4 to 3 as the complexion of this game has been completely changed!

—JOHN CARMICHAEL, October 6, 1938.

Wrigley Field, Chicago, IL. "I may not have been the greatest pitcher ever, but I was amongst 'em," boasted Jay Hanna (Dizzy) Dean. He may have also owned the greatest heart. In Game Two of the 1938 World Series, wearied by age and injury, Ol' Diz—throwing only what he dubbed his "nothin' ball"—muffled the Yankees on intransigence and control. Pitching for the Cubs, ahead, 3-2, Dean faced Frank Crosetti with one out in the eighth inning. The Crow's ensuing home run downed Chicago; it also marked the last grand moment of Dean's sun-dazzled career. "You never would have done that if I'd had my fastball!" Diz screamed as Crosetti circled the bases. Replied the New York shortstop: "Diz, damned if you ain't right."

RAPID ROBERT

And down goes Chet Laabs for the third strike! That makes it eighteen for Bob Feller—a new major-league record!

—BOB NEAL, October 2, 1938.

Municipal Stadium, Cleveland, OH. From Bob Feller of Van Meter, Iowa, baseball evoked more than gingerly enthusiasm. Still only nineteen, the sharp-edged prodigy bested Dizzy Dean's single-game strikeout record (seventeen, set in 1933) on the last day of the regular season. Ironically, Feller was the losing pitcher, bowing to the Tigers, 4-1.

Grannie Mack is on the ground with one knee, scoops it up with his glove hand, flips it over to Trosky at first. A close decision—and he's out! Bob Feller has his first no-hit game. Boy, listen to that crowd!

—JACK GRANEY, April 16, 1940.

Comiskey Park, Chicago, IL. Feller began this season with comparable austerity—throwing the first opening-day hitless game in American League history. His triumph pierced the White Sox, 1-0; he would pitch two additional no-hitters; twenty-two years later, he entered the Hall of Fame.

5
Stargazer
(1940–50)

"Why, man, he doth bestride the narrow
world/ like a colossus;"
—William Shakespeare, *Julius
Caesar*

BETWEEN 1939 (BASEBALL'S FIRST SEASON OF TELEVISION) AND 1951 (VIA THE
kinetic tube, its first truly national World Series), twelve teams won at least
a single pennant; the other four grasped the first division. Recalling and ap-
preciating the time — the last decade to have a .400 hitter or a pitcher complete
more than thirty-five games in a season or the Cleveland Indians win a World
Series; the first (excluding the Cubs) to have all teams play at night (the Tigers,
straggling, installed lights in 1948) and broadcast virtually every game on radio
and televise (if infrequently) and have a black major leaguer (Jack Roosevelt
Robinson) and a one-armed outfielder (the inherently heroic Pete Gray) and
a team that drew more than 2 million spectators (in 1946) and a pennant race
that ended in a tie (same year); the first *and* last in which a "Subway [here,
Streetcar] Series" rose west of the Mississippi River and a batter hit safely
in fifty-six consecutive games — one marveled at the anniversaries in which
baseball has been rich.

Eight times, a league championship was decided in the final game of the
final week; on twelve occasions, the winning margin was three games or less.
As they developed, the years 1940–50 became baseball's most competitive
epoch. One did not go to Ebbets Field, Comiskey Park, or Municipal Stadium
to witness thick-haired mascots, Antaean promotion ploys, and exploding
scoreboards that lit fireworks in the night. Riveting baseball was the major-
league attraction, and a wonder of the 1940s was their entanglement of
cacophony and detail.

The decade rose with catharsis. In 1919, Cincinnati had won its first pennant
and World Series; the Classic, belatedly, was seen as fixed. Now, twenty-one
years later, Paul Derringer and Bucky Walters won forty-two decisions and
the Reds, blitzing second-place Brooklyn by a dozen games, became the first
contemporary team to win successive pennants without one future Hall of
Famer on its roster. At Briggs Stadium, four regulars hit more than .300,
Hank Greenberg led the American League in home runs and RBIs, and the
much-traveled, roguishly round Louis Norman (Bobo) Newsom (who moved
from one team to another *sixteen* times, caused a teammate to warble, "Bobo

45

has a rubber arm and a head to match," and was [re]acquired by Washington in five different seasons; "the reason's simple," a writer said. "Clark Griffith just loves to play pinochle with him") won twenty-one games as Detroit, axing Cleveland on the final weekend, won its sixth league title and third in seven years: a partial recompense for past Tigers' decades of glutting decline.

Sans Yankees for the first time since 1935, the World Series of 1940 still flaunted New York announcers: the literate, observant, Mississippi-born Voice of the Dodgers, only thirty-two, of whom a Brooklyn taxi driver groused, "That Barber, he's too fair," and a former speech instructor and recent law graduate of the University of Alabama, at twenty-seven now the Voice of the Yankees, whose "Hello there, everybody, this is Mel Allen" would become a national idiom and whose voice was the voice of a friend.

Batting for the Mutual Broadcasting System, in its second year of exclusive coverage, and selected by Gillette, the Series' radio sponsor, they expanded the perimeters of play-by-play fluency; as one decade supplanted another, they earned the appellations *folk hero* and *avatar*; and in a nation where baseball was a meritocracy, they fostered, in a rich and even magical way, a golden age of broadcasting.

Between them, announcing for fifty-nine years, they covered thirty-three World Series and twenty-nine All-Star Games. "Even now, when Americans talk about baseball voices, you have to start with Mel Allen and Red Barber," said Vin Scully, a Dodgers' announcer since 1950. "And there are a lot of folks who believe that when you think 'truly great,' you stop there too." They stirred a country. Among contemporaries in the life of baseball, they, alone, became *bigger* than life. They dimmed banality's spirit and spoke — years later, after their exit from daily coverage, to former listeners grown old — of common memory, distant childhood, and a yearning for a sense of time standing still.

They also appealed, more often than not, to different constituencies. Barber was the critics' choice; Allen, the orb of Everyfan. Detached, Barber reported; involved, Allen roared. The Ol' Redhead broadcast as a prim and orderly phoneticist, born of the South's polite, decorous respectability; The Voice cheered even a hard-hit ground ball. Barber was white wine, crêpes suzette, and bluegrass music. Allen was beer (Ballantine, naturally), hot dogs, and the United States Marine Band. Barber's voice was cultured, silken; Allen's was extraordinary. Barber etched; like Astaire, he was a poet. Allen roused; like Sinatra, he was a balladeer. Red sat back on the small of his chair, flanked by a three-minute eggtimer (a reminder, to give the score), and chatted, as around a pot-bellied stove, soft-voiced and evocative. Mel moved up to the edge of his seat — "You just couldn't get into the game as well if you leaned back" — and filibustered, often brilliantly, for hours.

"Barber was a professional *southerner*. He used all the phrases they had down there — 'rhubarb,' you know, or 'the catbird seat,' totally foreign to Brooklyn — and he *worked* at being a personality. But when Mel came up with 'How about that!' he was just using a phrase they'd had in the South for twenty years. His sayings came naturally to him; they weren't put on. And neither was his knowledge." Pause. "He was the best *ever* to broadcast the game. It wasn't Barber — it was Mel," said Lindsey Nelson, formerly the Voice of NBC's "Major League Baseball," then of the New York Mets, and among the most appealing of announcers.

Fastidious, more shy than stuffy, Barber was a rationalist in an emotive profession. Luminous and unrelenting, Allen's broadcast mien had a swagger to its stride. Off-air, Barber was more reserved than solicitous; Allen, more gentle than hard. One applauded Barber. One remembered Allen. One admired Barber as a theatre would a soloist. One felt for Allen almost familial affection. The Ol' Redhead advised, "Never raise your voice. Never yell. When the crowd yells, shut up." The Voice countered, "The waves of noise shoved you up. When the crowd shouted, you would too." With Barber, the radio/television booth turned lyrical platform. With Allen, one could become excited to a ridiculous extent. Barber was full of rectitude and repulsed by prejudice; "to care, to root," he said, "they are not the rights of the professional announcer." Allen believed, "Of course, I had to be partisan." Millions of Yankees' fans regarded him as a Valiant. Others, echoing Irving Howe (a Yankee-hater?), thought of the Big Ball Park and jibed of its showman, "We know the nightmare is ours."

Listening daily, you were driven toward one or the other. You paid your money (or rather, sponsors did) and you took your choice (or rather, in Brooklyn, "cherce").

"Red played it consummately down the middle, an impeccable broadcaster with his down-home charm. Allen was the more volatile — just a tremendous voice, with a flair for the moment; he came on the air, right off the bat, that voice — boom, it just grabbed you," said Bob Prince, the long-time Voice of the Pirates, *his* voice strong and familiar, to whom the contrasting styles hid a private irony. "Red was less melodramatic than Mel, but no less a student of the game. Barber would give biblical allusions. Mel'd give you his terms and catchwords."

"You know them both," I said. "When they signed off, how did they compare?"

Brushing against his desk, the Gunner smiled. "*That's* the interesting part," he said. "Red was more standoffish — it was a struggle to get to him, but once you did, it was worth it. He was just very much a loner. Mel, on the other hand, wasn't always confident of himself. He could be easily hurt, exactly the opposite of his image — to the nation, he was crowing, assured — and he was tremendously sensitive and had a humanity that isn't always true of broadcasters. It was amazing, for a guy that went as high as Mel did — as high as you can go — that he had almost a total lack of ego, which, of course, is one reason his peers were so fond of him."

John Hutchens, former book critic and radio editor of the *New York Times*, enunciated another school. "I liked him," he said of Barber. "I sat in his booth at Ebbets Field, came to know him, and to me, he was a good, competent, straightaway announcer. Allen had some screwy phrases, and people would make fun of them. That was never true of Red." Joe Falls, the Detroit columnist, agreed. "It's Barber—he was the best baseball broadcaster I ever heard. He taught me about the intricacies of the game while giving me a feeling for baseball that I have never lost. This man introduced me to baseball in a way that was simply beautiful."

Jim Woods, who joined Allen and Barber in 1954–56 to form the most elegant (as opposed, with "Monday Night Football," to notorious) trio in the history of broadcasting, plucked at their complexities. "Red was more outwardly religious than Mel," he said. "At Cincinnati, he'd been pretty loose, but when he got ill [in 1948, of a hemorrhaged ulcer], he found the Word and his personality changed. After a game, he'd go up to his room; Mel would circulate in a restaurant, table-hopping; he loved the attention. On the air, yes, both were professionals—one was a machine-gun; the other, a violin. But privately, Mel had a more exuberant sense of fun, sort of on the corny side. Red's humor was more, well, sometimes you had to think for a moment and wonder, '*What* the hell'd he say?' Once I asked him, 'What you been up to, Red?' He said, 'Oh, I've been killing rats.' So I said, 'How do you do that?' And he came back, 'You see, you kill one here and you kill one there.' " The gravel voice exploded. "You know, Red's a friend and I *still* don't know what the hell he meant."

"Mel had a style and delivery, a certain something, that made you want to listen to this man," mused Nat Allbright, who re-created games for thirteen years (1950–62) on the Brooklyn (then, Los Angeles) Dodgers' Radio Network. "Red's approach was more homespun, less rapid-fire. But the biggest difference was that Mel was easy to talk to—very lighthearted." Finally, Scully, hired by the Redhead and, quite literally, his protégé: "I worked with Mel," he related, "and he was excellent. But Red, when he's said I'm like the son he didn't have, he was my teacher—and my father. It wasn't so much that he taught me how to broadcast. It was an *attitude*. Do your homework. Be prepared. Be accurate. He was a stickler for that. He was very much a taskmaster."

By his second season with the Dodgers, Barber towered, enlarging Brooklyn's vocabulary and touching the borough, the most respected announcer in baseball. "He and I were very much alike," Bob Elson, immodestly and perhaps inaccurately, proclaimed. "We both made a *living* from baseball, and we both followed the box scores. But we were first and foremost *newsmen*, not some jock announcer, and we both followed the news of the front page and outside world more continually, more avidly, than anything some sports page might headline."

In 1940, the Old Commander asked, as Barber did also, whether America could survive its isolationism. From Aid-the-Allies and America-First, answers cleaved. Because they saw the world differently, they would not concede the other's sight. The new census waggled, "131,669,275." Thomas Wolfe's *You Can't Go Home Again* appeared posthumously. Did politics stop at the water's edge? "That Man" thought so, naming Republican secretaries of the navy (Frank Knox) and war (Henry Stimson). James Stewart won an Oscar for *The Philadelphia Story*. Carl Sandburg won a Pulitzer for *Abraham Lincoln: The War*

Years. As the year's shadow lengthened, American "neutrality" became a sham: Congress approved the sale of surplus war materiel to Great Britain; Roosevelt transferred fifty overaged destroyers. In Washington, debate assaulted the Burke-Wadsworth Act. "Enact peacetime conscription," wailed Montana Senator Burton K. Wheeler, "and no longer will this be a free land."

Dominoes littered the European continent: in April, Norway and Denmark; in May and June, the Low Countries and France. In Rome, Italy declared war on France and Britain. "On this tenth day of June," said FDR, "the hand that held the dagger has struck it into the back of its neighbor." On June 22, the Third French Republic surrendered at Compiègne; for the world's "finest army," encamped behind the world's "most impregnable line," humiliation. Only England, its character formed from welded steel, stood between Hitler and "the abyss of a New Dark Age," warned its new prime minister, Winston Churchill, "made more sinister, perhaps more protracted, by the lights of perverted science." Leon Trotsky, the exiled Russian war minister, was murdered with an ice pick in Mexico. The American electorate confronted a different pick: the 1940 presidential election. Seeking a third term, Roosevelt faced, said Harold Ickes, "a simple, barefoot, Wall Street lawyer." The Republican galleries in Philadelphia thundered, "We Want [Wendell] Willkie." Not enough Americans did; FDR peppered the Hoosier scion, 449 electoral votes to 82.

On the November day of Willkie's heartstorm, Barber had already aired six World Series on network radio, a National Football League championship game, the Sunday skirmishes of the football Dodgers, the first televised football game, and less than one year earlier, to fewer than four hundred sets with flickering picture and uneven sound, the major leagues' television premier.

"The players were clearly distinguishable," Harold Parrott, writing in *The Sporting News*, observed of the August 26, 1939, pageant, "but it was not possible to pick out the ball."

It *was*, however, possible to see Barber, up in the second deck on the third-base side, encircled by rowdy, sweat-drenched fans — with only two cameras ("One was up by me, the other near the box seats behind home plate, and I had to watch to see which one's red light was on," he said. "Then, I could only guess where it was pointed at. We were making history and we were flying blind") and with no monitor — shilling for the game's three sponsors: Ivory Soap (Barber held up a bar), Mobil Gas (he donned a service station cap), and General Mills (the camera showed him open the Wheaties box, unfurl a bowlful, slice a banana, add sugar, leaven with milk and say, a smile splitting his face, "Yes-suh, that's a Breakfast of Champions").

After March 1940, when Old Gold cigarettes replaced General Mills as a Dodgers' radio sponsor, it was possible to hear the Ol' Redhead celebrate home runs with "Attaboy! That was a real Old Goldie! And just to show our 'preciation [Andy Griffith, rejoice], we're sendin' off a carton to Dixie Walker, that southern boy come north."

As the Yankees clinched the pennant in their 136th game, the earliest terminative ever, it was also possible to share the gut-wrenching *angst* of the

1941 season. Ted Williams went six-for-eight in a season-closing double-header (his final average, .406); Number Nine's patrician rival, the glossy, lank-edged DiMaggio, made "56" a keepsake; and without one regular from their farm system, the Dodgers of Kirby Higbe and Whitlow Wyatt (winning twenty-one games apiece) and Billy Herman (who better to hit behind the runner?) and Camilli (the league's Most Valuable Player) and Reese (the glove, the glue; "he came here a boy," Barber later liked to say, "and wound up a man") and the sparkling Reiser (hitting .343 to win the batting title and stealing home seven times) won a hundred games and their first pennant since the last full year of Woodrow Wilson's presidency.

"Lord, those years were exciting. Everybody talked baseball. If a million people went to Ebbets Field to see the Dodgers play, ten million listened to Red broadcast the games," Robert Creamer wrote in his preface to Barber's auto-biography, *Rhubarb in the Catbird Seat.* "Everybody knew who Red Barber was, even my maiden aunt — literally. The language he used in his broadcasts be-came part of everyone's speech. James Thurber used some of it in a memor-able short story that was later made into a motion picture. Much of it sounds dated now — sittin' in the catbird seat (the radio booth), tearin' up the pea patch, walkin' in tall cotton, we got a rhubarb (an argument) growin' in the infield, the bases are FOB: Full of Brooklyns — but a cliché is essentially a phrase that is so good everybody keeps repeating it. And Barber was good. Mixed in with all that southern corn were felicitous phrases like 'advancing to third on the concomitant error,' which flattered his ever-more-knowledgeable audience, an audience that was ever-more-knowledgeable primarily because of him.

"I was a Yankee fan in those days — but I never listened to Yankee games. I listened to Barber and the Dodgers. Everybody did. In the summer of 1941 you did not need to own a radio to hear Red broadcast. You could thread your way through the crowd on a beach and get the game from a dozen different portables. In traffic you'd hear it from a hundred different cars."

Over the bulky console while sitting at home, you also heard *another* voice daunt illusions, for even as "Barber's impact on New York," said Creamer, "was extraordinary," so was Roosevelt's upon the nation — defining *The Four Freedoms* and, with Churchill, the Atlantic Charter; signing the Lend-Lease Act and a freeze of all Japanese credits; engineering the American occupation of Green-land and Iceland; extending $1 billion credit to the Soviet Union. That sum-mer of 1941, Germany invaded the Motherland; "the world will hold its breath," Hitler waxed of Operation Barbarossa, "and make no comment!" In September, a Nazi U-boat attacked the U.S. destroyer *Greer* off Greenland; retaliation flooded Washington. "When you see a rattlesnake poised to strike," said the president, ordering the Navy to shoot on sight, "you do not wait until he has struck before you crush him." In early October, German tanks drove within forty miles of Moscow; Josef Goebbels proclaimed Soviet defeat. On December 6, a Russian counterassault ravaged the Wehrmacht. Forty-eight hours later, after "a day that will live in infamy," FDR asked Congress to declare war "on the Empire of Japan"; his audience required little prodding.

On December 11, before a clamorous Reichstag, Adolf Hitler declared war on Roosevelt, his "Jewish clique," and the United States of America.

The Dodgers lost the 1941 World Series, four games to one (over Mutual, Barber again matched strengths with Allen), and Mickey Owen (of his Game-Four, ninth-inning passed ball which breathed life into the Yankees, one writer said, "The condemned jumped out of the chair and electrocuted the warden") vaulted hidebound into baseball's pantheon of goats. On January 15, 1942, with the globe in wanton degradation, FDR asked baseball to elude a wartime mausoleum. "I honestly feel it would be best for the country to keep baseball going," he wrote Judge Landis. "There will be fewer people unemployed and everybody will work longer hours and harder than ever before. Here is another way of looking at it — if 300 teams use 5,000 or 6,000 players, these players are a definite recreational asset to at least 20,000,000 of their fellow citizens — and that, in my judgment, is thoroughly worthwhile."

That same year, the White Sox' forty-one-year-old Ted Lyons, in his twentieth season, started twenty games, completed twenty, and led the American League with a 2.10 earned run average. Owen's Dodgers, winning 104 contests and leading the league by 10½ games in mid-August, became the first team to capture more than 100 games and *not* win a championship. Instead, with 106 victories under manager Billy Southworth, the Cardinals of infielders Whitey Kurowski and rangy Marty (Slats) Marion — of whom Barber said, "He's out there at shortstop, movin' easy as a bank of fog" — and outfielders Terry Moore, rookie Stan Musial (.315), and Enos (Country) Slaughter (hitting .318, leading the league with 188 hits, and saying, after his twenty-two-year career, "That '42 team, it was the best I ever played on") and the battery of catcher Walker (.281) and pitcher Mort Cooper (molding, as the MVP, his first of three straight twenty-victory years) won forty-three of the last fifty-one games and their sixth National League pennant. Then, in an unforeseen turnabout, in the third consecutive Series broadcast by Allen and the Redhead, with a team averaging only twenty-six years of age, St. Louis elbowed the favored Bombers (a record *nine* Yankees' players graced the 1942 All-Star team) of Charlie (King Kong) Keller, Most Valuable Player Joe Gordon (an absurdity; Williams won the Triple Crown), Red Rolfe ("the best third sacker," Ed Barrow said, "the Yankees ever had"), rookie Phil Rizzuto (of whom pitcher Vic Raschi later chortled, "My best pitch is anything the batter grounds, lines, or pops in his direction"), and pitchers Red Ruffing, Spud Chandler, and Atley Donald (transporting a team-record thirteen victories in a row) to win its fourth World Series, four games to one. "The Yankees," Frank Graham wrote after the Cardinals downed New York, "have finally found a team they can't frighten half to death just by walking out onto the field, and taking a few swings in batting practice."

For Barber — something of a mystery, a future lay preacher, at once remote and courteous, an odd prism and progenitor of the archetypal Dodgers' fan's fuming, cursing, whining hope — the torrents of 1942 shaped a visible and crowded year. The preceding summer, the Brooklyn Chamber of Commerce had cited him as "the young man who has made the largest civic contribution to Brooklyn's betterment." Now, over WHN, the team's flagship station, the Redhead pioneered appeals for Red Cross blood donors—"a sample of radio at its best," he said of the wartime effort, "saving human lives"—and the blood of Brooklyn overlapped his booth. He began the War Bond Radio Telephone Sale, and after the final day of a four-day program, journeyed to Washington; there, summoned by officials of the Treasury Department, a baseball announcer detailed his procedure. Greeted by shopkeepers and passersby as he neared the ball park, the symbol of a ball club and, even more, its choir, Barber could say by the 1942 World Series, "Brooklyn had 3 million people and needed a voice, and the fates had made me that voice."

For another voice, that Series, originally, seemed more mortification than pleasantry. "I'd already been in three World Series, and in about five minutes, was about to begin my fourth," Mel Allen was saying in his thick, slightly slurred southern drawl. "Even today I remember sitting up there above old Sportsman's Park in St. Louis, along with Red and Bill Corum [columnist for the *New York Journal-American*], as the Cardinals prepared to take the field."

"This was before Game One," I said.

"Yep," he said, "and I was about to provide my opening remarks. I had the microphone close to my chest, as was my custom, hoping, that way, to call any play a split second before the crowd actually roared. And I was thinking, as I always did, about one solitary fan—Ralph Edwards taught me this—who I imagined sitting just a few feet away from me. In my mind, that one guy—a blank face, maybe, but one person—was my audience. I was talking to him."

"Did Edwards say if he'd talked back?"

"No," Allen said, "but I 'bout fell out of the booth." The Voice formed a Jimmy Carter smile. "I'd just read an article in *TIME* magazine, and remembering it now, that solitary guy of one became a multitude. The story was titled, 'Fifty Million Ears,' and it started out, 'In U.S. drugstores, barbershops, lunch wagons, parlors, and pool halls, over 25 million radio listeners will cock their ears next week to listen to three men—the sportscasting trio that broadcasts the World Series.' "

"And that about did you in."

"As you know, I like to talk," he said, laughing, in the understatement of the century, "but thinking about that number '25 million'—all of a sudden I was terrified. And I just bumbled along for a while until finally, somehow, I got my wits about me and went on from there."

Composed, Allen survived the Series. The next month, over WABC (ironically, the CBS Network's then-flagship station), he told of Branch Rickey, who resigned as Cardinals' general manager, and the Army-bound Larry MacPhail, whom Rickey succeeded at Brooklyn, and Judge Landis' mandate, responding to Roosevelt, barring night games in 1943, and early that year, The Voice himself, leaving for the Army. "I'm not saying they were *totally* related," Allen said with mock malevolence, "but in the same year I went into the service, the Yankees and Giants weren't even on the air. They couldn't find a sponsor," leaving to Barber the sacred tableau of exclusivity. "If you lived in New York and wanted baseball on radio that year, you had to turn to Red."

In 1943, many turned. Again, Barber broadcast the Series, and in a Classic equally dull and motionless to the season as a whole, New York ambushed the Cardinals, four games to one. Soon afterward, awash with presumption, Gillette — intent on sponsoring Yankees and Giants' home games in 1944 — asked Red to break his Dodgers' contract. Offended, Barber balked: "It was," he said, "a sleazy, unethical thing to try"; the Redhead meant to stay in Brooklyn. Gillette's shock was all the stronger; who said "no" to baseball's Sugar Daddy? Against Barber's refusal, Gillette trenched itself in hostility, hiring Bill Slater and boxing's Don Dunphy; they, in turn, drowned in Brooklyn's popularity. "When they asked me to come over and handle the Giants and Yankees, I told them it was a losing proposition, that nobody'd listen," said the son of a locomotive engineer. "I told 'em they should put their money on Brooklyn." Barber's remembrance masked fierce pride. "They didn't believe me and they went ahead and we slaughtered them in the ratings. Funny thing, you know — Gillette dropped their broadcasts, got out of local radio altogether, after that one, long, telling year."

Perhaps Barber was impenetrable. Perhaps the Dodgers' 154-game continuity encased rival teams in a brooding streak of failure. Perhaps Slater and Dunphy, to many baseball fans freighted with obscurity, veered memory toward the monarch *in absentia*: the first to call Joe DiMaggio "Joltin' Joe" and Tommy Henrich "Old Reliable" and dub International Falls, Minnesota, "the coldest spot in the United States — temperaturewise, that is" and "transcend the drama and excitement of the game," Mel's 1978 Hall of Fame plaque decreed, "in a cultivated, resonant tone — uniquely his own."

Allen was born on Valentine's Day, 1913, thirty-six days after a Californian named Richard Nixon; he was the oldest of three children; his parents, Julius and Anna Israel, both natives of Russia, owned a women's clothing store in Johns, Alabama, twenty-five miles from Birmingham.

Tall and bright and curious ("He had a brilliant mind," Nat Allbright said, "the kind you'd expect from a lawyer"), he graduated from grammar school at eleven and high school at fifteen. "It wasn't that I was a genius or anything," Mel allowed. "You have to understand, Johns was so small that we had outhouses back then, and so whenever I had to go to the bathroom — this was when I was four or five — I'd take either a Sears or Montgomery Ward's catalogue and I'd look at the pictures. Then, when I was done, I'd go inside and have dad or mom read me what was underneath this or that picture, and as a result, I learned to read before I even got to kindergarten. So I ended up skipping three or four classes in elementary school — I just had a head start."

In school, Mel Allen played, without distinction, the magic triangle of baseball, football, and basketball; as a teenager, he was a bat boy in North Carolina in the Piedmont League; on vacation, visiting his aunt, he even sold hot dogs at Navin Field.

"I went on to become the Voice of the Bronx Bombers, and Joe Louis became the Brown Bomber," he announced, "and when I was a kid, I'd take a train from Alabama, where Joe grew up, and shoot up to Detroit, where Joe now lived."

"And you'd head for Michigan and Trumbull," I said.

"Dadgum, who wouldn't?" he said. "Once I went out to Navin Field and saw Babe Ruth catch a fly ball for the last out in the last of the eighth inning. The Tigers were way ahead, and after Babe caught the ball, he trotted into the Tiger dugout and then decided he was going to stay there during the top of the ninth."

"Didn't the umpires object?"

"Nah, he wasn't supposed to come to bat. Anyway, this was Babe Ruth; he could do anything he liked. Well, so help me, the Yankees come up, start a rally, and they bat around."

"And Ruth came to bat," I said.

"Hell, were you there?" he laughed. "What happened was that Ruth left the Tiger dugout, crossed the field to the Yankee side, grabbed his bat from the rack, came up to the plate, and—this is the God's honest truth—he belted a home run over the center-field fence with two men on base, and the Yankees ended up with six runs and the game."

"How'd the crowd respond?"

"They couldn't believe it," Mel said, his head bobbing like Louis Armstrong's. "But then, neither could I."

In 1928, majoring in political science, Allen enrolled at the University of Alabama and, younger than his peers, rambled to the football field. "Even as a law student, I wanted my varsity letter in the worst kind of way," he said, "but it didn't take very long to realize that I wasn't going to get it. I'd gained all my height. I'd lost all my weight. So I became a student manager." Mothering the Crimson Tide's equipment, he also grabbed a microphone.

"Student managers," I said, "usually don't have to handle the P.A. system too."

"*I* did," he replied. "I was sort of football's answer to the utility infielder. And believe me, it wasn't glamorous—all the public address announcer did was give opening lineups and substitutions. Back then, there were hardly any substitutions to worry about."

Two weeks before the start of Mel's second year in law school, the Tide's radio announcer left for a better-paying job. The exodus worked in Allen's favor; when the station manager asked head coach Frank Thomas to suggest a replacement, the old Notre Damer tapped The Voice.

Gratitude split Allen's face. "Thomas didn't know one announcer from another, and to that I say, 'Thank God!' Because, you see, he knew *me*, he knew I'd done P.A. work, and he didn't see any difference between that and broadcasting. So he asked me to audition for the job."

"Did you have any experience?" I asked.

"Broadcasting? Not an inning's worth. My only experience was in listening to Graham McNamee and Ted Husing. But even so, I passed the audition."

His eyes danced. " 'Course, from what I understand, I was the only one *to* audition."

At age twenty, the new Voice of the Tide, Allen broadcast over the CBS Birmingham affiliate, station WBRC.

"By now," I said, "you must have had broadcasting ambitions."

"Damn, that seemed further away than the Eiffel Tower. I still hadn't changed my plans," and completing his law degree in 1936, Allen gravitated toward the law. "That same year I passed my bar exam and, man," a Perry Mason at twenty-three, "was I on Cloud Nine."

Weary, Allen began a vacation. "I thought I'd just enjoy a few days off," Mel said. Journeying to New York, he set upon the CBS offices.

"For a job?"

"No, for a lark," he said. "Husing had heard me on an Alabama game; they'd expressed some interest in me. So while I was up there anyway, I thought, 'Oh, why not?' and I went over for an audition."

Remembering, The Voice amplified his cadence, like the rise and fall of a breaker. "I told them I wasn't really interested," he said, "but I recalled some wild stories I'd heard about those auditions — they were supposed to put you into a room with no windows and make you improvise for an hour or something."

"So you decided to find out."

"And when I did, I found it wasn't true. Instead, they gave me different sheets to read — a commercial, a symphony program to see if I could do the composers' names correctly, things like that." Allen *could*, and on New Year's Eve 1937, leaving his hotel room to celebrate, he received a telegram from CBS "saying I'd got the job."

"Did *that* convince you?" I said.

"No, because I still had to teach a final semester at the university [Allen had won a fellowship as a speech instructor], and my thinking hadn't shifted: stick to what you know. But CBS was persistent — they let me go back and take care of everything." In early 1937, moving to New York, Mel Allen became a staff announcer for $45 a week.

Over WABC, as the understudy to Ted Husing in sports and Bob Trout in special events, in the infancy of a career that was still impossible to guess at or foretell, Allen hosted a nightly sports program, covered the Vanderbilt Cup Races (with its start delayed, he ad-libbed for fifty-two minutes in a helicopter) and the 1938 World Series (with France Laux, adding color), interrupted the "Kate Smith Hour" to read a bulletin that the *Hindenburg* had burned and crashed at Lakehurst, New Jersey, aired the International Polo Games, Kentucky Derby, and the 1939 All-Star Game, and introduced, to a national audience, on the U.S. Tobacco Company's "Pick and Pat Minstrels Show," singers like Jo Stafford and Perry Como and bands like Harry James', Sammy Kaye's, and Benny Goodman's "for your listening and dancing pleasure."

"Jiminy Cricket, those days were fun," he said, quietly now, almost as in a whisper. "The more broadcasting I did, the more I liked it. Things got to the point where I was covering political conventions, inaugurations, presidential elections, you know, not the same as in Johns. And the money — well, 'Pick and Pat' alone paid the magnificent sum of $50 a week. So now I was making $95 fifty-two times a year — I mean, that was *good* in those days."

"You just said good-bye to the law?"

"I just stopped and thought, 'If I go back to Alabama, the most I'll make clerking in a law office is ten bucks a week.' You can see why I decided then: radio's for me."

So too was baseball, for "I loved the game, ever since I'd learned, almost, to talk," and on soft, springy-green afternoons, recalling Ruth and Navin Field and the red soil of the Piedmont League, Allen drove uptown to Yankee Stadium and the Polo Grounds. He sat alone, apart from the crowd; he loved the vociferosity which filled the chambers; he watched the players, isolated in his attention, and broadcast *sotto voce*, a semi-Marceau at ease.

"I know this," Allen said. "As I sat in the ball park and broadcast, really, to myself, I thought, 'God, I'd give up about anything to broadcast in a place like this.' "

"Your chance came soon enough," I said. In 1939, the Yankees and Giants' first year on radio, he assisted Arch McDonald, as bucolic as New York was cold.

"Yeah," he said, turning in his chair, "and I've often thought back on how it happened. It was almost a miracle, the way it came about. Sometimes, when I'm just sitting around Yankee Stadium, waiting for a game to start, I look around and it hits me. Talk about being in the right place at the right time. I was so damned fortunate."

Allen looked at the ceiling. I looked at his face. His countenance was wistful; the product, one gleaned, of an earlier milieu.

"Wheaties was the main sponsor, and when CBS signed a two-year contract to do the Yankees and Giants' home games, McDonald agreed to come on board," he said. "Even so, I took an audition. I didn't know what for, but a few days later I found out. CBS called me in the early part of '39 and said, 'Mel, will you go down to Washington and replace Arch?' "

"A trade-off in the booth?"

"Very much so," he agreed, "and it *was* kind of unusual. I said, 'Sure, I'll do it if, when the season ends, I can come back to New York and practice law.' We were all set — I was going south — when one day Walter Johnson happened to walk into Clark Griffith's office, and a brainstorm hit Clark: what a wonderful idea it would be for Washington's greatest baseball hero to do the games. At that time, he was probably more popular there than Roosevelt. A few minutes later, Clark calls New York and that did it." Allen brushed a forearm with his knee. "It's kind of a thrill," he said, "to think I was nudged out of something by Walter Johnson."

"Suddenly, you were out in the cold."

"From baseball," he said, "yes," but not for long.

Six weeks into the regular season, McDonald's assistant paused for a between-innings commercial. Barking for Ivory Soap, the miscreant said, "Ovary

Soap," and by twice repeating his E-B (error, booth), made unemployment certain. He was replaced by Allen, and in late 1939, with McDonald tired of New York, and New York already tired of McDonald, The Old Pine Tree, replacing Johnson, cut a path back to Washington.

In every way, as Melvin Allen Israel, raised up by the calendar, his precocity chided and extolled, became the principal announcer of the Team of Champions, a season of excess had dawned. Within a year, so far, so fast, too fast, he often worried, for his own good, he had vaulted from baseball anonymity to partnership with the *New York Yankees*, six states and a world away from Johns, Alabama.

Pouring coffee, Allen looked past his cup. "Thinking back, I still sometimes don't believe it," he said, slowly. "A guy made a mistake and is let go, Arch doesn't like his new city and goes back to the old, for some reason they pick me to succeed him. Everything worked out — everything *had* to work out — for me to get the chance I did."

As a young announcer, The Voice realized what he had. Sipping Maxwell House, I remembered Nick Mileti, former owner of the Indians, saying, "My years in college were the finest of my life. What was unusual — that wasn't — was that I knew so at the time." Mel Allen *knew*. He loved Yankee Stadium, with its insatiable mass, sloping shadows, and skim of smoke covering the field, and the English language, with its most deadly sin (to Mel) of silence, and The Game, which he cloaked in a mythic posture, and the ballplayers, his heroes even then, like the Great DiMag, whom he called "the Yankee Clipper," and the acrobatic Rizzuto, whom he dubbed "the Scooter," and the dying Iron Horse, whom he knew as "Larrupin' Lou," and the manager (1931–46) whose Yankee teams won eight pennants and seven World Series and who, as a leader, was unyielding: "the best," Ted Williams would say, "I heard of, or played against, or played for, or could imagine."

When Joe McCarthy's temper blazed, some sensed that not only jobs or careers were imperiled, but also arms, legs, jaws, and possibly life itself. "He had a lot of Irish in him," Allen said, "and was a stern disciplinarian. But I also found him fair." Marse Joe dealt with colleagues on a no-nonsense basis founded on respect and authority. Some called it fear, or complexity, or the resultant stirrings of a troubled man. Few doubted that he was hard.

"To the public in the forties," I said, "listening on radio, you were their window on McCarthy's club. How did he relate to you?"

"To someone just breaking in, he was as accessible a baseball man as I've ever known. That first year, he came up to me and said, 'Don't worry about Murderers Row. We win on defense.' And as he explained it, it worked two ways: The Yankee gloves kept the other team from scoring, and the Yankee hitters put pressure on the other team, so that when *they* cracked, that's when you broke through."

"And McCarthy personally?"

"He had a great sense of pride, dignity, and of what the Yankees' history meant. And he instilled that in his ballplayers."

"Like Gehrig," I said.

Allen's soft, large eyes searched the window. "No," he said, "Lou already *had* those things — nobody had to instill them. I remember my second year with the Yankees [1940]. Lou was dying [of amyotrophic lateral sclerosis], and he was almost bedridden, always keeping to home, except that this one day he paid a rare visit to the ball park. He came into the dugout and, as you can imagine, was mobbed. After a while, he shuffled over and sat beside me on the bench. We didn't say anything for a bit — just looked out at the field. Finally, he turned and patted me on the knee. 'Mel,' he said, 'I never got a chance to listen to your games before because I was playing every day. But I want you to know they're the only thing that keeps me going.' " He paused. "Then Lou left and I went over by myself and started to cry."

"And McCarthy loved him."

"They were so much alike," he said, "private people, great values, all-baseball. And that was so typical of Joe's players. They were always in the game. If a guy wasn't hustling, another'd go over to his locker and read him the riot act — 'You're taking money out of my pocket, you so and so.' They'd take their lead from Joe."

"How?"

"McCarthy'd be in a ball game, standing in the dugout, and he'd yell down at a player, 'What's the score?' Or he'd see a guy sitting on the bench with his arms stretched out, and Joe would shout at him, 'Where the hell do you think you are, in a canoe?' Keeping players alive, thinking, alert — that's why he was so great."

"But not as expressive as a Stengel?" I said.

"No, but put him in a bar with a couple belts," Allen grinned, "and he'd loosen up. He had a brother who was in vaudeville, and that was his hobby. He'd name an act and see if you could describe it, or describe the act and see if you could name it. And he loved to talk baseball. But otherwise, from the players, he maintained a distance — and he was the boss. He'd have a tough time managing today, with the rise in players' leverage.

"I remember," he said, "when Ben Chapman, a good player, made some insults against a fan in the stands — some minority slurs — and McCarthy traded him, pronto. Didn't matter what Ben was hitting, he wasn't a *Yankee*," and reciting those syllables, Mel Allen flushed with pride. "Another time, Joe walked into the clubhouse and saw a card table. Right away, he threw it out. It was all business with McCarthy. He *was* a Yankee."

In 1940–42, Allen broadcast, he claimed, in a "partisan" but not "preju-dicial" manner, a Yankee, one suspected, down to his pinstriped underwear. The next three years, he broadcast not at all. Instead, restlessly awaiting the renewal of a peacetime spring, he heard and read about players for whom even obscurity was too good-humored an end. By 1944, most teams were stocked with has-beens and never-weres, wizened castoffs and marginal rook-ies, and men rejected by the service; rosters pulsated with the phrase, "4-F." "The game being played on the field was recognizable," Douglass Wallop wrote, "but many of the players were not." Among those who were, the Tigers' Dizzy Trout won twenty-seven games and MVP Hal Newhouser, twenty-nine;

the Red Sox' Bobby Doerr (six times, he drove in more than 100 runs; six times, he led the league in fielding) hit .325; the fielding blur of Marty Marion ("He's a regular floating ghost," rhymed Bill Dickey) hit .267, lofted only six home runs, led the Cardinals to a third straight pennant, and was named Most Valuable Player; and in Marion's own Sportsman's Park, its other resident (nine years earlier, the Browns drew 80,922 fans for an entire *season*) attracted their first home sellout in nineteen *years*.

The only team in either league, not surprisingly, still without a championship, the Browns of 1944 beat the Yankees in the concluding game of the regular season to, *quite* surprisingly, win their first and only pennant; facing the Cardinals in the last World Series where both teams shared a common site, they reverted to form as America's most app(e)alling incompetents, making ten errors to the Cardinals' one and losing, four games to two. The next April, baseball welcomed a one-legged pitcher (Washington's Bert Shepart), the Browns' one-armed Gray ("He didn't belong in the majors," said his manager, Luke Sewell, "and he knew he was being exploited"), and a Senators' team that would smack precisely one home run (hit inside-the-park, by Joe Kuhel) in *seventy-seven* home encounters. "He is a modest man," Churchill once said of Clement Attlee, "but then, he has much to be modest about." So too the average wartime major leaguer.

Like other owners, Horace Stoneham, who, when sober, was more than average (and whose 1945 Giants, placing fifth, were somewhat less), ached for the end of war. "When you getting out?" he asked a friend at the long bar of Toots Shor's restaurant in late 1945, a year in which a comic-opera World Series (Detroit v. Chicago) matched teams of such similar defects that Warren Brown, sports editor of the *Chicago American*, professed, "To tell the truth, I don't think either team can win." (In seven games, the stolid Tigers did.)

Mel Allen shook his head. "Horace, I don't know," said Stoneham's former broadcaster, in New York on furlough from Fort Benning, Georgia. "Depends on how soon, I guess, they start releasing the troops."

"Well, Mel," Stoneham said, drink bringing color to his cheeks, "if you get out in time for the '46 season, how would you like to have your old job back?"

"Sure, Horace, I'd love to," the Alabamian said. Reliving the episode four decades later, Allen explained, "When he offered me the job, I stopped thinking about Larry MacPhail and the Yankees and I 'bout jumped twenty feet in the air."

On January 25, 1945, MacPhail, Dan Topping, and contractor Del Webb had purchased the Yankees, for $2.8 million, from the heirs of Jacob Ruppert. Explosive, the ex-Dodgers' president was also cunning, and MacPhail—still in the Army, a colonel on the staff of General George C. Marshall—soon blazed with a new contention: to erase the radio noncontinuity buffeting the franchise since 1939. In 1946, he informed the Giants, the Yankees would no longer share their broadcast package; they would carry all 154 games, home and away.

"We're going strictly on our own next year," MacPhail told Stoneham. "What you do is strictly up to you," adding, almost as an afterthought, "Horace, one more thing. To make sure the Brooklyn broadcasts aren't going to run this town anymore, we're going to have a new announcer [in 1945, Slater and the beefy, glad-eyed Al Helfer aired Giants and Yankees' games]. We're going to do every game live," even on the road, the first time in baseball history. "No more Western Union, no more re-creations. Every pitch of every inning, from wherever it is."

Thereafter, chess. First, the séance at Toots Shor's. "It was just accidental, me bumping into Horace," Allen said, "and it was he that first told me about MacPhail splitting off on his own." Next, MacPhail secured a station, WINS, and merging change with constancy, asked his former Voice at Crosley Field and Ebbets Field to reshape the Yankees' broadcast world.

"You must have been terribly tempted to take the job," I told the Ol' Redhead.

"Mr. Rickey used to say, 'If something overwhelming comes along, I am willing to be overwhelmed.' Well, this was pretty overwhelming," Barber said. "The most successful team in sports. The great stadium in the Bronx. Total continuity, as we had in Brooklyn. A three-year contract for $100,000. And history in the making—no more wire reports, use my own eyes, my own mind."

"All that and MacPhail."

"Yes, and that wasn't the least of it."

"So why didn't you do it?" I said. "MacPhail at Cincinnati, as in Brooklyn, and now New York. You could have completed the cycle."

"Everything you mention did appeal to me," he conceded, "but Mr. Rickey, you may recall, was a very persistent man. He offered me a three-year contract, he matched MacPhail's salary offer, and it came down to this: I had a civic involvement with Brooklyn. I had roots. I loved the borough and it needed me. I loved the park and the first-name dealing with everyone. And I admired and respected Rickey." By and by, after a tidal bout with conscience, where the future vowed enticement, Barber remained at Ebbets Field, where the past overwhelmed.

With the Ol' Redhead's rebuff, MacPhail summoned Allen in early 1946. The Voice blinked and called Stoneham, who suggested another conference at Shor's.

"My problem is simple," Allen said. "MacPhail wants to talk with me, and it ain't about croquet. There's only one reason he'd want to see me, and that's about broadcasting. Horace, he's going to offer me the Yankee job."

Stoneham mixed Scotch and consolation. "Then you may not *have* a problem, Mel, and the reason is because I *do* have a problem."

"What do you mean?" Allen said.

"Look," Stoneham said, "MacPhail has a station and all he needs is a broadcaster. I have a broadcaster—you. But I don't have a station and I may not be able to *get* one. You just keep your appointment and if he wants you, then . . ."

"But I have a moral obligation," Mel interrupted. "I promised you I'd do your games."

"I can't guarantee you a single thing," Stoneham said, "and you can't promise to do games that may never get on the air."

The Giants' owner pursed his lips. "As of this moment, you no longer have a moral obligation to my team or to anyone but yourself." It was then, Allen knew, that he was the Voice of the Yankees still.

*   *   *

Back from the scars of World War II, the soldiers of baseball's green and tended fields reassured a nation starved for peacetime heroes — "Oh, man, we were fearless," related Joe Garagiola, then a twenty-year-old catcher. "Anything you did, you felt you were ahead of the game. Not that you'd been in the trenches necessarily. No matter *what* you'd done, you were so glad to be back" — and from the eastern to westernmost settlements of the major leagues (aptly, Boston and St. Louis, the foils of the first postwar World Series), deeds and reaffirmation busted out all over.

In Pittsburgh, Ralph Kiner began the first of seven consecutive years in which he led the National League in home runs and the Pirates in RBIs. For Cleveland, where the Indians (for the first time) drew more than a million spectators, Bob Feller threw thirty-six complete games, the most since Grover Cleveland Alexander's thirty-eight in 1916; three weeks after Allen's discharge from the Army, Rapid Robert no-hit the Yankees. At Griffith Stadium, where the Senators passed 1 million in 1946 for the first and *only* time, Mickey Vernon hit .353 to win the batting championship. Jackie Robinson, starring for the Dodgers' Triple-A affiliate, the International League Montreal Royals, led the high minor leagues with a .349 average. Hank Greenberg bashed forty-four home runs. Stan Musial (later, Warren Spahn would say, "Once he timed your fastball, your infielders were in jeopardy") won his second batting title. Tying Brooklyn for the pennant, the Man's Cardinals swept the best-of-three play-off, and behind Garagiola (hitting .316 and throwing unshakably) and Harry Brecheen (the first left-hander to win three World Series decisions since Stan Coveleski in 1920) and Country Slaughter (racing wildly around the bases to score Game Seven's climactic run), the Redbirds succeeded where five other N.L. teams had failed: in a manic set of games, they beat the Boston Red Sox. Afterward, boarding a train at Union Station for the long ride home, Ted Williams bolted shut the door of his private compartment and began to weep; preoccupied, he did not realize the Boston train had not yet left the station. Moreover, the compartment blinds were open; in his distress, Williams had failed to draw them; later, looking toward the platform, Ted met more than two thousand eyes. Private grief turned public mourning, as public, almost, as Teddy Ballgame's .200 Series batting average, or Slaughter's mad dash for home.

In 1946, both leagues pummeled their all-time mark for paid admissions; overall attendance topped 18 million, 80 percent above the previous high. In what even moppets called the "Junior Circuit," every club but the Browns and

Athletics broke its single-season record. The Yankees, finishing a distant third, attracted 2,265,512 people. Even New York's Nationals, placing last, lured 1,219,873 customers, and while many chose to *see* the Giants fumble, still more were allowed to *hear*. Horace Stoneham had been only semiprescient. Though as late as February 1946, no New York station would transmit his games, enter WMCA and its rich-man, owner Nathan Strauss. His station would carry the ball club, Strauss said, if Stoneham placed its sports director, Steve Ellis, on the Giants' radio team. Ellis had never broadcast a pitch of play-by-play.

Lacking options, Stoneham agreed and, scurrying to find a principal announcer, fastened on Jack Brickhouse. "The whole thing was just so incredible," Brickhouse said, rolling his eyes. "First, you had Strauss, who owned a wealthy clothing store and his twenty-four-hour independent station, WMCA. He was a well-meaning man who couldn't *spell* baseball, and the only reason he had the game on the air at all was to make enough money for him to broadcast his more highfalutin tastes."

"Highfalutin?" I asked.

Grimacing, Chicago's Mr. Baseball slowly shook his head. "This guy thought baseball was lowbrow; it was beneath his dignity. 'Sometimes,' Strauss said, 'you have to do business with the devil.' The guy was a boob. And then you had Ellis, the so-called 'sports director,' who had a fine voice, good delivery, but who was totally ignorant of the game."

"And you spent all year with him."

"All of 1946. It was the longest season I ever had. Steve's the only guy I've ever worked with in more than forty years of broadcasting that I disdained. Steve, please understand, was Number Two, and he resented that fact. He didn't know baseball, and he certainly resented *that* fact." Jack smiled, wanly. "So that's part of the story."

"What's the rest?"

"How I came to the Giants in the first place. You see, I'd originally auditioned for the *Yankee* job — behind Mel, as his assistant. But I lost out to another guy you may have heard about — somebody by the name of Hodges. When that happened, I was set to go back to Chicago in '46. But Horace beat me to it and offered me his top job."

" 'And the last shall be first.' "

"That's what made it weird," Brickhouse shot back. "The guy who *lost* the Yankee audition got the Number One Giant job — me. The guy who *won* the audition got the Number Two Yankee job." Asod in baseball's 1946 prosperity, Brickhouse and Ellis stirred like seedlings against the intensely forested Barber and the resonant Connie Desmond, Red's associate since 1943, and The Voice and *his* assistant, Russell Patrick Hodges.

Born in Dayton, Kentucky, Russ Hodges earned varsity letters as a schoolboy athlete and attended the University of Kentucky, playing halfback on its football team until a broken ankle dissolved the scholarship and kicked him to the radio booth. He became a spotter and sometime assistant to the Wildcats' chief announcer — "The guy had never done a football game before," Hodges recalled, "so he let me do part of the play-by-play. I was terrible, but I got the bug real bad" — and later on, a peripatetic and barrister, combining jobs (on various radio stations) with night classes (at the University of Cincinnati) that led (like Allen) to his law degree. "And I passed the bar examination too," he said, "but never practiced law. In those days, lawyers were jumping out of windows."

From Covington, Kentucky, where, in 1932, the twenty-year-old, $25-a-week announcer asked station manager L. B. Wilson for a $5 raise — "You know what Wilson said? 'Hodges, I can go down any alley, fire a shotgun, and hit thirty guys who are better broadcasters than you' " — the bug-bitten middle-brow shifted to Rock Island, Illinois, and Chicago (over WIND, airing the White Sox and Cubs) and Charlotte, North Carolina (from a studio, using telegraphic reports to re-create Redlegs' games), and nearby Washington, D.C. (1938–45, with the formidable McDonald, ruminating the Senators' claus-trophobic foibles), and, finally, in April 1946, to the tradition and autumn *hubris* of the most imperious franchise in America.

"Russ joined me that first year back from the Army," I heard Allen say, "and he helped broadcast our games through '48," a span in which the Yankees won a single pennant — for New York, an almost exhortatory crash.

"How'd you decide on Hodges?" I said.

The Voice shrugged. "In early '46, just before I went back to the Yankees, I was transferred from the infantry to the Armed Forces Radio Service, and they put me on detached service in New York. One of my duties was to intro-duce the big-league games that went through us to the soldiers overseas. And listening to some tapes, I heard Russ."

"When he was doing Senators' games with Arch."

"That's right," Allen said. "Russ sounded very warm, very pleasant. At this time we were looking for an assistant to join me at Yankee Stadium, and Jack Slocum, who worked for the Yankees, was going to Chicago to talk with Brickhouse. So I asked Dan Topping if Jack could detour by way of Wash-ington and see Arch as well."

"What did he discover?"

"The same as when I called Arch to check Russ out — that he didn't have a hell of an ego, that he'd fit in, wouldn't be disruptive, that the players liked him immensely. Russ flew up to New York and we talked," said the Hall of Famer. "Again, we went to Shor's and we just hit it off beautifully. People used to say we formed a great team. I know this — there was a marvelous chem-istry between us. It got to the point where we could almost read each other's minds."

In 1947, following a salary dispute, Brickhouse returned to Chicago. He was replaced by Frankie Frisch, recently fired as Pirates' manager, who now, with Slater, saw their club of bulging, lead-footed sluggers — "the window breakers," sportswriters called the Giants — homer in eighteen straight games, bomb a major-league-record 221 home runs in a 154-game season, steal twenty-nine bases and lead the league in errors, and finish fourth, thirteen games behind the Dodgers. The next year, stunning all of baseball, Leo Durocher fled Brooklyn to succeed Mel Ott as New York manager. "This is not my kind of team," he prattled, and as if to prove the Lip's reproval, the Giants fell to fifth.

Then, in 1949, Hodges vaulted across the Harlem River, flowing slowly to the sea, and dwarfed by the tenacles of his two splashier colleagues, this gentle-voiced, round, teddy bear of a man began a nine-year run above the pop-gun foul lines and Sahara of a center field of the bizarre and beautiful, mis-shapen and majesterial Polo Grounds. There, while "Barber of the Dodgers . . . gave his listeners corn-fed philosophy and humor . . . and Allen of the Yankees told you more about baseball than you cared to know," columnist Wells Twombly wrote in *The Sporting News*, "Hodges of the Giants . . . told it the way it was."

As Voice of the Stonehams, in a park with a crazy name (polo was never played there; in 1891–1957 and 1962–63, baseball was), even crazier dimensions (the left- and right-field foul poles hovered 279 and 257 feet from home plate; the center-field bleachers, topped by the "Chesterfield" sign, stood a fearsome 483 feet away), patchwork quilt of girders, pigeon stoops, and roofed bull pen shacks, and vast emerald turf that shrouded the horizon, Hodges recited as Durocher roared — trading the lumbering John Mize, Walker Cooper, and Willard Marshall; nourishing Monte Irvin and Henry Thompson and Willie Howard Mays; luring second baseman Eddie Stanky and shortstop Alvin Dark and reacquiring Sal (the Barber) Maglie; building and screaming and moving, in the most memorable of pennant races, toward the last pitch of the 1951 National League season.

At 3:58 P.M., October 3, 1951 ("D-Day" to Brooklyn-born comedian Phil Foster, which is to say, "Dat Day"), at the Polo Grounds, off Dodgers' pitcher Ralph Branca, in the ninth inning of the final game of a best-of-three playoff series, before 34,320 witnesses to the "Miracle of Coogan's Bluff" and millions more who, serious-faced, would piously claim that status, Bobby Thomson lashed a line drive into the lower deck of the left-field stands. The Giants won the game, 5-4, and the pennant; Thomson's homer became frozen in amber, like Pearl Harbor and November 22, 1963; and up in the WMCA Radio booth, amid tension thick enough to chew, Hodges five times cried, "The Giants win the pennant!" and chanted, "They're going crazy! They are going crazy!" and shouted above the hysteria: the Home Run of the Century, the Shot Heard 'Round the World.

"It was an incredible thrill, and there are a couple of stories behind it," mused Ernie Harwell, who had been Hodges' partner with the Giants since April 1950.

While Hodges shook the Giants' Radio Network, Harwell, a Dodgers' announcer in 1948–49, telecast the Shot over NBC. "This was the first baseball ever televised on a truly *national* basis," he began. "The 1951 World Series was *scheduled* to be the first, but the playoff beat it."

"There had been championship fights, two All-Star Games, and the Kentucky Derby on network TV," I said.

"Yes, but not from one coast to another," he reminded me, "and to begin with the Thomson homer — unbelievable. In fact, this kind of national coverage was so new, so unprecedented, that when we went on the air we didn't even have a sponsor."

When Thomson's blast began its arc toward delirium, "I said it was gone," Harwell said. "Then I saw Pafko [Andy, Brooklyn's left fielder] going back to the wall and I began to have second thoughts. My wife was watching on TV and when I got home, she said, 'The only times I've seen you with that dazed look is when we got married or when our kids were born.' "

"What's the other story?" I said.

"Most people don't know this," he said, "but it's a miracle we even have a recording of Russ's call. We didn't tape things back then, keep that in mind."

"How did it survive?"

"Russ got it in the mail that winter, months after the season ended. And he got it — if you can possibly believe this — from a *Dodger* fan," Harwell said. "The fan said he taped Russ in the ninth inning for the sole purpose of hearing him *cry*. Then, I guess, he felt guilty and sent it on to Russ." A fleeting smile. "Russ sent him ten bucks."

A.D. ("After Dat") Thomson, Hodges telecast a rising network mix: three World Series (1951, 1954, and 1962, involving the Giants) and the first 1961 All-Star Game, college football and the Wednesday night "Fight of the Week." Daily, yearly, his club more unfortunate than not, he also sculpted — though no one believed it, not even Horace Stoneham, on October 3, 1951 — the final six seasons of the entity born on May 1, 1883, christened the New York Gothams, and often known, fondly, as the Old Towne Team.

Of each Giants' home run, Hodges declaimed, "Bye, bye, baby" — his rejoinder to "How about that!" In 1953, Durocher grated, *"Compassion? In baseball?* Hell, in this game compassion is for toads." People laughed. One year later, with Dusty Rhodes pinch-hitting, Johnny Antonelli pitching, and the heroic Mays flaunting the Catch (over the shoulder, on instinct, in Game One of the World Series, in the remotest extremity of the Polo Grounds, off the Indians' Vic Wertz), one could see the Giants beat Cleveland, four games to none. Watching Willie, people gaped. The following season, the Stonehams collapsed. Durocher was fired. Said the Lip: "Following us this year, how could people not fall asleep?"

Over WMCA (all 154 contests) and television outlet WPIX (home games only), Hodges and sidekick Bob Delaney watched their 1956 club finish twenty-six games behind the Dodgers. Attendance plummeted to 629,267; nine years earlier, in postwar, pretelevision prosperity, the Giants drew 1,599,784. "Most people knew they were leaving," mourned Jim Woods, who worked with Allen in 1953–56. Fired to create a broadcast vacancy for Phil Rizzuto, the ex-Yankees' shortstop released on August 25, 1956 (and, therefore, looking for a job), Woods leaped to the Polo Grounds in March 1957. "It was a strange time to be with the Giants," he said, "me coming in as they were skipping town.

"When you get caught in a vise like I did — when a Rizzuto came into the Yankee booth — somebody had to leave, namely me," Jim related. "You need a helping hand. And the hand that reached out was Russ's; he pulled me to safety. I'd known him long before I worked with him, and he was doing that all the time. Nobody will ever know the thousands of dollars he gave to charities and to other people, especially guys down on their luck."

"You were part of an interesting trio," I said. "You worked with Allen, with Hodges, and you went directly from one to the other. How would you compare them?"

"Mel had all sorts of rules for the guys he worked with. And he was the absolute master at Yankee Stadium; whatever Allen wanted, Allen got. He was extremely demanding, but it made better announcers out of all of us," Woods said. "Just look at the people he worked with — they all went on to bigger things: Gowdy, me, Russ. We all learned from him — and I include Russ here — he thought a lot of Mel." He laughed. "You know Mel. He'd argue over the air with the fans who'd sent him letters or wires, just controversial as hell. No one was in his league. And probably no one was as thorough, much more so than Russ, who was like the Giants' whole marketing approach: low-key everything."

"Meanwhile, Allen was in high gear."

"Oh, was he ever. After we did a game," Woods said, "Mel'd want to sit in the booth for half an hour and pick it apart — the great plays, what we said, what we could do better, the good, the bad, the indifferent."

"And Russ?"

"Hell, we'd sign off and the first thing Russ'd say was, 'OK, that's enough of that. Let's go get some booze.' "

"What about personally?"

"On the air, Russ had an easy-going style. Compared with Mel, it was like the minuet and the twist. And he was very unaffected — what you heard was what you got. To know Russ was to love the guy. Mays did, I know; Lord knows the times Russ helped him out with money or advice. I happened to be in San Francisco with the Cardinals in 1971 when Russ dropped dead of a heart attack. I was just stunned; I felt like I'd lost a brother. And I was a pallbearer at the funeral." Sadness matted his voice. "There were women trying to get *autographs* of Giant players at the funeral," Woods said, finally. "What a horrible thing for a man like Russ. He was the greatest human being I ever knew."

On August 19, 1957, torching his franchise's first seventy-five years, Horace Stoneham passed forth the pronouncement: for baseball, Moving Day had truly come. "We're sorry to disappoint the kids of New York," he claimed, wed to disingenuity, "but we didn't see many of their parents out there at the Polo Grounds in recent years."

The Giants fled to San Francisco. Woods left for Forbes Field, joining the maniacally riveting Bob Prince. "Sure, I would have liked to have gone with the Giants," Jim said, "and earlier that season, when it looked like the Giants were going to Minneapolis, Russ and I had a contract all worked out with the Hamm's beer people. I was all set. Then Stoneham decided, 'It's San Francisco,' and they wanted to link Russ up with a guy out there who was already a local personality. So enter Lon Simmons and exit me to Pittsburgh."

Racing west, Hodges erupted for the next thirteen seasons over station

KSFO, a liegeman on the Bay. He remained the team's announcer, but with the Polo Grounds condemned and then demolished, the Giants were no more the team.

*   *   *

On September 29, 1957, as the Giants, before 11,606 mourners, played their final game in the oblong cabash at 157th and 159th Streets and Eighth Avenue, the first professional baseball team — born, 1869 — bowed to the Braves, 4–3, at Milwaukee County Stadium.

High above the field, possessed of a precise, exhaustive lexicon, rasped the pioneer whose tenses always matched and who never split an infinitive and who was rousingly a professional: a former ballplayer turned announcer, Waite Charles Hoyt, the Voice of the Cincinnati Reds, 1942–65.

He was spiky, urban, and urbane — "the aristocrat of baseball," chimed the late New York writer, Will Wedge — and, as a pitcher, was even better than his record, for important games inspired him, their pressure refocusing his energy.

In nine seasons with the New York Yankees, he helped fashion six pennants and three world championships, won six World Series games with a 1.83 earned run average, and held Ty Cobb to a .167 average (eight hits in forty-eight at-bats). In the 1921 Series, he pitched twenty-seven innings and yielded no earned runs, tying the 1905 record of Christy Mathewson. Cerebral and sinewy, he was the Ace (a term born in 1860, when Asa Brainard pitched every game for the unbeaten Cincinnati Red Stockings) of the Bronx Bombers: a peer of Gehrig, whom he admired, and Miller Huggins, his first of a dozen managers, and Lazzeri, whom he patronized, and Ruth, his senior partner in aplomb.

Born in Brooklyn on September 9, 1899, the son of a vaudevillian, Waite Hoyt belonged to a comfortable middle-class family, starred as a pitcher for Erasmus High School (a newspaper, in the dialect of its borough, headlined a future injury, "Hert Hoite"), and at age fourteen, trudging to Ebbets Field, attended a Dodgers' tryout. Except for a garrulous outfielder named Stengel (called "Casey" or "Dutch" by his teammates; years later, he remembered Hoyt as "the big kid in a pair of bloomers his mother must have made"), anonymity muzzled him, and tired of condescending amusement, Hoyt talked of becoming a college man.

"I would have gone too," he said, his eyes brown and hard, his build more fragile than before. "In fact, I was already checking colleges out" when Giants' manager John McGraw, piercing Hoyt's school-league obscurity, signed him to a contract (or rather, Waite's father, since Hoyt *fils*, at fifteen, was a minor).

"It was a long ride from our part of Brooklyn to the Giants' office in Manhattan," he mused, "and to make the contract legal, money had to change hands. So McGraw handed me a $5 bill, like you'd give a kid a Christmas present."

"What did you buy with it?"

"I stuck it in my pocket, thanked McGraw, and we left. We walked down the stairs to the street where my father turned to me and said, 'Let's have the five.' "

Sent South for "seasoning," Hoyt trained one spring with the Little Napoleons, moved to New England for more minor-league maturing, and in September, in his only deed as a 1918 Giant, pitched one inning and struck out two. That same year, the Giants finished second; perturbed, McGraw turned to veteran players and traded the right-handed rookie to Rochester of the International League. "I don't go to the bushes," Hoyt said. Instead, rebuffing his sudden fall, he caught on in Lynn, Massachusetts, where, pitching for a semipro club, Waite's leggy stride piqued the Boston Red Sox — then, the baseball champions of the world.

In two years (1919–20), Hoyt won ten games for the Red Sox; sold to the Yankees (with Ruth, Herb Pennock, and other underlings) by Boston owner Harry Frazee (a wanton promoter who needed money to finance Broadway plays), he wove a 19–13 record in 1921, his first season in New York. Three times, Hoyt would win nineteen games; in 1927–28, he went 45–14. "The secret of success as a pitcher," he often said, sober *or* drunk (an alcoholic, Waite flogged the bottle), "is getting a job with the Yankees."

Like his city, streetwise and opportunistic, Hoyt wrote and painted, composed and sang — often loudly, not always well — under the bright lights of the Palace Theatre. "Wives of ballplayers, when they teach their children to pray," he uttered, "should instruct them to say: 'God bless mommy, God bless daddy, God bless Babe Ruth! Babe has upped daddy's pay check by 15 to 40 percent!' "

Time rested lightly on him, and on the road, rooming with the fine-gloved, dancing-tongued third baseman, Joe Dugan, Hoyt sampled its desserts. Not all were erotic. One wind-blown morning, Dugan left the hotel lobby and, unknowingly shadowed by his roommate, walked to a nearby church. Inside, Jumpin' Joe devoutly lit a candle.

"Hi, pal," said Hoyt, surprising him in the vestibule. "What's with the candle?"

Dugan scowled, his profile marked by creases. "I've tried everything else," he explained. "I thought maybe with this I'll get some help with my hitting."

"Then light one for me," Hoyt said. "I'm pitching today."

Dugan lit a second candle. Hoyt assumed the pitching mound and was blasted to the dugout.

"What gives?" Waite demanded upon the shelling. "I got killed out there — what happened to the candle?"

Dugan eyed him solemnly. "Some bloody Protestant," he said, "sneaked in and blew the candle out."

Hoyt's candle flickered in 1930. Shipped to Detroit, he later bounced to the Athletics, Dodgers, Giants (again), Pirates, and finally, clasping the last of his 237 victories, to his native Brooklyn, where English was the only foreign language. He retired in 1938, a twenty-one-year icon, and was signed by the Brown and Williamson Tobacco Company.

"By now, I'd developed something of a name in New York," Hoyt said, "and this company thought I could help their sales. So, in the off-season, they put me on WMCA, the station where I started and where I did a three-hour program called 'Grandstand and Bandstand,' introducing all sorts of people — theatrical and radio stars, opera bigwigs, hoity-toities coming over on boats from Europe."

"Had you ever done radio?" I asked.

"Well, back a ways, I'd done a baseball program in September of 1927 for NBC in New York. And I was used to appearing. I'd done the public bit before," on and off the diamond. In 1929, he shared a bill with Jimmy Durante, Eddie Jackson, and Lou Clayton. Another time, he scolded umpire George Moriarty for missing a pitch. "You're out of your element," Hoyt shouted, glibly, sarcastically, walking toward the plate. "You should be a traffic cop so you could stand in the middle of the street with a badge on your chest and insult people with impunity." *Element? Impunity?* From a *ballplayer?* On the *ball field?* Where, as author Roger Kahn once wrote, "English is superfluous to baseball profanity"?

Hoyt paused, reaching for several pills (one month after my visit, the ex-pitcher died, at eighty-five, of heart trouble). "From WMCA, I went to WNEW, and then I jumped ship in 1939 to WABC," he said, "but my show was canceled after three weeks because the network had priority, and they wanted to substitute a national program. Mine was local."

"From there, WOR."

"You got it," he said. "But first I tried to get the Yankees' job. This was when, as you'll recall, they were going on radio for the first time — and I knew my real goal was to be a baseball announcer. I really pushed. But Wheaties wouldn't even let me take an audition because they didn't think we baseball players had enough of a vocabulary to do a decent job."

"And Arch McDonald got the job."

"Yes," he said, "and *then* came WOR," the Dodgers' station, where, in 1940–41, in the same park as Barber ("He'd never done baseball before," the Ol' Redhead said, "and it didn't take long, or a genius, to see that he took to it naturally"), Waite aired pre- and postgame features and commentary.

Pleased, Hoyt was not content, for, at forty-two, he panted for play-by-play.

"I enjoyed those programs with the Dodgers, but I still wanted to be the big cheese — I wanted to do balls and strikes," he said. "So I went to William Morris, the talent agency, and they took me on," and in the awful winter of 1941–42, with constants uprooted and the world inflamed, Hoyt heard from Barber's former turf, Cincinnati, Ohio.

Outside, July beckoned, warm and bright. The Queen City glistened in the sun. "I've been here now for more than four decades," Waite announced, a half-smile pasted to his face.

"What was it like when you came?"

"Let me explain what happened," he said. "Back in '41, two stations were already doing the Cincinnati games — WSAI and WLW. They both were owned by Powel Crosley."

"Barber's old stations," I said.

Hoyt's eyes grew merry. "And they were still at it," he said, embracing the then-defending champion Reds. "Well, now along comes a third station wanting to do the games, WKRC [the William Howard Taft Company station], and they were looking for a broadcaster."

"And you applied."

"You bet I did," he said. "I had some big deals in my corner—J. G. Taylor Spink [from 1914 to 1962 the publisher of *The Sporting News*] was for me and talked with folks out here."

"And you won."

"Yep."

"And went," I said.

"Yep. When they offered me the job of play-by-play, it took me about half-a-second to yell 'yes,' " he said. "Originally, I'd had a few qualms about going; after all, Cincinnati was the only place in the majors that closed down after dark. But I went and, when I did, I found a level of happiness I'd never known anywhere else, young or old."

For twenty-four seasons, over four different flagship stations, Waite Hoyt outlasted sidekicks Lee Allen ("He was around six weeks; then he tried to get a raise, go the union route, and they canned him") and Jack Moran (1957–61) and Gene Kelly (1962–63) and Claude Sullivan (1964–65; doomed by cancer). In his first eleven years, brought to the entire Ohio Valley, *always*, by Burger beer, he was the loneliest man in announcing, the entire Reds' broadcast team —"After Allen went, I did it solo, by myself, every inning, every year"— cadging climaxes and amenities and Yankees past and Redlegs present and making baseball rise before us.

"He had a million stories," Gabe Paul said, caressing a phone at Municipal Stadium. Now a consultant to the Indians, in his sixth decade of professional baseball, Paul served the Reds from 1937 to 1960, graduating from publicity director to traveling secretary to assistant to the president to vice-president and general manager.

"What kind of stories?" I said.

"Any kind you can imagine," he whistled. "Waite would talk about his days with Colonel Ruppert and how he pitched to Cobb and Speaker. He'd talk about Ed Barrow [also borrowed from the Red Sox] and how Earle Combs could fly around the bases. Then he'd go on about how the Iron Horse would never let you down."

"And Ruth?"

"Well, of course, he was always there—don't forget, Hoyt ran with Ruth at night before he took the pledge. On, on, Waite would go—Ruth, Ruth, and then *more* Ruth." He marveled at the Babe's skills, weaknesses, his love of children and love of drink. He told of how, when Ruth took batting practice, silence seized the field; how, further, in April of 1925, fleeing spring training, the Babe ate—what was it?—a half-dozen or dozen or two dozen hot dogs (as the story grew older, the number grew larger) and suffered, as the baseball public fretted, "the stomachache heard 'round the world"; and how in August 1948, as a sweltering pallbearer of Ruth's cancer-wracked remains, Hoyt heard Joe Dugan whisper, "Lord, I'd give my right arm for an ice-cold beer." Nodding, Waite murmured, "So would the Babe."

At Crosley Field (born 1912, died 1970, the 1935 site of Ruth's second-to-last game), with its terrace before the left-field wall (the better, on opening day, to implant temporary bleachers), its double-decked grandstand and sun-deck pavilion, and its equally modest seating capacity (generally, 27,603) and out-field dimensions (328 feet down the left-field line, a paltry 387 to the deepest corner of center field), Hoyt, like the Ol' Redhead, broadcast from an open rooftop booth.

"Jesus, we could have been killed," Hoyt was saying. "It was always jammed 'cause it was so goddamned small — you could hardly crowd three people in it. You had these steel chairs with pads on the seats, and when rain came in the booth, the floor got flooded and you were scared to death some thunder was going to hit your microphone."

"A little different from today," I said.

"When I think back, when the wind started to blow, the booth would sway back and forth. It's a miracle it didn't collapse." Waite's face softened. "But, you know, it's an interesting thing. It was better then — and I don't just say that because I'm an old son of a bitch."

"Then, why?"

"Which I am, incidentally," he said in his self-mocking way. "What I mean is this: You were *close* to the fans, you *knew* them. Crosley Field bred intimacy. You were right on top of the place, you recognized a lot of the people there, and they'd be calling right up to you. I mean, you could hear them on the air."

"And now," I said.

"The moment you enter Riverfront Stadium or Three Rivers Stadium or any of these places, you feel like you're witnessing an exhibition, a spectacle," said Hoyt, who retired after the 1965 season — joining Burger as a public-relations spokesman — when Wiedemann beer became the Reds' radio sponsor. "It's like a giant coliseum. You feel *alone*. There's not the companionship — it's cold, sterile. And it extends to the players."

"How so?"

"You'd see guys like Ernie Lombardi [the Reds' two-time batting champion] and Johnny Temple [their second baseman of the 1950s] and so forth," he said. "They were familiar faces. They got involved in the community. Everybody knew 'em. The players now — they go to the game, go home, and when the season ends, they get the hell out of town quicker than a Feller fastball."

Familiar, the Redlegs were often also nondescript, and as the retired pitcher expounded over a five-state network, listeners endured a succession of losing teams. In Hoyt's quarter-century of play-by-play, Cincinnati finished fifth, sixth, or seventh fourteen times; in 1945–55, the Reds were condemned to the second division.

"Remember this," Hoyt told me. "Allen and Barber always had great material to work with — they were the *good* news broadcasters. The fellows with the winning clubs — a Scully with the Dodgers — they have the top banana fiber."

"And you?"

He smiled, after a fashion. "I was a *bad* news broadcaster."

"Not all the time."

"Mostly, anyway," he said. "I remember when Warren Giles, this was back in

'46, when he was president of the Reds, and he called me in and said, 'Waite, why aren't you more enthusiastic about the Reds? Why are you always low-keying it?' He mentioned Bert Wilson of the Cubs and a couple others, and he said, 'Why don't you cheer like they do?' "

Hoyt's frame tightened. "I got mad as hell," he said. "I told him, 'Why in the shit *shouldn't* Bert Wilson cheer? They won the pennant last year, didn't they? They've got a great park to play in'—everybody called it 'Wrigley's Doll-house' back then—'and they've got some stars, they win some games,' " and reliving the story, he bristled. " 'But us,' I said to Giles, and I got so damned upset, 'your top hitter's a lousy .267 or whatever the hell it is. Your top pitcher's won eight games. What is there to *cheer* about?' "

"What did Giles say?"

"Not much," Hoyt said.

"And you?" I said.

"All I left him with was, 'Christ, if I cheered like Bert Wilson with the bums we've got, people would think I was blind or the village idiot.' " Waite paused, dramatically. " 'Or maybe both.' "

Bewildered by the National League, their shade a dour gray, the Reds were not devoid of gifted individuals. "That was the saving grace," Hoyt said of the exigencies of the occasion. "I would have been a jerk to talk about our *teams*; we were almost always hopelessly out of it. So I spun some stories and built up the *stars* worth talking about," recounting the feats of Lombardi and Der-ringer and Walters, of Joe Nuxhall (at age fifteen, debuting on June 19, 1944) and Ewell Blackwell (winning sixteen straight games in 1947) and Jim Maloney (hurling a ten-inning no-hitter on June 14, 1965, and losing in the eleventh inning) and the muscle-bound Ted Kluszewski, bursting through his sleeveless uniform (and hitting .300 or more seven times with 254 home runs), and of the wrecking crew of 1956 (which clubbed 221 home runs and *almost* won the pennant) and the unsung throwaways of 1961 (who couldn't win the pennant and *did*) and the near-miss Reds of 1964 (losing the pennant, to St. Louis, on the final day of the season).

"Those three years were the only times we ever even *thought* about a cham-pionship," Hoyt said. "And the funny thing is that the '56 club was a *hell* of an outfit. We had Frank Robinson—he was Rookie of the Year—and Gus Bell, Wally Post, and Big Klu, Temple, Roy McMillan."

"But no pitching," I said.

"You can say that a million times. *None*. If they'd had even an ounce, they'd have won the Series. Then came 1961, and we had good pitching but, Christ, the rest of the team was like the Reds of today—totally unreliable. We could look terrible, just the shabbiest bunch you ever saw, and then somehow, for some reason, they put it together," the Reds of Robinson, the Most Valuable Player, and Vada Pinson, Gordy Coleman, and Gene Freese, and pitchers Joey Jay and Jim O'Toole, winning thirty-nine games, "and they just took off."

"Not a ball club for the Hall of Fame."

"Hell, they didn't have half the talent our old Yankees did," said Hoyt, himself a Hall of Famer. A Dodgers' official called the 1961 Redlegs "a con-glomeration of castoffs who have banded together for one last stand."

Born to reminisce, the ex-Yankee found sweetest memories in his steadfast companion, time. Did he remember, I wondered, how Faulkner said, "The past is never dead. It's not even past"? Announcing, even Hoyt's delivery evoked a vivid, exemplary yesterday. Unlike any broadcaster in the totality of baseball, Waite Hoyt aired play-by-play in the past, not present, tense. He was a chronicler, not sportscaster; he narrated action *after* the fact; on radio, his accents, like his life, bridged, not disengaged, the years.

Hoyt stared for an instant. "Instead of saying, 'The batter hits a ground ball to shortstop. The fielder catches it and throws to first. He's safe,' I'd turn around and say, 'He hit a ground ball to the shortstop. The shortstop caught it and threw to first base. The runner beat the throw—he was safe.' "

"All right," I said. "How about, 'Here's a pitch across the plate. Snider bombs it to left field. And Post goes way back—he makes the catch'?"

"That would come out, 'The ball was across the plate. Snider belted it to left field where Post made the putout.' " Pause. "Not everything would be in the past, naturally, but a lot was," he said. "And the reason was simple: *accuracy*. As I speak to you now, what I said to you two minutes ago is gone. When a batter hits the ball, the announcer is always a bit *behind* the action in describing it—he was in the past; he *had* to be; it couldn't be otherwise. Any broadcaster tells you what the athlete *has* done, not what he's doing or is going to do."

"I guess so," I said, "but wasn't it all unusual?"

"Oh, it roused a great deal of conjecture," he said, "as to why I did it. But I was just being precise."

Waite Hoyt grinned at my laughter. "Even back then, I was pretty adamant, set in my ways, wasn't I?" he said. "Well, it's like I told you earlier."

"I know," I said. "You're just an old son of a bitch," dying to be sure, but still an institution and grammarian and the always-Voice of the Reds, among the very first ex-athletes to enter the broadcast booth and, quite possibly, the best.

*   *   *

While Waite Hoyt meandered through endless summers of conviviality, his tense a metaphor for an unrecoverable time, farther east, amid the pine cover and fallswept streets of the Oakland section of Pennsylvania's second-largest city, in a neighborhood shadowed by the University of Pittsburgh's forty-two-floor Cathedral of Learning and a park—a park built for *baseball*, Forbes Field, at once sensual and recognizable and kind—which glistened in the dusk and was, as Theodore Roosevelt once wrote of his summer White House, Sagamore Hill, "the offspring of the years as surely as is a reef of coral," a 112-pound baseball fanatic worshiped at the shrine of his beloved Bucs.

An informal and cheerful man, orphaned as a child, he sat in a radio booth to the left and high above home plate, surveying (and breathlessly detailing) the left-field wall ringed with ivy, enormous dark-green outer garden, and taunting, sun-baked infield where shortstops (as Tony Kubek, in 1960, discovered) feared for the certitude of their lives.

He was a humorist, a writer, and penned four books of sayings and poetry; he could have lived on his earnings as an after-dinner speaker. Thousands of shut-ins wrote him letters; housewives would not begin dinner until he signed off each day. For nineteen years (1936–54), Albert Kennedy (Rosey) Rowswell held sway as the first Voice of the Pirates, Pittsburgh's ultimate baseball celebrity, and his revival hour blanketed western Pennsylvania, eastern Ohio, and most of West Virginia.

"There'll never be another like him," proclaimed Bob Prince, a bucketing, opinionated, and expansive personality who became Rowswell's sidekick in 1948 and who once won a $20 bet by diving from his third-floor window into the pool of the Chase Hotel in St. Louis, clearing twelve feet of concrete. Upon Rosey's death, at seventy-one, in early 1955, Prince was named the Pirates' principal announcer.

"They say that about you too, Bob," I said.

"Yeah, but they *mean* it about him," he winked, not without a measure of self-deprecation. "First of all, he was a very unusual man, very gentle, sensitive, and he put together a poem once that was absolutely magnificent."

Sitting in a New York hotel room, Rowswell wrote "Should You Go First" after he and his wife discussed what one would do without the other:

> Should you go first and I remain
> To walk the road alone,
> I'll live in memory's garden, dear,
> With happy days we've known.
>
> In Spring I'll wait for roses red,
> When fades the lilac blue,
> In early Fall when brown leaves fall
> I'll catch a glimpse of you.
>
> Should you go first and I remain
> For battles to be fought,
> Each thing you've touched along the way
> Will be a hallowed spot.
>
> I'll hear your voice, I'll see you smile,
> Though blindly I may grope,
> The memory of your helping hand
> Will buoy me on with hope.
>
> Should you go first and I remain
> To finish with the scroll,
> No length'ning shadows shall creep in
> To make this life seem droll.
>
> We've known so much of happiness,
> We've had our cup of joy,
> And memory is one gift of God
> That death cannot destroy.
>
> Should you go first and I remain
> One thing I'd have you do;

Walk slowly down that long, long path,
For soon I'll follow you.

I'll want to know each step you take
That I may walk the same,
For some day down that lonely road
You'll hear me call your name.

"See what I mean," Prince said. "That was one side of him — for a long while, in fact [1909–28], he was secretary of Pittsburgh's Third Presbyterian Church."

"And the other side?" I said.

"The other side was that every afternoon Rosey'd go to the ball park. Every year, on his vacation, he'd travel with the club on an eastern trip. And he was just *wild* as a fan — the 1925 world champions even gave him a gold baseball watch charm. So when, in '36, the Pirates finally decided to broadcast their games, he was the logical choice by far. You see, to Rosey, there may have been sixteen major-league ball clubs, but there was only one major-league *team*."

"Baseball was his religion," I said, "and the Buccos, his Good Book."

"That's it," he said. "That sums it up. Here was a guy who looked about as far from an athlete as you'll ever see. He was a Gomer Pyle kind of guy. He looked like a toothpick," his features more linear than Don Knotts'. "But he *loved* baseball, and to him, the Pirates *were* baseball. And he's mostly responsible — when I took over in '55, I found this to be true — for the fans of this entire area feeling, 'Hey, we don't *want* an announcer who plays it right down the middle. We want him to *root*, to live and die with the Pittsburgh Pirates,' " and during Rowswell's longevity, mostly to die.

"I'll never forget," Prince said, "how one time the Dodgers came to Pittsburgh, and Barber was their announcer. And Red, like Mel with the Yankees and Russ with the Giants — they *had* to sound almost disinterested, more of a reporter."

"Even Allen?" I asked.

"Even Mel was no homer compared with Rosey."

"Why the impartiality?"

"Two reasons," he said. "First, New York was such a gigantic place, you had people from all over the country, and a lot of them still followed their old teams. And even more, each of the New York clubs was sponsored by a different brewery — you can be damn sure they didn't want their announcers being so biased that they ticked off guys who might otherwise take their swigs."

"But Rosey."

"Oh, God," said Prince, and he started laughing. "He was the first to pioneer the Midwestern Cheering School — the Rowswell-Prince-Caray-Bert Wilson camp where you weren't impartial, you *roared*. I asked Red once if he'd put Rosey on for an inning on the Dodgers' Network that was piped back to Brooklyn — to show 'em, you know, a little different type of twist. Well, it was *hilarious*. They couldn't believe it back in Brooklyn — they must have thought an alien had seized the broadcast booth. Believe me, they'd never heard anything like *this* guy."

Mild and frail and eloquent, exuding a sense of playful companionship, Rosey Rowswell described some of the truly enfeebled teams in the history of the National League. In ten of his nineteen, eight of his last nine, and all six of his final years, the Pirates — Rosey's "Picaroonies" — graced the second division; in 1952–54, they finished last, a collective 144½ games from first place. The 1952 entry won 42 outings and lost 112 and pain-gnarled Tri-State rooters; their October burial ground lay 54½ games behind the champion Dodgers.

Still, to Pirates' listeners, Rowswell purged ennui on the field, telling of graphic and rewarding situations, lauding the vapid quality of the team's play, leaving, as Prince would also, a compendium of memories.

In Erie, Wheeling, Oil City, and Ashtabula, one heard the quintessential fan hail Paul and Lloyd Waner (spraying Forbes Field with hits to its yawning gaps and "old iron gates") and Rip Sewell (he of the blooper or "Ephus" pitch, splitting the plate on its downward arc) and the All-Star Game that *was* (in Pittsburgh, July 11, 1944) and the World Series that *wasn't* (leading the league in late September, the 1938 Pirates fell to Gabby Hartnett's Cubs) and eight Pirates' managers (one, Bill Meyer, becoming Manager of the Year, and two, Pie Traynor and Frankie Frisch, later adopting radio). One heard too such antiquities as "the bases are FOB" (an acronym, altered by Barber, meaning "Full of Bucs") and the "doozie marooney" (a Pirates' extra-base poke) and the "dipsy-doodle" (a strikeout by a Pirates' pitcher) and "put 'em on and take 'em off" (a Pirates' double play) and "oh, my aching back" (after a Pirates' loss) and "put on the lamb chops, I'll be home soon" (after a Pirates' victory).

"The guy could have been a novelist, he had the imagination for it," Bob Prince related. "You know, I was born in California, went to school in Oklahoma and a couple other places, then on to Harvard before I dropped out of law school — in other words, before deciding to go into baseball, I'd been around — and I'd never heard anything like it. Remember, our teams were almost always lousy, and we'd get way behind in the second inning, and Rosey'd just start talking about poetry and these crazy sayings of his — they all came from his head — and it was like a little kid who gets wound up when he's tired, and off he went."

"Sort of stream of consciousness."

"I used to call it a 'Rosey Ramble,'" he said. "I mean, he'd be chirping about the 'doozie marooney' and the 'dipsy-doodle' and about the weather and art. *Anything* but the game. I used to ask him, 'Rosey, how can you *talk* about this stuff?' And he'd come back, 'Bob, we have sponsors that deserve fans, and we've got listeners that deserve a show. Now, if I just sit up here and talk about the facts, we ain't gonna have either — fans *or* a show.' And, Jesus, he was right. You can't just ho-hum it; you have to *entertain*. 'It's not just play-by-play that matters,' he'd say. 'It's what you say between the pitches that counts.'"

Rowswell's catchwords, critics groaned, demeaned and trivialized the game. Even so, the moonlighting bard relished them, and his radio pupils recited them, and *everyone* loved Aunt Minnie.

Far-fetched and dazzling, Aunt Minnie surfaced in 1938, when, as a Pirates' home run cleared the Forbes Field scoreboard, Rosey stood up and implored, "Get upstairs, Aunt Minnie, and raise the window! Here she [the baseball] comes!" Seconds later, to Rowswell's rear, an assistant shattered a pane of glass; to partisans at home, the broken glass meant Aunt Minnie's window. "That's too bad," Rosey sobbed. "She tripped over a garden hose! Aunt Minnie never made it!"

"By the time I got there," Prince said, "the routine had changed a bit. Instead of glass — it was too messy — it got to the point where I had this big dumb-waiter's tray, and on that tray were bells and nuts and bolts — *anything* that would make a noise. And when a ball was belted, I'd grab the tray and stand up on a chair."

"Unbelievable," I said, pausing between syllables.

"Listen, you haven't heard anything yet," he chorused, shaking his head. "See, Rosey had this slide whistle around his neck. And when a Pirate hit a pitch Rosey thought was going over the fence, he'd start blowing that damn whistle like crazy and he'd say, 'Hurry up, Aunt Minnie, raise the window!' And he'd nod at me, and when he nodded, I'd drop the tray from about six feet off the floor."

Prince chuckled, softly. "To the guy with a radio, it sounded like an earthquake, like the whole window had been smashed to hell. And there'd be Rosey saying, 'Poor Aunt Minnie. She didn't make it again.' And while he was talking, I'd be crawling on the floor — picking up the nuts and bolts."

"And bells," I said.

"That's right," he said. "I had to have the tray ready again, just in case the *next* guy hit one out."

"And you got a lot of practice."

"Who wouldn't," he recollected, "with Ralph Kiner around?"

Returning from war in 1946, Ralph Kiner became cosmic in Pittsburgh's concourse; he also attended regularly to Aunt Minnie's glass. In September 1947, he blasted eight home runs in four successive games; for the year, he clouted fifty-one. In one month (September 1949), the stout-legged staple bashed sixteen baseballs over National League fences. On the Fourth of July, 1951, Kiner exploded for seven RBIs in two innings. The next year, he clubbed thirty-seven homers and asked Pittsburgh general manager Branch Rickey, recently moved from Brooklyn, for a raise. "I know you hit all those homers," Rickey replied, "but remember, we could have finished last without you."

Kiner's many wallops failed to check the Pirates' buffoonery. But as the outfielder lashed, Rowswell blew his whistle, Prince scraped the floor, and Aunt Minnie moaned, a curious equation invaded Forbes Field. Losing, the Buccos won. Struggling to plant mediocrity, they flowered at the gate. In 1947, dropping ninety-two games, Pittsburgh attracted a record 1,283,531 customers. The 1948 team, an ordinary fourth-place assembly, drew an audience of 1,517,021.

"You know, Pirate officials used to say, 'Thank God for Ralph Kiner!'"

Prince said. "And I have to tell you, the most surprising . . . I'm looking for a word here . . . no, the most *bizarre* thing I've witnessed in the broadcast booth concerned me, Ralph, and Rosey."

"When?" I said, playing Bergen to Prince's McCarthy.

"In 1948, my first year, and I was still scared to death. Rosey was at the far end of the booth," he said, "and Bing Crosby, who'd come in as a part-owner of the ball club a year or two before, was sitting between us. The Cubs were playing — I'm sure Doyle Lade was the Chicago pitcher — when Kiner snaked one to left."

"And away we go," I said.

"Oh, Kiner ripped it, *creamed* it, and off it went into Schenley Park."

"What did Rosey say?"

"He wasn't supposed to say *anything*," Prince said, thoroughly relaxed, "because *Bing* was at the microphone. He'd been doing play-by-play for an inning or two and doing a damn good job. So Crosby starts describing the trajectory of the home run, and he's talking beautifully, and nobody *hears* him."

"The mike," I guessed, "went dead."

"No," he insisted. "Rosey got so excited about Ralph's shot that he grabbed the microphone from Bing — stole it right from him — and started yelling, 'Open the window, Aunt Minnie, here it comes!' " (The recorded text. Crosby: "I'd like to see Ralph improve a little on his showing so far this afternoon. Against Rush he couldn't do much. He's facing Doyle Lade now — maybe he can do a little better. And he did! . . . " Rowswell (interrupting): "There goes a long one — open the — it may go in there! Aunt Minnie! [shouting now] Boy, it goes clear out over the scoreboard." B.C. (barely audible): "Oh, what a blast . . ." R.R.: "Over into Schenley Park, a long homer for Ralph Kiner — his first of the 1948 season!" B.C.: "Oh, did he . . ." R.R.: "Let's hope that it's the first of sixty-one!")

"When all this was going on," I said, "did you get ready to unload the tray?"

"No," he said. "I was laughing so hard — I just stood there dumbfounded."

"What did Crosby say?"

"Well, he was looking at the home run and talking — he didn't realize Rosey'd stolen the audio. And I said to him, 'Sounds great, Bing, but you haven't had the microphone now for ten seconds.' "

"And Rowswell?"

Prince looked at me whimsically. "I had tears in my eyes from laughing. All I could say was, 'My Lord, do you know who you just stole the mike from?' But that was Rosey. When you upstage Bing Crosby, you've really pulled the cork."

In 1939, Prince's only year at Harvard Law School, Rowswell and a plump, sodden-faced woman named "Aunt Minnie," promoting a KDKA television demonstration, drove into Forbes Field in an Austin car. The belle was authentic; her golden name untrue.

"There were those who claimed that the lady was Aunt Minnie, and there was another lady who died in 1983 at a nursing home here," Prince said in his pleasant baritone voice, "and her friends claimed that *she* was Aunt Minnie. I'm sure, though, that he invented it, like he made up everything else — he had that kind of mind. And I think everybody in Pittsburgh *knew* that. But they didn't object — in fact, that's what made it great."

"What did?" I said.

"The fact that it was so absolutely, so whackily spurious and wild. It was like the emperor having no clothes — and folks applauding the nudity." The Gunner flashed a grin. "You know, I've been in broadcasting for more than forty years, and I can honestly say I've never heard of anyone with a home run call in the same league with Rosey."

"Not Allen's 'Going, going, gone'?"

"It was fantastic," he said, "but the answer's still the same — a big, fat no."

"Not Russ Hodges' 'Bye, bye, baby'?"

"Nope."

"How about Harry Caray's 'It might be, it could be, it is'?"

"Not even close," Prince countered. "Think of it. It was totally fictitious and understood as such. It was a chant women liked especially — it drew them out as fans. And it came out of the blue, weirdly, totally off the wall," enduring after the February of Rosey's final year, when he died of a heart attack, a paean to any pitch wafted over any wall in the sunlight or outer darkness by any Buccaneer of the National League Baseball Club of Pittsburgh, PA.

*   *   *

In Pittsburgh, where townspeople venerated his evangelism, Rowswell united generations. He had, as families envisioned it, always been among them; they knew him, or at least his caricature; he was a part of their lives. On November 10, 1939, Jim Britt became a part of New England, and until March of 1953, when the National League deserted Boston, he aired the triumphs and cataclysms of the Red Sox and Braves, ending each broadcast with his compact tag line, "Remember, if you can't take part in a sport, be one anyway, will ya?"

Born in San Francisco, he grew up in Detroit, the son of wealth and uninhibited ambition; his father was board chairman and chief executive officer of the Burroughs Corporation, the maker of computers, cash registers, and calculators. After graduating from the University of Detroit (his brother, a priest, would become its president), Britt earned his law degree at the University of Southern California.

"Never took the bar exam," he told a reporter.

"Why not?" the writer asked.

"Because I'm an idiot," Britt countered. Actually, like Allen, Prince, and Hodges, he preferred microphone to bench.

At twenty-six, Britt was hired by a small radio station in South Bend, Indiana, then moved to Buffalo and wandered to station WKBW, where, reigning over wooden Offerman Stadium, he covered the International League Bisons: "the pride," to quote their publicists, "of western New York."

"We announced together all during the mid-and-late thirties," Leo Egan, a native Buffalonian, said with good-natured affection. "We did home games live, naturally, and road by re-creation."

"Any great memories?"

"I'll not soon forget," he said, "the couple days when Newark's Bob Seeds hit seven straight home runs in seven times at bat. Never happened before, never since, and in my time with Jim we had a lot of hard-to-forget days. Britt was very meticulous, hard to work with, and he didn't take kindly to criticism. But why should he? To a neutral observer, he didn't do much that was wrong."

In February 1939, Leo Egan liberated himself and fled to Boston. Eight months later, his new employer, the Yankee Network, began a search to replace Fred Hoey's successor, Frank Frisch, leaving to manage the Pirates.

"As you'll recall," Egan said, "Hoey had been fired in early 1939 and Frisch, who'd recently been canned as Cardinals' manager, took over on radio."

"To do both of Boston's teams," I noted.

"Well, Frisch was here for only that '39 season," after which he was quixotically recalled for his anguished byword, "Oh, those bases on balls!"

"And then the Pirates grabbed him."

"Frisch wasn't that big a radio hit here," Egan said, "and when Pittsburgh wanted him as their manager, he jumped. So I got hold of Jim—he was still at WKBW—and told him about the opening. 'Get the hell up here,' I said. He did, took the audition, and got the job," signed by WNAC as sports director of its Yankee Network. He was twenty-nine years old.

By the time Japan defiled Pearl Harbor, Britt had served for two years as the Voice of Boston baseball. Turning to the Pacific, he entered the Navy as an intelligence officer in a 1942 of crossroad, unknown, and heightened superlative—of precedents like the first U.S. jet plane tests, self-sustaining nuclear chain reaction, and Allied bombings deep inside the pockmarked Reich (Americans flew daylight sorties; the British, nightly saturation blasts); of sunbursts and tragedies like the United Nations Pact (in Washington, twenty-six nations signed its charter) and the Cocoanut Grove fire in Boston (491 died); of names like "White Christmas" (by Irving Berlin) and *The Robe* (by L. C. Douglas) and Bataan and Corregidor (tipping to the Japanese) and Midway and Guadalcanal (falling to the Allies) and Tobruk and El Alamein and Field Marshal Bernard Law Montgomery (the hero of North Africa; the subduer of the Desert Fox) and James Cagney (the hero of *Yankee Doodle Dandy;* the Best Actor of the Year). At year's end, with German troops trapped at Stalingrad, one marveled at the resiliency of the Russian people. One also recalled FDR's pledge of February 18, 1942, when darkness terrified: "Soon we and not our enemies will have the offensive."

Stationed in the Ellice Islands in the South Pacific, Britt was fortunate to emerge alive. On a run over Japanese-held Naura, a nearby isle, his bomber collided in mid-air with another American plane. While his craft limped back to base, Britt learned that he was among only eight survivors.

In 1946, after the rotgut of war, he returned to undulate over WHDH, the new flagship station of the Red Sox and Braves.

"I grew up listening to his broadcasts," said Red Sox' announcer Ken Coleman, "and after hearing a bunch of guys fill in for him in '42, say, to '45, you especially appreciated his coming back."

"Why?"

"Because there's no doubt in my mind that of all the broadcasters I've ever heard, and this includes network newspeople, no one had more of a command of the English language than Jim."

"How'd that grab folks around here?" I said.

"Some," Coleman observed, "thought it was great. 'Finally,' you know, 'an erudite announcer.' But there were also a lot of people around Boston who thought he was talking down to them, that somehow Jim felt he was better than the average Joe."

"Did he?"

Coleman paused. "In a way," he said. "You've got to keep in mind that Jim was used to being sort of a top dog, above it all, I guess. And that spilled over to the booth, to a kind of patrician view."

In the 1940s, the Braves (née Boston Bees) were infrequently patrician. For six straight years, they wallowed in the second division. Then, in 1948, one year after third baseman Bob Elliott won the MVP Award, he, Tommy Holmes, Eddie Stanky (traded by the Dodgers), and Alvin Dark (the Rookie of the Year) fielded and hit effectually; Warren Spahn and Johnny Sain ("Spahn and Sain," the jingle went, "and pray for rain") won forty games; and the Braves greeted their first World Series since 1914.

At Fenway Park, the Red Sox were no longer clowns. "By the time the press of Boston has completed its daily treatment of Theodore S. Williams," John Lardner, returning from an aircraft carrier in the Pacific Theatre, wrote in the jubilant summer of 1946, "there is no room in the papers for anything but two sticks of agate about Truman and housing, and one column for the last Boston girl to be murdered on the beach." Leaving the Naval Air Force, Williams batted .342 and smacked thirty-eight home runs. Johnny Pesky hit .335. Bobby Doerr and newcomer Rudy York — "that big old Indian," Britt caroled — knocked in 116 and 119 runs. Dave (Boo) Ferris won twenty-five games, Cecil (Tex) Hughson added twenty, and before nearly a million-and-one-half fans at home, Boston played 60–17 baseball. Superior at the plate, the '46 Red Sox won 104 games. Razing the American League, they won their first pennant in twenty-eight years.

"See, Jim was really in an ideal situation," Leo Egan said. Britt became, as the late Ray Fitzgerald, the literate columnist of the *Boston Globe*, recalled, "for almost a decade, the biggest name in Boston radio" and the first broadcaster to be associated with the young, struggling Jimmy Fund, New England's charity against cancer. "He did the Braves and Red Sox' games at home," Egan mused. "He did some away re-creations too, though a fellow named Tom Hussey did most. Hussey did them in a very staid way — no crowd noise, a ticker tape in the background, saying, 'Ball one, strike one,' and that was it. But what *Jim* did, he did well."

"Did you like him?" I said.

"I'd helped bring him into the big leagues, helped him get his job here," he said, "so yes, we were close, played golf together. And I'd be there to listen if he had drinking and marital problems." Egan wavered. "Which he did."

"Any effect on his work?"

"No," he answered, quickly. "Jim was still the same — very professional, very difficult. But, God, he was articulate. He did college football, and he'd go up to Dartmouth and paint a picture of the New England autumn — a classic description."

"But still thin-skinned."

"Absolutely. Sort of a Felix Unger type — quirksome, picky," he said. "I remember one day at Fenway, we were doing a broadcast and a northeasterly was blowing in a gale from left field. So a Boston batter hits a fly ball toward the wall and Jim says, 'That ball is smashed and it's gone!' But it wasn't — it blew back and was caught. A little later, *another* Boston hitter belted one to the wall, and Britt yells, 'Yes, it's gone!' But it wasn't. Same thing — the wind blew it back for an out."

"How did Jim handle it?"

"Oh, he was peeved. So a little later, a *third* guy tattoos one to the wall and Jim roars, 'It's really smashed and I don't care what *anybody* says! It's gone!' But," and now, he was laughing, "it wasn't. *Another* out, and now Jim is beside himself."

Egan took a deep breath. "Let me show you what I mean about Jim being persnickety," he said. "Once, at Braves Field, a guy hit a pitch over the left-field wall, and Britt misspoke, saying, 'It's way outa here! It's gone *under* the fence!' I started to break up, laughing like hell, and I began to walk out of the booth to regain my composure."

"Did he stop you?"

"He saw me and turned the mike off and asked me what was wrong — Jim really didn't know what he'd said. So I told him, 'Nothing, Jim, nothing,' but he kept at me. 'What's wrong?' he kept saying. Finally, I tell him, 'You said *under* the fence,' and he said, 'I did not. I did not,' like a little kid. What it comes down to: He couldn't admit he'd made a mistake."

Jim Britt announced six All-Star contests and two World Series, nine Sugar and two Cotton Bowls, one East-West and four Blue-Gray Games on network radio. He covered the 1951 All-Star Game and three World Series (1949–51) for NBC Television. He also made "a mistake."

For years, Narragansett beer — "the beer," ads bellowed, "with the seedless hops" — had sponsored radio coverage of both Boston baseball clubs. But in 1950, P. Ballantine & Sons pirated the Braves' broadcasts and Britt must choose: stay with Narragansett (and the perpetually contending Red Sox) or opt for Ballantine (and the ambulatory, again-struggling Braves).

"What happened," Coleman said, "was that Lou Perini [the Braves' owner] suddenly took off on his own. He decided to leave WHDH and take Braves' games back to the Yankee Network — and go head-to-head against the Red Sox. Which was, of course, a terrible misjudgment as to the relative popularity of the teams. Well, to his later regret, Jim decided to go with the Braves, and the Red Sox countered — Tom Yawkey wanted to do this anyway — by starting, for the first time, live coverage of *away* games," and from Yankee Stadium, artful as Mel Allen's assistant, rose the new Voice of the Red Sox, Wyoming's Curt Gowdy. Dave (the Colonel) Egan, the acerbic *Boston Daily Record* columnist, had tagged the balding Britt "Meathead" or "a radio Rollo" or "Tuft" (i.e., a thin wedge of hair). Now, he wrote: "That beer salesman who for years has been trying to sell the beer that *doesn't* have seeds in it is going to try to sell us beer that *does* have seeds in it."

The contest became no-contest. "Curt had the top product going for him," stated the *Globe*. "Britt had the Braves when they were cracking up." In 1951, Britt's first year as Voice of (only) the Braves, Holmes replaced Billy Southworth as Boston manager, and the next season, drawing so poorly that the new manager said, "We were playing to the grounds help," Charlie Grimm succeeded Holmes. On March 18, 1953, the Braves, of Boston since 1876, absconded for Milwaukee; Earl Gillespie and Bob Kelly, officials said, would broadcast their games.

"Now he had nothing," I said of Britt.

"Yes," Coleman exclaimed, "and for Jim, it was quite a shock. He never really recovered from what he'd done — it was like going from the sublime to the ridiculous. And when the Braves left town, Jim knew he'd have to too. He wanted to do play-by-play, and there was just nothing left. So he stumbled around for a year, and then came out to Cleveland, where I already was, and in 1954 and '55 we did Indians' TV for Carling Brewery — about a hundred games in all."

"Had he changed much?"

"Not really," he said. "I remember one weekend, Jim gave the attendance and said, 'There are twenty-seven thousand *persons* here today.' Off the air, I said to him, 'Jim, you always say *persons*. Is there a reason you don't say *people* or *fans*?' And Jim became very proper and said, 'Yes, Ken, *people* is correct. And *fans* is correct. But *persons* is *more* correct.' "

Forthright and civil, his nature earnest, Coleman basked in memory. "The Indians had a second baseman and his name was pronounced Bobby Avíla [Ah-VEE-la]. I called him that — everyone did," he said. "But not Jim. He called him Ávila [AH-vee-la]. We got a lot of letters and people calling in — they didn't like it. So one night at the ball park, the chairman of Carling said to Jim, 'You know, in view of the local colloquialism, we should probably call him Avíla, like most fans prefer."

"What was Britt's response?" I said.

"Well, the chairman's name was Ian Dowie, as in *row* or *dough*. So Jim looks at him and says, 'No problem. It's perfectly all right with me, Mr. Dewey.' "

In 1958, he returned to Boston, laboring as a local sportscaster, and watched a dreary series of Red Sox' teams perform with hypnotic monotony. Fired at WHDH, Britt moved to Detroit, then St. Petersburg, then Sarasota, and endured a divorce, arrests for drunkenness, and clinging unemployment. He died on December 28, 1980, at seventy, at his home in Monterey, California, less tragic than forgotten, his command of the English language less diminished than his career. "In truth," Fitzgerald wrote, "life had turned its back on him a long time ago."

*   *   *

For nearly four decades, *his* history was Philadelphia's *baseball* history. He was styled "The Man of a Zillion Words," and his listeners felt a personal communion. "Would you please talk a little louder?" wrote a woman from Red Bank, New Jersey. "My radio battery is getting very weak."

He was unflamboyant, uncharismatic; decidedly not, in his pejorative phrase, a *glamour boy*. Yet reaching across artificiality, he not so much triumphed over, as *outlasted*, the sketchmarks and reservations of his critics, and looking back, his presence intruded upon Philadelphia much as the World Series does October—his words draping saloons and drawing rooms; his play-by-play heard as cars moved through Center City; his talented instrument of a voice rising from the ancient booth at 21st Street and Lehigh Avenue.

Arriving from WCCO, the 50,000-watt CBS station in Minneapolis, Byrum Fred Saam broadcast Athletics' games in 1938, aired the Phillies and A's from 1939 to 1949, reverted to the American League in 1950–54, and after the A's traded Philadelphia for Kansas City, revisited the Phillies for twenty-one often interminable years.

"Rosey Rowswell described some terrible teams," I suggested, "but you make him look like the guy who won the million dollar lottery."

"Yeah, I had some clunkers, but believe me, they weren't of my doing," he said, at seventy-one, at his home in the Philadelphia suburb of Narberth. "And anyway, it wasn't *all* bad."

"Pretty much," I said.

"No, there were always interesting events going around. Fights in the stands. Or debates with my broadcast partners, guys like Chuck Thompson, Lee Vines, Taylor Grant, Bill Campbell. Or I'd be hearing some guy say what a dump our ball park was. Or something would be going on in the press box at Connie Mack Stadium. Remember how rickety it was?"

"And way high up," I recalled. "Up at the roof."

"Well, Russ Hodges was so scared of heights that he tied a rope around his waist so that when he looked out of the booth, he wouldn't collapse and tumble out on the field."

"But what about *upon* the field?"

"There were always guys on our teams you could talk about—even when we were stinking up the joint. Switching to our opponents, I remember Williams and DiMaggio and Roberto Clemente—he could miss a pitch by a foot and look terrible, you'd think he'd never hit it in a million years, and then Clemente'd wiggle those hips and slam the next pitch, the same pitch, to left-center field for a double."

"Still," I said, "those same opponents would beat your brains out."

"True," he agreed, "but they looked so good *doing* it."

"You must have ached, though, for some excitement on the Philadelphia side."

Seconds elapsed. "Sure," he said, "you *wanted* to get excited. Sometimes you had to feign enthusiasm when you didn't feel any. And I can tell you: With some of the clubs we had, you had to do a lot of feigning."

Broadcasting the equivalent of a half-century of baseball, Saam enjoyed only *twelve* years in which his teams surpassed .500. Across seventeen seasons, his A's sleepwalked to a 1,057–1,553 dead end; in 1954, they plunged to sixty games from the lead. Over thirty-two years, his Phillies' won-loss tableau was 2,182–2,842; in 1961, they lost twenty-three matches in a row. Eleven times, Saam's teams dropped more than a hundred games; nineteen times, they finished last; in his forty-nine seasons of play-by-play, baseball's Gibraltars of degradation refused to claim a single pennant.

From the summer dark, the record book emits this frightful pounding: Byrum Saam of Ft. Worth, a personable man who deserved better and who belongs (as of this writing, his noninduction baffles) in the Hall of Fame, announced more losing baseball games than any man in history.

"Did you get used to it?"

"The losing?" he asked. "No, you just got inured. And it wasn't all that easy to stick in there some hot Sunday in the second game of a double-header when you're getting blasted out by fifteen runs, and everybody else is at the Jersey shore guzzling down the beer. But you *had* to sound interested in your work. That's what you'd been trained to do."

Saam was trained in central Texas. He attended Central High School (the factory spawning golfer Ben Hogan, singer Tex Benecke, and quarterback Tommy Thompson) and received his diploma in bed (running track, he had ruptured his appendix). Entering Texas Christian University, he broadcast Southwest Conference football (over the Texas Network) and played varsity basketball (like teammate Sammy Baugh, at guard) and, in November of 1935, on the weekend "CBS Football Roundup," aired TCU's battles with Rice and Southern Methodist Universities. "SMU beat us and went to the Rose Bowl," he reminded me, "and TCU beat Rice and went to the Sugar Bowl." Only twenty-one, Saam went to Minnesota.

"How'd it come about," I said, "your going to WCCO?"

"It goes back to public address announcing," he said.

"Meaning?"

"An owner of a radio station in Ft. Worth heard me running up and down the sidelines of a TCU game, carrying the mike with me as I ran and handling the P.A. system," Saam stated. "So, he apparently thought, 'This kid is better than anyone I've got at the station,' and he put me on the air."

"And that led to the 'Football Roundup.' "

"See, each weekend CBS scheduled several games for its coverage, one following the other, and my two games came right after Ted Husing's," he said. "For instance, he did the Army-Navy Game, and then they'd switch to me with TCU-Rice. Before long, I got heard around the country, and WCCO wanted me to come up and audition."

"For football?"

"No," Saam said, firmly. "They wanted me for baseball. I flew to Minneapolis and they asked me to re-create the 1935 World Series in their studio—not for over the air, but just"—he laughed—"for their listening pleasure. Only one problem: I'd never *done* a baseball game. But I did it and they liked it, and Husing put in some words as well. So 1936 rolls around and I'm up doing both the Triple-A baseball team's games and football at the University of Minnesota," where he transferred as a student.

In 1938, he proceeded to Shibe Park, the first steel-and-concrete baseball plant, where the press box was small (and sweat-infested), the outfield was large (a fifty-foot-high wall hovered above right field; a two-tiered pavilion stretched from the left-field pole to straightaway center; to clear the distant fence, one must arch a 468-foot wallop), the viewing was intimate (total capacity: 33,608), and the fans made boo-birds famous, sullied Dick (Don't Call Me Richie) Allen, and failed to exorcise misfortune. By 1949, Saam's last year of dual coverage, the scoreboard read: In *twelve* of By's first twenty-three seasons, the A's and Phillies finished eighth in an eight-team league.

"Did you know," I said, "that in this 1938–49 period, only three clubs in the big leagues *didn't* place even a single player on *The Sporting News* All-Star Team? The Browns were one. Guess the other two."

"I don't have to guess; I *know*. Yes, Philadelphia had some teams for the ages," he said, halting, and then, "the Middle Ages."

The next year, 1950, Saam (temporarily) divorced the Phillies and became (exclusively) the Voice of the A's. "It wasn't really my decision," he noted. "Don't forget, I was under assignment to N.W. Ayer & Son, the first advertising agency in the country. Now they're in New York; then they were down here. Anyway, in early 1950 it was decided that we'd travel to away games and not do them by re-creation."

"In the years before," I said, "you'd done only home games of both clubs live."

"Yes," he said, "and then we'd added whatever road re-creations we could. That way, you could do a home game of, say, the Phillies in the afternoon and the road re-creation of the A's from Chicago that night."

"But the new policy screwed that up."

"Actually, it was better," he said, "because now you'd have live, more intimate, colorful coverage from the road. The fans loved it. But it put me in a sticky situation because I had to make a choice. Now that we were going with a team on road trips, it was impossible to handle both teams."

"And you chose the A's."

"At the time, it made sense. After all, I had a close relationship with just the kindest man who ever lived, Mr. Mack," Cornelius McGillicuddy, the Athletics' manager, owner, aging patriarch, and Great White Father, for whom Shibe Park was renamed in 1952. "So I supported the move. But what made it kind of ironic, though," he nodded, "is what happened later on."

What happened was that, implausibly, the Phillies—the Whiz Kids of Curt Simmons and Richie Ashburn and Granny Hamner and Willie (Puddin' Head) Jones, all under twenty-five—won the 1950 pennant, their first in thirty-five years. Robin Roberts won twenty games, the Phillies' most since 1917. Ashburn, roaming across center field, and Del Ennis, whacking 126 RBIs, hit more than .300. Ennis, Jones, and Andy Seminick teamed for eighty home runs. Only one regular, relief pitcher and Most Valuable Player Jim Konstanty, admitted to thirty years of age. Eddie Sawyer managed, the club set a new attendance record, and over station WIP, Saam's successor, Gene Kelly, rode Philadelphia's rolling swell of applause.

"By always made light of the fact that the year he left, the Phillies won," said Ashburn, a Phillies' announcer since 1963. "Instead, he'd talk about his enjoyment at doing the A's," and of how Connie Mack deflected praise, Jimmy Dykes amputated tension, and, in 1952, the Athletics' Bobby Shantz earned twenty-four victories and the MVP Award while Roberts, a domineering 28–7, earned little but distinction.

The former Phillies' All-Star paused. "Still," he said, slowly, "the whole thing must have bothered him. I mean, to announce all those years and then just miss a pennant. It *was* unjust."

"So," I said, "was 1964," when the Phillies, armed with a six-and-one-half game lead with twelve games left, lost ten and, to St. Louis, the pennant. "Then By was even closer."

"Yes, and in the final blow, to top everything off, damned if By doesn't retire in 1975 [plagued by dimming vision, Saam had a cataract] and the very next year the same thing happens. The Phillies won *again*," edging Pittsburgh for the Eastern Division title, their first of three straight championships.

"How did By react to *that*?" I said.

"He didn't have to," Ashburn exclaimed. "We were up in Montreal to play the Expos in '76 and with a win we'd clinch the division. So we had By fly up there even though he'd retired. He broadcast the game. And we clinched with him on the air."

"You weren't going to have him go out a loser."

"No, sir," he said, abruptly, "and why *should* he? You know, By broke me in as an announcer after *I'd* retired as a player. He interviewed me, gave me the job, and we had a hell of a good many years. He was a comfortable guy—the good voice, he did his homework—and I don't think any announcer was as big a part of the same city for as long as he was here."

"But not as notorious as, say, a Bob Prince."

Ashburn laughed. "Who in God's sake was?" he said. "Actually, By had the image of being real laid-back, but I have to tell you—he had a great sense of humor."

"Which rarely surfaced."

"And do you know why?" he said. His voice was severe. "Because he was such a professional that he didn't think joking around belonged in a booth. Only later in his career did By start to unwind a little, to consciously provoke some laughs. Of course," Richie muttered, "a lot of it *was* unintentional."

At Memorial Coliseum for the 1959 World Series, one of two (the other, 1965) he covered, Saam listened as his colleague on NBC Radio unfurled a supple introduction. "And now here's the very fine announcer from Philadelphia, the very engaging Byrum Saam," Mel Allen cried during Game Three, to which Saam, not hearing, whistled, "Right you are, Mel." Twenty-one years earlier, crackling in the pressure of his first major-league broadcast, the Voice of the A's began his career by saying, "Hello there, Byrum Saam, this is everybody speaking." Upon another afternoon, with heat squatting over Shibe Park, Saam severed Athletics' outfielder Bob Johnson. "There goes a long fly to left," he roared. "Johnson is going back, back to the fence! He bangs his head against the wall, picks it up and throws it to second base." Even now, Ashburn gulped at the memory of a weary, road-splattered Saam, late at night from Candlestick Park, explaining variations of a run-down play. "And now," he intoned, "for all you guys scoring in bed . . ."

The Phillies' all-time leader in games, at-bats, consecutive games played, and total hits blared approval. "You can just imagine the stir *that* caused," he mused. "But how can you not love a guy like that? He just had the knack of saying the wrong thing at the wrong time — totally innocent, of course, and he wouldn't realize what he'd said."

"The master of the malapropism."

"Or the *non* se*quitur*," Ashburn said. "We were playing the Montreal Expos in 1969, in their first year at Jarry Park, and By says, 'You know, 85 percent of the people up here speak French, but they're nice people anyway.' The two parts of the sentence were totally unrelated. But that was By — he'd say these innocuous things, and when they caused a fuss, he would wonder why."

In the 1970s, as Saam's eyesight quivered, the use of Astroturf blossomed, and more clubs played increasingly at night, he often wondered too: Where is the ball?

"I think had By taken a leave of absence and got his cataract taken care of," Ashburn was saying now, "he could have come back after '75 and he'd be broadcasting today. But I think he just got tired of broadcasting; he knew he was going to retire, and he didn't look after his eyes, and as a result, in those last few years, he had some real problems."

"Prince told me," I said of the Pirates' sphere, "that in Rowswell's final seasons, he had to point out to the field — this is when the play was going on — and show Rosey the location of the ball."

"There was some of that," he confided. "I'll tell you, when Astroturf gets faded, it's real hard for *anyone* to see the ball, especially in night games. And By had it even worse. So to adjust and find the ball, he had to develop a great technique. He'd watch the fielders moving on the grass or artificial surface, and look at the umpire's call, and he'd take his hints from there."

"Did it work?"

"Not always," Ashburn warned. "Once we were in the new St. Louis park, where sometimes you can't pick up the ball at all. And this Cardinal batter — I can't remember who it was — smashed one way back toward the bleachers. But

By didn't see the ball. He thought the guy had hit a grounder. After he started talking, he realized, finally, what had happened. I'll never forget By's call. 'There's a ground ball to shortstop,' he said, 'and it's gone!' "

The two-time batting champion roared at the remembrance. "See what I mean about Byrum Saam?" he said. "Who else do you know like that, who could go on, year after year, still booming out that great voice and entertaining the fans?

"Now you tell me," Richie Ashburn demanded. "Why isn't that guy in Cooperstown?"

*   *   *

Six hundred and fifty miles west of Cooperstown, in a *ball park* (not to be confused with *stadium*) that first welcomed the National League on April 20, 1916, a five-foot-nine, 190-pound, brown-haired and blue-eyed compatriot of Byrum Saam's, the endearing Bert Wilson, held a pencil before the microphone ("I keep it in my hand the whole game. Don't write with it, but I like to know it's there") and inhaled beer during double-headers ("I'd look over there on a hot August day," gushed Russ Hodges, "and he'd be drinking up a storm") and, expelling neutrality, shouted, "I don't care who wins as long as it's the Cubs!"

A native of Columbus, Ohio, Ralph Bertram Puckett moved to Iowa as a child. He attended high school in Cedar Rapids, the state's second-largest city, where, with a deep indrawing of breath, his father played trumpet (his hobby, in the local symphony), and, with a pliant owner, Bert finagled a noontime series on a local station (his musical debut, in 1930). Attracted, like Saam, to a Big Ten college (the University of Iowa), he broadcast and sang on the school's pilot station, WSUI, and willed (to quote a 1950 news release from WIND, Chicago) that "instead of an engineering career he'd been considering, sports announcing was for him."

At twenty, Wilson left the university and joined commercial station WMT. "Though the local baseball games had never been broadcast, Bert convinced the station to air them," WIND blew frontally, "and when the season opened, Wilson sat on a housetop across from the center-field fence bringing listeners play-by-play descriptions of all games."

From there, a trek to Olympia (or at least a knothole pass to Wrigley Field): play-by-play, *live* coverage, of Iowa football and Indianapolis Class-AA baseball, hockey, roller derby, semipro basketball, and, in 1941, the Indianapolis 500, the last until the first May of a troubled peace. Cheers and upward mobility. Who would not hire this persistent, tuneful man? Bless the poetic Wilson. Bless his beloved Cubs.

Enter 1943. The war pushed on. The Axis burned. The Casablanca Conference—held in the same year *Casablanca* was named Best Picture—demanded "unconditional surrender." The Cairo Conference, starring

Generalissimo and Madame Chiang Kai-shek, plotted strategems for the Pacific Theatre. The Teheran Conference appointed date and commander for the Normandy Invasion. The New York theatrical season hailed *Oklahoma!* the Mecca of Broadway musicals. Sicily welcomed the Allied amphibious force. Unions welcomed an influx of members; by late 1943, the rank and file totaled 14,146,000, more than one-third of the nonagricultural labor force. Americans did not welcome their new paycheck withholding tax. Ernie Pyle released *Here Is Your War*; Betty Smith, *A Tree Grows in Brooklyn*; Wendell Willkie, the influential (and, with sales exceeding 2 million, inordinately profitable) *One World*. Bert Wilson, who craved recognition more than profits, thrashed militantly toward the major leagues.

His "break into the big time came when Cubs' sportscaster Pat Flanagan [formerly, of WBBM] needed an assistant," the WIND broadside continued. "One of Bert's former sponsors recommended him for the audition, and despite a bad attack of laryngitis he managed to talk his way into the job. At the end of the 1943 season, Flanagan retired and Bert took over Chicago's number one sportscasting job — airing the Chicago Cubs' games — and went on to become the team's most enthusiastic supporter."

Enthusiastic, bombastic, or distinctly rhapsodic? Even if the Cubs weren't all *that* intriguing, how could you tell with IDCW^{2}ALAITC behind the mike?

Jack Rosenberg chuckled. "That's what he was always saying," the WGN executive said. "I Don't Care *Who* Wins As Long As It's The *Cubs*.' "

"Recount," I urged, "his announcing style."

"Bert was always charged up for his games," he said. "You have to understand — Chicago's broadcasting is a little different than in other cities. We don't *want* our radio-TV guys to kneel in a chapel and sit on their hands. Here, fans *expect* their announcers to get involved, to be part of the show. They want 'em to fit into a certain mold — exuberant, gung ho, go get 'em, Cubs."

"A la Harry Caray," I said of the yeoman who, leaving the White Sox, meandered to Chicago's North Side in late 1981.

"Harry's in a league by himself, but he also was made for the mold. Before him there was Jack Brickhouse and Vince Lloyd and others. And Wilson, of course. A lot of the rah-rah started there."

For twelve (1944–55) seasons, the Voice of the Chicago Cubs rooted boisterously for the oldest continuous member of the National League.

He pricked deadly smugness.

"He freely admitted that he sat and listened to Bob Elson [long-time Voice of the White Sox] and copied him. He was a souped-up Elson," said Brickhouse, who in 1940 became Elson's assistant and, before retiring, aired 5,060 games in forty-two years. "He was more excitable than Bob, and he was incredibly conscientious. He was always around the players, always at the park. He did his homework, he knew his baseball. You could have buried him at Wrigley Field."

He broadcast alone.

"How he ever did it, I don't know," Saam said, fetching incredulity. "I kept telling him, 'Bert, you gotta get some help.' But he never did. He took care of the commercials, the play-by-play, the anecdotes and stories — what we call color today. Maybe he had more stamina than the rest of us. Maybe he just loved the game more."

Round-faced and sweltering, Wilson straddled a chair in the radio booth which overhung the backstop and, smacking nonchalance, sketched grass that was real and bleachers that were full and ivy vines that climbed the brick outfield wall. "There isn't," he liked to say, "a bad seat in the house," nor for other spectators, watching from adjacent rooftops. Two tiers of grandstand flanked all of foul territory. Winds off Lake Michigan made every fly ball an adventure. After each home contest, a flag with a white "W" (upon a blue backdrop) or blue "L" (set against white) rose atop the scoreboard to elucidate the result. "The Cubs are [Ronald] Reagan's kind of team," political columnist David S. Broder wrote on June 6, 1984, the fortieth anniversary of D-Day and, rather less pivotally, Wilson's first year as a midwestern dominance. "They prefer not to work at night. They believe that three hours of labor in the afternoon are enough for any job. They know the old ways are best. God intended baseball to be played on grass and under the sun, so they play it that way. They appreciate beautiful surroundings. There is no more gracious ball park than Wrigley Field."

In 1944, as Broder entered the University of Chicago, Reagan, an Army Air Corps captain, made films "the producers didn't necessarily want *good*. They wanted them *Tuesday*," and paratroopers, filtering into Normandy, dropped like avenging angels, Wrigley Field was gracious yet. Often, the outside world was not. Wading in one of Italy's winding streams that had to be crossed repeatedly, a GI said, "Damn it! Every son of a bitch river in this country is named Volturno." On June 5, General Dwight D. Eisenhower, the commander of Operation Overlord, told his troops: "If you see an aircraft flying over you, it will be ours." Eighty days later, Charles de Gaulle entered Paris. Germany bombed London with V-2 rockets. B-29s began raids on Japan from nearby Saipan. In December, the Battle of the Bulge, fought amid the incongruity of luxuriant stands of wood, ensured the Third Reich's demise. At home, women stampeded the work force, producing armaments (U.S. plants made more than 41 billion bullets) and newly rife synthetics and, less than three years after unemployment topped 10 percent, making the economy swell. Americans bought war bonds (in all, $100 billion), grew fresh vegetables in "victory gardens," and donated scrap metal (to huge collection tureens), time (to USO canteens), and 13 million pints of blood (to be administered as plasma to the wounded). Housewives withstood cigarette, liquor, and paper shortages, endured food and gas rationing and citywide dimouts, and understood, as Hitler never could, a poster reading, "Use it up — wear it up — make it do! Our labor and our goods are fighting!" Only Black America, understandably, seemed immune from contagion. At Red Cross quarters, their blood was segregated; when white soldiers boarded troopships, a band played "God Bless America"; when black recruits trudged up the plank, they heard "The Darktown Struters' Ball." During 1940–44, federal spending leaped from $9 billion to $95 billion. Twenty-seven million people moved. "Looks like the war," a farm

agent said, "has speeded every kind of process, good and bad, in this country."
Returning from war, soldiers would confront old, unfamiliar places.

For all these itinerant writhings, the beckoner of Chicago baseball was
fiercely disinterested. The 1944 Cubs, however, won seventy-five games, their
most since 1940. With *that*, Bert Wilson was transfixed.

"I've been in Chicago now for almost fifty years," Brickhouse acknowledged,
"so maybe I'm not the most objective guy in North America."

"I've heard that," I said of the Voice whose robust "Hey-Hey" after a Cubs'
home run joined generations of listeners.

"It's true," he laughed. "I've always considered sportscasting first and above
all entertainment. I'm like Harry Caray — I couldn't be dry, didn't want to be.
I liked the 'Let's forget our troubles and have some fun' approach."

"And that's what Chicago wanted."

"The people in this whole area don't want the sophisticated, 'What difference
does it matter who wins?' attitude," he said. "Baseball's a religion here, it's a
way of life. It's a lot, I suppose, like Red Sox' fans in New England, passed
on from father to son, mother to daughter. It's like a dowry."

"Was Wilson part of it?"

"Oh, he was wild. I recall once how he and I were going out to dinner
someplace, and we got in a massive traffic jam. Didn't go anywhere for hours.
And some guy about eighteen cars away started honking an SOS on his car
horn."

"And Wilson was a ham radio operator," I remembered.

"Yes, and he started honking back in code. It was like a Mardi Gras — a
carnival of noise. But that was Bert — he did *everything* with gusto. And he was
so typical of the kind of style that broadcasters here have adopted," Brickhouse said. "Of one thing I'm positive. You had in that era [the 1940s] the one
city with the most colorful collection of broadcasters anywhere."

Among this collection, Brickhouse and Elson (more formal than his sidekick) gabbled over WGN, the siren-sweet Jimmy Dudley over WCFL (until,
in 1947, he left for Cleveland), and Hodges, the pre-Wilson Working Man's
announcer (like WGN's coupling, a future Hall of Famer), over WIND, 560
on your dial. The hit parade also featured Hal Totten and Lew Fonseca and
sunny Charlie Grimm, "Jolly Cholly," baseball's ambassador without *vitae*, who
worked as a player and coach, scout and broadcaster, and whose managerial
creed enshrined, "Keep 'em happy."

"We all like to think of ourselves as the sum of our parts," mused Caray, at
ease in public, at home in crowds. Debuting in St. Louis in 1945, he starred
for twenty-five years as Voice of the Cardinals. Fired on October 9, 1969, Caray
spent one year at Oakland before ambling to Comiskey Park in 1971. "But if
that's true of Joe Blow, it was magnified with Charlie Grimm. He had more
parts than most of us, and he did in baseball about everything it's possible to
try."

As a child, Grimm loved baseball, banjo, and the stage; as a twenty-two-year
major leaguer, 1925–36 with the Cubs, he batted .290 with 2,299 hits, played

in two World Series (hitting .364), and led the league's first basemen in fielding for nine consecutive seasons; as a scout, he tried, vainly, to enhance the Cubs' rag-tag teams of the fifties; as a coach, he once feigned a seizure, toppling over backward in a dead faint, when a Cubs' pitcher whacked a home run. "When a Cubs' regular also homered," author James Enright wrote, "Charlie whistled all of the bench warmers out of the dugout, each with a bat in hand, and lined them up in two rows with bats upraised to form an arch for the homer hitter to pass underneath as he returned to the dugout, accompanied by Grimm in a suitably majestic manner." In 1961, Grimm served as one of the eight original members of the remedial (in theory) and inept (in fact) College of Coaches. "The Cubs have been playing without players for years," one critic patronized. "Now, they're going to try it without a manager."

Against this heterogeneity, the Grimm of stronghold memory occupied the dugout. "As a manager," said Vince Lloyd, a Cubs' announcer since 1965, "that's how most people recall him," shepherding the Cubs in 1932–38 and 1944–49 and for seventeen games in 1960. In thirteen years, Charlie won three championships. Three times, he was fired. Twice, he bounded to the broadcast booth.

On August 4, 1932, Grimm replaced Rogers Hornsby, won thirty-seven of the last fifty-seven games, and finished first: the first manager hired after mid-season to clasp a pennant. Three years later, winning twenty-one games in a row, Jolly Cholly pounced again: the Cubs' third flag in seven years. In 1938, he yielded to Gabby Hartnett; rallying, the Cubs won *another* pennant. Booted upstairs, Grimm broadcast for three seasons, managed the American Association Milwaukee Brewers to a 1943 championship, and awaited the Cubs' next call for help.

Under Hartnett and Jimmy Wilson, the 1939–43 teams placed fourth, fifth, sixth, sixth, and fifth, and after the 1944 Cubs lost thirteen of their first fourteen games, the cry went forth: *get Grimm!* In 1945, the Cubs led the league in hitting, pitching, fielding, and the standings. At .355, Phil Cavarretta won the batting title. Stan Hack hit .323, Andy Pafko drove in 110 runs, and two Hanks, Wyse and Borowy, combined for thirty-three victories. On September 29, the Cubs beat Pittsburgh to clinch the pennant. "At the team victory party," Enright glowed, "Grimm had a pair of shears. Everybody who had a necktie on contributed. He had a quilt made. It's probably the oddest pennant souvenir in the history of the game."

Fired (for the second time) in 1949, hired (for the third time) in 1959, and fired on May 5 (who would believe it?) after the 1960 Cubs crawled to a 6–11 start, Grimm was banished to the WGN Radio booth, replacing announcer Lou Boudreau, who, in turn, replaced *Grimm* as *manager*.

"Phil Wrigley called me in, this was in May," said Brickhouse, "and he said, 'Jack, I want to make a trade, and I want you to take care of it.' I said, 'Oh, who's involved?' And Mr. Wrigley looked at me and said, 'I want to trade Boudreau for Grimm.' "

" 'Boudreau for Grimm?' " Brickhouse repeated.

" 'Yes,' Wrigley answered. 'Charlie's worrying himself sick over the team. He's out walking the streets when he should be resting. And between that and his coaching first base, if the Cubs don't kill him first, his sore feet will.' "

What a team, I thought. "So you went to both guys and arranged a trade."

"Yep," Brickhouse said. "A manager for a broadcaster." Only with the Cubs.

On November 15, 1983, at eighty-five, the unsinkable and eminently recyclable Jolly Cholly finally sank. His body was cremated, his ashes scattered over Wrigley Field, his career a creature of (baseball's) habit, as renewable as the morning sun.

Grimm's fairy tale of 1945, said Wilson, proudly, "provided me with the greatest thrill of my career." In truth, he had few. After 1945, the Cubs plummeted. In Mr. Puckett's last ten seasons, the National League's once-luminous Chicagos (in 1906–10, four pennants) won 598 games, lost 786, and three times finished last; a generation matured never knowing the first division. One expected *Webster's* to patent the term "Cubs' fan: To suffer, to be inflicted upon. A derivative of the old proverb, 'Being Irish means laughing at life knowing that in the end, life will break your heart.' Being a Cubs' fan is twice as hard (at least)."

Frustrated, Wilson's tenor must chatter ceaselessly about Hank Sauer, "the Mayor of Wrigley Field" and 1952's Most Valuable Player, slamming a league-co-high thirty-seven home runs, and new manager Cavarretta, whose team that year went 77–77 (in 1947–62, the Cubs' only .500 season), and the small-gloved third baseman, Stan Hack, who batted .301 in sixteen seasons with Chicago, and a sad-faced man named Sam (Toothpick) Jones, the first black to no-hit a major-league opponent (on May 12, 1955, against the Pirates), and a gangling, quick-wristed shortstop plucked for $20,000 from the Kansas City Monarchs: Ernie Banks, the greatest Cub of all time.

Still, the team fumbled, and as its misery deepened, its following grew, full of listeners, viewers, and far-off fans who loved sunlit ball games ("Hello, this is Bert Wilson saying good afternoon on a beautiful, cloudless day") and endemic exuberance ("Let's play two!" cried Mr. Cub) and the rich antiquity of Wrigley Field, with its baseball, real baseball, as it was *meant* to be played, and who, by the 1980s, avowing America's ardor for any dog that was under, had made the ageless, peerless, Grand Eventless (for four decades now) Chicago Cubs, arguably, America's most irresistible team.

"I've had a good chance to see all the promising young rookies who'll be fighting for a job this summer, and believe me, they look great," reported Bert Wilson, dreamily, one March day in 1955 (or was it 1965, 1975, or 1985? Only the seasons, not illusions, change). "The Cubs' infield generally is recognized as one of the best in the big leagues already, and there are several outfielders who look like real major leaguers. Pitching is a cinch to be better, and the catching department was given a big boost when Harry Chiti [who would hit all of .231], a fellow built like Gabby Hartnett [and who played like Gabby Hayes] came back from the service. Yes, it looks like a very interesting season [do you believe in Peter Pan?] for the Chicago Cubs this year."

This "promising . . great . . . one of the best. . . . real major leaguers . . .

very interesting" team won seventy-two outings, lost eighty-one, and finished twenty-six games behind the Brooklyn Dodgers. It also finished off "the biggest Cubs' fan I've ever known," said Jim Gallagher, the team's business manager. In Wrigley Field, hearts are broken every year. On November 5, 1955, Bert Wilson's heart stopped beating. He was forty-four years old.

*   *   *

"This was a sports rivalry unlike any that ever was or probably ever will be," is how columnist Steve Jacobson, writing in 1974, catalogued the holy wars between Brooklyn and New York. "The fans rode the subway from their homes to the turf of the other team and cheered their raving hearts out. Each meeting was an angry collision. And sometimes it was close to hatred."

During Bert Wilson's tenure, the Cubs' fiercest rivalry entailed a short trip from the pleasant meadows of Wrigley Field to the boxy ball yard at Grand Avenue and Dodier Street. There, less than six hours by rail from the North Side of Chicago — The Chicago & Alton linked the cities daily — the St. Louis Cardinals touched an entire region, with the heartland of America bestirred.

"Swarming up from the Texas wheat fields, the Georgia cotton lands, the West Virginia coal mines, the Oklahoma cow ranges, the Ozark farms, [they] redramatized for the public that old traditional story about the talent of common men," drama critic Lloyd Lewis said in 1942. "They fit the historic pattern of the American success story, the legend of the country boy who, on native wit and vitality, crashes through, clear up to the top."

By the time Lewis was writing, *they* meant the St. Louis Swifties, as newsmen called them, or the Runnin' Redbirds, or, less affectedly, the Gas House Gang. (Research intimates that the latter name arose when Willard Mullin, cartoonist of the *New York World-Telegram*, painted two large gas tanks on the indigent side of railroad tracks. In the 1930s drawing, several ballplayers crossed over into the good part of town, carrying big clubs, not bats, on their shoulders.)

The Gas Housers baited fans and rivals, flung dirt at umpires, scratched with teammates, mocked league officials, and embronzed themselves. They carried workmen's tools on road trips, disrupting hotel lobbies with their pranks. They formed a band, the Mississippi Mudcats — carting fiddles and harmonicas, washboards and guitars; playing entries like "Rock Island Line" and "The Wreck of the Old '97" on long train rides to Cincinnati and points east. In 1930-31 and 1934 and, when that gang grew old, in 1942-44 and 1946, they "crashed through, clear up to the top," winning seven pennants and five World Series. They made aggression a symphony. They were raucous, defiant, and sleek.

"Hold that success against the tone of the country," said Bob Broeg, and, unguardedly, he twirled his glasses in one hand. The author of twelve books, recipient of the University of Missouri's medal for distinguished service to journalism, and former columnist for *The Sporting News*, Broeg became *St.*

Louis Post-Dispatch sports editor in 1958. Twenty-two years later, he entered the writers' wing of the Baseball Hall of Fame.

"I remember when I took tickets at Sportsman's Park in the mid-thirties," he said. "The country was on its knees, especially in the states around St. Louis, and you wouldn't draw flies all week. But then came Sunday."

"And the habitual double-header."

"You know," Broeg remarked, "Sam Breadon [the Cardinals' owner] was condemned for playing two games on Sunday. He actually *started* the practice, and for his trouble, people called it synthetic. But by nine A.M., when the gates opened on Sunday, the whole section instantly filled up with brown-bagging out-of-towners."

"Sunday was the only day," I guessed, "when fans from outlying areas had the time to make the trip."

"That," he said, "and the fact that they were almost certain to see Dizzy Dean pitch — all during the thirties, the Cardinals staggered it that way. But the point is — this ball club really pulled them in from the hinterlands."

"Becoming a regional team."

Bob Broeg nodded. "They were that," he mused, "and they were *more*. Don't forget that in the thirties and forties, in fact, up until the late 1950s [when the Dodgers and Giants carpetbagged to California], St. Louis was the majors' westernmost club. You could almost say it was the most southerly too. So the Cardinals had all this area — more than half of the *country* — to themselves, and their spiritual following was enormous.

"I recall so well two names you may have heard of. Bob Feller grew up in Iowa and Mickey Mantle in Oklahoma, and they both told me years later that the big event of their young lives was when their dads mustered a couple dollars to bring them hundreds of miles to St. Louis for a Cardinal game. And that was characteristic. This was the focal point for an entire part of America."

Like Wrigley Field, the Xanadu of these "brown-bagging out-of-towners" had personality. A double-decked grandstand extended fully along both foul lines. A high screen covered the right-field pavilion. Left field stood 355 feet from home plate, a hefty shot even for power hitters; right field (pre-1953) was a more accommodating 320. To reach the center-field bleachers required a prodigious blast of 430 feet; the pasture's size gave Terry Moore (1935–42 and '46–48) a perfect showcase for his fielding. Seats were splintered, comfort uncommon, and parking, unfailingly minute. Yet with its scarce foul territory, steep-rowed sweep of stands, and clamorous, knowing celebrants, Sportsman's Park became a Midwest bathhouse, and as the Cardinals of the early 1930s — Frisch and Martin, Durocher and Medwick, Rip Collins and the brothers Dean — yielded to the Cardinals of Branch Rickey, with his farm system and shameless profiteering, and the tightly wound, uncoiling Stan Musial, escaping the poverty of Donora, Pennsylvania, and Albert (Red) Schoendienst, a freckle-faced boy from southern Illinois, and Country Slaughter, who played every inning with the full measure of his strength, going to St. Louis, for generations of Middle Americans, proceeded to suggest: coming home.

In 1928, Pepper Martin played his first game as a major leaguer. St. Louis first baseman "Sunny Jim" Bottomley whipped thirty-one homers and won the MVP Award. Musial turned eight years of age. Dean (the elder, Dizzy) endured his first year in the Army. The Redbirds drew 778,147 customers, more than they had ever drawn (and ever would, until 1946), and finished two games ahead of the second-place Giants. From the subtle beauty of rural Oklahoma, deep in Cardinals' country, wandered the strapping Elven (Mutt) Mantle, father of the unborn Mick, and a thick-lipped, stubby-haired former high school coach and part-time referee.

Loping separately to Sportsman's Park, Mantle visited the left-field bleachers and France Laux, the narrow, seat-soiled press box. In 1927, Laux had joined station KVOO, Tulsa, as a $30-a-week sports announcer; in 1929, he would jump to St. Louis' 50,000-watt KMOX. "I went up there," he often said, "for a thirty-day trial." Laux's trial lasted until 1953, when Anheuser-Busch Brewery bought the Cardinals, the errant Browns fled to Baltimore, and, at fifty-five, France retired.

For eighteen years (1929–46), Laux vibrated over KMOX as the Voice of St. Louis baseball, dismissing pomposity and elaboration.

"When he was young, he was pretty aloof, but he warmed up as he came to know St. Louis," Broeg said. Then very slowly: "Remember, he came from the country, and it took him time to adjust. Eventually, he did *that*, but he still always spoke in a flat, metallic southern type of accent. It was accepted in the thirties, but later on, when competition hit him in the war years — keep in mind that other stations could broadcast too — it was really quite a drawback."

"Laux wasn't the stylist of the year," I said.

"No, and it cost him," he counseled. "France had his strengths — players and managers liked him, and he was impartial to the bone. He was even OK on live home games [from Sportsman's Park, Laux aired the Cardinals and Browns]. But when the team hit the road, trouble."

I stopped. "But he handled away games through re-creations."

"Oh, he handled them," Broeg jousted. "It's just that they were deadly dull."

Laux's narration was constrained, laconic; ardent praise embarrasssed him, jarred the modesty which cloaked his self-esteem. "Let me put it this way," I said. "He was a quiet, low-key guy, which worked for him *away* from the mike and worked against him *behind* the mike."

"Bingo," Bob said. "The truth was that when France had the field to himself, he could just *be* himself — there was no one to compare him with. Be a reporter, just tell the facts, and he could do that well. But when he had to entertain — jazz up the away re-creations or be flashy like his competitors, the Deans and Harry Carays — he couldn't do it. People said that he was too old-timey."

"What did they say when the Cardinals decided to grant exclusive rights to just *one* announcing team?"

"What happened there," he said, "was that Sam Breadon got fed up with sharing KMOX with the Browns. He was sick and tired of only having his home games covered live. The Cardinals didn't do *any* live away feeds, and not even all their road games were carried."

"So he beat it," I said, "and tried to find a station that would do all 154 games."

"He wanted more money for the rights," Broeg noted.

"He wanted more exposure with the money," I said.

"Yes," Broeg said, "and when that became clear, France didn't have much hope. Breadon was going to award the games to the guys who could do the most to promote his team," and when, in 1947, the Cardinals' owner awarded exclusivity to Caray and partner Charles E. (Gabby) Street, the ex-St. Louis manager, "France wasn't just old-timey, he was done. In the next few years, he did a few Browns' games when their regular broadcasters had a scheduling conflict and were off doing something else. But even then, because almost no one was following the Browns, almost nobody was listening to Laux."

In Laux's first six seasons, the Cardinals won three pennants; in his last five, they notched four more. France wondered at Marty Marion's range and durability, the Man's obliteration of Brooklyn pitching, and Dizzy and Daffy's 49–18 benchmark in 1934. On May 24, 1940, in the Grand Dame of Grand Avenue's first night game, he recorded the Browns' 3–2 loss to Cleveland. On April 17, 1945, he related the one-armed Pete Gray's debut against the Tigers. Over CBS Radio, he broadcast the World Series from 1933 to 1938 (the year before Mutual's co-option), and the All-Star Game from 1934, when Carl Hubbell, a fellow Oklahoman, fanned five consecutive American Leaguers, to 1941, when Teddy Ballgame's ninth-inning drive, soaring high into the second deck of Briggs Stadium, downed the Nationals, 7–5.

"I've got to be honest," he often said, post-1946. "Watching that '34 game from the Polo Grounds, I was describing the same guy that I'd batted against in Oklahoma bush baseball so many years before. So you can imagine my thrill when I told them: 'Now Hubbell has struck out Ruth; fans, he puts over the third strike on Gehrig,' and so on down the line."

"And what," a reporter asked in February 1945, "is your greatest World Series thrill?"

"Just three months later," he said, saturnine in the past's implacability. "In that '34 Tiger-Cardinal Series, the late Will Rogers, a great fan and our most famous Oklahoman, was attending the games in Detroit, and I managed to get him on the mike. Maybe I had mentioned to him that I was an Okie. Anyway, with the whole nation listening in, he asked, 'You don't happen to know Judge Laux out in Oklahoma, do you?' I replied, 'Just slightly; he's only my dad.'"

At about the time Laux was glimpsing effulgent memories, America was nearing what one observer called the "blessed hush of history." On both fronts, victory seemed inevitable. Chester Nimitz, commander-in-chief of the Pacific Fleet, explained: "It's simple arithmetic to fight the Japanese: subtraction for them and addition for us." General Carl Spaatz of the Eighth Air Force asked: "What's the use of bombing rabbits in Italy when you can bomb wildcats in Germany?" George S. Patton, vowing, "Battle is the most magnificent competition in which a human being can indulge," swept eastward toward Berlin. One read of Yalta and Okinawa and Iwo Jima and Remagen, where a platform platoon from the Ninth Armored Division crossed the Rhine, and the Elbe, where American and Soviet troops toasted one another with captured German champagne. Roosevelt died, at sixty-three, at Warm Springs, Georgia, of a cerebral hemorrhage. "Boys," his successor told reporters, "if you ever pray, pray for me now. When they told me yesterday what happened, I felt like the whole moon, the stars, and all the planets had fallen on me." On April 30, 1945, Hitler shot himself. The first atomic bomb was detonated at Alamogordo, New Mexico. "I am sure," a scientist said, "that at the end of the world — in the last millisecond of the earth's existence — the last man will see something very similar to what we have seen." General Douglas MacArthur became Grand Overseer of Japan. Churchill became an ex-prime minister; Clement Attlee succeeded him. On Broadway, critics found fashionable *Carousel* and Tennessee Williams' *The Glass Menagerie*.

"It was a glorious time," Laux later said of the mid-1940s, his peroration as a Cardinals' announcer. "To err is Truman," cracked sophists, but not the son of the Oklahoma Lauxes. "Had enough?" asked radio spots in the 1946 election. The electorate responded; for the first time since 1928, Republicans won control of Congress. Rationing and price controls ended; the Greek Civil War began; in Nuremberg, nineteen of twenty-two high German officials were found guilty of "crimes against humanity." Traveling to Westminster College in Fulton, Missouri, Churchill ordained: "From Stettin in the Baltic to Trieste in the Adriatic, an Iron Curtain has descended across the continent." At New York's Imperial Theatre, in the first of 1,147 performances, *Annie Get Your Gun* opened with Ethel Merman as Annie Oakley. Was the musical old-fashioned? a critic asked its lyricist and composer. "Yes," replied Irving Berlin. "A good old-fashioned smash."

For France Laux, shed from Redbirds' play-by-play and assigned to boxing, wrestling, basketball, and hockey, the years after 1946 were neither glorious *nor* a good old-fashioned smash.

"I knew him quite well," said Jack Buck, the irreverent son of Holyoke (Massachusetts), graduate of Ohio State University, Voice of Columbus and Rochester minor-league baseball, and member of the Cardinals' broadcast team since 1954.

"As a broadcaster?" I said.

"No," he said. "When I was coming in through the door of KMOX, he was going out. But I got to know him personally. And even after he retired in 1953, he was very visible around the area. He owned a bowling house, did a hell of a lot to publicize the sport. He was secretary of the American Bowling Congress. He even did tournament reports for the station."

"When he went around, did listeners remember him," I said, "or was he just some voice from the bygone past?"

Buck's voice lowered. "Who'll remember any of us a hundred years from now?" he asked. "First of all, don't forget that we've always had colorful announcers here, so it's not like when Laux left, there was a void."

"Not with Ol' Diz and Caray still around."

"They obscured his memory," he said. "And there was also a generation gap-type of thing, the reality that in the last couple of decades, folks even the age that I am [now, sixty-one] either were aware of France only as a bowling promoter, blotting out his baseball work, *or*, if they remembered him in baseball, it was mostly in the sense of, 'Gee, he was a pioneer, one of the first,' and then they'd talk about all the stories he told of his days in Oklahoma, of the World Series he did, or even the fact that for a city of St. Louis' size, one of the smaller towns in baseball, France became one of the early big names in network broadcasting."

Laux had two sons (Roger, a high school principal, and France, a pathologist), and "he was very proud of them," Buck recollected. "They were a success — they did it on their own."

Elsewhere, though, as Curt Flood sued baseball and Lou Brock retired and Bob Gibson, the Prometheus of the pitching mound, ended his remarkable career, Laux met a somerset of adversity — losing several fingers in a lawnmower accident and, in 1976, his wife, Pearl, of forty-seven years; moving to a nursing home, where he died two years later, of a heart ailment, at eighty.

"He went out pretty shabbily," said Buck.

"A far piece from starring at the World Series," I proposed.

"The *Series?*" he said, sadly. "Or even from what he'd been *here*," with his familiar soft tones, clipped precision, and relaxed, imperturbable air.

"I just lived too long," Laux told a friend in 1977, forty-eight years after first gripping the KMOX microphone. The world he now encountered was not the world he knew.

*   *   *

What world did Jay Hanna Jerome (Dizzy) Dean, born in a rickety shack to indigent Arkansas sharecroppers, realizing the American Dream when many Americans had abandoned it, *not* know or encounter or confirm on faith?

Triumphant, this bolt of Americana in baseball flannels, tall and lean and loose-jointed, was as much a Falstaffian legend as any ballplayer who ever lived. "Fogging" his "good ol' country hardball" past opposing batters, or saying of his fractured grammar, "A lot of people who ain't saying *ain't* ain't eatin'," or prompting a newspaper's double-edged headline, "X-Rays of Dean's Head Show Nothing," Ol' Diz ratified his manager's 1930 prophecy: "I think he's going to be a *great* pitcher," Gabby Street told St. Louis Mayor Victor Miller, "but I'm afraid we'll never know from one minute to the next what he's going to say or do."

He was the son of a migratory cotton picker, rough and ready and slightly tattered. His formal education ended in the second grade, "and I wasn't so good," he added, "in the first grade, either." At eighteen, ignoring curfew, Dean bumped into the president of the Texas League at 4 A.M. "Good morning, Mr. President," he is supposed to have said. "So the old boy is out prowling around by hisself, eh? Well, sir, I'm not one to squawk. Us stars and presidents must have our fun."

Ol' Diz won his major-league debut, 3–1, over Pittsburgh, on the final day of the 1930 season. In 1932, he won eighteen games; the next four years, he won twenty or more. "Me 'n' [brother] Paul," he said in 1934, "will win forty-five games this year," and in fact they won forty-nine. Late that September, he threw a three-hit shutout in the first set of a double-header. Paul no-hit the Dodgers in the second game. "Dawgonnit," Diz protested. "If I'd-a knowed Paul was gonna throw a no-hitter, I'd-a throwed one too."

By 1936, Dizzy Dean, only twenty-five, owned 121 major-league victories. "He threw so smoothly and efficiently," said Broeg, a teenager when Dean won thirty games in 1934, "that my guess is if he'd stayed healthy, he'd have used that resilient right arm to pitch into the bigs into the early fifties. That way, he'd have opposed the black stars he met on barnstorming tours — and respected — at a time they were locked out of the major leagues."

"You're talking about a career for Dean of over twenty years," I said.

"Yes," he said, "and I really believe Dean could have won more than four hundred games."

"Even Christy Mathewson won fewer than that [373]," I pointed out.

"True, but as a pitcher, this guy had it all," Broeg said. "I was twelve years old when I first saw him throw, and even then, it hit me: this big, strapping right-hander with high cheekbones and that flowing delivery who threw a ball — well, when it popped into catcher Gus Mancuso's glove, it was like a high explosive."

More than Gomez or Feller or "King Carl" Hubbell, Dean was "the stunning comic heroic," wrote Lloyd Lewis, "most famous of all living pitchers," and on July 7, 1937, pitching the All-Star Game at Griffith Stadium, he met an Achilles end. Shaking off Gabby Hartnett's signal, Diz threw a fastball to Earl Averill, the Cleveland outfielder, who lashed a drive that struck a glancing blow off Dean's left toe.

"Your big toe is fractured," a doctor told Jay Hanna.

"No, it ain't," said Ol' Diz. "It's broke."

Too soon, Dean returned to the Cardinals' rotation, his broken toe still in a splint. Favoring his arm, he hurt his arm. Proud of his fastball, he lost his fastball. A pillar of St. Louis, he was traded by St. Louis — to the Cubs, in April 1938 — and reduced, Broeg said, to Diz's "nothin' ball," to "slow-balling everybody to death. No fast stuff. Just great motion, control, and heart," he retired on May 14, 1941. Who can't go home again? Diz might have stammered, aping Thomas Wolfe, had he *heard* of Thomas Wolfe. Tomorrow, Dean told reporters, he would visit St. Louis' Falstaff Brewery, the Cardinals' radio sponsor. "Think I'm going to like this here play-by-play," he said, adopting his favorite hillbilly role. Baseball on radio, still maturing, would never be the same.

Ol' Diz first faced the microphone one sleepy afternoon in June. "I hope I'm as good a sports announcer as I was a pitcher," he said, brusquely. "Now I know how a prisoner feels walking to his death." His concern seems modest now, for by August 1941, several surveys gauged, Dean owned an astonishing 82 percent of the Cardinals' baseball audience. Saucy and ad-libbing, with a generous spattering of gall, he charmed Mound City listeners. Runners "slud," Dizzy's personal past tense. Batters "swang." Pitchers "throwed" the ball with

great "spart." ("Spart," he confided, "is pretty much like gumption or fight.
Like the Spart of St. Louis, that plane Lindbergh flowed to Europe.") A hitter
could look "mighty hitterish" or "stand confidentially" at the plate. Faking a
double steal, two players "are now returning to their respectable bases."

"What I remember about Diz is that he was a personality more than an
announcer," mused Mel Allen, Dean's 1950–51 broadcast partner, and reliving
the Great One, The Voice flashed a smile. "Oh, he could get serious with you
once in a while when *you* were talking, but once *he* took off solo, doing what
passed for play-by-play, it was show biz time. Missing a pitch or two—it never
fazed him. And he was smart, intelligent, and how he loved to sing that song.
What was it? The artillery . . ."

" 'The Wabash Cannon Ball,' " I said.

"That's it," he said, his jaw jutting forward, "that's what I meant. Diz had
a method and a style all his own. Nothing like it before."

"Just look around. Nothing like it since."

"That's because you couldn't get away today with the stuff he did then,"
Allen countered. "They'd throw you out of the booth with the mike strangled
around your neck."

"Were his mistakes preplanned?"

"Some were, they must have been," he said. "Diz always knew what he was
doing. The things he came up with—a guy 'sludding' into third—they were
professional. I'll never forget: Once he said 'slid' correctly, by mistake, and he
corrected himself. He *wanted* to goof up—it was a part of the vaudeville. But
even more of his mistakes, I'm sure, were natural—the guy just didn't have
much of an education. But he had an excitement about him, and he was a great
name, especially in St. Louis. And Good Lord, he was an extrovert."

To fans at home, Ol' Diz urged, "Don't fail to miss tomorrow's game." To
batters in the on-deck circle, he called loudly, "Well, here's Enos Slaughter, my
ol' pal. Come on now, knock the ball down this guy's throat." To Cardinals
in the dugout, Dean conversed by signals from the booth. To critics who disparaged his colloquialisms, Dean observed, "When I tell people that the score
is nothin'-nothin' and nobody's winning, why, folks know exactly what the
score is. I just talk common sense." Each game assumed the air of fresh performance, its set of realities choreographed by the Ozark encyclopedist. "I
never keep a scorecard or the batting averuges," he said. "I hate statics [sta-
tistics]. What I got to know, I keep in my haid." Supposed spontaneity became
pervasive; what *new* atrocities, fans wondered, would Ol' Diz orchestrate? This
batter had an "unorsodock stance." Give that shortstop "a sist." A play made
adroitly was "nonchalloted." A one-handed catch was "a la carte," a pop fly
a "can of corn." Swinging at a bad pitch comprised a "fishing trip"; a strikeout
victim strode "disgustilly back to the bainch." When Cleveland loaded the
bases, "That loads the Injuns full of bases." A critic was, if practiced, a "what's
whatter." A manager "argyin' with an umparr [umpire] is like argyin' with
a stump. Maybe you city folks don't know what a stump is. Wal, it's somethin'
a tree has been cut down off of."

Merging malapropisms and dialect, Dean invaded Missourians with a regiment of promiscuity. About a sordid colleague, Diz proclaimed, "He's just a *main* [mean] guy." With a game approaching midnight, he revealed, "We've got less than an *are* left." Walked intentionally, Johnny Mize was *purply* passed. Like slud, "tell" too acquired a past tense: "I *toad* Frisch not to yank me." St. Louis heard *karm* ("He karmed a double off the wall") and *airs* ("Three runs, five hits, no airs") and *thang* ("The only thang wrong with him's his arm") and *tetch* ("Ol' Diz'll tetch him what's what") and *pose* ("Why do the Browns always lose their pose?" he asked), which converted, naturally, to "poise." Like verbs, nouns, and adjectives, proper names imbued the cutting block. "They got to be my words," Diz said, " 'cause no one else would have 'em." Mort Cooper became "Cupper," Stan Musial "Moo-zell," Phil Rizzuto "Rizzooti" or "Rizzoota," Chico Carrasquel "that hitter with the three K's in his name." Tony Giuliani, a Washington catcher, was rechristened "Julie-Annie." With Chicago pitcher Ed Hanyzewski, Dean shifted oral tactics. "I liked to have broken my jaw tryin' to pronounce that one," he said. "But I said his name by just holdin' my nose and sneezing."

While Ol' Diz rambled, the Cardinals thrived. In 1942, St. Louis won the World Series, and Dean was judged "baseball's announcer with the worst diction." By 1944, a Voice of the first-place Browns and Redbirds, he had "become even more a terrific radio favorite in St. Louis than ever before," said *The Sporting News*, naming Diz its Announcer of the Year, "an accomplishment all the more remarkable because his broadcasts were carried over only stations with limited power"—WEW, St. Louis, a daytime station, and WTMV, East St. Louis, at night.

"He was poles apart from other announcers," I said to Robert (Buddy) Blattner. A native of St. Louis and, at sixteen, the world's doubles table-tennis champion, Blattner played five years with the Cardinals, Phillies, and Giants. Perishing as an athlete, he then solicited the broadcast booth. In 1950–53, he covered the flagging Browns. In 1955–59, he teamed with Dean on the CBS Television "Game of the Week." "Given that, how did Diz know he'd succeed?"

"He related to people because he was Dizzy. He's going to say anything because he's dizzy, and he *was* dizzy," said Blattner, tall and genial. "He didn't do baseball games like anybody else. He didn't want to. He was loved in St. Louis, and he knew that. He had been, and would remain, a Hall of Fame pitcher, recognized as such. And I think he'd always had such overwhelming ability to back up everything he'd done, such total confidence."

"Unbridled?" I asked.

"Oh, yes," he said, "and as a result, I'm positive he believed he'd succeed on the air, even with the incredible spectacle he made of the King's English. After all, there was a certain command he possessed. The possibility of failure probably never entered his mind."

"But still, at the start, he didn't know whether he'd be good, bad, or indifferent."

"Not for sure," Blattner conceded, "but he knew he had the powerful personality. And if he didn't make it big in radio, so what? He cared how he did, but he still had the indifference that could be enjoyed only by one who knew he could make a living in some other way. Even back then, he didn't need the money. I think he made enough from golf alone to last him the rest of his life."

Ol' Diz, though, *made* it big, and by the time Germany surrendered and Bess Myerson became Miss America and the world awoke to the dewy nightmare of the Nuclear Age, even golf, among Dean's variety of eclectic skills, paled beside his transcendent sense of comedy.

Already, in early 1944, when announcers (by government decree) could not give weather news (lest that scorecard help the enemy), Dean had skirted caution. "I can't tell you folks why this here game is stopped," he said as rain pelted Sportsman's Park, "but I'll tell you what. If you just stick your head outside the nearest window, you'll know what I mean." Now, Diz grew more restless as games grew dull, roaming far afield to tell a community of stories. "Me 'n' Paul was always set down first at the spelling bees," he announced one August afternoon. "The best spellers on our bench was Lydie and May George— they'd be up there spelling and they'd butt heads to see who won. What was I talking about on them Red Sox? . . . Oh yeah, if Williams will cut more of them fouls into singles, he will be batting a million."

Chatting torrentially, submerging play-by-play, a plain-spoken, portly Dean (by the mid-1950s, almost three hundred pounds) adorned lax Browns' attendance ("The peanuts vendors is going through the stands. They is not doing so good because there is more of them than there is of customers") and baseball's finest catcher ("Yogi needs a half-dozen hot dogs and three or four bags of popcorn just to keep going during a game. I'd rather take a span of mules to feed than him") and the joy of travel ("I think I'll take a trip to Nofus Scofus") or bird-hunting ("Wish my old Texas meat dog, Suds, was here. The skillet never gets rusty when Suds is around") or umpire-baiting ("They shot the wrong McKinley!" he turned on Bill McKinley, whose *out* call Dean dismissed) or familiar, pleasant "hillbilluh" music. "Man, Roy Acuff is what I love best, not your kind of slop," he roared when a St. Louis station, offering an off-season position as a disc jockey, asked Dean to comment on classical music. "You want me to play this sympathetic [symphonic] music and commertate about these Rooshian and French and Kraut composers? *Me* pronounce them composers' names? Why, I can't even pronounce everybody's name in the Cleveland Indians' infield!"

When Judge Landis removed him from the all-St. Louis 1944 World Series, dubbing his diction "unfit for a national broadcaster," Diz replied: "How can that commissar say I ain't eligible to broadcast? I ain't never met anybody that didn't know what ain't means."

When Dean turned to football (for the first and only time), he rolled a die of murmuration. The officials were "umparrs"; referees, "those guys wearing striped pajamas"; the head linesman, "a guy who must be low on ammunition or a poor shot because I ain't seen him hit nobody."

When the English Teachers Association of Missouri—terming Diz a cultural illiterate—demanded his removal from the air, Dean's home station (now WIL), the Association, and the *St. Louis Globe-Democrat* (whose editorial attacked the teachers' "smugness") received a righteous train of letters. "I see where some of the teachers is saying I'm butcherin' up the language a bit," Dizzy said, awash in redemption. "Just remember: When me and Paul was picking cotton in Arkansas, we didn't have no chance to go to school much. All I've got to say is that I'm real happy them kids is getting a chance today."

When, finally, in 1947, Sam Breadon chose Harry Caray and Gabby Street as the Cardinals' on-air magnates, Ol' Diz and his straight man, Johnny O'Hara, careened to St. Louis' raggle-taggle American Leaguers.

"Our radio surveys showed Dean has the largest baseball following in St. Louis," said Bill DeWitt, the Browns' general manager. "We're happy to offer Dizzy the opportunity to continue his contacts with his large local following." Writing in the *Chicago Sun*, Jack Clarke supplied an afterword. "All who cherish the inalienable rights of free speech and abhor censorship, as well as students of Elizabethan English," he said, "view with dismay Sam Breadon's decision to let Diz go [his reason: Dean's obstreperous candor]. Blessed with the gifts of tongues, Dean proved to be an extraordinarily popular announcer. When Dean did not have at his disposal a word suitable for the occasion, he simply invented one."

For three insignificant and frustrating years, Ol' Diz lambasted the patchwork Browns over station KWK, an Olivier in Podunk. In 1950, he dissolved the partnership.

"I slud along with them as long as I could," he said, "but I eventual made up my mind to quit. I was tired of being asked to talk up 'the great Browns' [in 1947–49, they finished eighth, sixth, and seventh] and being called a liar by the standings. One day I said the Browns were nothing but a lot of Humpty Dumpties. And that was the end of the Dizzy Dean broadcasting career in St. Louis."

Flapping with prosperity, Dean deserted radio ("I'm through talking about things," he pledged, "that folks ain't seein' ") and meandered to New York, where, as Allen's television sidekick (and for $40,000 a year), he would conduct (by design) a pre- and postgame program and syntax-maul (by inclination) the aloof, boundlessly arrogant, defending world champion Yankees.

Would New Yorkers accept (or even understand) the hawsers of Dean's ministry?

"Don't know if they'll get my meaning, but if they cain't, that just evens up the score," he said in his full, twanged voice. "I played here lots of times as a pitcher, and I never could make out what they was saying, either." Tit for tat? Quid pro quo? Not without conviction, this son of the lower South would soon be without a home.

*   *   *

Ol' Diz left the National League as baseball's electronic signposts were perceptively changing — from an emphasis on local broadcasting to a diversity of sounds and networks; from World Series marked *radio only* to Oktoberfests with extensive television coverage; from a 1945 populace that owned only 16,500 TV sets to an America, in the early 1950s, buying almost that many each day.

The medium "I'd say is pretty good," Bing Crosby once said of television, "considering it's for nothing," first greeted the public in 1936; three years later, at the New York World's Fair, regular program service was born; and by a point in the 1940s, when RCA unveiled the first color TV, "producing images," it said, "by electric and optical means," the kinetic fun house turned and seemed certain to become a household core. If we were not yet a global village, experts predicted, at least television might soon supplant radio as the nation's lynchpin.

"I don't think there's any question about the way a lot of television people felt back then, in the late thirties, the early forties, before we went to war," said Harry Coyle, the dean of television sports directors, debuting with the DuMont Network, an industry pioneer, in 1947.

"And how was that?" I said.

"They believed that before long TV would be top dog, or at least a strong contender, that it would be in everyone's living room," he said. "And it's easy to see why. The strides in TV had just come along so tremendously fast."

Then, with Pearl Harbor, civilian production withered, and for the next forty-five months, television channeled labor and technology into "Dr. Win the War." Between December 7, 1941 and September 2, 1945, the date of Japan's surrender, CBS Radio broadcast an astonishing 35,070 war *programs*, both news and entertainment, the equivalent of nine *months* of normal programming. NBC applauded its "outstanding advances achieved in radar, loran, shoran, radio communications, and other military systems"; over CBS, in twenty-four hours, Kate Smith sold $108 million in war bonds. Radio listeners heard "The Hit Parade" and "Suspense" and "Molly Goldberg" and "Lux Radio Theatre." Bathed in income, the medium could afford discretion. For nearly four days after the death of Franklin Roosevelt, and then, again, on V-E Day, all commercials were banned.

Only in 1946, as RCA introduced the first postwar sets, the Yankees became the first professional sports team to sell video rights (to DuMont, for $75,000), 56 million radios served 140,480,000 Americans, and Red Barber (who said, "I am a child of radio. Radio is my leather") was named director of CBS Sports, did the promise of television reawaken. A global pyre had stunted its rise; the sunburst of peace would nurture it.

The next year, television occasioned a series of firsts: from Capitol Hill, on January 2, the opening of the eighteenth Congress; from the White House, over a seven-city hookup, a presidential address condemning the world food crisis; from New York and Washington, "Kraft Theatre," "Howdy Doody," and "Meet the Press"; from Ebbets Field and Yankee Stadium, beamed to a network linking Washington, New York, Philadelphia and (say what?) Schenectady, the World Series, in its forty-fourth year.

"That was it," said Harry Coyle, "the length and width, the entire universe of televised sports in October of '47 — four cities, with a scattering of sets, along the East Coast. And those of us putting the Series together, we were just as newborn — just a bunch of amateurs trying to capture the action on the field of a bunch of professionals."

"And for the small number of viewers at home?"

"It must have been something else," he said. "Placing a cardboard cone on a lens and making the most of rubber bands and masking tape, we tried to create a split-screen shot. We had the camera out of service for a time while fumbling with the rubber bands and masking tape. It seems like a lot of nonsense now, but back then, it was pretty serious stuff."

"What was the reaction?"

"I guess anybody watching could have reacted in one of two ways. He could have been amazed — at the simple fact of this new toy called television itself. Or he could have been appalled — in that Series, we had the 'please stand by' sign on the screen almost as much as the ball game."

"Either way," I said, "it was uncharted terrain."

"Either way, it was remarkable."

It had already been a remarkable year. The thirty-third president pronounced the Truman Doctrine. Congress passed the Taft-Hartley Labor Act. At Harvard University, the secretary of state proposed to heal war-torn Europe. "Marshall aid," the *London Economist* said, "is the most straightforwardly generous thing that any country has ever done for others." *A Streetcar Named Desire* lifted Broadway. World War II veterans flooded colleges and universities. An explosion at the Texas City, Texas, pier killed 561. Air Force captain Charles Yeager made the first deliberate supersonic flight. Palestine was partitioned; its future, like its past, meant encircling debris.

For those whose world meant baseball, the rookies of 1947, like the clamor they loosed, lit the scene: at Shibe Park, Ferris Fain; at Yankee Stadium, the rounded, gnome-like figure of Lawrence Peter (Yogi) Berra; at the Polo Grounds, Larry Jansen, he of the slider and handsome 21–5 record, and a third baseman named Bobby Thomson; and at Ebbets Field, a second baseman who could — and this year, did — play first. Jackie Robinson was a Negro and a symbol and "the first of his race," sportswriters condescended, to play major league baseball. He was also a crucible, the lightning rod of millions, of whom Charlie Dressen (his manager, 1951–53) later said, "He's the best ballplayer I ever managed, anywhere," and Bob Feller chattered, "If he were a white man, I doubt if they would even consider him big-league material," and Branch Rickey sensed, "Here is a man whose wounds you could not feel or share." As Rookie of the Year, Robinson hit .297, stole a league-high twenty-nine bases, and led the Dodgers to the pennant. Brooklyn won without its manager, the harsh-edged Durocher, suspended (in April, for the entire season, by A.B. [Happy] Chandler, Landis' successor as commissioner) for consorting with known gamblers (his Scarlet Letter, "conduct detrimental to baseball"). Rickey and reporter Dick Young were frightful opposites, and when the Dodgers' president picked Burt Shotton as Leo's "temporary" replacement, Young's employer, the *New York Daily News*, took to censuring the venerable gentleman; banned from its pages, Shotton's name was referred to, obliquely, only as KOBS, for "Kindly Old Burt Shotton," the acronym immersed in sarcasm.

"By gosh," Shotton might have gaped at 1947's other feats. The Reds' whip-armed Ewell Blackwell almost threw two straight no-hitters. Williams became the first American Leaguer to win a second Triple Crown; incredibly, DiMaggio was named Most Valuable Player. In Cleveland, Larry Doby wore the press sobriquet, "First American League colored ballplayer"; only twenty-three, he hit .156. In the Bronx, without a pennant for four years, the Yankees won nineteen straight games in June and July — matching the 1906 White Sox — and behind Joe Page, their late-inning gladiator, and starter Allie Reynolds, acquired from the Indians, waltzed into the World Series. "We'll beat those guys," growled Dodgers' captain Harold Reese, not *next* year but *now*. Ten days (and Bill Bevens, Cookie Lavagetto, Al Gionfriddo, and a Yankees' victory) later, Pee Wee's optimism had sensibly withdrawn from the fore; not for another three World Series setbacks and 2,939 days, until that spectral Indian Summer of 1955 when the Dodgers finally won their first world championship, would Brooklyn expunge its image as Sad Sack of the Globe.

"You can see what I mean," Coyle was urging now, the memories gentling his voice. "That '47 Series was following on the heels of a hell of a year," as improbable, almost, as Harry's own career: before World War II, a project engineer for Wright Aero; in 1942–45, a bomber pilot flying thirty-five missions; back home, a member of the remote crew for DuMont, television's postwar experimental body; and the codirector of NBC, CBS, and DuMont's joint coverage of the first televised Series.

"Did you think it could top the regular season?"

"Man, we didn't know exactly what to expect," he said. "We just didn't want to be embarrassed — after all, this whole television thing was so unknown"; in Fred Allen's *mot*, resembling "a collection of passport photos." But Coyle was less concerned with novelty than with the lure of the game, and for seven almost surreal contests, with only three cameras (compared with twelve in 1982) and with Bob Stanton, Bob Edge, and Bill Slater (now of DuMont) airing play-by-play, the "Michelangelo . . . Cecil B. DeMille . . . Hall of Famer . . ." of baseball directors, whom NBC producer Mike Weisman would call "the Abner Doubleday of televised baseball," made of television's first sports fragment less embarrassment than success.

Still, in 1947, it was *radio*, like railroads, that fused the nation, and on September 30, before 74,765 spectators in Yankee Stadium, The Voice and the Ol' Redhead conveyed a World Series welcome from Mutual.

"We'd been together in 1940, '41, and '42," said Barber, "and then, as you may recall, after I told Gillette I wouldn't break my contract [at Brooklyn, in 1944] and come over to the Yankee and Giants, Gillette didn't ask me to broadcast any more Series."

"An interesting coincidence," I said.

"You could call it that," he said, "and there's no doubt in my mind that except for one thing, I would never have been asked to do another. But what Gillette hadn't reckoned with was that later on, the commissioner ruled that the principal announcer for the Series *teams* had to be on the broadcasts."

"So with the Yankees and Dodgers, Gillette got you by default."

Barber's voice revealed traces of amusement. "They probably would have picked Mel anyway," he said, "but Gillette, who certainly knew how to hold a grudge, obviously wouldn't have named me."

Now, however, in a Fall Classic that was Barber's tenth and Allen's seventh, whose radio and television rights totaled $175,000 and $65,000, and which marked the Pickett's Charge of radio's pre-eminence, one heard these national celebrities recount Gionfriddo's sixth-affair robbery of Joe DiMaggio (exclaimed the Redhead, indelibly, "Oh-ho, Doctor!") and Joe Page's Game-Seven sundering of Brooklyn bats and Bevens' luminary bid, three days earlier at Ebbets Field, to pitch the first no-hit game in World Series history.

Baseball tradition, with its sterling and Byzantine past, dictates that no one (except, naturally, the opposition) mention a no-hitter while it is still in progress, lest he jinx the pitcher (from the dugout or on the air). "Obviously what I said or didn't say in the booth wasn't going to influence anything that happened on the field," Allen conceded. "But I've always known that players on the bench don't mention a no-hitter; they respect the dugout tradition. And I've always done the same. It's part of the romance of the game; it's one of the great things that separates it from the other sports, like the seventh-inning stretch or 'Take Me Out to the Ball Game.' " He halted. "Or the biggest difference of all in a World Series or any other baseball—the lack of a clock."

On October 3, 1947, the obscure Bevens yielded ten walks and no hits in his first eight-and-two-thirds innings, and in a Game Four requiring two hours and twenty minutes and tissues to dry moist palms, the baseball was forever caught by time.

Allen, who broadcast the first four-and-one-half innings, respected the baseball tradition. Barber, granting himself the title of "reporter, not a dealer in superstition," did not. Upon grasping the microphone, Barber told his audience the Dodgers' totals: one run, two errors, no hits. Allen gasped. The Redhead shrugged. Wild inside and high, Bevens dismissed the plate. With two out in the ninth inning, Lavagetto lined a one-strike fastball off the concrete right-field wall just above a sign that said, "Watch for Danny Kaye in *The Secret Life of Walter Mitty*." On their only hit, the Dodgers won, 3-2, tying the World Series. A day later, confronting Bevens, Barber confessed his heresy. "You didn't jinx anybody," replied the ill-starred right-hander. "It wasn't anything you said. It was those bases on balls that killed me."

It was a time of transition and, not incidentally, trivia (Lanny Ross singing, "Let's Have Another Cup of Coffee") and bickering ("I am not now, nor have I ever been, a member of the Communist Party") and of vectors intersecting, cramming 1948's existence. *Born*: over WGN, with Jack Brickhouse and Harry Creighton, televised games of the Chicago Cubs; the NBC Midwestern Network (its outlets: Buffalo, Cleveland, Detroit, Milwaukee, St. Louis, and Toledo); in April, the Organization of American States; on May 14, the state of Israel; and the New York flagship station of the American Broadcasting

Company, founded when the Federal Communications Commission forced NBC to sell its "Red" or "Blue" Network. *Died*: Mohandas Gandhi, of an assassin's bullet, and on December 15, the primacy of Alger Hiss, indicted for perjury. *Abandoned*: by CBS, its early indifference to network programming; it would build, announced William Paley, "the world's biggest TV studio" in Grand Central Station. *Roused*: the baseball reservations of Boston, where the Braves won their first pennant in thirty-four years, and Cleveland, whose Indians, minus a championship since 1920, buffeted their league. Gene Beardon and Bob Lemon each won twenty games. Doby hit .301. Lou Boudreau batted .355 and, against the Red Sox in the A.L.'s one-game playoff (its last until Bucky Dent trampled Boston), wafted two home runs. Wrote Rud Rennie of the Indians' player-manager: "Boudreau can't run and his arm's no good, but he's the best shortstop in the league." *Nonplussed*: Chiang Kai-shek, fleeing to Formosa from the Chinese mainland, and the Soviet Union, whose blockade of Berlin's Allied sectors ended after 321 days. *Deplored*: the Communist coup in Czechoslovakia. *Obscured*: by Boudreau, Joe DiMaggio's 155 runs batted in; by the Braves, T. Williams' .369 average. *Astonished*: the major-league establishment, as Cleveland passionately embraced the oft-skulking Tribe, filling Municipal Stadium with 2,620,627 spectators. *Marketed*: 33⅓ rpm phonograph records. *Invented*: the transistor radio and "Going, going, gone!" Allen's calling card of a home run. (Roaring, " 'It's going, going,' " on a line drive to right field, "then I started to slow up because I saw DiMaggio and Tommy Henrich still playing the ball," The Voice recalled. "I thought it was gone, but it was one of those rainbow-type drives that sometimes sail back in. Then I saw them drop their gloves, and I continued, 'gone!' While the crowd was cheering, I leaned over to Russ [Hodges] and said, 'Jiminy Cricket, I sounded like an auctioneer trying to call that one.' I never thought anything more about it, but the fans picked up on it and started writing letters.") *Debuted*: television's "Toast of the Town," with the pleasant, stone-faced Ed Sullivan; "Talent Scouts," with Arthur Godfrey; "Broadway Open House," starring Jerry Lester, Morey Amsterdam, and Dagmar; and "Texaco Star Theatre," whose Mr. Television, the former Milton (Uncle Miltie) Berlinger, embodied the pie-flinging, makeup-doused, baggy-pants clown. *Bombarded*: New York's baseball public. At 7 P.M. each weekday, over station WMGM, having heard, perhaps, that afternoon's regular broadcast, one could inhale "Today's Baseball," a thirty-minute program re-creating the same Dodgers, Giants, and/or Yankees' games. *Deluded*: Thomas E. Dewey, the Republican presidential nominee — "an authentic colossus," quoth Lowell Thomas; a sure bet, George Gallup said — who campaigned as though already coronated and whose "humorless calculation," one reporter wrote, mirrored nothing as much as "a certified public accountant in pursuit of the Holy Grail." *Welcomed*: Ty Tyson, who returned to broadcast the Tigers' first televised games, and Jimmy Dudley, a former World War II glider pilot, starting a twenty-year assignment as Voice of the Indians. *Stricken*: in June, with a hemorrhaged ulcer, the Ol' Redhead. Barber nearly died; his injury recast the CBS Summer Olympics coverage; his convalescence effected a Dodgers' broadcast vacancy. *Dealt*: to Brooklyn from the minor-league Atlanta Crackers, Ernie Harwell, their broadcaster since 1946. "Kiki Cuyler [the Crackers' manager] and our players heard so much praise about his work," said Atlanta owner Earl Mann, "that they put a radio in their dugout and listened to his descriptions. He was that good." Via tape, Branch Rickey listened too, and when the Redhead's ulcer ruptured, the Dodgers' president asked Mann to release Harwell from his contract. "All right," Mann agreed. "I'll let you have Harwell; I won't stand in his way. But, as a precondition, I'm going to ask you a favor." The favor unlimbered a historic first: the only announcer ever traded for a player. "Atlanta wanted a catcher in the Dodgers' farm system, Cliff Dapper, to succeed Cuyler as its manager," Harold Rosenthal said, "and since the Dodgers already had Roy Campanella behind the plate, Rickey said OK," and from Ponce de Leon Park, William Earnest Harwell, only twenty-nine, vaulted to the broadcast booth at Ebbets Field. *Expanded*: television exposure of the 1948 World Series, sprouting though not yet comprehensive, brought to you, ironically, at Gillette's bequest, by a still-recovering Barber. "What happened," Red told me, "is that Craig Smith [Gillette's advertising director] conveniently forgot the curveball he'd thrown four years earlier. He called me up and bled. He said, 'Red, we've been friends for many years now, and I really need you. I want you to do the television. It's getting big, and you're the only guy who can make this go.' I mean, he just *pleaded*, got on his knees, and I finally said OK. And every hour I was worried I would hemorrhage again." *Dismissed*: the incumbent president, "Give 'em Hell, Harry," who spoke of his opponent as the "front man" endorsing Hitler, Tojo, and Mussolini ("Truman Likens Dewey to Hitler as Fascist Tool," headlined the *New York Times*), etched the GOP as "gluttons of privilege . . . bloodsuckers with offices on Wall Street" who "stuck a pitchfork in every farmer's back . . . silent, cunning men, who have developed a dangerous lust for power and privilege," and whose campaign was shrill and intemperate, basely vituperative, and, above all, cheap. "If anybody in this country is friendly to the Communists," Truman thundered in one of his more moderate attacks, "it is the Republicans." If any president demeaned his office, it was Harry S. Truman in 1948. *Evoked*: America's affection for the underdog. The *Washington Post*, predicting, like Wall Street's 1–15 odds, a Dewey victory, now hung a bed sheet: "Mr. President, we are prepared to eat crow whenever you are ready." In Nassau County, Long Island, a Republican women's group replaced its planned talk, "Our new Republican president," with a more vinegary commode: "It Pays to be Ignorant."

In 1949–50, it paid to be a fan (who, in truth, need not pay at all) — for even as cities in both major leagues enjoyed daily radiocasts and, in pockets of the East, the increasing regular-season mirth of television, other parties (like the pastime itself, motivated by self-interest) began to serve areas a light-year distant from Brooklyn, the Bronx, and the unseen geometry of the diamond.

In Portland, Oregon, and Portland, Maine, in Nebraska and Ohio, and, not incursively, in the gas stations and Grange halls of upstate New York, forces converged to satiate non-major-league America with a breadth of daily exposure, an empathy with the game, so generous, obliging, and memorable, that years later, enriched beyond other decades, enriched much more than scarred, listeners would think back upon the mid-twentieth century and say of its baseball coverage, "It was a magic place." Magic might come again.

Lindsey Nelson, for whom these years marked a pivot in his life, replayed them with his usual well-proportioned urgency.

"Up until now," he explained, "the only baseball available to fans not living within reach of local broadcasts was the World Series and the All-Star Game — the network events, the ones carried across the nation. But during the regular season, these folks were out in the cold."

"What part of the country are we talking about?" I said.

"That didn't have access to local broadcasts on the big-league level?"

"Yes."

"Oh, it was a huge percentage, at least half the country," he said. "Don't forget, this was before expansion and before established teams started shifting around. If you looked at the major-league map, the existing teams were all clustered in ten cities — the upper right quadrant of the country — and the area that they covered was from Boston only as far as St. Louis to the west, and Cincinnati and Washington to the south."

"All the rest was virgin?"

"Virgin *and* ignored," said Nelson. "When you went west of the Mississippi and south of, say, Virginia, there was practically no way people could hear major-league ball."

"Unless their local station was part of a team's far-flung network," I said, "or they had a strong radio at night."

The Tennessean chuckled. "That being true, it was only a matter of time before someone got the golden idea: 'Gee, whoever brings baseball to these folks on radio — people, remember, panting to follow big-league games — is going to make a whale of a lot of money.' All it took was to look at a map."

Gordon McLendon, who called himself "the Old Scotchman" and was, at times, called much worse by others, was not a cartographer. He was, however, talented (graduating from Yale University; attending Harvard Law School) and fluent (in World War II, he was a Japanese interpreter) and bold (like his father, who bought Gordon a radio station, KLIF, in the Oak Cliff suburb of Dallas).

"Gordon went on to make a ton of money," Nelson said, "and became a fabulously wealthy guy. But he always maintained that his very happiest days in life came in the late forties, the early fifties, when he was a broadcaster." Humor touched him. "The problem was, later on, he just couldn't afford the luxury of broadcasting. He was too busy looking after his empire."

In 1949, the Old Scotchman was busy too. Recently, from flagship KLIF, McLendon had formed the Liberty Broadcasting System; not incidentally, the FCC had accelerated licensing. Since the newly licensed stations needed vivid programming; since most resided in the South, Southwest, and West, far from the nearest major-league ball park; since McLendon was ardently fond of baseball and broadcasting; and since the sport was enormously popular, a cynosure of sponsors, these absolutes fathered a *Wunderkind*: "the second-largest network, we used to call it," Nelson announced, "in the entire nation.

"Looking back, it was so simple in concept," he said, "but at the time, it took a great imagination to think it up. You see, McLendon used these stations' void in programming, and the fact that radio was the closest these areas would ever get to a big-league game, to build his network, to create that empire."

The Old Scotchman's economics, which assaulted fair play, amplified profit. For a fee of $27.50, KLIF received a complete game of Western Union's play-by-play summation. McLendon must also pay his announcers; otherwise, Medina.

At the same time, each station in the Liberty Network covered all line charges, sold its own commercials, and paid McLendon $10 per contest. "We had a tie-in with every major-league park," said Nelson, who worked for Liberty Broadcasting in 1951–52, "and so every day, courtesy of Gordon McLendon, we would do for all of these stations in our network the creation of that afternoon's 'Game of the Day.' "

"Did you do every game by Western Union?" I asked.

"One out of every four weeks, we'd go do the 'Game of the Day' live," he said. "We'd go to Wrigley Field or Crosley Field or go to Briggs Stadium, and we'd do these games from there. The network would have to pay our transportation and other costs. But the other three weeks, we'd do the games by re-creation — the Western Union coming in to us; we'd convert it into the action — and, you know, we had the sound effects, the whole deal."

"And McLendon had no other expenses?"

"The $27.50 and our salaries, that was it," Nelson said. "They didn't call him the Old Scotchman for nothing."

By October 1949, the Liberty Baseball Network included more than three hundred stations. In the previous six months, if one followed the Scotchman, one heard him describe, on July 8, in the Dodgers' sandbox of a park, how the Giants' Hank Thompson faced Don Newcombe, Brooklyn's towering right-hander: a meeting of fervid rivals, yes, but more than that, the first time in major-league history that black hitter and pitcher blazed *mano a mano*. One listened as Jackie Robinson won the batting title and the MVP Award. One feasted as George Kell led the American League at .343. One asked, as McLendon did, "How could the 1949 Red Sox *lose*?" Four regulars batted more than .300. Williams and Vern Stephens each knocked in 150-plus runs. Dominic DiMaggio shaped a thirty-four-game hitting streak. Left-hander Mel Parnell, with twenty-five victories, and righty Ellis Kinder, with twenty-three ("Ellie could drink more bourbon, and pitch more clutch baseball," a teammate said, "than anyone I ever saw"), were the most successful pitchers in baseball. Boston even had Joe McCarthy as manager. By reputation, McCarthy's foil, the first-year manager of the Yankees, was a jester and semigrammarian. Only once in nine previous big-league seasons had Casey Stengel finished above .500; *never* had he placed higher than fifth. "I became a major league manager in several cities and was discharged," he later told a U.S.

Senate committee. "We call it discharged because there was no question I had to leave." Yet here the Yankees were, blunted by age and injury and a patch-work lineup—no regular hitting above .287, only Phil Rizzuto appearing in more than 130 sets, and DiMaggio missing the first sixty-five games—one game behind the Red Sox with two left to play: before gigantic home audiences, Boston at Yankee Stadium on October 1 and 2. They were austere and tightly played; they stirred these famous old contenders; and after Joe Page and Vic Raschi unhosed the Red Sox, the second straight pennant to elude Boston on the final day, Williams sought isolation and McCarthy, a flask. "When those two games were over, I just wanted to go and hide somewhere," the Splendid Splinter mourned twenty-five years later. "They really tore me up inside." His face grew pensive. "Christ, I wanted to beat the Yankees!" So did all of baseball in 1949. Brooklyn clinched the pennant in its 154th game. Chandler disclosed the broadcast teams for World Series 46: on television, Jim Britt; on radio, Allen and Barber. In the third chapter of the two clubs' serialized novel, New York won the Series, four games to one. Of America's 39 million home radios, an all-time record of 26 million heard the Brooks and Yankees duel.

"You can see why so many stations wanted baseball—the interest was enormous," Nelson declaimed. "And so was Liberty's profit. Figure it out: McLendon's outlay was $27.50 a day. His income was three hundred stations times $10 a game. Gordon was *making* $3,000 each day."

The Liberty Broadcasting System, being new, extensive, and profitable, fenced with an old conundrum.

By baseball edict, which was not to be mistaken for baseball sense, all stations within a seventy-five-mile radius of the closest major-league field were barred, legally, from airing network broadcasts. That way, for all of Liberty's appeal, the local team would remain reasonably sure of its audience, and safe.

"Baseball said, 'Hey, with this seventy-five-mile limit [later changed to fifty],' and I mean," said Nelson, "the language was exact, seventy-five miles from *home plate*, 'we can protect ourselves in two ways.' The first, of course, was protecting home attendance. Otherwise, fans, say, thirty miles outside of Pittsburgh might stay home and listen to two good teams play instead of going out to see the Pirates."

"And the second?" I said.

"To protect the local radio networks. Imagine you had a strong station sixty miles away from Detroit and they covered a Yankee-Red Sox' game, and let's assume both teams were good. Well, where did that leave the Tigers' radio outlet and the other stations in *its* network? If the Tigers were lousy, listeners would tune in to the other game in Detroit's own back yard. You'd kill off local interest."

"But doesn't the record show that most markets can support a local and network broadcast at the same time?"

Nelson began to laugh. "We know that now," he said, "but back then, there wasn't enough network evidence around to know much of anything."

Liberty's "Game of the Day" was banned in Boston and in much of seventeen states, its off-limits forming a rectangle from southern Maine to western Wisconsin to southern Missouri to eastern Virginia.

"Even here, we had some outlets," Nelson said. "There were some big stations in western New York where we went into; they were more than seventy-five miles from a park. And if you got into central Ohio, that was more than a hundred miles away from Cleveland and Cincinnati."

"But still, most of the Northeast was blacked out."

"That's because back then that's where the major leagues were," he said. "So McLendon remembered Horace Greeley, and, oh, did we go west."

By 1950, 431 stations transported McLendon's upstart; in Texas, more than fifty outlets broadcast the "Game of the Day"; on the West Coast, Liberty dotted San Diego, Los Angeles, San Francisco, and Seattle. Dismissed by corivals as either a buffoon or leper, the Old Scotchman bore the weight of a pioneer, and the warring made him glad.

"He just *loved* it, creating something the big guys had called impossible," said, in retrospect, his most successful announcer. "Two things I remember especially. One, we were almost always battling for credibility against the giants — the Paleys and the NBCs. All the big advertisers in New York were going into TV. They thought radio was on the downslope. And then McLendon came along."

"And said, 'It ain't necessarily so.' "

"He surprised a lot of people," Nelson said. "And McLendon delighted guys who announced for him — Jerry Doggett, Don Wells, Buddy Blattner, and the rest. And the reason is because if we had an idea — you know, broadcast this game out of Detroit or maybe interview that guy in Cleveland — you could do it. It was sort of anything goes, a great training school, especially for young guys like I was then [in 1951, thirty-two], and really, the stage you were training on was the nation."

Liberty was instantaneous.

"We started off only broadcasting games in the afternoon and then we got smart. We'd have a 'Game of the Day' from a Wrigley Field, starting at two-thirty Eastern Time, and then a few hours later, we'd do a 'Game of the Night' from Philadelphia. And there wasn't any tape delay; to the audience, even on re-creations, we seemed *live*."

Ubiquitous.

"We did every team in each league, and if it started to rain, at the end of the third inning, we'd shift to another game, because we'd have a standby Western Union line linked up to another park. We'd have two games on holidays. And if there was only one game scheduled and *it* got rained out, we'd re-create games from the past — Murderers Row in 1927 or a game from the old Brooklyn Trolley Dodgers of the Teens."

And, finally, a verisimilitude in the small towns of America, in the prairies and the provinces, *out there*, beyond the Alleghenies and Ohio Valley and Dakota uplands.

"It was amazing, really," Nelson said. "Even after you blacked out the Northeast, you still had a listening potential of between 60 and 90 million

people. And of that number, it was like a Messiah to those who listened —
because, except maybe for the Series once a year, they'd never heard *any* baseball before."

"And now they were getting seven, ten games a week," I noted.

"Not only that," he said. "They were luckier than fans in major-league cities.
Listeners in a Boston — they'd only get the Braves and Red Sox; Pittsburgh,
only the Pirates. But if you lived in Butte, Montana, or Amarillo, Texas, or
in some dinky town in Louisiana, you got to hear every club in baseball."

"It made a few fans."

"It also made for coverage like no sport has ever had — day in, day out, team
in, team out — and it created just a storm of baseball enthusiasm. These people
you're talking about — I don't think interest in non-major-league areas has ever
been as high."

"But what do *you* remember?"

Nelson paused for an instant. "I guess its impact, because I'm constantly
being reminded of it. Even now, it's incredible — and it happens all the time —
I'll be in some obscure place somewhere in the country, and out of the blue,
people of middle age will come up and say, 'I used to listen to you every afternoon.' And I was only at it for two years," he recalled. "The whole experience —
it was just a very memorable time."

The 1940s, which were nothing if not memorable, receded. Patches of the
1950s dawned. On April 18, the Red Sox and Yankees began their 1950 season.
They also launched the longest-running network radio series in the history of
professional baseball: a lateborn, stronger sibling of Liberty's only child, the
Mutual Broadcasting System's "Game of the Day."

The phenomenon was the creation, ironically, of McLendon and chance.

Condemned, in 1949, to an outsider's role, Mutual officials watched the Old
Scotchman thrive beyond anyone's fantasies. His starburst gnawed; with 520
stations, MBS was the nation's largest network; it was *they*, affiliates pressed,
less out of pride than commercialism, who should broadcast the game's blend
of sudden outburst and ballet.

Mutual's interest also derived from a long-distance phone call one evening
in August 1948, placed by a Yankees' fan in Louisiana to station WOR in New
York. The call was routed to Paul Jonas, the sports director of Mutual. "Listen,
bud," Jonas heard a voice plead at the other end of the phone. "I'm in a hotel
suite down here in New Orleans. My damned radio can't pick up the broadcast
of the Yankee game that started a few minutes ago."

"So, what do you want me to do about it?" Jonas said.

"Do me a favor and leave your phone receiver right beside a radio tuned in
to tonight's game. You do that and I'll take care of the phone bill when the
game's over."

Nine innings, $340 in phone expenses, and a New York victory later, the
vicarious Yankee let out a yell; he won his bet. Twelve hundred and fifty miles
away, Paul Jonas let his intellect run free. Like the wealthy caller, there must be
millions of listeners, he reasoned, outside the radio range of major league

baseball; like McLendon, soaring on intuition, he sensed that network broadcasts would enlarge America's family album of eager big-league fans.

"In a way, it was both easier and tougher for Mutual to put this thing together," said Al Wester, lurching for perspective. Born in Brownsville, Texas, Wester now lived in New Orleans. The long-time MBS Voice of professional golf and Notre Dame football, he once aired play-by-play on the "Game of the Day."

"It was easier because Mutual already had hundreds of stations which were part of our network," Wester allowed, his voice cheerful and animated, "and the 'Game of the Day' was our incentive for still more to come aboard. I remember just in that first year of the series, we added over a hundred affiliates — they wanted baseball, and so many were in the Deep South. There, the reaction was just tremendous. They already had excellent minor-league teams, and now we became their link to the bigs. It was a rabid baseball area. If you look at any old rosters of the fifties, you'll see so many dotted with players from Texas, the Carolinas, Florida, Mississippi."

"You're saying Mutual was a cause of that?"

"Not necessarily," he said. "It just showed how receptive the region was. And because we were thriving, we had a leg up on landing their affiliates. McLendon had it more difficult; he had to build a network, to *find* the affiliates to carry his games."

"But how was it tougher for you?" I said. "You had more money than Liberty. You were an established network. It should have been a breeze."

"That's just it," he riposted. "Because we *were* established, Mutual had to be very careful about undertaking the project. That first year, Mutual figured the bill for network time and production costs would come to $4 million. McLendon could just wing it — what'd he have to lose? But if we failed, we *had* a lot to lose. That's why we had to study every aspect — and that took some time — before Mutual leaped into the water. They knew that if they got into it, they wanted to do it right."

In 1949, Mutual's leading executives, President Frank White and Programming Vice-President William H. Fineshriber, Jr., visited affiliates in the South and West. They caucused with businessmen. They targeted advertisers. They asked if regular exposure would blunt interest in Mutual's twin tiaras: the World Series and All-Star Game, each carried exclusively. They evaluated, finally, that a "Game of the Day" would lure sponsors, delight fans, and enhance the corporate ledger. Late that year, MBS officials signed a contract for a daily "Game of the Day" broadcast, Monday through Saturday, every afternoon, over 350 eligible affiliates. They would "do it right." They would also do it *live*.

"Unlike Liberty, we decided not to broadcast Sunday and not to go at night — and it was really at baseball's urging; they didn't want the minor leagues' attendance to be cut to the bone," said Wester. "You see, we worked *with* baseball. We paid for the rights to do the games. We had a rapport with the sport. And Mutual didn't care about the restrictions. That still left six afternoons we could air games all over the country to the stations who weren't blacked out by local broadcast rules."

"And the other differences?" I said.

"There were many instances where Liberty, who didn't pay baseball a penny for its rights, *pirated* games. I mean, they literally had someone in the ball park flash signals to a guy outside in a telephone booth, and then he'd transmit that stuff to the studio for re-creations."

"An interesting technique."

"*Shabby* is the word I'd use," he said. "Well, no re-creations for us. We were there, boy, we were there. Everything *as* it happened, from *where* it happened." In 1950, Mutual aired a minimum of ten games from each American League facility; broadcasts emanated too from all National League parks. Every game supped of interviews with players, managers, and coaches. "And every pitch brought the real excitement, not Western Union's, into the living room. We spread into every nook and cranny. That guy in Fargo who'd only known baseball through magazines and his daily paper; man, now he was hearing it day after day after day."

For its Voice, Mutual turned to a portly, theatrical ex-Navy commander. By the time George Alvin Helfer — "Brother Al" — joined the "Game of the Day," the former college football running back had already served for three-and-one-half years aboard destroyers and destroyer-escorts in the North Atlantic, Atlantic, Mediterranean, and Caribbean Theatres; won hurrahs for his 1943 landing in Sicily (Helfer's signal touched off the first fire of the Allied invasion) which, a decade later, was dramatized on the "Cavalcade of Sports" television program; and, almost secondarily, announced for the Pirates and Reds (airing re-creations), Dodgers (with Barber in 1939–40), Yankees (Slater, in 1945), and Giants (as Hodges' partner in 1949). His voice was rousing, distinctive; he struck one as robust and self-assured, and should be remembered more for what he was than what he did — broadcast, as no one else ever has, for all three major-league baseball teams in the city of New York.

Tall (six-foot-four) and russet-peaked, the 275-pound Helfer reveled in "my checkered career," a board catapulting the eldest son from his family in western Pennsylvania ("My father was about five-eight, and my mother was about five-three. They could never understand why their children were so big") to Washington and Jefferson University (where he graduated) to the University of Pittsburgh Medical School (leaving, after one month, to support his parents) to a small station in nearby Silver Haven (his salary, $5 a week) to Cincinnati and New York, where serenity disdained him.

He remained "always controversial," Helfer agreed in 1951. "People have always reacted strongly, not blandly, to what I had to say."

There was a time, for example, when six-day bicycle races were inexplicably chic. "We broadcast a lot of 'em, and this one day they were having a jam," he said, "and one guy was really going. I guess I got carried away because I yelled, 'And here comes DiBaggio going like a bat out of hell!' " His laugh approached half-curse and half-command. "Well, then *I* caught hell. But the sponsor backed me up. He said, 'You've got to admit, the fellow has enthusiasm.' "

Helfer linked a polemic nature and a Dutchman's temper. Once, he was scheduled to announce the inaugural of a plush room in a hotel on NBC's old "Red" Network. After the opening cut was delayed three times, Helfer flared to an engineer, "Are we going on this goddamned network, or is this all a gag?"

It was no gag; Helfer was on the air. "At the end of the program, in those days you had to sign off with your name. I said, 'This is . . .' and I gave a phony name," he sparkled. "The boys in Cincinnati, where I'd just come from, covered up for me and said I was still back there. But what about that phony name guy? He was fired from New York real quick."

"He was a monster of a man," Wester said, easily. "He dominated scenes he touched, and when he was in the same room as Jonas, who in his very natty suits and Homburgs weighed about eighty-five pounds, the contrast was stunning. One spring training, Jonas and Helfer came walking into the lobby of the Tampa Terrace Hotel and somebody cried out, 'My God, here comes Jonas and the whale!' "

"Some biblical scholar, probably," I said.

"Well, it was a hell of a line," he said, "and *true*. Everything about Helfer was big. He was huge. He was married to a five-foot-ten brunette, Ramona — the professional pianist with Paul Whiteman's Orchestra who did command performances at Buckingham Palace. She even had her own band and, believe me, she assuredly knew how to manage Helfer. Then, of course, he also had that great necessity of his time."

"Namely?"

"He had the great voice [and a generous ego, Blattner would tell me]. Al could make it do wonders, recognizing the action and vividly portraying it. I've worked with some superb announcers — Nelson, Gowdy, Van Patrick — and Al's voice was the best. Back then, unlike today — when it's basically your contacts among network bigwigs that affect your future — you had to have the resonant, deep, dramatic tones to be a success — a Husing, for example, or an Allen. *That* was the key. And no one's was better than this big, flamboyant, man's man kind of a guy."

By April 1950, now the consuming tongue, at forty-three, of the most notable series of America's largest network, Al Helfer had traveled far. In the next five years, before leaving the "Game of the Day" to rejoin the Dodgers, he traveled, "I'd guess, about 4 million miles in the air," and reminded colleagues, with a delivery that was quick and croaky, how a prolific writer named Dan M. Daniel cried of baseball's itinerance: "The road'll make a bum of the best of 'em." Silence. "And kid," he added, sagely, "you ain't the best."

In St. Louis for a Monday game, Helfer might dart to Cincinnati of a Tuesday, then to Wrigley Field for a 2:30 "Ladies Day Special," then to Detroit and Fenway Park and Yankee Stadium before, finally, on Sunday, sighting rest. For six days a week, twenty-five weeks a year, he boarded a plane once or twice a day. He became a household word for those he called the "regular Americans": men, one supposed, who drank beer and cherished Chester A. Riley; women who scrubbed floors and laughed at Eve Arden; people who watched

"December Bride" and loved their country, and whose eyes misted shamelessly as the flag marched by. In his own household, however, he became "the Ghost of Hartsdale," his home outside New York. "I was the only guy I ever knew," Al said, "who would come home, pick up fresh laundry, and get out the door before it would swing shut." His large cheeks flushed. "The only time I spent with my wife was on the long-distance telephone. My daughter was growing up and I didn't know her."

What he knew, of course, was baseball, and flanked by sidekicks Art Gleeson and Gene Kirby, among the communal megaphones of his time, the clear and gifted raconteur untangled for America the initial season of the most lingering decade ("batting eighth, the immortal Sibby Sisti") to ever grace the institution of baseball.

Early that first year, while bacon sold for 49¢ a pound, National Airlines trumpeted, "Our new service ships you from New York to Tampa in five hours and five minutes," and television thrust the split screen forward ("showing two images," NBC said of Coyle's embryo, "at once"), the Dodgers' bony left-hander, Edwin Charles (Preacher) Roe, unleashed his own declaration: "I got three pitches. My change, my change off my change, and my change off my change off my change." He had also mastered a fourth: the spitball. In 1950, Hank Bauer hit a career-high .320; Raschi, as in 1949, banked twenty-one victories; Rizzuto collected two hundred hits and a .324 average; staving off Detroit, the Yankees won their sixth pennant in the last ten years. The Phillies beat Brooklyn on the final day to win their *second* pennant, the first since 1915. On October 7, Whitey Ford styled the first of a Series-record ten victories; in four games, the Whiz Kids scored five runs, three of them earned. Soon afterward, Branch Rickey—"El Cheapo" to Dick Young and "the Mahatma" to Tom Meany, thefting John Gunther's witticism of Gandhi as "a combination of God, your own father, and Tammany Hall"—sold his share of the Brooklyn National League Baseball Club; the price, $1,050,000. "Comest thou here," he asked reporters on October 26, 1950, "to see the reed driven in the wind?" Walter O'Malley—"a man," intoned Mr. Rickey, in an extempore pronouncement, "of youth, courage, enterprise, and desire"—became the Dodgers' new president. Ten years later, wreckers invaded Ebbets Field and crumpled it into rubble.

In the distant, contented shelter of 1950, as Barber and Allen chorused and McLendon and Helfer stirred what, in 1968, columnist Joseph Kraft would divine as "Middle America," and the Bronx-born, Fordham-bred Vin Scully, at twenty-two, became a Dodgers' announcer, replacing Harwell, who joined Russ Hodges at the Polo Grounds, few could foresee or distinguish the upheaval—the piercing of baseball's geographical and broadcasting heart—that, from long perspective, would ultimately singe the fabric of America's then-unrivaled game. Baseball seemed invulnerable. Did Lincoln, on his deathbed, *really* say to Abner Doubleday, as children of the forties often learned, "General, save baseball. Protect it for the future"? How *could* he—and yet, why not? From the Black Sox Scandal to October 24, 1929, to the draft-ravaged rosters of war, baseball had endured all there was and found that it survived.

The 1950 census reported, "150,697,361." Mrs. I. Toguri d'Aquino — "Tokyo Rose" — was sentenced to ten years in prison. The Grand Army of the Republic staged its last encampment. The State Department released a 1,054-page white paper; "the Nationalist [Chinese] Armies," wrote Dean Acheson, George Marshall's successor as secretary of state, "did not have to be defeated; they disintegrated." Harry Truman said: "The buck stops here." *TIME* said: "Truman's first term is Roosevelt's fifth term." Senator Hugh Butler said: "I look at that fellow [Acheson], and I watch his smart-aleck manner and his British clothes and that New Dealism, everlasting New Dealism, in everything he says and does, and I want to shout, 'Get out! Get out! You stand for everything that has been wrong with the United States for years.' " Although the Korean War darkened and Truman flung air, ground, and naval forces into the Oriental breach, in Bangor, Boise, and Baton Rouge, the living was easy, and across America, the comfortable were joined. Arthur Miller gloried in *Death of a Salesman*. Rogers and Hammerstein presented the magnificent *South Pacific*. Norman Vincent Peale and Bishop Fulton Sheen championed sentimentality and inner peace. If one observed the round tube's compound, one saw "Broadway Revue" and "Garroway at Large" and "Kukla, Fran and Ollie." With Jim Britt and Jack Brickhouse airing play-by-play, the World Series was televised west to Omaha; 38 million watched. Even Wisconsin Senator Joseph McCarthy, waving a list of 205 State Department employees who "belong to the Communist Party," seemed more curiosity than threat. In Stockholm, William Faulkner received the Nobel Prize for Literature. "I decline to accept the end of man," he said on December 10, 1950. "I believe that man will not merely endure, he will prevail." Wanting to believe so, many did.

6
Happy Talk

"Then shall the eyes of the blind be
opened, and the ears of the deaf un-
stopped. Then shall the lame man leap
up as an hart, and the tongue of the
dumb shall sing."
— Isaiah 35: 5–6

FIFTY-SIX IN 'FORTY-ONE

*Sixty-seven thousand fans here at Municipal Stadium in Cleveland to see if Joe DiMaggio
can keep his fifty-six-game hitting streak alive. Jim Bagby on the mound works the count
to one and one. A runner on first base. Here's the pitch. Joe DiMaggio swings. There's a
ground ball out to short to Lou Boudreau. He flips the ball to Grannie Mack for one out.
The relay to Grimes at first . . . It's in time for a double play! Joe DiMaggio's fifty-six-
game hitting streak is stopped!*

— MEL ALLEN, July 17, 1941.

Municipal Stadium, Cleveland, OH. In the last summer of an uncertain truce,
his nation turned "its lonely eyes to you" — No. 5, Joltin' Joe, future husband of
Marilyn Monroe, and the once-and-always Mr. Coffee, his tableau explored in
Mrs. Robinson, the Greatest Living Ballplayer (so proclaimed by baseball in 1969).
For sixty-two days, starting May 15, Joe D's immemorial feats enthralled America;
they ended (momentarily) before the then-largest crowd to see a big-league night
game — 67,468.

THE "OUT" THAT BROKE BROOKLYN'S HEART

*It's the first half of the ninth inning. The Dodgers are leading by a score of 4 to 3. There
are two out and nobody on base. . . . Tommy Henrich is up and the count is three balls and
two strikes. Reliever Hugh Casey is on the mound. He's walking around behind the hill
now, getting set for the payoff pitch. . . . This is a big one. . . . Now he turns around. He
looks in toward the plate to catcher Mickey Owen to get the sign for the next pitch. . . . He
shakes it off. . . . Owen gives him another sign. . . . Casey OKs this one . . . steps on the
rubber. He's all set to go. Three and two the count on Henrich. Joe DiMaggio on deck.
Casey goes into the windup, around comes the right arm, in comes the pitch! A swing by
Henrich . . . he swings and he misses, strike three! But the ball gets away from Mickey
Owen! It's rolling back to the screen. Tommy Henrich races down toward first base! He
reaches it safely! And the Yankees are still alive with Joe DiMaggio coming up to bat!*

— MEL ALLEN, October 5, 1941.

122

Ebbets Field, Brooklyn, NY. Here, in the Cathedral of the Underdog, where innumerable Dodgers' hopes succumbed, Mickey Owen's muff prompted almost hallucinatory grief. Within a single strike of winning Game Four (and tying the Fall Classic at two games apiece), Brooklyn saw the Yankees score four runs, secure a 7–4 victory (and, next day, their ninth world championship), and renew an entire borough's wailing call: "Wait Till Next Year [again]!"

COUNTRY'S MAD DASH FOR HOME

Enos Slaughter is on first base with two away. Harry Walker at bat. Bob Klinger on the mound. He takes the stretch. Here's the pitch . . . there goes Slaughter. The ball is swung on — there's a line drive going into left-center field — it's in there for a base hit! Culberson fumbles the ball momentarily and Slaughter charges around second, heads for third. Pesky goes into short left field to take the relay from Culberson . . . And here comes Enos Slaughter rounding third, he's going to try for home! Here comes the throw and it is not in time! Slaughter scores!

—MEL ALLEN, October 15, 1946.

Sportsman's Park, St. Louis, MO. In a World Series where the Boston Red Sox were 7–20 favorites, and where its leading totems, Stan Musial and Ted Williams, hit .222 and .200, Enos (Country) Slaughter electrified a nation. He was rancorous, belligerent; his was a heroic resiliency; and as he tore around the bases to score in the eighth inning of the seventh game, giving St. Louis a 4–3 victory, Slaughter "was like a steam engine racing his way across the country," George Vecsey wrote, "telling the people: 'Look — look — the men are back — the war is over — baseball has survived!' "

COOKIE JARS THE YANKEES

Two out, last of the ninth, 2 to 1, New York . . . Well, Eddie Stanky's stepping in . . . You know, Ewell Blackwell had pitched one no-hitter . . . and was on the verge of pitching a second successive one against the Dodgers. He had gone eight-and-a-third innings . . . and Stanky broke up Blackwell's bid for two straight no-hitters. So Stanky's up with the idea of trying to . . . Wait a minute! Stanky is being called back from the plate and Lavagetto goes up to hit . . . Gionfriddo walks off second, Miksis off first. They're both ready to go on anything . . . Two men out, last of the ninth . . . the pitch . . . Swung on, there's a drive hit out toward the right-field corner. Henrich is going back! He can't get it! It's off the wall for a base hit! Here comes the tying run and here comes the winning run!

—RED BARBER, October 3, 1947.

Ebbets Field, Brooklyn, NY. In this, the fourth contest of a madcap covenant of games, Yankees' pitcher Floyd (Bill) Bevens played Tom Dewey to the Dodgers' "Give 'em Hell." Despite a World Series-record ten walks, Bevens was within one out of the first no-hitter in Classic history: Enter Cookie Lavagetto, his pinch-hit double that transported Brooklyn, and a Grand Event now tied, two sets apiece.

"OH-HO, DOCTOR!"

*Joe DiMaggio up, holding that club down at the end. The big fellow, Hatten, pitches . . .
a curveball high outside for ball one. So . . . the Dodgers are ahead, 8 to 5. And the crowd
well knows that with one swing of his bat, this fellow is capable of making it a brand-new
game again . . . Joe leans in . . . He has one-for-three today, six hits so far in the Series.
Outfield deep, around toward left, the infield overshifted . . . Swung on, belted! It's a long
one! Deep into left-center! Back goes Gionfriddo! Back, back, back, back, back, back! . . .
He . . . makes a one-handed catch against the bull pen! Oh-ho, Doctor!*

—RED BARBER, October 5, 1947.

Yankee Stadium, New York, NY. Superlatives lit Game Six of the 1947 Oktoberfest: a record postseason crowd (74,065), the longest time for a nine-inning World
Series pageant (three hours, nineteen minutes), a rapt display of extroversion
(after Al Gionfriddo's catch) by an intensely private man (the Yankee Clipper,
kicking the dirt), and, most improbably, the Catch itself—"a truly impossible
catch," said Barber—by a reserve outfielder playing in (who could have guessed
it?) his final major-league game.

TRIBE SI, BOSOX NO

*Here's the pitch and Tebbetts swings and there's a hot shot down the third-base line. Keltner
moves in, knocks it down, picks it up, finds the handle. Here's the throw to Robinson at
first and Tebbetts is out! The ball game is over! The final score: Cleveland 8, Boston 3.
Yes, the Cleveland Indians win their first American League pennant in twenty-eight years!
And, man, oh, man, how I'd like to be down on Euclid Avenue right now!*

—JIMMY DUDLEY, October 4, 1948.

Fenway Park, Boston, MA. History will little note (though Red Sox' fans will long
remember) how Lou Boudreau canceled an all-Boston World Series. The Braves
had already won the National League pennant when the Indians and Bosox staged
the first-ever A.L. playoff game. Boudreau, the Cleveland player-manager whom
owner Bill Veeck had sought to trade (until fans, protesting, threatened to boycott
Municipal Stadium), climaxed an estimable season (.355, Most Valuable Player
Award) by going four for four, blasting a pair of homers, and driving in five runs.
"He may have been the greatest shortstop ever," Veeck said upon L.B.'s retirement. He surely was in 1948.

7
Sweet Seasons
(1951-64)

"He may live long. He may do much. But
. . . he can never exceed what he does
this day."
— Edmund Burke

THEY BEGAN WITH — WHAT? — THE TWENTY-SECOND AMENDMENT LIMITING A
president to two terms, or the April 13, 1951, FCC mandate voiding a ban on
new television stations, or Douglas MacArthur's address, six days later, before
a joint session of Congress, in the aftermath of his removal from command, or
even the October 15, 1951, inaugural of "I Love Lucy," starring perhaps the
best slapstick rhetorician, outside of Curley Howard, in America's comic
suzerainty. They ended, as in a bleary mist, within a year of that sun-glint Texas
afternoon in November 1963. "Maybe they were just another decade," a friend
said of the 1950s and their cultural extension, the early 1960s. "Maybe. But
somehow I think those years meant more."

Looking back, they comprised a time frame, an age of lushness and unprecedented tranquility. "Fighting on Sunday," television's Andy Griffith counseled son Opie in 1961, "I mean, that's disgraceful." Even now, something was
left, if but an oblique recollection, of their sober, more silent poise — the irenic
wont and tended lawns, the seeming warmth and propriety — a closeness that
Ronald Reagan, among others from an earlier steppeland generation, also felt
toward his childhood home. "Everyone has to have a place to go back to," he
said of his heartland Pleasantville. "Dixon [Illinois] is that place for me."

It appeared, of course, as it always does, less simple at the time. *Living*, as
opposed to reviewing, the years 1951–64, one focused on polarity, not uniformity, and upon how America changed: from a country founded on tradition to a society which thrived on youth; from an administration led by Main
Street and businessmen to a government laced with academicians, unionists,
and civil rights activists; from a presidency reserved for Protestants to an
office Catholics were not denied; from politicians who equated success with
legislative policy to leaders believing, even after Dallas, that among all the
attributes of Camelot, none mattered more than style.

In shorthand code, those who disdained the straightforward fifties — like
Norman Mailer, scoring "one of the worst decades in the history of man"; or
Adlai Stevenson, tarring their "green fairways of indifference"; or John Ken-
neth Galbraith, he of the mercifully resistible eloquence, torching "the bland

125

leading the bland" — most regarded the early sixties as an epoch that captured one's imagination. America before the advent of Kennedy, they said, had been hypocritical and puritanical, somnolent, inhibited. As a young, small-town, and Presbyterian boy growing up in the 1950s, on the other hand, *my* people discerned in the age of Eisenhower a domesticity and Norman Rockwell nostalgia, a time graced by self-restraint and a shy, Fred MacMurray-type of affability; inadvertently ennobling, and possessed of an innocence that seems now — after the cataclysms of the past two decades — almost artlessly kind.

Only later, in a time when perspective was in season, would one see the close working agreement — unacknowledged yet real — which bound both then-opposing camps. Under Ike or JFK, their pillar was the keeper of the faith and defender of the peace, the guardian of West Berlin and scourge of "Godless Communism." Who could doubt — in fact, few did — that upon the alluvial terrain of America lay the last best hope of freedom? For most of the Republic, especially its burgeoning middle class, theirs was the most euphoric community in the melting pot of nations. Doing good, they did elaborately well. They helped perpetuate — and, righteously, found their bliss divine — a system that would feed better, feed more, clothe better, clothe more, house better, house more than any other system ever devised by man. "I cannot now deny my recognition that Eisenhower's years in Washington from 1954 [post-McCarthy] through 1960," historian Theodore H. White conceded, "were the most pleasant of our time." In what Archie Bunker would call the "good old U.S. of A.," it was a good time to be alive.

In an America bereft of wild eccentricities, the sustaining norm of baseball was the finest game in the land. "Back home, even among the adults," Willie Morris reminisced in his affectionate autobiography, *North Toward Home*, "baseball was all-meaning; it was the link with the outside." From faraway places with their rich, imposing names — Memorial Stadium, Wrigley Field, Candlestick Park, and the Los Angeles Coliseum — simian sounds and static-lapped voices draped a thousand games with a mythical life of their own. Comparing batting averages, watching the churnings of the American and National Leagues, trudging to the American Legion sand lot for an afternoon of fungos, or trading an assortment of Red Sox' playing cards for a dog-eared Mickey Mantle, my friends and I thought of little else. In the happy, endless existence of rural and suburban humanity, baseball was not a diversion; it was a dominance, aural and wondrous.

From a distance, do I exaggerate the influence of what was, after all, only a sport? Across the America of 1951–64, even cursory glances at its literary paraphernalia provide definition. In daily newspapers (with their ornate prose detailing the major leagues) and weekly periodicals (like *The Sporting News*, the self-proclaimed "Bible of Baseball," or the newly born *Sports Illustrated*, which devoted entire issues to "Our National Pastime") and yearbooks, annuals, and guides, the acreage of baseball's turf was considerable.

Unlike the precocious Mel Allen, who read box scores at age five, I was at least seven or eight before devouring the baseball of the printed page. Yet already, for several years, and for rhythmic decades afterward that swooped to the limits of the horizon, it was the *broadcasters*—more than the players, managers, or even the glorious ball parks—that set one's sense of fancy rippling and proselytized, as the most fervent newspaper never could, the ethos and characters of the game.

By the end of 1951, when I was slightly less than ten months old, living in western New York, as my parents did, or eastern Ohio, as my favorite college teacher would, or eastern Maine, as did an aunt on my mother's side, or western Florida, as would my father's parents, or central Texas and Southern California, as did the future thirty-sixth and thirty-seventh presidents of the United States, or the upper Midwest and red-clay parts of Georgia, as had their two successors, you heard—if one were so inclined, in these places more than the magic seventy-five miles from the closest big-league city—ferried on past you, from small shops and gas stations and gentle back yards, a galloping world of baseball vibration.

In just that one year, the '51 festival of the Yankees' third straight pennant, Preacher Roe's .880 winning percentage (highest ever for a National's twenty-game victor), Bobby Thomson's rock of ages signature, and the debut of two rookies, Mantle and Mays, the Mutual "Game of the Day" aired 145 major-league contests—more than four hundred *hours* of play-by-play. The Liberty Broadcasting System was even more indomitable, covering nearly two hundred games, showering the pastime with almost six hundred hours, and more than *quadrupling* the total network time—via radio and the television web—that baseball would command in 1984.

Writing about the territory, Yazoo City, Mississippi, which embroidered and curbed his youth, and its summer priest, Gordon McLendon, Morris revealed more than he intended when he said: "By two o'clock almost every radio in town was tuned in to the Old Scotchman. His rhetoric dominated the place. It hovered in the branches of the trees, bounced off the hills, and came out of the darkened stores; the merchants and the old men cocked their ears to him, and even from the big cars that sped by, their tires making lapping sounds in the softened highway, you could hear his voice, being carried . . . in the delta."

Morris' regionalism was narrow-lensed, but his corridor was fish-eyed. For in the Mississippi of his puberty, indeed, in the America of 1951—more diverse and shadowy, less homogeneous than today's McDonaldsland—in Yazoo City, hearing the Old Scotchman, and Mitchell, South Dakota, hearing Al Helfer, and Philadelphia, where By Saam described the first of Ferris Fain's two straight batting titles, and Cleveland, with Jimmy Dudley narrating the twenty-victory seasons of Bob Feller, Early Wynn, and Mike Garcia, and the Polo Grounds, where Russ Hodges recounted the inside slants of the Rasputin-faced Sal Maglie ("He was so mean," warbled an anonymous Dodger, "that you'd lean forward and think you were safe, and his slider would break off your neck"), and the sprawling scepter of Comiskey Park, as Bob Elson's White Sox—forlorn no more—led the major leagues in stolen bases, and, finally, at Yankee Stadium, over television, where Allen and Dizzy Dean matched accents, ballooned bank accounts, and told of players named Gil McDougald and Gene Woodling and Billy Martin and Tommy Byrne, here, baseball *mattered*, an amalgam of memories, vernal and intense.

"There was—what would I call it?—a hubbub, an excitement to the time," said Allen, who would televise, with Hodges and Jim Britt, the 1951 World Series, his first of eleven video Classics, and who, because the Yankees regularly visited the Series, welcomed himself into America's October living room for ten of the next twelve years.

"Not more so than at other times," I said.

"Oh, I think so," he said, "and the reason is because everything was up in the air. It was a kind of experimental era—anything goes. And keep in mind that radio was still a powerful force, so that even though television was roaring in the early fifties, they were very close in stature."

"Not like the forties, when radio was king."

"Or today with TV," he noted. "But the thing is, in '51 and '52, they were both giants—both hating the other's guts. And the competition was conducive to baseball because they were both great vehicles for the game."

"Nationally?"

"On a network level, just beginning, but back then, more locally." The Voice reached for a Coca-Cola. "I may be a little prejudiced," he said, subduing a grin, "but during that time, even more than now, what happened in New York affected the nation. So our broadcasts here had a great influence on the game as a whole. Not me, necessarily, but all of us. It was just one hell of a town."

In 1951, if one resided in the forty-eight states, you saw NBC trumpet its "TV Network, now up to sixty-four stations, including the first foreign affiliate in Matamoros, Mexico." America welcomed the paperback book and long-playing-record industries; Britain, the aging Winston Churchill, re-elected prime minister; and even Mencken's "great unwashed," Menotti's *Amahl and the Night Visitors*, the first opera produced for network television. Harry Truman was booed at Griffith Stadium. Critics hailed James Jones' *From Here to Eternity*. Congressman Dewey Short called MacArthur "God in the flesh, the Voice of God." Said a GI of the Korean conflict: "It's the war we can't win, we can't lose, we can't quit." Husbands, housewives, and students followed *another* kind of conflict: a Cuban bandleader v. hellbent redhead in the wild and landmark "Lucy." If one also lived in New York, you heard Allen of the Yankees, Hodges and Ernie Harwell of the Giants, and Red Barber and Vin Scully of the Dodgers—in one city, at one time, five of the first six broadcast inductees in the Cooperstown Hall of Fame. Was this monopoly a testament to chance, or talent, or, less probably, the political machinations of New York's baseball lobby? No matter; in the early 1950s, it was one area's fortune to experience the most memorable of teams.

All that, and the giant, churlish, and bombastic figure of Yankees' announcer Jay Hanna Jerome Dean.

Arriving in the Bronx the previous April, Ol' Diz had chosen Casey Stengel, the Bombers' manager, as the guest for his first pregame television show.

"Mr. Stingle," Dean opened the program, "I'm a stranger around these parts, and I'd 'preciate it if you'd sort of give me a hand in this interview."

"Sure, son," replied Casey, whose 1950 Yankees won their second of five straight World Series. "I can see where you'd feel like a stranger in Yankee Stadium after all your years in the National League."

"You ain't just a-woofin', Mr. Stingle."

The Ol' Perfessor, sitting to Dizzy's right, twirled his gnarled fingers near the microphone. "Well, boy," Stengel said, "you ought to begin this interview by asking how my ball club is shaping up. And I ought to answer you by saying we got pretty good pitching and pretty good hitting. And then, son," his monologue persisting, "you ought to ask where I figure we'll finish up in the race. And I ought to answer you that . . ."

Within months, dashing counsel that he change his style — "You know what some of these advertising guys are trying to do?" glared wife Pat. "They're trying to get Diz to speak English" — Dizzy Dean corkscrewed into "the hottest thing in television," wrote Vincent X. Flaherty. "I'm not taking anything away from Milton Berle or others, but Ol' Dizzy Dean is the kingpin of TV." To columnist Ed Sullivan, "The story of Dizzy Dean would be a natural for Hollywood — a composite of Will Rogers, Mountain hero Sgt. York and Frank Merriwell. Baseball, the American game, has no more truly American saga than his." Sportswriter Hugh Bradley wrote of how Diz already had "wrestlers writhing jealously and is causing the maidenly mayhemers of the Roller Derby to spill new buckets of blood in order to compete with Diz." To Frank Conniff, Diz was "the next big rage of television. He'll be the video's delight in a matter of weeks."

In a city characterized by harsh empiricism, incivility, and an often cliquish brilliance, Ol' Diz, in those first ineffaceable days, seemed less alien than accepted, a triumphal Ozark in New York.

At times, he reminded one of Mailer's depiction of Ronald Reagan as "a tripped-on-my-shoelace, aw-shucks variety of confusion." In 1950, Diz and concert singer Jessica Dragonette performed a duet of "The Wabash Cannon Ball." When the music stopped, Dean asked blithely, "Is it true you girls are real temperamental?"

By rote, he could also play the good ol' boy. In the early fifties, Ol' Diz appeared on the television program, "What's My Line?" Seeking his identity, a blindfolded Arlene Francis said, "The guest could be Dizzy Dean." Startled, fellow panelist Dorothy Kilgallen declaimed, "Oh, no, this man is much too intelligent." Later, when she apologized, Diz did a semibow and said, "That's perfectly all right, ma'am. You never meant no harm."

Another voice riveted indignation. One afternoon, four balls were called on a Yankees' pitcher. From the booth, Dean objected; the umpires, he said, were parodying the sport. "You know what I'd do if I was out there?" Diz admonished viewers. "I'd take offen my glove and I'd give it to the umparr and I'd give him the ball and I'd tell him, 'Say, Mr. Umparr. You know so much about how a fellow ought to pitch, well, sir, you pitch and let me umparr.'"

When the need demanded, Diz could author a virtuoso ad-lib. "This ain't no job they give me," he said of his "commertating" assignment. "It's a sentence. I feel like a mortar." Ted Williams "reminds me of a long-legged pelican." Of a dispute jostling the field, Dean burlesqued, "That batter shakin' his head down there — he don't know what's going on. I don't know what he don't know, but I *know* he don't know. Look at the umparrs," he roared. "*They* don't know, either. If I knowed what they don't know, folks, I'd sure tell ya," after which a writer rasped, "Diz just says whatever comes into his head — even if it's nothing."

Still, towering above this babbitry of roles stood the fracturer of syllables. Reading the spring training roster in March 1950, Diz spotted Clarence Wotowicz, a rookie Yankees' outfielder.

"You gotta let him go," he implored the Perfessor. "I'll never be able to say that."

"He's gone, Dean ol' boy," Stengel replied. "When I heard you were going to do our games, I knew I couldn't keep him. Now, look our lineup over carefully and anybody you can't pronounce, I'll trade."

Tommy Henrich emerged as "Hendricks" or "Henry." Yogi Berra was re-named "Barry" or "Barrow." Roy Campanella was christened "Campanellie"; Brooklyn pitcher Willie Ramsdell, "Ramsdale." Once, Dean narrated the opera *Carmen*. The toreador became "tudor"; Carmen, "common." Upon hearing commentator H. V. Kaltenborn denigrate his diction, Diz responded, "Wal, Mister Kaltinbomb, I listened to you once and I couldn't find a word you used in the dickshunary."

Critics laughed. Reviews sparkled. Unstirred and relentlessly unimpressed, the New York baseball public, as in a chasm, yawned.

"He bombed," Allen was admitting now. "For the first and, I would suspect from his later success, the only time in his broadcast career, Dizzy laid an egg. A lot of the reporters liked his way with words, but fans just didn't take to him. And I guess it comes down to this: Diz was too folksy, too rural — maybe he was before his time. I know that in 1951 country and western music would never have gone over in this area. Now it does."

"What about his style?" I asked.

"Don't forget, Dean broadcast daily here — not twice a week, like later with CBS. Singing a song constantly, mispronouncing names all the time — people got tired of it. And it's strange that a guy like Diz, as popular as he was, wasn't a hit. It just goes to show how tough this business is."

"It also says something about this market," I said.

"What it says is that it's full of demanding, knowing fans," The Voice said. "You've got people here from all over the country — you can't fool them; they know baseball."

"And their announcers."

Allen dabbed at his drink with a plastic spoon. "I think," he supposed, "if I'd had the chance to work with Diz directly over radio as opposed to just TV, where he wasn't under my control, he could have developed into an excellent guy. He could call a play, don't misunderstand me — it was the *way* he called it.

You couldn't fault his enthusiasm, the feeling he put into the game. If only he'd been a little more sophisticated."

I hesitated. "And a little more honest?"

"What do you mean?" he said.

"Diz came to the Yankees because owner Dan Topping was a great friend of his," I said. "Well, there are many who swear that Dean would set Topping and other people up — the presidents of Goodyear and J. Walter Thompson, people like that. They were all avid golfers, and what Dean would do is shoot a terrible round one day when there was no money on the line. 'Boy,' his partner would think, 'this guy is duck soup.' Then they'd make a $2,000 wager the next day and Dean'd shoot an eighty-two and clean up the pot."

"I've heard those stories too," The Voice said, "and the bad blood that came about. How much that went into Dean's leaving after '51, I don't know. Probably not much. See, the real reason the Yankees dumped him — and it was mutual; Diz wanted out of New York — was that Joe DiMaggio had just retired that winter and Topping wanted *him* to do the postgame television show."

"A slightly different image."

Allen laughed. "Well, in New York anyway, just a slightly bigger name," and in 1952, as DiMaggio grappled, not always securely, with the foreign microphone, Ol' Diz broadcast Browns' games, with Blattner, over Falstaff Brewery's twenty-station network.

The Voice of the Browns since 1950, Blattner had watched his woebegones thrash vainly against the rapids of the second division. Seventh that first year with a 58–96 record, the Browns were even more vapid in 1951. "We finished dead last. Not surprisingly, most of the laughs were at *our* expense," Buddy said. "Then one day we were able to turn the tables."

On August 19, in new owner Bill Veeck's golden anniversary celebration of the American League, a crowd of 20,299, exotic for a team thirty-seven games behind league-leading Cleveland and New York, trooped into the iron and concrete grandstand of Sportsman's Park to sample ice cream and souvenirs and watch Eddie Gaedel, a three-foot, six-inch midget, wielding a miniature bat, spring from a three-tiered paper mache birthday cake between sets of a double-header. In the second game, fans jerked with shock as Gaedel, a vaudeville actor, marched toward the plate. "It was all Veeck's idea," Blattner marveled. "He'd inked Gaedel to a contract, and when the midget got to the plate, he showed it to the umpire. The crowd, naturally, was going bananas, and all Gaedel did — again, at Veeck's instructions — was stand up there, motionless, in a deep crouch, and take four straight balls."

"They weren't even close to the plate," I recalled.

"Bob Cain [the Tigers' pitcher] didn't know whether to laugh or cry — we'd heard of small strike zones before, but this was ridiculous. But that was Veeck — I respected him tremendously, and he thought well of me. He'd call me late at night, early in the morning, and he'd explore promotional ideas with me, bounce around trial balloons. A great mind, a brilliant promoter."

"And despised by his peers," I said.

"A lot of them, yes," Blattner said, "but it was jealousy more than anything.

Here's a guy who brought up Satchel Paige into the bigs [with Cleveland, in 1948] and then acquired him for St. Louis when Veeck bought the club. He had Zack Taylor, his manager, sit in a rocking chair while the fans were asked to manage by waving placards from the stands — you know, 'hit away' or 'bunt.' *Anything*, Bill figured, to take your mind off the incompetence on the field."

"Including Dean."

Blattner looked at me and winked. "Especially him."

Even with the Brownies, pre-CBS "Game of the Week," listeners appointed Dean to the limelight, Blattner to the footlights, and thought them both content. In the public's eye, Diz became bizarre and fiercely rambunctious; his sidekick, Rotarian and well-informed. Dean was a household word; Blattner, the neighbor next door. The pair cut wildly disparate figures — a snapshot, ironically, less illusory than real.

"We *were* different," Blattner said. "We complemented each other. I think one reason is that I'd known him so long, ever since his days with the Cardinals. I suppose he thought he could trust me. After all, he didn't want anyone prying into his popularity or feeling that someone would pull the rug out from under him."

"How could he?" I asked. "By the early fifties, *you* were the Browns' principal announcer."

"Yes, but this was St. Louis, and he was the star — forget what our press releases said. And I didn't mind, really, because I knew that we made a good team. If listeners wanted his humor, fine. But even in our first years, we also knew, from our mail, that people wanted some relief. Diz gave everything but the ball game, which they liked, but then I'd come back on and explain what had happened during Diz's innings. I'd give the averages which he hadn't and so they got both sides of the spectrum. And it worked well. We played off each other, 'cause I knew Diz like the back of my hand. I knew when he'd react. I knew when he wouldn't."

"Did he know what he was doing?" I said. "You know, his killing of the King's English?"

Blattner chuckled. "Exactly," he said. "Diz was, in the expression of many athletes, 'dumb like a fox.' He made sure, with rare exceptions, that he *didn't* prepare, because people didn't want him to be a polished, prepared broadcaster. They expected him, they *wanted* him, to demolish the game."

"And Diz aimed to please."

"Did he ever. I remember one day in 1952. Diz had begun to do some games, as I had, for Mutual's 'Game of the Day,' and one afternoon he called and convinced me to fly to Detroit. That's where the game was, and the press box back then was about nine thousand feet in the air. It looked like the Singer Midgets were performing. Anyway, I told Diz to do the first two innings. You had to get his part in there quickly because at any time he might get up and leave. So he did the first inning and, I tell you, he actually did a standard play-by-play and put things together pretty well. The actual structure was good, so unlike all the chaos he usually specialized in."

"What was the response?"

"People were surprised," Blattner said, "but for Diz, it was a lark—he wasn't about to spoil a good thing. So he leaned over to me and said, 'That's enough o' *that* poop. Now I'm going to start making money.' And he slaughtered the next inning above and beyond recall."

"Back to business."

The ex-Voice of the Browns pressed his lips and sighed. "He started talking about his friends down in Texas and about quail- and duckhunting. Everything *but* the game. And he brought in a few products that weren't to be sponsored—like Grandma's Biscuits or something. I guess he'd just gotten in five hundred pounds of meal or biscuit mix from Grandma's and he wanted to thank her."

"So," I said, "he *did* prepare."

"In a sense, yes," Blattner said. "He would actually preplan his mistakes, which shows quite an intelligence. 'I'm goin' to butcher this up today—it'll be in the second inning,' he'd say. He would program when he was going to mention so and so, and how he would tie it in. At home, you'd roar—folks had never heard anything quite like it. But he was good, and he knew what he was doing."

In 1952, apparently, the Old Scotchman did not. Planning Coronado, McLendon doubled, to $20, his per-game fee (which angered many Liberty outlets in the South and Southwest) and expanded network programming beyond the perimeters of baseball (which ensured soaring expenses). Worse, under ex-sportswriter Ford Frick, since September 1951 the game's new commissioner, the major leagues moved to bar Liberty from its lifeblood, recreations; local broadcasts must be protected, Frick said, even from the remote wanderings of McLendon.

On February 21, 1952, the Liberty Broadcasting System filed a $12 million damage suit, charging major league baseball with "illegally hindering and restricting a free and natural flow of commerce." Through the next few months, disaster turned a somersault. On April 14, a federal judge denied McLendon's request for a temporary injunction allowing broadcast rights. In mid-November, baseball answered the suit. "We don't deny," said attorney E. S. Baker, "that we have agreements [between major-league clubs and their local stations], but they're not agreements made behind the barn. They're agreements we sat down and thought out, printed, signed, and sealed with the corporate seal. Our basic defense," baseball's brief concluded, saying Liberty had presented "no claim on which relief" could be granted, "is that they're reasonable agreements." From Oak Cliff, Texas, McLendon professed caravans of unconcern. "They admitted all that we have charged them with doing," he said of baseball. "That is, the major leagues had agreements and rules which hindered and restricted Liberty Broadcasting System from carrying on a free and natural flow of commerce," but by 1953, only bankruptcy was natural, and soon the Old Scotchman was still.

Traversing three decades, Lindsey Nelson found old memories reemerge. "I'd have to say 1952 was a better year for me than it was for Gordon," he said. "That year I broadcast a few 'Games' and then stopped doing them—and the reason I stopped is because everything fell on Gordon when he decided to broadcast nonbaseball games. His costs climbed, and he lost even more stations; all *they* were interested in was 'Game of the Day.' "

"And baseball dropped the final bomb," I said.

"They were just worried about McLendon hurting their local networks, and when they shut him out of the big-league parks, just locked him out — Gordon couldn't get Western Union to supply him with re-creations and even named *them* as a codefendant in his suit — it was Katie bar the door," Nelson mused. "Without the product Liberty had been founded on, how could there be any Liberty? It was all over, curtains."

"But the Old Scotchman survived."

"McLendon had other interests," he said, "and so he prospered very nicely. But when his network died, it was a sad thing, really, because so many of us had enjoyed it and in coming years, people in the hinterlands missed it. Their reaction had been so warm."

In 1952, minus, temporarily, the warmth of radio employment, Nelson watched television accent "The Life of Riley" and "Our Miss Brooks." The FCC begot the rise of ultra-high-frequency (UHF) channels; of that year's more than seventy new outlets, many used big-league telecasts to forge a local identity. Cried Adlai Stevenson: "Let's talk sense to the American people. Let's tell them the truth." Said Richard Nixon: "He is Adlai the appeaser, who got a Ph. D. from Dean Acheson's College of Cowardly Communist Containment." Vowed Dwight Eisenhower, post-Checkers Speech: "Dick, you're my boy." Declared the populace, giving the war hero a thumping victory, 442 electoral votes to 89: "We Like Ike."

More personally, Lindsey witnessed a season of the Cleveland mound firm of Lemon, Wynn, and Garcia, each with twenty or more victories, and twenty-eight-year-old rookies — the Giants' Hoyt Wilhelm, going 15–3 and leading the league in earned run average and winning percentage, and Joe Black, the Rookie of the Year, the catalyst in a Brooklyn pennant, the first black pitcher to win a World Series game — and of the Yankees, winning their fourth Classic in a row, and their agile, diminutive shortstop. "If I were a retired gentleman," said Stengel, "I would follow the Yankees around just to see Rizzuto work those miracles each day." In 1952, the Tennessean also joined NBC as its assistant director of sports, working for Tom Gallery — said Nelson, "a blarneyed, extroverted, free-spirited Irishman" — who succeeded Bill Stern as the network's director and who unleashed an alliterative blitzkrieg at his CBS counterpart, the elegant Barber: " 'I hate,' Gallery used to say, 'that Psalm-singing, sanctimonious son of a bitch.' "

With Allen, the Redhead broadcast the 1952 World Series, a seven-game convention crowded with names like Erskine, Reynolds, and Mize. That fall, the NBC Television Network linked eighty-two affiliates; on radio, in Mutual's fourteenth year (and first in a five-year pact negotiated by Chandler) of Classic exclusivity, Al Helfer and Jack Brickhouse resounded over more than seven hundred stations. At his home in Dallas, Dean followed the Oktoberfest solely via TV, for he despised Brother Al, and Helfer disdained Diz, and "Dean would have as soon cut off his right arm," said Al Wester, blithely, "as he'd have listened on radio to what he called 'that bastard.' "

"With Dean and Helfer, was it a tale of two egos?" I said.

"They just couldn't *stand* each other," Wester said. "After Liberty bowed out, we at Mutual had the only network radio game in town, and here you had two giant men with two giant self-esteems. For the rest of us involved in 'Game of the Day'—Art Gleeson, who never married, was an exceedingly nice man and a close friend of Helfer; Bud Blattner did some games; you had Gene Kirby, almost a caddy to Dean, catering to him constantly—every day was very unpleasant. The whole thing was over, 'Who'd be the star?' "

"You couldn't have two."

"That was the problem," Wester agreed. "Dean, especially starting in '52 and '53, was determined it was going to be him, and *nobody* could be Dean's boss. You mentioned egos; his was like a blimp. And to be honest, the same was true of Al—except for Ramona, he was unmanageable. Once, Diz started to sing 'The Wabash Cannon Ball,' and Helfer said—this was on the air—'If you want to be a damn comedian, go out to Las Vegas.' "

"Was the problem *all* personal?"

"Some of it was professional—Diz was off-the-wall, Helfer more traditional. But most of it was just them rubbing each other the wrong way. They wouldn't even ride on the same plane." A wave of disbelief swept over Wester's voice. "Talk about fighting the other networks. In our booth, we had a heavyweight fight each day. You'd do a whole series, say in '53, in the Braves' first year in Milwaukee, with the two of 'em on play-by-play—and at first, with those two tubs around, the booth seemed much smaller than it was."

"And after a while?" I said.

"After only a few innings, you'd say to yourself, 'We don't need a color man. We need a referee.' "

As the Braves, worshiped in Wisconsin, more than quintupled Boston's 1952 attendance, Washington's Mickey Vernon won his second batting title, Brooklyn's Campanella won his second Most Valuable Player Award, and Al Rosen of the Indians led his league in home runs and runs batted in, one also needed a 1953 scorecard.

On July 14, Brickhouse (for the fourth straight year) and The Voice (his second) telecast NBC's coverage of the All-Star Game. . . . For the first-place Dodgers, seven regulars played in more than 130 games; the club scored 955 runs, only twenty fewer than Murderers Row. . . . In St. Louis, Dean and Blattner presided over the last ignoble chapter in the entirety of the eighth-place Browns: a 54–100 record, 46½ games from first place, fewer than four thousand spectators per date. . . . For the Yankees, again world champions, platooning reached the truth of extremity. Three players shared the first-base position; only Whitey Ford threw over two hundred innings; only Martin and McDougald graced more than 140 games. Did irregularity annoy the Bombers? "When you're walking to the bank with that World Series check every November," Hank Bauer groused, "you don't want to leave. There were no Yankees saying play me or trade me". . . . At the Polo Grounds, obscured by

Russ Hodges, the Fordham Flash was vivid yet. "The best postgame show on the air locally is that of Frankie Frisch, who appears after each Giant home game," beamed the *New York Times*. "Most baseball players are not looked upon as performing talent except on the diamond but, as a former player and manager, Mr. Frisch knows how to talk in front of a camera." So did announcers like Curt Gowdy, in his third season with the Red Sox, and Bob Wolff, in his seventh year at Griffith Stadium, and the Cubs' troika of Brickhouse, Bert Wilson, and Harry Creighton, and the raging Helfer, consigned to nomadism, to whom no encomium seemed misplaced. "People knew me, whether they liked me or not," said Brother Al, years later, after rejoining the Dodgers, "and I'd get letters, cards, and telegrams."

"Like what?" a reporter asked.

"I used to get a bunch of letters from a boy in Durham, North Carolina. Bucky Braham was his name, and he wanted to be a baseball player. He'd write me once a month or so, and I'd say things on the air to kind of answer him. Then, after a while, I stopped getting letters."

"For good?"

"In 1953 I was in Detroit, and I got this telegram. I don't remember the exact words, but it said that Bucky had polio. He was paralyzed from the neck down and wasn't expected to live. It asked if I'd say a few words to cheer him up. And I did—it was against FCC regulations—but I talked right to him."

"What happened to the boy?" the writer said.

"That's the wonderful part," Helfer announced. "The next day I was in Chicago, and there was a telegram from Durham. I was sure it would say Bucky was dead, and I felt terrible. But he wasn't dead. 'We don't know what you did,' the telegram said, 'but you have done something medical science couldn't do. The boy will live.' It was signed by the kid's father, a doctor himself."

"Have you heard from him since?"

"You bet," Al said in a burst of emphasis. "The last I heard, Bucky was playing baseball in college. You can't ask the Good Lord for much more than that."

*　　*　　*

While Helfer implanted himself against obscurity, another voice, less full and intimidating, vibrated over the largest single-team network of re-created games in baseball's more than sixty years of broadcasting. Originating in a studio in Washington, D.C., and linking 117 outlets by 1953, its stations reaching from the northernmost settlement of Cleveland to seventeen cities in North Carolina to the facade and fluff of Miami Beach, the Brooklyn Dodgers' Radio Network became a seminational vehicle for what Roger Kahn termed America's "national team." In the South, the Dodgers' Network rivaled Mutual, for its stations dotted Maryland and Virgina, the Carolinas and Mississippi, and its announcer was the siren-sweet, quick-cadenced Nat Allbright, who was born in Dallas and whose tongue scented of antebellum.

The Dodgers' Network began in late 1950, when general manager Emil J. (Buzzie) Bavasi, listening to tapes, summoned Allbright from Columbus, Georgia, to Brooklyn. It tore apart in 1962, after the Dodgers' pennants of 1952–53, 1955–56, and 1959, two playoff catastrophes against the Giants, and a dozen seasons in which the O'Malleys delighted, disappointed, and helped a country fall in love.

"What killed us in the end was the Dodgers' move to California. Their home games would end about one-thirty in the morning, and you'd lost your audience. It was just too late for the network affiliates back East," said Allbright in his soft, Dixie way. "But until then, and especially in the mid-fifties, we had something going that no club in baseball could equal—a public relations arm which put the Dodgers into every nook and cranny of half the country."

"Describe," I said, "how it started."

"When Walter O'Malley bought the club from Branch Rickey, he came up with this idea: In addition to the regular Dodger broadcasts with Red, Vin Scully, and Connie Desmond, why not set up a network of those same games by re-creation, thereby saving the line charges from Brooklyn or wherever it was that the team was on the road?"

"That way, you could reach outlets in states other than the Northeast."

"Exactly," he said at his Arlington, Virginia, home, "and at this time, I'd done two years of re-creations with Columbus in the South Atlantic League. So Bavasi told me, 'Take it over, re-create it, and see what happens.' "

"You weren't long in seeing," I said.

The past buoyed Allbright's face. "By '52, we had over a hundred stations, and soon we were getting almost fifty thousand pieces of mail a year," he said. "We sold a lot of yearbooks, we promoted upcoming tryout camps in a Jacksonville or Savannah. Every game home and away, and re-creations were natural, really, because I'd been doing 'em since about seven."

"Where, in Dallas?"

"No," he said. "As a kid I moved to Ridgeway, Virginia, about nine miles away from Martinsville in the Class D Bi-State League. Enos Slaughter played there. Rizzuto and Ken Keltner played in the league. And I'd go to the game—it cost me a dime to get in—and announce games to myself."

"But your bag became re-creations, not live."

"Sure. Because that was the quickest ticket to the bigs. All the regular jobs were locked up—Barber, Mel, Hodges. And I like to think I was one of the best at re-creations. I'll say this—it was more fun than *being* there. You could make baseball more entertaining, you could build up, not just report, the excitement."

By 1953, no franchise was more exciting than Brooklyn's. Reading the newspapers, one could glimpse the death of Joseph Stalin, the conquering of Mt. Everest, and—to Eisenhower, "my worst damn mistake"—the nomination of Earl Warren as chief justice. George C. Marshall won the Nobel Peace Prize. The Korean War ended. Over CBS, 44 million viewers watched "Lucy Goes to the Hospital." On ABC, "Kraft Theatre" dominated Thursday nights. The next evening, one could see "Topper," starring Neil, the boozy Saint Bernard whose ice bag on his head dulled a weekly hangover, or NBC's masterful "Gillette Cavalcade of Sports"; when, eleven years later, it finally left the air, it was the longest-running series in TV history. One could also see how the Dodgers won 105 games and lost 49, ending 13 lengths ahead of the Braves.

With a set lineup that was virtually an All-Star team, the Dodgers made the already-paltry dimensions of Ebbets Field seem incongruous — slashing drives into the deepest corner of right-center field, 399 feet from home plate; wafting fly balls into the upper deck of the left-center-field bleachers; lining shots over the combination cement wall/scoreboard/wire-mesh screen in right. Duke Snider hit forty-two home runs; Campanella added forty-one; eight players reached double figures; manager Chuck Dressen's club bombed 208. Five regulars hit more than .300. Carl Furillo won the batting title at .344. With Don Newcombe in his final season of military duty, Carl Erskine won twenty games, had the league's best winning percentage, and struck out a record fourteen men in Game Three of the World Series. The Bums led the National League in runs, home runs, and runs batted in, slugging, fielding, and batting averages, stolen bases, and strikeouts.

"They were a great club," Allbright said, "and even in the South, almost a matter of life and death. You had whites who were praying for big Newk and Jackie Robinson to lose. You had blacks who wanted them to win. Just in Washington, D.C., for example, you had three stations doing the games — WINX; WOOK, the black station; and for the white audience, WEAM. And here's a fact: People don't know this, but all throughout the fifties, our Dodger re-creations had higher ratings in Washington than the *Senators* did."

"Says a lot for the Washington club," I said.

"Says even more about the Dodgers," he said.

"But what happened to the seventy-five-mile limit forbidding other teams' games — here, the Dodgers — from coming into another market?"

Allbright laughed. "O'Malley just ignored it," he said. "Even then, Walter had the power. I remember how Clark Griffith wrote to Bavasi and said, 'Get your games out of here.' And *years* later — they waited that long — a telegram was sent to Mr. Clark Griffith: 'No one tells me what to do with my baseball broadcasts. Sincerely, E.J. Bavasi.' The Senators, after a while, got so desperate that Gunther beer, Arch McDonald's sponsor at the time, told him to get on the road and do all the games live, try to make them more interesting, get more listeners from us."

"How did listeners respond to the fact that your games weren't live?" I said.

"Most people never knew," he said, again laughing. "They couldn't *tell* it was a re-creation — they were that vivid. All our mail went to, 'Nat Allbright, c/o Brooklyn Dodgers, Ebbets Field,' and the club bundled it together and sent it down to me. So in the minds of most people, I was up on Flatbush Avenue."

"Where did . . ."

"For six years we were carried on WMCK, McKeesport, Pennsylvania," Allbright said, "and, ultimately, Rickey told Bavasi to remove the games — we were beating the *Pirates*. Once, Mel Allen told me, 'Nat, you have the best baseball job in the major leagues. You go to the studio, it's all baseball, you've got huge pictures of the National League parks all around you.' "

"Pictures?" I said. "Why?"

"To make it authentic," he jibed. "I'd want to make it as life-like as I could. We even had the National Anthems recorded differently. In Brooklyn, Gladys Goodding played it on the organ. In Pittsburgh, you had band music. In Milwaukee, even in the first year of '53, everybody sang it. In the Polo Grounds, during the games when the Dodgers played, we had the crowd noise amplified, fights in the stands, people going wild — in other words, just like it *was*."

In 1954, as the Dodgers finished second, it was Erskine winning eighteen games, Campanella hitting .207, Hodges and Snider parking eighty-two homers, and Newcombe returning from the service. "I'd say of Don, 'There stands big Newcombe on the mound, perspiration dripping down his face, trying to get through this tough game, firing missiles at the batter at close to a hundred miles an hour.' And people would tell me, 'Boy, Nat, I like you because you put me right in the ball park.' Well, that was the whole *idea*," he glowed. "To the guy at home, I wanted him to think I was sitting in the radio booth, bathing in the sunshine, just the Ol' Redhead and me, talking about the Dodgers, *our* team."

The remarkable news of 1954, of course, was that the Ol' Redhead, the *real* Voice of the Dodgers, was now Mel Allen's "associate."

A fifteen-year pantheon of Brooklyn, with his melodic precision and crisp voweled lilt, his *voice*, even divorced from his *name*, recognizable to generations of Americans, Barber had broadcast his first World Series in 1935. As early as 1939, however, the first year of Gillette's and Mutual's exclusivity, he began to bridle, Red later wrote of that four-game Oktoberfest, his fifth consecutive on radio, at the almost insulting fee — "Seventy dollars a game . . . for the biggest job in my business . . . the World Series . . . exclusive to one sponsor, on one network . . . and to get two hundred eighty dollars. I began to wonder what was going on" — and, even more, at the brashly lucid dynamo who dictated that amount: Gillette's advertising director, the redoubtable A. Craig Smith.

"Anything I wanted handed to me at Gillette, I got," Smith told me more than forty years later. "I could get away with any project, any idea, any venture at all."

Craig's leverage arose from his astonishing success, which, in turn, began that summer of 1939, when Gillette, floundering (the inventor of the safety blade at the turn of the century, it now owned only 18 percent of the market), paid baseball $100,000 for exclusive Series sponsorship. Baseball radiocasts, Smith said, would generate sales, and in the October wake of Gillette's sixty-four minutes of commercial announcements, Americans, squelching disbelievers, bought nearly 4 million World Series Special razor sets. The company became a sports institution; its advertising director, an Apollo — and in 1946, with

Gillette's annual profits topping $10.5 million, A. Craig Smith, his position ferociously secure, gilded the major leagues with $14 million for ten years of exclusive radio rights to the World Series and the All-Star Game.

Then, even before its release from the wartime licensing freeze, Smith sank his teeth into television. In 1947, with fewer than 160,000 sets in use, Gillette cosponsored, for $30,000, with the Ford Motor Company, to an audience estimated at 3 million, the second Yankees-Dodgers' World Series. The next year, for $175,000, Gillette seized exclusivity; the year after that, Smith flaunted $800,000 — an unheard-of figure for the primordial medium — for the privilege of sponsoring the Grand Event. Craig was not troubled by the sum; 10 million would watch the first of Stengel's seven world championships. By 1952, Gillette, NBC, and Mutual basked in the splendor of their brilliant October idiom; on radio, the Helfer-Brickhouse team transmitted its autumn sounds to almost six hundred Mutual affiliates, one hundred independents, the Dominion Network outlets of the Canadian Broadcasting Corporation, and the Armed Forces Radio Service; on television, Allen and Barber packaged play-by-play in the first of a five-year, $7-million contract. Later, Mutual J. A. Ward, Inc., a research organization, reported that of the 44 million homes in the United States, more than 31 million owned a television set, radio receiver, or both, and that among *them*, more than 49 and 65 percent of the television and radio households, respectively, watched/listened to part or all of the 1952 World Series. On Madison Avenue, if the results astounded, the cause did not: America's Fall Classic was better than Ike, brassier than Uncle Miltie, the Biggest Enchilada in town.

Sponsor, pastime, networks — the assemblage felt "swell" or "peachy-keen" or "A-OK" about the Series, to repeat three watchwords of the time. Everyone was happy.

Except Red Barber.

"Gillette was growing an empire, NBC and Mutual were getting rich, baseball was getting better contracts every year, and the announcers — their *link* to the public, the men who *sold* the event — were getting stiffed," Barber said. "We were lackies. We were being taken."

"Exactly how?" I asked.

"As you know, the Commissioner's Office had decided that the principal announcers for the teams in the Series would *do* the Series," he said, "and would be selected by Mr. Craig Smith, and he alone. But the problem was that he also decided how much you would be *paid* for this — by far, the most glamorous assignment in sports. I negotiated with everyone else — the ball club over my salary, with people for outside interests, but not with Craig Smith. It was a case of, 'If you want to do the Series, you'll take what we give you,' and they counted on your being afraid to balk for fear of losing the Series."

"No leverage," I said.

"None," the Redhead said, "and the degradation began to eat at me. We were stripped of any kind of human dignity — we were coolie labor, and we were getting coolie wages."

He paused. "In 1939 I got $280 total. By 1952 I was geting $200 a game, but it was still ridiculously low, demeaning for the biggest sports event in the world." When, that October—following the Yankees' victory over Brooklyn, his thirteenth and, as it evolved, final Series—Barber received a check from Gillette for $1,400, he decided, in a rising coil of bitterness: *no mas.*

The 1953 Dodgers clinched the pennant on September 12, in Milwaukee, in their 143d game. The Ol' Redhead had enjoyed the season on the field; above it, he met unrest. For he and Wesley Branch Rickey had been friends, and Rickey hated O'Malley, and the Dodgers' owner hated the Bible Belt oracle, and the unpleasantry poisoned Barber. "I think that baseball broadcasters generally run the risk of being unaware of their vulnerability," Lindsey Nelson, replying to a letter, observed. "And I think that owners do in some cases grow envious of the stature of their broadcasters. The owner doesn't want the broadcaster to become the symbol of the team. I think Mel Allen erred in not realizing that Dan Topping wasn't exactly fond of him [in 1964, it was he who fired The Voice]. And I think that Red Barber made a mistake in not realizing that, perhaps because of his prior closeness with Rickey, Walter O'Malley didn't like him very much, either."

Thoughtful and reflective, Nelson crystallized the Redhead's vise.

"He was on his own; when push came to shove, O'Malley would never support him," Jim Woods added in 1985. "Red was *Rickey's* boy, not his; if Barber was going to challenge the Series' broadcast setup or anything else, man, he was going out there without any help from the Dodgers."

Woods, called "the Possum" since that day in 1954 when Enos Slaughter saw his burr haircut and said, "I've seen better heads on a possum," laughed. "I'll never forget drinking one night at Toots Shor's in I think it was '53," he said, "and there's Topping and O'Malley at the bar. And Walter says, 'Goddamn it, I hate that son of a bitch,' meaning Barber. And Topping, who, of course, with MacPhail, had tried to get Barber to do their games [in 1946], started talking about Allen. 'I can't stand him,' Dan roared. Here we have the owners of the two biggest teams in baseball berating their *own* announcers—who in themselves were the two biggest names in announcing."

"What happened?" I said.

"The strangest goddamned thing you've ever heard of," Woods said in his friendly, familiar bass. "They'd both been drinking a bit, and O'Malley turned to Topping and said, 'I'll trade you the son of a bitch.' And Topping says, 'Hell, I'll go you one better. I'll give you Allen.' You talk about your deals that would have shocked the country—Allen for Barber, at the top of their careers."

The next morning, "sans booze," to quote Jim Woods, both reconsidered. But O'Malley's rancor, unlike his hangover, persisted, and when "push came to shove" in autumn 1953, in an epilogue laced with irony, the Dodgers' honcho pushed the Dodgers' Voice from the borough of Brooklyn to the Home of Champions.

On September 14, two days after Brooklyn won its pennant, Barber received a call from New York; with Allen, he had been chosen to announce the fiftieth World Series. "I must have the right to negotiate. Yes—I am sure," the Redhead told his agent, Bill McCaffrey.

At Gillette's offices in Boston, A. Craig Smith, raging, insisted on $200 a game. "Take it," he told Barber, "or leave it."

Barber left it, and O'Malley left him, saying of Gillette's rigidity, "That is *your* problem. I'll nominate Scully to take your place." In Red's autobiography, this literalist, reporter, and uncompromising don related, "As I heard Walter say, 'That is *your* problem,' I said to myself, 'From now on, Walter, the Dodgers are *your* problem.' I was finished at Ebbets Field by the time I placed the telephone in its cradle."

Three weeks later, on the morning of Game Six (won by the Yankees and, with it, the Series, on Billy Martin's single in the bottom of the ninth inning), Barber accepted general manager George Weiss' offer to join the world champions as The Voice's colleague. Over WINS, he would broadcast two-and-one-half innings of each game on radio; over WPIX-TV, in every Yankees' home outing, he would air several innings on that medium come of age; he would host (replacing comedian Joe E. Brown, who succeeded DiMaggio after the 1952 season) a fifteen-minute pre- and postgame television program; he would (and did) achieve what, earlier, he had at Brooklyn and Cincinnati — bring a magical property to the microphone.

With a new team, in a new league, a self-professed "child of radio" now reliant on TV, Barber arrived in the Bronx the year the Yankees, despite a Stengel-high 103 victories, *failed* to win the pennant. Instead, the Indians unveiled Bobby Avila's .341 average, Larry Doby's thirty-two home runs and 126 RBIs, and the greatest pitching staff in the totality of baseball. Rookies Don Mossi and Ray Narleski anchored the bull pen. Art Houtteman won fifteen games, Mike Garcia nineteen, and three future Hall of Famers — Wynn, Lemon, and Feller — compiled fifty-nine victories. In the regular season, the Indians won an American League-record 111 games. Against New York in the World Series, they won exactly none.

For the Ol' Redhead, 1954 was the season Yogi Berra was named Most Valuable Player; Virgil Trucks, thirty-five, won nineteen games for Chicago; the cleavage between the third- and fourth-place White and Red Sox totaled a startling twenty-five laps; and of Willie Mays, October's child, Leo Durocher remarked, defiantly, "If somebody came up to me and hit .450, stole a hundred bases, and performed a miracle in the field every day, I'd still look you in the eye and say Willie was better." It was also the season, in Move Two of The Great American Hopscotch Game, of the St Louis Browns' trek to Maryland; a year earlier, the Brownies lured only 297,238 people; as the Baltimore Orioles, their 1954 attendance would leap to 1,060,910.

The new principal owner of the Orioles was Jerry Hoffberger, for in the aftertaste of the Cardinals' 1953 purchase by the Anheuser-Busch Brewery, Bill Veeck — realizing, as Bud Blattner said, "that on the one hand, he'd be outgunned in St. Louis forever and that, on the other hand, he'd be blocked from moving the team by league owners who hated him" — had sold the franchise, in late October, for $2,275,000.

The following April 15, the first American League game in Baltimore in fifty-two years squeezed 46,354 fans into Memorial Stadium. Up in the

WCBM Radio booth, balls and strikes were called not by the past Voice of the minor-leagues Orioles, Bill Dyer, who left Baltimore in the early fifties, nor the past Voice of the Browns, whom Hoffberger pursued and whose exquisite loyalty to St. Louis lay griefs on an intent to leave—but, rather, by Russ Hodges' analytical former assistant, whose depths were as real as his Georgia accent and whose voice was as warm as coals.

"The Orioles' officials, the people in Baltimore, were so nice to me," Blattner was saying. "They wanted me to come east and broadcast. Hoffberger even picked out a home for my wife, Babs, and me. But as we were driving back after our visit we got to talking and, well, St. Louis was my *home*. I was born there. I grew up there. I couldn't move."

"So you recommended Ernie Harwell," I said.

"The Orioles didn't want an Allen or a Bill Stern, someone real controversial who'd be bigger than the team itself. They wanted someone steady," Blattner said, "a professional, a low-key kind of guy the community would accept."

"Did they get him?"

"I told Hoffberger, 'You can't do better than Ernie.' And I was right. From Day One in Baltimore, he was a smash."

For six years, Harwell burned brightly as the Voice of the Orioles. That first season, back in St. Louis, his career alive and widening, Blattner resonated over Mutual's "Game of the Day." He often worked with his former partner—"pod-nuh," the friend pronounced it—from their days with the Neanderthal Browns. In the mid-fifties, however, the friend was not always available. He was busy on a more massive stage, a homespun hillbilly who became a happening and, later on, a myth—the hero of the first network baseball series ever telecast, a pioneer who was always a personality, the prodigious Dizzy Dean.

*   *   *   *

The most transforming baseball series in television's show of shows—the 1955–64 CBS "Game of the Week"—first appeared, strangely, on another network, before the Network of the Eye backed by floating clouds grasped the lure of its bodacious, bubbling star.

Dean was not, as a fellow southerner once told me while wheezing between guzzles of a gin and tonic, "television's gift to the gods." Rather, he was the advertising agency of Dancer Fitzgerald and Sample's gift to the Great God Television.

Bethlehem beckoned in early 1953, when a minor player at Dancer Fitzgerald, which listed among its accounts the Falstaff Brewing Company, chanced upon a triangle linking his agency, its client, and the American Broadcasting Company.

The employee's name was Edgar Scherick, a native of Long Island, graduate of Harvard, and slave/master of an indiscriminate creativity; in time, he would sire ABC Sports, invent "Wide World of Sports," and form his own production company, Palomar. At twenty-eight, Scherick knew that Falstaff, a regional, Missouri-rooted beer, yearned for a national market; that the brewery valued sports sponsorship; that ABC, only ten years old (born when the FCC—fearing a monopoly by behemoth RCA—forced subsidiary NBC to sell its "Blue" [public affairs] Network), lacked capital to invest in television programs; and that, minus the identity of an NBC or CBS, it would look more favorably upon prepaid programming. He had also experienced, on radio and in person, the rustic unorthodoxy of Ol' Diz.

"Diz was Falstaff's boy. They'd sponsored him on Browns' games, they'd encouraged him to do 'Game of the Day.' He was, even before the term came in vogue, the brewery's 'superstar,' " recalled Gene Kirby, Dean's long-time colleague. "So when Dancer began to think of how they could make Falstaff a national proposition, with Diz in the back of their minds, they thought of sports—Falstaff was very heavily involved all through the Midwest—and of TV, which had easily surpassed radio as your primary vehicle."

"And they looked toward ABC," I said.

"NBC and CBS were giants. They *had* great programming," Kirby said. "With them, Falstaff might never have broken through. But ABC was almost a nothing network—not as many outlets, especially in the big markets. And Dancer thought if they could somehow put together a sports concept, get Falstaff to sponsor and pay for it in *advance* so all the commercial time was sold, the network might jump."

Scherick then thought of baseball, for no sport more appealed to beer-gulping males, and of his firm's most outrageous figure, already a national avatar on "Game of the Day." Why could Dean not thrive weekly, on *television*, as he had daily, on *radio*? Why, midwifed by Dancer and Falstaff, could ABC, which *needed* attractive programming, not join with Dean, this attractive mega-force, to bear a "Game of the Week"?

The concept was novel; except for the World Series and All-Star Game, baseball had always been a local, not network, product.

"Historically, that's the way it is," said Harold Rosenthal, who joined the *Herald Tribune* as a general sportswriter and became a baseball writer after World War II. For the next fifteen years, he covered the Dodgers, Yankees, and Mets. "In baseball, not many clubs are nationally oriented. The Cubs, Yankees, Red Sox—but they're the exceptions. Baseball today—and this was true even in the fifties—is still a regional game."

"Unlike, for example, the NFL, " I said.

"There's the difference," Rosenthal said. "Football fans growing up were sold as National Football League fans—network television *made* them that way. That's the genius behind [Pete] Rozelle as commissioner. Because some guy in Appleton, Wisconsin, had been brought up to be interested in all pro football, not just his local team, he'd turn on the tube and watch the Giants play the Browns. From one decade to another, you followed the game, not a club."

"But not baseball."

"*Their* fans were brought up to follow the Cardinals or Giants or Tigers," he said. "It was the local coverage that mattered, the local announcer. That's why even the 'Game of the Week,' post-Dean, that is, hasn't had the impact baseball officials had expected. It didn't have the national allegiance to begin with."

How, Scherick wondered, could a televised "Game of the Week" between, say, the Tigers and Senators seize the interest of viewers in an Appleton or Lubbock, Texas? America watched the Series and All-Star Game because the outcome mattered; even with glittering announcers, it was the *game* that transcended. A network telecast each Saturday would be an altogether different beast. "Dancer realized, and this was brilliant on their part, that to make this thing work, you needed a continuity from week to week that was bigger than the teams involved," said Blattner. "They knew that a guy in Missouri wasn't going to watch the Dodgers and Reds necessarily because of who *they* were— he'd watch because it was the 'Game of the Week.' You had to build that habit. And they knew that would happen only if you got someone to be the announcer who was so entertaining, so uproarious, that people would tune in regardless of who was playing."

"Enter," I said, "Ol' Diz," whom, in a 1984 book, *Supertube*, critic Ron Powers dubbed "straight out of James Fenimore Cooper by way of Uncle Remus."

"He didn't simply *provide* the program," Blattner said. "He *was* the program. It was like a prime-time series—you didn't tune in because of who the guests were; you tuned in to see the star. And likewise for Dancer and Falstaff. The teams that were going to be featured every week were almost incidental. To get around these local loyalties that fans had long built up required a totally different kind of packaging. It was show biz more than sports. And the 'Game of the Week' came packaged in that big white Stetson wrapping of Ol' Diz."

Still, to realize the "Game," Dancer must buy network broadcast rights from the individual teams; only then could ABC televise from their remote, almost fictive parks. In early 1953, touring each big-league locality, Scherick convinced a mere three clubs to sell: the A's, White Sox, and Indians. Worse, Ford Frick and the owners had enacted a blockade: The ABC Network, *any* network, could not broadcast its "Game of the Week" into *any* major-league city—the first of many harpoons with which baseball knifed its own network coverage so that by 1965, when ABC finally televised weekly games into big-league areas, ratings were dreadful; in American and National League cities, no viewer loyalties could be drawn upon.

"They wanted a blackout," Blattner explained, "to protect local television coverage—that way, if the Reds were playing on a Saturday afternoon and the game was televised in Cincinnati, you wouldn't have a 'Game of the Week' cutting into the audience."

"But the blackout was unconditional," I said. "Even if no Reds' game was scheduled that afternoon, or if they played and the game wasn't on TV, the 'Game' still couldn't come into Cincinnati."

"Yes," Blattner said, "and, in coming years, I often wondered how big we'd have become if we were permitted into big-league towns. It was a shame, really—there was a big percentage of America that never saw us. 'Course, there was a bigger percentage that *did*," for despite the blackout, Dancer Fitzgerald persisted; in early 1953, with sixteen big-league clubs clustered in only eleven cities, "Somebody looked at a map of the country," Blattner mused, "and it hit them: 'Hey, most of the U.S. is still up for grabs.' "

On June 6, 1953, the Falstaff "Game of the Week" debuted; by the end of the season, its results waved a cock-a-hoop welcome to prosperity. Over a network whose local stations were often their market's weakest and least-watched, and broadcasting only from Connie Mack Stadium, Municipal Stadium, and Comiskey Park, Dizzy Dean attracted an 11.4 national rating (one point reflects 1 percent of all households with television sets). More remarkably, 51 percent of all sets in *use* each Saturday turned to Ol' Diz, and this total came *solely* from the 68 percent of viewers who lay outside of major-league cities (and, therefore, received "Game of the Week"). The upshot staggered: During that first pivotal season of 1953, a gleaming *75* percent of sets in use in non-big-league areas gaped weekly at Dean's appeal. As Blattner would wonder, years later, in a secular vein: "It was like the Second Coming."

The next year — as Puerto Rican nationalists shot five Congressmen, the Supreme Court ruled that segregation in public schools was unconstitutional, and Joseph Welch, a quiet-spoken Brahmin, asked Senator McCarthy, "Have you no sense of decency, sir, at long last?" — America looked in a mirror and saw lines of discord in its face. Viet Nam was partitioned. RCA produced the first commercial color sets. Of the secretary of agriculture, a Missouri tenant farmer spit: "We've been plagued by one year of flood, three years of drought, and two years of [Ezra Taft] Benson." Died: McCarthyism, condemned by the Senate, 67–22. Born: the Air Force Academy, the Newport Jazz Festival, and the proper, cheerful "Father Knows Best." In the 1950s, if Ike was President, Robert Young was Dad.

The Game, of course, as its ruling cadre termed the pastime, was baseball, and *its* fans were more intrigued by how the Giants and Dodgers, succeeded by other clubs, now allowed Diz to penetrate their ball parks. In 1955, becoming, to quote Powers, the precursor of television's "rendezvous with billion-dollar league contracts and ultra-tech saturation coverage of media megagames," the Saturday telecasts moved to the larger, richer, and more prestigious household of CBS. There, for the next ten seasons, the "Game of the Week" evolved into a phenomenon; and its epitome — not delicate like Barber, or bleached like Laux, or eastern like Husing, or compulsively dramatic like The Voice — into a cavalcade of Ma Kettle, Tennessee Ernie Ford, and a John Huston western: a "mythologizing presence," sayeth *Supertube*; arguably, the most beloved broadcaster in America. "He created the audience before we ever said a word," said Blattner, who was replaced in 1960 by Pee Wee Reese as Ol' Diz's TV sidekick. "It was going to be Dizzy Dean on the 'Game of the Week' with me, or, like, with 'pod-nuh.' "

From 1955 to 1964, Dean and "pod-nuh" formed sportscasting's most extraordinary duo. During the first two seasons, a Saturday game arose each weekend; in 1957, a Sunday game was added. Before Diz, no baseball, football, or basketball series had been broadcast nationally; Dean and Company charted virgin ground. Had the series folded, its failure might have punctured the future of televised sports. Instead, the reverse sprung forward, and a cult of spectacular legitimacy unfurled.

In the "Game of the Week," Falstaff found profits, Reese and Blattner affluence, Dean celebrity status, and CBS an audience that astonished industry brass. "The reaction was stunning. Just stunning," said the director of CBS Sports during Diz's reign, Bill MacPhail, once portrayed by William O. Johnson, a *Sports Illustrated* writer, as having "pallid blue eyes, gray hair . . . a mild, nearly bland manner that seems better suited for the head usher at—well, at an Episcopal Church."

By 1957, numbly aware of Dean's success, NBC began its own Saturday series; two years later, it entered the Sunday field. The outcome was preordained; CBS's ratings often tripled its rival's. "We'd get reports from towns like Cedar Rapids, Iowa, or Little Rock, Arkansas," MacPhail related, "and they'd simply close down in the afternoon when Dean was on." Diz and Blattner, then Dean and Reese, bordered on the invincible, and the tides, once behind them, were never turned aside. "Dean's popularity, and thus his broadcasts, were enormously powerful in the small cities," said the son of the Dodgers' ex-president. "And in the small towns and rural areas, when they talked about sports on television, it was all that was discusssed."

Denver, Dallas, and Miami—immune to baseball's blackout—rolled with Dean's network comedy, but Washington, Cleveland, and Chicago were condemned to weekend pabulum. "We used to have split programming. The major-league cities got golf or tennis or stuff like that," said MacPhail. "Today, you couldn't do it. You couldn't leave out New York and Detroit and the other big towns. But back then—the fifties and sixties—network sports weren't that powerful yet. At CBS, and even before then, at ABC, you could take more chances. You could afford to be daring."

Week after spirity week, Middle America unlatched its gratitude: the West and Southwest, the Rockies and Midwest Plains and Dean's natural constituency, the South. Until 1958, when what New York giveth, California taketh away, even Los Angeles and San Francisco shared in the "Game's" delight. "All this land was untapped territory," said the former CBS director. "It wasn't until much later that these places began to get major-league teams. Before that, they were ours. We hit them every week."

Only in the centers of the teeming Northeast, the loci of the big-league sphere, was "Game of the Week" concealed. "Because it didn't come into Manhattan, they didn't know there *was* a 'Game,' " MacPhail said of CBS's executive elite. "I'll never forget a sales meeting we had just after I came to CBS in the mid-fifties. We were talking about sports, and somehow up popped Dean's name. That prompted one of Bill Paley's aides to swear up and down that CBS would never stoop to hiring such a clod—*ever*. There then transpired what seemed eternal silence. Finally, a guy who was representing Falstaff looked around the room and told this aide: 'But he's *on* your network. Each Saturday. He's doing the Falstaff "Game of the Week." ' "

As far as the public of New York, Philadelphia, and Boston knew, "Game of the Week" did not exist. But beyond baseball's now-fifty-mile television black-out limit, in Buffalo, Harrisburg, Rochester, and Albany, Dean enjoyed a cornpone continuity. Entering New England, the split continued: Hartford and Montpelier *had* access; Worcester was without. Whatever the affiliate division, "Game of the Week" demolished opposing programs that had the bad fortune to appear. "I didn't care for him personally," MacPhail continued, "but on the air you had to like him. During any broadcast you had to laugh nine, ten times." At the least, memory claimed.

Dean's esteem, which was not to preclude his *self*-esteem, rose yearly above a taut, engrossing decade. By 1955, Mutual's baseball network (its broadcasters, Art Gleeson and Bob Neal) had swollen to more than five hundred affiliates; an additional eight hundred stations saturated the country with local-team play-by-play. The Dodgers, over WMGM, flowered with Scully, Desmond, and Andre Baruch; the Reds, over WSAI, with Waite Hoyt and Jack Moran; the Cubs, with WIND's Wilson; the Giants, with Hodges and Bob Delaney, over WMCA. In Milwaukee, Earl Gillespie and Blaine Walsh boasted two originating radio stations, WEMP and WTMJ. The Phillies had one flagship, WIP, and three announcers, Saam, Gene Kelly, and Claude Haring. With Rosey Rowswell's death, WWSW's Bob Prince ascended as Voice of the Pirates. Over KMOX, Harry Caray, Jack Buck, and newcomer Joe Garagiola made the Cardinals a regional obsession. At Memorial Stadium, Harwell, Bailey Goss, and Chuck Thompson covered the second-year Orioles; from Fenway Park, Gowdy and Bob Murphy vibrated over WHDH. On WCFL, "The Voice of Labor" in Chicago, Elson and Don Wells narrated the goings-on of the good-pitch, no-hit White Sox. Chilled by winds off Lake Erie, WERE's Dudley and Ed Edwards warmed the Indians' cavernous yard. Over WJBK, the upper Midwest heard Van Patrick and Paul (Dizzy) Trout hail the fifth-place Tigers. Recently moved to Kansas City, the Athletics used KMBC's Merle Harmon and Larry Ray to enliven their sixth-place hodgepodge. The Yankees flashed Allen, Woods, and Barber. The basement Nats countered with WWDC's Wolff and The Old Pine Tree.

Meanwhile, baseball's other electronic communications vehicle had moved far beyond the experimental form. In 1955, only four big-league teams — the Braves, Pirates, A's, and Indians — disdained the vessel of television. The Cubs and Dodgers (WGN and WOR, Channel 9) and Yankees and Giants (over WPIX, Channel 11) broadcast every home encounter; the Cardinals aired each road game on UHF station WTVI. The Reds' flagship outlet, WCPO, covered all weekday afternoon home games; the Phillies televised twenty-nine home and twenty-seven road contests; two Baltimore stations, WMAR and WAAM, carried sixty-five "selected home and road" sets; and Tom Yawkey allowed a small number of Red Sox' outings to permeate WBZ and WNAC. In Washington, showing what the station termed "a limited number of road and home" matches, WTTG linked the Senators and their despairing fandom. In Michigan, a six-station network telecast forty-two Tigers' games. Over WGN, one could view each afternoon pageant from the boxy interior of Comiskey Park; arriving from Wrigley Field, Brickhouse and Creighton did double duty.

"That's how TV was *locally* back then," Blattner noted. "*Nationally*, it was even better." In 1957, 74; in 1959, 98; and one year later, 123 games aired from coast-to-coast. By 1960, when ABC began a Saturday series, all three networks had invested in The Game. "Radio had always sold baseball so beautifully as a commodity," Bud said. "Now, in the fifties, its influence changed. It was *television* that took top billing — *television* that became the fans' addiction. That's why it was so ridiculous later on [the mid-1960s] for baseball to reduce its network schedule — that move alone cost the major leagues a major part of their popularity." During the years immediately after 1955, however, few thought of such decline or fall. Television was new, an infant still breast-fed on daring, and as baseball tumbled into the living room, into the weekend cycle of their lives, viewers came to suppose that style eclipsed substance, and that an announcer must be part-informer, part-observer, part-Broadway marquee, e.g., Ol' Diz.

Instinctively, Dean sensed what, a decade later, a division of Sominex voices failed, mystically, to grasp. "Baseball's fundamental weakness on TV is the long wait between pitches," columnist Jack Craig has written in *The Sporting News*. "And for most kids, the slow pace is intolerable. . . . If a sport turns off youngsters at the TV level, it seriously reduces efforts to lure them later on." Baseball does not inherently televise well. The "long wait between pitches" irritates; the "slow pace" endures; unlike the mind's meliot of radio, the TV screen negates the sweep of ball field and diamond. Football telecasts more fluidly — both teams are viewed in their entirety; the action is synchronic; its core develops whole. As opposed to football, baseball cannot "sell itself" on television; the game's *announcers* must be its Force. Muffled by mouthpieces who dryly, sparsely, merely *report*, baseball's video clash between hitter and pitcher can dissolve into a blazy stupor. But enlivened by voices who *use* the sport's languid tempo to mix drama and hilarity, who entertain, not simply parrot, baseball can be riotously vibrant, unsurpassed among its peers. Above the batter's box, as inside it, the lone artist excels.

Few proved more artful than Dizzy Dean.

"Our success wasn't that we were smarter than NBC, or that our production was better. It was Dean," said MacPhail, dismissed by CBS in 1974. "He was just very homey. It was warm, very warm, and very much accepted."

Few procured more wealth.

"It was a funny format, the 'Game of the Week.' Falstaff owned the broadcasts — we didn't. We aired the shows, but the rights were theirs. They made a mint; we got the ratings."

Few tapped more humor, either.

"This," said MacPhail, reverting to a cigarette and adjusting his tie, "is where Dean's pioneering took effect. He was the first announcer *ever* to inject comedy into a game. Don Meredith, Bob Uecker — they're clones of Dean. And I think an overriding concern now is that too many guys take themselves too seriously on televised sports. Of course, there was always a question of when Diz was acting and when not — some of his funnies on the air were put on. But we never discouraged it, because it added to the color."

"Was Dean's humor as evident off the air?" I said.

"He was two different people," MacPhail said, coldly. "He was much warmer, in fact, on the air. I'm not saying at times he wasn't funny in person, even though it might disgust you how he was constantly played up to—Gene Kirby [who produced the "Game"] barked at his slightest whim—but on his broadcasts, it was impossible not to sit there and roar. Colorful, funny, even knowledgeable."

"But you weren't enamored?"

"Personally, no. I wouldn't say he was only a big hillbilly, because he could be very cunning." He paused, looking much like his father. "He was just not my type of person. Very hard to handle—he'd do what he wanted to. I also recognized, of course, that there was never any thought of getting rid of him and replacing Ol' Diz. None at all. Never."

Americans saw only the public Dean and thought they knew the private, for intuitively, without backstage counsel, Ol' Diz realized the essence of his pull. "The thing I've got to guard against," he confided as 1955 began, "is improvement. If I start talking better," citing a nonexistent peril, "they'll throw me out."

That first year, quiescence dressed the country. Once McCarthy had been eliminated, an era of Good Feeling settled over its national life. In 1955, a Gallup Poll revealed that 60 percent of *Democrats* wanted Ike as their nominee. Said the man who, in reflection, emerged as a superb and civilizing president: "Everybody ought to be happy every day. Play hard, have fun doing it, and despise wickedness." Marian Anderson appeared at the Metropolitan Opera. Newscasts reported the Salk polio vaccine, a summit conference in Geneva, and the resignation of Winston Churchill. More than three times as many passengers now preferred planes to trains. One of Bill Paley's favorite radio shows, an "adult western" called "Gunsmoke," began a twenty-year run on CBS-TV. Viewers howled at "The Honeymooners" and "Private Secretary." Other prodigies included "Jane Wyman's Fireside Theatre," "Sergeant Preston of the Yukon," with the wonder dog Yukon King, and "The Lone Ranger," starring Clayton Moore, Jay Silverheels, and, most unforgettably, Silver.

In baseball, Diz danced upon a stage of stars. Al Kaline hit .340 and became, at twenty, the youngest batting champion since Ty Cobb in 1907. Robin Roberts led the National League with twenty-three victories. Herb Score of the Indians struck out 245 for the then-rookie record. Otherwise, the 1955 season nested in New York. Whitey Ford won eighteen games, Tommy Byrne led his league in winning percentage, and Mickey Mantle took the A.L. home run and slugging crowns. At Ebbets Field, Campanella won his third MVP Award, Snider knocked in 136 runs, and with the worst regular-season ERA among Flatbush starters, Johnny Podres won two World Series games and the Dodgers, implausibly, the Series. In the *New York Daily News*, Willard Mullin's sassy caricature, the Brooklyn Bum, exploded: "We dood it! We beat 'em! We beat them Yankees! We spot 'em th' foist two games . . . an' we beat 'em! That Podres! Woil Cham-peens! Me!" On page 1 of the October 5 *New York Times*, John Drebinger sent forth a more stately digest. "Far into the night rang shouts of revelry in Flatbush," he wrote. "Brooklyn at long last has won the

World Series and now let someone suggest moving the Dodgers elsewhere." In two years, someone did.

Depending on time (Diz tired easily), colleague (Blattner energized his excesses), and the ex-pitcher's abrupt change in moods, Dean could be the pitcher's ally, pleading for a legalized spitball: "A pitcher these days really needs a shotgun out there, but I guess that's against the law. The ball they're playing with is not just lively, it's hysterical." He could befriend a fading player. "I ain't hesertant to knock," he said, "but not a guy who's slipping. Time like that, a feller needs a lift." He could praise the grace of baseball — "It's what made me what I was" — then assault the sport as cold. "It's strictly a business. You see the same thing at the park every day, and that's why people stay home and watch TV. I'm talking against my livelihood now, but that's the truth."

Truth was an attribute Diz could safely flaunt; financially, he hardly needed CBS's presence, though his full-sized ego did. Annoyed by Dean's autonomy, MacPhail yet required him; to hamstring the Great One would enrage hundreds of affiliates. What, fans asked, would Ol' Diz say next? Who knew? muttered Bill MacPhail. "We had no control — *none* — over what he'd say or do. I'd sit there in front of the television and cringe — just watch in suspended terror."

Why "purty up" a game? Dean asked. A mediocre pitcher had "nothin' on the ball 'cept a cover"; a hapless batter "couldn't get a hit with a hoe." Umpires were assailed from Ol' Diz's turret. "I kept disputing the umparr's call one afternoon," he said of a long-ago incident, "and that evening I run into the umparr at a chop house. 'That was quite a game out there today, wasn't it?' I asked him. 'What a shame you didn't get to see it.' "

Once, Dean refused to do a Falstaff commercial — because the date was Mother's Day. Over CBS, he praised "The Dinah Shore Show," one of NBC's most valued ventures. "It's the best variety show on TV," Diz said, moving MacPhail to shudder, "These things just weren't *done*, plugging a rival network. But we couldn't tell Dizzy not to do it, because if you did, he'd get more determined that he would." An ardent airplane-hater, Dean condemned them on the air. "Here CBS is selling time to American and United Airlines," said MacPhail, "and Dean says, 'Pod-nuh, I hate to fly, but if you have to, Eastern is much the best.' And I'd die. Just die." Hostile to the sport's tailend clubs, CBS purchased games from its ruling powers. "We didn't want to televise losing teams, so we showed lots of Yankees' games, the Cardinals, etc. But we didn't have the rights to all the teams. It would have been economically infeasible." Thus occurred one of Dizzy's Herculean barbs. "I don't know how our folks come off callin' this the 'Game of the Week,' " Dean told CBS viewers during a one-sided monotony. "There's a much better game — Dodgers and Giants — *over on NBC*."

Even unapologetic candor shrank beside inflections which, at best erratic, turned draconian on the "Game." Diz achieved what was impossible for most baseball teams almost to imagine — make a shambles of the New York Yankees. "Tony Kuebaak" replaced Tony Kubek; "Bobby Risharsen," Richardson. Mantle became "Mannle"; Moose Skowron, "Scarn." Enos Slaughter, the former

Cardinals' warrior, was converted into "Enose Slooter." New York's battery changed from Jim Coates and Elston Howard to "Jim Coots" and "Estone Howard," with "Ryn Duurn" (formerly Ryne Duren) in relief. From the dugout, "Casey Stingle" (Stengel) shouted advice to reserve "Marv Thornberry" (Throneberry), counsel the future Met never failed to miss. Yet verbal transplants were not a Yankees' monopoly; mangled vowels were nonpartisan; they could suffuse any name with two or more syllables. Once Diz and Kirby, subbing for Blattner, aired a game from Cincinnati. "They had all kinds of guys with long names," Dean said. "Ted Kluziwskir [Kluszewski] was on third. Somebody like Odrowski on second, maybe Timowitz on first. Boy, was I sweatin', hopin' nobody'd get a hit and I wouldn't have to call all them names." It was then that a Reds' batter lashed a line drive toward left-center field, worth two bases and sure to score three runs. "There's a long drive," Dean screamed, sensing danger as the fractured runners streaked toward home. "Yep, it's a long drive — and here's Gene Kirby to tell you all about it." Which, of course, Gene did, friend and caddy still.

Earthy and uninhibited, Ol' Diz aligned himself with the image of agrarian jester. "In states where the 'Game' appeared," recalled MacPhail, "if you asked folks what their top ten programs were all week, even including prime-time, he'd be right up there."

To denizens of Booneville, Arkansas, or Raleigh, North Carolina, or the sweeping farmlands of Ohio, Dean was more than "right up there"; each weekend renewed itself as his image paraded across the screen.

Saturday broke hot and steamy; why was the sun always present? Sand-lot games came first, a rite of grass stain, ground balls, and broken windows. Each player aped a major-league universe; some chose Roberto Clemente, others Mantle or Mays. Late-morning television followed. For hours my friends and I sat transfixed, enamored by the deeds of Sky King, Dennis the Menace, and Woody Woodpecker, and Roy Rogers and Dale Evans, giants among the heroes we craved, and guileless Pat Brady, their bedeviled cohort. Lunch came next, quickly ordered and hurriedly consumed. Then more television — Cliff Arquette as Charlie Weaver, Dennis James and his Saturday newsreel, cartoons combed from forgotten files. At 1:45 "Baseball Leadoff" surfaced, hosted by Kirby or Blattner or Ol' Diz himself. Two o'clock meant the "Game of the Week." Viewers loved Dean's plots and scenes, the postcards read to "my friends down in Mississippi," "The Wabash Cannon Ball" sung — it seemed, back then — impulsively, the nostalgia which clothed his stories. Sunday's world too hailed strictly patterned parts. The morning paper. Church. A wild scramble as the benediction ended. The short path home.

The game began and you were "pod-nuh" once more. Dean made you laugh. He made you listen. He made life gentle. He let you love.

*   *   *

For twenty-six years, Buddy Blattner broadcast major league baseball. He began in 1950, among the first ex-athletes to invade the booth. After "Game of the Week," he televised Cardinals' games in 1960–61, fled to the West and the expansion Angels, and returned in 1969 to Missouri, site of his youth and family.

A mature, cultivated announcer, Blattner spent the next seven seasons as the Voice of the Kansas City Royals. His ratings were healthy; he won critical applause. "Like the Angels, we were a rag-tag outfit," said a former Royals' official. "I'd like to have a dollar for every listener Buddy taught the fine points of the game."

In October 1975, he was fired, abruptly, and exchanged the jockocracy for commercial development. Since 1976, he told me now, the ex-Cardinals' infielder had lived in Lake Ozark, Missouri, three hours from both Kansas City and his former cabash at Sportsman's Park.

"When the Royals' thing happened," he said, "I could have gone a couple places, broadcasting games, and made a lot of dough."

"Bob Prince was fired in Pittsburgh about the same time you were," I said.

"I could have gone there, interestingly enough," he said. "It was offered, but they wanted me year round. I'd have been on the banquet circuit all year; it would have meant starting over. And to leave this area — away from my family, my grandchildren — it wasn't worth it."

"So instead you shifted gears."

"In my last year with the Royals," Blattner said, "I began to put together an idea I had — a dream to build the finest tennis complex in the Midwest; a place where I could live, sort of run things, and be creative, fulfilled."

"Are you?" I said.

"It's like a child being born to see it take shape. We've got a complex now with between three- and four hundred villas. We have indoor and outdoor tennis, a stadium court that seats three thousand people, racquetball, aerobics, swimming. Every day, you see new buildings go up. It's one of the damndest, most satisfying things I've ever done."

"What are you saying, that the Royals did you a favor?"

"Inadvertently, they did," he said. "They enabled me to get into all of this a lot sooner than I'd ever been able to if I was still in play-by-play."

I hadn't seen Bud Blattner since December 1975, when, over Scotch and peanuts, he first talked of the possibility of entering private industry. "That way I could stay around here," he said at his St. Louis home. "Certain guys have to be before a microphone — their egos drive them there. I hope I'm not like that. I've always broadcast because it was a way of making a living. I enjoy it — but I don't need it."

Even then, I was struck by Blattner's casual, unself-conscious manner; there was in all he said, even in appraising his misfortune, an absence of bitterness, of the pity and hostility which might have pierced his *Weltanschauung*. "There are things you can't buy with money," he remarked that December evening. "I don't have a dime, but I've lived like a millionaire."

At sixty-five, overseeing an $80-million project, he *had* a dime, but physically, and in his strong, midwestern voice, Blattner had changed little since Kansas City or, for that matter, his electric entwining with "Game of the Week."

"How," I said, "did you happen upon the series?"

"I was doing Browns' games when Falstaff got this property and put it all together. And it was quite an undertaking," Blattner said in a rising tone. "When, in '55, they decided to go over to CBS, they came to me, in large part, because I worked for them and because, I would guess, now the stakes were higher; they were with a network giant. By the time I was approached, Diz had done a couple games in the season with other men around the country, but I started in right after I was hired."

"The broadcasts," I began. "What'd you expect?"

"We had no idea," he said. "I do know Falstaff started with fear and trepidation. But only for a year. By the end of '55, they knew they had a gold mine. Dancer Fitzgerald put four or five men full-time on the account. They really promoted the series, and always in conjunction with the brewery because Falstaff owned the 'Game' lock, stock, and barrel. And I knew Falstaff cherished it. They made a lot of money, and they paid well, as breweries are prone to do."

At first, recalled the white-haired maven, no friction trampled sidekick and star. "It was so gratifying. All the way down the line—CBS, the viewers, us. And there was never anything negative. We had no axes to grind."

"Recount that first season for me," I said. "Nineteen fifty-five."

"Oh, see, it just took off like gangbusters," he exclaimed. "It was like feeding the multitudes, like being Fishers of Men. As you'll remember, people were getting baseball in the hinterlands, major-league style, for the first time in their houses. These fans, except for the Series, had never *seen* a major-league game. Now they're suddenly getting a game, then two, each week. And we knew the people out there were accepting what we did. I mean, our mail was incredible."

"From where?"

Relaxing, Blattner poured coffee. "Surprisingly, our biggest fans were those in the movie industry," he said. "I recall Clark Gable telling me that when he played golf on Saturday, he'd start at something like six in the morning. Why? Because our games came into Los Angeles real early. So he'd play nine holes, then go into the saloon and grab a sandwich and watch the game. Then he went out and played the *last* nine holes. We got bundles of mail from the entire entertainment industry—musicians, actors, and actresses are often great sports fans. And many at that time, most, in fact, were all baseball because it was really the only game in town."

By Blattner's second season, if a fan of "the only game" had grown insatiable, 1956 further bulged his interest, for in a year of Hungarian revolt and civil war in Cuba and "I Like Ike" (again), America witnessed a promenade of old heroes, new names, and endearing play.

"Ratings were even higher than the year before," Bud recollected. "And they stayed tremendously high for the rest of the fifties in every market we were in. And beer sales, in every market *they* were in, Falstaff led, like, two to one. [After a decade of declining profits, the brewery would die in 1980.] These marked the vintage years—a year like '56—for Falstaff as well as for 'Game of the Week,' and that event, I believe, made them."

That year, Americans watched "Your Hit Parade" and "Playhouse 90" and the "U.S. Steel Hour" and, already, at five, my personal favorite, the incomparable "Tales of the 77th Bengal Lancers." They watched too as Don Newcombe (of whom Ernie Banks shuddered, "Once he got out on that mound, he was a monster") won twenty-seven games, Banks (of whom Jimmy Dykes said, "Without him, the Cubs would finish in Albuquerque") blasted twenty-eight home runs, and Snider, Musial, and Hank Aaron led in homers (43), runs batted in (109), and batting average (.328), respectively. The Braves placed second, one game behind Brooklyn; the Reds, climbing to third, clubbed a major-league-record-tying 221 home runs; and Stan the Man saluted Warren Spahn. "I don't think Spahn will ever get into the Hall of Fame," Musial joked. "He'll never stop pitching." In 1956, Mickey Mantle seldom stopped hitting: his statistics, fifty-two home runs, 130 RBIs, and a .353 average; his reward, the Triple Crown. Frank Lary, soon to wear the shield of "Yankee-killer," and left-hander Billy Hoeft won forty-one games for the fifth-place Tigers. Yet, inevitably, events encroached on even *these* priorities. Egypt nationalized the Suez Canal. Nikita Khrushchev denounced Joseph Stalin. A fifty-four-week boycott, begun the previous year, forced Montgomery, Alabama, to integrate its city buses. One heard the names of Maria Callas, Alan Ginsberg, and Dr. Martin Luther King, Jr. On Broadway, you could see O'Neill's *Long Day's Journey into Night* and Paddy Chayevski's *Middle of the Night. The Diary of Anne Frank* won a Pulitzer Prize. On the book page of New York's seven dailies, reviewers trashed *Peyton Place.* The World Series was telecast over 201 stations in the U.S. and seventeen in Canada; in it, Don Larsen *was* center stage as the Yankees and Dodgers presented the last "Subway Series." They "had played each other so often, it seemed safe to assume that everything possible had happened. What more could happen?" Stan Isaacs later wrote. "Don Larsen had an answer. . . . He strolled to the mound and retired twenty-seven straight Dodgers. That effort must have destroyed the script maker. There was indeed nothing else to say. So the Yankees and the Brooklyn Dodgers never played another World Series after 1956, at least for the price of a subway ride."

Pleased with such postseason wizardry, NBC plunged into the 1957 *regular* season. "Tom Gallery and I would meet with affiliates," Lindsey Nelson told me, "and they would say, 'Look, if you guys don't put baseball on Saturday, we'd might as well close down. 'Cause there ain't nobody watching us.' We were getting absolutely terrible ratings against Dean. No, let me amend that: We weren't getting *any* ratings. So we decided, 'If we don't want to get off the air, we have to do *something.*' "

That something was NBC's Saturday "Major League Baseball."

"Their threat never bothered us," Blattner observed. "And they brought the big guns in — Leo Durocher, Fred Haney, Lindsey. I just figured, 'Let's don't change a thing, just do what we've been doing.' And we did, and we just overpowered them. But again, by that time we'd been with the people in America two or three years. We'd become a part of their weekend schedule. People arranged their outings around our Saturday game. Maybe they set Sunday aside to go boating. Then we went Sunday too, and maybe they didn't go boating at all."

"Dean and the series," I said. "Which made the other?"

"*Each* did," he replied. "The 'Game of the Week' was a tremendous vehicle for Diz, who in the mid-fifties was almost at his zenith of popularity. He was doing television specials out of Hollywood. He was a national figure, one of the best known, most loved people in the nation. Not just in sports—in the entire *nation*. He'd made national polls showing him to be on the 'Most Recognizable' list. And the 'Game of the Week' gave him a forum to remain so."

"Yes," I said, "but what accounted for his appeal?"

Blattner stopped, momentarily, and cleared his throat. "Well," he said, "Diz had certain expressions which people took to. He had stories, little anecdotes that he would tell—about the Gas House Gang, about different pitchers. And he could use me as a crutch. You know, here I was, a little .250 hitter, and I was made to order for him. 'Pod-nuh,' he'd say, 'you'd be duck soup for me.'

"Diz loved to agitate, although Diz didn't like to be agitated. That was one quirk of his personality that people didn't really know about. For the public, Diz had a ready smile. Privately, his temper was a little short. And he didn't argue, per se. He'd walk away, like, 'Get me outa here, pod-nuh.' Diz liked the adulation of the crowd, and then, after that, he wanted to get the hell out. In other words, get your ovation and scram."

"What's the label you would use?" I said. "Arrogant?"

"No," Blattner said, "for the simple reason that he never really assaulted viewers. I don't think he ever walked with me to 'Game of the Week' and said, 'You lucky slobs, you around the country, I'm going to attack you,' or, 'I can say anything I want.' Sure, he said things that once in a while would bother people, but we all do. The only time he'd really get upset during a game is when he'd told a person how to bet on a game and then his advice turned sour."

"How often did *that* happen?"

"People were forever calling Diz—they'd call him from Texas and every-where—asking, 'Who's going to win?' And he'd say, 'Well, I think the White Sox are going to win.' So if the White Sox' pitcher was doing badly, Diz would get mad. You know, he'd just rip him. 'Can't see how a fella can pitch like that,' Diz would fume," and here Blattner's voice became hurried and animated. " 'Come on, throw the ball over the plate,' or, 'Pod-nuh, throw the ball. Nibble. Nibble.' "

"The dark side of the moon."

"For the listener, it was kind of different," Bud said. "He enjoyed it. But the amazing thing was how little Diz knew about baseball. As far as being a man-ager to construct the game, when to bunt, when to hit and run, how you put the lineup together so that, for instance, the second batter could push the ball around—no, Diz didn't know. And he didn't want to discuss the inner work-ings of baseball. 'Score some runs,' he'd say. Man, Diz was just down to the basics. And he always had to have somebody who could come back, put the game in perspective and give the right score. That's where I came in."

At the time he kept coming back, coming in, and nursing perspective,

Blattner's role, some wrote, verged on condescension. How could the ex-infielder not bristle at playing second fiddle to the Great One's Lear?

"Oh, no, no," he protested. "I never felt that way. You see, if the roles had been reversed, if I'd had the name and image and following that Diz had, I would have expected someone working with me to perform the same function. He'd be grumpy, and I could say something that would allow him a line to get on me, and he would brighten up just like a new penny. That was his crutch. I never felt like an interloper. I knew I made a definite contribution. We made a good team because I really didn't care what Diz did."

Blattner paused and sipped a drink. "That's why some things fell flat when Dean worked with Pee Wee in the sixties," he said, haltingly. "Pee Wee was an outstanding hitter. So there was no need to play my .250 against Diz's thirty wins in 1934. See, with Reese and Dean, Pee Wee didn't want him to talk about, 'That's how they got you out, pod-nuh,' because maybe they *didn't* get Pee Wee out. Or Reese would say, 'I hit guys like you, Diz, like I owned them.' And Diz didn't like it. Those things didn't play well."

"How did they play with you?"

"I actually received," he said, "a degree of a sympathetic audience. Diz knew he couldn't bury me, and he didn't try. I would say things that I knew would get a charge from him, phrases that I knew he'd pick up, because he was just waiting for a crumb he could really run with. All the public saw was Diz making cracks at my expense. But these things were important to him — he had to get a laugh. Maybe it was at your detriment, but you were primarily being a straight man for his part of the performance. He needed those laughs."

The man described by Blattner diverged, incongruously, from the jaunty qualities usually ascribed to Dean. "You make him sound wary, almost insecure," I said.

"There was some of that," he said, "and a lot of it came from not having an education. He was very aware of what he'd missed. But more of it came from selfishness. Having always been the big man, he was determined to remain so. And he respected me because he never told me a lot of the stories he had told others. He knew I'd never buy them. He knew I knew him too well."

"And to people that didn't know him?" I said.

"Then he told stories that he knew you wanted to hear. He pleased you and built himself up. And it wasn't a bad way, really, because everybody was happy. Off the air he might tell me, 'Those clowns on the field, those humpty-dumpties,' but on mike the only guys he'd really get on were the pitchers."

The night unfolded. A large smile split Blattner's face. "The general public never really understood Diz," he said. "Dean was a character. He enjoyed being a character, and he was smart enough never to get *out* of character. That was the most important thing he did in his life. When you're tabbed with the name of Dizzy, you're not expected to have a Phi Beta Kappa key dangling from your watch-fob."

"But he knew enough," I said, "that the techniques that worked for him, he continued to use."

"Yes, and a reason is that he was in a different locale for most games, so he could get away with the same expressions week after week," Blattner said. "Diz was not, by nature and education, a linguist. Names were a little difficult. But he had a homey voice, a certain command, and a good memory. People don't realize that. Going into a given area, he remembered particular things that he'd said to a particular writer ten years earlier. He might have told fifty other local writers a different story — but he remembered which story went with which guy."

"Financially, what did it bring him?"

"He was in six figures all the time," he said. "Diz picked up so much money, or as much as he wanted to, with all the network TV specials. Every two weeks or so, there'd be someone in from New York or Los Angeles coming to Diz with a script for a television series. Hermione Gingold, for one. Diz would get all excited about that for a while and then he'd drop the idea. He didn't want to work that much — it was really his wife, Pat, and his own love of being recognized, that drove him into broadcasting in the first place. So he'd relegate himself to three specials a year, but he could have done as many as he wanted."

In early 1957, according to *The Sporting News*, what Ol' Diz wanted was out. "If I'm ever going to start enjoying life," he said, vowing retirement, "the time to begin is now." But by Opening Day, CBS (and Diz's $62,500 salary, Blattner noted) had renewed Dean's appetite, and in a daybook of Sputnik, racial violence at Little Rock, the Asian Flu epidemic, and "Leave It to Beaver," of McCarthy's death and Jack Kerouac's *On the Road*, a postwar high 7.7 percent unemployment rate, and Congressional probes of labor racketeering, of shivering silence and unquenchable joys, Ol' Diz saw how baseball too was not without its contrasts.

New York lost the Giants to San Francisco, the Dodgers to Los Angeles, and the World Series, stripped from the city for the first time since 1948. Herb Score, struck in the face by Gil McDougald's line drive, almost lost an eye. The Senators' Roy Sievers blasted forty-two home runs and 114 RBIs; as in 1956, Billy Pierce was a twenty-game winner; Mickey Mantle hit .365, the highest for a Bomber since 1939; and Ted Williams, at thirty-nine, with heavy legs and a peerless stroke, bashed a monumental .731 slugging percentage and a .388 average, the best since T. Ballgame's .406 in 1941. In their fifth year, the Milwaukee Braves dominated the year, winning ninety-five games and the pennant, then thwarting the Yankees in October. Despite the glowing baseball, though, the season's big loser, strangely, *was* baseball, for by leaving New York, the Dodgers and Giants betrayed two of the game's most fervent followings, demolished the bromide invented by baseball executives — "Baseball is a sport, not business" — and permanently axed, among millions of fans, their affection for the pastime.

"Who said the National League *has* to have a team in New York?" blustered its obtuse and corpulent president. What Warren Giles was incapable of understanding was that upon baseball's near-desertion of the nation's leading city, its cultural, communications, and advertising hub, a sports vacuum would occur; some entity must rise to fill it; in the late fifties, shedding its underdog mentality, that body became the television-inspired phenomenon of the National Football League.

"It's interesting," said Harold Rosenthal, "that in these years of 1957 and, of course, '58, with its sudden-death [Baltimore's 23–17 overtime victory in the December 28, 1958, championship game over the New York Giants], pro football really took off nationally, and it started in New York. And it started only *after* the Dodgers and Giants left town. You see, the newspapers, radio, and television stations had always been baseball, baseball, baseball. Now there were only the Yankees left—not nearly enough to write about or to fill their sports pages."

"And into that void marched the NFL," I said.

"One of the greatest ironies of our time," Rosenthal said, "is that pro football, which baseball would come to fear so greatly in the sixties and seventies, had its birth, really, in baseball's raping of New York."

"In effect," I said, "baseball ignited the NFL's explosion."

"Not intentionally, of course, but that was the result," he said. "With three baseball teams here, there wasn't time or space to pay attention to something called pro football. Baseball wasn't just the biggest here—it *owned* the city. And people were too busy hating or loving the Dodgers and Giants to bother with the NFL. But with only one team, there was plenty of time *and* attention, and people became aware, as they'd never been before, of how exciting pro football could be."

If baseball lost, so did Dean's traveling evangelism, for with Los Angeles and San Francisco major-league (and subject, therefore, to unconditional blackout), the CBS series watched its then-third- and tenth-largest markets dissolve. "The amazing thing was that while folks in these cities were obviously delighted to have live big-league ball," said Blattner, "they were absolutely up in arms over not seeing us each week. I mean, letters, phone calls, petitions to the stations. And, naturally, we were upset ourselves, because it meant that a smaller part of the country would see us."

With the National League's upheaval, fifteen cities were blacked out—four more than in 1953—and by April 1958, only 59 percent of all households could feel the fortuitous blasts of "Game of the Week." Yet geography, Blattner added, was not among Dean's workaday concerns, and as Khrushchev became Soviet premier, de Gaulle returned to power, Harry Golden released *Only in America*, Sir Edmund Hillary reached the South Pole, and, visiting Caracas, Nixon was stoned by a Communist mob, "Diz didn't change as the '58 season went along. He was the same—possibly less warm in person than on the tube, because, you see, the Dean on air wasn't his real personality."

"Examples?" I said.

"Diz created many illusions that he didn't try to eliminate," Blattner said. "One was that he was a big drinker, which wasn't true. Diz worked for Falstaff, and you got the impression, just from his innuendoes during the course of the afternoon, that he'd had fourteen beers during the game. Well, I never saw Diz take a drop prior to or during a game in all my years with him. But he got so big, and he was always mentioning booze, that you thought, 'Boy, this guy's a big drinker. He can really handle it.' "

"What were other illusions?"

"That he was a mammoth eater. You know, Diz talked about food *all* the time. He wanted to get all the plugs in — from biscuits to corn meal to steaks to a certain kind of pork chop that he'd had somewhere. And when you looked at him, you swore he really did gulp all those things down. But the truth is that he'd just become too inactive. The only thing Diz did was golf, and even there, he rode the cart. And he never had to walk fifty feet, 'cause he hit the ball down the middle. Plus, he was one of the greatest putters I've ever seen."

"Any more?"

"People thought of Diz as everybody's friend, as a guy surrounded by a close circle of real pals," Blattner said. "*No*. People all knew Diz and he always had a smile and he'd take off the sombrero and use that famous expression of his, 'Hi, pod-nuh.' He didn't know *anybody's* name, of course, but people thought, 'Oh, my God, he remembered my name, 'cause he called me pod-nuh.' So in this regard Diz was very private, selfish even. He was prone to indulge himself — and because he had no children, he and Pat showered their attention on themselves. He was outgoing only when it was a matter that he should turn it on to please his fans."

"Did Diz know," I said, "and enjoy what his veneer became?"

Blattner's response was slow to start, then came rushing forth. "Diz's image was, and he *loved* this, the guy that just dropped off the back of the truck, barefooted, and wandered into town, saying, 'Fellas, what's it all about?' But he was just about two steps ahead of you all the way."

" 'Dumb like a fox.' "

"Precisely. He knew of his great popularity and became lazy with it. All of us started doing more work because we were doing his." Bud hesitated. The smile faded. "There was this conflict between the on- and off-air Dean. There was also an amazing complexity to the man. He could be quite bright, quite knowing, and on the other side of the coin, he could be so naive about things, it would stun you."

"The guy, barefooted, wandering into town."

Ebullient, Blattner refilled my coffee mug. "I can't say he was basically kind, either. He wasn't. Yet there were times when someone touched him, and Diz could be almost tender — whether it was show or not, I don't know. He'd spend a half-hour with a kid, then say, 'Let's get out of here.' Diz was not a reader, and yet he'd crop up in his bed in the hotel room when we were on the road and start reading a paper. Just at the time, incidentally, when you'd think Diz would be out on the town."

"But still a Public Man," I said.

"He was instantly capable of the lure," said Blattner. "That was his image — the people's choice. When we walked down Broadway or Lexington Avenue in New York, there'd be a mob around him. And he'd say, 'Hi, folks,' then grab a cab and beat it. He wanted out. He wanted that sanctuary — to get away from people. On the 'Game of the Week,' we'd get in a town on Friday, and Diz would get a suite and he wouldn't leave. We'd even have dinner up there. So there were conflicts. And America still thought of him, nonetheless, as a wild man, a harmless, lovable wild man, drinking and eating up a storm."

By year four of the CBS series, with a majority of "Game of the Week" broadcasts emanating from Yankee Stadium, Diz ate most of his storms in the Apple. "Those Damn Yankees, why can't we beat 'em?" cursed Joe Hardy, the grizzled epicenter of the 1958 movie. That season, few did. The Bombers ambled to a fourth straight pennant, their ninth in ten years, and rallying from a 3-1 games deficit, ousted the Braves in a fascinating Series. Richie Ashburn won his second batting championship; at .328, Williams won his sixth; and Ted's outfield playmate, Jackie Jensen, was named Most Valuable Player. Aside from Milwaukee, accents echoed around Ernie Banks, the National League MVP, and the Pittsburgh Pirates, vaulting to second place from the 1957 cellar. At shortstop and second base, the Bucs' Dick Groat and Bill Mazeroski made of baseball a theatre. At first base, Dick Stuart, who was dubbed "Dr. Strangeglove," played only sixty-four games, and *still* led the league in errors, made of infielding a joke.

"I may be biased," Blattner observed, "but I don't believe baseball has ever been more exciting to broadcast than in the 1950s." They ended, then, correctly, in the final year of Blattner's connecting threads to CBS.

On Sunday, September 27, 1959, winning their last games of the season, Milwaukee and Los Angeles tied for the National League pennant. "Because of an NFL conflict, we weren't scheduled to do a game that day," Blattner said, "so I was at home in St. Louis and Diz was in Chicago. Falstaff had already told us that if there was a playoff, they'd sponsor it. About four o'clock I got a call from Falstaff — the playoff is on. So I telephoned Diz, who suggested that we meet in his hotel," then drive the ninety miles to Milwaukee, where the best-of-three series would begin in twenty-one hours.

"While I was driving to Chicago," he continued, "unbeknownst to me, Diz and Gene Kirby had gone to a place to eat," and Falstaff — having pledged to sponsor the playoff — found itself unable to underwrite the costs.

"They needed another sponsor," I guessed.

"Yes, and after a couple hours Falstaff discovered that L&M cigarettes would come in for half the costs, which was great except for one thing — for years, on almost every game we did, Diz'd talk about, 'Man, I never felt so good since I threw that last cigarette away.' "

"Trouble in River City."

No, Blattner said, the trouble struck at Dean. By telephone, a Falstaff spokesman explained, "Listen, Diz, we can't hack this thing alone and L&M won't take you. Bud'll do the games, and we'll get [Tigers' broadcaster] George Kell to help him out. But not you, Diz. Sorry. You're off the broadcast."

In early evening, reaching Chicago, Blattner arrived at the Knickerbocker Hotel. "Funny thing, I found out that Diz wasn't there. So I sit in the hotel lobby, waiting like a little boy. Finally, about eight o'clock, here comes Diz flying across the lobby, knocking old ladies down with their packages, and right by me he goes to the phone. And there he starts screaming at these agency people in New York. He was just out of his mind. And all I found out is that L&M is going to be one of the sponsors, which was fine with me."

Twenty-six years later, the silences were still tense. "It was a little while later when I heard Diz say, 'Well, I'll tell you one thing. They're not going to get away with it.' This was the first inkling I had that maybe cigarettes wouldn't want him. And when the agency told him to return to Dallas, just to forget the game — well, now he's really burned; his pride's been hurt. So Diz comes back," Blattner said in a way that was wavering and slow, "with a statement that anybody who appeared in the playoff would be off the 'Game of the Week' forever."

"Blackmail," I said.

"It was obviously aimed at me. I told him, 'For God sakes, Diz, why don't you just forget it? You don't want to do the playoff anyway.' Pat was there and it was just a very bad scene."

"Did he understand *your* position?"

"Sure. My point to Diz was, 'If you want to go with me, fine. Gene, the same with you. But I'm going to grab the rented car and get to Milwaukee. I have a job to do.' Gene thought if we discussed it more, maybe Diz would drop the whole thing and go back to Dallas. But all I said was, 'Diz, there's not a thing I can do.' So Kirby went with me, and Diz said he was going to stay up all night calling the people at Dancer Fitzgerald. I couldn't imagine him doing that, but in the end, he did."

Blattner's smile grasped the middle road between compassion and disdain. "We got to Milwaukee at two in the morning," he said. "I got up five hours later to try and find someone who could pull the whole show together. I find George Kell, and we got to the park about ten. I'm heading toward the broadcast booth, and I was halfway up the ramp, and Gene Kirby is coming down. And he said to me, 'Pod-nuh, can't believe it.'

"I don't know what made me say this, but I said, 'Well, Gene, am I off the game?' And Kirby said, 'Pod-nuh, yeah.' What Dean had done was say that if I was on the playoff, he'd never come back for 'Game of the Week,' which, of course, terrified the Falstaff people."

"So Dean forced you out," I said.

"Yes," he said, "and Falstaff misjudged me badly. They thought I'd be happy to return to St. Louis and get paid for these games I hadn't broadcast. After all, they thought, what did *I* care? So I came down the ramp and called New York and dictated my resignation as of right there. I had a couple years left with Falstaff and CBS, but after several thousand dollars in lawyer fees and three months of hassle, I finally escaped the contract."

Civilly and directly, Blattner adhered to an uncomplicated code of character and intuition. "Why didn't you accept the money and stay with CBS?" I said. "Why leave the series you loved?"

His manner resorted less to pomp than matter of fact. "It was strictly a matter of pride," he said. "It was something I just *felt*. I never could have looked in the mirror again had I said, 'Well, I'll take the dough and flee and then come back in the booth with Diz next year.' And I left, quite bluntly, the best job in the country, but it all evened up as the years went by."

"What was Dean's reaction?"

"I think he was very sorry, even though he really was behind it," Blattner said. "Again, he acted in that selfish vein of his. Falstaff said to me, 'Stay on. You know Diz didn't mean what he said.' I told them, 'Quite likely he didn't,' but in no way was I about to be dictated to. I never blamed Falstaff—they never tried to hurt me or take me off the playoff. But Diz was self-centered, and this got to him terribly—that he could be kicked off and I would go on."

"You must have felt some bitterness," I said.

"I never held any great hatred for Diz," he insisted. "He did something that was a big hurt to me, and that's partly why you're the first person I've ever told this publicly to. I didn't want to air my grievances out loud. But I reacted in 1959 in a way I knew I had to."

"Did your paths cross much later?"

Blattner pulled up in his chair and set his lips. "Not often," he said, "and whenever we did, he always made out like nothing had ever happened. And Diz could do this so beautifully. You know, bad things that he'd done, he'd forget tomorrow. And I never looked back, never second-guessed myself. Even if I *had* gone on the playoff games, and Diz had in the end relented, there would have been an uneasiness all the time. So once he dropped the hammer, I had to leave."

Blattner's "pod-nuh" rarely knew contrition. "Oh, he never apologized," the sidekick said of Dean. "His only reaction was utter amazement, as though I'd lost my mind. And the country was surprised. That's why I kept my story to myself, because I didn't think it was a story for public consumption."

From Milwaukee, the former table-tennis champion left for the emphatic comfort of home.

In December 1959, Reese was named his replacement; four months later, Ol' Diz and Pee Wee went forward to daub the major leagues.

Leaving Blattner now, a quarter-century after contention rent the "Game of the Week," one drew toward a word conveying more than any invented on-air persona.

Gentleman.

*   *   *

In Blattner's last season with Dizzy Dean, the Cleveland Indians enjoyed—dare one say it?—their final pennant race, conceivably, of the twentieth century. Five years after winning 111 games, the Tribe, now chasing the Chicago White Sox, matched strength so lyrically that years later, in the trail of almost three decades of scorched earth, Ohioans would regard 1959 and say, "There was our last hurrah, if only we had known it."

That year, I was eight, the Indians finished second, and Jimmy Dudley

made a city leap to its feet and cheer—and not just a city but a state, and beyond that state, over the club's then-sixty-eight-station radio network, anyone
who loved a story, beautifully told, by a voice that was soft and lilting.

I was never an Indians' fan (no masochist, me), but from the moment I first
caught his rhythms, two springs later, in April 1961, on a clear nighttime
station which boomed into western New York, I was always a Dudley fan.

More than any contemporary, he reminded me of Barber. Quiet, earnest,
he exuded light, rich tones, and as the Indians reverberated inside the walls
of mediocrity, his rhetoric made signal sounds in the dreary somnolence.

He was pleasant, seldom petulant, and pleasant to listen *to*, and I would
listen not out of interest in the ball game—except when the Yankees played—
but rather, because it seemed to me that here was a voice who had fathomed
the mystery of baseball and whose sprightly expressions etched the poetry of
its core.

"I never saw a bad game, only a few long ones and a few slow ones," he said,
at seventy-one, at his home in Tucson, Arizona, the Indians' long-time spring
training site.

"The long ones must have happened in the sixties," I said. In its first eight
seasons, lurching to a 635–652 record, Cleveland placed fourth once, fifth four
times, sixth twice, and eighth in 1967, Dudley's last year. In that same time,
the Indians never drew a million people, never finished less than fifteen games
from first place, never *suggested*—not even in 1966, winning their first ten
games—that they would somehow contend, *this* year, at *last*, past the end of
June, the annual meridian of the Wigwam's collapse.

"Now that you mention it, they did seem to get worse the longer I was
there," laughed Dudley, for two decades, starting in 1948, the Voice of Cleveland baseball. "What do they say on television shows? 'Any relationship between the facts is wholly incidental'? I hope that was true of me."

He was born in Alexandria, Virginia, three miles from my present home.
Remembering, I turned back to his colleagues—Allen, from the factory stench
of Johns, Alabama, and Barber, from the lush hills of rural Mississippi, and
Nelson, from South Main Street in Columbia, Tennessee, and Ol' Diz, from
the primitive terrain of Lucas, Arkansas. Why were all the great broadcasters
southern?

"I think our accents appealed to people—they were sort of graceful, they fit
in with the game," Dudley mused. "Dixie speaking is slow, leisurely, it sort of
moves with the weather. And baseball is that kind of game. Plus, southerners
love to talk, as you know, and nothing anywhere is as verbal as baseball."

"That's not so true today among announcers, the southern link," I said.

"No," he said, "and I'll tell you why. The professionals—the Allens, Barbers,
Lindsey Nelson, me—we were southern, yes, but even more, we were trained.
Today's broadcasters, with the notable exception of my dear friend in Los
Angeles . . ."

"Vin Scully."

"Except for him, they've gone more to ex-players, and it doesn't matter
whether they're from the South or not, they can't do the job because they can't

set the mood. They're not *prepared* in their vocation. We *were*. Broadcasting is acting. It's a show-time mode. And those that you speak of — the reason they were good was due to the nature of the game, our voices that fit in, and the fact that it was our life, not something we just stumbled onto when we threw down our bat."

From Alexandria, Dudley moved ninety-five miles to the southwest, playing football, basketball, and baseball at the University of Virginia while majoring in chemistry. After graduation, he worked, briefly, for DuPont, but boredom forced a clear break with his past. In 1937, at twenty-three, he took a job broadcasting for WCHV, Charlottesville, and in the next four years ricocheted to stations in Washington, Syracuse, and Pittsburgh. "Then, I went to Chicago," he said, and in 1941–42 bounced from WCFL to country music WJJD to giant WIND.

"They used to say Jack Brickhouse was Bob Elson's brief case carrier," Dudley said. "Well, when he was a Cubs' announcer in those days, I was Hal Totten's brief case carrier. I was sort of his 'gopher' — I'd do the odd jobs — and once in a while he'd let me do play-by-play."

"For how long?"

"Not more than an inning, tops," he said. "Totten closely guarded the mike. He was like Ted Husing, who I knew in the early forties and who told me, when I was trying to get on the air, 'Hey, kid, you're good. I let you do a little baseball and football and the first thing you know, you'll be taking my job.' That's the way Ted was — blunt — and it's one reason I admired him so."

Theatrical, Husing was also shrewd: the Virginian *was* good. In 1942, he was inducted into the Air Force. Stationed in India, he entered innumerable GI bull sessions, vowing to re-enter radio after the war. " 'What do you do, Jimmy, sell 'em or repair 'em?' one smart-ass second lieutenant asked me." Unrattled, Dudley emigrated to Cleveland in 1947.

"I went with the hope of doing some Indians' games or at least some minor-league action," he said, "but as nothing opened up, I got more frustrated. I kept thinking about how I'd listened to Elson, Brickhouse, and Totten and how much I was in awe of them — and how I'd give up *anything* to have the job they did."

"Soon you would," I said.

"Yes," he said, "and it was like going to heaven."

One day in June 1947, Jimmy was assigned to broadcast a sand-lot match at Municipal Stadium before the Indians' regular game. "I thought," he said, "this might be as close as I ever got to the major leagues," but Dudley's luck would prove uncanny, for listening over the club's flagship outlet, WJW, and impressed by the sweep of the announcer's voice, was George Creedon, head of the beer company which recently had purchased the Tribe's radio rights.

On June 21, 1946, Bill Veeck had bought the Indians. Approaching baseball's Barnum, Creedon now insisted, "That's the guy I want to do the Indians' games — the guy I just heard on the radio," and climbing the Standard Brewery Company's ladder, Dudley went "to heaven" in April 1948.

That first season, Dudley resembled, more than obliquely, a singles hitter who, after punching a home run in his major-league inaugural, finds that, years later, anticlimax had settled in his bones.

With Bob Lemon throwing ten shutouts, Bob Feller whiffing 164 batters, and Gene Bearden compiling a 2.43 ERA (all league bests), Lou Boudreau scoring 116 runs, Joe Gordon banking thirty-two home runs and 124 RBIs, and the Indians drawing an exorbitant (for 1948) 33,598 spectators per date, Cleveland won ninety-seven games in the regular season, beat the Red Sox in their one-game playoff, and clubbed the Braves in the Fall Classic before record-toppling crowds at the lakefront bowl.

"It was like living a dream," Dudley marveled. "Talk about being at the right place at the right time. It was so hard to believe—the crowds flocking to the park each day, the pressure, the Red Sox and Yankees nipping at our heels."

"And then the playoff."

"Going into Fenway Park that day was like throwing the Christians to the lions. I was fortunate enough to do the radiocasts on sort of an ad-hoc network around the country. It was free to clubs who wanted to pick it up and carry the game on their networks. The Reds, the Pirates, the Tigers all did."

"Did you think you could beat the Sox?" I said.

"Lord, they were so good at home!" he said. "The Boston crowd alone had to be worth at least a run. But we won and then came the Series and, my, how that huge stadium was packed. No park in baseball is as dramatic as Municipal Stadium when it's jammed to overflowing. And for someone thirty-four years of age, it was truly a Utopia."

In 1949–50, the Tribe fell to third and fourth. In 1951–53, under the gallant-mannered Al Lopez, Cleveland finished second: five, two, and eight-and-one-half games behind New York. Then, in the summer of '54, the Indians broke through: a .721 winning percentage, only forty-three losses, and the largest regular-season throng in baseball history (84,587 for a double-header, on September 12, against the Yankees).

"Rizzuto said it best about all those wonderful years," Dudley was recalling. "Phil stated, 'The Yankees always had the great balance of youngsters and older players,' the kids and the veterans. And every year, come September, George Weiss and Stengel would make magnificent and wise moves with all that money they had."

"They'd pick up a Country Slaughter."

Dudley sighed. "Or a Johnny Mize—you could name as many as I. They'd go out and replace a Bobby Brown with a Billy Martin. Or, the perfect case is, of course, replacing a Joe D. with a Mantle. We were so close. A fringe player here, an injury healing more quickly there, and we could have won—I counted up once—about six or seven pennants in a row during the fifties."

"Forget the six pennants," I said. "I'll bet you'd have traded 'em all for four victories in October of '54."

"No one could believe it," he said. "We'd been this juggernaut all year, the great pitching, the record number of wins, and we came into the Series as a heavy favorite when—boom! Dusty Rhodes gets a couple pinch-homers and Mays makes that amazing catch and we're swept before you know it." His voice softened. "In some ways, the franchise was never quite the same."

After October's shock, banality ringed the Indians.

The club contended in 1955–56, resurfaced in 1959 as Rocky Colavito whacked forty-two home runs and Tito Francona hit .363, and played out the sixties in virtual anonymity. From 2,620,627 in 1948, Tribe attendance shrunk to 1,335,472 in 1954, 725,547 seven years later, and only 662,980 in 1967, second lowest in the league. In 1963, luring 562,507 people in seventy-seven home dates, Cleveland averaged 7,447 spectators in its 74,208-seat yard.

"You've got to remember," Jimmy Dudley said, "that those immediate post-war years were inflated. A lot of that 1948 total had to do with the fact that with the fighting over, people were looking for something that was fun to do, somewhere to throw their money—and because baseball was the only sports show around, it got chosen. Check the figures of the major leagues: almost every team went wild at the gate, say, between '47 and '49."

"But in Cleveland," I said, "wasn't a lot of the gate caused by Veeck?"

The ex-Voice grinned. "Was it ever," he said. "I was a homer on the air—Veeck wanted you to be, to promote. 'Get the fans interested!' he'd say. 'Baseball belongs to them.' Bill would stick S&H green stamps—thousands of them—under certain seats at the park. Then, at a given signal, everybody at Municipal Stadium—there could be eighty thousand people there—would jump up and close their seat to see if they'd won. Ever hear eighty thousand seats crashing at once? And he'd have orchids at the park—'Flown directly to you from Hawaii,' he'd say—and the ladies went bonkers."

"Don't forget Joe Earley," I added.

"Joe was a guy," he said, "who wrote in and said that he was the average fan and it wasn't right that the average fan wasn't honored with days—just the big shots. So Veeck had a night for *him*, gave him a car, a boat, showered him with gifts. And those crowds we used to have! Cleveland in the late forties was unlike anywhere in baseball."

"And the fifties decline in attendance?"

"We still drew all right as long as we were winning," he said. "It was later on, when we hit the skids, that naturally the crowds weren't there. But even then, it wasn't *all* bad. We had some great moments in that old canyon of a park." In late 1949, after the Indians were eliminated, Veeck held a ceremony in which the club buried its 1948 championship pennant behind the center-field fence. On June 23, 1950, Luke Easter, the Tribe's huge first baseman, unloaded a 477-foot home run, the longest ball ever hit at Municipal Stadium. It was on August 14, 1958, that Vic Power stole home twice against the Tigers; June 17, 1960, that Teddy Ballgame hoisted his five hundreth home run; and July 31, 1963, that Woodie Held, Pedro Ramos, Francona, and Larry Brown lashed consecutive home runs off the Angels' Paul Foytack. "That's the stuff *I* remember," Dudley said. "Not the empty seats and the rest."

At the double-decked stadium, with its mammoth capacity and short foul lines, its vast outfield acreage and interior fence, and its green seats rolling away, row upon row, in perfect, straight lines, Dudley paired with Jack Graney (1948–54) and Tom Manning (1956–57), Harry Jones and Herb Score, Ed Edwards, whom he disrespected ("Ed wouldn't know where the hell home plate was"), and Bob Neal, whom he despised.

"Jack was my first air partner and the one that did the most to help me," Dudley said. "He told me that 85 percent of the people who listen to baseball broadcasts either know more about the game or *think* they know more about it than you do. And I never forgot what he said."

He never forgot Neal, either, but for reasons set apart from fondness or past help. "They didn't get along *a*-tall," a former Indians' producer told me. "I'd sit between 'em up in the booth — almost like an umpire, like a different round every day. But at least they were consistent. They didn't speak to each other *off* the air. They didn't speak to each other *on* the air."

Dudley's third straight year with Neal was his twentieth with the Indians. "I was looking forward to going on, to being their Voice for who knows how long," he said, quietly. "I loved the games. I loved those letters people wrote."

"From where?" I asked.

"Go back to about 1950, when WERE outbid WJW to get our games. From then on, we built up a network which reached way outside Ohio to all over the Midwest and East," he said. "We had a 50,000-watt station in Wheeling, West Virginia, named WWVA, and it carried our games throughout the South. But I guess the ones that meant the most to me are the ones from a little blind boy in Brantford, Ontario. They were written in braille and were transcribed for me by his family. He always wound up by saying, 'God bless you, Jimmy, and remember, you are my eyes.' And I applied that to all my audience. I was the eyes of all the people who couldn't be there."

On January 19, 1968, at a press conference at Municipal Stadium, Jimmy's eyes went black. "I would not say we were dissatisfied," Harry Dennis, WERE's vice-president and general manager, remarked of Dudley's firing. "It's just a changing world."

Even now, the memory made Dudley's nerve-ends sting. "They may have had their reasons for firing me, and that was Gabe Paul's privilege [as Indians' president], but I certainly didn't like his methods. They waited until almost February — too late even to find a job for the coming season. They knocked me out of a year's occupation."

"Why'd it happen?" I said.

"I think because Paul had been friends with Neal," he said, "and one of us had to go. It was strictly politics. At least that's what the writers told me — Gabe never bothered to give me a reason. I know that between Neal and me, the chemistry didn't mix. We both were talented. We both were envious of the other. I was the Number One guy and Bob wanted to be, and he knew as long as I was there, he wasn't going to be." From WJW-TV, the nasal-singed Score, an Indians' television commentator since 1963, jumped into Dudley's vacuum, to be replaced by Mel Allen, commuting from New York.

Dudley, unsurprisingly, soon assured himself of employment, and on April 6, 1968, Dewey Soriano, president of the Seattle Pilots, the American League's new expansion team, announced the news of Jimmy's 1969 coming. "We are indeed fortunate," said Bert West, vice-president and general manager of TVI, the Pilots' flagship station, "to get a man of his caliber."

They did not have him for long.

Stumbling through their only year as the Northwest's team, the Pilots, penniless, escaped in April 1970 to Wisconsin, where, renamed the Brewers, they succeeded the Braves as Milwaukee's team.

When the baggage cleared, Dudley was among the missing.

"I'd made a stupid mistake," he said. "When I signed with the Pilots, my contract was with the Golden West Network, which owned TVI. Gene Autry owned it, and I knew Gene very well. But there wasn't any stipulation that in the event the team moved, they would be obliged to take me as their announcer."

"How could you have expected them to move?" I said.

"Especially after only one year," he said. "In any event, when the Pilots vamoosed to Milwaukee, I was left with no paddle. They were under no obligation. And there was no way I was going to get the Brewers' job. Merle Harmon was established in the area, he'd done baseball for the A's and the Braves, he was a natural. I just hadn't been careful enough."

Thereafter, a bright flowering of promise. In late 1970, rumors populated baseball that Dudley would become the next Voice of the White Sox, or in early 1976, the new Voice of the expansion Blue Jays or Mariners, or in the late seventies, the next radio signature of the Pirates or A's. "Yes, I heard those stories going around," an American League official said, sharply, "and Jimmy *should* have had any *one* of those jobs."

"Why didn't he connect?" I said.

"He didn't have the mod, preppy look. He wasn't an ex-ballplayer. He was in his sixties by then. The demographics weren't right. Oh, there was always promise—just no delivery at the end."

He returned home to Tucson, where, in 1976, as a semiholding action, Jimmy called the games of the Pacific Coast League Toros. "Sure, I'd like to do big-league play-by-play," he said then, "and if it's the Lord's will, He'll give me a ring." A decade later, his number was deifically unlisted, and only semi-retirement had called.

It remained, perhaps, for Joe Falls to sketch Dudley's postgame éclat. "He spoke about the game with understanding and intelligence," the columnist wrote. "The thing I liked most is that when you listened to him, you knew he was a baseball broadcaster broadcasting a baseball game—not a soap salesman—and he always made me feel as if I were right in the ball park with him."

In Cleveland, that park was often empty, but with Dudley, its booth was full. "I thought Jimmy was a great anouncer," Falls observed, "and I still do."

He fashioned his career with dignity. Like Byrum Saam, he belongs in the broadcast wing of baseball's Hall of Fame.

* * *

On July 31, 1983, near "the mountains [which] stood in their native dress, dark, rich, and mysterious," James Fenimore Cooper wrote in his rude and soulful *The Deerslayer*, "while the sheet glistened in its solitude, a beautiful gem of the forest," on a bright, seamless upstate day in the recesses of the Mohawk Valley, Jack Brickhouse was inducted at Cooperstown.

Revisiting the Glimmerglass, he found, as Natty Bumppo had, that "here all was unchanged," and reading his acceptance speech, set his heart upon the beauty and sublimity of the game of baseball; its parks alight with greenery, its order and variety, its sawdust memories mixed with unexpected turns.

To the rear of the Hall of Fame Library, Brickhouse faced more than ten thousand spectators crowded into Cooper Park and gave a talk bereft of dogma and clichés. Instead, in a moment rich with feeling, he described his experiences as a young and restless boy, unaware, possibly, of himself and yet, through radio, aware of a world beyond his childhood imaginings, a world that, ultimately, would immerse him in sportscasting and Chicago and "the game I love."

"I stand this day on what I consider the hallowed ground of Cooperstown. I feel at this moment like a man who is sixty feet, six inches tall. On a clear day in this quaint central New York village, you can hear and see and feel the echoes of baseball's storied past. The atmosphere is breathless and humbling," he said in what, later, many locals called the finest speech in the nearly fifty years of the Hall of Fame.

"The trains, the planes, the cabs, the buses — they have carried me millions of miles through the years to get me where I most wanted to be — the ball game. A reporter once told me that even if *I* didn't make Cooperstown, my suitcase probably would. Fortunately, for me, we arrived together. . . . Here on this memorable afternoon, my heart tells me I have traveled the ninety feet from third to home and scored standing up."

A big man with a big voice, a ruddy personality with a round face and an infectious enthusiasm that brought to mind the maxim, "I have never known a stranger — only friends I haven't met," Jack Brickhouse burned himself into more than four decades of Chicago's consciousness. Dominated by fresh vigor and always, it seemed, exuberance, he became, in a vivid exercise of romantic hope, the television Voice of the Cubs and White Sox and, even more, their roaring, dreaming, groping minions. With his graphic rhetoric and a very presence that seemed to say, "Wait Till Next Year," he touched — how many? — humid nights and rain delays and hot, dusty Sunday afternoons.

"If you're from the Midwest, given the words 'Hey-Hey,' who comes to mind in an instant? Unless you have spent the last thirty-plus years under an Arctic snow drift, the answer is elementary — Jack Brickhouse," read an early-1980s Cubs' program.

"His exclaiming the famous 'Hey-Hey' following a Cubs' home run has become synonymous with Brickhouse not only in Chicago, but throughout the baseball world. It was Jack . . . who taught the generations of the 1950s, 1960s, and 1970s about baseball. He was an extension of a baseball fan's learning experience."

Born on January 24, 1916, Brickhouse "was still a growing boy in Peoria when a group of trailblazers in broadcasting introduced me to the Chicago Cubs," he said at a table in the press room of the Hyatt Regency Hotel in

Washington. Later that day, Hey-Hey would air a cable telecast of the annual Cracker Jack Old-Timers Baseball Classic.

"Quin Ryan, Hal Totten, Pat Flanagan?" I said.

"Yes," he replied. "They were some of the ones I listened to. And also the guy who was without doubt the most imitated, creative baseball broadcaster who ever lived. When he started, there was nobody to copy. He was the scout on the frontier drive, a pioneer by the name of Elson."

Four decades before Nixon aide John Ehrlichman etched the phrase on an earthen urn, Bob Elson "played in Peoria." Listening to the Old Commander in the early sixties, his pristine, laconic delivery transmitted over WCFL, I found him ungodly dull. Brickhouse thought him a god.

"Elson was a man for his time," he mused, opting for a sip of diet Coke. "As a teenage fan, I thought so, and from a different perspective, as an announcer [entering radio at eighteen, over WMBD in Peoria], I thought the same. In fact, I can play records of at least half a dozen guys — Bert Wilson, Milo Hamilton, Earl Gillespie with the Milwaukee Braves, Gene Elston with Houston — who've sounded like pups out of Bob."

"Different time, different style."

"Oh, it's true that Bob was more laid-back — broadcasting's become more entertainment since then. But he still had an excitement to him; his voice cut through the air. And it wasn't just announcers — it was the fans in Peoria. Bob got us to identifying with baseball and, more particularly, the Cubs."

"Why more than the Sox? After all, he did home games for each."

A soft edge crept into Brickhouse's face. "Easy," he said. "Because they *won*. In those days, every kid on the block knew the Cubs had to win the pennant every three years. Like clockwork. They won in 1929, in '32, in '35, in '38. To us in Peoria, it was almost providential."

The Cubs did not, however, win in 1941, the year after Elson, then a WGN staff announcer and, outside New York, baseball's pre-eminent voice, asked Hey-Hey to converge on Chicago. "The timing was right," Brickhouse said. "Bob was looking for someone to help him, and I was itching to move on. After all, I'd been in Peoria for six years. I'd gotten to know Bob when he came down for personal appearances and we got to be friendly. So, without me even knowing about it, he arranged an audition."

Leaving for spring training in California, Elson wired a March 1940 telegram to Peoria: "Expect call from WGN as a staff announcer and sports assistant. Remember, if asked, you know all about baseball. Best of luck. Bob Elson." Brickhouse, who later framed and hung the telegram in his Wilmette home, drove to Chicago, auditioned for Ryan, and was hired for the job.

"*Had* you done baseball before?" I said.

"Oh, I'd done some Three-I League games. I broadcast, for example, the day that Phil Cavarretta broke in with us and hit for the cycle. My thought was, 'Jesus, we're not going to keep *this* guy very long.' " Brickhouse spoke whimsically, his voice calm and amused. " 'Course, maybe I hadn't done *quite* as much baseball as Quin Ryan thought."

For three years, Brickhouse helped Elson re-create Cubs and White Sox' games. "I've always contended that if Bob had lived in New York, he would have been the first, not the third, to be inducted [1979] into the Hall of Fame," he said. "Barber and Allen could never carry his microphone."

I contrived a laugh. "Some folks would disagree," I said, mildly.

"Not those who knew them," he argued. "When I joined Bob at WGN, I had to fight the urge to say things just the way Elson would. I was determined not to say simply, as Bob would say it: '*He's* out.' But how many other ways can you say: 'He's out'? So I tried not to copy him, and it wasn't easy. Sitting alongside him at the parks or for re-creations, I found him to be an overwhelming personality."

In 1942, a central point in Brickhouse's life, Elson drifted into the Navy as a public-relations specialist, thereafter dubbing himself the Old Commander. At age twenty-six the sports nabob of Mutual's Chicago affiliate, Brickhouse became WGN's Voice of baseball in baseball's twin Meccas of the Midwest. "How fortunate I was," he said from behind his glasses, "to broadcast from two grand places like Wrigley Field and Comiskey Park. Sure, they look different, they've got varying dimensions, one holds more people. But to me, they've always been alike."

"Parks, not facilities."

"These sterile new stadiums," he said, grimacing. "You don't know whether you're in Spokane, Dallas, or Disney World. They've got no personality. But Chicago's — God, they're built for baseball, and how I loved them." No cookie cutters, they.

From Wrigley Field, with its animal-cracker dimensions, hand-operated scoreboard, and nearby L tracks and corner saloons, and the white cube of symmetrical Comiskey Park, now the oldest stadium in the major leagues, Brickhouse lionized the game. "I never thought you couldn't have excitement and integrity at the same time," he said, "or that if you were accurate, it meant you had to be boring."

"People said you were 'gee whiz,' " I noted.

"I was!" he said. "I don't think the dry documentary narration — the humdrum approach — does one single thing for the sport. All it does is put you asleep. And anyway, it wasn't my style. I figured as long as I was working, I might as well have some fun."

"You didn't mind the 'We School'?"

Hey-Hey tilted his head. "Not at all. Chicago is a very proud city. It loves its teams, and it has a fierce loyalty. So for me to say, 'Come on, let's get a run,' or, 'Boy, do we need a hit' — it wasn't just accepted or not frowned upon. It was *expected*. It came with the turf."

By 1944, the Cubs' turf belonged to Wilson, succeeding Flanagan as Voice of the Wrigleys. The very next year, station WJJD gained exclusive rights to White Sox' games.

"What happened is kind of interesting," Brickhouse said. "For years WGN had done the Cubs. Now, at the end of the '43 season, they gave it up. And the reason was economics. The Mutual Network had a great series of late-afternoon kids shows — they made a bundle off these programs; they were a great sponsor buy. But they had a problem in Chicago, namely baseball."

"But your ratings were good."

"They were *great*," he announced, "but you have to understand — back then, afternoon games started at three P.M. and would last through about six o'clock. The result was that they wiped out the whole block of kiddie shows. And this was brutalizing Mutual because it meant the country's second-largest market was wiped out. So WGN acted like a good team player and dropped the Cubs — even though it killed us to do so."

"But how did Wilson and WIND gain exclusive rights?"

"Jimmy Gallagher, the Cubs' business manager, saw WGN's exit as the perfect time to do what he'd wanted to anyway — put the Cubs' games up for bid. WIND won and got exclusivity — something Chicago hadn't had since games first began in the twenties. When that happened, WJJD grabbed the Sox, and I went over to do *their* games. Nineteen forty-five was the first year I hadn't done the Cubs."

Like By Saam with the 1950 Phillies, Brickhouse's transfer grew infested with reverse; while the 1945 White Sox, sick with ordinariness, finished sixth, the Cubs — surprising all of baseball — won their first pennant since 1938. "So there I was," Brickhouse said, "the Cubs closing in on their pennant at home — and Bert Wilson going berserk on every pitch — while yours truly is calling a double-header between the Sox and Connie Mack's old Athletics by ticker tape."

In 1946, Elson returned from the service. "Naturally, he got his job back with the Sox," Hey-Hey recalled. "I became 'at liberty,' as they say." Brickhouse wandered to New York, where, after his one-year interregnum at the Polo Grounds, he reverted to a Chicago world not of ticker tape but of the protean landscape of the rectangular tube. He did a scattering of 1947 games with WBKB's Joe Wilson, then shifted the next season — television's World Series breakthrough year — to WGN, Channel 9, debuting as the visual appendage of the Second City's two baseball teams. "Later on, in the 1980s, Chicago would be way behind other cities in being wired for cable," explained Chuck Schriver, the Cubs' 1967–75 public-relations director who later worked for the White Sox, "but the fact is: The same city was a TV pioneer."

"DuMont bought Yankee games in 1946," I said.

"Maybe," Schriver said, "but its audience was small; its impact was nothing. WGN, on the other hand, was a station that had money behind it; it was a power. Even in '48 there was a disproportionately high ratio of sets in Chicago. From the first, TV had an influence, and from the word 'go,' Brickhouse was a hit."

Without knowing it, in that remote, infantile year, like Donner harnessing the Pass, Brickhouse began a continuum — an intimacy between ball club and viewer — that decades later, in the wake of cable and, thus, WGN's intrusion into millions of American households, fostered for the Cubs an enormous national sect.

"Every year," Schriver observed, "at baseball's winter meetings, the public-relations people ask a Triple-A affiliate to report on what they're doing. In 1983, Bill Valentine, the ex-umpire who now owned the Little Rock team, came before us and talked about the concessions sold at his park."

"How did the Cubs come up?"

"Bill asked us, 'Of all the shirts and helmets and pennants we sell at our place, do you know what the hottest-selling item is?' "

Little Rock was Cardinals' country. "A Redbirds' hat?" I guessed.

"Well," Schriver said, "you're right about the hat but wrong about the team. It's the Cubs. And it's all because in Little Rock, homes are wired for cable."

Intuitively, Cubs' management felt that television would make fans of viewers and, eventually, patrons of fans. "Phil Wrigley has done a better job of selling baseball on TV than anyone in the majors," former Phillies' owner Bob Carpenter chimed in 1965, long after Wrigley allowed WGN to televise his club's entire home schedule. Pre-McLuhan, the Cubs' Father looked at television and saw that it was good and that its message, with age, could nurture the need of Chicago parishioners to frequent his North Side chapel.

"Like his dad, who'd recognized, early on, what radio could do as a promotional tool, Phil Wrigley did the same in television," Brickhouse was saying in the Hyatt press room. "Other owners refused to let home games be televised — they thought it would cut down on attendance."

"In New York in the fifties, that's exactly what happened," I reminded him. The 1949 champion Dodgers, for example, drew 1,633,747 customers. Three years later, with each home game televised, first-place Brooklyn barely passed the million mark. "Or take the Yankees. They won pennants from '49 through '53 and their attendance fell by half a million."

Brickhouse nodded. "With those clubs, that's true," he said, and waving to ex-Dodgers' infielder Ron Fairly, now an Angels- and, later, Giants' broadcaster, he hurried back in time. "But don't forget that in the New York market, you had three clubs and a corresponding glut of TV games. In Chicago, and I think this is the case in other towns more often than not, there wasn't an overlap and the tube helped more than hurt the gate."

"Why?"

"Oh, maybe on a given, specific Tuesday in June at Wrigley Field, you'd draw a thousand less because the game was televised," he said. "But over a period of months and years, you gained far more than you'd lose. And the reason is because TV's continuity made the Sox and Cubs a part of life. It *made* fans. The broadcasts built loyalty and stirred interest. In the long haul — and this was Wrigley's thinking in '48 — the guy that became a Cub fan as a result of television was going to sooner or later come out to Wrigley Field."

The apposition of 1948 and 1952 startles; in five big-league seasons, paid admissions tumbled by 6,287,798 — but why? Had home telecasts blunted motivation to attend the ball park, or were the pennant races somehow less riveting, or had baseball's postwar novelty waved a last farewell? Were all of these indictments valid, or were none, as the pastime's poo-bahs claimed? The case of *Television v. Home Attendance* would filter, unanswered, into our own media-saturated present, and more than three decades after Chicagoans first saw Brickhouse bid a video "Hey-Hey," the evidence still contraposed. In 1982, allowing no home telecasts, the Dodgers packed a major-league-high 3,608,881 people into their palatial gulley. Over conventional TV, the 1983 Mets aired forty-one games from Flushing Meadows; their attendance plunged to 1,112,773. At the other end, the Braves that season televised seventy-seven home sets and drew a record 2,119,035 patrons. One year later, barring all free telecasts in the Tri-State Area, the Pirates, veering toward enfeeblement, lured only 773,500 stragglers to the cold drabness of Three Rivers Stadium.

Brickhouse motioned to a waiter and ordered me a drink. "That's the debate," he said, "and it's been going on for years. Does home TV hurt attendance? Or does it promote the regional interest? Does no TV make you go to the park to see your favorite team? Or does it kill off interest so that you don't *care* about going? You can find figures on both sides of the aisle."

"But in Chicago?" I said.

"No question," he said. "TV meant manna from above. What made it work for us is that the Cubs, in those days before expansion, were never at home at the same time as the White Sox, so there wasn't the problem with television conflicts. WGN could do the home games of both teams."

"Plus, the Cubs played only in the day."

"That's why WGN didn't have to disrupt prime-time programming. We televised every game from Wrigley Field. With the White Sox, we'd televise all day games and some at night. When Bill Veeck bought the club in '59, he wanted to black out the home night games to protect attendance. So, instead, we televised thirteen games from the road. Either way, for almost forty years we've had baseball on TV almost every day of the season."

"And the result?"

"It's made Chicago the best baseball town in the country."

His first year of television, Brickhouse covered two last-place teams; joined by common failings, the Cubs and White Sox lost 191 games and played before more than 2 million people. Four years later, in Chicago's resurrection of the dead, the Cubs shotput to fifth place and the Sox to third; even with (indeed, because of?) the showing of daily telecasts in this baseball stronghold, home attendance climbed to 2,256,501.

"In those early days, there wasn't a lot usually to cheer about *on* the field," smiled Brickhouse, who in thirty-four years at WGN-TV broadcast with Harry Creighton and Marty Hogan, Vince Lloyd and Lloyd Pettit, Jim West and Lou Boudreau, and, finally, Milo Hamilton. "But people watched anyway; why, I don't know. Mostly, I guess, because people loved the Cubs. They loved baseball. And in those first years, mostly, I suppose, because of the simple *fact* of TV—the fact that it existed. To people in those days, that in itself was stunning. People would sit and stare for hours, just gawking at the set."

"What was it like?" I said.

"Those early years?" he said. "You busted your ass. We had eighty people doing four hundred people's work. I mean, if you worked an eighty-hour week, you were dogging it. I'd do a ball game in the afternoon, come to the studio for the sports, then go out and broadcast wrestling three nights a week and boxing too. We were working seven-day weeks. If you ever got a day off, it was like finding a golden nugget."

"Did you mind?"

"Oh, sometimes you'd get down — not too often. After all, I was a lot younger then. What made it so wonderful, though — sometimes, we'd work a hundred hours a week — is that I loved my job. I feel awfully sorry for people stuck in a job because of security." The waiter returned. Brickhouse paused. "Plus, we knew we were on the ground floor of something tremendously important," he said, his eyes widening. "I'm very proud that I wasn't just the first Voice of the Cubs — I was the first voice ever heard on WGN, airing a boxing tournament from Chicago Stadium. So, we were making history. We could sense it, even then."

For Jack Brickhouse, the fifties were a lovely, consequential time. With Jim Britt, in 1950, and Russ Hodges, four years later, he telecast the World Series. He called NBC's coverage of the 1950–53 All-Star Games. He dotted the "Gillette Cavalcade of Sports," aired "every sport imaginable except for hockey and horse racing — which makes sense," he said. "I have enough trouble *picking* a horse without trying to broadcast it," covered national political conventions and other newsworthies for the Mutual Broadcasting System, and beamed his husky voice through the window of Eisenhower's America.

Sadly, the same decade also mousetrapped the Cubs. "We had some great *performances*," Brickhouse would note — one recalls Dick Drott striking out fifteen Braves on May 26, 1957, or Hank Sauer, Lee Walls, and Ernie Banks making the All-Star team, or Mr. Cub pounding more than forty home runs in four different years — but as a *team*, a mural the Wrigleys rarely resembled, Chicago dredged the second division for each 1950s season. "And that's not the worst of it," the ex-Voice said in a facetious way. "Starting in 1947, for twenty straight years — I'm sure it's the longest streak in baseball — this wonderful, indescribable ball club never *once* finished in the first division."

A Cubs' town at heart, Chicago now turned to the White Sox, for in 1951–58, rising to second the last two years, the South Siders fielded a sequence of winning teams.

Then, in 1959, The Game witnessed a historical anomaly, like Monaco winning the Olympics. On paper, the Braves again were baseball's best. Aaron won a second batting title, Eddie Mathews belted forty-six long balls, and Spahn and Lew Burdette each won twenty-one games. Yet on October 1, accustomed to fifties Oktoberfests from ports like County Stadium, Ebbets Field, and The House That John Lindsay Would Rebuild, it was the "Go-Go" White Sox and the Los Angeles Dodgers that fans saw open the World Series — for the Sox, their first pennant since the Black Sox Scandal of 1919; for the California Dodgers, a world championship in their second year.

"God, those Sox were a fun bunch to watch," Brickhouse said. "They'd beat you, two to one. A big rally, for them, consisted of an infield single, a stolen base, a passed ball, and a sacrifice fly."

"Not a lot of punch," I said.

He scratched his ear and leaned across the table. "They wouldn't remind you of Murderers Row, but they had great pitching, a hell of a manager, and marvelous defense. Just a very enchanting team."

The '59 White Sox shared headlines with Alaska and Hawaii, the newest stars on an altered flag, and Fidel Castro, Cuba's new *duce*, and Lunik III, a Russian satellite that orbited the moon. "You send up oranges," the Soviets' bulbous leader jeered, "while we send up tons." That May, John Foster Dulles died of cancer. Steel workers struck for four months. Touring Moscow, Richard Nixon dueled Khrushchev in the "Kitchen Debate." Two scandals rocked broadcasting: Network quiz shows had been fixed, and disc jockeys had played records in exchange for "payola." The last veteran of the Civil War died at age 117. Popular were two of the new TV season's novel tastes: "Dennis the Menace," starring seven-year-old, forty-nine-pound Jay North, and "The Many Loves of Dobie Gillis," with its beatnik orb, Maynard G. Krebs, the symbol, somehow, of the decade's pleasant, driftless life.

Against such competition, the White Sox — the "Pale Hose" of quaint childhood usage — more than held their own. Managed by Al Lopez, they broke their all-time attendance record. At 22–10, Early Wynn received the Cy Young Award. Luis Aparicio, a palatine at shortstop, stole fifty-six bases to lead the majors. Jim Landis patrolled center field with solidity and flair. The tobacco-chewing, iron-willed Nellie Fox, sport's pre-Pete Rose emblem of "Charlie Hustle," was named Most Valuable Player. The Sox won thirty-five games by a single run.

In 1959's other flourishes, Banks, the only shortstop to top his league in home runs and fielding, won his second straight MVP Award; Pittsburgh's Elroy Face, he of the daunting forkball, won eighteen games and lost only once; Detroit's Harvey Kuenn hit .353 and Ted Williams batted .254; and on June 10, Rocky Colavito bashed four home runs against the Orioles. In Washington, Harmon Killebrew emerged as the first player to lead his circuit in homers (forty-two, tied with Colavito) while hitting less than .250 (quoting Ol' Diz, "Yeah, pod-nuh, but it's a *hard* .242"). In New York, the Yankees crashed to third; for the first time since 1918, no New York American collected more than seventy-five runs batted in. In the World Series, the Sox' Ted Kluszewski homered thrice, the Dodgers' Chuck Essegian clubbed two pinch-hit home runs, and Los Angeles reliever Larry Sherry, winning and saving two decisions each, was named the six-game pageant's Outstanding Performer. Despite three crowds exceeding ninety thousand which filled the Los Angeles Coliseum, baseball watched its Grand Event — "the greatest show on earth," cried Mel Allen during Games Three, Four, and Five — unfold in a gaping, ill-contoured cave where bleacherites, needing portable radios to follow the play-by-play, sat nearly seven hundred feet from home plate.

Apart from "Game of the Week" fragments in August and September 1959, that Series remains my first memory of televised baseball. In 1955–56, Allen and Vin Scully; the next year, Allen and Al Helfer; and in 1958, Allen and Curt Gowdy had telecast the Classic. In July of each year, The Voice and

Brother Al aired NBC's coverage of the All-Star Game. Presently, for its Chicago-Los Angeles convention, NBC flung forth not "blow-dried pretty boys," in Nixon's tart phrase, or, worse yet, flaccid ex-ballplayers who strangled the language, but rather, a quartet of *professionals*: on radio, Mel and By Saam; on television, Brickhouse and Scully. Even from a distance, now, of more than twenty-five years, I remember that autumn — its leaves and splashing hues and spooked-up nights that cradled the imagination. I remember, also, how to a tow-haired child in the second grade, these voices made a simple game the era's guts and heart. I would never wander very far away.

"Believe me, we took great pride — painstaking care — in our choice of announcers," related Lindsey Nelson, then in his eighth year as NBC's assistant director of sports. "Back then, the Series was the blue-chip event in all of sports. Nothing rivaled it. Nothing was remotely *close*. It was the Chinese New Year of athletic events — each season's Fourth of July."

"This would have been, what, your twelfth year of exclusive TV coverage," I said.

"Yes," he said, "and in 1957 we'd gotten the radio rights of the Series away from Mutual, so it was our third year of exclusivity there. And wanting to do it justice, we naturally went for the best. In those days, that meant Allen, and since, for a change, the Yankees hadn't made the Series and, therefore, Mel wasn't assigned to TV, we grabbed him with By."

"How'd you settle on Scully and Brickhouse?"

"Vin, of course, was the Dodgers' principal announcer, so his choice was obvious. But the Brickhouse story is more involved, and it revolves around an absolute disdain — bordering on hatred — that Tom Gallery felt toward Bob Elson."

Since 1956, replacing Wilson, Jack Quinlan, Elson's contemporary, had absorbed Chicago as radio's Voice of the Cubs. A glib and friendly man, exuding mirth and an easy literacy, he broadcast, first, with WIND's Hamilton and, when WGN seized exclusivity before the 1958 season, with the celebrated ex-shortstop, Boudreau. "Quinlan was my protégé," Brickhouse informed me. "I was involved in that deal that brought the Cubs to 'GN, and one reason it pleased me was that Jack came along. He was quick, polished, had a great Irish sense of humor, and we would never have been able to keep him — Jack [killed in an auto accident in 1965] would have been a network star, for sure."

It was said, oddly, that Quinlan, like Brickhouse, admired the Old Commander — odd because I have talked with many who state, categorically, that his was the most dramatic presence in Chicago's tide of broadcasting. I will admit that Elson, as devotees insist, was crisp, meticulous, and Old World in his approach, but he no more emitted drama than Guy Lombardo reeked of punk. Elson observed; Quinlan heightened. One reported the game; the other stimulated it. "You can't really say that one was better than the other, or that Quinlan or Elson called a superior game," said a former *Chicago Tribune* columnist. "I knew them both closely — and they both knew their baseball. It's like comparing hard booze and Dr. Pepper — how can you tell a fan of one that the other has a greater taste?" Clamoring for a Scotch and water, the writer revealed *his* predilection. "What you *can* say, however, is that by the time the Sox' pennant rolled around in '59, whatever Bob Elson's many assets, his style had gone *out* of style."

At his 30 Rockefeller Plaza office, Thomas Patrick Gallery agreed.

A large and unmorbid figure, Gallery arrived at NBC Television in 1952, at fifty-four, almost as an afterword to a theatrical career. As a young veteran of World War I, he had shuffled west to Hollywood more than thirty years earlier. There, he appeared in fifty-six movies ("One critic termed me 'the Gabby Hayes of the B's' "), starred in the first Rin-Tin-Tin series ("The damn dog went for my ear the first day we met," he said. "We never got along too well"), and married the movie actress Zasu Pitts, the 1956–60 costar (as Miss Esmeralda "Nugey" Nugent, a ship's beauty salon operator) of TV's "Oh! Susanna." Profiting from movies, Gallery was consumed by sports, and in the 1930s, now an ex-cowboy actor, he began promoting prizefights. From boxing, he meandered to the Rose Bowl (making it a national event) and the NFL's Pro Bowl (organizing its beginnings) and pro football's Brooklyn Dodgers (during World War II, managing the team for his friend Dan Topping) and the DuMont Network (where, in the late forties, he tried to steal the World Series from NBC) and, finally, in 1952, the National Broadcasting Company.

With Gillette's intercession, NBC became The Sports Network — and as the decade proceeded, Gallery could boast (and, not infrequently, did) of his "Gillette Cavalcade," with its Friday night fights and sports anthologies, and the Saturday college football "Game of the Week," with Nelson and Red Grange, and such eminences as the Rose, Orange, Sugar, and Cotton Bowls and East-West Shrine and Blue-Gray Games, with their pageantry and upscale demographics, and the weekend "Major League Baseball," enriched by the musical gyrations of Lindsey's range, and, above all, the All-Star Game and World Series, flaunting the announcer of Gillette's and Gallery's preference: the Voice of the Yankees, calling all nine of the 1952–59 Mid-Summer Classics and seven of the eight 1951–58 Fall Classics and evolving into a broadcast institution.

To the larger American fifties public, far beyond New York itself, the World Series *meant* Mel Allen. Now, in September 1959, the six-foot-four length of Tom Gallery raised two feet onto a desk and asked: "Bob Elson?"

"It's hard to believe today," Nelson said, "because rights fees have gone so high that no one sponsor could even dream of owning a property. But back then, until 1965, Gillette owned exclusive rights to the All-Star Game and Series. So Craig Smith would choose announcers, and we'd approve them, along with the Commissioner's Office. And there was never any problem, because Smith and Gallery had similar tastes in announcers."

"Allen," I said.

"Smith thought — and Tom did also — that Mel was perfect for a showcase, that there was something about him, something in his voice, that brought a special drama to the moment."

"But in '59," I said, "when the White Sox made it, it was Elson's turn. He was their daily announcer. What happened?"

Laughter washed Nelson's voice. "We had trouble, first, because this gregarious, colorful, and totally delightful and decent man named Tom Gallery thought Bob Elson wasn't even in the same ball park as Allen," he said. "And Tom didn't want him intruding on our biggest show of the year."

"Any other reason?"

"The big reason is that, amazingly, Tom Gallery had grown up on the same block in Chicago as Elson, and he *detested* him. For what reason, I'm not precisely sure — I think they'd rubbed each other the wrong way even as kids — but Tom couldn't stand Elson even more than he disliked Barber, which is saying quite a lot. He said to me one day in September, 'I'm not going to let that bastard on the Series' — and yet, as you say, the commissioner had insisted that the White Sox have their own announcer on NBC."

I grew silent. Then, "So how'd you get out of it?"

"We were sitting in his office," Nelson said, "and I said to him, 'Well, Tom, you may have an out. Jack Brickhouse is the principal TV guy for both the Cubs and White Sox. You could always pick him.' And Gallery's face lit up like a Christmas tree. He thought Brickhouse was a class act — which, of course, he is. So that's what Tom did, choose Brickhouse to go along with Scully." Angry, bitterly depressed, Elson aired the Series over WCFL Radio.

The White Sox-Dodgers' dramaturgy was the third Series to accent the center-field camera shot, first introduced nationally by Harry Coyle. "In those days," recalled the NBC director, "your mind was going crazy because everybody was trying to find the answer to improve baseball's coverage. So when we showed the pitcher-batter shot in the '57 Series — formerly we'd featured shots from way up above the catcher, focusing on the infield, or just gone in the boxes behind home plate and shown the pitcher throwing the ball toward you — it was the turning point in getting the right coverage." After 1957, most clubs followed Coyle's lead. "They found that you could get more intimacy that way. Now you could see the pitcher, the batter, and umpire the way a center fielder would."

"Why hadn't you gone to the shot before 1957?" I said.

"In the early years, you couldn't run camera cable to center field. Once the technology allowed a camera to go there, we did," Coyle said. "Having said all this, I still think Camera 2 [from the press box behind home plate] is the best for keeping up with the action." Tacitly, I agreed.

By the early 1960s, the center-field shot had graced the last decade of WGN's coverage. "I don't understand why others were so late," Brickhouse said. "We'd featured it as far back as the early years of the fifties. One of our cameramen got the idea from watching a schoolboy game. He noticed the scoreboard out in center field and thought, 'If we put a camera out there, you'd get a great shot of the hitter and catcher.' So we tried it a couple of times in about 1951."

"What did Chicagoland think?"

"The public liked it, but there were some purists who thought all your cameras should go the same direction — from behind the plate toward the outfield. We picked a democratic solution: putting it to a vote of the fans. They wrote in and the result was ten to one in favor of the center-field shot. Coyle may have done it first with the nets, but when the 1960s popped up, we'd been at it for ten years. We were just far, way ahead."

The White Sox, unhappily, were not, and as Fox and Aparicio were dealt away, Gary Peters and Tommie Agee became Rookies of the Year, Joel Horlen no-hit the Tigers at Comiskey Park, and the '64 model missed the pennant by a game, the Pale Hose's sixties melted into what-if, how-close, what-might-have-been years. Then, suddenly, in 1967, Arthur Allyn, Jr., a butterfly collector, amateur pilot, pianist, and former chemist, and the White Sox' owner since 1961, stunned the Cubs by signing a television contract with WFLD, Chicago's first UHF (ultra-high-frequency) station. Channel 32, he said, would air all Sox' games, home and away. WGN was surprised. Phil Wrigley was livid.

"Wrigley thought Allyn had stabbed him in the back," Chuck Schriver said. "See, there had been a handshake agreement between Phil and the White Sox' former owners, the Comiskey family, that they would not televise away games while the other was at home. When the Sox were aired on the road, it was usually at night, and the Cubs played under the sun; that's how they were able to share one station and not hurt each other's games."

"Did Allyn ever mention the UHF possibility to Wrigley?" I said.

"It came as such a shock," Schriver said, "that when Allyn dropped his bomb—this was in the middle of '67—Wrigley called up WGN and said, 'If they're going to put every game on TV [broadcast, in 1968, by Jack Drees], I am too. I'm not going to charge you any more for the TV rights, but as of this moment, you have my permission to televise every inning of all of our games."

"War."

"Yes," he said, "and I have to say: The White Sox started it."

Thrown by the Pale Hose, Brickhouse rode the lure of the Cubs, still buoyed by "that boyish enthusiasm that nothing could seem to shake," said WGN's Jack Rosenberg. "He was just as excited in the ninth inning of the second game of a double-header as in the first inning of the first game. Didn't matter whether the team was in first place or the cellar. After five or six hours of broadcasting, he'd just be catching his second wind."

In 1969, it seemed possible that the Cubs had too.

Cast in incompetence, the 1966 Wrigleys had finished tenth. The next two years, they rose to third, their first bolt from the second division since 1946. On April 8, 1969, before 40,796 denizens of Wrigley Field, in the club's last at-bats on Opening Day, pinch-hitter Willie Smith—a fringe player who loved high fastballs—lofted one into the right-field bleachers to give the Cubs a 7–6 victory. Soon after, as Ferguson Jenkins, Bill Hands, and Ken Holtzman blotted opposing hitters, and sinkerballer Phil Regan pitched magnificently out of the bull pen, and Banks, Glenn Beckert, Don Kessinger, and Ron Santo formed the league's finest infield, and outfielder Billy Williams activated the "Bleacher Bums" to applause, euphoria blossomed. On June 1, Leo Durocher's Cubs were 32–16; in mid-July, they were 56–34; in mid-August, they led New

York by 9½ games. Here, at last, was the Promised Season, the Jerusalem when the Chicago Nationals became the best baseball team on earth. Who imagined that the Mets — that symbol of indigent striving, as harmless as a housebroken puppy — would stir like swelling to win thirty-eight of their last forty-nine games and, eventually, the World Series, while the Cubs — addled, exhausted — would surrender to the idea of a miracle and freeze, like artifacts, in shock and disbelief?

"Thank God I've loved my work," Brickhouse said, "and one reason is because I love this game — ever notice how baseball keeps those around it young? I have respect for my profession too — when a pennant race like '69 comes along, what material you have to work with, win *or* lose. And you never know the ending — you ad-lib the script. That's why if I were going to start an announcing staff at a radio station, I'd start with the sports announcer — he can do anything. The sports announcer can ad-lib; he's a reporter at heart. You can put him on a parade, a disaster, a political convention [Brickhouse covered five]. He can read copy, do a commercial. Look at the number of jobs he can do without the text."

"Broadcasting in the sixties," I said, "who were some of the best?"

"In no particular order," he warned, "I remember, of course, Barber — the complete stylist. Caray — a better baseball authority than some claim, and probably as great a fan as we've ever had. Bob Prince, with that marvelous voice and a guy who never took himself too seriously. And Allen — the kind of electricity that if he walked into an audition and you'd never heard of him, you'd still say, 'God, I want him on my staff.' "

"By Saam?"

Brickhouse's face brightened. "He put the rest of us to shame. By carried around a brief case everywhere he went — did more homework than anyone I've ever known. Scully, right now, is the master, the best around, for his ability to put words together and draw a picture. Lindsey Nelson was the total pro — a wonderful technique. Ernie Harwell is one of the great gentlemen of sports — plus, he has that artistic bent the rest of us envy. And Garagiola — I love the guy."

"Why?" I said.

"Joe showed the good sense not to listen to my advice," Brickhouse said. "In the 1950s, Joe was winding up with the Cubs as a player when he came to me and said, 'Jack, I've got a chance to get into broadcasting. I wonder if I should do it?' And I told him, 'No, stay in baseball. This broadcasting is one tough field.' " The reminiscence pleased him. "So Joe took the opposite course, and you can see how totally brilliant *I* was."

"So far he's gone on to announce, counting radio, eight World Series [nine, as of 1986]."

"That many? Well, I was lucky enough to do four, and I would have had one more if the '69 Mets hadn't become Cinderella. Yogi Berra says, 'In baseball you don't know *nothin'*.' And brother, that's the truth. Forty years around the game and I still can never tell."

After 1969, the Cubs deteriorated, though not to the extent one might expect. They finished second in 1970, a year punctuated by Banks' five hundredth home run, and 1972, the year marred by a needless players' strike. In the seasons of the seventies, contending frequently, they appealed as light adventure. Even their timing intrigued; would the Cubs fold this summer in early June, or wait till late July? From 1970 to 1972, Jenkins three times won twenty or more games; in 1972, second in the MVP balloting, Williams had his greatest in a rolling stone of unsung years. That same season, on September 2, Milt Pappas no-hit the Padres. Two years later, the large-bellied Rick Reuschel tossed a twelve-hit shutout, and on August 21, 1975, Rick and brother Paul became the first siblings to hurl a combination blanking. The next month, the Pirates bombed Chicago, 22–0, as Rennie Stennett collected seven hits in as many at-bats. On April 17, 1976, Philadelphia's Mike Schmidt unleashed four home runs in an 18–16 triumph. "Hey-Hey," Jack Brickhouse; in these "friendly confines" of your parlor of a park, the wind was blowing out.

The decade ended as it began; "with the feeling," said Brickhouse, "that a guy once expressed: 'A Cubs' fan is born so that he can suffer.' " Then, in 1981, having mitigated the futility of Chicago's baseball globe and become — to millions of Middle Americans — a diversion, jongleur, and moving smoothly among the events of both leagues, friend, the Voice of the Cubs retired.

On the afternoon of his final game, more than a thousand fans flocked to the concourse below the front-office level, gathering to cheer and remind him, as Sherwood Anderson had in *Winesburg, Ohio*, how "at the same instant, and if the people of the town are his people, one loves life so intensely that tears come into the eyes."

"I loved every day coming out to the ball park," Jack said, sounding, eerily, like Mr. Cub. "And that last game, that really touched me. I was holding out pretty good until then."

"What do you remember?" I said. "And how are *you* going to be remembered?"

Brickhouse leaned back in his chair. "The people," he said, "the fans and colleagues, the ballplayers. I've always been sort of an idolater, I guess. If I mentioned fifty players, I'd leave out a hundred more."

I sipped my drink. "And if you moved outside yourself, how would you regard Jack Brickhouse?"

"He regards himself as a professional broadcaster and, secondarily, as a sports announcer," he said. "And he thanks God every day that apparently the Good Lord gave him the ability and the voice to make a living in this business."

"Regrets?" I said.

"Yes," he said, "that I didn't learn another language. Plus," and here he chuckled, "I always wanted to hit the vaudeville circuit."

"Weaknesses?"

"I blew hot and cold on homework. Sometimes I went after it. Other times, I was as lazy as you can get," he said.

"Biggest thrill?"

"Personally, it has to be Cooperstown."

"Do you have the epitaph written for your career?"

He looked at me and made a grin. "Yep," Jack Brickhouse said. "On my tombstone it's going to read, 'Here lies the guy who could do the best soft-shoe anywhere for "Tea for Two."'"

A Hall of Famer in love with life, Brickhouse resumed his attack on the diet Coke. The waiter approached our table. "Is your entertainment all booked up for tonight?" I asked him. "If not, I know an act that'll knock your socks off."

*　　*　　*

In 1982, for Jack Brickhouse a pastoral voyage in extravagance, Hey-Hey was inducted into the National Sportscasters and Sportswriters Association Hall of Fame in Salisbury, North Carolina.

Learning of the selection, newsmen asked who would introduce Brickhouse at the awards dinner. Motioning to a phone, Jack surrendered to a smile. "There's only one person I'd want to present me," he said. "My good and dear friend Lindsey."

At his home in Knoxville, Tennessee, Lindsey Nelson warmly retrieved that night. "When the Salisbury people asked me to present Jack, I was naturally delighted and flew down to be there," he said.

"Brickhouse says the highlight of the evening was when you two teamed up to sing 'Nothing Could Be Finer [Than to Be in Carolina in the Morning],'" I reported, southern laughter gurgling in the background. "He says it's a tradition."

"Yes, but that's his old midwestern hyperbole talking," Nelson said. "The next year we also sang it, and when I mentioned that we'd only done it twice, Jack said, 'Hell, in Chicago two years *is* a tradition!'"

Across more than three decades over the national airwaves with, progressively, Liberty and NBC, CBS and ABC, C. D. Chesley Productions and the Mutual and Turner Broadcasting Systems, and the radio/television networks of the New York Mets and San Francisco Giants, Lindsey Nelson *himself* became a tradition.

Unmistakably lower-Border, at once crusading and exact, his voice sashayed down four Rose Bowls, one All-Star Game, two World Series, nineteen years of the National Football League, five seasons of "Major League Baseball" and the National Basketball Association "Game of the Week," twenty-six Cotton Bowls and a decade of National Collegiate Athletic Association football, and, finally, the University of Tennessee '41, his alma mater, where, after quasi-retiring in 1981, he taught seminars in broadcasting.

Not, like Allen, intractably public, or, like Rosey Rowswell, a rising chorus of hometown glee, he was every bit as ebullient, and his speaking style became a national signature, clear and urgent.

"You'll find that as you go talking to different broadcasters," said Mutual's Al Wester, certain in his recollections, "that nobody in the business has a bad word to say about Lindsey Nelson. You may doubt me on some other things, but trust me on this. I know."

The fact is that Wester knew. In a profession, like politics, rife with intrigue and betrayal, of the self-serving pretense of self-serving men, Nelson was, as far as one could tell, remarkably devoid of broadcasting's self-congratulation. Like Saam, he did his homework. Like Hodges, he knew his teams. Like Dean, he found himself—increasingly—lauded for his hale, expressive commentary. Like Brickhouse, he was, it seemed, *everywhere*.

"I know you're a child of the Great Depression," I found myself saying, "but your schedule was ridiculous."

"I know," he said. "It's an interesting thing, and I've often thought about it lately, sort of after the fact—'How did I do it all?' I don't know why, but I've always been overscheduled. I've always had about twice as much work as I could get to. Once I did four bowl games in six days. For so many years, I'd be running around the country, doing a football game on Friday, baseball on Saturday, then off to a basketball game. I'd sleep in airports, get by on an hour of sleep."

"Didn't you say once that it all caught up with you at Notre Dame?"

"Yes," Nelson said. "See, every Notre Dame football season from 1967 through '79, I did that taped delay play-by-play for C.D. Chesley, and I enjoyed it. But when I went to live in San Francisco and do the Giants [in 1979], I found out, 'This has got to stop.' I was flying from the Coast to Chicago and then on to South Bend every week—you lose a day each way—and it was killing me. So I had to end it."

"And lose the exposure it brought."

Laughing softly, he volunteered perspective. "You know, of all the stuff I did over the years, the greatest identification I had wasn't with the Mets. It wasn't the NFL or CBS, or college football per se. It wasn't 'Monday Night Football' [in 1974–77, he called Mutual Radio's coverage; Wester added color]. It was *Notre Dame*. I remember once doing a Packers' football game in the sixties at Milwaukee," Lindsey said, "and I went out for a morning walk with Vince Lombardi. We came back to the Pfister Hotel and some kids see us, and one yells, 'Hey, here comes the Notre Dame announcer!' "

"For once, Lombardi was overlooked."

"True, and I'm sure it shocked him. But that was the identity. Notre Dame, the national team," he said.

"How would the good Bible Belt folks of Tennessee feel about that?" I said.

"If you won't tell 'em, I won't, either."

Born in Pulaski, Tennessee, in 1919, Nelson remembers sitting in his family's living room eight years later, after a move to nearby Columbia, and hearing Graham McNamee tell how he was close enough to the boxing ring "to reach out and touch the canvas." There was something in the parlance of the greatest announcer that then existed in the Republic, something vivid and transforming, that linked Lindsey—forever—to McNamee, speaking from Chicago, and the boxers, Jack Dempsey and Gene Tunney, and the instrument through which the King spilled into the Nelsons' living room—a rectangular box called an Arbiphone.

"It was the strangest looking thing you've ever seen," he said, recalling its form to consciousness. "To tune it so that you could hear more than a jumble, you had to adjust—exactly—three different dials. The speaker itself rested on top of the box."

"What did the box look like?"

"A big question mark," Nelson said.

"What did it sound like?"

"A big question mark. But it also made me aware—as I hadn't been before—that there was such a *thing* as broadcasting. And I was drawn to it from that day."

A decade later, after covering sports in high school for his local newspaper, Lindsey bundled up his possessions and drove to Knoxville, where he enrolled in the state university, majored in English, and became a student spotter.

Nelson's voice grew wistful. "From that McNamee fight," he said, "I was hooked on radio, and at the university, the best way to get into that field was through the football broadcasts. Now, to understand this story, remember, first, that our games were aired from the second deck of a wooden shack on top of the stadium's left stands. And the only way to reach this shack was by climbing a stepladder—it too was wooden; it swayed; it was like what Jack must have endured vaulting up the beanstalk. And once up here, you were stuck, because it was more terrifying coming *down* than it was going up."

In November 1939, Nelson was the spotter for Jack Harris, the play-by-play announcer of the Tennessee-Vanderbilt game over WSM ("The Station of the Grand Ole Opry") in Nashville. "Keep in mind that swerving stepladder," Nelson said, playfully, "and also know that there were no restrooms inside the broadcasting shack. One fact meant that you found it hard to leave the shack; the other meant you'd better have a strong constitution."

"Did Harris?" I asked.

"That's the story. At half time of the Vanderbilt game, I climbed down the stepladder to get the statistics from the Tennessee athletic department, as I always did, and then took them back to the booth. When I got there, Harris was staring at me with a pained expression on his face. 'Here are the stats,' I told him. 'You do 'em,' he said, and with that he was off."

"To find a restroom?"

"Yes," he said. "Jack had had a second cup of coffee at brunch that morning, and the extra cup, I guess, was too much. So I had to read the stats over WSM, and I was into broadcasting. If Jack Harris had been content with just a single cup of coffee, my life might have gone off in an entirely different direction."

After graduation, Nelson taught English and entered the Army, where—over four years—he served as a liaison officer with the French Foreign Legion; traveled with the Ninth Infantry Division through North Africa, Sicily, and Hitler's *Festung Europa*; worked as an Army public-relations officer with such correspondents as Ernie Pyle, Bob Capa, Hal Boyle, and Ernest Hemingway;

and was attached as a war correspondent to General Eisenhower's headquarters, earning the friendship of Ike, Omar Bradley, and William Westmoreland.

"In 1979," Wester said, "Lindsey was inducted into the Salisbury Hall of Fame, and he asked General Westmoreland to introduce him. So Westy got up and looked at the audience — the place was packed — and said simply, after which the place erupted, 'I am here only because I am a friend of Lindsey Nelson.'"

Pride slanted into Nelson's voice. "What an incredible time that was," he said of the early- and mid-forties. "Under Army auspices, I had a brief educational stint at the University of Paris. I was involved in the early link-up of that grand and historic day when the United States and Russian troops met at the Elbe. And I broadcast some Army baseball games in Linz, Austria."

"Where Hitler grew up," I said, "and where he planned to construct his Model City."

"He hadn't bargained on the U.S. Army," Nelson bandied. "After the war, of course, we became the occupying force and during our time there, we put together some baseball teams. And we had a lot of former and future major-league players there — Harry Walker, for example, was our manager."

"Had you met Walker before the war?"

"Walker, no, Westmoreland, yes," he said. "Westy and I had first met in 1941, when we both reported to the Ninth Infantry Division in Ft. Bragg. At the time, we were both bachelors. He was about five years older than I was, and later we became very close. In fact, in the fifties, when he'd been assigned to West Point, I broadcast some Army games up there, and we kept in contact even then."

Released from the service, Nelson hurried back to Knoxville. He wrote local news for its morning and afternoon papers and "was bored stiff. After you'd moved through Europe, I couldn't get too excited about a drunk in city court." Frustrated, he recalled the Arbiphone, and from 1947 to 1950 touched Tennesseans over WKGN and WROL. Then, Gordon McLendon summoned him to Dallas, where he discoursed for two years on the Liberty Broadcasting System. In 1952, Nelson left this place, which he enjoyed, to unloose his color in New York City and, more tangibly, as NBC's nonesuch. If Mel Allen stood out as the network's World Series, All-Star Game, and Rose Bowl Voice, the symbol of its big *Events*, Nelson became the squire of its weekly continuity, the conveyer, in what seemed an omnipresent manner, of its almost infinite variety of *events*.

"Mel, of course, was doing Yankee games every day, so he couldn't have done for us what Lindsey did, anyway," Tom Gallery was saying at his home in Encino, California. "Even if he had been available, I don't think he would have worn as well as Lindsey did."

"Why?" I said. "Allen came at you daily in October. He wore well then."

"I'll buy that," Gallery said, "but even though the Series might run seven games, it was still one event. Mel was great for those kinds of broadcasts. He was a free-flowing kind of guy with a great knowledge of baseball, and I personally liked him. In fact, two or three times when Dan Topping fired him — they didn't always get along, to put it mildly — I intervened to get his job back. But as far as his impact was concerned, if he'd been coming at you across the country *every* six or seven days all year, as Lindsey was, he might have grated. Lindsey could be dramatic too, but he was more low-key and very easy to take. And the great thing about him was that he shouldn't have been called a *professional* announcer — he should have been called a *professor* of announcing."

"Why?" I said.

His admiration almost whistled. "Because when you got him, you got a writer, an editor, an educator, a guy who would study an event from top to bottom — he was such a damn perfectionist," Gallery said. "The incompetent broadcasters on the air today — they should all hire Lindsey to coach 'em from the ground floor up."

"How did *you* wind up hiring him?"

"It goes back to a guy named Bill Stern, who was my predecessor at NBC, and who by this time [the early 1950s] was one of the first users of what we call 'dope.' It changes you completely and its effect on Stern was that it made him a horrible person as well as a horrible announcer. He was a monster — literally."

"He'd had an amputated leg," I said. "Some said he used the stuff to dull the pain."

Gallery's voice was devoid of pity. "That was his *excuse*," he intoned. "Stern just enjoyed being cruel, vicious. When I was at NBC, he'd disappear for two, three days on assignment — just go off and get doped up. To answer your question, Stern was covering a golf tournament for us in 1952 when, all of a sudden, he checked into a hotel, locked the door for two days, wouldn't answer the phone — got drugged to the gills. He'd do this all the time — it was a nightmare."

"So you called for Nelson?"

"I was desperate — we had a golf tournament and no one to cover it," Gallery said. "I called a friend of mine in Dallas and said, 'Do you know someone who can cover golf?' And this guy knew Lindsey through his McLendon and Liberty connections. I called Lindsey in Tennessee and said, 'Would it be possible for you to get to Dallas, like tomorrow?' and he said, 'Sure,' and that was the start of it all." He laughed. "Best damn phone call I ever made."

In 1955, with Red Grange, "the Galloping Ghost," Nelson aired NBC's coverage of the NCAA "Game of the Week"; with Curt Gowdy, he anchored the NBA telecasts. Two years later, it was Saturday baseball; in 1959, stealing a monopoly from Dean, he added Sunday.

"What *didn't* you do?" I said.

"Rest," Nelson answered, dead-pan.

"Did you realize the kind of pace you were setting?"

"Not at the time — it just became a part of you," he said. "And I'm glad I did it. I'd just hate to have to do it again."

From 1957 to 1961, Nelson's psychedelic sports coats and his rhythmic country gabble transported themselves into the American bosom as the trademarks of "Major League Baseball." With Leo Durocher (1957–59), then Fred

Haney (1960), and, finally, Joe Garagiola, Nelson discharged charm and accuracy as, playing the Polish Cavalry to Ol' Diz's Wehrmacht, he collided with CBS for the loyalties of the largest single baseball audience in the country.

"I thought I'd been through a lot in the war," he said, "and then I get back to the States and by the mid-fifties, I'm with Grange and Durocher. Now *there's* an experience."

"How'd you enjoy Leo?"

"He was a delight—the most energetic guy you'd ever see in your life. But he had this great reluctance to say on the air the outrageous things he'd say anywhere else—he had a great fear of offending people," Nelson noted. "In 1960 he left to join the Dodgers as a coach and we got Haney, who'd just been fired as the Braves' manager. Fred was sort of coasting, at the point in his life where he just wanted to take it easy. Then *he* left to join the new American League team—the Angels—and we got Joe to replace him."

"How aware were you of CBS?"

"We just figured, 'Let's keep it straight.' We knew we couldn't match their comedy. We didn't *want* to. And we got a good reaction *our* way. That's probably true because after years of pressing us—of telling horror stories about Dean's popularity—our affiliates were just glad we finally got baseball on the air."

"Did you have any problems *getting* on?" I said.

"Well, Dancer Fitzgerald never thought we'd make it past that first year," Nelson said. "They bought all sorts of games from different teams and figured there wouldn't be enough left for NBC to put together any kind of decent package. But they hadn't bargained on Tom Gallery. In early '57 he put me on the road and the first place I went was Milwaukee—a team CBS hadn't bought and which was a terrific team. I paid them $25,000 for each of eleven games. Then I went to Pittsburgh, and we got eleven Pirates' games. We bought four Cubs' games—to them, it was the difference between being in the red and black. To balance it off with an American League twist, I bought four Senators' games, and believe me, with their terrible clubs, I picked the dates *very* carefully—one with the White Sox, one with Boston, and two with the Yankees."

"Was it any easier the second time around?"

"Night and day," he said. "Understand that, originally, CBS had bought rights to a lot of teams for the sole purpose of freezing us out. Once they saw we were going to get on regardless of what they did, they found their protection was useless, so they didn't buy from as many, and we picked them up. In '58, for example, we bought Red Sox' home games, the Tigers. We were on our way, and from then on it was just a question of which you liked—baseball with us, or song and dance with Diz."

My first whole season of watching network baseball was 1960, a time in which, for many, the Kennedy-Nixon election, won with distinction and lost with honor, left America limp. Like the year itself, the campaign assigned fire to its blood, and as the Soviets shot down an American U-2 plane, torpedoed a Paris summit conference, and enjoyed their leader's truculence—"Only my face is ruddy," Khrushchev scoffed. "Eisenhower's is white. And [Harold] Macmillan's has no color"—men of substance wondered if the Free World, by lack of will and initiative, must abide a foreign policy of shrunken ambitions. Less balefully, the number of families with television sets had soared from 4.4 million in 1950 to 40 million, or 88 percent of all American households. From their black-and-white screens burst forth "The Flintstones," the medium's first prime-time cartoon, and "The Huntley-Brinkley Report" and "Route 66" and "The Andy Griffith Show," debuting on October 3, a warming evocation of small-town life. Burt Lancaster won an Oscar for *Elmer Gantry*. Rafer Johnson took the decathlon at the Rome Olympics. Floyd Patterson pummeled Ingemar Johansson to win back the heavyweight boxing championship. Jack Lemmon and Paul Newman animated *The Apartment* and *Exodus*.

Equally memorable was the season's baseball, for by 3:36 P.M. on October 13, the moment Bill Mazeroski's Game-Seven, ninth-inning Pirates' blast beat New York, 10–9, in possibly the most theatral of all World Series contests, fans had traveled through a year that, decades later, would be worthy of recall.

In early April, the Tigers traded a batting champion (the steady Kuenn) for a home-run titleist (Cleveland's Colavito). Acquired from Kansas City, Roger Maris whacked thirty-nine home runs, Mantle added forty, and winning the regular season's last fifteen games, the Yankees won Stengel's tenth- and final pennant. The Orioles—Paul Richards' "Baby Birds"—placed a surprising second. In his final at-bat, Williams retired with an electrifying home run; in Pittsburgh, marching toward their first pennant in thirty-three years, the "Beat 'Em Bucs" electrified a city. On Tuesday, November 8, 1960, John F. Kennedy, at forty-three, was elected president. Twenty-four days earlier, because of "his advancing age," Yankees' officials argued, the game's most voluble and magic manager was unamiably sacked. "I'll never make the mistake," said Mr. Stengel, "of being seventy again."

That year, I would catch snatches of Nelson dispensing counsel from Forbes Field, County Stadium, or Fenway Park. After a few innings, I turned back to Ol' Diz—not merely, I believe, out of loyalty but because, in the finite breadth of my attention, he answered a need for dashing and opinionated entertainment.

I was struck, *then*, by Dean's indomitability. Viewing preserved broadcasts of the two series from that age before videotape, I am impressed, *now*, by another perception. To Ol' Diz, glorying in the spoken word, what cognoscenti viewed on the screen was abstract irrelevance; "up in the booth," said Blattner, "he almost never even looked at the monitor. The camera could be showing Mickey Mantle or Al Lopez chewing tobacco, and Diz'd be talking about game-hunting in Texas or the catfish streams in Mississippi. Eisenhower could have been at the game and Diz still would be talking about how great Roy Acuff was. Man, he didn't care. His personality was the show."

Nelson, at another extreme, was among the first TV broadcasters to grasp the importance of marrying what viewers saw at home to the images stamped-ing from his tongue. Unlike Husing, he adapted from radio to television. Unlike Barber, his career blossomed postwireless. Unlike Stern, he made few errors for the camera to illuminate. "I'll never forget," Gallery said, "how a guy at a rival network paid Lindsey the ultimate compliment. 'If a cameraman tipped his lens down by mistake to a rolled-up gum wrapper on the floor,' the announcer said, 'Lindsey would come up with something apropos to say about that bleary wrapper.' "

To the 1955 and 1963 National Sportscasters and Sportswriters "Sportscaster of the Year," the radio-television fissure was hardly bleary. "Some didn't adjust to the great differences between the mediums," Nelson said, "but to do them justice, you *have* to."

"What kind of differences?" I said.

"I love radio—you're totally in charge. To me, broadcasting baseball all season that way is a delight. You just let yourself roam. And you're the entire show—you paint the picture. If you get in trouble, you can get out of trouble just as easily—and because there's no picture, *nobody knows it.*"

"But TV?"

"Much more stressful," he said, quickly. "Sure, to be successful in this business, you have to do it, but I think most announcers prefer radio. You have much less freedom in TV. You're at the mercy of what pictures the producer and director show. In language, you have to be more selective. And always, your destiny is in someone else's hands."

"True in all sports," I said.

"Especially in baseball," he said, "and I guess I notice it so sharply because there's no radio sport better than baseball to do stream-of-consciousness—the slow pace, the time to improvise. It's an English major's dream."

Nelson's fifth year on "Major League Baseball" marked Garagiola's first. A funny, biting analyst, the ex-Cardinals' catcher, thirty-five, had emerged from his six years with Harry Caray as a hugely popular iconoclast. "He'd become very much accepted," said Nelson. "He was a smash for Anheuser-Busch on the banquet circuit. He'd done some guesting on Jack Paar's 'The Tonight Show.' They loved him on the St. Louis Network," and now, a certified regional success, Joe drew weekly *network* exposure as the Tennessean's sidekick.

He began in a season of change and circuit clouts, and in which critics treated generously his puckish knack. *The Sporting News*, based in St. Louis, hailed Garagiola's "wit and expertise . . . his usual quippy self"; the *New York Daily News* loved "his radiant sense of humor." In 1961, critics also surveyed new cars (the Valiant, Corvair, and Falcon) and movies (*The Guns of Navarone* and *West Side Story*) and television programs ("Ben Casey," "Dr. Kildare," the domestic "Hazel," with Shirley Booth, and "Mr. Ed," who died in 1979, at thirty-seven) and, moreover, a president who began the Peace Corps, created the Alliance for Progress, endured the Bay of Pigs, and presented "a picture of total urbanity," one writer said, "the first true reflection in the presidency of America at the mid-century, a country of city dwellers long gone from Main Street."

From the capital, where Kennedy's inauguration was softened by twenty inches of snow, the Senators moved to Minnesota and became the Twins. The

American League expanded to add teams in Washington and Los Angeles; its schedule inflated to 162 games. Killebrew and Baltimore's Jim Gentile each walloped forty-six home runs. The Tribe's impertinent Jimmy Piersall batted .322. The Tigers' 101 victories marked their most since 1934. But almost no one noticed, for the 1961 Yankees and, more specifically, the M & M core of Maris and Mantle, staged clammy warfare on the Shrine of Ruth. Maris offered up sixty-one blasts; Mantle smacked fifty-four; six Yankees unloaded more than twenty; all told, the Bombers hit 240 homers. Bolstered by Luis Arroyo's twenty-nine saves and a lineup appreciably superior in the field, the cannonading allowed Whitey Ford to win twenty-five games, rookie manager Ralph Houk a regular-season 109, and in October, against the docile Reds, a World Series victory, four games to one. Still, it was the home-run derby fans recalled. "In all my years," said Allen, "for pure excitement, the day in and out thrills that lift the sport, there may not have been a season like it."

Unlike most, Lindsey Nelson was wedded to *all* of this—the national pastime, the universe of both leagues—through the link of "Major League Baseball." What did it matter that NBC was waylayed weekly in the ratings? At some point, thought network executives, even Dean must succumb to Nelson's ad-lib brilliance and elaborate resourcefulness. Who would chance such a prospect—such assurances of national reputation—on something called the Metropolitan Baseball Club of New York, Inc.?

Lindsey Nelson would. In January 1962, the National League's newest franchise announced that Nelson—like Allen and Barber, a southerner come north—would reign as the first Voice of the New York Mets. Resonating over WOR-TV, the Brooklyn Dodgers' old station, and WABC, 770 on your dial, he would work with Bob Murphy, Gowdy's former colleague at Fenway Park and Harwell's at Baltimore, and Ralph Kiner, Elson's 1961 sidekick at Comiskey Park; recount the strategies and untangle the incoherences of what writer Joseph Reichler called "the most memorable man to ever wear a baseball uniform"; and collide with his friend and NBC colleague, the Voice of the Yankees, for the baseball fealty of America's most discriminating public.

"That was quite an assignment," I said. "What in the world possessed you to take it on?"

"It was a challenge," he said, "the money was good, and it meant that when the Mets were home, I could commute from my home in Huntington [on Long Island]. Plus, my whole family was baseball-oriented. My wife, who'd grown up in Detroit, was a great Tiger fan—her nickname was 'Mickie,' after Cochrane. I had a lot of baseball friends—Russ Hodges, whose wife was close to Mickie. Al Helfer lived nearby. Mel and I worked together. My two kids loved the game. And the family talked it over and agreed, as I've always thought, that a baseball announcer has the best life in the world. He works one month of spring training and six of the regular season—that's it. The rest of the year's his own."

"What happened to the football?"

"When I took the Mets' job, I really felt that I'd never do any more football," he said. "In fact, I was so sure that I put all my spotters' charts in storage. But by June of '62, I was getting the itch again, and I wound up doing college ball the next four years [1962–63 for CBS; 1964–65, NBC]."

"Which brings up a point," I said. "Your baseball broadcasts had been blacked out in New York. Did this city think the Mets were getting a football announcer?"

Nelson broke into a chuckle. "The regular baseball beat writers knew my NBC work. But the New York columnists, TV critics, and so forth didn't. Believe me, I remember how they said, 'What in the hell are the Mets hiring a *football* guy for?' And my response was, 'Well, if this is Broadway, I've had the longest-running tryout in history—five years of network baseball.' "

"What did they say about you against Allen?"

"It wasn't just him, it was Mel and Barber," Nelson said. "But we couldn't worry about them—we knew *we* were going to have enough troubles of our own. We had *our* job to do, and early on Ralph, Bob, and I sat down and decided we were going to level and be straightforward—we had a bad club and we had to say so. And it seemed to work. The Yankees were winners, we were losers, and yet by July 1963—and the critics couldn't believe this—we passed them in radio and TV ratings, and we stayed ahead."

"What caused it all?" I said.

Lindsey Nelson beamed. "A man who spread more happiness than any man I've ever known. The *happiest* man I've ever known—because he was doing exactly what he wanted to. A guy I would have hated to go through life without meeting. Mr. Stengel."

On April 11, 1962, in St. Louis, in the Metropolitans' opening game, an 11–4 debacle, there arose among the first in the club's hurricane of Casey Stengel jokes. "They were at Busch Stadium," said Nelson, "and Casey was giving the opening-day lineup. He got through the names of most of the players until he got to the right fielder. Then he stumbled and fell over his name, chatted on as only he could and finally said, 'And when he hits the ball he rings the bell, and that's his name, Bell' "—as in Gus.

Touching the Big Apple's need for a ready and unifying eloquence, as would the Mets themselves in 1969, Stengel retook New York in the year the first Negro student enrolled at the University of Mississippi, John Glenn became the first American to orbit the earth, the Cuban Missile Crisis shrouded October, and a Californian stormed, "You won't have Nixon to kick around anymore." It was a year of John Steinbeck, who won the Nobel Prize for Literature, and "The Beverly Hillbillies," the oasis of camp, and Johnny Carson replacing Paar on "The Tonight Show," and Wilt Chamberlain, scoring 100 points against the Knicks. It was a year of peculiarities (Bo Belinsky no-hitting the Orioles; Dick Donovan winning twenty games for hapless Cleveland; the Angels, in their second season, placing third) and home runs (Killebrew hitting forty-eight; the American League, a record 1,552) and high skills (the Dodgers' Tommy Davis plating 153 runs; Maury Wills stealing a record 104 bases; Don Drysdale posting twenty-five victories) and a certain haughty charm ("I've got one way to pitch righties," snarled Big D—"tight"; asked how opponents should pitch him, the Giants' Willie McCovey said, "I'd walk me"; admitted the Tribe's fast and scatter-armed Sam McDowell, "Almost every batter guesses a few times. This is an advantage for me. Hell, most of the time I don't know *what* I'm going to throw"). Above all, 1962 was a year of National League baseball, as practiced by the Ol' Perfessor, returning to New York.

"The fans, they took to us like we were urchins left in the rain on a front step," Nelson said, "and Stengel gets the credit. He took their minds off defeats while retaining his own sanity, one of the greatest double plays the old man ever pulled off. If Al Dark or Gene Mauch had been the manager, they would have jumped off the bridge, but Casey knew how to handle it. He knew he was in show business."

"Did you get tired of the pantomimes?" I said. "You know, Casey's verbal gymnastics, the same stories, the winks, the grimaces?"

Nelson grimaced. "God, no," he said. "Everybody laughs about it now, tells funny stories about how awful the team was in those early years. I tell the stories myself. But they were gruesome years. Thank heavens for Stengel—he kept us alive. I remember a sellout that first year and Casey standing on the dugout steps in disbelief. He said, 'We are frauds. Frauds for this attendance, but if we can make losing popular, I'm all for it.'" So were the Mets, who strove to please.

The early Mets were so pathetic they turned and became an enduring fashion in the ephemera capital of the world. Their inabilities were, literally, historic. "They were the last age of innocence," vowed Lindsey Nelson. "They played for fun. They weren't capable of playing for anything else." That first year, the club lost its first nine games, later suffered a seventeen-game losing streak, and tested the limits of hilarity with a 40–120 record, the worst in baseball's modern longevity. Roger Craig lost twenty-four games and Al Jackson, twenty; only one pitcher, Yale's Ken MacKenzie, had a winning record (5–4). With Rod Kanehl (receiving fifty thousand King Korn Trading Stamps for the Mets' first grand slam) and Clarence "Choo Choo" Coleman (answering the question, "What's your wife's name and what's she like?" by saying, "Her name is Mrs. Coleman and she likes me, Bub") and Piersall (running his one hundredth career homer, one July day in 1963, *backward* around the bases) and such unforgettables as Bill Wakefield, Tim Harkness, Jesse Gonder, John Lewis, and pitcher Galen Cisco—so wretched he was banished by the *Red Sox*—the Mets heaped ingenious layers of new connotation upon Barber's exclamatory "Oh-ho, Doctor!"

For seventeen years, Nelson glossed the Mets' image and skidded on their roller-coaster. In 1962–63, a collective 108½ games from first place under the tutelage of "the most amazing person I've ever known," the Mets waddled upon the enormous tundra of the Polo Grounds; from 1964 to 1978, under no less than eight managers, the Gotham Nationals—Stengel's "Metsies"—swung from tenth (in a ten-team league) to first (in 1969 and 1973) and back to sixth (in a six-team division) in the cold and circular Queens orb of five-tiered Shea Stadium, twenty-five minutes from Kennedy Airport and a million years from Ebbets Field.

"Shea had all the conveniences—good facilities for radio and TV, great parking, easy to get to, a prototype of the modern stadium," Nelson said. "And, of course, it opened all of Long Island to the Mets' market. So in a sense, it was nothing like Ebbets Field. Having said that, let me add that the Mets' *fans* were *indeed* like the Brooklyns," spawning Metsomania, a favorite allegory of the time. Fans scribbled messages on bed sheets and banners. Exhibitionists waved placards before the roving WOR camera eye. The chants of "Let's Go Mets!" pierced the jammed and hopeful grandstand. The millennium of a Mets' loud foul met a full, steady roar. These were, writers clamored, the excitables of "the New Breed," shouters to rival Hilda Chester and her bell.

"Did they come to see or *be* seen?" I said. "Did they come to roar or hear themselves be heard?"

"A little of both," the once-Voice of the Mets replied. "Dick Young and some others wrote a lot about it, and that, in turn, made its stream a flood. The fans loved the attention, they became even louder, and I don't believe they were ever more incredible than that first Mayor's Trophy Game against the Yankees in 1963."

"But that was just an exhibition game."

"*Just?*" he said. "Not to Mets' fans. It was a holy war, a crusade. The game was at Yankee Stadium, and this was Stengel's first return to the park where he'd been fired. Oh, how he hated the Yankees—*despised* them—and so did our fans. My wife and two daughters came with their cowbells and horns and the Yankees stopped them at the gate—stopped anybody with any kind of noise-makers and confiscated the stuff. And you wonder why the Yankees were despised? There were fifty thousand people there that night and forty-nine thousand were probably rooting for the Mets. So we come to the sixth inning and—incredibly—the Mets are ahead. The stadium is in a din of frenzy, and Stengel calls down to the bull pen for a pitcher. 'Who do you want?' the bull pen coach asked him. 'Ken MacKenzie?' "

"The epitome of blah," I said.

"A thousand times, yes. But in a normal exhibition game, that's the kind of humdrum pitcher you expect to see. Well, not in *this* game. 'No,' said Stengel. 'I don't want him.' 'Then who?' the coach asked. 'You want Carl Willey?' Casey answered, 'You're damn right I do,' " Nelson said. "Carl Willey was probably our best pitcher, and Casey was using him to nail down an exhibition."

"And the Mets won," I said.

"Yes, and in forty years of broadcasting I have never seen *anything* like the reaction of the Mets' fans that night. A second-year, truly deplorable club beating the *Yankees*—to our fans, it was unbelievable. It took me two hours that evening to get from Yankee Stadium to the Triborough Bridge—traffic couldn't move, people were dancing, it was a spirit of David killing Goliath. But that was Stengel—that's what he brought to the Mets."

As Pee Wee Reese, said Barber, *was* the Brooklyn Dodgers, Stengel became the New York Mets. But it was a player, *Marvin Eugene Throneberry*, a microcosm of rapt initials, who came quickly to embody their childhood; if buffoonery is an art form, Throneberry was the Rembrandt of his age.

Throneberry—"Marvelous Marv," naturally—struck out with comatose regularity. He made screenplays out of muffed ground balls. Seeking to impress, he continued to amaze. "Throneberry looked like Mickey Mantle hitting," teammate Richie Ashburn, sold by the Cubs to the Mets in December 1961, said charitably, "but he didn't get the same results." Lacking gravity, the Marvelous at least knew self-effacement. "Hey!" he yelled once at a Mets' infielder who dropped a fly ball. "What are you trying to do? Steal my fans?"

"I've often said," Nelson observed, "that no money can replace the joy and the experience of being with the Mets. To me, baseball has always been theatre. It has all the elements—drama, comedy, tragedy, all of it, and I was a lucky stiff to be on the Mets' stage. With Throneberry, you didn't have much drama, but there was both comedy and tragedy in his performances. I remember how Ralph Kiner would say, 'Marv never made the same mistake twice. He always made different ones.' "

On June 17, 1962, after bashing an apparent triple, Throneberry was called out by umpire Dusty Boggess for missing second base. Stengel rushed from the dugout, only to be intercepted by Cookie Lavagetto, the first-base coach. "Don't bother, Casey," said the Cookieman. "He missed first base too." Later, Marv explained his quandary. "What does everybody want me to do?" he asked reporters. "I hit the ball a long way. I just had a little trouble because I haven't been to third base in a while." He threw to the wrong base, allowed runners to elude the run-down play, and became the seal—the living, swinging, missing imprint—of the '62 Mets' disastrous silhouette. "Marv was upset the other day because the writers gave me a birthday cake," said Stengel in early August. "He asked how come they didn't give him one. I told him, 'Marv, they would have, but they were afraid you'd drop it.' "

Missing—impressively, given his schedule—only twenty-five Mets' sets in his seventeen seasons, Lindsey Nelson watched the New Yorkers lose an average of ninety-one games a year. Yet, after Stengel, breaking his hip in 1965, retired, and as the front office signed players like Tug McGraw, Bud Harrelson, Tom Seaver, Ron Swoboda, and Jerry Koosman, the Mets, still a poor ninth in 1968, began to feel the winds of *respectability,* an upwardly mobile Yuppie in blue and white pinstriped cloth.

"That whole decade, the sixties, was absolutely, to quote a phrase, 'amazing,' " said the man who, with his artful banter, was often the Mets' least pejorative lure. Once, Nelson broadcast a game while riding in a blimp. He flung down his three basic rules of life: "Never play poker with a man named Ace, never eat at a place called Mom's, never invest in anything that eats or needs painting." He collected what would become, surely, the world's largest single coterie—by 1979, nearly *seven hundred*—of plaid, wild, crazy, chartreuse, loud, and louder sports jackets.

The first time the Mets visited the Astrodome, he even called play-by-play from the *roof*—in a gondola, towering high above second base.

"What about my man up there?" Stengel asked umpire Tom Gorman.

"What man?" Gorman said.

"My man Lindsey. What if the ball hits my man Lindsey?"

Gorman looked up, stared wide-eyed, and shrugged. "Well, Case," he said, "if the ball hits the roof, it's in play, so I guess if it hits Lindsey, it's in play too."

"How about that?" Casey said, returning to the dugout. "That's the first time my man Lindsey was ever a ground rule."

On May 26, 1964, the Mets scored nineteen runs against the Chicago Cubs. Asked a fan, calling WABC, "Yes, but did they win?" (They did, 19–1.) Five days later, in the second game of a Shea Stadium double-header, the Mets fought the Giants for twenty-three innings and seven hours and twenty-three minutes. Jim Bunning hurled a perfect game on the third Sunday in June, and on July 7, its NBC voices Nelson and Blattner, the All-Star Game visited Shea. "And that was only one *year*," Lindsey noted. "Believe me, their troubles would continue. Sure, in the mid- and later sixties, haltingly, like a child, you could see them throw off some bad habits — in their case, bad ballplayers — and learn at least a few social graces like how to hit and catch the ball and, most of all, how to succeed in life: *pitching*. Still, there wasn't even a *hint* of what was to come. I began to think, personally, they'd stay near the basement forever."

Enter 1969, the city of New York's most explosive season since the last "Subway Series" and Don Larsen's perfect game.

In baseball's first year of divisional existence, a whole country was stirred by the Mets' bizarre sensation of invincibility. A 100-to-1 comic entry to win the pennant, New York joined Seaver's twenty-five victories, Tommie Agee's twenty-six homers, the .340 average of Cleon Jones, and manager Gil Hodges' brilliant platooning at four positions with what Swoboda later dubbed, "still magic to me, a fairy tale," to rush past the Brickhouse Cubs, clinch the Eastern Division on September 24 against the Cardinals, sweep Hank Aaron's Braves in the best-of-five playoff series, and float into the World Series against the arresting Orioles. "We are here," pronounced Baltimore third baseman Brooks Robinson, "to prove there is no Santa Claus." Seven days later, after a five-game Oktoberfest which suspended believability, a ticker tape parade rivaling Lindbergh's snaked through Manhattan. M. Donald Grant, Mets' chairman of the board, explained, "Our team finally caught up with our fans." The Ol' Perfessor was yet more indefatigable. How had they done it? someone asked of the Miracle Mets. "They did it," Stengel said, "*slow*, but *fast*."

This Metsian sense of fantasy, with its flamboyant tenacity, far outlived 1969; even in the mid-1980s, with Hodges dead, Jones retired, and Seaver and Koosman still pitching, its glow would remain in exaggerated form, a perceptible, inexplicable thing.

"What do you remember about '69?" I said.

"Those last three months," Nelson said. "You know, we were almost ten games out in mid-August — we weren't even in the race. Then the Cubs started falling apart, we got hot, and we passed them so quickly that once they got behind, they weren't even in the pennant race, either. We wound up winning by eight games."

"No time to savor being in front all year."

"No," he laughed. "I've never been with a club ahead all year, where you just looked forward to going to the park every day and being with baseball's best. In '69, it just happened so abruptly. The Mets saved their miracles for the last part of the year and then it was like the 'Miracle of the Day' from then on."

"First, the division clincher against St. Louis."

"You know, in love, in baseball, whatever, there can only be one first time, and this was it — fifty thousand people in absolute delirium," he chimed. "A few weeks ago WOR was cleaning up some old stuff and sent me a tape of a show we'd done after the clinching. It was entitled, 'To the Mets with Love,' and it looked at that game and at the whole season. In a book he later wrote, *Joy in Mudville*, George Vecsey said that he saw more honest and enthusiastic joy in the crowd that night and on that program than in anything he'd ever seen on television."

"And the team," I said. "As I recall, they reacted after that game like something out of *Night at the Opera*."

"The night we clinched," Lindsey Nelson mused, "the writers were asking a storm of questions, and when they'd subsided, someone said, 'Gil, how did it happen? Tell us what all of this proves.' Hodges sat back, stared a while, and spread those meat hands wide. 'Can't be done,' he said, and this giant, gentle man just laughed. Years later, I thought of this when I asked Walt Alston, the Dodgers' manager, 'Walt, what's the greatest thing you've learned in all your years in baseball?' He said, 'You just make out your lineup card, sit back, and some very strange things happen.' "

"To quote a cliché, 'That's baseball.' "

"And that was the Mets — there's no way any of us could have believed it, could have dared dream that the butt of everybody's jokes was finally going to win. We'd always been an unbelievable team, all right — but now we were winning the improbable games, not losing them. Like the night Steve Carlton of the Cardinals struck out nineteen Mets — and *lost*. Or the night Seaver pitched a perfect game [on July 9] until the ninth inning against Chicago. Or the day when Al Weis, a banjo hitter, bombed a homer to beat the Cubs. Or, of course, just the madness of the night we clinched."

"And then the Braves."

"Even now, I don't believe anybody thought we'd win the playoff. I know I didn't. Then we won in three straight. And then came the Orioles with their marvelous team and pitching staff. And I don't know anyone who even *fantasized* we'd beat *them*."

The Amazin's lost the Classic opener, then rode a hidden influence to four victories in a row. On October 16, 1969 — to Nelson, "The most memorable event I've ever covered. It is so far ahead of anything else that I couldn't even imagine which event is a distant second" — the New York Mets, the Tiny Tim of Baseball, became Champions of the World.

"I was telecasting the Series on NBC with Curt Gowdy," Lindsey said, "and in the fifth game, the Mets were leading in the eighth inning. As we'd agreed before the game, I left the booth and headed for the elevator to get to the clubhouse for the victory celebration. That's when it hit me — the whole enormity of the thing, this dream that for so long had been a nightmare."

"Standing, waiting for the elevator."

"That's when I thought, 'My God, this is what we've been hoping for all these years.' And my next thought was, 'What if this damned elevator gets stuck and I'm pinned in there for hours and miss the whole party?' The elevator had done that in the past."

"Did you take the chance?"

"No sir," he said, rather formally. "Not this day. I turned away from the elevator, raced down the ramp, fought my way through the fans going out of their minds, and reached the dressing room for the celebration."

Over NBC, Nelson communicated the Mets' victory party to a nation which, after several years of negative prognoses — rising, like much of the late 1960s, out of uncalculated ignorance — to the effect that baseball was dead, now found, to its unexpected pleasure, that the patient lived. Washing the champagne from his hair (and sensing that *this* sports coat, stained and dripping, must be dry-cleaned tomorrow), the planet's foremost interpreter of Stengelese waited for Shea's delirium to subside and then drove around the island of Manhattan.

"Why'd you do it?"

"I had my wife and kids with me," he said, "and it just seemed so *right*. There was a party at seven o'clock for players, their families, and the rest, and by the time I got done with the postgame craziness it was past four. I said, 'We don't have time to go home and, anyway, if we don't go into Manhattan, we'll have missed the celebration.' So we went into town and, boy, it was marvelous. Dancing in the streets, throwing confetti. Every once in a while a cop would recognize me and go wild. It's a cliché, I know, but this was truly — if there has ever been such a thing — a once-in-a-lifetime happening."

How could the 1970s match such a festival? "The answer was," said Nelson, wryly, "they couldn't." On April 22, 1970, striking out nineteen Padres, Seaver fanned the last ten batters. In 1972, shelved by the Giants, "Say Hey" returned to New York. The next year, after a wagon train of three third-place breakdowns, one could see the Yogi Berra Metropolitans, built of pitching and defense and a misfit league, win another pennant. But there would be no *Second* Coming for this middleweight pleasantry without a .300 hitter, twenty-game winner, or totem to drive in a hundred runs; against the curmudgeon Athletics of Charles O. Finley, the Mets lost the Series in seven. "You gotta believe!" cried Tug McGraw, the Mets' irrepressible reliever, to his 1973 mates. Few believed, however, during Nelson's last five years at Shea Stadium, for as Yogi was fired, attendance slid, and the Mets twice finished last, interest again swooped to the Bronx. By the late seventies, New York, New York was once more a Yankees, Yankees' town.

Then, one day in early January 1979, baseball fans awoke to an even more jarring experience, something for which not even the perils of Marvelous Marv had prepared or conditioned them. After almost two decades of growing, deepening affection, Lindsey Nelson was no longer the Voice of the New York Mets.

"I went into the Mets' offices, and the first person I encountered was an old friend, Jim Thomson, the business manager," Nelson related. " 'I want to make a speech,' I told him, and Jim invited me to go ahead."

"Did anyone have an inkling of what you were about to say?" I said.

"I don't think so," he said. "I know Jim was surprised. As best I can remember it, this is what I told him: 'I have loved every minute of my long association with the Mets. I will never forget it. Even the bad years were memorable. The happy years outweighed them. I am fond of everyone in this organization. I could not have asked for better treatment. I say all of this, Jim, because, *despite* all that, I would like to be released from the remaining year of my contract—for personal reasons which have nothing to do with the Mets.' And Jim said in response, 'That's quite a speech,' " as was its primary cause.

Six years earlier, Nelson's wife had died of a cerebral hemorrhage. Their younger daughter, Sharon ("She knows things about the Mets *I* don't," Lindsey said. "Every breakfast, lunch, at dinner, we'd talk baseball, baseball, baseball"), was mentally and physically handicapped and lived in a residence in Middletown, New York; the other child, Nancy, now worked as a page at CBS while attending graduate school at the University of Southern California. It was Nancy who prompted Nelson's exit from the Mets; by early 1979, "She was twenty-four," he said, "and I wanted to be closer to her. I planned to move to the West Coast, which I did, and to do football, which is not as time-consuming as baseball, and to share some time with my daughter, which, happily, I was able to do."

"But why the timing? Why not wait a year or two?" I said.

"It was so difficult leaving the Mets, but I think the way I did it was right," he said. "Over the years I've encountered many sportscasters who were long associated with one organization. I kept thinking how bitter Red Barber was when he was let go [by O'Malley] and Mel's inglorious end [in 1964]. I didn't want that to happen to me. Their reaction had always startled me, and I wanted to make sure that everyone knew that there would be no bitterness from me toward the Mets."

"Did you think you'd stayed too long?"

"No, but I've seen an awful lot of people who have. I just didn't want them to have to cut the uniform off me. I had absolutely *loved* New York, but I came to the point where I'd really done everything in broadcasting there that I could." He paused. One wondered what his thoughts were. "Actually," he said at last, "maybe I should have gone earlier. When the announcement hit, the phones started ringing off the hook. I was offered more jobs than I knew existed."

For Lindsey Nelson, in the beginnings of his post-Mets' age, the peregrination west led to San Francisco. "The Giants had just signed a contract with a new station," he said of KNBR, "and they were looking for a new announcer."

"And that was the one offer you *did* accept."

"It just worked out so well. I told the Giants I'd come out there and do the games for three seasons, and that was it. I didn't want to move there permanently. But I had always been fascinated by the city—I went basically for the experience of living there. Plus, of course, there was Nancy. If I had any doubts about taking the Giants' offer, that fact erased them," and through

1981, over KNBR and television station KTVU, Nelson and his associate, Hank Greenwald, called the Giants' plunge into the second division.

The year afterward, Nelson returned to Knoxville.

"The University of Tennessee's dean of its Communications College had asked me if I was interested in lecturing and conducting some classes. I told him it was something I'd always looked forward to. He said basically, 'We're ready whenever you are,' and so in the winter of 1981 I said, 'I guess I'm ready.' "

Nelson's voice announced, if not sentimentality, an allegiance to old loyalties and loves. "Well, something like that," he said, pleasantly. "Of course, there are times in the year when I'm teaching very seldom."

"During college football season?"

"Yes, but I hope to be back to it full-time as soon as that's over. I've always enjoyed the give and take, no matter where I've been. And I've always felt that college offers a marvelous forum."

In his sixties now, isolated from Gordon McLendon and network baseball and the kaleidoscopic Casey, Lindsey Nelson found the classroom tugging at his calves; one recalled Maury Allen, the profound and gentle columnist of the *New York Post*, writing, "How strange it was to see Nelson in a bus filled with ballplayers studying the latest centerfolds as he read a heavy tome on World War II."

But it was not, alone, the teaching that had brought him back to Knoxville, to the university where, more than four decades earlier on a football afternoon, a second cup of coffee conspired to change his life. It was the place itself, and its symbols and memories, and how to this gifted and private man, walking among them, he felt almost capable of voiding the intervening years. Mets' fans missed him, and I, for one, missed his "Major League Baseball," but who could fail to understand the changing arc of his direction?

Lindsey Nelson was home.

*   *   *

At NBC and Shea Stadium, Lindsey Nelson expanded his sphere of lifework possibilities. Yet there were *other* announcers, less nationally known perhaps than a Nelson or Blattner or Scully, who enriched the years 1951–64 and made them, if not a Beulahland, precisely, at least among the hardest to forget, pilfering from John Winthrop, in baseball's "Shining City on a Hill."

Their inflections roused the major leagues' local and network coverage; at their incisive best, they engendered tension and regional pride. Over radio, that movable feast, available *anywhere*, and even television, whose two-dimensional screen often subdued baseball's clarity and charm, they converted nuance into poetry, tedium into absorption, and made the game seem aflight with belonging.

"I've followed broadcasting since I was a kid," observed Pirates' broadcaster Lanny Frattare. "I've made it a combination hobby-vocation. When I was growing up [in the fifties, in western New York], to be a local radio big-league announcer was the pinnacle — the terrific job fans would dream about."

"You had your 'Game of the Week,' " I pointed out.

"Yeah, but only a couple games a week, and even then, only in the so-called 'sticks,' " he said. "And that was it — no cable, no proliferation of games, nothing to dilute the local team's power. And the Number One guy — a Gowdy in Boston or Bob Prince — was unchallenged. Today, you may have three announcing teams for one club — one to do radio, a second for conventional TV, a third for cable."

"And you're saying, back then, that a Van Patrick and Dizzy Trout, for example, at Detroit, would handle everything, radio *and* TV."

"Just remember the names — in their own region, they were *king*," said Frattare, a KDKA announcer since 1976. "An Allen, a Barber, a Caray at St. Louis, a Hodges — you could go down the list. Sure, they were different — some better than others, some dry, some rapid-fire, some talked too much, others not enough. But they had the best jobs not just in baseball — in sports. *The absolute top of their profession*."

Growing up in upstate New York, conditioned to the tango of sleepy midsummer afternoons and the roaring jolt of play-by-play, we were, I think, more fortunate than any section of America, for we heard — as no other region did — Dean and Nelson on the weekend, and Allen and Barber every day. "Ain't that something?" glowed a drinking companion, years later, as we stumbled upon the truth. "*Only* part of the country. In Iowa and Arkansas, they saw Ol' Diz but not Allen or Red. In New York City, they got Mel and Barber but never even heard of 'Game of the Week.' In Cleveland, you didn't see *anybody* [with apologies to Jimmy Dudley]."

Allen and Barber, both baseball Hall of Famers, and Nelson, who should be, and Dean, who would be were he not already in the players' wing, combined to vitalize baseball's discoveries and freeze its permanence in the mind so that by the 1980s — years after their divorce from daily broadcasts — the game remained cyclical and timeless for those who heard them, often taken for granted but somehow never reduced.

"Not even in Washington?" Bob Wolff said in his erudite way. "Good grief, if we couldn't kill baseball off with the teams we had, I guess what people say is true. Baseball *must* be immortal."

For fourteen years (1947–60), Wolff barbed and laughed and interviewed his way through teams whose God-awfulness rivaled the Mets'. Airing the 1984 Cracker Jack Old-Timers Classic with Chuck Thompson, a former Washington colleague (1957–60, post-Arch McDonald's fall), he recounted their facility at warming the Senators' chill. "As I remember, Chuck," he said, "we rarely gave the score of the Senators' games in those long and losing years." Replied his ex-associate: "That wasn't an oversight, Bob; that, as you know, was well-planned, believe me."

Now the television Voice of Madison Square Garden, calling events from college basketball to the Millrose Games to the Westminster Kennel Club Dog Show, Wolff was born in New York City, grew up listening to McNamee and

Husing, and after batting .583 as a senior at Woodmore Academy (NY), entered Duke University, then a leading big-league factory, on a baseball scholarship. "In both my career and my life, I can say, 'If it ends tomorrow, I've been blessed,' " he told me. "Everything that's happened has been through a great break." He paused, with the actor's timing. "At Duke, as you'll see, that was *literally* true."

Wolff hit nearly .300 as a college freshman. But early in his sophomore year, the center fielder broke his ankle sliding into second base. Healing, he began broadcasting — "They had a local CBS affiliate, WNDC, in Durham," he said, "and when I was playing, I used to hang around there being interviewed. Now that I had a cast on my leg, I ended up the year announcing our games" — and at the start of his junior season, Bob sought out counsel and his coach. Should he return as a player? Should he return to the mike?

" 'I've never seen an arm or a pair of legs outlast a voice,' the coach, Jack Coombs, told me," Wolff recounted at his home in South Nyack, New York, forty minutes from Grand Central Station. "He said, 'If you want to get to the big leagues, I suggest you keep talking.' Well, that was pretty plain — it hurt my pride. But it was another break — the best advice I ever got."

"No more hopes of replacing DiMaggio?" I said.

"No," he said. "Except for spring training with the Senators every season when I was with them, and a few years of extracurricular activity as their batting-practice pitcher, I've been talking ever since."

A Phi Beta Kappa graduate, Wolff earned his diploma in 1942. The next day, he received his naval commission and, following an indoctrination course at Harvard Business School and with the Seabees at Camp Perry, Virginia, flew as a supply officer to the Navy's most advanced base in the Pacific. It was here, in the Solomon Islands, that supplies and ammunition converged to accompany the seaborne troops on invasions farther north; here, also, that Wolff, extemporizing, wrote a manual. "I thought the seaborne procedures there were a mess — totally alien to what I'd learned at Harvard," he said. "So I wrote this manual, and it said basically that the whole Navy Base Supply System should be revised." Mailed to the Navy Department, the book, to his astonishment, resulted in Wolff's transfer to Washington — "to be in charge of writing training books and movies for use by the entire Supply Corps" — where, at war's end, he assembled his Duke scrapbook, visited commercial radio stations, and soon gripped the medium of television.

"Basically, like so many veterans, I was looking for a job, so I hit the streets, showing stations what radio stuff I'd done in college and hoping, yes, for a break," he declared, a hint of satisfaction in his voice. "Finally, in 1946, I was hired as sports director for WINX."

"Owned," I recalled, "by the *Washington Post*."

"Not bad!" Wolff said. "Then comes 1947 and this new thing called television. DuMont had the first station here — WTTG — and they took me on as the first telecaster in Washington. There were so few stations anywhere, and so I also did the first network broadcasts between Washington and New York. That year I did the first Senators' TV games, the first Washington Capitols' basketball games — they were Red Auerbach's team. I was doing University of Maryland basketball and football."

"You were the Gil McDougald of Washington television," I proposed. "You know, a utility infielder."

"More like Elston Howard," he said. "Always in the lineup, but shifting from left field to first to catcher. My lineup was sports — that's all WTTG did back then. And my God, for a kid in his twenties, it was fantastic training."

In 1950, Paul Jonas tapped the TV Voice of the Senators to call Mutual's "Game of the Day." The same year, Wolff added radio to his Nationals' *vitae*, joining WWDC as McDonald's colleague. "What happened was that Chesterfield cigarettes began sponsoring the radio *and* TV side," he said, "and so I'd do the first three and last three innings on the tube and the middle three on radio. With McDonald it was reversed." By the next season, steadily maturing, Wolff covered boxing and special events, the Gator Bowl, and Mutual's football "Game of the Week"; locally, one could hear him on *six* Washington stations.

"I was with the *Post* when he first came to town," explained Morris Siegel, later of the *Washington Star*, "and I remember several things. First, he never became as popular here as Arch. Second, Bob became much bigger on the national level. Third, maybe as a result, Arch resented him deeply, thought he was trying to steal his job. They had a running feud, and even on the air, barely spoke. When Arch was dropped after the '56 season [the Nats' new sponsor, the National Brewing Company, selected Thompson], he blamed Bob, I think unjustly. And fourth, Bob was somewhat insecure, probably because of his youth, but a terribly hard worker. He was an interesting blend — suspicious but nice."

"How do you mean?" I said.

"You'd be talking to Pete Runnels, who played with the club, and after you were finished, Bob would come over and say, 'What were you talking about?' There were things like that." Lighting a cigarette, Siegel allayed abuse. "But I don't want to sound like I'm knocking the guy. On the air, he was aggressive, did a thorough job. And he got a *lot* of assignments."

At Griffith Stadium, where losing clubs and vacant seats were perpetually bound, Wolff hosted a pre- and postgame television show. Sponsored by such entities as Countess Mara neckties and George's Radio and TV, the narrative ran simultaneously with Wolff's pre- and postgame *radio* programs, taped earlier that day. "It made for a rather full time," Wolff said of the early 1950s. "Four shows a night, plus the radio and TV game itself, and that was just with the Senators."

"But you enjoyed it."

"Oh, it was my life," he answered, quickly. "For over forty years I've been interviewing — God knows how many thousands I've done. And I don't really interview; it's not an interrogation. If I always had a strength, it's been my ability to converse, just to talk casually with a guest, all the while knowing, hopefully, where I wanted the talk to go."

What Bob Wolff wanted, of course, was stardom, and, slowly, his reputation climbed. "Still," he said, "I'd go to the Gillette people in Boston and say, 'How about some network work?' and they'd answer, 'If your name gets big enough, we'll put you on.' And I came back, 'If you put me on tonight, my name will be big enough tomorrow morning.' "

"You were frustrated," I said.

"Yes. My path seemed to be going horizontal, not vertical."

Then, in the last year of Ike's first term, the vagaries of saliva exploded the New Yorker's career.

On August 7, 1956, in the eleventh inning of a scoreless game against the Yankees, Ted Williams was jeered by the Fenway Faithful for misplaying a fly ball, made a diving catch for the third out two batters later, and upon nearing the home dugout at the end of the inning, launched spittle toward occupants of the ground-level box seats. "Ted Spits at Fans!" screamed the *Boston Globe*. Joe Cronin, the Red Sox' general manager, was said to be furious. Hub radio and television stations raged unmercifully. Owner Thomas Austin Yawkey burned.

"After leaving Boston, the Red Sox' next stop was Washington," Wolff said, "and by the time they got here, Williams' spitting had become a sensation. The club had fined him [$5,000]. The sports pages, the *front* pages across the country, everybody was talking about 'that Williams, there he goes again.' "

The first big-league game I ever attended was August 30, 1960, Teddy Ballgame's forty-second birthday, at Fenway Park, against the Tigers. Except from my father, I knew almost nothing of Williams. I remember that he pinch-hit, met a prolonged ovation, and lofted a long out to right field; I took home with me that night a charged puzzlement as to his voltage upon the crowd. Only retrospect would tell me that in my day, or, should I say, my father's, he was the most volcanic athlete since the Babe; even now, I think that except for Ruth and, perhaps, Ali and Jackie Robinson, Williams was the one sports figure of this century who developed into an epic. "It's his presence, that's the word," T. Ballgame said of Joe McCarthy, explaining Ted's admiration. One need not explain Williams' presence to see its aureole; when No. 9 entered the batting cage, reverence enswathed the field.

This was the man whom, two days after the *Globe* headline, Bob Wolff approached at Griffith Stadium.

"Ted and I had a run-in, for lack of a better term, earlier that spring," Wolff said. "I'd asked him to go on my TV show, and he said, 'Hell, I don't want to do that, don't bother me.' So after that, every time I'd go near him to say hello, he'd start grimacing. He'd recoil. After a while, I got tired of being treated like a leper, and I forced the issue. 'Look, Ted,' I said, 'most of the time I'm just coming over as a friend to say hello. I'm not trying to get you on the show.' "

"What'd Williams say?" I asked.

"You know Ted. He sort of muttered and half-cursed. He looked at me, I looked at him, and I said—this was in spring training of '56—'Let's get this thing behind us. Why not agree that if you're hitting, say, .340 at the beginning of June when you come into Washington, or have thirty homers by the end of July—whatever it is—you'll come on the show.' In other words, if he was *going* good, he'd *feel* good and come on with me. 'That'll be our agreement and then you won't have to worry about me bugging you.' And Williams agreed."

"And then unloads the spit."

"He'd spat a couple times earlier that season, and the press was just *murdering* him," Wolff said. "After the latest incident in Boston, Ted said he wasn't going to talk to any journalists, which obviously included me. But when he came into Washington a couple of days later, he had great statistics for the year, even though he'd had a recent slump, so our agreement — as far as I was concerned — was on. I went to him and said, 'Ted, I imagine you don't want to go on with me and honor your agreement. If that's the case, I'll understand. But if you do honor it, then I'm going to have to ask you about the spitting or else people will say I'm dodging the issue and being a lousy journalist.' "

"I'll bet Williams honored it."

Wolff chuckled. "Well, he was a man of the old virtues — a deal's a deal. I mean, he *hated* doing it, but he came on the show and, looking at the ground as he spoke, expressed remorse about the incident and said he was doing the show only because of his 'friendship' with me. It was, if I do say so, quite a coup. So what I did was put together the clip of Williams with a shot of Mantle I'd done previously — at this moment, they were the two biggest athletes in America — and come up with an idea that I took to New York."

The offshoot was a syndicated TV program bought, first, by the Yankees and, then, the Red Sox and A's. "I'd do the tapings, put the shows together — a different one for each club — and mail them off for their use," he said. "The teams used them before or after the games, and by late in the '56 season, I was doing seven or eight shows a *day*."

"Another break," I said, if self-created.

"Yes," he said, "and just a few weeks earlier, another one happened, a big one — again, a simple matter of timing."

On July 10, 1956, in, improbably, the only game where the decade's four brightest lodestars — Mays, Mantle, Williams, and Musial — all bombed home runs, Wolff aired Mutual Radio's play-by-play of the All-Star Game at Griffith Stadium, a National's triumph, 7–3.

"The fact that it was in Washington got me the job," he admitted. "Jonas wanted a local favorite, one who knew the town and its park, and after I did the broadcast, Gillette, as I'd hoped, began to pay attention."

It was at this time that Wolff began to sense an immediate kind of network fulfillment. Assigned, with Bob Neal, to Mutual's coverage of the 1956 World Series, he called the last four-and-one-half innings of Larsen's perfecto, the last, Game-Six hit of Robinson's career, and the Yankees' seventh-set demolition of Don Newcombe and the Dodgers. For NBC, he did radio play-by-play of the 1958 (with Earl Gillespie) and 1961 (with Waite Hoyt) Autumn Occasions. From 1962 to 1965, he hosted that network's World Series pregame television shows. He also broadcast the 1962 Giants-Dodgers' playoff, won by San Francisco in the ninth inning of the third- and final game. "One game I did solo, another with George Kell, another Joe Garagiola," he said, "and it's the second game I remember. It started late in the afternoon, Eastern Time, and turned out to be the longest nine-inning game in history [four hours, eighteen minutes] and ran into NBC's prime-time schedule. I loved it. Every half-hour the network would say, 'This program will not be seen tonight because of the baseball game,' then another thirty minutes later they'd come on and chop off another show."

"So you were the guy who shot down 'Laramie'?" I said.

"The ballplayers helped," he said, generously.

By the late fifties, his voice and person sharing the great axes of Washington and New York, Bob Wolff had arrived. He announced the East-West and Blue-Gray Games, two Rose and Sugar Bowls, and the 1958 Colts-Giants' championship game. Except for Allen, he called more World Series in 1956–61 than any broadcaster. Nationally, the Republic learned what its capital already knew: Wolff was not simply driven and aggressive. He was also very good. "Let's face it," I recalled a friend saying of 1947–60. "In those years, with those teams, he *had* to be."

Not once in the Wolff administration did the Senators escape the second division. They won 883 games and lost 1,270. They tunneled 482½ lengths from first place. Twice, the Nats lost more than 100 games. Four times, they finished in seventh place; four times, they finished last. They drew as many as 850,758 people (in 1947) and as few as 425,238 (in 1955). They failed to pass the half-million mark four consecutive years.

With the Senators plumbing the depths of abysmality, Wolff must somehow divert attention. "Did I have a *choice?*" he quipped. "No, I couldn't laugh it off when the shortstop kicked one that let in the winning run — although I was laughing inside. Humor, to work well, must be timely. But believe me, there were plenty of times it was tough to keep a straight face and tell the fans, 'Now, the Senators need eight runs in the last two innings to pull it out.'"

Mocking, teasing, bemoaning over WWDC and television's WTTG and, later, WTOP, Wolff conducted pleas for bottle openers, coat hooks, and hangers for the broadcast booth. Before a night game or between contests of a twin-bill, he managed interviews with players and scouts, season- and irregular ticket holders, dignitaries and concessionaires. Wolff tabbed them "fans in the stands"; often, their identity, when revealed, described men who had *made* it. "I'd talk with anybody," he said. "Sometimes they'd be regular fans from Bethesda or Chevy Chase. And sometimes, when I collared a well-known celebrity, I'd just let them talk and I wouldn't say who it was until the interview was over."

One 1957 afternoon at Griffith Stadium, after the homestanders had, surprisingly, won the opening game of a double-header, Wolff ventured into the box seats and accosted a student of The Game. "I went down toward the field and went up to the guy and said, 'Sir, I'd like you to be on my show. Will you?' He said, 'Sure.' And I went on, 'But let's play a game. Don't say your name until we're finished talking.' And this was total ad-lib," Wolff related. "For seven minutes my guest carried it off with a professional's flair — talking about baseball, the Senators. It was amazing. And so, finally, we came to the last exchange. Here's how it went:

"And I think that I'll ask this first gentleman here who has been watching the ball game how *he's* enjoying the game," the Voice of the Senators began. "Sir, how'd you like the first game today?"

The guest, a frequent visitor to the Senators' yard, replied, "Well, of course, being a Washington fan, I thought it was great."

"Are you originally from Washington, sir?" Wolff said.

"No, I'm a Californian."

"What sort of work do you do, sir?"

"I work for the government," said the fan, age forty-four.

"Oh, for the government?" Wolff said.

"Yes, yes, I work for the government."

"What sort of work do you do, sir?" said Bob Wolff, probing.

"Well," said Richard Milhous Nixon, "I'm the vice-president."

Sixteen years later, when NBC Television, seeking novelty to help Curt Gowdy and Tony Kubek, began a regular Monday night "Game of the Week," the network stumbled on the concept of guest appearances; each week, officials said, domos like Howard Cosell, Pearl Bailey, and Joe Namath would inhabit the TV booth.

Though the former Sports Network was ignorant of the fact, the format had a precedent; Wolff had used it successfully from 1955 to 1960 and, after the Senators moved to Minnesota, in the first year of the New Frontier. "Proof that it worked was the fact that I used it so long," Bob noted. "The key was to exercise discipline with these stars during the broadcast [with NBC, it wasn't], which meant that their vanity couldn't be the main ingredient [in 1973, frequently, it was]."

Unlike NBC's "Game of the Week," where celebrities staged a nine-inning marathon, Wolff's guests, whether on radio or television, only shared the mike in innings four through six. "You were too busy setting the scene in the first three innings," he said, "and you were too involved reporting changes in pitchers and climactic plays of the game in the final three."

"Who were some of the people you had on?" I said.

"We had Don Adams, Danny Kaye [also gracing NBC in 1973]. We had Buddy Lester, Jerry Lewis, Jonathan Winters. Shelly Berman was on."

That had been my first thought, I told him. "Mostly men and comedians."

"And some women," he said. "Most of the spots came from getting to know the personalities when they were in town on night-club tours or when they stayed at the same hotels on the road."

"With NBC, the guests talked about baseball. Did yours?"

"Oh, no," Wolff protested. "Our people *entertained*. Adams did, as I recall, an umpire skit. Danny Kaye, who, of course, was a big baseball fan, mixed English and Spanish. Lewis did a routine about a bleacher fan. And Bill Dana did a half-inning using a different language than usual baseball jargon. They were all funny."

So, unintendedly, were the Senators. "Not only were they bad," Wolff remembered, "they were embarrassing." Until 1956, when Calvin Griffith, the adopted son of Clark Griffith, became the Nats' president and shortened the park's dimensions, the Senators played in a yard which virtually outlawed the long ball; it was a trolley ride of 387 feet down the left-field line, 422 and 435 feet to left- and right-center; one must unload a chasm of a shot — 457 feet — to reach the home bull pen near dead center field. Pre-Calvin, Roy Sievers and Mickey Vernon, with twenty-five and twenty, held the single-season records for home runs by a right- and left-handed batter; in 1955, Carlos Paula led all Washington outfielders with *six* home runs. Griffith reduced the distance to the left-field bleachers, installed a screen in front of the stands, and (re)signed Sievers, Jim Lemon, and a free-swinging Idahoan named Harmon Killebrew to hit balls over it. In 1959, two years after Sievers belted forty-two home runs, Killebrew did the same. That very season, outfielder Bob Allison was the Rookie of the Year, and in 1959–60 Lemon drove across two hundred runs. Even the Nats' pitching impressed. Camilo Pascual, blessed with the majors' best curveball, led his league in 1959 shutouts; the next year he, Pedro Ramos, and Chuck Stobbs merged for thirty-five wins.

The 1960 Senators finished fifth, only eight games below .500; they also drew 743,404 customers, the most since 1949. "They were bad, but they were getting better," Bob Wolff said, "and they were more entertaining, scoring more runs, and people were starting to say, 'Hey, these guys — I can hardly believe it — might win something some day.' "

That was exactly, of course, what happened; in 1965, after an interval of thirty-two years, the Senators won the American League pennant. By then, however, they were known as the Minnesota Twins, for on October 26, 1960, convulsing a sixty-year-old franchise, Griffith moved the Nats to Minneapolis-St. Paul.

From 1955 to 1960, the Senators attracted 2,722,790 fans; the Twins lured almost half that number in 1961 alone. "Calvin asked me to go with him to Bloomington [site of the Twins' park, Metropolitan Stadium], and so I figured, 'Why not?'," Wolff said, "and I had a ball out there," as over WCCO Radio and WTCN-TV, he unfolded as the Boswell of Killebrew, hitting forty-six homers, and Allison, banking twenty-nine, and the Ramos-Pascual ticket, losing thirty-six games, and shortstop Zoilo Versalles, batting .280 and fielding with Marion-like range.

Yet, removed from the East, Wolff felt the pain of that alienation, and in 1961 George Weiss, the Mets' new general manager, contacted him about returning to New York. Wolff's response flew back to unforgotten years. "Here I was, a native of New York City, and just after I get to Minnesota, George — who, like Stengel, had just been fired by the Yankees — started talking about me becoming the Voice of the Mets."

"How serious did things get?" I said.

"We talked rather extensively," he said. "It was all over the papers — 'Wolff Coming to New York,' that type of thing. But George, being very meticulous, wanted everything in order before he offered anybody the job, and the problems were that the team didn't have a sponsor or a station yet. The thing kept dragging out, and now the *Twins* were anxious. They were looking ahead to '62, and they wanted to know my plans."

"How hard did Griffith press you?"

"They finally said, 'Look, we need a yes or no.' I went to Weiss, and he couldn't make a firm commitment. I had no choice. I couldn't wait. I went back to Minnesota, signed my contract there, and a couple months later, after the Mets grabbed WABC and got a sponsor, Rheingold beer, out comes the news. They've signed Lindsey Nelson as their Number One announcer."

After Nelson's leaving, his "Major League Baseball" required a Voice. "That's the irony, another break," Wolff said. "When Lindsey wound up getting what might have been *my* job with the Mets, a couple weeks later NBC came to me and offered me *Lindsey's* job on the network baseball."

"Did you hesitate?"

"Are you kidding?" he said. "The Twins let me out of my contract—they insisted that they be able to save face by saying they'd released me—and I moved back to New York, took my family there, and during my next three years [1962-64], I did the play-by-play every Saturday and Sunday. And my partner was Joe [Garagiola], of course, who lived in the same place that I did, up in Scarsdale."

"How did you find him to work with?"

"I thought we formed a great team," he volunteered. "I've always prided myself on accuracy and conscientiousness. Joe provided the humor and color. And working with him was a positive delight. Some announcers you feel you're in rivalry with—they're envious, there's friction. But I always felt that Joe was exceedingly caring about his partner."

"And the competition?"

"Well, Dean had a wonderful personality. But his approach to the game was more country-type. Joe and I were bigger in the cities. And, you know, the great thing about Garagiola was—people don't know this—that he was a very erudite fellow. He'd bring new words to the booth. Instead of saying, 'A runner almost slid into the shortstop,' Joe'd say, 'He almost stapled him to the bag.' "

The post-Dean manifestation of the ex-athlete behind the mike, Garagiola would go higher, more quickly, than any former jock in baseball. Too easily dismissed as a conglomerate of one-liners, he was both clever and ambitious— "not a bad kind of ambition," Wolff observed, "just a desire to improve"—and retiring as a player in 1954, Joe set about to create a following and become its high-wire to sports. Practicing, critiquing, listening to tapes, he fashioned an avuncular style. He worked. He advanced. He worked. He became a versatile, capable announcer. By the 1970s, he had evolved—few had foreseen it, even Wolff, in 1962—into a network heavyweight, a Bob Hope of the resin bag.

"He had this great gift for the phrase," Wolff was saying. "Each of us depended heavily on stories on our games, and on a Saturday, we'd get to the park about three hours before the game. Then we'd go to the players. I remember Joe cracking, 'You work your side of the street, and I'll work mine.' "

"Each week, your street was different," I said.

"Yes, we moved around. We did a lot of games from Forbes Field. Some White Sox, Cleveland. We did some games from Lindsey's Polo Grounds. And

ABOVE – On August 5, 1921, Harold Arlin aired radio's first baseball game. Forty-five years later, he returned to Forbes Field, that baptismal site, where, flanked by long-time Pirates' announcer Bob Prince, Arlin (on the right) called play-by-play over trailblazing station KDKA. Said the pioneer of baseball broadcasting: "No one had the foggiest idea, the slightest hint of an inkling, that what we'd started would take off like it did."

RIGHT – To Red Barber, he was "the greatest announcer we ever had"; to millions of Americans, he was sportscasting's first/most recognizable name. In 1923, Graham McNamee broadcast his first World Series; over the next decade, vivid and theatrical, he became the Classic's unrivaled Voice, a celebrity among celebrities. (Photo: National Baseball Library, Cooperstown, NY)

ABOVE – In April 1924, over station WMAQ, Hal Totten, then twenty-three, aired the inaugural radiocasts of the Cubs and White Sox. He helped turn Chicago into the Main Street of baseball broadcasting (at one time in the 1920s, seven stations carried big-league ball), covered five World Series and Mutual Radio's "Game of the Day," and fled the wireless in the 1950s to become president of the Three-I League. In 1960, Totten moved to the Southern Association. (Photo: United Press International)

BELOW – In the late 1920s and early thirties, covering the Tribe over WTAM, Tom Manning spiraled into a Cleveland institution. Vocal and extroverted, he made radio baseball come alive, even when the Indians weren't. (Photo: *The Sporting News*)

ABOVE LEFT – When WHK replaced WTAM in late 1931 as the Indians' flagship station, left-fielder Jack Graney succeeded Tom Manning as the franchise's Voice. The first former athlete to broadcast major league baseball, Graney excelled at re-creations, calling balls and strikes from the showroom of an auto dealer. On October 2, 1935, from Navin Field, the act turned live and national: Jack became the first ex-player to announce a World Series. (Photo: *TSN*)

ABOVE RIGHT – A football official, sportswriter, and native Bostonian, Fred Hoey was already a Hub heavyweight when he entered radio in 1925. For the next fourteen years, often simulcasting games over the Colonial and Yankee Networks, he detailed the feats and foibles of the Red Sox and Braves. Said the *Boston Traveler*: "To thousands of listeners, he *was* New England baseball." (Photo: *TSN*)

BELOW LEFT – When Baseball Commissioner Landis dropped Tigers' announcer Ty Tyson from the 1934 World Series for "excessive partisanship," Michiganders, protesting, collected a petition with more than six hundred thousand signatures. "His appeal," said the Bengals' post-1959 mouth-piece, Ernie Harwell, "was, and remains, in retrospect, extraordinary"; from 1927 to the early fifties, Tyson, the first Voice of the Tigers, helped make the upper Midwest a baseball hotbed. (Photo: *TSN*)

BELOW RIGHT – Five-foot-six and 320 pounds, Harry Hartman waddled into Cincinnati's base-ball heart in 1930. Doubling as the Reds' radio domo and P.A. announcer, Hartman favored such catchwords as *socko, whammo, bammo,* and *belto.* When, in 1934, Red Barber debuted on a rival Reds' network, it was Harry who was belted into the Rhineland darkness. (Photo: *TSN*)

Yours For Kentucky Winners and Kentucky Club
Dutch Reagan

Who is that piped man? Looking back, who could have believed it? In the mid-1930s, holding forth over WHO, Des Moines, Dutch Reagan re-created White Sox and Cubs' games during the worst of the Depression. Said America's fortieth president in 1986: "How could I not love baseball? After all, it made me what I am today." (Photo: *TSN*)

RIGHT – He was termed the "Rembrandt of the Re-Creations"; his moniker was "The Old Pine Tree"; he was a huckster, a hustler, and his broadcasts, a midway. For twenty-two seasons, Arch McDonald was also a capital presence as Voice of the hapless Senators. "At his peak," said *Washington Times* columnist Morris Siegel, "Arch was probably the most popular announcer this city has ever known." (Photo: NBL)

ABOVE – How often have you heard, "Never say never"? There has *never* been a more uproarious home run cry than Rosey Rowswell's, the 1936-54 radio seal of the Pittsburgh Pirates. A 112-pound poet, humorist, and baseball zealot, Rosey charmed Tri-State listeners with his homespun bywords (e.g., a "doozie marooney [Buccos' extra-base hit]"; "the bases are FOB [Full Of Bucs]"). He also fathered The Game's pre-eminent long ball salute. Whenever a Pirates' blow was about to clear the fence, Rowswell stood and implored of an imaginary damsel, "Get upstairs, Aunt Minnie, and raise the window! Here she comes!" Seconds later, to Rosey's rear, an assistant either shattered a pane of glass or LEFT (standing, Bob Prince) dropped a dumb-waiter's tray laden with bells, nuts, and bolts. To Pirates' fans, the crash signaled Aunt Minnie's window. "Oh, that's too bad," Rowswell mourned between blows of his slide whistle. "She tripped over a garden hose! Poor Aunt Minnie! She didn't make it again!" (Photo above: *TSN;* at left: NBL)

ABOVE – Literate, quirksome, and, to New England, ubiquitous, Jim Britt (left, with assistant Tom Hussey) imparted both Boston baseball teams from 1939 – the Red Sox through 1950; the Braves until their March 1953 exodus to Milwaukee. He was the Voice of NBC-TV's 1949-51 World Series coverage. (Photo: *TSN*)

BELOW LEFT – Ralph Bertram Puckett (alias, Bert Wilson) was not, nor professed to be, an Everest of neutrality. "I don't care who wins," he told listeners, "as long as it's the Cubs." For eleven 1940s and fifties seasons, what one team official called "the biggest Cubs' fan I've ever known" vowed, annually and relentlessly, that *next* year would be *this* year; sadly, Wilson's *final* year was 1955, when he died of a heart attack, at forty-four. (Photo: *TSN*)

BELOW RIGHT – Why is this man smiling? After all, Byrum Saam announced more losing baseball games than any man in history – 4,935. Still, he persevered and, ultimately, broadcast seventeen- and thirty-two seasons of the Philadelphia A's (1938-54) and Phillies (1939-49 and 1955-75). He was dubbed "The Man of a Zillion Words." (Photo: NBL)

LEFT – From 1949 through 1970, Russ Hodges was the Voice of the New York (then San Francisco) Giants. He broadcast with gentle tones and a reporter's bent, at once dispassionate and droll. Even now, many remember his "Bye, bye, baby," Russ's inevitable home run signature; many more, his clarion call of Bobby Thomson's October 3, 1951, pennant-winning thunderclap. (Photo: *Rochester, NY, Times-Union*)

BELOW – After winning 237 games as a big-league pitcher, Waite Hoyt turned to radio and, eventually, television. There, for a quarter-century, calling Redlegs' games into the mid-sixties, the son of a vaudevillian described mostly inferior clubs and broadcast in the past tense. Related the Brooklyn native: "Instead of saying, 'There's a line drive to center field, and Mays makes the catch,' I'd say, 'There was the pitch, the batter hit a ball to center field, and Mays made the putout.' It's a matter of accuracy." (Photo: NBL)

ABOVE AND CENTER RIGHT – In 1934, a distant relative of writer Sidney Lanier became a Cincinnati Reds' announcer, and for the next thirty-three years, Walter Lanier (Red) Barber made of baseball almost existential pleasure. In 1939, he moved to Ebbets Field; in 1954, to Yankee Stadium; and on August 7, 1978, to the Hall of Fame – the first broadcaster, with Mel Allen, to be inducted. Precise, rhythmic, and understated, Red brought eloquence to language, appreciation to sport, and respect for his audience. He aired thirteen World Series, five All-Star Games, and college and professional football, and towered in the 1930s and forties as the pastime's leading Voice. Moreover, Barber introduced millions of Americans to the game of baseball, making listeners of fans, and fans of listeners, and became a synonym for broadcast objectivity. (Photo above: NBL; at right: *Rochester T-U*)

BELOW RIGHT – For three seasons in the late 1940s and early fifties, Gordon McLendon – "The Old Scotchman" – linked more than 430 radio stations with his Liberty Broadcasting System's "Game of the Day." The series served territory far removed from the nearest big-league stadium; made regular-season baseball available to listeners once limited to the All-Star Game and World Series; and created a storm of enthusiasm. (Photo: Associated Press)

LEFT – Like fellow southerners Mel Allen, Red Barber, Dizzy Dean, and Lindsey Nelson, Jimmy Dudley was a superb baseball mouthpiece. He was the Voice of the Cleveland Indians from 1948 through 1967, and his calls reached states from Maine to Mississippi over the Tribe's spiring radio network. (Photo: *TSN*)

RIGHT – A Second City potpourri. Before retiring in 1943, Pat Flanagan (standing, with Charlie Grimm) did Cubs and White Sox' games, and three World Series for CBS. Grimm, a 1925-36 Wrigleys' first baseman, broadcast for the Cubs in the late 1930s and early forties. He also managed the North Siders on three different occasions; fired for the third (and final) time on May 5, 1960, Jolly Cholly returned to the radio booth, BELOW, replacing Cubs' announcer Lou Boudreau (on the right), who, in turn, replaced Grimm as manager. The next year, Charlie did time as an original member of the Cubs' eight-man College of Coaches, and Boudreau again became a Chicago mouthpiece. For the past quarter-century, the Hall of Fame shortstop has resonated over 50,000-watt WGN. (Photos: AP)

He was the Master, the Great One, the *nonpareil* – the "Pod-nuh" of millions, warbler of "The Wabash Cannon Ball," and star of baseball's pioneering network TV series, the 1950s and early sixties "Game of the Week." As a 1930s pitcher, Jay Hanna Jerome (a.k.a. "Dizzy") Dean had been "a folk hero," wrote *St. Louis Post-Dispatch* columnist Bob Broeg, "capturing the country's fancy during the Depression." In 1941, Ol' Diz switched to broadcasting, where, airing the Browns and Cardinals, he told of runners who "slud," pitchers who "throwed" the ball, and batters standing "confidentially" at the plate. In 1950, it was on to Yankee Stadium, then Mutual Radio's "Game of the Day," and, in 1953, television's "Game of the Week." (Photo: NBL)

LEFT – Its first two seasons, "Game of the Week" burst forth over ABC; in 1955, it moved to more prestigious and widely-watched Columbia. Seen in non-major-league cities, the "Game" originally reached more than half the country. Before Dizzy Dean, no major sport's series had been televised nationally; his success presaged today's MediaAge. From 1955 through 1959, Ol' Diz was aided by former Browns' radio colleague Robert (Buddy) Blattner (right). (Photo: CBS-Television)

BELOW – After the 1959 season, Dean, in effect, forced Blattner off the "Game of the Week." His successor at CBS was the Dodgers' celebrated ex-shortstop, Pee Wee Reese, who teamed with Diz into the mid-sixties, then moved to NBC as Curt Gowdy's 1966-68 partner. (Photo: NBL)

ABOVE LEFT – "Hey-Hey!" Jack Brickhouse proclaimed to millions of Midwesterners. Hearty, buoyant, and indefatigable, Brickhouse became WGN's baseball Voice in 1942. Over the next four decades, he cheered for Chicago's two big-league franchises, told of players like Appling, Fox, Jenkins, and Banks, and energized network coverage of the World Series and All-Star Game, political conventions and presidential inaugurations, and the "Gillette Cavalcade of Sports." He was inducted into the Baseball Hall of Fame in 1983. (Photo: WGN-Chicago)

ABOVE RIGHT – His voice was vivid and unmistakable, and his very name spoke of Notre Dame and NFL football. Few remember, perhaps, that Van Patrick handled the 1948 World Series, or was the Voice of the Tigers for eight 1950s seasons, or buoyed Mutual's 1960 "Game of the Day." In 1974, Patrick died, at fifty-eight, of cancer; he spent his last hours, aptly, at South Bend, IN, covering the Fighting Irish v. Purdue. (Photo: *Rochester T-U*)

BELOW LEFT – The fifties Milwaukee Braves bathed in Wisconsin's love from the first awakening of their 1953 arrival. Their Voice was the colorful Earl Gillespie, who livened Braves' games over a huge five-state network. Screaming "Holy Cow!," trapping foul balls in his fish net, or calling the 1957-58 World Series on NBC Radio, Gillespie helped make the team a Midwest happening. (Photo: *TSN*)

BELOW RIGHT – Wending your way down Pennsylvania Avenue, traversing the U.S. Capitol, or enjoying a sunglazed afternoon at Griffith Stadium, you could not escape the glossy, fluent play-by-play of Bob Wolff, the Senators' 1947-60 announcer. When the Nats moved west, Bob did 1961 balls and strikes from Minneapolis-St. Paul, then enriched the final three seasons of NBC's "Major League Baseball." (Photo: *TSN*)

Lyricist, musician, essayist, and, above all, baseball man — Ernie Harwell "has worn better, more durably," the author writes, "than any announcer I can think of." Ernie began in the 1940s, a small-town Georgian airing the Atlanta Crackers. In 1948, he flew to Brooklyn, then the Polo Grounds, Baltimore, and the Motor City; from 1960, vibrating through America's most fervent baseball town, Harwell made Detroit even more a Tigers' lair. On August 2, 1981, Ernie became the fifth announcer to be inducted at Cooperstown.

Erudite, meticulous, and possessed of a vibrant voice, Lindsey Nelson has broadcast more than forty years, covered every major event and sport imaginable, twice been named National Sportscaster of the Year, and flaunted what may be America's largest collection of outrageous sports coats. The 1957-61 Voice of "Major League Baseball," NBC's first baseball series, Lindsey later aired two World Series and presided over the first seventeen seasons of the New York Mets. (Photo: NBL)

LEFT – Calling nine NFL title games and four Super Bowls, Ray Scott became linked, nationally and invariably, with the Green Bay Packers. Few recall that Scott also sparkled on balls and strikes. He was the 1961-66 Voice of the Minnesota Twins, and later worked for the Senators, Brewers, and Pirates. (Photo: *TSN*)

LEFT – In 1965, baseball welcomed its first sustained "national" regular-season TV exposure – the ABC "Game of the Week," and featured as its No. 1 announcer the breezy and amiable Merle Harmon. The then-Voice of the Milwaukee Braves, later to broadcast for the Twins, Brewers, and Rangers, Harmon embossed ABC's coverage with clear, perceptive commentary. (Photo: *TSN*)

When ABC's big-league coverage ended in October 1965, the "Game of the Week" moved to NBC, where Curt Gowdy emerged for an entire generation of listeners as the national embodiment of baseball broadcasting. From 1966 to 1975, he called the play-by-play of every All-Star Game and World Series, and virtually every regular-season game. Three times, Curt was voted National Sportscaster of the Year; in 1970, he was the first sports-caster to receive the George Foster Peabody Award for excellence in broadcasting; fourteen years later, he entered Baseball's Hall of Fame. (Photo: *TSN*)

wherever we were, Joe would amaze me with his recall. We'd be driving home from the airport on Sunday night, and he'd say, 'You know, Bob, you said "so and so" in the third inning today and I came back with "such and such," and I think it would have worked out better if I'd said "this or that" instead.' He had the sequences memorized word for word. His concentration was absolutely stunning."

Live, infrequently (after all, Ol' Diz), and later, by recording, I enjoyed Garagiola's sting and insight and Wolff's preparation and, to mouth a platitude here becoming truth, his total professionalism. From Municipal Stadium, Comiskey Park, or the Polo Grounds, Wolff painted clear portraits; his voice seldom grated; he was among his time's most fluent rhetoricians.

After the 1964 season, ABC acquired TV rights to major league baseball; the next year, Wolff aired a handful of its games. In 1966, he began a distinguished stint in public relations for the new Madison Square Garden; later, he taught sports journalism at Pace University and sports broadcasting at St. John's University and attended to his family. "*Finally*," he said, "I was home enough to be part of what I'd never had time to before." At his peak in the early seventies, broadcasting almost entirely in New York, Wolff called the play-by-play for as many as 250 events a year.

"But no baseball," I said.

"Hockey and college and pro basketball, the National Horse Show, tennis, track," he said. "Everything *but*. Madison Square Garden just doesn't have a team."

"Any regrets about leaving the game?"

"I still love it," he maintained. "It nourished me when I was young. But the travel just kills you, and I've been loving the last couple of decades too much to regret much of anything."

"What do you . . . ?"

"Retract what I just said. I *do* have a regret. It's about Washington. That town deserves a club," said the man who embodied a team which is dead in a park which has been destroyed in a city which now, *again*, for the second time in twenty years, yearned for the label 'major league.'

"You don't approve of city-hopping?"

Characteristically, he proffered fundamental advice. "For franchises, no, but I sure do for human beings. That's how breaks occur. Not from one city to another, necessarily, but from one opportunity to the next," Wolff said. "Fresh starts bring on brand new lives," and leaving me, the once-Voice of the once-Nationals, who each year opened the baseball season and by September had become its door mat, left for a drive into the city and a meeting with the points of his past.

*   *   *

In 1958, the season Tab Hunter foiled Ray Walston in *Damn Yankees* to win a fanciful pennant for the Senators, Bob Wolff's Nats televised forty-eight games over WTOP, the city's CBS affiliate. In all, thirteen big-league teams —

only the Giants, Braves, and A's abstained—beamed 781 telecasts, a beaten-down sum against the 1957 high of 883. "The figure dropped because in '57, the Dodgers and Giants were still in New York and televising heavily," said Tom Villante, baseball's 1978–82 director of broadcasting. "In '58, on the West Coast, the only TV they allowed was by the Dodgers in a few away games from San Francisco." A year later, although the Cubs and Yankees televised every home match and, for the first time, Kansas City used the medium, showing ten road games, the total dropped again, to 669; one American (the Athletics) and five National League teams (the Dodgers, Braves, Pirates, Cardinals, and Giants) forbade *any* home coverage.

If exposure fluctuated, rights fees clashed wildly. In 1959, a truly *national* television pact, with each club sharing equally its revenue, lay out there, unseen, beyond the sports horizon; every team negotiated separately its own radio/TV contract. At bottom, KSFO paid the Giants $125,000; the Senators pocketed a mere $150,000. On the other hand, the Phillies led the National League with a $600,000 arrangement; WIP Radio and WFIL-TV recouped investment from such sponsors as Atlantic Refining Company, Ballantine Ale and Beer, Tastykake Bakery Company, and—naturally—Phillies Cigars. Looking at the Yankees' numbers, other clubs could hardly keep down their jealousy; in a year when CBS owned a program called "The Millionaire" and, as the saying goes, a million *meant* a million, the Bombers took in $875,000. From first to eighth, the A.L. financial ladder read: New York, Cleveland, Detroit, Boston, Baltimore, Chicago, Kansas City, and Washington. The National's pecking order listed Philadelphia, Chicago, Cincinnati, St. Louis, Pittsburgh, Los Angeles, Milwaukee, and San Francisco.

"This kind of imbalance kept the rich teams—the Yankees, above all—on top year after year. That, and some wise moves by the front office," then-Baseball Commissioner Bowie Kuhn remarked to me in 1979. "It was absolutely terrible for competition. How could *my* Senators, for instance"—and here the native Washingtonian smiled—"possibly contend when they were getting Army rations for their radio/TV rights while others were getting steak?"

"Which, of course, is why you went to a 'share the wealth' network series in the sixties," I said.

"Yes," he said, relaxing his countenance and smoothing his button-down shirt. "Later, some of my more unenlightened critics would call it 'thinly-veiled Communism.' "

"What do *you* call it?"

"I call it horse sense," Kuhn asserted. "Unless we have more and more of this revenue sharing, the sport as we know it will give way to a cannibalism in which the weak die out and the rich teams in the rich markets win forever."

Motivated, like their sponsors, by a passion for greater profits, big-league clubs grabbed $11 million in 1959 for radio/television rights—$250,000 and $3 million from NBC for All-Star and Series exclusivity; $6,125,000 from local stations for distinct and varying coverage; and the rest of this roster of prominence ($1,625,000) from the CBS "Game of the Week," NBC's "Major League Baseball," and the Mutual Radio "Game of the Day."

"Nationally too there was no uniformity whatsoever," said Bill MacPhail, then amid his oligarchy at CBS. "Some clubs made a mint from 'Game of the Week' — the Yankees, above everyone. Some clubs made less, because they weren't on nearly as often as New York. And there were some teams so unattractive or in such small markets that NBC and CBS weren't interested in buying their rights at all."

In 1959, Columbia telecast from Wrigley and Crosley Fields and Yankee, Municipal, and Connie Mack Stadiums. Over its network linking 120 cities, NBC staked out Busch Stadium, Fenway Park, and that Peacock perennial, Forbes Field. "See," MacPhail continued. "In that particular year, network games were aired from only eight parks. The rest were shut out."

"So you saw a few teams have a disproportionate number of games."

"Hell, the networks didn't care," he said. "CBS showed the Yankees all the time for a simple reason — they were the big team, they got the big ratings, and the network made a lot of dough."

At the same time, *advertisers* spent $36,200,000 to propel just that fixed ambition; baseball's 1959 commercial chart featured the hit tunes of cars, beers, and tobacco. Phillies Cigars cosponsored NBC telecasts and three teams' radio/TV exposure; Atlantic Refining Company helped sponsor four. One remembered announcer Bob Delaney, the Yankees' appendage on their four-state radio network, shilling for "Red Ball Service" and how, as in a greasespot intellection, "Atlantic Keeps Your Car on the Go." One remembered too, from a hundred heat-dappled nights, Atlantic's theme song, more brisk than the Gillette Blue Blades March, or KMOX's Caray, chortling over Budweiser, or WERE's Dudley, extolling Carling's "Mabel, Mabel, Black Label," or The Voice himself, a sponsor's Stradivarius, exclaiming that I should assault the refrigerator, at age *eight*, and "go get yourself a Ballantine."

Outside the fifteen big-league cities, everyone could watch a new high of ninety-eight network telecasts. It was *within* these cities, though, where one's link with baseball was *personal*, that you were more or less fortunate than outlanders. By 1959, the number of local telecasts oscillated from the zero of Milwaukee and San Francisco to Pittsburgh's twenty-seven to Boston's and Cincinnati's fifty-one and fifty-three to the 123 of the Team of Champions. "And it wasn't just the *amount* of exposure that differed," said MacPhail. "It was *how* they were presented on both radio and television — the voices and the men behind them."

Like many fans, in those colonial days of presupercable and micropenetration, I never heard announcers from distant places like Baltimore, where Harwell and Herb Carneal entertained over WBAL Radio and WJZ-TV, or Kansas City, where WDAF's Merle Harmon and Bill Grigsby taught Missourians the technical aspects of the game. In New Mexico, it was impossible to know what Cleveland's Dudley sounded like; in Washington state, Cincinnati's Hoyt and Jack Moran were foreign matter; in rural Georgia, one knew the Red Sox' Gowdy, Bob Murphy, and Bill Crowley only (at best) by name. It was as if they did not exist; they never made a ripple. In upstate New York, however, one could touch a majority of the communities of the world of baseball. Switching the dial, I picked up games of the Red Sox, Indians, Reds,

and Senators; heard the White Sox' murmurings of WCFL's Elson and incessant social intercourse of KDKA's Prince and Woods; and if reception clarified
their play-by-play, admired the propriety of the Phillies' Kelly, Saam, and
Haring. On a clear evening, I came across stations of twelve of the game's sixteen big-league teams.

It was about this time that in the town where my father's parents lived, about
sixty miles south of Rochester, I recall watching the "Game of the Week" one
Sunday afternoon.

Turning to my grandfather, I asked which major-league club he rooted for.
He removed his cigar and thought a moment, and I expected him to name
either the Yankees or the Cardinals, whose Rochester Red Wings were their
Triple-A affiliate. Instead, he said something about *excitement*, and then named
a team which, a decade later, would not exist. "Guess," he nodded, "I like those
Milwaukee Braves."

In the late fifties, the two most thrilling franchises in sports were the Baltimore Colts and Milwaukee Braves. Treated as a nonperson in Boston, the
Braves had bathed in Wisconsin's love from the first awakening of their 1953
arrival. They enthralled a city. They touched a state. Their civic embrace
astounded reporters and executives, and for a few, glorious years — so few, in
retrospect, they seem almost mythic — they became a fashionable team; and
their fans, the envy of every club in baseball. In their first seven years, the
Braves won two pennants and narrowly missed two more, set a National League
single-season attendance record, and regularly enjoyed paid admissions in excess of 2 million per year. The Braves sold out night after night. One wit
called Milwaukee County Stadium "an insane asylum with bases." More chillingly, the Braves were the first big-league franchise to change cities in half a
century. Their success ensured that they would not be the last.

"I've been in baseball for more than three decades, and I've never seen anything remotely close to Milwaukee in the fifties. They were wild, incredible
years. Nobody cared in Boston whether we lived or died. Then, in Milwaukee,
the town went bananas. We couldn't buy a thing — fans would give us everything *free*. The players were treated like royalty. Every day was a feast," observed Ernie Johnson, a Braves' pitcher in the fifties and their announcer since
1962.

"What do you remember specifically?" I said.

"The news of the shift had come in spring training down in Bradenton," he
said. "When we went north to Milwaukee, they had a huge parade and we went
downtown. When we got there, I'll never forget how the people put up a
Christmas tree — in *April* — inside the Schroeder Hotel. They were so beautiful.
They said that since we'd missed Christmas with them, they wanted to celebrate it with us now. So there were hundreds of presents under the tree —
shaving kits, toiletries, radios, appliances. Just ga-ga from the first day."

Outside the ball park, fans camped out on freezing nights to buy tickets to
Opening Day. They arrived three hours before games to watch batting practice; they brought cowbells and picnic lunches; they endured rain and snow
to roar for the Braves. At County Stadium, with its then-35,911 capacity, Milwaukee drew 1,827,397 fans in 1953. Braves' players were given free gas, milk,

and beer. Each summer, they received cars rent-free. Perhaps the best of the conquerors, Warren Spahn, already *had* a car, so fans gave him another one — for his *family*. "It was like a small town," said Johnson, the Voice of the Braves since 1976. "Some of us lived five minutes from the park. In those first few years we'd go around town, and even when we tried, we couldn't pay for what we bought — the fans wouldn't let us."

From 1954 to 1957, in the major-league city with the smallest population, the Braves *averaged* nearly 2.1 million customers per year, almost doubling their nearest competitor. After losing the 1956 pennant by a game to Brooklyn, Milwaukee the next season won its first league- and world championship, and drew a National's record 2,215,404 people. Spahn won the Cy Young Award. Bob Buhl and Lew Burdette teamed for thirty-five victories. Wes Covington, leaping from the minors, hit 21 homers in 328 at-bats. Hank Aaron bombed 44 homers, knocked in 132 runs, and was named Most Valuable Player. Surveying the lineup, one saw almost an All-Star team — Eddie Mathews, Johnny Logan, Red Schoendienst, and Joe Adcock in the infield; Covington, Billy Bruton, and Aaron from left- to right field; and Del Crandall behind the plate. Called "Bush League" by New Yorkers, Milwaukeans cheered when their newspapers headlined the World Series: "Bushville Wins!" One writer recollected: "It was the season of light."

"The whole phenomenon was very hard to put into words, and, Lord knows, I've tried often enough," confessed the warm and emotional Earl Gillespie, the Voice of the Braves from 1953 to 1963. "They were the toast of Milwaukee — the whole region lost its marbles. And it was like that all over. We'd go into Pittsburgh — they had a last-place team, they weren't drawing — and there'd be thirty thousand people there. We'd go into Chicago and Brooklyn — the parks would be packed."

"Because you were winning."

"Not just that," he said.

"Then why?" I said.

"There was a madness about it. It was like a fairy tale — this small city became the capital of baseball, winning the Series or not." Each day the *Milwaukee Sentinel*, the city's morning newspaper, ran a front-page cartoon. Had the ball club won the previous day? The sketch showed a Brave smiling, weeping, or defying a downpour; after a double-header, the cartoon sometimes had a split head. "At County Stadium, it was a party every night. It was the place to be. And the nation really identified with us, I think, because what sports is all about is *belonging,* and this city took the Braves in their arms."

Gillespie grew up, ironically, a Cubs' fan, playing first base at Chicago's Lane Tech High School. Nicknamed the Lip, he played three seasons for the Green Bay team in the Wisconsin State League, entered the Marine Air Corps, returned after the war for a final year of Class-D ball — "I must be the only guy in history," he said, "who played four years in Class D without advancing" — and vaulted to real estate in 1947, selling properties with his father-in-law.

It was a field, however, far removed from baseball, and soon Gillespie applied for — and won — a job in sports announcing at WJPG, Green Bay's newly opened station. Radio nurtured his voice and shaped him into maturity;

"Earl would work alone in an empty studio for hour after hour," said the station manager, John M. Walker. "And he'd be screaming into a dead microphone." As loud, chorused a friend, "as a carnival barker," Gillespie won an audition and became the Voice of the American Association Brewers. Moving to Milwaukee in 1951, he called the team's games for two years: That first season, the Brewers won the Little World Series; a year later, the A.A. pennant. When, on March 18, 1953, the Braves first stirred in Milwaukee's future, the Miller Brewing Company — the likely sponsor of the National Leaguers — decided that no matter which station aired their regular-season warpath, Earl Gillespie must broadcast the games.

"Two radio stations wanted to be our flagship outlet," said Gillespie, now sixty-two and the sports director of WITI, Milwaukee's CBS television affiliate. "So Miller announced that they could *both* be the flagship." For eleven years, over 50,000-watt WTMJ and weaker WEMP, the Brewers' once-originating station, Gillespie rafted down a river of anxiety and handclapping over a huge network linking Wisconsin, upper Michigan, and parts of Minnesota, Illinois, and Iowa. He was assisted by Blaine Walsh; he belonged to the Bert Wilson School of Hometown Rooting; he was "excitable, he pulled for the Braves," Ernie Johnson said. "He was a homer, yes, but fair. I remember the night Warren Spahn won his three hundredth game [August 1, 1961]; it almost brought tears to Earl's eyes."

From the first, as Milwaukee came to share the Braves' expansive sense of identity, Gillespie enjoyed a love-hate relationship. "When the team won, I got the sweetest kind of mail," he told me. "I was a great guy — my broadcasts were wonderful. But if they went into a slump, I was the Boob of the Year." Because Braves' defeats were judged calamitous, a tailspin converted Earl "into the bubonic plague." Still, partisans listened and waved their pennants, mailed "lucky pennies" to County Stadium, sent along miniature china cows with halos suspended over their heads — a tribute to Earl's epithet, "Holy Cow!" (later borrowed by Phil Rizzuto) — and gave Gillespie the trademark fishing net (also adopted by compeers) he used to ensnare foul balls.

"Earl was pretty rabid," Johnson admitted, "but, then, it was pretty hard for anybody to stay neutral in those years." In 1958, the Braves took hold of a second straight pennant; Spahn and Burdette went 42–21; in October, Gillespie's second Series on NBC Radio, the Yankees won in seven games. A season afterward, Milwaukee lost the pennant in its 156th game. "With victories on the last day of the 1956 and '59 seasons," said Gillespie, "I'd have been in four World Series in a row." He would not be in another.

In 1960, the Braves, aging, finished second, then fourth the next season, then fifth, then sixth. Milwaukee traded local favorites: the brawny Adcock to Cleveland, the fleet Bruton to the Tigers, the scrappy Logan to Pittsburgh. Attendance slid from nearly 2 million in 1958 to less than eight hundred thousand four years later; the Twins, moving to Minnesota, slashed the Braves' drawing area; the football Packers, winning under Vince Lombardi, became Wisconsin's team.

"Lou Perini sold the club in the early sixties," Gillespie said, "and the new owners did everything they could to wreck the team. They shipped out the popular players. They didn't move to field a winner. I think from the moment they bought the club, they were looking to skip town."

When the 1963 Braves drew 773,018, Milwaukee—no longer suffused with love—watched the club's chairman of the board, Bill Bartholomay, cast lengthening sighs at a future stadium rising in Atlanta. "It was so obvious, even as they denied it, that that's where they were going," said Earl Gillespie, and in October 1964, marching toward Georgia, officials conceded that the Braves would become the first team to move its franchise *twice*.

By then, Gillespie was the ex-Voice of the Braves; he had resigned, for personal reasons, in late 1963. "My wife had raised four kids on her own," he related, "and when I got the chance to go with WITI—I've been here for more than twenty years—and get weekends off, be with my family, have what I hadn't known for years, a summer vacation, I jumped." He also sensed (and resented) the Braves' impending move—"If any city ever deserved to keep its team, this one did"—and relieved and angry, Earl watched his successor, Merle Harmon, endure two years of catcalls, suffering, and rage.

"How was it around here?" I said.

"When Bartholomay announced his move in '64, a judge ruled that they couldn't leave immediately, that they'd have to play here in 1965 and only *then* go to Atlanta," he said, "so Harmon had the great nonpleasure of broadcasting for a team in a city where they weren't just unpopular—they were *hated*. They were pariahs. I felt sorry for Merle. He deserved better. But so did Milwaukee."

On September 22, 1965, before a paid crowd of 12,577, the Wisconsin Braves played their last home game. In eight years of self-destruction, the National League had ripped to shreds the fan loyalties of, arguably, its three most pivotal franchises: Brooklyn, New York, and Milwaukee. "Even when the Brewers came here five years later," Gillespie contended, "there were a lot of us who could never forgive baseball for the meanness and cruelty it showed."

"Now, so long after the good years, what do you remember?" I asked.

The man once known as "the Pied Piper of Milwaukee" formed a sad, slow smile. "Every year Miller would put together a half-hour Braves' highlight film, and in it we'd show people all around the city in boats, on bikes, at sidewalk beer cafés, in polka halls. And there was one common element in all these scenes—people had their radios on. They were listening to the games," he said, firmly, proudly. "Like Brooklyn with the Dodgers, Milwaukee came to *mean* the Braves. That's what I'll remember."

Hearing again the noisy, knowing, and hopelessly sentimental creature that remains the Milwaukee fan, it occurred to me—and, perhaps, should he reminisce, to my grandfather—that Earl Gillespie was not alone.

*   *   *

On any question pertaining to geography, Gillespie would have cast his lot with the Chicago Cubs as the Braves' most vengeant rival. The two cities lay only ninety miles apart; at weekend series, adherents jammed the other's ball park to boo and holler and make out like reprobates.

In those years, the Cubs' radio emperor was Brickhouse's self-styled "protégé"—the hefty, dulcet Jack Quinlan. Turning to WGN, I would lie in bed at night, mindlessly content, and hear him and Lou Boudreau serenade the people of their town. The Wrigleys of the late fifties and early sixties were bad and getting worse, and I dismissed Quinlan, accordingly, in the ignorance of my youth, as an apologist for the Cubs' perduring woes. Jack was that, perhaps, but he was also a facile man, as adept at words and gestures as his charges were barefoot in the standings.

"He didn't broadcast in New York, so he didn't get a lot of eastern ink, and this great friend was taken so far before his time," said Boudreau, his 1958–64 partner, "so he didn't have time to build a reputation. But he was an exceptional broadcaster. He carried me for years and helped me in a strange field. It's like Brickhouse says: 'When Jack died, it was like losing a younger brother.' "

Quinlan attended New Trier High School in Winnetka, Illinois, played basketball, baseball, and football, and rejected an offer from the Brooklyn Dodgers; he intended to enter Notre Dame. At South Bend, he amused classmates with simulated broadcasts of imagined events, and after graduation, took jobs in Tuscola and Peoria and, in 1952, at WIND. It was here that he assisted Wilson, became the principal announcer in 1956, and left for WGN two years later. "And it was in Chicago," declared Vince Lloyd, "that he became as talented a link as you could find between the pioneers of the twenties — the Tottens, the Flanagans—and our broadcasters today."

In the evaluating and rubbing together of Quinlan's nine seasons as Voice of the Cubs, the Chicago National League Baseball Club ignored all invitations to vacate its enclave of demise. The box score reads: one ninth-, two eighth-, four seventh-, and two fifth-place finishes. The Cubs changed profile more slowly than an Alabama autumn. Quinlan had less to talk about than Herbert Hoover's speechwriters. Yet talk he did, flowingly, informally, and with a ubiquity that made Cubs' baseball his preserve. Do the good die young? On March 18, 1965, Quinlan was returning from a round of golf near the team's spring training site in Mesa, Arizona. When the wheels locked on his rented convertible, the car skidded nearly two hundred feet and hit a semitrailer truck parked at the side of the road. Jack Quinlan was thirty-eight years old.

Job-hunting, the Voice of the Cubs had hit the big time at twenty-five. "Three years out of Notre Dame and I'm working at Wrigley Field," he said once, impishly, before pausing. "Only in America."

Another Midwest catalyst wondered for years whether he would even *make* the big time. "You go along so long," Jerry Doggett said in his Dodgers' final year at Ebbets Field. "When you realize your life's ambition all of a sudden, you can't hardly speak. It's a funny feeling. Incredible, really."

Like Quinlan, Doggett was never forced to come to terms with national estimation; Jerry's was a *regional* following, his name unknown, largely, in provinces beyond New York and, then, Los Angeles. But in a way, his was a national *parable*, for Doggett broadcast in the minor leagues for eighteen years until, in 1956, Brooklyn tapped him as Vin Scully's colleague (replacing the man who, in the identical phrase of three ex-peers, "drank himself out of a job": the estimable Cornelius Desmond).

Doggett was born in Moberly, Missouri, and after his father died, moved to Iowa as a child; following high school, he joined his mother (working in Chicago), went to radio school for a year, answered an ad in *Broadcasting Magazine*, and snagged a job in Longview, Texas, at $80 a month. "That was in 1938, remember," he told a reporter, "and it seemed like a million." In 1941, he moved to Dallas, where his voice turned progressively southern and he appeared on Liberty's "Game of the Day" and aired Texas League play-by-play through Brooklyn's Independence Year of 1955.

"Jerry probably doesn't know to this day how he got hired," Tom Gallery said, warmly. "When I phoned Lindsey Nelson in 1952 and I got him to cover his first event for NBC — that golf tournament in Dallas — I said, 'Oh, by the way, if you know someone to go along as your assistant, take him' — and sure enough, he got Doggett."

"He'd worked some with Lindsey on 'Game of the Day,' " I noted.

"Did a hell of a job on the tournament," Gallery said, "and I remembered that fact years later when Buzzie Bavasi called me up and said, 'Tom, we're down to four finalists to replace Desmond. I've got the tapes here, and I want to play 'em for you. Then tell me what you think.' And the first tape he played was Jerry Doggett. I butted in and said, 'Buzzie, you don't even have to play the other three tapes. You've got your man right here.' "

At Ebbets Field, his first-year salary was less than $15,000. "Naturally," he said, "I hope to be able to make more eventually." In Southern California, the ineluctable pull of the Dodgers' turnstiles reclaimed that hope, and by the Los Angeles pennants of 1959, 1963, and 1965–66, Jerry Doggett, like the dye of Dodger blue, impregnated the fabric of O'Malley baseball.

I heard of Doggett only later, in the fourth of his five decades of broadcasting. Recalling his two years in Brooklyn, several college professors praised his calm and unflappability; in the 1980s, looking at his past and hearing his resonance by short-wave radio, I came to think of him even more as a survivor, enduring the flea-bag hotels, splintered press boxes, and eternal bus rides of the minors. "He's like the Billy Williams of the booth," mused a colleague. "Just a guy who goes out there every day and does his job."

He had paid his dues. He had dreamed his dreams. Now, as ever, he gave his audience $1.10 for every dollar of its time.

Once the Dodgers changed their home, an easterner might follow them, with varying degrees of difficulty, through the daily paper, several National League radio/TV networks, the CBS and NBC weekend telecasts, and Mutual's "Game of the Day." To fill New York's baseball void, Budweiser even televised forty-four Giants and Dodgers' road games back to what Thomas Wolfe called the Fabulous Rock.

"The brewery sponsored it in 1959," said Jack Buck, the series' play-by-play announcer, "and the games were carried over WNAT in New York City. Then you played twenty-two games against each opponent — eleven at home, eleven on the road — so whenever the Giants and Dodgers came into Pittsburgh and

St. Louis, we'd televise back to New York. And the reaction was just dynamite —
so good, in fact, that the Yankees threatened to televise *their* games into St.
Louis if we didn't end the broadcasts."

"Which you did after one year," I said.

"We didn't have much choice," Buck said. "There were all sorts of possible
legal problems if we didn't. The series was great for me, of course, because it
gave me entree into *the* market. And I know the fans loved it — it was by far
their best link to teams who'd once been in their back yard."

Bleeding slowly, one might hear Buck unearth self-termed "funnies," or
hear Saam, Hoyt, and Gillespie narrate Dodgers' visits to Philadelphia, Cincinnati, and Milwaukee, or listen to Ol' Diz mangle the Angelenos' invasions
of Wrigley Field, or explore the borders of reminiscence as such Mutual pun-
dits as John MacLean, Joe Wilson, and Gene Elston renewed affection for
ballplayers now remembered as Ozymandian figures.

MacLean (who eventually joined the Senators), Wilson (Brickhouse's TV
partner in that first television year of 1947), and Elston (landing, in 1962,
as the first Voice of the Houston Colt .45s) were, if not network-, at least
heartland stars. Bob Delaney, who knit his shadow onto hundreds of big league
broadcasts on the Bronx Bombers' Network, was not. He was, however, a
curiosity.

"Here was a guy who, when I worked with Russ Hodges in 1957, would spend
most of his time, when he wasn't on the air, muddying up his scorebook with
profanities and doggerel about Horace Stoneham," laughed Jim Woods. "He
hated baseball, was bored to death by it, and was one of the strangest damn
ducks that ever wandered into a studio."

Raised in Elmira, New York, Delaney attended Syracuse University's School
of Speech and Dramatic Arts, took his first full-time radio job in Syracuse —
making $125 a week — and by 1950 was calling Red Sox' games. "I just hap-
pened to be standing on the corner," he said. "The hook pulled me up." After
four years on WHDH, Bob shifted to the Giants and, when the Polo Grounds
emptied in 1957, to the colossus across the river. "There's one thing I know
I do well," he said upon his arrival at Yankee Stadium. "I can sell." Saying of
himself, "I don't like mediocrity," Delaney did little play-by-play. Rather, he
introduced Yankees' games and, after the inevitable victory, signed off; did
between-innings commercials for Atlantic Refining, Ballantine, and Winston
and Salem Cigarettes; and to millions of network listeners, became nearly as
familiar as The Voice and Ol' Redhead, a vivid tatter of the time.

"It was odd," said Woods, "that a guy with a good voice, which he had, and
with a great team, which he was, was in the *sport* that he was." Few remember
Bob Delaney; possibly, even fewer should. But in the late-fifties orbit of The
American Game, his radio presence occupied the platform of springtime
memory, as brief, almost, as it was bizarre.

*   *   *

The career of Van Patrick was neither brief nor bizarre. It was, instead,
eclectic. "In the end, he became probably better known for his pro and Notre

Dame football broadcasts," said Al Wester, Patrick's successor as sports director of the Mutual Broadcasting System. "But those who knew him realize that
he could do it all. Golf. Basketball. Auto racing. Van did everything and did
it so well."

A lineman in football, catcher in baseball, guard in basketball, and shotputter
in track, Van Patrick, like Byrum Saam, attended Texas Christian University.
By stages, he called baseball in the Three-I League, Texas League, Southern
Association, and International League. In the late forties, he moved from Buffalo to Cleveland—"Veeck brought him," said Wester, "to do some television"—
and broadcast, with Barber, the 1948 Indians-Braves' World Series. Patrick
hosted a daily sports program on MBS. He did play-by-play for the NFL
Lions, the Michigan Wolverines, and, ultimately, the Fighting Irish. In 1949,
he joined Harry Heilmann on Tigers' radio, and following the Old Slug's death,
was named Detroit's primary announcer.

From 1952 to 1959, the burly, balding Patrick filled the broadcast booth at
Briggs Stadium—a wondrous playpen which held more than fifty-two thousand fanatics and yet, because of its boxy configuration, fairly reeked of intimacy;
as a Red Sox' fan, let me admit it: the best damned ball park in America—
and endured possibly the most inglorious stretch of seasons in the proud history
of this uproarious and human town.

Van's "Tiges," in the derivative of his successor, Ernie Harwell, won 570
games, lost 662, and finished 208½ games from first place. "He had less to
broadcast about in a decade," said Harwell, "than some guys do in a year." But
only in 1953, a 60–94 nightmare capped by a 23–3 June loss to Boston, did
attendance dip below 1 million. Detroiters proved as patient as they were depressed; they were consoled, to some degree, by Kuenn and Kaline batting
titles, Virgil Trucks' two 1952 no-hitters, and a prodigious thirteen-player deal
in 1957 with the even lowlier A's; and for eight years, people either made a
beeline for their dowager park or heard Van etch Bengals' pratfalls on the air.

"There are some announcers," said Wester, "who know a lot about one or
two sports. Then there are others who know a little about everything. But Van
was fascinating because of his fantastic range of knowledge. Plus, unlike a lot
of guys, he was extremely well-attuned to the financial part of the business."

"He was part-owner of four radio stations," I said.

"Yes, he invested well. And this big, smiling Irishman lived in what you'd
have to call a chateau overlooking a golf course in Dearborn."

"Tough, overbearing?"

"Oh, I suppose so," Wester said. "I'm probably not the best guy to ask. You
see, Van was as close a friend as I had. He was the brother I never had. He'd
be up at six in the morning and still going at midnight. He had amazing resiliency—absolutely nothing seemed to faze him. And the people he knew—in
Canada or Mexico, in South America—*everywhere*. I treasure every day of our
relationship."

Over radio stations WJBK and—at night—WJR, the latter's signal sweeping
to the Atlantic, and a six-station television network fusing most of Michigan,
Patrick worked with such compatriots as Ty Tyson, Dizzy Trout, Mel Ott, and
after No. 4's November 1958 death in a car accident, the quiet-voiced George

Kell. "I came on at a terrible time," Kell said in the Ozark accents of his native Arkansas. "We'd all been stunned by Mel's death, and I was so new at broadcasting, that only added to the trauma."

"What was Patrick like?"

"To me, he was the epitome of success, and he took me under his wing," said the former Tigers' third baseman. "I was in sort of awe of him. He was such a talented announcer — too big, really, for Detroit."

As if weary of provinciality, Patrick left Briggs Stadium for MBS after the 1959 season, replacing Paul Jonas as sports director. His going invited bluster: Some said the Tigers' new radio sponsor, Stroh's beer, wanted its own mouthpiece ("Hell, if it hadn't been for that," Wester explained, "he'd have been there forever"); others, that Patrick's ego had become an annoyance to his employers ("The beer change was a cover," said a current major-league Voice. "Tiger officials were just fed up with his loudness").

In 1960, Patrick called Mutual's "Game of the Day"; later, he aired several Olympics, the Monte Carlo Grand Prix, the network's extensive coverage of tournament golf, and the 1971–73 radio side of "Monday Night Football." Then, as Wester's wife died on December 7, 1973, of cancer, the same disease maneuvered Patrick into its clamp. "When my wife was dying," Wester said, "Van tried to alleviate my pain. Maybe he gathered strength from her — I don't know. He spent that whole last year of his life fighting it off — he thought he could beat it, like he'd beaten everything else."

Van Patrick died on September 29, 1974, at fifty-eight, of complications from cancer surgery. Like a soldier in his pillbox, Patrick spent his last hours on earth in South Bend, on Game Weekend, as Notre Dame went forth against Purdue (the Irish were upset, 31–20). "It was a horrible *way* to die, but it was the right *place* to die," said Al Wester. "You see, Van truly loved sports — this happy, beautiful hulk of a man — and to live his final day near both the Fighting Irish and Mutual, then leave us a few hours later" gentled the final gasp of a man, it is easy to forget, who was respected by his colleagues; a patriarch to the end.

*   *   *

"It's always been my belief that people tune in to hear a *game*, not the broadcaster, and I think that was Van's belief," observed a Voice of the 1958–78 Giants and of the cross-bay Athletics since 1981. "I mean, some guys announce because their very souls demand it — they have to be behind the mike. Patrick wasn't like that. He had an ego, yes, and he enjoyed the business. To him, it was a living — an *excellent* living. But to do play-by-play — it wasn't an absolute necessity to the essence of his core."

"Do you see some of that in you?" I said.

"God, I hope so," he laughed. "Just as soon as I can afford it, I'm going to give all this up and make an exit — permanently — to the nearest golf course I can find."

Lon Simmons was a baseball, track, and football letterman at Burbank High

School who earned a scholarship to the University of Southern California, went instead to World War II, returned to baseball in the Phillies' organization, injured his back, became a civilian carpenter, and decided that if he meant to make the major leagues, he would need a more sturdy set of credentials.

"After my hopes of being a big-league player went down the drain," he said at the Pontchartrain Hotel in Patrick's Detroit, "I went into construction and as a carpenter I was getting $1.90 an hour."

"This would have been in the early fifties," I said.

"I remember, even now, how I used to pray it would rain so that I didn't have to work — I disliked it so. Then I'd pray it wouldn't rain because I needed money for my family."

"Either way, not a long-term commitment."

"I just knew it wasn't what I wanted to do the rest of my life," Lon said, "and sometimes, I remember that fact when I have frustrations as an announcer. As you go into other fields, it's always a good idea to keep in mind from whence you came."

In 1954, Simmons was hired as the sports director of KMJ in Fresno, California, ripening into a fresh, intelligent broadcaster and seizing the attention of the Gene Autry-owned Golden West radio station, San Francisco's KSFO. "Autry had bought the station in '56 and under the direction of a bright, tough general manager by the name of Bill Shaw, KSFO was putting together an aggressive sports staff," he said. "To head it up, they tried to get Chick Hearn from L.A., but he couldn't get out of his contract. Then they turned to me to do the 49ers' football games — which they'd bought the rights to — and hopefully, to the Giants' baseball team, still in New York."

"Whom they were *hoping* to acquire the rights to," I said.

"They were having discussions with the team when the Giants were still back East," and against this backdrop Simmons joined KSFO as *its* sports director in July 1957. Eight months later, the new sidekick of transplanted Russ Hodges began Year One of the California Giants.

From their playground at the Polo Grounds, the Giants settled, a continent away, in their temporary home, tiny, attractive Seals Stadium, a steep-rowed tenement which held fewer then twenty-three thousand fans. Celebrated for its polite reserve, "San Francisco went absolutely bonkers," Simmons said of the 1958 welcome. "This had always been a good minor-league baseball town. Now, what impressed me was that women, especially, went batty. Shopping in a supermarket, they'd hear the game on a radio at the meat counter, and they wouldn't leave for the vegetable aisle until, say, a Duke Snider went down on strikes. Then, satisfied, they'd leave."

Rousing curiosity, The Russ and Lon Show became a household hit, and its broadcasts caused one visitor to tab San Francisco "the City of the Deaf"; everyone, he said, walked around with a hearing aid — in reality, a transistor radio.

Their first year, the Giants finished third. By the end of 1959 — The Year the Giants *Almost* Won the Pennant — more than five hundred thousand transistors had been sold in the Bay Area. Over KSFO's fourteen-station network, they carried a streamer of home runs, slugfests, and cliffhangers to a public so bloated with baseball interest that one holdout muttered, "Good God! People will think we're like *Milwaukee* or something!"

"Those years seem like a million years ago," said Stu Smith, the Giants' director of community and public relations, who worked for KSFO from 1959 to 1974. "There are more than a few of us who wish we could retrieve them."

"For yourselves?"

"Well, that too," he said. "But I was thinking more about the ball club. As an outsider, you just can't believe how emotional it was. Russ and Lon were heroes. And from April through September, even if you wanted to, you couldn't escape their voices."

"True in a lot of cities," I said.

"If you'd been here," he suggested, "you'd know what I mean. You couldn't go anywhere and not hear them. You'd walk down the street and hear Lon and Russ from a dozen different directions. A restaurant—they'd have it on. Go to the opera—people would be wearing earplugs from their transistors. And because we played so many games then in the afternoon, it just flooded offices, bars, cable cars. It was absolute lunacy."

Not everyone felt such fervor. One sports columnist, Charles McCabe, of the *Chronicle*, spiked the Show as "a model, Madison Avenue style. Hodges . . . is, I fear, bush. Bush and out of date. And that goes for the junior partner too." Another scored "the duo's insipid Boy-Scoutry, just plantation slaves to the Good Master Horace." Replied Hodges, dismissively: "McCabe also called us shills—and he's right, we are. But as far as bush, it takes one to write one."

Hodges, legendarily untailored (several designers asked Russ, facetiously, to remove their labels from his clothing; that way, their image would be preserved), and the thick-framed, six-foot-four Simmons, whose ex-jock informality masked a knowledge of the game, formed an appealing and, by any standard, consciously humorous body. Once, after the team's third announcer, Bill Thompson, finished two innings of play-by-play, Simmons sighed and told his audience, "Lord, am I glad *that* dull stretch is over"; later, referring to a note on the ball park message board during the Giants' dreadful 1976 season, he confided, "It says, 'Happy Birthday, Debbie.' Too bad she left in the third inning"; and of a 49ers' game against Green Bay, he said, "You've heard of games that are a toss-up. This is a throw-up."

In the seventies, upbraiding the Giants' pallor, Simmons turned more severe. "What many owners have never understood is that you can't announce for them. And you can't be a salesman for teams that don't deserve it," he was saying. "When the team became lousy later on, you had to say they were lousy." But in 1958–59, added Smith, "The club was good, meaning there was no *need* to be severe. Even more, they were novel. And because Russ and Lon came on the scene at exactly the same time as the Giants, they were looked on—as the team was—not as a religion, necessarily, but as entertainment."

"Which they were," I said.

"They weren't expected to solemnize. They were expected to invigorate," Smith said. "And because in those days the Giants *meant* San Francisco, this city — which thinks very highly of itself and, above all, is lively, like the team was then — took exceptionally well to that."

In those carefree, leather-lunged years, with a club more stagy than splendid, San Francisco made the Giants' Westward-Ho transfer look permeated with foresight. Northern Californians, naturally, cheered the brilliant Mays, migrating from New York. But they became positively *blasted* — as did the newspapers, referring to "our Giants" — over players like Orlando (Baby Bull) Cepeda, with his wild and violent swing, and Jim Davenport, Felipe Alou, and the leggy 1959 phenom, Willie McCovey: players who matured there, in Baghdad on the Bay, and who, without the sapping effect of ties to New York, were, without apprehension, *theirs*.

Despite the park's thimble seating, Giants-watching at Seals Stadium was insouciant fun. "There was a freshness to it," Simmons said. "We knew there were worse places we could have found to play in." Improbably, the Giants managed to *find* a worse place, and opening on April 12, 1960, Candlestick Park quickly earned more contempt in this hotbed of critical review than Don Drysdale at the height of his supremacy. One writer dubbed the team's new home "a cancer ward," and plagued by freezing nights, peanut shells that eyeballed infielders, and sudden sandstorms that hindered play, Candlestick unfolded as a memorial to endless, relentless, carnivorous wind.

"The whole thing was a nightmare," said Lon Simmons. "To begin with, Seals Stadium was a San Francisco trademark, and this town is very provincial, maybe less now than then, but still proud and protective of its heritage. The park had been used for minor-league ball; it was part of the city. It had tremendous charm."

"Why didn't the Giants just expand Seals and stay there?" I wondered.

"There was a lot of talk about just that possibility, but there wasn't much parking around it," he said, "and the biggest problem was, even if you did, say, double its capacity, where would you put the club while the park was being renovated? So, without thinking, the city just rushed pell-mell into building a new stadium. And why they put it near the water, out on Candlestick Point, where it was as cold as anywhere else in the city and where the winds were terrible, no one with any brains will *ever* know."

I retreated nearly three decades. "Think back to when Candlestick opened. Was it a disappointment even then?"

The memory jarred him. "People were so enthused about this park — and they came out those first few months and already it was an embarrassment. 'Jesus,' you know, 'is that all there is?' "

"Was it just the wind?"

"No," Simmons argued. "There was hardly anything good about it. If it's cold at the Oakland Coliseum, it's bitter at Candlestick. If it's a breeze at the Coliseum, it's a gale at Candlestick. The access around the park was — and remains — terrible. I can get home in a few minutes from the A's. From Candlestick, with a big crowd, it takes forever. It's dirty, not well-kept. Now you've got rowdyism, thugs, just utter decay."

"And back then?"

"In most parks, you get some fans that'll say on a beautiful evening, 'Let's go out and see a game tonight.' It's a pleasant time. With the Giants, yes, you'll get people to go out when they're winning, but nobody in their right mind would go out to Candlestick and expect to have a pleasant time."

Brushing up against the elements, the Giants thumped back. In 1961, the season Candlestick hosted the All-Star Game and pitcher Stu Miller was blown off the mound, Cepeda bashed forty-six homers to lead the league. A year later, San Francisco caught the Dodgers in regular-season game No. 162, won the playoff series in the final inning, and extended the Grand Event to McCovey's Game-Seven final out. The next season, Stretch whacked forty-four home runs and Juan Marichal no-hit the Colt .45s; in 1965, pounding fifty-two over the wall, Mays was named Most Valuable Player; the year afterward, the Giants placed six players on the All-Star team, Marichal hurled his fourth twenty-victory season in a row, and Say Hey hit his 512th homer to break Mel Ott's National League record. "Today, the Giants have no superstars, nobody worth going out to see," said Simmons. "Back then, they had almost too *many* superstars. You almost didn't know where to look first." Five straight times, the Stonehams finished second. Fans grew restless. Attendance fell. Past his prime, Mays became merely excellent. In 1968, the Athletics invaded the Bay Area, dividing the market. On April 19, 1971, Russ Hodges died.

"The tragedy is that Russ had just retired," said Simmons. "He'd just had enough of the traveling, the constancy, the physical and mental punishment of play-by-play. It just caught up with him."

"But he was still doing some P.R. work for the Giants—appearances, speeches," I said.

"He hadn't totally shut down," mused the Glendale, California, native. "He was going to do TV games and radio when I was busy doing the 49ers. But it wasn't the same, and I think Russ knew it."

"How so?"

"He came to me in March and said, 'Now, let's see. You'll be doing football on August 4 and 11'—he was looking forward to doing radio so much. And I really *feel*—I don't know this for a fact—I just feel that in his mind, Russ felt it was over. I think Russ Hodges died of a broken heart."

"Does he belong in the Hall of Fame?" I asked. "He got in in 1980, ahead of some guys that broadcast a lot longer and, frankly, as Russ himself said, had much better voices."

Recently, two Voices of big-league teams had privately blistered Hodges' ability. His selection, they said, ahead of Saam, Caray, Prince, or Nelson, reflected "politics, pure and simple," claimed the more emphatic of the pair. "Russ broadcast in New York, made a lot of friends, was a nice guy. But he no more belongs in the Hall of Fame—especially when you consider the truly great ones they've left out—than my Aunt Agnes. It's the New York baseball lobby. If Russ had broadcast in Cincinnati, he wouldn't have made it even now."

Simmons turned wintry. "That's the most ridiculous thing I've ever heard of," he said, angrily. "Russ was outstanding. I think he was the most accomplished broadcaster I've ever heard. You can take your Scullys and Barbers. I'll take Russ any day. And even more than that, he was a friend — just wonderful character. We used to call him 'the Fabulous Fat Man' — and, believe me, he was more fabulous than fat."

"Not the ego of a Cosell?" I said.

"Christ, I'll never forget 1958, when he welcomed me so warmly into the booth — there was no star/partner complex. He never *thought* of himself as a star," Simmons said. "Once, I was doing play-by-play for the 49ers, and I needed someone to do color. Russ said, 'Hell, I'll do it,' and this came from the Number One broadcaster. But that was Russ — to help a friend, he'd take a secondary role."

"A Hall of Famer."

"In *and* out of the booth," he said. "You talk to anyone he ever worked for or with. They'll tell you the same."

Six months after Hodges' death, the Giants won the Western Division title and drew a million people for the first time since 1967. But by 1974 attendance dropped to 519,997; two years later, Horace Stoneham offered the club to Labatt's Brewery of Toronto; it took two businessmen, Robert Lurie and Arthur (Bud) Herseth, to match Labatt's price and rescue the franchise from Canada.

"In a way," said Simmons, "I was sorry to see Horace go. He and I were friends. But we had our differences."

"Like when Stoneham [upset over Simmons' "ripping the team"] almost fired you?" I said.

"See, and this is true for more owners than just Horace — he didn't mind me telling the truth in those early years. Why? Because when I did, out came good news. But when we got bad — and, boy, did we get bad — and I told the truth, he called it getting on his players."

"What'd you tell him?"

"I just went to him and said, 'Look, Horace, I wasn't hired to be your P.R. agent. My first responsibility is to the station that pays my salary. Then it's to the people listening and sponsors. Only then comes the team. And I can't be worried about what you're thinking. If we're getting our brains beat out, that's when I'm going to start having a good time, tell jokes, do anything to keep the people listening. Roaming from the action, ripping errors — in the long run, 'cause it retains fan interest, it builds credibility and *helps* the team.' Well, Horace said he agreed. But he didn't like it."

Then, in a combustible 1978, the Giants led their division in August before finishing a vigorous third; more than 1,740,000 customers filed into the Wind-O-Rama. For Lon Simmons, sharing the nineteenth season of Candlestick's disreputable life, the club's brief, unlikely contact with the blue-chip stocks of first carted him back to the good days, to a simpler kind of happiness.

"Everything means more when you're younger," Simmons, sixty, explained. "When we first enter a situation, we feel that that's how it's done best. It's closer to our understanding. For instance, now I find that kids making noise, screwing around on the bus, bugs me more than it did twenty-five years ago. Yet I don't think the players have changed that much. *I've* changed. I've gotten older. Well, it's the same with the Giants — it would be difficult to get anything closer to your emotions than their early years in town."

"Did '78 come close?"

"In a sense, it was semi-*déjà vu*. It's always that way when you're in a pennant race. At least there was one side benefit. With bigger crowds, if you sat in the upper deck and died, somebody'd actually find you before an entire week was gone."

Before the *year* was gone, the Giants were pirated by KNBR, the Bay Area's 50,000-watt NBC station. "What happened is that KSFO lost Bill Shaw to retirement and had some other changes, and the station went downhill. And Lurie and the station's new people didn't mix — it wasn't the right chemistry. So here comes KNBR, and they sold Lurie a bill of goods. They offer more money for the rights. They tell the Giants that because they're more powerful than KSFO, they'd do a better job of promoting."

"So the Giants bit," I said.

"Yes, they went over in 1979 and for the next two years, for the first time in twenty years, on KSFO — no baseball."

Deprived of its back-yard commodity, KSFO belatedly activated itself and paid a visit to the American League side of San Francisco Bay. There, in 1981, the long-time station of the Giants became the flagship outlet of the green-and-gold Athletics. More astoundingly, the long-time Voice of the Giants, still employed by KSFO, excited conversation by chattering as a new Voice of the once-menacing A's.

"Your going from one club to the other," I said, "is like Caray going cross-town from the White Sox to the Cubs."

"Well, the only difference," Lon said, "is that there was that two-year gap in '79 and '80 when I didn't do baseball. So the reaction wasn't that strong. The real reaction came when KNBR *didn't* take me when the Giants went over there — after all, I'd been with the team ever since 1958, with the exception of two years in the mid-seventies [when Simmons' wife died, and Lon took a two-year leave of absence]. It made it sort of tough for Lindsey Nelson when he first came to town."

"How did the A's' fans accept you?"

Simmons chuckled, faintly. "The only problem there was came from the boosters' fans — you know, the real hard-core. They didn't see *how* the A's could take that Giants' SOB. But they sort of calmed down, as those types are prone to do."

"If Charlie Finley still owned the club, would you be doing the games?"

"The A's wouldn't even *have* a station," he said. "The story is that when Walter Haas bought the club from Finley, Roy Eisenhardt, his president, started a tremendous promotional, marketing, publicity campaign. And it was only after Finley left that KSFO was interested in the A's. Hell, there were years that the club was winning championships when their games had been on a college station. And the topper is that after the A's went with KSFO in 1981, our station stole practically all the stations in the entire Giants' Network from *their* new flagship."

"KNBR didn't know how to package the network?" I said.

"Not only that, " he said, "but now, for the first time ever, it was the *A's* that people began to talk about in this entire area — especially when, under Billy Martin, they started to win. You saw Oakland caps on the street. The crowds were great. And today, now that both clubs have slumped off, the area is up for grabs. Whichever team is on top's going to be the team that draws."

"Which wasn't true in the A's' first years."

"Oh, no," Simmons said. "Up until very recently, no question that even in their lousy years, the Giants were the Bay Area's team."

A security blanket for Northern California's baseball public, Simmons had lived almost three decades rich in lingering experience — a 1968 Gaylord Perry no-hitter against the champion Cardinals, the uppercut pyrotechnics of Dave (King Kong) Kingman, a mystical early-eighties fad dubbed "Billy Ball," the celebratory terror of Cepeda, McCovey, and Mays. I wondered, though, if anything had been more indelible, more terminally stamped on his mind, than those first crazy and anticipatory years? "God, no," Lon Simmons said. "The Giants *owned* this area then. And they own a lot of my memories today."

*   *   *

If a baseball broadcaster is good enough, lasts long enough, and is possessed of an easy familiarity, he becomes almost an extended member of the family. He evolves into a friend, a reality/rehearsal repeated daily, into a form larger than some Voice of an organized and mercenary team.

Throughout broadcasting, no baseball manner has spoken more distinctively of *friendship*, as opposed to stagecraft or egomania, than that of the lyricist, poet, and historian also known as Ernie Harwell.

By the 1980s, after a quarter-century as the Voice of the Tigers, he had emerged as the upper Midwest's diocesan tongue, his company beheld by more people, possibly, than any man or woman in the suzerainty of Detroit. Sensitive, he was — and *is* — not self-centered; effective, he was not affected; ingenious, he was not disingenuous; he would not enter a room and fleece it.

"Ernie Harwell is a professional," Bengals' fans like to say. Yes, but there are many professionals. "Ernie's got a great voice," they add, unerringly. Yes, but from McNamee to Scully, great voices abound. "He's got the experience too," they say, fleshing out his skeleton. Yes, but as Curt Gowdy showed in the 1970s, broadcasting experience is not an unfettered shield. It can abruptly convert itself to overexposure, an ennui of "Oh, not him again!"

What is it, then, that has made Ernie Harwell the Ronald Reagan of baseball broadcasting — a man almost impossible to dislike, even if one despised his Tigers/politics? From Brooklyn in 1948 to the 1950 Giants to Baltimore four years later to Briggs Stadium in 1960, he has worn better, more durably, than any announcer I can think of. "Eisenhower has, and retains, a magic . . . that is peculiarly his: he makes people happy," Theodore White wrote in a passage reminiscent of Harwell. People meet Ernie — and they are happy. Listeners hear his disarming voice — and they are reminded in a twinkly way, I believe, somehow like personae from a Pepsi commercial, how constant baseball/America remain in a strange and turmoiled world.

"He probably could be elected mayor of Detroit, if not governor of the state. He has that hold on people. Ernie Harwell is probably the most popular and best-known voice in all of Michigan — more popular and better-known than the governor," *The Sporting News* rhapsodized in 1981. "Kids, mothers, grandfathers, cops, firemen, teachers, bankers, and insurance men spend their summers with Ernie Harwell. He has been in their lives for more than two decades, a cherished friend who brings them the sounds of baseball."

How many barkers, shysters, and charlatans use the word *special* in ushering to one's attention a deodorant, program, or politician? Ask anyone who knows him: *This* man with the slight frame, thinning hair, and Magnolia-scented accents, whose idea of a magic off-season evening is to sit at the organ in his living room and compose a melody — *this* man is special.

Nice is as nice does, a high school teacher advised me. In a profession where, miming Marion Marlowe in the musical *The Sound of Music*, "Nothing is as wonderful as I," Ernie Harwell was special, largely, because he was almost extraordinarily *nice*. At spring training or on the same Detroit city corner where Ty Cobb played, seeing you after a lapse of days or years — it never mattered — he would smile and have something pleasant to say. After more than four decades of broadcasting, he still delighted in self-deprecation, still retained the polish and subtlety that had always marked his narrative. He was not a hater; he sought endlessly to understand other points of view. More than any contemporary I knew, to evoke real anger, one must fearfully provoke him; even his jibes and put-downs were whimsically cast.

What compounded this sense of wonderment was Harwell's versatility. At age sixteen, he was a sportswriter for the *Atlanta Constitution*. In World War II, he was overseas sports editor of the Marine magazine, *Leatherneck*. He contributed regularly to *The Saturday Evening Post, Esquire, Collier's,* and *Reader's Digest*. His essay, "The Game for All America," is perhaps the most stylish tribute ever paid to baseball. He compiled one of the most complete personal collections of baseball records and memorabilia in existence. In the eighties, the composer of nearly fifty recorded songs, he had written lyrics for Merilee Rush, Barbara Lewis, Tommy Overstreet, and B. J. Thomas. "That's the amazing thing — of all the announcers I've met, none is more talented beyond the microphone or has more of a *reason* to have a big head than Ernie. And yet his feet are planted on the ground. He likes everybody. Everybody likes him," said Red Sox' announcer Ned Martin. "You see some guys who haven't done a damn thing by comparison and still they think they're God's gift to creation. Then you look at Ernie, who's a giant and who has time for everyone. The comparison makes you laugh."

Harwell was born in Washington, Georgia, on January 25, 1918, and influenced, one mused, by its lush density and steamy, romantic past, reveled in early fantasy. With wit and osmotic imagination, he fastened on the métier of broadcasting—more literate than the movies, more mystical than print.

"I'm not sure when it happened, when this sort of lifeblood ambition started," Ernie was explaining. "I think, in fact, it may have been at a hobby fair as a kid. I remember there was a puppet show with a boxing exhibition featuring Young Stribling and Max Schmeling."

"Your first stab at re-creations," I suggested.

"I wasn't simply behind the curtain," he said. "I was beneath the stage. That's where I gave the blow-by-blow from. Stribling was a native Georgian and a great favorite, and we usually managed to have him knock Schmeling out. It was the first meeting for me of speech and sports, and I think I got the idea that I wanted to be a broadcaster."

There was incongruity in Harwell's hope, for as a child—talking baseball in Doc Green's drugstore in Washington and striving to imitate McNamee— the tow-head stuttered and "mangled the letter *s*." His impediment frustrated but did not overcome; through special speech lessons—"expression" lessons, they were called in the South—Harwell clobbered self-consciousness, entered debate and declamation contests, and graduated from a hawker of soda, pop-corn, and newspapers in Ponce de Leon Park, home of the Southern Associa-tion Crackers, to bat boy in the visiting team's dugout to regular writer, as a sophomore in high school, for "The Bible of Baseball."

"I was fifteen at the time and I *loved* baseball. In fact, I tell people that I haven't paid to see a game since I was ten," he observed. " 'Anything to get in free'—that's been my motto. And at this time I'd already been reading *The Sporting News* for years. I also thought their coverage of my Crackers was, to say the least, inadequate."

"This would have been about 1934."

"The year of the Gas House Gang," he said. "So, in the 'anything goes' spirit of one's youth—and with no experience as a baseball writer—I sent off a letter to Edgar G. Brands, then the editor of the paper." Thinking of the signature, he laughed. "To appear older than I was, I signed the letter 'W. Earnest Har-well,' and, naturally, I didn't dare tell my age. Later, from *The Sporting News* I get this letter back. Mr. Brands asked me to 'shoot some stuff along.' "

Harwell's first article adorned *TSN* of August 6, 1934; for the next fourteen years, he was its Atlanta correspondent. He also wrote for *Baseball Magazine* and part-time—"for a whopping $10 a week"—for the *Constitution*, and won a nationwide contest for the "best high-school column." Echoing with esoteric, unheard-of ("for central Georgia," a friend tut-tutted) words, his prose paid the way to Emory University, near Atlanta, where Harwell met Lulu Tank-erseley, the Hazard, Kentucky, beauty queen he would soon marry, followed sports as the college newspaper editor (*The Saturday Evening Post*, then the Queen Mother of weekly periodicals, termed Ernie "one of America's top young writers"), earned his bachelor of arts degree in 1940, and one day that spring—watching an Emory track meet—received a call to report immediately to station WSB, Atlanta.

"A classmate of mine, Marcus Bartlett, I guess liked my voice in speech class, so without me being aware of his shenanigans, he got WSB to ask me to come over there," he related. "Once I got to the station, I was hustled into a deserted studio and told to read the baseball scores and other sports news out of that morning's *Constitution*."

"What's the catch?"

"That unbeknown to me, station officials were listening in an adjacent room."

"In effect," I said, "an audition."

"That very day I was offered a job as sports editor. The next week I started a fifteen-minute daily sports program, and before long I was doing Georgia Tech football games."

Before long, the young polemicist was also in the Marines, and in those forties years of death and expectancy he doted on *Leatherneck*, wrote articles from the Near East for "The Bible," interviewed Eleanor Roosevelt, and covered the retaking of Wake Island. In 1946, he returned — to Georgia, where he visited hospitals and talked baseball with sick and wounded servicemen; to radio, broadcasting Crackers' games for two-and-one-half years; and to an enviable vantage point as, arguably, the most credible sports voice in the entire South.

Then, in August 1948, as we have seen, Harwell traveled to Ebbets Field; the next year, he formed a sensitive complement to Barber. On the recommendation of his savings account — "I just got a better deal; it was strictly commercial; Mr. Rickey was kind enough to let me out of my Brooklyn contract" — he moved to the Polo Grounds in time for the 1950 season; there, for four happy and often compelling years, one heard a superior Giants' broadcast team, distinguished also by its modesty. "God, when I think of the weird and obnoxious people who go into this vocation," Jim Woods said, "it's a miracle to have in one booth two such soft-spoken guys as Ernie and Russ."

In the early fifties, Harwell and Allen, Barber and Woods, and even the Kentuckian Hodges comprised a southern expatriate community. "How'd you folks all wind up in the same city?" I said.

"Well," Harwell responded, "I could say it proves we were all too lazy to work for a living. But, of course, that would be facetious. It would be specious too. I don't know — it's a tantalizing question. I think it goes back to the fact that we grew up in the same kind of semirural atmosphere of the South. We came from a story-telling, anecdotal background — the kind of stories that fit in so well with a leisurely game like baseball. We learned early on how to tell a tale."

"Any other reasons?" I said.

"Don't forget that along with our backgrounds, we also grew up in an educational type of climate where we learned how to use the language. We all went to college — not so common in those days. I know there were many professors that Red admired. Melvin had his law experience. And I grew up with a lot of people who loved literature. Really, it so happened that in this particular time, all of these announcers were quite erudite."

"And you worked with two of them."

"Yes, with Russ and Red," he said.

"Compare them."

"Barber was much more demanding, very strict with the people around him, on and off the air. Russ was more of an Everyman's announcer," said Harwell, "not as flashy, no gimmicks, just sort of talked the game. And he was *very* relaxed — not as prepared as Red, but he sort of said, 'It's a game. Let's not take it as life or death.' "

"Who was better?"

"Oh, Red."

"The best *ever*?" I asked.

"I think, interestingly enough, it's a guy who entered the big leagues when I did and who's still going," he said. "Vin Scully has a great voice and command of the language, and a penchant for detail that's almost intimidating. And I don't think he's lost a thing since he broke in in the early fifties."

Enter, in Scully's fifth year, 1954 and Baltimore's return (after an absence of *fifty-two* years) to a kind of major-league euphoria. On April 15, inheriting Bud Blattner's St. Louis Browns, more than three hundred thousand baseball- and (it would soon become apparent) victory-starved fans lined the route along Howard, Charles, and Baltimore Streets to cheer a melange of floats, bands, cheerleaders, Orioles' officials, and, finally, the ex-Brownies themselves. "It was a gigantic parade, one of the greatest thrills I've ever had," recalled the new Voice of the Birds. "An absolutely stirring welcome to Baltimore." More stirring, by far, than the season that was to follow.

That first year, Ernie, Howie Williams, and Bailey Goss — sorrowing over WCBM Radio and WMAR-TV; sponsored by the National Brewing Company — called each of the Orioles' 54 victories and 100 defeats. "We opened the season with eighteen old Browns," Harwell said. "It was obvious early on that the team wasn't going to overwhelm the world." Their household, more horseshoed than the Polo Grounds, was the then-47,806-seat Memorial Stadium, with its abbreviated foul lines (309 feet) and monstrous outfield expanse (center field stood 445 feet from home plate; the power alleys were a foot longer). In its early years, the stadium lacked a fence from left-center to right-center field; alone among big-league shelters, a hedge served as its barrier.

"It was wonderful," mused the liberated Georgian. "It never really entered the area of play — the hedge was too far away for anyone to hit. But, you see, where I'd come from — Ponce de Leon Park — had a magnolia tree growing in deep center field. What we had in Baltimore was similar — sort of Rhett Butler come north."

"The American League's answer to the ivy at Wrigley Field," I said.

"It was just such an unusual touch, so southern. I thoroughly enjoyed it."

In the mid-fifties, he enjoyed few home runs; Memorial Stadium was even more of a pitcher's refuge than Griffith Stadium, an hour's ride away. "Put together the long distances and our Punch-and-Judy attack," Harwell said, "and the long ball was like Prohibition — a forgotten tool." The 1954 Orioles bashed only nineteen home runs in seventy-seven home games; opponents

clubbed twenty-three; for the season, Vern Stephens led Baltimore with eight
home runs and all of forty-six runs batted in. Through the endemic mediocrity of the decade's heel — relieved only by such touchstones as Brooks Robinson's Orioles' debut on September 17, 1955, four straight Birds' shutouts in
June 1957 and a 19–6 August thumping of Cleveland, the signing of "Kiddie
Corps" pitchers Chuck Estrada, Jerry Walker, Milt Pappas, and Billy O'Dell,
and a cathartic 1958 in which Gus Triandos hit thirty homers, Hoyt Wilhelm
no-hit the Yankees, and the city hosted the All-Star Game — W. Earnest Harwell brought Baltimore as close to a state of joyousness as its forgettable clubs
would allow.

"He had more authenticity as an announcer than anyone I've ever heard.
Ernie could extrapolate on anything — poetry, history; if you talked to him
about baseball manufacturing, he'd be able to tell you what went into the
baseball, how many stitches on it, and how it was sewn," said John Steadman,
the long-time columnist and sports editor of the *Baltimore News American*.

"How was he received?" I said.

"If there was one word I'd use to describe Ernie, it would be *educational*. He
was a great teacher of baseball. And he was highly respected because he didn't
talk in clichés. When he said something, he said it authoritatively. People
said — and this was especially important since big-league ball was new here —
'This guy knows his sports.' "

"Thorough?"

"He was a modest guy, no extravagances of any kind," Steadman avowed,
"and when he was broadcasting Colts' games in the fifties — I was doing color
at the time — he was the only announcer I've known who wanted to look at the
game films. I'd drop them off at his home and he'd study, look, analyze. Plus,
Ernie had a wonderful tempo, a great delivery, and no controversy — just a lot
of laudable qualities."

Drawling and even-handed, Harwell found receptivity in willfully un-
fashionable Baltimore. "The ball popped out of Strickland's fingers like a wet
watermelon and everybody's safe!" he exclaimed of Cleveland's George Strickland, muffing a ground ball. Sincere and trustworthy, he was country in a way
that radiated affection. Yet there was an urbanity to his mind and an intensity
too, reflecting themselves most vividly in the 1955 panegyric which first appeared in *The Sporting News*, has been praised as a classic, and hangs today in
the Hall of Fame at Cooperstown: "The Game for All America."

> Baseball is President Eisenhower tossing out the first ball of the
> season; and a pudgy schoolboy playing catch with his dad on a Mis-
> sissippi farm.
> It's the big-league pitcher who sings in night clubs. And the Holly-
> wood singer who pitches to the Giants in spring training.
> A tall, thin old man waving a scorecard from his dugout — that's base-
> ball. So is the big, fat guy with a bulbous nose running out one of his
> 714 home runs with mincing steps.
> It's America, this baseball. A re-issued newsreel of boyhood dreams.

Dreams lost somewhere between boy and man. It's the Bronx cheer and the Baltimore farewell. The left-field screen in Boston, the right-field dump at Nashville's Sulphur Dell, the open stands in San Francisco, the dusty, wind-swept diamond at Albuquerque. And a rock home plate and chicken wire backstop — anywhere.

There's a man in Mobile who remembers a triple he saw Honus Wagner hit in Pittsburgh 46 years ago. That's baseball. So is the scout reporting that a 16-year-old sandlot pitcher in Cheyenne is the new "Walter Johnson."

It's a wizened little man shouting insults from the safety of his bleacher seat. And a big, smiling first baseman playfully tousling the hair of a youngster outside the players' gate.

Baseball is a spirited race of man against man, reflex against reflex. A game of inches. Every skill is measured. Every heroic, every failing is seen and cheered — or booed. And then becomes a statistic.

In baseball, democracy shines its clearest. Here the only race that matters is the race to the bag. The creed is the rule book. Color is something to distinguish one team's uniform from another.

Baseball is Sir Alexander Fleming, discoverer of penicillin, asking his Brooklyn hosts to explain Dodger signals. It's player Moe Berg speaking seven languages and working crossword puzzles in Sanskrit. It's a scramble in the box seats for a foul — and a $125 suit ruined. A man barking into a hot microphone about a cool beer, that's baseball. So is the sports writer telling a .383 hitter how to stride, and a 20-victory pitcher trying to write his impressions of the World Series.

Baseball is a ballet without music. Drama without words. A carnival without kewpie dolls.

A housewife in California couldn't tell you the color of her husband's eyes, but she knows that Yogi Berra is hitting .337, has brown eyes, and used to love to eat bananas with mustard. That's baseball. So is the bright sanctity of Cooperstown's Hall of Fame. And the former big leaguer, who is playing out the string in a Class B loop.

Baseball is continuity. Pitch to pitch. Inning to inning. Game to game. Series to series. Season to season.

It's rain, rain, rain splattering on a puddled tarpaulin as thousands sit in damp disappointment. And the click of typewriters and telegraph keys in the press box — like so many awakened crickets. Baseball is a cocky batboy. The old-timer whose batting average increases every time he tells it. A lady celebrating a home team rally by mauling her husband with a rolled-up scorecard.

Baseball is the cool, clear eyes of Rogers Hornsby, the flashing spikes of Ty Cobb, an overaged pixie named Rabbit Maranville, and Jackie Robinson testifying before a Congressional hearing.

Baseball? It's just a game — as simple as a ball and a bat. Yet, as complex as the American spirit it symbolizes. It's a sport, business — and sometimes even religion.

Baseball is Tradition in flannel knickerbockers. And Chagrin in being picked off base. It is Dignity in the blue serge of an umpire running the game by rule of thumb. It is Humor, holding its sides when an errant puppie eludes two groundskeepers and the fastest outfielder. And Pathos, dragging itself off the field after being knocked from the box.

Nicknames are baseball. Names like Zeke and Pie and Kiki and Home Run and Cracker and Dizzy and Dazzy.

Baseball is a sweaty, steaming dressing room where hopes and feelings are as naked as the men themselves. It's a dugout with spike-scarred flooring. And shadows across an empty ball park. It's the endless list of names in box scores, abbreviated almost beyond recognition.

The holdout is baseball, too. He wants 55 grand or he won't turn a muscle. But, it's also the youngster who hitchhikes from South Dakota to Florida just for a tryout.

Arguments, Casey at the Bat, old cigarette cards, photographs, Take Me Out to the Ball Game — all of them are baseball.

Baseball is a rookie — his experience no bigger than the lump in his throat — trying to begin fulfillment of a dream. It's a veteran, too — a tired old man of 35, hoping his aching muscles can drag him through another sweltering August and September.

For nine innings, baseball is the story of David and Goliath, of Samson, Cinderella, Paul Bunyan, Homer's Iliad and the Count of Monte Cristo.

Willie Mays making a brilliant World Series catch. And then going home to Harlem to play stick-ball in the street with his teen-age pals — that's baseball. So is the husky voice of a doomed Lou Gehrig saying, "I'm the luckiest guy in the world."

Baseball is cigar smoke, hot-roasted peanuts, *The Sporting News,* winter trades, "Down in front," and the Seventh Inning Stretch. Sore arms, broken bats, a no-hitter, and the strains of the Star-Spangled Banner.

Baseball is a highly-paid Brooklyn catcher telling the nation's business leaders: "You have to be a man to be a big leaguer, but you have to have a lot of little boy in you, too."

This is a game for America, this baseball!

A game for boys and for men.

"What prompted it?" I asked Harwell three decades later. "I've read a lot of tributes to baseball — none of them like this."

"I had a couple of speaking engagements in the winter of 1954," he said, "and this one day I just thought I'd sit down and jot out some notes on baseball. And they sort of came together in a prose poem, and after a couple days polishing up, it was finished. Then *The Sporting News* printed it in their Opening Day issue of 1955, and every year that J.G. Taylor Spink was publisher [through 1962], they ran it as an editorial."

"It's been translated into how many different languages?"

"About six, I guess," he said. "A few months ago, this fellow in Rome called me and wanted to put it in his baseball manual — you know, the game's taken off there like a rocket. But the reaction has always been heart-warming — and it wasn't for me, necessarily, but I hope for the sentiments people feel for the game."

From almost everyone in Baltimore, Ernie Harwell had known love. But in the schizophrenia of progress, beginning in 1960—at forty-two, already his seventeenth season in radio—he would know Detroit, with its blue baseball bloodlines; the picturesque Bengals' empyrean, with its center-field flagpole acres from home plate, an overhang in the right-field upper deck, and virtually every seat up close to the field; and the city's avid baseball fans, with their shared communion of lore. "When Van Patrick decided to go to Mutual," Harwell said, "the vacancy opened here. And I guess they wanted someone who would bring a low-key style and who was going to stay a while, provide a continuity and a link."

"What did you find the year you got here?" I asked.

"The Tiger fan is very knowledgeable," he said. "Knowledgeable and loyal, steadier than in most towns. The town is steeped in tradition, and that tradition is handed down from one generation to the next, so there is a strong sense of history, even among younger fans."

"No ballgirls or mascots. No instructions on the scoreboard to cheer."

"There would be a rebellion if there were," Harwell proclaimed. "Baseball's the show here. You go into a restaurant in the surrounding area, even during the off-season, and listen to the conversation at the next table. Before long, you'll hear baseball being discussed."

"You've broadcast for four clubs in four parks. What did you think of them?"

Briefly, he fell silent. "Ebbets Field meant a lot to me because it was the first big-league park I ever broadcast from," he said, curiously pensive. "It was compact, friendly—you were right on the field. And the fans were characters— it's the only place I've ever known where people made a *vocation* out of being a fan. Fanatically loyal."

"The Polo Grounds?"

"The seats weren't as close to the diamond. The fans were different—there was a tremendous history that was lacking in Brooklyn. And it was an older crowd—a lot of stockbrokers and actors who grew up on the Giants. The younger fans—the trendies—went to the Yankees. The real fans stayed at Coogan's Bluff. Then Baltimore—it had good fans but only a minor-, not major-, league tradition. And finally Detroit, an interesting blend."

"In what way?" I said.

"The park itself is like Ebbets Field—only bigger—and it's my favorite park ever to broadcast from. But the fans are more like the Giants'—a history there as well, even if it's a younger crowd. I may be partisan, but I think many baseball people would agree—combining fans and the ball park, there's no better franchise in sports."

Recalling the same pleasance where Gehringer cavorted and Cochrane dazzled and Al Kaline delineated the term *ballplayer*, the stardust of Harwell's second Tigers' season reappeared. Sixth the preceding year, the 1961 Bengals lost only sixty-one games, repelled the Yankees until early September, and attracted more than 1.6 million people onto the ramps and concourses of recently renamed Tiger Stadium. Rocky Colavito drove out 45 home runs and

knocked in 140 runs. Norman Cash — otherwise, never hitting above .283 in
a seventeen-year career — poked 41 homers and 132 RBIs, and at .361 was
baseball's highest hitter. Frank Lary won twenty-three games; Jim Bunning
and Don Mossi added thirty-two. Rookies Jake Wood and Steve Boros sparkled
in the infield. Kaline batted .324 and fielded superbly. A nebulous entity called
Terry Fox blossomed in the bull pen. "It was the most exciting season I'd
known since the Giants in '51," Harwell said. "This was the year Maris and
Mantle hit 115 home runs — more than Ruth and Gehrig in 1927 — and still,
with a couple breaks, we could have beaten the Yankees and edged them for
the pennant."

Today, I recollect that late summer vividly — how the Tigers, leading most
of the season, rolled into New York for a September 3–5 series; how enormous
hordes crowded into the triple tiers for a trio of Yankees' victories; and how,
over radio and television, Allen, Dean, and Harwell instilled the weekend set
with a grand and unleavened eloquence.

"On the night of the first game of the series, the Lions had a preseason
game scheduled back in Detroit," said Harwell. "But interest in the Tigers was
so high that the Lions postponed their game until three days later — when the
baseball series was over — so people could stay home and watch the series on
TV. That whole season was baseball at its best." It was also the Tigers' last
sustained gaiety until the next-to-last year of the 1960s.

"There are three years I remember in the decade," said the Voice of the
Tigers. "In '61, we came so close. Then, in 1967, the summer of the fires and
killings in Detroit [in America's worst urban riot, forty-three people died], the
Tigers came up to the final day of the season with a chance to win the pennant.
We had a double-header scheduled against the Angels."

"Win both games and you tied the Red Sox."

"Yes, and we would have forced a playoff. But we lost the second game. It
was a crushing heartbreak — to come all that way and lose."

"Then came '68," I said.

"A fabulous year," he said, fondly. "What I remember is that the papers were
on strike that year. A lot of players used to kid that the reason we won the
pennant is that there weren't writers around to bug them. But the fascinating
thing is that the whole season seemed like something a writer *would* invent. We
won games every way imaginable."

Entering 1968, no one was certain if the Tigers would win the pennant. Or
was it rather that everyone had focused on whether the city would burn? After
its awful summer of 1967, Detroit became an armed fortress. Men purchased
firearms; housewives bought triple locks for their suburban homes. Would
stores again be looted and lives erased? Would smoke again sway over the
streets ringing Tiger Stadium? The truth is that in the spring of 1968 — as
Martin Luther King and Bobby Kennedy were murdered, unrest tormented
168 cities, and America itself seemed a carnage — no one knew.

Too much can be made of a baseball team. It is not a social instrument; it
is not a crucible of world diplomacy; it is not a cure for Original Sin. Yet, in 1968,

in this terrified and troubled city, the Tigers lanced a people's wounds. "A strange thing happened" that summer, Joe Falls has written. "The ball club . . . started winning games. . . . Each game seemed to produce a new drama, a new hero. As the streets began to heat up, people began staying in at night to listen to the games on radio. You could walk through an entire alley and not miss one of Ernie Harwell's calls. And when the team was at home . . . there was something to do now — a place to go. A place where it was exciting. A place where a guy could let off steam."

The Tigers of that year were gifted as a team, helpful to Detroit's serenity, and — we have forgotten it now — beneficent to the sport of baseball.

The 1968 regular season, named The Year of the Pitcher, had been an interminable dud — only *one* American Leaguer hit more than .300; the two leagues sustained a record 339 shutouts; even to purists, it was obvious that a horrible imbalance had seized the game. While professional football flaunted its violence and Nielsen ratings, baseball — already smeared as inert and overly cerebral — endured a year in which, as though to reaffirm the critics' harshness, *nothing seemed to be happening.* Series after week after boring homestand, pack thinkers asked not whether baseball was dying — that conclusion, apparently, was foregone — but instead, why a mere decade after the Duke, Big Klu, and the Rock of Colavito battered pitchers, no one any longer could *hit* the ball? Over both leagues, zeroes assaulted the scoreboard; paid admissions and radio/TV ratings went the way of runs; and the pennant races were depressingly one-sided. Only in Cincinnati, whose Reds — *mirabile dictu* — batted .273; and St. Louis, whose champion "El Birdos" won ninety-seven games; and, most agreeably, Detroit — where Denny McLain won thirty-one decisions, Jim Northrup bombed four grand-slam homers, the "Tiges" won forty games from the seventh inning on, and this ancient franchise smashed its all-time attendance mark — did the excitement and daily goings-on even *resemble* The Game That Had Been (and, mercifully, Would Come Again).

"It was an interesting dichotomy," Harwell said. "For a lot of folks in baseball — as opposed to just Detroit — 1968 was a bad year. That following winter they lowered the pitching mound and reduced the strike zone — anything to restore some offense. For them, The Year of the Pitcher [hereafter, TYOTP] was The Year to Forget."

"But not for Detroit," I said.

"Who'd *want* to forget it? Every night a Jim Price or Gates Brown or Tom Matchick — not stars, for sure — would do something amazing to help us win. Interest probably wasn't quite as high as in 1984 [when the Tigers streaked to a 35–5 start] but it still was off the charts."

On September 17, in a moment as golden as any in the regular season, the Tigers clinched their first pennant since 1945. The final score, suitably, in TYOTP, was 2–1, over the Yankees, at Tiger Stadium. What followed was more revelrous than the 1954 Orioles' welcoming parade.

"Coming into the night, we needed either a Detroit win or a Baltimore loss to Boston to wrap it up," Harwell remarked. "And coming into the bottom of the ninth inning, with our score one to one, we learned that the Orioles had lost. The fans didn't know it yet—but we had already won the pennant."

"When did the crowd find out?"

"The stadium was packed, and Jim Campbell [the Tigers' general manager] felt that if we posted the score on our scoreboard, the fans were sure to pour out of the stands and we'd have to forfeit. So he held back the score and asked me to do the same."

"Which you did," I said.

"I didn't totally agree with Jim—it *was* kind of censorship—but I could see his point. So we let the bottom half of the ninth inning play itself out, and wouldn't you know it? Kaline gets on base, Don Wert's single knocks him in, and the old place exploded." (To quote from Harwell's play-by-play: "Let's listen to the bedlam here at Tiger Stadium!")

There ensued then a World Series which by itself, officials hoped, would redeem baseball's abominable pre-October. Following the first four games, that prospect seemed a riot of delusion; the Cardinals led, three sets to one, and the late columnist, Jimmy Cannon, rose from his press-box seat and pronounced of the Tigers, "I never saw anyone play so bad in the World Series. They're stinking out the joint is what they're doing." Before Game Five, Jose Feliciano sang the National Anthem in a folk-rock fashion some found novel and others obscene; when the Cardinals scored three runs in the first inning, it was the *Tigers* who looked obscene. But Detroit clawed from behind to win a fascinating match, 5–3—Kaline drove in the deciding run; Tiger Stadium was in an uproar—and two days later, the Bengals tied the convention with a 13–1 romp. The next afternoon, inconceivably, they beat St. Louis and Bob Gibson, 4–1, and as Tigers' fans erupted, the thank-yous began. Detroit, the doctrine claimed, had not merely captured the World Series; it had breathed life into baseball's corpse.

"When Bill Freehan caught the ball [a foul pop, by Tim McCarver] to end the Series, Detroit blew up," said Harwell, who broadcast the World Series over NBC Radio; George Kell did the video. "Block parties mushroomed. Confetti flooded downtown. People snaked their way through the streets. The whole occasion was memorable."

"So," I said, "was the Feliciano song," and not simply to viewers, whose complaints blitzed the switchboards of Tiger Stadium, the pageant's two local television outlets, and NBC, New York—but also to Harwell, whose suggestion had prompted the invitation.

Ernie laughed softly. "Well, at least when the club asked Jose to perform, we took him out of the record business and made him a national figure," he said. "Looking back, I'm not too sure I'd get involved again, although I think times and attitudes have changed considerably since 1968 and I really don't think that Jose would cause as much of a stir now as then."

"Don't you think a lot of the confusion resulted from people not knowing what was happening?"

"Of course," he said. "No one was sure what Jose was singing—whether it was the National Anthem or 'Ramblin' Rose.' And a lot of narrow-minded people equated his performance with hippies because he carried a guitar and wore dark glasses."

"He had to wear dark glasses."

"Naturally, he did—he's blind. I think a lot of people overlooked that."

After Feliciano, the Tigers' comeback, and baseball's avoidance of imminent morbidity—aided, one must acknowledge, by the 1969 Mets—Detroit felt its next undercurrent of delight in The First Strike Year of 1972.

Even now, I shiver at its feast of memory, for it was Boston that the Tigers edged to win the Eastern Division championship—beating the Red Sox twice in the season's final series; clinching the half-pennant on October 3, before 54,079 patrons, at Tiger Stadium, on a single (again, who else?) by Kaline. I remember sitting that night in an old yellow chair in my college dormitory, cursing Boston's eternal misfortune—a fusion of Calvinism and Murphy's Law—and hearing Harwell's voice drowned out by the noise of the crowd. I remember too a grudging sensation that if the Sox couldn't win, at least baseball *had*—for empathy links these two old-style franchises, and I hoped that the Bengals, advancing to the playoff (to Madison Avenue wit, "The Championship Series"), might purge the Oakland A's. That they did not—losing an extraordinary series by a single run—meant that the Tigers pounced upon 1984, when their famine ended, still searching for a pennant.

By then, his voice rushing through the bowels of sleek transistor radios as it had, almost a half-century earlier, in brown Philco models that tousled the carpet, Harwell had broadcast two World Series (in 1968, with Pee Wee Reese; in 1963, with Joe Garagiola. "It was my first introduction," said Ernie, "to the transistor craze in California. Even in the *Series*, people brought radios to the game. Joe would say something funny, and titters would go through the crowd"), ten A.L. Championship Series (for CBS Radio, 1976–83 and 1985–86; five with Curt Gowdy, three with Martin, and one each with Bill White and Denny Matthews), and two All-Star Games (in 1958, with Bob Neal; in the second 1961 Classic, with Blaine Walsh); worked with Tigers' partner Kell (1960–63), Bob Scheffing (1964), Gene Osborn (1965–66), Ray Lane (1967–72), and Paul Carey (since 1973); recounted Detroit's seven-hour, June 24, 1962, loss to the Yankees, McLain's thirtieth 1968 victory, Kaline's three thousandth hit on September 24, 1974, and Mark (the Bird) Fidrych's crash into the major leagues; and since 1964 crystallized play-by-play over flagship outlet WJR, feeding a network of more than fifty stations.

One year earlier, he called his last nonbaseball sports event. "Up until 1960, I'd done football every year," Harwell shrugged, "but when I came to Detroit, Mr. Fetzer [John, the Tigers' owner] said, 'I don't mind you doing that as long as it doesn't take you away from any baseball.' With the overlap of seasons, that pretty much decided things. I did Michigan State in 1963, but that was it. And I didn't really mind, because now the off-season time became my own."

The next season, Harwell also did his last baseball telecast. "I'd done TV and radio my first five years," he said, "but in '65, they split up. And I haven't missed TV a bit."

"Why?" I said.

"Because radio is the best medium for baseball — and television is the worst."

"Can you explain?"

"Sure," he said. "Imagine a basketball game on radio and the announcer says, 'And he scored on a twelve-foot jump shot.' Try to visualize that in your mind's eye — it's hard. You don't know where he shot it from on the court, what kind of motion he used, you don't know who was around him. Same for football. The action's jumbled in your mind. But baseball is perfect — sitting home, you can imagine it all. Everyone knows where first, second, and third bases are, where a shortstop plays for a pull hitter. The game is linear. The bags, the positions, the batter, the pitcher — they're all definite designations. You start with the bare bones, and your creativity fills in the rest."

"And the announcer too, if he's up to it."

"Exactly," said Harwell, "which is why I think the announcer *matters* more in baseball than in any other sport. But television is just the opposite. Unlike radio, which allows your mind to see *everything*, TV doesn't show you nearly enough."

"All it focuses on is the pitcher and the batter," I said.

"See, television accentuates the people, the individual — close-ups, for instance, of a hitter or a pitcher mopping his brow. But there's so much more to baseball than just the hitter-pitcher duel. The problem is that it's a small screen, it's a large area to cover, and the players are so far away from each other — TV can't show you the sweep of the field."

"Examples?" I asked.

"Say you're sitting in the park and a guy lines a double to left-center and a runner scores from first," he surmised. "At the ball park, we see it all at *once* — the runner tearing around the bases and the batter going for two, the fielder chasing the ball, the shortstop going out for the relay throw, the catcher getting ready for the peg — you see it as it's happening. But with TV, all you see are an individual *succession* of shots. It reduces baseball, makes it smaller than life, less exciting than it is."

Are you a media critic? For four decades, Harwell has understood that television does not equal simply radio plus picture. Are you a cinemaphile? Do you recall the nuthouse scene where Jack Nicholson, groping to hear the 1963 World Series in *One Flew Over the Cuckoo's Nest*, perceived a voice in the background airing the Dodgers-Yankees' dialogue? That was Harwell; "I loved appearing in it," he said. "I just wish I'd got a residual." Are you a curator, collector, or bibliophile? Have you heard of a thirty-six-year lode of baseball material donated in 1965 to the Burton Historical Collection of the Detroit Public Library? "The hobby had got so big that I was becoming a slave to it. I did some self-examination and saw I was collecting for collecting's sake," Ernie said of his nearly four thousand books and eighty thousand clippings. "I bought my first baseball books when I was a kid of twelve. The last time I moved, it cost me more to move the baseball items than it did my furniture." Have you dreamed, even in a remote, misty haze, of sinking a hole-in-one (Harwell did in 1965) or writing lyrics (he scored "I Don't Know Any Better" for Thomas on "an album that went platinum," collaborated with Sammy Fain of "I'll Be Seeing You" and "Love Is a Many-Splendored Thing," and crafted the 1973 paean to baseball's emerging home-run monarch, "Move Over Babe, Here Comes Henry," and the immortal "I'm Waiting for the Midnight Charter to Detroit and Last-Place Blues") or singing a duet with Pearl Bailey, giving Christian testimony on a Billy Graham TV special, being baptized in the Jordan River, and putting a hammer lock on Leo Durocher?

"Once Joe Falls asked me if I'd ever lost my temper," Harwell was saying. "I said, 'I don't think so.' Then I got to mulling it over and I said, 'Oh, I get a little mad when the traffic is heavy.' "

"That was it?"

"We kept talking and I kept thinking and it finally hit me. 'Hey!' I told him. 'I can tell you when I lost my temper,' " and Ernie started to laugh. "I was working with the Giants, we were coming back from Chicago, and I was sitting in a compartment with Russ Hodges. I was reading the newspaper when Durocher [the Giants' manager] came in and slapped the paper and it hit my face."

"Great guy," I said.

"Well, that was Leo. He'd do those things to see how far he could get with you. I jumped up and put him in a hammer lock until Russ broke us apart."

"You didn't write many songs on *that* train trip."

Harwell unpent an easygoing smile. "I loved the trains," he said, "but actually, I didn't start writing songs until the sixties."

"What started you on the binge?"

"I've always been drawn to words," he said, "in movies, the theatre, in musicals. There's poetry in them, and I began as a reporter, of course. So I guess it's only natural that I'd turn eventually to writing songs," and he went on to define where phrases and ideas struck him — in a hotel room or restaurant, mowing the lawn, or sitting on the team bus staring out the window. "Even more pop up in those long plane rides from one city to another city as we travel around with the Tigers. It's usually some expression which catches my attention, and I build on it from there. You just start with the phrase and go wherever your mind brings you."

On August 2, 1981, that mind brought him to Cooperstown. Not a showman nor a salesman but a play-by-play conversationalist, this "class selection," said Ed Stack, the Hall of Fame president, "kind, polite, and pleasant and as venerable as the game itself," became the fifth brother inducted into the fraternity's broadcast wing.

In his peroration, reciting a partial text of "The Game for All America," Harwell digressed to say, "Baseball is a tongue-tied kid from Georgia, growing up to be an announcer and praising the Lord for showing him the way to Cooperstown."

Sitting a short pop fly away, I retreated as if memory-logged to how, his tones crackling over the car radio, Harwell often called a batter out ("He takes the pitch for strike three! Just stood there like the house by the side of the road") and how he viewed his job ("You do the best you can, and do it the way that you can satisfy the most people") and his audience ("We've got truck drivers who may care about baseball, but not about grammar, English teachers who are just the opposite, young kids being introduced to baseball, and retired major leaguers who know a lot more about the game than I do") and the equation that older meant better ("We probably think stars of the past were greater because we were young then and didn't have so many things on our mind"), and how he delighted in life, from reading the morning newspaper to kibitzing in the press room, and how his voice, full of talcum and inflections and ancient rumblings of the South, made listening so *comfortable* — and as these images shimmered on a tempting mid-summer day, I thought of three five-letter words that would have seemed perfectly natural, I am certain, to everyone there.

The first was *Ernie*, as in friend.

The second, *Tiger*, as in baseball.

The third, *class*, as in Harwell.

"A tongue-tied kid," indeed.

*   *   *

As commerce, Harwell's first season in the Motor City — a year in which Barber lost two-thirds of his stomach to ulcer surgery, Herb Carneal replaced Ernie as Voice of the Orioles, Allen and Gowdy telecast All-Star Games from Kansas City and Yankee Stadium, and The Voice and Bob Prince called NBC's coverage of an autumn war wanting in neither drama nor development — was gladdened by the profits and exposure, the gumbo of the game, inherent in the growing receipts baseball derived from TV and radio.

In 1960, revenue from the majors' broadcast rights leaped to $12.4 million — exactly half from regional radio and television; $3.2 million from NBC's big-money packages of the All-Star Game and Oktoberfest; and a record $3 million from assorted regular-season network series.

"Each year there was more money to spread around, and depending on their perspective and financial situation, teams looked at the cash much differently," said Tom Villante. "Some clubs put as many local games on TV as they could. All they cared about was the television dough — to hell with attendance. Some went to the other extreme — no television whatever, even on the road. 'If you want to follow us,' they'd say, 'come out to the park and *pay*. When we're away, follow us by radio.' "

"And with no road TV allowed in a case like that," I said, "your radio rights would be worth more. There'd be an exclusivity — nothing to compete with."

Conceding the point, the ex-advertising employee of Batten, Barton, Durstine, and Osborn twirled a cigarette in his hand. "There was also *another* way to go," he explained. "A lot of clubs televised just a handful of home games — safeguard your attendance that way — and then allowed a heavy schedule of away games. That way, you kept up the interest. More and more in later years, teams went *this* way, and it made sense—you really got the best of both worlds."

"Looking back," I said, "what are the lessons of the early sixties?"

"That clubs were casting about, trying like hell to see how they could get the most loot," he observed. "Were you better off taking the local TV money and running? Or did you come out ahead by being judicious and trying to build a better attendance base?"

As if to confirm that polarity, 1960 American League teams—led by the Yankees' 123—televised 411 games; the National League, opting, generally, to protect home attendance at the expense of TV, limited its coverage to 276. Riding the television bandwagon, the Bombers lapped all clubs with $900,000 for local broadcast rights. Meanwhile, the Dodgers, allowing *no* home television, led the National League with $600,000. The money mushroomed from O'Malley radiocasts; Vin Scully acquired the tag-line, "the Transistor Kid"; as Barber later wrote of Southern California, "Vin merely owns the place."

"But there were other clubs too," I said, "like the Milwaukees and Kansas Cities, who were in such small markets that even if they wanted to flood the screen with games, weren't going to get as much in rights as a Chicago or New York."

Villante agreed, his voice hurried and aggressive. "And that's exactly why you had so much franchise-hopping in the sixties. Milwaukee moved. Kansas City moved. They saw the Yankees and Dodgers getting rich and they felt trapped—they hadn't had the same local radio/TV money available to them. So they said, 'Hey, maybe in a new market it *will* be available.' "

Nationally, the cleavage yawned wider than even these *local* disparities. The 1960 Yankees, who won the pennant, pocketed more than $600,000 from network television—a sum appreciably higher than any competitor's and which, in turn, helped them win future pennants. "There's no question—the clubs' regional differences, big as they were, were nothing compared to the gaps on 'Game of the Week' and the NBC series," spoke Bill MacPhail. "We paid more for our rights than NBC even though we televised the same number of games. The reason was simple: We had the Yankees. And the lion's share of our money went *to* the Yankees. This was in the era of the bonus babies, before the free-agent draft, remember, when the richest clubs had a tremendous advantage."

"And your network money helped perpetuate that advantage," I said. "You helped maintain the Yankees' dynasty."

The ex-director of CBS Sports turned in his chair. Through the office window, its skyline shrouded, mid-town Manhattan wilted in the rain. "That was not our *aim*," he said, slowly, "but it was obviously an effect. To us, honestly, it didn't matter. With the Yankees locked up for the more than half the country we reached by 'Game of the Week,' we had the show and we had the audience." He smiled. "*That* mattered."

In 1960, what mattered to non-major-league America (still more than 55 percent of all households) was its staggering multiplicity of games.

For the eleventh straight year, Mutual aired a daily "Game"; spinning balls and strikes were MacLean, Elston, and Patrick. "We thought the series might go on into eternity," said Al Wester, "but when the major leagues expanded [in 1961, to eighteen teams; the next year, to twenty] the new clubs expanded their own local networks so that they often fanned out into four or five states. Even before then, Mutual had a problem because you were blacked out in big-league towns and in minor-league cities where games were in progress. Now we had *another* problem — the local networks were taking away stations who'd always broadcast 'Game of the Day.' "

"You just ran out of country," I said.

"It became a case," Wester said, "of there being fewer stations every year who were available to carry our games. And, ironically, it was baseball itself who killed us — their teams kept reducing the market. They gonged the death-knell," and in 1961, aping the Gunner, "You could kiss it [the series] good-bye."

Yet even in 1960, it had been on *television*, not radio, that baseball's assembling crested, for if one lived outside the major markets — i.e., between California and St. Louis, almost *anywhere* south of the Mason-Dixon line and east of the Mississippi, and in large patches of the Northeast and industrial Midwest — he was assaulted by 123 network broadcasts in a twenty-five-week season.

"It was terrific coverage," remarked MacPhail. "If you were a fan of *baseball*, not just of one particular club, you didn't *want* to live in a big-league city; you were better off in the boonies. The kind of coverage the networks gave them — well, it had more hours per year of baseball than even the National Football League has today." In 1986, the NFL enjoyed fewer than three hundred hours of network exposure; the 1960 bigs boasted almost four hundred. Did such concentrated volume, as critics said, impair the minor leagues by curbing attendance? To a degree, although admissions plunged most sharply *before* the birth of network baseball. More probably, this same coverage — five network games a week, a breadth of viewing unrivaled by any sport — made mulish indifference toward the major leagues *im*probable, and planted (in the experience of many) a love and affection for The Game.

The magic 123 arose from ABC's decision to televise a late-afternoon Saturday series. Its games began at 4 P.M. Eastern Time — voiding conflict with earlier-starting NBC and CBS — and originated in San Francisco (thirteen games), Kansas City (six), Washington and Philadelphia (three apiece). "The other two networks never broadcast from Candlestick or K.C. and almost never from Washington, so we had easy pickings getting rights," said Jack Buck, calling play-by-play. "And that was Candlestick's first year, so we thought folks would be interested in what the hell it was all about."

"How'd you happen to broadcast the games?" I said.

"Easy," he said, mockingly. "When Bud Blattner left 'Game of the Week' in late 1959, he came back to St. Louis, and the Cardinals hired him. This meant we had four announcers to do our radio and TV — Caray, Bud, Garagiola, and me — and that was one too many. I guess the Cardinals weren't as impressed as some others by the job I'd done the same year with Budweiser televising the

Giants and Dodgers back to New York. Anyway, the upshot was that they fired me — and I was free and clear when ABC came along."

"How did you find it?"

"I loved working with Carl Erskine, who did the color and became a lifelong friend. But the series itself ran into some trouble," Buck said. "First, I was up against Dean and Nelson — there was already a glut of games. Second, we'd come along years after they'd got started. They'd become established; we weren't. They didn't need New York and L.A. markets to become a big hit; we *did*. And because we couldn't go into those markets, we couldn't *become* a big hit. In fact, the series had such little impact, you may be the only person in the country who remembers it."

Buck's network was also hampered (and would be, until the 1970s) by an audience- and, therefore, sponsor-killing problem: about 20 percent fewer affiliates than either of the two older networks. "In any given market," Buck said, "our numbers were OK. But when you went across the country and added them up, the totals just weren't there." The next season, sacking baseball, ABC unveiled "Wide World of Sports" and some motto hailing "the thrill of victory, the agony of defeat"; twenty-five years later, both were running each Saturday afternoon.

NBC, of course, in its fourth year of weekend baseball — "Join us for all fifty games this year," its advertisements bannered — had Nelson and his new sidekick, Fred Haney, succeeding the Dodgers-bound Durocher. Elsewhere in major papers, one could read promos urging, "See two games every weekend on the CBS-TV Game of the Week! Starting Saturday, April 16, Falstaff's eighth consecutive season of major league baseball. There's a big game every Sunday too. Stay tuned on CBS-TV and keep plenty of Falstaff on ice. That way you'll be set for the summer with baseball and beer at their refreshing best."

Above the text a headline blared, "Join Two Great Guys on CBS-TV," and to its right loomed the beaming visages of Dean and *his* new sidekick — "a captain among men," Barber had called him, the leader of the Dodgers for a decade-and-one-half; a southerner, his childhood home forty miles from Louisville, his aid a solace to Jackie Robinson; a pioneer in NBC's first truly *national* series, the 1966–68 "Game of the Week," reaping the laughter of many and respect of more; and who, a generation later, settled and assured in his sixties, flung aside these memories and said, slowly choosing his words, "My years with Diz — they were the best years of my life."

*   *   *

During 1940–42 and 1946–57, the shortstop of the Brooklyn franchise of the National League helped with his bat and glove, and more with his heart than either. Dodgers' fans, famous for their loud, harsh edge, reveled in his growth, his quiet humor, his tolerance and courtesy. In July 1955, on the night of his thirty-seventh birthday, more than thirty thousand of the congregation gathered at Ebbets Field and struck matches as the field lights dimmed, there to show their love. On a team of household names, Harold (Pee Wee) Reese wore No. 1 on his uniform.

"Just being in Brooklyn was amazing," he said as we sat in the Audubon Country Club. Outside, the Louisville summer poured forth its warmth. Reese's home was minutes away. "They'll never be anything like it — no sir, no way. The Dodger Symphony Band. The fans, you know, you joked with them on a first-name basis. You saw them ever' night."

"You *knew* these people," I said.

"Oh, did I," he said. "It's like walking into a bar like this and saying, 'Hiya, Ben,' or 'How you doing, Joe?' You were friends. And the ball park was so wonderful. The damn stands were right on top of you."

"Robinson," I said. "That must touch you too."

When Jackie Robinson joined the Dodgers in 1947, the first Negro to play major league baseball, he met beanballs and brushbacks, vitriol and obscenities; death threats became a weekly alarum. Even Brooklyn teammates, circulating a petition, demanded his return to the minors. Reading the petition, Reese refused to sign. More frontally than any Dodger, he befriended the embattled No. 42.

"Yes, Jackie's trials stick out," he said. "You know, people talk about that petition. Hell, I was in the service, coming home from the war, when Rickey first signed him. I knew I had to play. I couldn't sign that petition — I had a career to worry about. So when they came to me and said, 'Hey, we're getting things up — we're not going to play with that nigger so and so,' I said, 'I don't give a damn what you do.' And I wouldn't sign."

"Your refusal was financial."

"Sure," he said. "It wasn't any racial motives on my part. I wasn't out, consciously, at least, to promote integration. As I told Jackie, I was brought up in a very poor neighborhood. I didn't even come into contact with black people. I knew, as a youngster, what we'd been taught — Negroes were supposed to ride in the back of streetcars, speak when spoken to. I just wasn't around them. But after being with Jackie, seeing the kind of person he was, what he was going through, it didn't take long for me to have a great respect for him."

"But your refusal to sign the petition," I said, "broke its back." Reese's modesty was disarming.

"Look, if it helped him, I'm glad. It's just a situation I was in. Jackie and I became very close. He used to show me the hate mail he got. Once, in Atlanta, somebody threatened to shoot him if he played that day. During warm-up I said to him, 'Robinson, don't stand so damn close to me today. Move away, will you?' It made him laugh. I'll say this: He was one of the most dynamic people I've ever met. He could have made it anywhere, in any profession, at any time."

Jackie Robinson last played for Brooklyn in 1956; since 1945, the Dodgers had outdrawn every team in the National League. That autumn, Walter

O'Malley sold Ebbets Field. A year later, he sold out Brooklyn. As construction began on Dodger Stadium, the first privately financed ball park since Yankee Stadium opened in 1923, the club found refuge in its temporary shelter, the gargantuan Los Angeles Coliseum. "There's no doubt in my mind," Reese said, "that looking back, O'Malley always intended to leave."

"But you didn't think so at the time," I said.

"Never," he confessed. "In fact, I bet a couple players that we'd stay in Brooklyn. They said to me, 'We're moving.' I said, 'Man, what are you talking about? We're drawing over a million people ever' year.' Those people in Brooklyn would have done anything to keep them—build a stadium anywhere, even on Coney Island. It was a hell of a shock, us moving, I'll tell you that."

Reflexes fading, his legs soiled by wear, Reese passed forty in 1958. Walter Alston, ever unsung, remained O'Malley's manager. "I kept telling him, 'Walt, I can't play shortstop. Hell, I'm way too old.' But I think they wanted me for my name."

While memories of base hits crested three time zones and a ball park away, Reese, marooned in California, hit .224 and the Dodgers collapsed; third the year before, Los Angeles placed seventh, two games above the Phillies. The captain retired and became a coach; he had emerged, insiders said in 1959, as Alston's obvious successor. "Mr. O'Malley kept saying, 'Pee Wee, one day you're going to manage this club,' and I said, 'Mr. O'Malley, there ain't no way.' "

"Why not?"

"It's not that I disliked the idea of managing the club on the field," he said, "but all those extracurricular activities, going to banquets, this and that."

"B.S. and P.R.," I said.

"Jesus, that's right. And I knew that if I stayed with the Dodgers as a coach, they were going to get me. And to be honest," he said, releasing the inevitable truth, "after seeing Durocher and Charlie Dressen run the club, I just didn't feel like I could be that way."

"A sergeant."

"Well, so tough, you know. And it would have been hard for me to manage the Dodgers. I knew the players so well. I think I would have had their respect, but still . . ." Reese a martinet? Like Blattner, he was almost damnably pleasant.

With Maury Wills at shortstop, Los Angeles won the 1959 World Series. "I was making more money coaching than anybody in the majors," Pee Wee said, "and the only reason was because of my playing career. But where are you going as a coach? I would have floundered around in baseball, I'm sure."

Then, in September, Blattner resigned as "pod-nuh" to Dean. "We considered several people," Bill MacPhail told me, "but as Bud's replacement, Pee Wee always led the list. He had the following. He had a nice manner. We wanted him very much."

Seeking acquiescence, Gene Kirby and Dancer Fitzgerald executives flew from New York to Louisville; Patricia Dean also called, urging Reese to join Ol' Diz. Pee Wee balked; he had never done an inning of play-by-play. "I didn't think I was that much of an extrovert," he said. "I just didn't want to bomb."

Still, CBS persisted; unsure, Reese consulted Buzzie Bavasi. "Why in the hell don't you try it?" asked the Dodgers' general manager. "More than likely you'll screw it up, but even if you do, you can always come back and have a job with us." Amused by Bavasi's counsel, Reese endorsed it too. A neophyte to television, he would work with Dean, chancing face and reputation on a medium he barely knew.

"You bet I was frightened," he said as the afternoon unfolded. A waitress at the country club approached our table. "I mean, this was all new to me. All that winter, before the 1960 season, I'd have a projector and baseball tape set up in the basement. Kirby came here and worked with me. I worked on the video. Then I'd talk, talk, talk."

We ordered drinks. "Then comes spring training," I said.

"Yes, and we'd get a little tape recorder and use that. Then, at night, Gene and I'd go back to the hotel and we'd listen to what I'd done. Usually what I'd done *wrong*. And Diz," he broke off, laughing, "he'd come in some afternoons and say, 'Pod-nuh, having a little trouble? Let me show you how to do this stuff.' And he'd sit down and sing 'Wabash Cannon Ball.' He'd roar and say, 'That's all there is to it.' But mostly it was work — how to project, how to watch the game, when to watch the monitor, when not to."

"Harder than patrolling shortstop?" I said.

"Oh, baby," he said. "Tough? Are you kidding? I kept thinking, 'What happens if I can't say anything? What happens if the guy says, 'ten seconds till air time,' and I freeze?' We did all that work in the winter and then we went to New York before the season started and watched a game Mel Allen had done — I watched how he set the tempo — and with all this, the first game I did, I *still* had problems." He looked at me, easy, the dilemma reborn. "But I'll say this: Working with Diz, it was the best thing that ever happened to me."

Nervous, far from glib, Reese sputtered badly in early 1960. But Blattner's ogre turned tutor for the ex-Dodgers' shortstop, and by late season the pair teamed superbly — one from the mid-South; one, Ol' Diz, the deep. "I know that just being with Dizzy relaxed me," Pee Wee said. "He knew when I was out on a limb, when I was uneasy. He'd come in and kid me when I hesitated. 'Pod-nuh,' he'd say, 'let me take over here,' or, 'Pod-nuh, let me say something,' or, 'You got this all fouled up.' And we laughed about it, I guess, as only two former ballplayers could. You know, if there was a professional announcer up there and I goofed, it was terrible. Like when I worked later with Curt Gowdy. But not with Diz. We'd just sit there and laugh."

"So would your viewers," I said.

"Well, a majority of 'em anyway," Reese said, humility yielding to working pride. "To this *day* people talk to me about it. Yesterday a guy looked at me — I was at a filling station — and he said, 'You're not Pee Wee Reese, are you?' I said yes. And the first thing he said was, 'Baseball hasn't been the same since you and Diz left.' That's how it was — you either raved about us or said, 'Jesus, I can't *stand* these guys.' There was no middle ground."

A frown blackened Reese's face. "I liked working with both Diz and Gowdy," he said, "but it was so different. With Diz, we just kind of went on the air, pushed a button, and said, 'Here we go.' With NBC, it was a Cecil B. DeMille production. All these guys passing statistics and the rest — Diz used to call them 'statics.' It was just so much more *fun* the way we did it before."

"You termed them your most memorable years," I said.

"They *were*," he said. "I can remember one Friday night in Cleveland. And I got a call from Diz late at night — I was in the hotel room. 'Pod-nuh,' he said, 'guess who's in town?'

"I said to him, 'Diz, I have no idea. What in the hell you want?' We were kidding, of course.

"Diz said, 'We got Roy Acuff,' and I said, 'So what?'

"Well, Dean, he loved Roy Acuff. 'Let's go down,' he said, which meant, of course, we're going down. Because if Diz wanted it, I'd say, 'OK, Diz, let's go.' So I got out of bed, and we went to hear Roy Acuff. And I *enjoyed* it. Met Roy for the first time. A great guy, real country. But I loved those things — seeing Diz have a few drinks, have a few laughs."

"Which outflanked the other?" I said.

Pee Wee's frown reappeared. "I know what people said. But I swear to God," he vowed, raising his hand, "hope I drop dead. I never saw that man take one drink before a game." My smile suggested skepticism. "Never," Reese repeated. "Oh, he'd get a sandwich a lot of times during a game, especially if it was dull, and he'd make a big to do. They'd get a shot of Diz eating the stuff. Or we'd come into Philadelphia and they'd play up Diz stumbling down the rungs which hung from the booth. Diz would really put it on. He loved to play the ham." Diz with sandwich, Diz with beer, Diz atop the old steel ladder — the memories were even more real than today's dim shapes of reality.

"We were at the New York airport," he recalled, "and I was walking ahead of Diz. He had the hat, the big boots on. All the porters, everybody saying, 'Hi, Mr. Dean.' 'Hi, Diz.' 'How ya doing?' 'Hi, pod-nuh.' And Diz shouts to me, 'Pee Wee.'

" 'Yeah, what do you want?' " Reese said.

" 'How come you played in this town for eighteen years and nobody knows Pee Wee. Everybody knows Ol' Diz.' So I shot back to him, 'Hell, if I had that cowboy hat and boots on, everybody'd know me too.' He just laughed."

With Reese, like Blattner, Dean towered, unchallenged; even those repulsed by his power were fascinated by his crude and robust style. "He kinda ran everything," Pee Wee admitted. "The agency, CBS. Whatever Diz says, Diz does. As they often said, the network created a monster and they weren't too sure what to do with it. It was amazing, really — Dean could tell a giant corporation what he wanted, and what he wanted, he got. 'Course," he said, quietly, "I knew who was the boss. If Diz wanted me to come eat with him in the hotel room, I did. If he didn't, I didn't. There were the Kirbys and the Pee

Wee Reeses and all the people at CBS, and then there was Diz. We had no friction. Never." But Blattner, I protested, split violently with Dean; why was Reese's station more secure? "If Diz didn't like you, he'd want to see you fall on your ass. But he wanted to be sure I didn't. He didn't want anything to happen to me. He was kind of protective, really."

Drinks arrived. Reese unfurled his pipe. "Diz didn't resent me doing play-by-play. I remember when he first walked out of the booth and said, 'Pod-nuh, see you in two or three innings,' and then he'd go grab a steak. He let me do it solo. But," Pee Wee continued, laughing, "he didn't stay out too long. If I got in a tight spot, he wanted to be sure he was there."

"You mean after 1960?" I said.

"Basically, that first year," he said. "Sometimes I'd do a commercial or an inning of play. Diz'd come on the air and say, 'Pod-nuh, I'd better pick this thing up. I think you just lost some sales.' You couldn't keep from laughing at the guy. Or I'd do a live commercial and he'd say, 'Well, pod-nuh, commercial wasn't *too* bad' " — Reese paused — " 'but I think you better get with it next time.' Or we'd get through doing a game and as soon as it was over, he had to call his wife. 'How'd everything go?' I'd ask him when Diz got off the phone. 'What'd Pat say?' 'Well,' Diz would answer, 'she said I was terrific, but the other guy . . .' and of course, we'd roar. We went through the same thing every week. Yes, we really had a life."

Blattner chafed at Ol' Diz's blanket reach; Reese, more pliant, delighted in Dean's company and accepted his whims, forgave the boundless ego that soared yearly into new, more elevated orbit. "I wasn't overwhelmed by Diz," he insisted. "I never felt like a poor second cousin. I always felt comfortable. Why? Because I didn't have to cater to anyone. Not even to Diz. I was just myself. Just ol' quiet Pee Wee."

Reese reached for his tobacco reserve. "When I went to NBC in '66," he said, his tone strangely embittered, "they used to tell me, 'Pee Wee, don't forget the sponsors, the Gillette people, the agency people. Mention 'em on the air.'

"I'd tell 'em, 'Hey, wait a minute. I've been doing games for seven years. I don't have to start kissing anyone's ass.' And they'd come right back: 'Well,' they said, 'we're just telling you.' "

Pee Wee's smile surfaced. "Maybe they were right," he said. "A couple years later, I was fired," replaced by Tony Kubek in 1969. "That's what was great about Diz. I never felt I had to be a straight man. I only did what came natural. And I knew how much people enjoyed him. I just hoped I added something in my own way." Reese asked the waitress for roasted nuts; the drinks, he quipped, needed companion help. "I never did really figure the big ox out. He wore the hat and this and that, like he needed to be noticed. But sometimes people bugged him and he wanted to get away, though he'd never let on. At dinner, when autograph hounds pestered him, Diz'd never tell them to beat it. He wouldn't let anybody know that it bothered him, which is actually a tremendous thing. Sinatra, you touch his coat and he hauls off and belts you in the mouth. Not Diz. He was unflappable."

"Was it all a façade?" I said.

"No, no," Reese answered. "Diz always took time for people. He was extremely kind."

Kind? Blattner was not alone in calling Dean less warm and amiable off the air than on. "Oh, he had his moments," Pee Wee conceded, "but he was almost always the same — always kidding. I'll never forget saying to him in the hotel lobby, mocking-like, 'Dizzy Dean. High, hard fastball. I wish I could have had the chance to hit against that shit.' And he'd start bringing his arm up in the air, like he was going to pitch, and I'd start to duck. Just a little gesture. But Ol' Diz loved it.

"I remember once I told Diz a story I'd heard from a friend that I thought was great. This guy was coming out of this small town and he picked up an old farmer. 'Where can I take you?' the guy asked him. 'I'm going about a mile down the road,' the farmer said. 'I got a little work to do.' It was a real hot day," Reese observed, "and as the farmer got in the car, a big Cadillac, the friend had the air conditioning on. They went down the road about half a mile. The old man turned to the driver and said, 'Son, would you stop this car?' The guy said, 'Why? I thought you were going down a couple of miles and cut some tobacco.' And the old man looked at him and said, 'Yeah, but it's turned so cold that I'm going back and kill some hogs.' "

Pee Wee laughed gayly. "I gave Diz the story," he said, "and I told him, 'Diz, I'm going to tell this over the air.' But he said, 'What? You can't do that. You'll insult the intelligence of the farmer.' And he was *serious* about it."

It would have been, of course, a ghostly thing, even ludicrous, to regard Dean as the jockocracy's version of a Fulbright Scholar. For it was likeability, not cultural prodigy, that Diz brought to the CBS booth each weekend, and laughter too — always that.

"How else you gonna explain the effect he had?" Reese queried. "We didn't do that much homework. You can read all the statics you want, but if it's a dead game, all the homework in the world can't save you. And we had Diz. We didn't *need* statics."

Even dull matches seemed intriguing. Once, Diz consumed a watermelon while calling the play-by-play. Another Saturday, while Reese described the action, the camera shifted to a close-up of Dean slumped backward, snoring as he slept. After Reese boasted of a catfish, twelve-to-fifteen inches long, he had recently caught in Louisville, Diz unburdened his response: "Pee Wee, we've got 'em down in Mississippi like that too, but that's between the eyes!" One afternoon, Pee Wee turned to Dean, asking, "Diz, you watched the pitcher out there for about four innings and he's been throwing that ball and I mean doing a great job. What would you say he's throwing out there?" Unfazed, Diz surveyed the playing field. "Well, Pee Wee," he replied, "I *have* been watching him four innings and after watching him four innings, I believe that's a baseball."

Often Dean turned impulsive; "announcers are too dull," he sighed, a defect Diz tried weekly to remedy. On a dank 1961 Sunday, chilled by cold winds sweeping Wrigley Field, he grasped the mike in the seventh inning. "I've had enough of this," Diz said. "I'm going," and departed the park, leaving Reese to finish the broadcast. Other exits were less peremptory, and most served as the natural outcome of Dean's craving, like a mongrel on a leash, for the sumptuous tonic of ball-yard chow. I remember, even now, how Diz would amble downward from the broadcast booth, straining the ladder as he scented the concession stand; minutes or innings later, one saw him reappear, several hot dogs in one hand, a slab of pizza in the other — Everytub before the Scarsdale Diet Plan.

No game, no matter how riveting, deterred him. "Pee Wee, I'm going out for a hamburger," he said, the score tied, 1–1, in the bottom of inning eight. "You want one?"

"Yeah, I'll take one."

"Pickles, lettuce, or mustard?"

"See if they have some onions," Reese replied, the nation watching in half-amusement and half-disbelief.

For Reese, these were memories at their best, and the former shortstop's face burst into a grin. "He was a show in himself," Pee Wee said. "I'd say, 'Diz, do a little singing,' if the game was dull. 'Sing "Precious Memories" or something.' Or when I'd see him sleeping, I'd ask for a shot; then I signaled the monitor and nudged Diz. 'Pod-nuh,' I said, 'am I keeping you awake?' It was corny as hell, but people *loved* it."

Making $20,000 a year as coach, Reese cleared several times that sum with Dean. "I could have been paid a lot less and still enjoyed it. People would say to me, 'Does Diz bug you? Do you mind all the corn?' And I would say to 'em, 'Hell, no.' It relaxed me [as a player, Reese had developed a stomach ulcer] and it made me more at ease. No one sat there, just waiting for me to screw up. We'd just sit there and roar."

Few, as Reese would discover, roared when the CBS "Game of the Week" was swept into obscurity's dustbin, its obituary published as ABC (in 1965) and Gowdy's NBC (the following year) began primary/exclusive coverage of major league baseball. "Diz might have gotten a job with Curt," Reese said, his grin vanishing, "but he would have had to do color, not play-by-play. Diz didn't want that. And neither did I. I said, 'Look, I'd rather work with Diz on the backup game.' But that was out too. NBC just didn't want Diz, I guess, overshadowing its top announcer. So I gave up and went with Curt," acting as his partner — as opposed to "pod-nuh" — as ratings first rose and then skidded in 1966–68.

Years later, in a cycle of irony, Reese was inducted into the Hall of Fame the same day Gowdy entered its broadcast wing. This old friendship had not been publicly brought together in more than a decade, since that blood-crazy year of 1969 in which Reese learned of his firing by reading *Broadcasting Magazine*. "It was in March," he said. "A few months earlier Curt and I had done the World Series. I was looking through this article about how all the NBC baseball announcers would return this year — Gowdy, Kubek, Jim Simpson, and Sandy Koufax. But no Pee Wee. Can you imagine? I was the last to know."

Tom Gallery's successor, Carl Lindemann, was then vice-president of NBC Sports. Furious, Reese phoned him. "Oh, he apologized for me having to find out this way. But Carl and I never did get along too well. And he never did give me a good reason for firing me."

"Was it the ratings?" I said.

"Possibly," he said, as though quizzing himself. "I don't know. Maybe it was. Maybe they needed a scapegoat. They'd invested so much money in Curt, and they certainly weren't going to throw *him* overboard. I have to say Curt was always very nice to me, and I thought he did a good job. People around here criticized him something terrible, but the only problem for me is that he worried about everything—if he made a mistake, if he pronounced somebody's name wrong."

"Different from Dean."

"From Diz, it was like going from Ringling Brothers to a final exam." Reese picked at salted nuts. "Maybe," he said, "they figured Tony could liven things up more than I could."

Previously limited to backup outings, Kubek was elevated to the primary "Game of the Week." "I was never bitter at Tony," Pee Wee mused. "True, he wormed his way around NBC, but what the hell. I'll only say that if you don't have anything to contribute on the air, you should just shut your mouth. Some of these guys today—they just talk like there's no tomorrow. I wouldn't do that. Maybe I should have."

From NBC, Reese drifted to Cincinnati, doing television for the powerful Reds, and then back to Louisville. "After the Reds' TV games had a change in ownership," he said, "I was asked to leave. Then they came to me a few years later and wanted me back. I could have gone a couple other places too. But who needs it? Who needs the hassle?"

Not the man, I knew, whom reporters called "the Little Colonel." He owned a bowling alley and storm window business. He was part-owner of a wholesale grocery store. He also worked for Hillerich and Bradsby Company, a Louisville-based firm (later, in the 1984–85 off-season, Reese retired to his winter home in Venice, Florida, after sixteen years as a Hillerich spokesman). "Strictly a P.R. job, that's all."

"You don't need the money," I said. "Why worry yourself?"

"It keeps me around baseball, just displaying our bats," he said, some sadness to his voice. "I can go to the All-Star Game or World Series or exhibition games. Or I'll meet with some baseball people from the Orient. Anyway, what am I gonna do? Play golf ever' afternoon? Wash my storm windows? This way, with Hillerich and Bradsby, at least I got somewhere to go each day, some office to work in." Work was Pee Wee's catharsis, the balsam for cankers every athlete feels when his most satisfactory deeds belong to quondam years.

"You know," he said, slowly, "Diz missed the 'Game of the Week.' It saddened him deeply. He still had the ego, the need to have applause. Only the applause wasn't there any more." Reese brightened. "But he still kept the happy face, never stopped kidding. We were up to a golf tournament in Dayton, Ohio—this was a year before he died [in 1974]—and I hadn't seen him in a while. I was getting ready to tee off. Well, Diz was in back of me and he couldn't stay still. 'Pod-nuh,' he said, 'a lot of trees over on the right.' Couldn't stop needling. The next tee came up. 'What'd you get on that hole?' he'd shout after I messed up. The next tee — 'lot of sand traps on the left.' " A smile exploded across Pee Wee's face.

A meeting pressed, Reese explained; he must shortly leave. "We were just a couple of country boys that made mistakes, that said things about which people knew." The "country boys' " series was dead and gone; long live their "Game of the Week." Did he miss it? I asked. The exposure, the turmoil, the platform they owned two days each week?

"Naw, not the series," he said, adding softly, "not really. But I sure miss Ol' Diz."

*   *   *

In the florid days of the early 1960s, one recollects hoping that baseball's blast of network coverage would last forever. Few spoke then of underrated batters, or fielding blurs cloaked in anonymity, or stars who remained "the best-kept secret in baseball"; few believed — really — that you needed a scorecard to tell the players. With weekends burnished by the television camera, how could Jim Landis be a secret, or Julian Javier anonymous, or even the battered Pumpsie Green — that entrepôt of disaster — an unknown scrap of trivia? How could you not at least be *aware* of their parade of varying skills? It was a time, Roger Angell wrote, "when we knew all . . . big-league teams as well as we knew the faces and tones of those sitting around the family dinner table at Thanksgiving." It was a time, you sensed, you might not live again — and would not have missed living for the world.

One whose feelings ran strongest about this age was The Voice, involved, as he was, in renown (his own) and conquests (his team's). "Russ Hodges and I used to talk about Mel," Lindsey Nelson said, "and we used to say that he'd rather have his job than Eisenhower's or Kennedy's. I never saw *anyone* love his work more than he did — every part of it, he relished."

Over NBC Television, Mel Allen called every World Series during 1955–58 and 1960–63, twelve straight All-Star Games (1952–61), and the Rose Bowl through the most furious "Granddaddy of them all," Wisconsin's 42–37 loss to USC on January 1, 1963. When he was awed, his voice expressed it; when he was bored, it somehow never showed; and as the Voice of the Yankees, he almost *became* the Yankees — perhaps in his own mind; certainly, to his larger American retinue — talking, enthusing, presiding over the greatest moments of early-sixties baseball.

Allen was *there* for Mazeroski's home run deposing the Ol' Perfessor, *there* for Maris' sixty-first and the Yankees' long-ball thundering of 1961, *there* — with Vin Scully — for New York's five-game Series extinction that fall of Cincinnati, *there* as Ralph Terry won twenty-three games, Bobby Richardson got 209 hits, Mantle won his third MVP Award, and the Yankees won the 1962 pennant,

Thank you for choosing Radio Spirits!

We're delighted that you've purchased our Smithsonian old-time radio product. We spend countless hours creating these collections and hope you enjoy them as much as we do! To thank you, we're offering you a FREE 75-minute Smithsonian Special Edition cassette or CD featuring *Bold Venture, Lum & Abner* and *Escape*, a $12.98 value – FREE! Just fill out this pre-paid-postage card and mail it to us... we'll rush you your 75-minute Smithsonian Special Edition cassette or CD absolutely FREE!

YES! Please send me my FREE Special Edition *(check one only)* Cassette ☐ or CD ☐

Name _____

Address _____

City/State/Zip _____

We'd like to get to know our customers better! Please take a moment to complete the following information:

1. Where did you purchase this old-time radio product?

   _____

2. Male ☐ or Female ☐

3. Age _____

Return Address

BUSINESS REPLY MAIL

FIRST-CLASS MAIL   PERMIT NO. 16   FRANKLIN PARK IL

POSTAGE WILL BE PAID BY ADDRESSEE

RADIO SPIRITS INC
PO BOX 2141
SCHILLER PARK IL 60176-9962

and *there* — with Hodges — for the Bronx Bombers' rain-splashed victory over the Giants, New York's twentieth world championship, its last until 1977.

A year later, The Voice was also present as — for once — Yankees' pitching, not power, determined that victory was secure. The Twins wafted 225 home runs and, wasting Killebrew's forty-five homers, sank to third. In Boston, Carl Yastrzemski, at .326, won his first batting title; the Red Sox still finished sixth. But in the Bronx, without one regular hitting over .287, the Yankees won a fourth straight pennant. Whitey Ford fashioned twenty-four victories; rookies Jim Bouton and Al Downing went 21-7 and 13-5; and their battery mate, Elston Howard, became the first black American Leaguer to receive the Most Valuable Player Award. "We had a lot of injuries that whole year," Allen observed of the '63 Yankees, Ralph Houk's third league champion in a row. "Maris had every injury you can think of [he played in ninety games]. Mantle ran into a wire fence in Baltimore and broke his foot [he appeared in only sixty-five]. But we had a great infield [from left to right, Clete Boyer, Kubek, Richardson, and Joe Pepitone] and pitching that was marvelous."

It was in the temple of Chavez Ravine, however, where opponents' bats most receded. A magnificent pitcher in the early flower of his prime, Sandy Koufax won twenty-five games, threw eleven shutouts, compiled a 1.88 ERA, and won the Cy Young and MVP Awards. Then, in a 1963 Grand Event that was equal parts perfunctory (only four sets) and stunning (a Dodgers' sweep), he struck out a record fifteen men in Game One and twice beat the punch-drunk Bombers. For Yankees' fans, the outcome was both disgrace and disappointment — and for their Voice, long ago fusing the thoughts *victory, Yankees*, and *October*, it was even more of a puzzlement. In retrospect, then, who should have been surprised when in Game Four, calling — it would have been lunatic to predict so — his last inning of Classic action, Allen, his voice already exhausted from a season of play-by-play, commercials, and outside assignments, combined to express that shock and choke off, within a year, his World Series career.

On October 6, 1963, at Dodger Stadium, Ron Powers related, Allen "began to emit strange noises in his throat during the late innings . . . a series of croaking . . . sounds." Shortly afterward, Mantle smashed a long seventh-inning homer to temporarily tie the final game at 1–1. "The crowd roared," The Voice remembered, "and I started to roar too. Then I suddenly lost my voice."

Later, Dick Young wrote, "If you have a television set, you know of the emotional crackup that knocked him off the air in the fourth game last October. They said he had laryngitis, but if it was, it was psychosomatic laryngitis. Mel Allen couldn't believe his beloved Yankees were losing four straight to the Dodgers. His voice refused to believe it, and therefore he could not report it."

Ascribing tangible causes to The Voice's great silencing, critics favored the idea that, distraught over the Yankees, Allen had been left, literally, *speechless*. "If that were true," The Voice demanded, two decades later, "how could I have broadcast the Yankees' heartbreak loss to the Pirates in 1960, or when Sandy Amoros made that wonderful catch in Game Seven of the 1955 Series to break the back of the Yankees?"

"No psychoanalysis here," I said.

"I'm afraid to have to say that the speculation, as is almost always the case, was a hell of a lot more dramatic than the actual event," he said. "What had happened was that a nasal condition I'd had earlier that season flared up again. At the time, I'd had it treated by the same throat doctor who cared for Frank Sinatra, and we both thought we had it cleared up. But in the seventh inning, I felt the same problem coming on, and when Mantle hit his homer and I started to roar, I felt something drop down on my vocal cords, almost like a hand had been placed over my throat."

"Then Scully takes over," I said, "and the rumors begin."

"I tried to speak but only some rasping sounds came out," he said. "Vin saw that I was in terrible trouble, so he took over as I rushed out of the booth. [Gallery's remembrance differs: "When I saw what was happening, I reached into the booth and literally seized Mel with both hands, lifting him out of the booth."] Anyway, I went into the press box and got some hot coffee and lemon juice."

"Hoping to clear your throat."

"But it didn't work—not soon enough, anyhow. By the time I could speak clearly again, the ball game was over," and also, Allen's Oktoberfests.

Leaving 1963, Mel Allen visited his twenty-second year as the Voice of the Yankees.

Resilient, he had weathered the abrasion of laryngitis.

Distinct, his vocal cords still turned heads. "I always thought I had the kind of a voice that was not unpleasant," he said once in his human, not immodest way. "Then one year *Variety* ran a list of the most recognizable voices in the world—Churchill, Roosevelt, people like that. I was the only sports announcer on the list. I guess then I realized I had a special voice."

Well-known, he was, to quote a columnist, "Howard Cosell, Brent Musburger and Curt Gowdy rolled into one"—still as identifiable in 1964 as when, a decade earlier, the Broadway musical *Damn Yankees* used his taped voice-over in a non-baseball setting.

Well-read, it was possible that he remembered how Adolf Hitler, Churchill's and FDR's foil, said of Nazi Germany's Operation Barbarossa, commencing against the Soviet Union on June 22, 1941: "At the beginning of each campaign one pushes a door into a dark, unseen room. One can never know what is lurking inside."

What one recalls, today, of Allen's final two Yankees' campaigns are faint, often colliding images of hope and atrocities migrating through the darkened stretch—of segregationists who unleashed police dogs and fire hoses on demonstrators, beat civil rights workers, and, bombing a black church, killed four small girls at Sunday School; of a newly elected governor—honoring a campaign pledge—who "stood in the schoolhouse door" at the University of Alabama to briefly bar the admission of two blacks; of November 22 and its obscenity, and how Lyndon Johnson, five days later, in his first presidential address to Congress, declared, "We have talked long enough in this country about equal rights. We have talked for one hundred years or more. It is now time to write the next chapter, and to write it in the book of law"; of Pope John XXIII, affable and courageous, and Barry Goldwater, whose campaign of 1964, it must be said, endures as a monument to stupidity, and the Beatles, the Warren Commission, *Mary Poppins*, and Cassius Clay; of Khrushchev, who was driven from power, and the Supreme Court, outlawing the Lord's Prayer in public school, and the Nuclear Test Ban Treaty, "a step," said JFK, "toward putting the genie back in the bottle"; and, finally, of General of the Army Douglas MacArthur, whose pedagogy had opened this 1951–64 time frame and whose death, at eight-four, now closed it.

For baseball too, at the start of the 1964 campaign, what came bursting out from behind the door of its media closet mixed beginnings and imminent departure. Since 1960, Chuck Thompson and Frank Messer had succeeded Carneal and Bob Murphy in Baltimore; Ned Martin and Art Gleeson had joined Gowdy at Fenway Park; Milo Hamilton had begun rowing for the Old Commander in Chicago; and Monte Moore had become the Voice of the A's, replacing Merle Harmon, the luckless emblem of the almost lame-duck Braves. While Tom Collins assisted Harmon, Dan Daniels distilled wit and solace as the Voice of the expansion Senators. Ray Scott, having supplanted Wolff at Minnesota, called play-by-play over baseball's most expansive (fifteen stations) local TV network. Bud Blattner was entering his third year in the Angels' broadcast booth; Jerry Coleman had been hired as the Yankees' fourth sportscaster; and while Nelson, Murphy, and Kiner trenched themselves as a New York institution, the Colt .45s' Elston and Loel Passe schooled Texans in the rudiments of baseball.

In 1964, the Cardinals—with 100 stations—and the White Sox and Reds, with 90 and 60, claimed the game's largest radio networks; the Cubs, limited to WGN, and Senators, with a seven-station lineup, occupied the basement. The Mets and Yankees televised 126 and 124 games; the Cubs and White Sox beamed in the eighties; Houston and the Dodgers allowed only twelve and nine away showings; and for the seventh year in a row, the Giants vetoed the television spree. "It was the same story as when TV became a real force in the fifties," said Carl Lindemann. "There were some kings. There were some paupers. And the paupers were rot eating into the bottom of the game. But that was all right with the royalty. It was very much a case of don't rock the kingdom."

Similarly, creeping socialism was denied admittance to the majors' *network* table. The '64 Yankees received $550,000 from CBS for their dominance of "Game of the Week"—nearly two-thirds of the $895,000 that network spent on television rights; nearly five *times* as much as the next club received from CBS or NBC. "As I recall, we only bought the rights to about five clubs that year," said Bill MacPhail. The Cardinals and Phillies snatched $100,000 apiece, the Orioles $75,000, the Cubs $70,000. "And because we owned the home rights to the Yanks, NBC had to buy rights from more teams to come up with a package that was even *remotely* as attractive." The White Sox, Indians, Braves, and Pirates each grabbed $125,000; together, the Reds, Twins, and Tigers took $300,000 to the bank. "I can imagine that the glamor, big-buck clubs would have been satisfied with this set-up forever," he continued. In baseball, reality was survival of the fittest/fattest. "We've got ours," cried those self-deemed by lineage and ledger book to rule. "The hell with you."

None of this, naturally, clouded an American viewer awash in 1964's ninety-six network telecasts. "The guy at home belting down a six-pack," said Blattner, "didn't care which club was getting poor or rich or breaking even. He just gloried in the fact that every Saturday and Sunday, he could have a beer, rub his unshaven face, slouch down in his favorite chair, and slurp up the words, 'Here's the pitch.' "

Slurping, he also watched the final episode of this splendid fourteen-year affair. In August, ignoring *caveat emptor*, CBS bought 80 percent of the Yankees for $11.2 million. Under Houk's replacement, the comic Yogi Berra, the wheezing pinstripes, breaking up, outflanked the White Sox, whose Gary Peters and Juan Pizarro won thirty-nine games, and the Orioles of Brooks Robinson, the league's Most Valuable Player, and with a 22–6 September, won a last, dying pennant. Eight hundred and seventy-five miles away, the Cardinals, without a championship in eighteen years, edged Philadelphia and Cincinnati by a single game and, in a roughhouse round of seven sets, went on to win the Series. Then, in tumbling succession, Berra was fired as Yankees' manager and was replaced by Johnny Keanne, who had resigned as St. Louis manager (O tangled web!) and was followed at Busch Stadium by Albert Schoendienst, bleeding Cardinals' red. "It was an amazing, whacked-out campaign," said Bob Wolff, calling his last "Major League Baseball" season. "How lucky people were around the country every week to see it." In the fall-winter of 1964, that luck, as with a bloodied pitching staff, ran out.

"It wasn't that the novelty wore off of what we and NBC showed each week," MacPhail was telling me. "It's that other factors in this area became too important to ignore."

The most important, by far, was the emergence of the National Football League, its image as a contemporary force molded by the kinetic screen. Like baseball, each pro football club once had its own separate TV package, an ideal format for teams in the lucrative markets but deadly for most of the others. Then, in 1961, Pete Rozelle, the new NFL commissioner, lobbied successfully for Congressional passage of a bill which sanctioned television contracts between a given network and a professional sports *league*. For pro football, it was a liberating and profitable decision: Its enactment allowed Rozelle to negotiate NFL coverage with, say, a CBS; each club would share equally in network revenue, Green Bay no less than the New York Giants. By 1963, the NFL received $4.6 million a year — divided among its constituent members, almost $329,000 per team. "We were their network," said MacPhail, "and through us, the NFL created an enormous impact on the mass buying public."

"In that same year, '63," I said, "the Yankees got almost double what you paid each NFL team."

"Sure," he said, "but the total of our major-league rights didn't begin to approach the NFL's. That's what galled the baseball owners — they saw what football had done." Under a 1964–65 CBS contract worth $14.1 million annually, every NFL franchise reaped more than $1 million a year. "That was the crowning blow — when now the Washington Redskins were getting a million and the Senators are getting maybe one-fifth that much. So baseball decided, 'Let's do the same thing — get our national network together. Let's get all the teams involved.' "

"A great idea, in principle," I said. "When did baseball hit you on this new share-the-wealth approach?"

"In 1964," said MacPhail. "They said they were going to start the new series in '65 — and for the first time, unlike everything we and NBC had done since 1955, this new 'Game of the Week' would go into *every* city, including the majors'. Well, this was a hell of a departure — we'd, of course, always blacked out the big-league towns — and it meant that the national ratings, theoretically, at least, would be even higher than they had been."

"Which meant baseball wanted more for its rights."

"*That* was the rub. We hadn't paid much for the rights to Dean's series, or NBC for theirs. In fact, by getting great ratings outside big-league cities for peanuts, we were getting away with murder," MacPhail confided. "Now baseball comes to us in '64 and says, 'We want *millions* for our *new* package.' All three networks were invited to bid for the series — only one was going to win. We declined our chance to bid."

"Why? You'd prospered with baseball for a decade."

"Easy," he said. "Because there was no guarantee that this new baseball series would work. No one knew if fans in, for example, Cincinnati would even want to see the Orioles play the Yankees. It was too much of a gamble — we didn't know how the big-league cities would react. And baseball wanted one network to have exclusivity — in effect, whoever won the bidding would be saddled with the whole deal."

"What if baseball had negotiated with NBC *and* CBS so that you both could have done a series — one on Saturday, one on Sunday," I supposed. "Then each would have had to put up less money — but baseball would have got the same amount of cash and twice the exposure."

Reliving 1964, MacPhail stared out the window. "From their perspective, that might have been the way to go," he said. "Had they done that, we might have been more interested — and they'd have gotten double the number of games on network TV. But they weren't really concerned with what fans at home got to see. They couldn't have cared less. All they cared about was the profit margin."

On December 15, 1964, baseball proclaimed its first "national" television package (only the Phillies, whose new local pact barred network involvement, and the Yankees, bound for one more year to CBS, abstained). The following April, said the game's television committee, the ABC "Game of the Week" would air the first of twenty-eight telecasts — a selected game every Saturday afternoon and holiday telecasts on Memorial, Independence, and Labor Days —

and for the first time, cried Tigers' owner John Fetzer, a member of that committee, let "the common good" prevail; each of eighteen clubs would receive
$300,000 from revenue totaling $5,400,000. "The total money was pretty good,
by the standards of the time," MacPhail conceded, "so baseball was *very* happy.
And they knew that the package would have been worth far more than $5.4
million had the Yankees been able to be involved."

"Which they would be at the end of the '65 season," I said, "when the CBS
contract ran out."

"Knowing that—knowing that in another year, the Yanks would be available—baseball couldn't stop patting itself on the back. 'Finally,' they said, 'we're
in football's league.' They looked at the great ratings we'd got with Dean
through the years in the hinterlands and believed, naturally, that ratings now
would be as good in big-league cities too and thought, 'We've got it made.'"
MacPhail smiled. "Little did they know."

In early 1965, ABC revealed its grand design. Each week, the network
would telecast three regional matches; the East might see the Red Sox and
Orioles; the lower South, the Cardinals-Cubs. Chris Schenkel, Merle Harmon,
and Keith Jackson were to be its principal announcers; only Harmon had done
baseball play-by-play. Meanwhile, the Columbia System made ready to stum-
ble gimp-legged through a final, extemporary year; Dean and Reese would
broadcast all twenty-one Yankees' home weekend games, then mope helplessly
as the CBS-baseball marriage died a prolonged and needless death. "We would
have been happy to go on as we had for years," said MacPhail, shaking his
head. "We just got priced out of the market. And we were very sorry to see
it end."

Its end meant that by 1966, instead of watching as many as 123 games on
three networks, a majority of American viewers could behold only twenty-eight
telecasts on *one* network. For baseball, the policy of "the common good"
brought a turning point in its television life—though, in retrospect, hardly in
the direction it planned. For Dean, it brought stark removal from prominence.
"Baseball is getting itself in an awful fix," he said in December 1965. "There
used to be four, five games a week on network TV. Now there is one. What
is happening? *What is happening?*" For a public weaned on the Great Television
Culture, the banishment of Ol' Diz and, even more senselessly, baseball's folly
in reducing its national exposure—incredibly, at the very time of pro football's
full-blown media explosion—introduced The Game's decade of the broadcasting Middle Ages: an epoch in which sterility became the very substance
of network baseball's existence.

Like the "dying quail" he often hunted and joked about, Dean fluttered
above the 1965 season before collapsing; he had expired as a national celebrity,
however, as of late autumn 1964.

Entering that fall's "dark, unseen room," another of the age's electronic
superstars had called nearly 3,500 baseball games, reveled in eighteen Bombers' pennants, twelve world championships, and a quarter-century of near-
perpetual triumph, and denied that he was biased ("I never *rooted*," said Mel
Allen, "like, say, Bob Prince, who would say things like 'Come on, boys, we

need a run'") and a random chatterer ("There are a lot of things fans can't see—on radio, obviously, and also TV. So it's your duty to *tell* details, to *tell* stories, to be their eyes and ears") and the looking glass of Yankees' hauteur ("When fans got to meet me, they could see I wasn't some ogre. But over the air, I was the guy out front. They disliked me because they disliked the Yankees; it wasn't based on fact, just emotion." Once, a wire reached Allen during the second game of the 1958 World Series. "Allen, you Yankee-lover," it read, "shut up." The message was sent two hours *before* the game began).

By the mid-sixties, Mel Allen's innate enthusiasm and sense of drama had sold more cigars, more cans of beer, more Gillette safety razors, and, possibly, more fans on the game of baseball than any broadcaster who ever lived. It was *he*, not Gowdy, Nelson, or Reginald Martinez Jackson, who wore the sobriquet "Mr. October"; his tones, phrasings, the mere fact of his presence—like McNamee, attesting that this event *mattered*—became a paraphrase for the folkpassion symbol of 1951-64 America, "this country's greatest sporting spectacle," he often cried: the World Series. Now, several months before Dean skidded into oblivion, Allen's prepotency ended with a thud. "He gave the Yankees his life," Red Barber said, years later, "and they broke his heart."

It was a September day, The Voice observed, when Dan Topping asked to see him. "I walked in to sign what I thought would be a new contract, and Dan said, 'Mel, I'm afraid I've got some bad news for you.' I said, 'What's that, Dan?' And Topping said, 'Well, Mel, we're going to make some changes. We're not going to renew your contract.' "

"Did he give you a reason?" I asked.

Allen's voice grew soft. "None," he said. "Topping looked very unhappy. He kept lighting one cigarette after another and pacing in and out of the room. I think it was very distasteful to him. All I asked him was, 'Why?'

"Dan said, 'It wasn't anything you did, Mel, and it wasn't CBS,'" having recently purchased the club. "Well, that left only one possibility—the sponsor," Ballantine Ale and Beer, located in Newark, New Jersey, and seeking to expand. "They'd made a real bad mistake," Allen perceived. "Most breweries had built smaller affiliates around the country, cutting shipping costs. Ballantine hadn't. Instead, they enlarged their home brewery and produced all the stuff there. The transportation costs became bad, just awful, and they started struggling just to stay alive. They knew they had to cut the budget, and heads started to roll."

"And your head was among them."

"They never gave me a chance," he said. "If they'd told me they needed to slash costs, I'd have come down, taken a salary cut. I'd have done anything to stay with the Yankees. If we could have just talked, just could have—we could have worked something out."

In late September, Topping chose Phil Rizzuto as the Yankees' announcer for the 1964 World Series. He would work with Garagiola, Gowdy, and Harry Caray; it was the Bombers' first Classic minus Allen since 1943; The Voice's ghost hovered atop the event. The next month, with no explanation, not even an announcement, the Yankees released the former M. A. Israel. Proud of their immunity to surprise, New Yorkers found themselves, for once, truly shocked.

As the news of Allen's firing passed quickly into print, thousands of letters flooded the Yankees' offices. Disturbed by their intensity, team officials refused comment. Having stripped The Voice of the 1964 Rose Bowl, NBC Sports did likewise. So, ultimately, to his chagrin, did the principal. "The Yankees never even held a press conference to announce my leaving," Mel said, more in hurt than anger. "They just let it leak out. So there were all sorts of lies spread around. And when people are left to believe anything, they're going to believe the worst."

"Why didn't you issue a denial?" I said.

"Because they were never *printed*. They just sort of floated around," he said. "The lies that started — they were horrible. They said I was a lush or that I beat my relatives or that I'd had a breakdown or that I was taking so many medicines for my voice that I turned numb."

"Or that you'd become too windy — you know, digressing too much."

"Yes, but it obviously wasn't that," Mel remarked, laughing. "If the Yankees had objected to my talking a lot, I'd have been fired long ago."

Trudging back twenty years, Allen flushed color from his face. "Gossip flourished in a vacuum," he said. "People just couldn't accept that times change, I guess, that there are new trends — that our Number One sponsor was going under."

"Could you?"

Gently, firmly, The Voice looked me in the eye. "It took me a long while," he said of what became almost a phased withdrawal from baseball, reemerging only in the late 1970s. "When Topping dropped his bomb, I was stunned. I just sat there and listened. But eventually, I realized that you have to get on with your life."

"No more regrets," I said.

"Not about that," Allen vowed, smiling. "The Yankees and I get along very well — we always have," and then, with a nostalgic twinge. "Anyway, after all these years, they still call you the Voice of the Yankees." At peace, he thought — what? — of Johns, Alabama, or the origins of "How about that!" or, more probably, the breadth of the dynastic years. "The Voice of the Yankees, to this day," he repeated, quietly. "You can't help but feel proud of that."

One could not feel proud of the mid-1960s New York Yankees, nor of the major-league squirearchy, exiling two of the greatest actors of our baseball time. Recalling Allen, one returned to what was said of the old Greek playwright, Sophocles: He saw the world "steadily, and he saw it whole." Knowing baseball thoroughly, The Voice transmitted it whole, and like the Volpone Dean — the fox taken as a buffoon who winds up taking the taker — merged youthful fantasies and baseball's real life.

Both brought to mind Ralph Waldo Emerson's essay on Napoleon: "He was no saint — to use his word, 'no Capuchin,' and he is no hero, in the high sense." Both occupied, in involuntary retirement, a graphic place in sport's broadcast psyche, more vivid, even, than in the decade where, at moments, their very names seemed to denote baseball play-by-play—for half of America, Dean *during* the regular season; for all of the Republic, The Voice *after* it. Was it that their careers toppled in mid-passage—Allen was only fifty-one; Dean, fifty-three—so that, for years afterward, listeners were reminded of the hypothetical, of what might have been? Was it, as the late sixties evolved, that we looked upon them as badges of a better baseball past? Had their talent been so towering? Had their successors *really* been that dull?

A decade after Dean's departure, an Alabamian, writing in *The Sporting News*, capsulized the mythmaking that Diz himself, astute and self-aware, would have found laboriously overdone. "We simple people really miss Dizzy Dean," the reader confessed. "He added life to the game. Maybe not perfect English all the time, but hours of clean, wholesome fun. Baseball has always been just for ordinary folks like me. Please bring Ol' Diz back." And what of The Voice, disappearing as he had, so suddenly, inexplicably, from the playing fields of America, and who came to have even a higher reputation after his exodus from play-by-play than he enjoyed before? Fourteen *years* following his ouster, the *New York Times* headlined a story, "Mel Allen Legend Still: How About That?" Once, bewildered by how time and absence had turned him into a kind of Grand Old Man of Broadcasting, he turned to me and said, as his manner spoke of propriety and a wonderment, not newly formed, that was neither bogus nor offensive, "You know, I've never understood it. People are still writing the Yankees, asking where Mel is. And that's unusual. I mean, criminy, you take movie stars—three years of inactivity, and they're forgotten." Not Mel Allen; when, later, in the early- and mid-eighties, through "This Week in Baseball" and other television sorties, he again courted, partially, the status of national pronouncement, it was as if he had never been away.

Deflected, in late 1964, from what was, in a real sense, almost bardic idolatry, Dean and Allen left a game which, to many Americans, still endured as a kind of secular religion, a denominator to be shared in an age—even then—inflaming a mean and boorish division. Who needed *those* two guys? big-league executives chortled; was baseball not, after all, immortal? For that matter, where was it written that baseball enlist more than one TV network? The Game had survived before national television; it could surely satisfy without it.

They were, of course, as wrong as wrong can be, and in a decade which as it proceeded took to pummeling such traditional dogma with network publicity and hype—the Age of Aquarius, its disciples cradling the bumper-sticker mentality—the conventional theatre of baseball would earn, ironically, the very television pejoration its own officials affixed so glibly to Allen and Ol' Diz: decaying, old-fashioned, less pastime than passé.

After a fourteen-year gloriole in which almost all of baseball's great broadcasters reached their absolute peak of fame, casually, if not in hindsight, obliviously, the darkest media midnight of baseball's experience began.

8
Minute By Minute

"There is something that is much more
scarce, something finer far, something
rarer than ability. It is the ability to recognize ability."
— Elbert Hubbard

BEAUTY AND THE BUNT

*Bases loaded, last of the ninth, score tied, one all. Boy, both teams would love to have this
one. They need first place and they need it badly and they want it badly and they're after it
badly. Once again, Bob Lemon looks in, gets the sign. The three runners lead away.
Lemon all set to work. The runners widen their lead. Here comes the pitch—and here
comes Joe DiMaggio racing for the plate! He lays it down toward the first-base line. Bob
Lemon races over, picks the ball up, has got nowhere to throw it as Joe DiMaggio crosses
the plate with the winning run on a squeeze play as the Yankees win it, 2 to 1!*

— MEL ALLEN, September 17, 1951.

Yankee Stadium, New York, NY. Of Casey Stengel's ten Yankee pennants, none
were won more cerebrally than 1951's. In Joe DiMaggio's last campaign (and
Mickey Mantle's first), New York eschewed its favorite bludgeon (the home run)
for pitching (Vic Raschi and Eddie Lopat each captured twenty-one games; Allie
Reynolds threw two no-hitters), speed (the Yanks stole a Stengel-era-high seventy-
eight bases), and that most exacting of baseball artistries, the suicide squeeze. Phil
Rizzuto's bunt (above), scoring DiMag to win a crucial game with Cleveland,
propelled New York into first place (and toward its third successive title).

THE FLYING SCOTSMAN

*Bobby Thomson up there swinging. He's had two out of three, a single and a double, and
Billy Cox is playing him right on the third-base line . . . One out, last of the ninth, Branca
pitches. Bobby Thomson takes a strike call on the inside corner! . . . Bobby hitting at
.292 . . . He's had a single and a double and he drove in the Giants' first run with a
long fly to center. Brooklyn leads it, 4 to 2 . . . Hartung down the line at third, not taking
any chances. Lockman without too big of a lead at second—but he'll be running like the
wind if Thomson hits one.
Branca throws . . . There's a long drive! It's going to be, I believe! The Giants win the
pennant! The Giants win the pennant! The Giants win the pennant! The Giants win the
pennant! Bobby Thomson hits into the lower deck of the left-field stands! The Giants win*

266

the pennant! And they're going crazy! They're going crazy! Oh-ho! . . . [silence in booth, pandemonium in background] . . I don't believe it! I don't believe it! I do not believe it! Bobby Thomson . . . hit a line drive into the lower deck of the left-field stands . . . and this whole place is going crazy! The Giants — Horace Stoneham is now a winner — the Giants won it by a score of 5 to 4, and they're picking Bobby Thomson up and carrying him off the field!

— RUSS HODGES, October 3, 1951.

The Polo Grounds, New York, NY. Among baseball's millennia of singular occasions, none equals "the Shot Heard 'Round the World." On August 7, the New York Giants trailed Brooklyn by 13½ games; forty-four sets later (having won all but seven), they forced a best-of-three playoff for the National League pennant. The Dodgers lost the series opener, took the second contest, and led, 4–1, in the final inning of the decisive game. Where were you when Bobby Thomson lashed his timeless home run? The polar memories endure.

THE "LONGEST HOME RUN" EVER HIT

Yogi Berra on first base. Mickey Mantle at bat with the count of one ball, no strikes. Left-handed pitcher Chuck Stobbs on the mound. Mickey Mantle, a switch-hitter batting right-handed, digs in at the plate. Here's the pitch . . . Mantle swings . . . There's a tremendous drive going into deep left field! It's going, going, it's going over the bleachers and over the sign atop the bleachers into the yards of houses across the street! It's got to be one of the longest home runs I've ever seen hit! How about that! . . . [minutes later] . . . We just learned that Yankee publicity director Red Patterson has gotten hold of a tape measure and he's going to go out there to see how far that ball actually did go. Man, that's got to be one of the longest wallops I've ever seen hit.

— MEL ALLEN, April 17, 1953.

Griffith Stadium, Washington, D.C. If you couldn't fantasize about being Mickey Mantle, forget it, nerd; you were squaresville, freaked out, out of it (but good). Hero to an entire generation, the locus of myriad baseball-card conventions, the Mick was never more pre-eminent than eighty-eight days after Dwight Eisenhower's first inaugural, when — in the City of Presidents — he wafted an imperial home run. Mantle's behemoth — the first recorded "tape-measure" orb — cleared a fifty-five-foot-high left-field wall and traveled an estimated 565 feet. It also, almost incidentally, helped New York down the Senators, 7–3.

"OISK"

The fans know that Erskine has either equalled or bettered a record. You can sense it. They want to see him beat it now. You don't get this guy on strikes very often — but you never can tell. The big Cat is one of the best free-swingers in the business. The 0-two pitch to Mize from Erskine. He struck him out! . . . Carl Erskine has set a new all-time World Series record! He has struck out fourteen men! And to a man, woman, and child — they're up on their feet out here in Flatbush!

— AL HELFER, October 2, 1953.

Ebbets Field, Brooklyn, NY. Ronald Reagan tells of how a young boy, yearning for a present on Christmas morning, discovered a room of horse manure. "Yes," cried the child, like Dutch, an optimist, "but there must be a pony in here someplace!" During 1949–53, an epoch in which they monopolized baseball, winning five World Series in a row, life was a stable for the New York Yankees; only Carl Erskine bequeathed manure. In the chilly sunshine of Bedford Avenue, before the largest Classic crowd (35,270) ever to elbow its way into Ebbets Field, Erskine struck out fourteen Yankees, eclipsing the record of Philadelphia's Howard Ehmke (v. Chicago in 1929). For the inexorable Yankees, transient mortality. For the beloved Bums, a pony.

"SAY HEY," A MIRACLE

There's a long drive way back in center field . . . way back, back! It is . . . oh, what a catch by Mays! . . . The runner on second, Doby, is able to go to third. Willie Mays . . . just brought this crowd to its feet . . . with a catch . . . which must have been an optical illusion to a lot of people. Boy! . . . [ten seconds later] . . . Notice where that 483-foot mark is in center field? The ball itself — Russ, you know this ball park better than anyone else I know — had to go about 460, didn't it? . . . [Russ Hodges]: It certainly did, and I don't see how Willie did it — but he's been doing it all year.

— JACK BRICKHOUSE, September 29, 1954.

The Polo Grounds, New York, NY. Even now, the images reverberate — of No. 24 turning, racing, nearing the distant bleachers of the rectangular yard. "I don't want to compare 'em," he replied when asked to choose his most elegaic play. "I just want to catch 'em." In Game One, inning eight of the 1954 World Series, with the Indians and Giants tied, 2–2, Willie Mays made the most indelible "catch" of the ministry that was his career.

AT LONG LAST, WHO'S A BUM?

Johnny Podres on the mound. Dodgers leading, 2 to 0. Billy Martin leads off second base. Gil McDougald off first. Yogi Berra the batter. The outfield swung way around toward right. Sandy Amoros is playing way into left-center. Berra is basically a pull-hitter. Here's the pitch. Berra swings and he does hit one to the opposite field, down the left-field line . . . Sandy Amoros races over toward the foul line . . . and he makes a sensational, running, one-handed catch! He turns, whirls, fires to Pee Wee Reese. Reese fires to Gil Hodges at first base in time to double up Gil McDougald! And the Yankees' rally is stymied!

— MEL ALLEN, October 4, 1955.

Yankee Stadium, New York, NY. Who among us was not a Brooklynite in early autumn 1955? After seven straight October debacles, Cinderella's foundlings won their first World Series (and last in the Borough of Churches). Years later, following the franchise's trek to California, Pee Wee Reese recalled: "Those years in Brooklyn — I should have paid *them* just for the privilege of playing there."

PERFECTION IN THE FALL

Count is one and one. And this crowd just straining forward at every pitch. Here it comes . . . a swing and a miss! Two strikes, ball one to Dale Mitchell. Listen to this crowd! . . . I'll guarantee that nobody — but nobody — has left this ball park. And if somebody did manage to leave early — man, he's missing the greatest! Two strikes and a ball . . . Mitchell waiting, stands deep, feet close together. Larsen is ready, gets the sign. Two strikes, ball one. Here comes the pitch. Strike three! A no-hitter! A perfect game for Don Larsen!

— BOB WOLFF, October 8, 1956.

Yankee Stadium, New York, NY. Mercurial, a journeyman hurler, Don Larsen was a perplexing maze of undiscipline and potential. "He can be," vowed Casey Stengel, "one of baseball's great pitchers any time he puts his mind to it." In the last of the "Subway Series," in the smokey hues of a sharp-shadowed afternoon, the self-styled enigma did. He employed an unusual no-windup delivery; he needed only ninety-seven pitches; he threw the first no-hitter in World Series history (and the first perfect game in thirty-four years). "I was so weak in the knees out there," Larsen confessed afterward, "I thought I was going to faint."

J.R.

Robinson waits. Here comes the pitch — and there goes a line drive to left field! Slaughter's after it, he leaps! It's over his head against the wall! Here comes Gilliam scoring. Brooklyn wins! . . . Jackie Robinson is being pummeled by his teammates!

— BOB WOLFF, October 9, 1956.

Ebbets Field, Brooklyn, NY. A lion at the plate and a tiger in the field, "He lived a life richer in honor than happiness," wrote Heywood Broun. Jackie Robinson changed America more profoundly than any athlete of his time; this line drive, in inning ten, Game Six, of the 1956 World Series, marked his final hit in the major leagues.

FIRST INNING, NO SCORE

Now Herb Score is ready to go again. Looking in, taking his time. Takes his cap off, wipes the perspiration from his brow. Looking in now to Jim Hegan. Got the sign. Here's the

windup and the fastball comes down. There's the swing and a line drive right back to
Score! It hits him and he's down!

— BOB NEAL, May 7, 1957.

Municipal Stadium, Cleveland, OH. He was, the *New York Times* observed, "the
best pitcher in the majors"—a twenty-game victor in his first full season; a sling-
shot of a southpaw, his fastball darting and pure. When Gil McDougald's shot
ricocheted off Herb Score's right eye, fracturing his nose and shrouding vision,
Cleveland lost its most palpable commodity; and baseball, a future paladin.

A BRAVES' NEW WORLD

The pitch to Henry Aaron. A swing and a drive back into center field! Going back
towards the wall! It's back at that fence . . . and is it gone or not? It's a home run! The
Braves are the champions of the National League! Henry Aaron just hit his forty-third
home run of the year!

— EARL GILLESPIE, September 23, 1957.

County Stadium, Milwaukee, WI. Fleeing New England in 1953, the Braves found
Canaan in the upper Midwest. They became The Team That Made Milwaukee
Famous, and on Hank Aaron's eleventh-inning homer against the Cardinals, won
their first National League pennant.

———————

The outfield around to the left. McDougald is on at third, Coleman is at second. Tommy
Byrne the base runner at first. Hank Aaron is pulled around in left-center field. A breeze
is blowing across from left to right. Burdette's pitch. Swung on, lined, grabbed by
Mathews who steps on third—and the World Series is over and the Milwaukee Braves are
the new world champions of baseball!

— E.G., 10/10/57.

Yankee Stadium, New York, NY. By taking the World Series, four games to three,
Milwaukee became the first non-New York City National League team to win the
championship since 1946. October's Star was ex-Yankee Lew Burdette, who compiled twenty-four straight scoreless innings and won three games, the last on only
two days' rest. Braves' manager Fred Haney, who once mocked his lanky, long-
legged right-hander, saying, "Lew could make coffee nervous," now transformed
his verdict. "If that guy could cook," he said with fellow feeling, "I'd marry him."

FOR THE OL' PERFESSOR, AN A +

Bill Skowron steps into hitting position. A right-handed batter. Lew Burdette, a right-handed
pitcher, is on the mound. Two runners on base. Burdette looks in, gets the sign, is all set to

go. Takes the stretch. Here's the pitch. Moose swings. There's a long drive going out into deep left field! It's going, it's going, it is gone! A home run! And the Yankees lead, 6 to 2!

—MEL ALLEN, October 9, 1958.

County Stadium, Milwaukee, WI. For Casey Stengel, 1958 justified the blandishment *special*. His Yankees led American League rivals—the Sorry Seven—by an unprecedented seventeen games in early August; he won a record ninth pennant; against the champion Braves, New York became the first team since the 1925 Pirates to win a World Series after trailing, three games to one. Said the Ol' Perfessor, caustically, after Bill (Moose) Skowron's three-run, eighth-inning outburst punctuated Game Seven: "I guess this shows we could play in the National League."

"ABSOLUTELY FANTASTIC!"

The final out of the ninth inning was a strikeout on Lew Burdette. It was the eighth turned in by Haddix, and at that moment, he became the eighth pitcher in all the history of base-ball to pitch a perfect no-hit, no-run game . . . He then went on to get 'em in the tenth, and the eleventh, and the twelfth—retiring thirty-six men in order and, counting the final two outs he had against the Cardinals in his last victory at Forbes Field, he retired thirty-eight men in order before a man got aboard, and then only on an error . . . One out. Batter, Adcock. Here's the pitch. There's a fly ball, deep right-center. That ball may be on through and over everything. It is gone! Home run! Absolutely fantastic!

—BOB PRINCE, May 26, 1959.

County Stadium, Milwaukee, WI. No one had ever pitched a perfect game for more than nine innings; no one had ever pitched a no-hit game for more than eleven innings. On a cold, anxious evening in the hollow of Wisconsin, Harvey Haddix did both. He sculpted perfection, threw a dozen surreal innings, and lost, 1–0, in thirteen frames, because his teammates were unable to score. "It still hurts," purred "the Kitten" twenty-five years later. "It was a damn silly one to lose."

TEDDY BALLGAME'S GRAND FAREWELL

The count one and one on Williams. Everybody quiet now here at Fenway Park after they gave him a standing ovation of two minutes knowing that this is probably his last time at bat. One out, nobody on, last of the eighth inning. Jack Fisher into his windup, here's the pitch. Williams swings—and there's a long drive to deep right! That ball is going and it is gone! A home run for Ted Williams in his last time at bat in the major leagues!

—CURT GOWDY, September 28, 1960.

Fenway Park, Boston, MA. He was called the Kid, the Splendid Splinter, and in New England, simply Himself. He was part-child and part-Gibraltar, a John

Wayne in baseball woolies, an iconoclast, a rebel, and, quite probably, the greatest hitter who ever lived. In 1960, Ted Williams batted .316 and smashed twenty-nine home runs, and at age forty-two, still the cynosure of all eyes, declined to tip his hat. He also exited as only a deity could — with a home run, No. 521, in his final time at bat. "And now Boston knows," wrote Ed Linn, "how England felt when it lost India."

BEAT 'EM BUCS

And Coates into the stretch. He sets and the two-two pitch to Smith. He swings — a long fly ball deep to left field! I don't know — it might be out of here! It is going, going, gone! . . . Forbes Field is at this moment an outdoor insane asylum! We have seen and shared in one of baseball's great moments!

— CHUCK THOMPSON, October 13, 1960.

Forbes Field, Pittsburgh, PA. Next-day accounts told of how "his electrifying homer" sent fans "into a delirium" and "turned Forbes Field into a bedlam." The essentials: Reserve catcher Hal Smith, climaxing a five-run rally in the eighth inning of the Series' seventh game, clubbed a three-run blast to give Pittsburgh the lead, 9–7, over the errant/unfortunate Yankees.

———————

Well, a little while ago when we mentioned that this one, in typical fashion, was going right to the wire, little did we know . . . Art Ditmar [actually, Ralph Terry] throws . . . There's a swing and a high fly ball going deep to left! This may do it! Back to the wall goes Berra! It is . . . over the fence, home run, the Pirates win! . . . Ladies and gentlemen, Mazeroski has hit a one-nothing pitch over the left-field fence at Forbes Field to win the 1960 World Series for the Pittsburgh Pirates!

— C.T.

The Yankees won Game Two of the World Series, 16–3; Game Three, 10–0; and Game Six, 12–0. New York outhit the Pirates, 91–60, outaveraged them, .338 to .256, outhomered them, 10–4, and scored twenty-eight more runs. How, then, in Casey Stengel's last Fall Classic, did Pittsburgh take the seventh game, 10–9, and its first world title since 1925? "The question," counseled Abraham Lincoln, "is not whether God is on our side, but whether we are on God's side."

HIMALAYA TUMBLES

Here comes Roger Maris . . . They're standing, waiting to see if Maris is gonna hit Number Sixty-one. Here's the windup, the pitch to Roger. Way outside, ball one . . . And the fans are starting to boo . . . Low, ball two. That one was in the dirt. And the boos get louder . . . Two balls, no strikes on Roger Maris. Here's the windup. Fastball, hit deep to right! This could be it! Way back there! Holy Cow, he did it! Sixty-one for Maris! Look at 'em fight for that ball out there! Holy Cow — what a shot! Another standing ovation for Roger Maris. Sixty-one home runs! And they're still fighting for that ball out there. People are climbing over each other's backs. One of the greatest sights I've seen here at Yankee Stadium!

— PHIL RIZZUTO, October 1, 1961.

Yankee Stadium, New York, NY. By victimizing pitcher Tracy Stallard, Roger Maris exorcised a ghost. In 1927, Babe Ruth hit sixty home runs in a 154-game schedule; in 1961, the Rajah unloaded his sixty-first in Game No. 163 (the Yankees played one tie). After a frenetic season, his pursuit of the Babe marred by *angst* and cacophony, for Maris, a golden time. "If I never hit another home run," he said, "this is one they can never take away from me." He hit 117 more home runs; they never did.

VERILY, A GAME OF INCHES

Ralph Terry gets set. Here's the pitch to Willie. Here's a liner straight to Richardson! The ball game is over and the World Series is over! . . . Willie McCovey hit it like a bullet. A line drive straight to Bobby Richardson. Had that ball got out of his reach, the Giants would have been the winner! Now, it's the Yankees! The final score of the ball game: The Yankees win it, 1 to 0!

— LON SIMMONS, October 16, 1962.

Candlestick Park, San Francisco, CA. In their twenty-seventh Series, the Yankees prevailed, four games to three, by the webbing of a second baseman's glove. The pageant lasted thirteen days, longest since the A's-Giants' Olympiad of 1911; four games were postponed by weather, three in San Francisco. When, finally, rain yielded to Ralph Terry, the goat of the 1960 World Series, past suffering met surcease. "A man seldom gets the kind of second chance I did," said Terry after Willie McCovey's violent drive found Bobby Richardson's mitt. "Thank God the ball wasn't a foot either way."

UP ON THE ROOF (ALMOST)

Right-hander Bill Fischer out on the mound for Kansas City. He's looking in to get the sign. Mickey Mantle digs in at the plate, swinging that dangerous bat of his around. Batting left-handed against right-hand pitching. Fischer all set to go — goes into the windup. Around comes the right arm, in comes the pitch. Mantle swings . . . There goes a long drive going to deep right field! It's soaring up high! It's going, it's going, it is gone! A home run for Mickey Mantle — and it almost went out of the ball park! Mickey Mantle, for the second time in his career, has come within a few feet of becoming the first man to ever hit a ball clear out of Yankee Stadium!

— MEL ALLEN, May 22, 1963.

Yankee Stadium, New York, NY. Of Mickey Charles Mantle's 536 career home runs, none echoed more frightfully than the eleventh-inning monster (final score: Yankees, 8–7) that glanced off the Bronx yard's towering façade. Unimpeded, a scientist said, the ball would have traveled more than 620 feet. "How," Ralph Houk asked a sportswriter, "would you like to have that one chopped into singles for the year?"

No. 7 Cuts the Cards

Here's Mantle. He's grounded to short, he's walked, he's doubled to right. Facing thirty-eight-year-old Barney Schultz. The big Yankee crowd roaring now for some action. There's a high drive to deep right! And . . . forget about it! It is gone! The ball game's over . . . Mantle has just broken a World Series record. He now has hit sixteen World Series home runs. He and Babe Ruth were tied with fifteen apiece.

—Curt Gowdy, October 10, 1964.

Yankee Stadium, New York, NY. Against the Cardinals, Mickey Mantle played in his final World Series. Leading off the ninth inning of Game Three, the score tied, 1–1, Mantle whipped the first pitch into Yankee Stadium's second tier—his first of three 1964 Series home runs; a blow, rising when it hit the façade, that gave the Bombers a 2–1 games lead. Five years later, the Switcher retired. Among his Classic records: most runs scored (forty-two), homers (eighteen), and runs batted in (forty).

9
Down On My Knees
(1965–75)

"It is useless to close the gates against
ideas. They overlap them."
— Klemens von Metternich

WITHIN THE LIMITS OF MID-1960S SPORTS JOURNALISM, THE 1965 ABC "GAME OF
the Week" was something of a pioneer undertaking. For the first time, network
baseball channeled its Saturday way into every city. *Gone* was the unconditional
blackout. *Gone* was baseball's TV absence from the nation's largest markets.
Instead, one was reassured, baseball would be born again through the imaginative eye of the American Broadcasting Company, whose "up-close and
personal" treatment had already energized college football.

Critics heard pledges of tightly framed camera shots, visionary production
techniques, and the magic of the instant replay. Viewers were promised such
color men as ex-Yankee Tommy Henrich, Leo the Lip, and Jack Roosevelt
Robinson (they were *not* ensured, yet received, Howard Cosell as a pregame
interviewer). Advertisers met avowals of coverage so intimate and rapid, so
tireless that it would "take the game to the fan," resolved network impresario
Roone Arledge: coverage more "hip" than NBC, more "with it" than CBS,
more contemporary — Lord knows — than the barnyard bearing of Ol' Diz.

Indeed, as it motored through what became a first- and final season, the
ABC "Game of the Week" had only a single, slightly irritating flaw: Almost no
one watched.

Benjamin Disraeli, the nineteenth-century British statesman, once muttered, "It was worse than a crime — it was a blunder." By mid-1965, as sponsors
winced, ratings approached ground zero, and Arledge mentally dismissed the
series, he later said, as simply "not successful," one need not possess an over-
intellectuality to look at his network package and conclude that it was worse
than not successful — it was a bust.

Across non-major-league America, conditioned by a decade of Dean's
atavistic barbs, the ABC "Game of the Week" wrote a brutal poem of bleakness.
What kind of baseball was *this?* yokels cried; it was too dull, too nondescript;
where, land sakes, was the *entertainment?* In 1965, airing the sporadic CBS
"Yankee Baseball Game of the Week" to markets *outside* the big-league sphere,
Dean and Reese collided on eleven Saturdays with, theoretically, baseball's
dominant series; against the Great One, ABC was overwhelmed; its audience
totals were fearful. On fourteen other Saturday afternoons, with the Yankees

275

not at home, ABC's ratings rose but not appreciably; minus Ol' Diz, millions of viewers — literally — went fishing. "Something happened in the conversion," an NBC executive, watching with interest, said to me years later. "Somehow, it became clear in 1965 — as it hadn't been before — that being a *Dean* fan didn't necessarily translate into being a TV *baseball* fan."

"Why not?" I said.

"For years there had been this debate over why CBS's ratings were so great," said the official, leaving NBC in 1968. "Were their games better? Was their camera work better? Or was it Dean alone? Now, we started to find out. You could look at the times in '65, for instance, that the CBS and ABC games went up against each other head to head — Dean killed 'em. Then you could look at the times CBS didn't broadcast on Saturday — remember, they only had rights to Yankee home games that year — and ABC ratings still weren't good. Suddenly, it dawned on us. With Dean gone, there were a lot of people that used to watch network ball who just weren't watching anymore."

"And in the other half of the country," I recalled, "ABC had another problem."

"There, it was even worse," he said. "You didn't have Dean to contend with — instead, you had all the local networks. Sure, it was nice that for the first time, network baseball was coming into New York every Saturday. But if ABC was showing the Red Sox and Indians and a New York station was showing the Mets-Cardinals, who in the hell were people going to watch?"

"Not the network," I said.

"*That* was the dilemma," he said. "In '65, baseball had taken the good first step of coming into major-league cities. But it hadn't done a damn thing to restrict local coverage that, invariably, just killed the network ratings. You'd have ABC going into Cincinnati with 'Game of the Week,' and they'd get a two rating [of every hundred households with TV sets] and, let's say, a seven share [of every hundred sets in use]. A Reds' game on the local station at the same time might get six or seven times that audience."

Sitting in a Manhattan bar, the ex-Sports Network official peered at a lithograph of Tom Seaver hanging above the glasswork. "Given the chance, Mets' fans were going to watch *that* guy, or Red Sox' fans, Carl Yastrzemski. They weren't going to sit down and snore through the Orioles-Twins. Well, until the game finally woke up to that fact [in 1984, banning local telecasts on Saturday afternoon, it awarded NBC total exclusivity], their policy was absolutely suicidal. To go against individual teams in the home market — that was a battle the nets were never going to win."

A great irony beset the principal announcer of the 1965 "Game of the Week," for even as his series sank beneath an ocean of indifference, Merle Harmon *did* win.

It is true that alarmingly few saw Harmon "battle" the Ghosts of Ol' Diz Past and Present, or contend, futilely, with Prince and Caray for the fealty of Pittsburgh and St. Louis, or thrash upstream against the anonymity that clung like molasses to ABC's baseball coverage. Yet those who saw were tactilely impressed. Not spiky, like Garagiola, or theatrical, like Barber, Merle was "breezy, relaxed, and stylish," saluted *TV Guide*. He was a heartland announcer, like Brickhouse, who spurned clichés for sound reporting, like Gowdy, and who trampled prejudice, like Scully, in favor of telegraphic impartiality. "It was such fun. We had a sense of the 'first time ever' — that year, you know, was a prototype for all of baseball's network TV since," said Harmon, presently, of his aborted series. "And I wish it had gone on longer — early in the season, we thought it might. But even one year was a terrific break for me. Before that, I hadn't done much national television. Since then, there's hardly been a year I haven't."

Born in 1928, Harmon was raised in southern Illinois, near Salem, and when he was sixteen, enrolled at Graceland College. The next year, he enlisted in the U.S. Navy, then returned to Graceland, then transferred to the University of Denver as a radio major. He began his fidelity to broadcasting at station KSFT in Trinidad, Colorado, and broke through into play-by-play with the 1949 Class-C Topeka Owls. "The first game I ever did involved a doubleheader between Topeka and St. Joseph," he said. "I was the announcer, the engineer, and the sweeper. It was something like 104° and I had a terrible headache."

"From the baseball?" I asked.

"No, that just made it worse," Harmon said. "The first game went about thirteen innings. The score of the second game was something like sixteen to fifteen. It was an eight-hour broadcast. I remember I apologized for the broadcast and mentioned the headache, and the *first* letter I ever got is still the most *important* letter I ever got. It said, 'Don't tell us your troubles — just broadcast the game.' "

In 1955, he succeeded Byrum Saam as the Voice of the major-league Athletics, now of Kansas City, and for the next seven seasons — a durance in which the ex-Mackmen won 432 games and lost 652, never settled above sixth place, and under five managers finished 250 games behind the champions — Harmon detailed the miscues and unimaginable malaise of some of the most wretched clubs to emboss the American League. "I've always thought of myself as a low-key announcer," he told me. "That is, I've followed the philosophy of Cubs' announcer Lou Boudreau regarding objectivity. If your team is a good one, you can criticize more freely. If it's lousy, you exercise patience." His pitch trembled between facetiousness and long-felt suffering. "Believe me, in Kansas City I was the most patient man in the world."

The sturdy mirror of midlands' baseball, Harmon broadcast in a pitcher's park — at Municipal Stadium, the left- and right-field foul poles were 330 and 354 feet from home plate; center field loomed 422 feet away — where, at most, fewer than thirty-three thousand fans could jam the renovated grandstand. On April 12, 1955, after the Athletics' move from Philadelphia, he watched Harry S. Truman, flanked by Connie Mack, throw out the first ball at the team's first outing at 22nd Street and Brooklyn Avenue. Thereafter, Merle gaped at Gus Zernial and Elmer Valo, pardoned pitcher Arnold Portocarrero, and cheered as Vic Power hit .319 in 1955, Bob Cerv bombed thirty-eight home runs in 1958, and Bud Daley won sixteen games in both 1959 and 1960. In

April 1961, he marveled as the Athletics hit Minnesota for a twenty-run explosion. Five years earlier, he pinched himself as Kansas City tapped out twenty-six hits in a July 27 game against the manifestation of everything the A's were not. "We were playing New York," Harmon said, "and it was all during my years in K.C. that they became known as the Yankees' cousins. Arnold Johnson, the Kansas City owner, was a long-time friend of Dan Topping, and they traded all sorts of great players — Roger Maris, Bobby Shantz, Ralph Terry, Hector Lopez — the Yankees got every one."

"Didn't they call you the Yankees' 'American League farm club'?" I said.

"Oh, and how it goaded our fans," Merle said. "That's what made that July night so memorable — like we were unloading our frustrations in one fell swoop. For one night *we* felt like the powerhouse." Self-effacement was in the air. "'Course, that feeling didn't last for long."

In his last year at Kansas City, Harmon broadcast for Charles Oscar Finley, who — after buying the Athletics in late 1960 — threatened to move the club to Atlanta, Oakland, Louisville, or almost any burg that waved a rent-free ball park and budding gate. "It was just crazy," said the Finleys' then-announcer. "Charlie fired me after the '61 season because I'd refused to participate in a Poison Pen Day for Ernie Mehl, the sports editor of the *Kansas City Star*. And after that, it got worse. Charlie was forever coming up with crazy stunts like a mechanical rabbit popping out of the ground with balls for the umpire, or installing a 'Pennant Porch' in right field [its 296 feet matched the length of Yankee Stadium; the inviting distance, cried Charlie O., gave New York an unfair edge], or constantly harassing the city of Kansas City for a more lucrative deal on the stadium, and seeing that, I was glad I'd left," for in the winter of 1963–64, leaving one league's smallest market for the other's, Merle traded the turmoil of Kansas City for the grotesquerie of Milwaukee.

"In Kansas City I'd been a teacher," he said. "I was the first big-league announcer they'd heard — I was telling 'em, for instance, that with a runner on second and nobody out, the batter would try to hit to right, that kind of thing. Now I get to Milwaukee and it's like Alice in Wonderland — you just can't believe it."

"Nobody had to teach *them* baseball," I said.

"Gosh no," he said. "I think Milwaukee fans are probably the most knowledgeable in the country. And probably the most loyal — you put a contending team there and you'll hit 2 million every year. But that was just the most incredible situation I've ever been in. I took over from Earl Gillespie in '64, and we almost drew a million people. Then the team announced they're moving to Atlanta for the '65 season. Then the court order says, 'You can't do that. You have to stay for one more year and *then* you can go.' So we had the bizarre — unprecedented, really — mess where you had the Braves playing an entire season in a city which knew they were going to lose the club. It was like two people living in the same house knowing that they're getting a divorce — terrible, no-win. And I was their Voice."

In 1965, Merle and Blaine Walsh rode bareback over WTMJ and WEMP as the Braves — referred to by Milwaukeans as traitors, louts, or, more frequently, unprintables — mocked Wisconsin by packing for Georgia as their tepee of memories burned. "We broadcast the entire schedule over a forty-five-station Wisconsin network, and the games were sponsored by the First Wisconsin Bank and Milwaukee's three breweries — Pabst, Schlitz, and Miller. But there were no commercials — the sponsors didn't want guilt by association, didn't want to be linked in the public's mind to these thoroughly hated Braves. So Blaine and I taped sixty-second spots with ballplayers to be used between innings just so we could catch our breath."

"And the listeners?" I said.

"My seat was so hot it was on *fire*," he said, quickly. "We had a good team that year — Lord, the Braves were exciting." They set a National League record with *six* players of twenty or more home runs: Hank Aaron and Eddie Mathews (thirty-two each), Mack Jones (thirty-one) and Joe Torre (twenty-seven), and Felipe Alou and Gene Oliver (twenty-three and twenty-one). "It was hard for me *not* to get enthused. But if I did, the thousands of people who now detested the Braves would rip me: 'How can you root for them?' they'd say. On the other hand, if I didn't, the few die-hards who still liked the Braves would blast me. 'What are you trying to do?' they'd ask. 'Keep us from getting another team?' "

That same year, sponsored by Anheuser-Busch Brewery and the Coca-Cola Company, Atlanta station WSB beamed Braves' coverage (on television, seventeen games; over radio, fifty-three) to the ball club's *future* home. "What a weird condition," Harmon said. "One network doing every game for a state the team was leaving. Atlanta doing half the same games for a city the team was going to."

The announcers embodying this Georgia sanguinity were Hank Morgan, Ernie Johnson, and the Alabamian who hoped, insiders claimed, to emerge as the Voice of the 1966 Southeast Braves. "I've known him for over three decades — even now, we have the same agent," Harmon said. "And I'll never forget how I met him — it was in 1955, my first year in the majors, and I was shaking in my boots the first time I went to Yankee Stadium. I was a nobody, he was the most famous name in broadcasting, and as I was putting things in order in the visiting broadcast booth, I saw this man move toward me, and I thought, 'My God, it's him.' He put on a big grin, stuck his hand out, and said, 'Merle, I'm Mel Allen. Welcome to Yankee Stadium. Anything I can do to help you, just let me know — we want to make you feel at home.' He broke the ice so beautifully — if it'd been up to me, I might have waited a year before I'd had the nerve to go up and introduce myself."

"And your paths came full circle in '65," I said.

"Mel had just been fired by the Yankees, and it just killed him," he stated. "So when the Atlanta job jumped up, he grabbed it; partly, I think, to show people he could still broadcast — after all, there were so many rumors floating around as to why he'd been let go. Well, *Mel* didn't even know why he'd been let go. That year of '65 he'd be up in Milwaukee with Ernie and Hank doing Braves' games back to Atlanta, and I'd have cookouts in my back yard. Mel would come over and pour his *heart* out about why the Yankees fired him — he had no idea. 'They didn't even send me a letter,' he said, not knocking any-body—he's never done that—just wondering what no one else could tell him: 'Why?' "

Drawing 555,584 clients to County Stadium, the Braves contended until early September. "There were baseball people deathly afraid we were going to win the pennant," Harmon said, "and that we'd wind up in the World Series and County Stadium would be half-deserted." Then, one night in St. Louis, Aaron came to bat against Curt Simmons, the Cardinals' aging left-hander. "With his herky-jerky motion and great change-ups, Curt had driven Hank crazy for years," the once-Voice of the Braves recounted. "In fact, it was a running joke that Curt had thrown Hank exactly one fastball in his life, and Hank had promptly hit it over the roof at Busch Stadium." Accordingly, Simmons now lofted a change-up to the lofty No. 44, who promptly bashed the pitch over the right-field roof. The blow scored an apparent three runs; would the Braves yet tomahawk the Series? "We really felt we were on our way, and then, as Aaron crossed home plate, umpire Chris Pelekoudas called him out. Lunging at the pitch, Chris said, Aaron had hit the ball with his foot on home plate. He was that overanxious to finally get back at his tormentor, Simmons."

"The homer was disallowed?" I said.

"Yep, and although [Braves' manager] Bobby Bragan went absolutely ber-serk, protesting the game and the rest, the Cardinals went on to win the game," he said. "And that one moment really demoralized the team—it was all downhill from there."

So, for the ABC "Game of the Week," were the contours of 1965. Its baseball bus ride began on April 17—Harmon, Keith Jackson (the network's future college football domo), and the mellifluous Chris Schenkel (whom one knew as the then-Voice of the New York football Giants and who was decried in the December 14, 1970, issue of *Sports Illustrated* as bereft of "real opinions or honest criticism. Speaking of old speak-no-evil, [he] has attained new heights") called balls and strikes from Shea Stadium, County Stadium, and Fenway Park—and ended, symbolically, seven months later to the day, with an unex-plainable hiring: of William D. Eckert, fifty-six, a retired lieutenant general of the U.S. Air Force, as the pastime's new commissioner. "We'd already dropped baseball, so the Eckert hiring didn't have an *actual* impact. But we all got such a huge laugh out of it. It just seemed to signify so much," said a 1960s ABC publicist. "Here we'd gone into '65 with such high hopes for the baseball pack-age, and by the end of the year we'd gotten so damned frustrated trying to get people to watch what, increasingly, was regarded as an old-fashioned game with little sixties appeal. Then baseball goes off and hires this Neanderthal, who wouldn't know Madison Avenue from Madison, Wisconsin. Everything about him simply reeked of stodginess. For the sports people at ABC, it was the perfect way to tell the world, 'We told you so.' "

Absurdly unqualified, a baseball novice/figurehead who less resembled Ken-esaw Landis than the League of Women Voters did the Russian Politburo, Eckert was far more of an unknown soldier—sadly, his tenure would not *remain* unknown — than the entities already shadowing 1965: Tony Oliva and Roberto Clemente, batting champions for the second straight year, and Boston's Tony Conigliaro, at twenty baseball's youngest ever home-run titlist, and Juan Marichal, clubbing Dodgers' catcher John Roseboro over the head with a bat on August 22, and MVP Zoilo Versalles, the key to Minnesota's first pennant, and the "Say Hey Kid," leading San Francisco to an explosive near-miss. The Astrodome opened. The major leagues welcomed the first free agent draft. Over NBC, Jack Buck and Joe Garagiola broadcast the National's 6–5 All-Star Game victory; for the first time since its birthdate, the Senior Circuit grabbed the series' lead. Three months later, Vin Scully and Ray Scott aired a Dodgers-Twins' Fall Classic which, if not a classic, was a cabaret of at least satisfactory interest. To many Americans, even more satisfactory was the Yankees' plunge into the second division; pricked by age, injuries, and perhaps — after forty years — the law of averages, New York collapsed to sixth.

It was a season that, for baseball fans, led the sport away from everything they knew — from Dean and Allen and the Bombers' overpowering dynasty and the certitude that theirs, alone, was The National Game — toward something unknown and unrecognizable, a future hidden and vaguely disturbing, and in which old verities would be supplanted, old landmarks struck down. For Harmon too, it was an epoch of transition. "Not only was I revolving around in the Braves' Twilight Zone," he said, "I was in the middle of baseball's move toward what they hoped would be an NFL-like network boom."

"And you managed both," I said.

Twenty years later, he was completely at home. "Two things let me *do* both — my love of baseball and the friendly skies. I was on planes more that year than the president uses Air Force One. I'd do the Braves all week and then fly out to the ABC game on Friday night, say, and then back to Milwaukee the next evening."

"What do you remember about 'Game of the Week'?"

"Besides the ratings nuisance, we had two other problems," he said. "One was that ABC, trying to be innovative, set up cameras and mike wires in the team dugouts for pregame interviews, and that had never been done before. And the baseball writers hit the roof. 'You're invading our prerogative,' they said. 'You're getting an unfair advantage.' They filed a protest with the Commissioner's Office, some club officials got angry with us, and certain folks at ABC started to say, 'Hey, we don't need this grief.' "

"The second problem?"

"That ABC decided they were going to get college football back on their network [after a four-year absence]. They were very proud of the kind of intimate, pioneering coverage they'd given that game in the early sixties, and now they wanted it again. But they knew they needed a ton of cash to grab the package away from NBC, to get the rights. Well, where did that leave baseball? It came down to what could do more for the network, which could get a bigger audience, which the sponsors liked more," he said. "Without that factor, I think the network probably would have picked up their baseball option. They just didn't have the dough for both."

"Other memories?" I said.

"The best was the chance to work with Mr. Robinson," he said. "Broadcasting was new to Jackie to begin with, and '65 also happened to be the first year that I had earphones that linked me directly to the producer in the truck. In this case, it was Chuck Howard, and he'd talk to us while we were talking to the audience—you'd just do what he told you."

"How'd Jackie handle it?"

"Not too well at first," Harmon said. "Chuck told Jackie something in his earphone, and Robinson blurted out, 'OK,' in answering him—which, naturally, viewers heard at home. They must have wondered what was going on. But Jackie adjusted, eventually, and for me it was a marvelous experience working with one of the most important figures in American, not just baseball, history."

Later that spring, Harmon was covering a Senators-Twins' game when *another* important figure of the second half of this century invaded D.C. Stadium. "All of a sudden I saw these guys with cameras leaning out of the press box," he said, "and I thought, 'Boy, ABC is going all out for publicity shots of the broadcasters.' Then I saw this great commotion below. Well, it wasn't us at all that the cameramen were shooting—it was Vice-President Humphrey, who was a terrific baseball fan and, having been mayor of Minneapolis and a U.S. senator, was a Twins' nut to boot."

"Humphrey," I recollected, "joined you in the booth."

"He sat down with us, like a lot of politicians do, and I expected maybe Hubert'd stay for an inning or two. But he stayed and stayed and I finally said, 'Mr. Vice-President, why don't you join us for some commentary?' And he did and got a kick out of it."

"Did you ask him to do play-by-play?"

"Almost," he said. "I was so close to asking him, and then I'd think, 'No, it would be beneath him. It would demean the office.'" He should know more politicians, I thought. "Afterward, Chuck told me that two or three times, he'd had his finger on the button asking me to call the play. But he said, 'I figured that's one call, Merle, you had to make.' And, looking back, I think I made the right call—but I'd have loved to let him call a few innings."

"Rate his commentary."

Receding, Harmon's voice hovered barely above a whisper. "It was great—the man was so loquacious," he said of the irrepressible Minnesotan. "There was only one *faux pas*. Bob Chance came out of the Senators' dugout to pinch-hit, and Humphrey said, 'Is he related to Dean Chance?' At the time, of course, Dean was a great Angels' pitcher."

"And he was white."

"Yes, and Bob was very much on the black side. So I said, 'I don't think so, Mr. Vice-President,' and boy, did I quickly get back to the game."

The calendar drifted slowly to an easing of ABC's burden. On September 26, the penultimate Sunday of the regular season, Minnesota won the American League championship, bringing to the World Series a new face—in the same fall as the thirty-seventh Miss America Pageant—against "May we have the envelope, please?" The National's all year had been a jungle-like league: On September 1, Cincinnati led by 1 percentage point and one-half game over the Dodgers and Giants; the Braves trailed by a mere two games; the Pirates were only two-and-one-half sets behind. San Francisco promptly won fourteen games in a row, whereupon Los Angeles countered with its own thirteen-game winning streak. "So we come to the last week," Harmon said, "and it's still totally up for grabs. And this is playing havoc with our schedule, because we're supposed to televise our last game of the season on that final Saturday, and as the week went by I didn't know *where* I was supposed to go." By now, only baseball's Hatfields and McCoys remained as contenders, and on Friday, October 1, Harmon entered into the "craziest twenty-four hours of my life.

"That day, the Braves were in Los Angeles to start their final series of the year — and their final games, incidentally, as representatives of Milwaukee," Merle began. "The race wasn't over — chasing the Dodgers, the Giants were still alive. That night, the Reds were in San Francisco. And that morning I began to get phone calls from the ABC people as to how, where, when, and under what conditions I would broadcast the next day."

"What was the gist of your phone calls?" I said.

"At first the message was, 'Stay there by the telephone in your hotel room — we're going to get this straightened out,' " he said. "Then they started saying I was going to this game, or that one, or another."

"Did your signals finally get uncrossed?"

"Now listen carefully," Harmon said. "At last, ABC decided that if the Dodgers won that night and the Reds beat the Giants, L.A. would clinch a tie, and in that case I should go to Cleveland for a game. On the other hand, if the Dodgers lost, I should go to San Francisco because the race would still be on. There was also the chance I'd be going through Chicago to Minnesota, where ABC could highlight the Twins, who'd already won. The only place I wouldn't be on Saturday — even if the N.L. race was tied — was where I was, in L.A., since to cover the Braves would create a conflict of interest."

"We move to Friday night."

"By now, I had plane reservations to San Francisco, Chicago, Cleveland," he said, "and the planes are leaving, like, at a quarter past midnight. But I'll only know where I'm going when I find out how the Dodgers do. Wouldn't you know it, our game is scoreless. It goes into the ninth inning, then the tenth, and I finally say to Blaine, 'I've got to get out of here.' So I rushed out, caught a cab, and told the driver, 'Put the game on, will you?' By the time we got to the airport, the game's in the twelfth inning and it's still scoreless. I *still* don't know where I'm going."

"What'd the cabbie say?"

Bathing in self-wonderment, Harmon fastened on the moment. "I'll never forget his reaction — he just couldn't believe it. He said, 'Which terminal you going to?' I said, 'I don't know. Let's pull over to the side of the road and listen to the game.' He probably thought I was either putting him on or over the edge, but finally, we're sitting there, the meter is going wild, and at last L.A. wins — they've clinched a tie. I look at my piece of paper with various flight possibilities written all over it, and I think, 'Let's see, Dodgers win. That means I go to Cleveland.' So I say, 'Take me to United, quick.' "

"And you made the flight?" I said.

Merle Harmon tackled a grin. "Barely. I checked in and the flight's ready to leave. I jump over the conveyer belt, vault through the baggage room, run up the steps to the plane, the doors close, I sit down, and the plane taxies down the runway. I say, 'At last I've made it.' Then I look at my paper again and I can't believe it. 'God, I'm going to the wrong *town*,' I said. 'I'm supposed to be in *San Francisco*.' And with that, I panicked — the whole thing was so confused."

"Hours later, you touch down in Cleveland."

"Yes, and the first thing I did — by now, I didn't know where I was supposed to be; I didn't know who I was — was call the hotel in Cleveland where the ABC people stayed. When I got through to some of our folks they told me, 'Yes, Merle, this *is* your right destination.' So in the wee hours of the morning [a day in which Sandy Koufax four-hit the Braves to clinch the Dodgers' twelfth pennant], we finally resolve this theatre of the absurd," its last act having banished the Giants (from contention), the Braves (from Wisconsin), and "Game of the Week" (from a grateful ABC).

Two years later, Harmon moved to the Twins' radio/TV booth, working with former Orioles' announcer Herb Carneal and the septuagenarian ex-sports-writer, Halsey Hall. Their Griffiths were a lively, mound-bashing team; the upper Midwest felt a sense of belonging with such stalwarts as Killebrew, Oliva, Tovar, and Carew; and that sense fell to *longing* when on the final day of the 1967 season, Minnesota lost a pennant its assemblage should have won. "If we'd beaten the Red Sox that last game, we'd have won the flag," Harmon observed of October 1st's hopes and heartbeats. "But when it became apparent the Sox were going to win it, I was determined not to moan. The excitement that day at Fenway Park was enormous, and I tried to report on it. When I got a letter that week from a woman criticizing me for not rooting for the Twins, I decided that I held up as a professional in a time of great personal stress — even now, Minnesota losing that game is the biggest disappointment I've ever had."

During 1967–69, the Twins boasted four twenty-game winners; in 1967, Dean Chance, obtained from California, no-hit the Red Sox and Indians; that same season, the franchise set a then-attendance record (1,483,547); two years later, the former Nats won the first of two straight Western Division titles. "It was a time when baseball was still relatively new, and thus the game was tremendously popular," Harmon said. "Plus, we had a lot of big-name players, and the games at Metropolitan Stadium were usually heavy-bombing affairs." Still, it was no County Stadium, and in early April 1970, as the Seattle Pilots became the Milwaukee Brewers, Merle fairly leaped at the chance to reign (again) as the Gauleiter of Wisconsin baseball.

"Schlitz was packaging the Brewers' Network, I'd worked with them before, and I really wanted to go back to Milwaukee," he said. "Calvin Griffith understood the situation and let me go. I got there five days before the start of the season."

"Still, those first years," I noted, "they were hardly shades of Spahn and Burdette."

"It was terribly difficult for our fans to adjust—they were used to success. For them, the Brewers being bad was hard enough to take. But for me, it was doubly tough—because even with a good team, I've always felt that broadcasting baseball is harder than football," related Harmon, having done play-by-play for the New York Jets and Pittsburgh Steelers, called American Football League games for ABC in the early sixties, broadcast college matches for several networks, and served as the Voice of the mid-seventies World Football League, causing the *Los Angeles Times* to opine that "his distinctive voice smacks of those golden days of Red Barber, Mel Allen, and Ted Husing"; and *TV Guide* to gush over "maybe the best radio play-by-play football man ever."

"Harder, how?"

"In football, you get up for a game the same way a player does. It's once every week—you build toward it," he said. "But in baseball, you have to remain interesting for the listener, even as you say more than two hundred times in a game that the pitcher is throwing the ball. You have to bear down all the time."

"Especially for a team that's out of the pennant race."

"Yes, and it was a long time before they were *in* one."

In 1972, the Brewers finished last and attracted barely six hundred thousand spectators; the year afterward, Milwaukee won ten straight games in early June, briefly occupied first place, and passed the million mark in home attendance. By the late seventies, as Henry Aaron returned to play his last two seasons, Cecil Cooper and Ben Oglivie arrived via trade, Paul Molitor and Robin Yount blossomed into genuine brilliances, Mike Caldwell won a franchise-high twenty-two games in 1978, Gorman Thomas pounded forty-five home runs the next year and knocked across 123 runs, and the Brewers drew nearly 2 million burghers, Milwaukee had regained its cachet in baseball's ruling aristoi.

"It took the team a whole decade to get back near the mountaintop years of the late fifties," Harmon said of his career as Voice of the Brewers. "It would have been nice to be there the year we finally got *to* the top." Milwaukee got there in 1982, winning the Eastern Division, edging the Angels in a spirity playoff, and carrying St. Louis to Game Seven of the World Series. By then, however, Merle had fled the Brewers for gold and freedom and The Event That Never Was, and his play-by-play speckled the dismaying swelter of Southwest terrain 850 miles from County Stadium.

"In late '79, I signed a multi-year contract with NBC Television," he said, "and its keystone was that I was going to cover the 1980 Summer Olympics in Moscow. That would have taken me out of the country in the middle of the baseball season—I'd have missed probably a dozen Brewer games. Bud Selig, our owner, was happy for me—he thought it was fine. But our station [WTMJ] said, 'No go. You do all the games or none of them.' So I was forced to choose—and I chose NBC. I didn't quit the Brewers, and I wasn't fired. It's just that we reached an impasse. There was no other way out."

On January 27, 1980, the *Milwaukee Journal* surmised, correctly, "Harmon will make more money, he will get more exposure, he will do less traveling, and he won't have to work seven days a week." With ex-umpire-turned-color-man Ron Luciano, Harmon aired NBC's secondary "Game of the Week." He broadcast college basketball and varied segments of the weekly "SportsWorld." That fall, deeper into what should have been his season of triumph, Merle described regional NFL games over the Peacock Network. He did not, sadly, broadcast from Moscow, since the Soviets' invasion of Afghanistan prompted the United States to withdraw from the 1980 Summer Games. "To all of us, of course, it was a terrible disappointment," he said, "even though let's put it in perspective — my letdown was nothing compared to the athletes'. Still, I had no great regrets about leaving the Brewers to go with NBC. It was fun being a neutral announcer again. If somebody kicked a play that cost a game, I didn't have any feelings at all about it. But even at NBC, I missed the hubbub — from 162 games a year with the Brewers, I'd gone cold turkey. I was only doing one baseball game a week; I was going bananas Monday through Friday — just nothing to do. That's why I knew that I could go back tomorrow and do the daily grind all over again and love it."

In early 1982, he returned to that grind. "NBC suddenly found itself with more baseball announcers than they knew what to do with," he said. "They had Garagiola, Kubek, Dick Enberg. They were about to hire Vin Scully," and ironic only in retrospect, Harmon took his tolerance and amenity to the tur-quoise skies and endless real estate of central Texas. For two years, he an-chored the Rangers' free TV coverage; in 1984, he converted to cable. "We do about a hundred cable games a year — it's just about right," Merle added. "On the one hand, it's not as boring as doing games only on Saturday, like with NBC; on the other hand, it's not as hectic as a game each day."

His arrival at Arlington Stadium intrigued cyclical students of the calendar, for shortly after Harmon left NBC, the Rangers announced their new director of television planning and evaluation. Nearly two decades earlier, in effect, this man had replaced Merle as the pastime's network Voice — the cowboy who came to define and, in a way, embody the contemporary craft of baseball broadcasting: Curt Gowdy.

*   *   *

I first heard Gowdy one late afternoon in 1960, in my family's car, over a Nashua, New Hampshire, affiliate on the Red Sox' Radio Network, as my father drove toward Nova Scotia and an August vacation.

Boston, I distinctly recall, was hosting the Yankees, and hurtling east from Albany, I heard Allen record the early innings on the Home of Champions Network. By central Massachusetts, The Voice's voice was blurred by static, and turning the dial I chanced upon a new voice — not inferior but so dis-similar — who spoke clearly of such names as Williams, Stengel, Malzone, and Mantle, and who transported me to the coast of Maine.

Unlike Allen, evoking, as he did, an exuberance, a response to personality, this announcer brought his audiences together in an informative and more somber mass. As a broadcaster, there could be no doubt of his cogency and knowledge; his play-by-play echoed with regular fellowship, and his persona bespoke the sturdy, handsome people of his Wyoming childhood with whom —even now, decades after leaving the territory—Curt Gowdy was thoroughly at home. He was, at heart, a small-town boy, and his style was a basic, earthy one. It was streaked with numbers, anecdotes, and a penchant for fact; and if less poetic than Scully, or exciting than Prince, or dependent on punchlines than Garagiola, revealed a natural, honest delivery that made one intersperse the terms *meticulous, professional,* and *fair*.

For fifteen years, arriving from Yankee Stadium in 1951, Gowdy resounded from the jut-jawed and antique park at the intersection of Landsdowne and Jersey Streets. Working for a club whose enduring mediocrity maddened loyalists and for an owner—Thomas Yawkey—who towered, the finest man in baseball, and presiding over the changing of the guard (from No. 9, 1939-60, to No. 8, Carl Yastrzemski), he became a near-institution for a franchise that *was* an institution: a regional team, the pride of Portland and Providence and Presque Isle, the arrant and ambrosial Sox.

"By the time Curt went to NBC [in March 1966, as the No. 1 announcer of "Game of the Week"], he was already one of the top announcers in sports," said Ned Martin, his 1961-65 colleague. "In football, he'd done TV games for colleges and the American Football League. In baseball, he'd done some World Series and All-Star Games. Plus, of course, he'd done play-by-play so long for the Red Sox."

"Which brought him the most attention," I said.

"Don't forget, this was in the era of the unquestioned power of local teams' chief announcers. The networks weren't so strong then, and other sports weren't as popular—if you wanted prestige and the big bucks, you pointed to local baseball. There was Allen with the Yankees and Caray with the Cardinals—you said one, you thought of the other. Vin Scully *was* the Dodgers, just like Prince with the Pirates. And there was Curt with the Red Sox— enormous stature throughout New England."

"Even if his weren't enormous teams."

"The ironic fact is how he barely missed out on both ends of having championship teams to cover. In '46 the Sox won the pennant, then almost won it in '48 and '49, then two years later Curt comes on the scene. He leaves in '66 and the next year the Sox win another title. I'm sure their listlessness in between made him a better broadcaster—he had to work harder to make his games interesting. Maybe those teams," Martin said, wryly, "were God's way of evening things up for all the fame and fortune Curt, deservedly, got later on."

Fame found Curt Gowdy in eastern cities far removed from his own best America of virgin terrain and sprawling newness—an America lying west of the Mississippi whose locals, in the Cowboy's sight, forged the country's backbone and formed, emotionally, its most vital flock. There, growing up in Cheyenne, the son of a Union Pacific Railroad superintendent hunted, explored local hills, played ball—"My dad used to say, in these years long before

TV brought baseball into the living room, 'Curtis, some day we're going to get to a big-league game' " — and fished in the sylvan waters he later brought to televised sympathy in the long-running network series, "The American Sportsman."

In 1938, Gowdy entered the University of Wyoming, earning six letters in varsity baseball and basketball, and after joining the Air Force, was discharged because of an injured spine. A doctor pointed him to surgery, where an operation, it was hoped, would repair Curt's ruptured disk. "I had it performed at the Mayo Clinic," the Cowboy said at his Wellesley Hills, Massachusetts, home, "but we didn't get the result we'd hoped for, and this was just the start of a painful back condition that would bug me for years. So the doctor said, 'Get the hell home. Just bum around, don't do anything strenuous for at least six months, and with luck you won't be a cripple.' "

It was an order no sane man could ignore, and, restless, Gowdy found that back in Cheyenne, "I was the only guy my age who wasn't in the service — all my friends had left town. I was pretty desolate until I heard that the local radio station needed a football color man to come in at the half and talk about what had happened."

"Then came your big break," I recalled from Curt's autobiography, *Cowboy at the Mike.*

"They gave me my first play-by-play," Gowdy said. "The story is that the station had sold the sponsorship for $50 in merchandise for a game between two schools too small to play regular football, Pine Bluff and St. Mary's. So the event became a six-man football game, and it was played in a vacant lot four blocks from my home. It was in sub-zero weather. There were about fifteen fans on hand and fourteen relatives of the players and me. Some start, huh?" He laughed, softly. "You know what my facilities were for that first indelible game? I stood on top of a wooden grocery crate and talked to the world — or as much as I knew of it."

"But it went well," I said.

"I guess so, even though to this day I don't know if anybody heard me," he said. "The next day our boss, Jim Ballas, asked me to do the play-by-play of a high school basketball game."

"How quickly did you say 'yes'?"

"That was the beginning of my sportscasting career, the only job I've ever had the rest of my life. And what a schedule — during the winter, seventy to eighty basketball games, then major league baseball — re-creations from our Western Union ticker — then back to college- and high school football." Even in 1944–45, radio consumed the marrow of his bones. Gowdy opened the station in the morning, read news and played records, and covered what passed in this time and spot for "the big events. There were prairie fires, bank robberies. I remember how we made a big to do over the arrival of Santa Claus for the Christmas season."

At twenty-five, Curt Gowdy was a rising presence in his native place. "I loved what I was doing," he said. "I thought, 'Lord, I'd love to do this forever' — I was so busy, involved."

Then, one night in early 1945, that intent to stay forever fell before events that led Curt to a place where he did not know a soul. Driving through Wyoming, the owner of station KOMA in Oklahoma City turned on his car radio and heard Gowdy's play-by-play of a high school basketball game. Impressed, Ken Brown stayed overnight in Cheyenne—"He stopped just to see me," said Curt. "He called my house that evening, dropped by the station next morning to say hello, talk about my broadcasting, and explain some problems he was having with his sports director"—and the next month, offered the Cowboy a job on Brown's 50,000-watt outlet.

"Any hesitation about leaving?" I said.

"A few, but the more I thought about it, it seemed to be the time to take a step and move up to the major leagues in sports," he said with that characteristic sense of unjaded wonder. "And the time I spent in Oklahoma City—it was the best on-the-job training for broadcasting that a person could have. When I got to KOMA, they told me I had only one job—to cover athletics. That meant two sports shows a day, plus the play-by-play on football and basketball."

"Quite a change from your balancing act in Wyoming."

"Yes, and I like to think this is the way every sportscaster should work, go up through the minors, get experienced, so that by the time you reach the majors, you can do the job," he said. "I'm not like [Howard] Cosell—I don't think every ex-jock's a bum. Pat Summerall, Kubek, they're fine. But too many are on the air just because of their names, and they can't hack it. They may know the sport, but they sure as hell can't articulate it. And it's too bad—they get employed while a young guy whose career *is* broadcasting finds doors slammed in his face. A young Curt Gowdy today—someone whose field is announcing—he couldn't find a job."

"What's the solution?" I said. "The public wants big names."

"You know what I'd do?" Gowdy said. "I'd have the network have a training program for athletes who want to enter broadcasting. Just don't put 'em on the air right off the bat and embarrass them nationally. Make 'em serve an apprenticeship—have the ex-jocks do some local games, learn the ropes, learn how to speak proper grammar, how to do play-by-play—and then bring the guys to the networks. This way the nets would subsidize their training—and by the time they reached the big time, they could do the job. Hell, as it is now, from the time they open their mouths, it's obvious they're out of their league."

"Coming from Cheyenne to Oklahoma City," I said, "did you feel out of *that* league?"

"No, and I'll tell you why," he said. "I had the fortune of people helping me, folks who made me feel at home from the first day I was there. So often we hear about the louses, the sons of bitches in sports. Well, I think that's wrong—I've found coaches, particularly, to be among the most wonderful people anywhere. I arrived in Oklahoma just at the time that Jim Tatum was coaching at the university and was building the football dynasty that Bud Wilkinson would continue. No one ever taught me more about football than Bud."

"And basketball?"

"At the same time, Hank Iba had one of the great all-time teams at Oklahoma A&M, and he was like a second daddy to me," he said. "He had a basketball program to rival Bud's in football—two marvelous teams to broadcast, how lucky could I get? My first year, Hank took that '46 team all the way to the NCAA championship against North Carolina at Madison Square Garden." Alive with intensity, the Cowboy related every bounce of the way.

Still, what Gowdy termed, "looking back, my *biggest* break," involved a *lesser* team—the Oklahoma City Indians of the Texas League. "This is where I got my start in live baseball broadcasting," he said. "Someone once asked me if I had to take a young broadcaster and mold him from scratch, what would I do? I said, 'I'd make him handle minor league baseball. It's the greatest teacher there is.' "

"Not as prestigious," I said, "as an Iba or Wilkinson."

"No, but it prepares you so beautifully," he said. "First of all, you cover 150 games a year, all by yourself. You're there with a pencil and a scorecard—you'd even be your own engineer. You do the balls and strikes, read about twenty commercials, and get practice selling a product. In the two- to three-hour period of a baseball game, all the demands of the sports broadcasting business are wrapped into one."

In his third year of Indians' play-by-play, Gowdy, already pining for the bigs, met the man who gratified that urge. At the time, Jack Slocum was touring the nation for General Mills. "He handled its promotions," said Curt, "and more to the point, he was in charge of orchestrating the tie-ins between baseball broadcasting and their breakfast foods—namely, Wheaties." Slocum felt buoyed by resonant comers. "He had an ear for young talent, and as he went from one city to another, he'd be on the lookout for guys who could sell baseball and, even more, his products." In 1946, it had been Slocum who ratified Allen's choice of Russ Hodges as the Yankees' second announcer; now, in late 1948, with Russ moving to the Polo Grounds, he anointed the Wyoming Cowboy. Arriving in Oklahoma, Jack heard Gowdy's play-by-play, hurried back to New York to confer with Allen, called the Cheyenne émigré and told him "to put together a brochure with some tapes and records. It cost a hundred bucks, and I had to borrow the money," and after receiving the package, telegrammed Curt in Ft. Worth. "That's where I was for a Texas Christian-Oklahoma game. And the telegram told me to come to New York where I was supposed to meet with Dan Topping and George Weiss."

Instead, leaving Grand Central Station, Gowdy stopped first at The Voice's hotel. "I had lunch with Mel in his suite, and he told me, 'Curt, I've gone over all these tapes and you're my choice. But you've still got to go through protocol, have your interview with Weiss, and get everyone to OK you.' "

"Obviously, you passed," I said.

"I guess so—I don't know if it was unanimous. Anyway, we finally had a conference with everybody and at the end the Yankee radio director, Trevor Adams, who became a good friend and whom I named a son after, got up and asked, 'What kind of money do you want?' " said Gowdy, not entirely without levity. "I would have settled for nothing. Fortunately, I didn't have to."

As Allen's assistant, drawn by New York's wanderlust, the Cowboy met both favor and maturation: favor, because in the sports capital he did not only the 1949–50 Yankees but also outside assignments in basketball, baseball, and football; maturation, because of what The Voice, indirectly, taught him — "There's tricks," noted Casey Stengel, "to this here game."

"When I came to New York, my basketball announcing was already pretty good, and the football had come along," said Gowdy, nearly four decades later. "But what Allen showed me, by example, was how bad I was in comparison at baseball. Under him, I found out quickly how far from a hot shot I was. Timing, organization, reading a commercial — I had so many bad habits, but Mel's polish helped me learn. He had that wonderful attention to detail, and he knew how to weave in the commercial naturally, which was done all the time back then."

"How was he to break in under?" I asked.

"I think I felt like Russ and Jim Woods — it wasn't very easy to work for him, but when it was all over, you were glad you had. He was the best man at my wedding [June 24, 1949]. I've always said what success I had is due basically to three men — Carl Lindemann [replacing Tom Gallery at NBC in 1963], Tom Yawkey, and Mel."

For generations of New Englanders, Yawkey epitomized, in the most legitimate manner, the stereotype of *sportsman*. He was patient (*too* patient, jabbed Red Sox' fans) and tolerant (with many of his players, he *had* to be) and as a person, unlike almost all his compeers, was someone to emulate. "Just one of the most marvelous men I've known in sports — except for my late father, he had a greater influence on my life than anyone," mused Jim Britt's successor as Voice of the Sox. "After we moved up to Boston, he treated my wife and me like members of the family. What a blessing to come here — and yet it almost didn't happen. I was really torn about leaving New York. I liked it. I was doing all the basketball games at Madison Square Garden. My career was growing. The Yankees were the greatest name in sports."

"Why leave?"

"I wanted to be some club's top announcer," Curt said, "and I knew Mel would be at Yankee Stadium forever. Plus, Ballantine was raising a stink about me doing the Garden's games — another beer was sponsoring them. And the more I thought about the Red Sox, the more I liked it — Ted Williams, Fenway, six states, all those great fans. This wasn't some Mickey Mouse operation — this was a core of the league. And the interesting thing is that when the Red Sox approached me in early '51, I had a year left on my Yankee contract. Topping released me so I could go. 'If it was anybody but the Red Sox, I wouldn't let you out of it,' he said. That just shows you how much the two clubs respected each other."

With Martin and colleagues Bob Delaney (1950–53), Bob Murphy (1954–59), Bill Crowley (1958–60), Art Gleeson (1960–64), and Mel Parnell (1965), Gowdy watched the Bosox place third three times, fourth four times, fifth once, sixth, seventh, and eighth twice, and ninth in 1965, his last year at Fenway Park. Under seven managers, mostly lamentable, Curt's teams compiled a 1,147–1,199 record, never finished fewer than eleven games from the top, played before diminishing hordes at their Back Bay beerhouse (in 1951–65, attendance fell from 1,312,282 to 652,201), and, not incidentally, grew progressively worse — by five-year intervals, 400–369, then 385–385, then a dreary 362–445.

Over WHDH Radio and its more than fifty-station network, and a seven-outlet television arrangement linking such burgs as Kittery, Maine, Hartford, Connecticut, and New Bedford, Massachusetts, the Cowboy recited the soaring deeds and lowest comedy of New England's household words. Was this the year Tom Brewer and Frank Sullivan untangled the Bosox' pitching staff? Gowdy asked. ("Maybe," cried the Cape Cod vacationer, swizzling down his Narragansett, but what did it matter if they did? "Who the hell is this Pumpsie Green is what *I* want to know, and where the hell'd we get him?") Was there a better outfield *anywhere* than the mid- and late-fifties trio of Williams, Jimmy Piersall, and Jackie Jensen? ("No," agreed the shoe salesman in Manchester, New Hampshire, "but as usual, it's not enough.") Would the Red Sox *ever* land a decent stopper? Would they *ever* break .500 on the road? Would the epochal Don Buddin, fielding a grounder in the hole at shortstop, *ever* manage not to throw the ball in the box seats beyond first base? Could new skipper Pinky Higgins (or Billy Jurges or Rudy York or Billy Herman) inspire the Boston regulars, and could Sox' starters challenge the hated Yanks? (Amid hoots and grinding teeth, other questions posed themselves. When would the Red Sox steal a base? When would the bull pen not self-immolate? Why did Felix Mantilla treat ground balls like untouchables at a bazaar? Could the gangling Dick Stuart, jibed an early-sixties adage, even pick up a hot dog wrapper without dropping it?) Was this the biblical season when Williams, Jensen, Billy Goodman, and Frank Malzone — the Bostons' outstanding heart — received even the shadow of a supporting cast? ("Sure," said residents of the Berkshires, "the same year Vermont goes Democratic.") What *was* it with these guys, anyway? In Calvinist New England, did the Red Sox disprove the doctrine of "life after death," or did they simply invert it?

Curt Gowdy was not haunted but, rather, moved by the texture of such memories. "We didn't do much in the standings — but what personalities we had! The Parnells, the Bobby Doerrs. And Williams — where would you find an imitation in another million years?" he said. "That's why broadcasting the Red Sox was so fascinating. In a way, they were *like* baseball. It's not really a team game, like football. It's a game of individuals."

"No team in baseball was as mediocre for as many years and still won as many individual championships," I said.

"Sure, and that's where the mistaken notion of the Red Sox as a 'country club' came about, that they were overpaid, that they all played only for themselves," he said. "Today people say the Red Sox are too cheap, too hard, to keep their players. Back then, people said Yawkey paid them too much, that he was a pushover, too soft on the players. With the press here in Boston, you can't win."

Williams won batting titles in 1957–58; Pete Runnels, in 1960 and 1962; Carl

Yastrzemski, the season afterward. Three times, Jensen led the American League in runs batted in; in 1963, Stuart achieved a replica. Across 1951–65, Yaz, Jensen, Piersall, Dom DiMaggio, Tony Conigliaro, and No. 9 led in other offensive categories; lyrical and asymmetrical, its Green Monster smiling wryly at home plate, Fenway Park muffled pitchers with a blanket of gloom. "And yet it's not the numbers, as much as baseball is a statistical game," the Cowboy continued. "You can't have broadcast as long as I did with the players I did without remembering the moments — individual dramas. In football, you remember entire games as great — the Jets' win over the Colts in 1969 to win the Super Bowl; the Giants-Colts in '58. In baseball, it's the crashing home run, the lightning catch, or the incredible inning or entire year" — snapshots, e.g., of the Red Sox' June 18, 1953, splurge against the Tigers, scoring seventeen runs in the seventh inning, and Piersall's six hits in a game that year at Busch Stadium; Boston's 20–10 victory the next season over Philadelphia and its 19–0 buffeting by Cleveland in 1955; the phenomenal 1957 in which Williams twice slammed three home runs, batted .403 at Fenway Park, and was intentionally walked a club-record thirty-three times; the team's three consecutive round-trippers in September 1959 against the Yankees, Yastrzemski's first hit on April 11, 1961, and the Sox' ninth-inning rally two months later from a 12–5 deficit to edge the Senators, 13–12; and the Splendid Splinter's splendid farewell, belting his five hundredth home run on June 17, 1960, at Cleveland and unfurling his final blast September 28, on his final at-bat, before 10,454 Fenway (dis)believers whose tonsils were redder than T. Ballgame's hose. "I guess my thinking was a lot like before I left Cheyenne for Oklahoma — that is, I wasn't desperate to move on," Curt Gowdy was saying now. "I could have gone on a contented man having spent the rest of my life doing the Boston Red Sox. I never thought I'd go — or had to go — with a network to do baseball."

Carl Lindemann, however, intended otherwise, and when the chairman of the major-league radio/television committee, John Fetzer, disclosed on October 19, 1965, that baseball and NBC had signed an exclusive three-year contract — through 1968, said the Tigers' owner, NBC would annually televise twenty-eight regular-season games, the All-Star Game, and the World Series — the network's thoughts settled not on Harmon, still bound to ABC, or Allen, still hoping for Atlanta, or his replacement that year as Voice of the Yankees, Joe G., or Scott and Scully, whose Series coverage that month had been sophisticated and inventive, or even the colorful, broadsiding Dean. "Diz and I were at Lake Tahoe when the news broke that only NBC was going to broadcast baseball," remembered Pee Wee Reese, who twenty-four days earlier had aired his last CBS "Yankee Baseball Game of the Week." "So I went to Diz and said, 'Hey, this could be serious. They're only going with one network — we could be in trouble.' He told me, 'Don't worry about it, pod-nuh. We'll be all right.' And Diz had been doing this for years, so I figured he knows what's what." Reese flashed his whimsical smile. "It turned out that for once, he didn't."

A minority sponsor of NBC's new series was Falstaff Brewery, and its officials pushed and prodded the Ozark showman; hire Dean, they hinted, or their money might evaporate. *"Hinted?"* laughed Lindemann. "Their pressure was almost brutal. 'Take Diz,' they kept saying. 'Look at his ratings, his audience appeal.' " But that very appeal clashed baldly with NBC's monetary interests, for having plunked down $18 million for the three-year pact, the network meant to change baseball's TV demographics and upscale its image. "Increasingly, because of its marvelous ability to self-promote, the NFL was a hit with upper-income, well-educated, suburban viewers — a sponsor's dream," a former NBC producer said. "And at the same time, Madison Avenue was more and more saying, 'God, baseball's becoming a turn-off to the affluent. It has a terrible following: the rural, low-income, the elderly, grade school graduates. What television sponsor wants them?' Dean's problem was that this was exactly the kind of people who adored him," and rejecting the bucolic Diz, The Sports Network summoned to mind the Rocky Mountaineer whose style was homestyle and whose name connoted respectability, good manners, and pluck.

Later, Red Barber would write, "In my measured opinion, the greatest television sports announcer of today is Curt Gowdy . . . He has amazing versatility and authority . . . who knows his business . . . I rate Gowdy the top man in televised sports." In March 1966, naming Curt as the Voice of "Game of the Week," Lindemann was content to say, "Anyone who knows him respects him. I can't think of anything in broadcasting Curt Gowdy could not do well."

"Why Gowdy?" I asked Lindemann. "There were other guys you could have chosen."

"Couple reasons," said the former head of NBC Sports at his home in South Freeport, Maine. "First, I'd lived in New England, and I was familiar with Curt's work — even now that he's gone from network TV, they love the guy up here. He's a hero. I walk with him on the streets of any city, he's mobbed. Plus, I didn't think there were many candidates anywhere who were as solid. I was a tremendous admirer. There was also the fact that NBC had just signed a huge contract [$42 million over five years] with the American Football League, luring it away from ABC, and we'd inked Curt to a contract to handle its play-by-play."

"Then you get baseball too."

"I still remember how it happened," he said. "The date was October 1965, and we're bidding for the baseball package at an owners' meeting in Chicago. It's late at night, and I'm asleep when I suddenly get a phone call — Walter O'Malley wants to see me downstairs at the bar. I go down and he says that if we could just raise our bid by a million bucks, we'd get the package away from ABC, who despite their ratings problems that year were interested in keeping the rights as long as they didn't have to pay too much — their enthusiasm was, to say the least, restrained."

"Was yours?"

"No," he said, "we wanted it — in those days NBC was trying to grab all the sports it could. So we picked up the phone in Chicago and called Bob Kintner [the network's president] in New York. He said, 'Hell, go ahead.' We go down in the hotel to tell O'Malley — how could you find a shrewder one than him? —

and Walter has already arranged for a press conference to announce the news. He was that confident we'd come up with the extra bucks."

By then, Gowdy had already televised college football on three networks and the AFL, with Paul Christman, on two; the East-West Shrine Game, Rose Bowl, and NBA "Game of the Week"; the first 1959, both 1960 (with Allen), and second 1961 and 1962 (with Garagiola and Scully) All-Star Games, and the 1958 and 1964 World Series. In 1958, his voice was first heard on baseball's network airwaves, and paired with his mentor on Fall Classic play-by-play, the Cowboy lured flattering reviews. "He turned in a real pro job," one writer said of Gowdy, who missed the 1957 and part of the '58 seasons because of his injured back and who reminisced, a quarter-century later, "Mentally, I'd been pretty low through the whole ordeal. That's why I'd have announced that '58 Series if it meant traveling back and forth by ambulance." Another critic remarked that while "Mel Allen, the other half of the team, is a professional but too obviously so—talking too much for TV," Gowdy "is our type of announcer—restrained, newsy, interesting. Just enough chatter."

"And in 1966," I said to Lindemann, rereading that critique, "you asked Curt to chatter for NBC."

"Chet Simmons [then director of NBC Sports] came to me one day and said, 'You know, about this baseball thing—Gowdy would be a natural,' " Lindemann stated. "I got to thinking about it and remembering New England and it hit me. Chet was right—he was. With Curt, we got one guy to handle our two main sports—we saved money that way [trading the Red Sox for NBC, Gowdy took a pay *cut*]. People talk about all the dough Curt made with us— shit, they're wrong. I know for a fact that in all the years he was at NBC, he never earned more than $200,000 tops."

"Looking back, a steal."

"Hell, it was a steal even then."

Originally, the Cowboy sought Ted Williams as his 1966 network partner. "Who knew more about baseball?" Curt asked me. "Who in the whole of sports television was more outspoken, flamboyant, well-spoken, handsome? He'd have been terrific. So Simmons and I fly down to Florida in March [1966] and Ted says, 'I'll do it only because I get to work with Curt, who I trust implicitly, and if I don't have to wear a tie.' After that, the only thing worrying him was that he'd use bad grammar or forget himself and start swearing on the air. I said, 'Don't worry about that—we'll be fine.' I thought Ted was all set."

"What happened?"

"A couple of things happened before the '66 season started. First, there was a fracas with Chrysler, one of the 'Game's' major sponsors," Gowdy said. "Somebody came up with the rumor that Ted had done a Ford commercial, which wasn't true; all he'd done was be photographed putting Sears sporting goods—he was their spokesman—into the back of a Ford truck. Until the truth became known, Chrysler was pretty upset. Then another of our sponsors, Falstaff, started putting the heat on NBC, and they caved in—and when they caved, they fell on top of Ted."

"How so?" I said.

"Falstaff wanted me to take Dean as my partner. 'No sir,' I told 'em. 'Look, Diz is a boyhood idol of mine. I love the guy, but I can't sing "Wabash Cannon Ball" and all that craziness—our styles are different,' " Curt averred. "I didn't have it in my contract that I could choose my partner, but the network respected my feelings—they rejected Diz. Then Falstaff came up with Pee Wee, whom they also had under contract, like Dean. I guess they figured he'd be more acceptable to me and they'd still have their boy on the games. And the network went for it."

NBC gushed with pleasure; Pee Wee projected continuation; he was a safer link than Dean back to baseball's most *beguiling* "Game." And what of Gowdy? He was a *reporter*, NBC said with evident satisfaction; his work bubbled with detailed preparation; to be accurate and inform the public was to put first things first. What did it matter that his performances were not dramaturgical (hey, sporto, whose were?), or his voice was not a fever-swamp (what d'ya want, fella—a Jennings Bryant in the booth?), or that the Cowboy was not hypnotizing as a speaker? He was objective; he did his homework; he had few peers as an observer. He was a man who knew baseball and who honored truth, and who was not bereft, spontaneously, of charm. Surely, that would be enough.

It cannot now be denied that Curt Gowdy emerged for an entire generation of listeners as the national signature of baseball broadcasting. From 1966 to 1975, he called the play-by-play of every All-Star Game, every World Series game, and virtually every regular-season network game. In exposure, he eclipsed Dean and Allen; in influence, he emerged as his contemporaries' response to McNamee; wherever front-stage baseball was, *he* was, and because his talents also draped the non-big-league world, he became sports television's correlate of commercial shilling's Bruce Jenner: Versatile, the Cowboy was also ubiquitous.

"Curt's had a rough last few years," Lindemann said in early 1985. "First, NBC reduced his schedule, and he left there in 1979. Two years later the same thing happens at CBS Television. All of a sudden the big events weren't there anymore—it's like the entire industry was saying, 'All right already, you've been on long enough.' He doesn't know why television just decided to jettison him—*I* don't know, and I've thought about it often. He feels badly about it, and I try to tell him, 'Look, there'll never be another like you. No network will ever have all the big events to itself the way we did at NBC, and no guy'll ever get to announce them all like you did.' "

"Today, the big events are split," I said. "The World Series between two networks, the Super Bowl among three, college basketball and football on two. It's more compartmentalized."

"Exactly," Lindemann said. "That's why I tell Curt, and I believe this: 'Nobody ever did what you did—not McNamee, not Husing, not Allen—*nobody*. And nobody's ever *going* to.' " All told, Gowdy televised an unmatched twelve Fall Classics and fifteen All-Star Games (one and two more, respectively, than The Voice), seven Super Bowls and seven Olympic Games, twelve NCAA basketball championships, thirteen Rose Bowls, the Pan-American Games, the

Sugar, Cotton, and Orange Bowls, and twenty years of "The American Sports-man," winning, personally, four Emmy Awards and hosting such totems as Phil Harris, Bing Crosby, and Andy Devine: circa, the mid-1950s, from *The King and I*, "etcetera, etcetera, etcetera."

Three times, Curt was voted National Sportscaster of the Year by the National Association of Sportscasters and Sportswriters. In 1970, he became the first sportscaster to receive the coveted George Foster Peabody Award for excellence in broadcasting, which praised his "versatility . . . and blend of report-ing, accuracy, knowledge, good humor, infectious honesty and enthusiasm." Two years later, on March 27, in Cheyenne — "the greatest day of my life," he said. "How could you beat it?" — Wyoming named a state park after him and his alma mater presented an honorary doctor of laws degree. Before environ-mentalism was fashionable, Gowdy had enlisted; "it's something I was brought up with — that the outdoors is sacred." He was elected president of the Basket-ball Hall of Fame in Springfield, Massachusetts, and entered the Sportscasters and Sportswriters, the International Fishing, and, in 1984, the Baseball Halls of Fame. "Gowdy was from the 'old school,' " said the latter's president, Ed Stack, in Cooperstown. "He concentrated on the game and never confused his own importance with that of the event he was covering."

In a profession where careers are transient, Gowdy's network longevity was remarkable (in the mid-eighties, divorced from national television, Curt still aired baseball play-by-play for CBS Radio). "He may not have many ups, but he doesn't have many downs," a columnist once wrote. "His approach is smooth, but knowledgeable. He may not excite you with a flamboyant phrase, but neither will he bore you." In an age that maligned responsibility, Gowdy preached self-discipline. "You have to be right on top of everything. You can't go on the air without knowing just about everything regarding the teams that will be playing," Curt said in 1982. "When I was doing the top events for NBC, I bought twenty-two different out-of-town newspapers every day and read them all." At one point in the early seventies, he aired a daily morning show for NBC Radio from his home in the Boston suburbs; to accommodate him, the network built a studio in Gowdy's basement. At times, he traveled 350,000 miles a year — vaulting in a given week from regular-season baseball to pre-season football to a dinner for the committee on the Atlantic Salmon Emer-gency to leisure fishing in a Wyoming trout stream; conferring with coaches, managers, players, and executives; before an NFL game, closeting himself in a hotel room for hours to memorize the numbers of every player; becoming such a peripatetic that Jerry Lister wrote, "A typical week in Gowdy's life is like a chapter in Jules Verne's 'Around the World in Eighty Days,' " and Carl Lindquist added, "Putting a town into a piece about Curt Gowdy is like trying to establish residence for a migratory duck."

Recalling, especially, Gowdy's 1966–75 decade as the quintessence of major-league announcing, one thought of Ralph Houk telling Howard Cosell, "You're like shit — you're everywhere." He was a superb professional, network officials and nearly all of Curt's colleagues agreed, a nice guy who finished first—and yet, this too cannot be denied: The Cowboy's reign on network television coincided, lucklessly and almost exactly, with the most barren period in baseball history.

In 1965, the fourth season of two ten-team leagues, the bigs gloried in a then-record attendance of 22,441,900 people. The year afterward, paid admissions reached another high of 25,182,209, or 15,544 spectators per game; two years later, the average crowd totaled 14,261; in 1970, 14,788; in 1972, 13,872; in 1975, a still-flagging 15,324. Under Gowdy, the twenty-five Saturday and three holiday 1966 "Game of the Week" telecasts averaged an 8.9 Nielsen rating (2.5 points less than Dean's ABC network norm thirteen years earlier); in 1967, the figure rose to 9.4, then dropped like a parachute—to 8.6 in 1968, 8.5 in 1969, and 8.1 in 1970. At the same time, NBA basketball on ABC jumped from a 7.4 rating to 9.3; NCAA football, 12.2 to 13.3; and CBS-NBC's pro football, 23.7 to 24.2. All-Star numbers, it was true, leaped from 1967's 25.6 to 1970's 28.8—but post-September, baseball also stumbled; as the decade shook America's once-transcendent interest in the sport, the World Series toppled from 25.7 in Curt's first season to 21.0. "In TV, like anything else in life, once a reputation is established, it's awful hard to tear down," perceived an early-1970s CBS director, "and as people began saying that baseball was a loser, that it was over the hill, the networks began to believe and, then, to spread it." But it was not on television alone that baseball suffered—though it *was* there, perhaps, on this medium increasingly understood to be the Main Street of America, that the pastime's distress seemed deepest. To those who discussed such things, it became an article of faith that The Game was too slow and tranquil, too stable and establishment to survive an age nurtured on violence and an ethical laissez faire. Its condition was obviously terminal; with luck, the patient would live out the seventies.

Among New York's creative colony, network baseball became a pariah— "Baseball is a game that was meant to be played on real grass and during lazy afternoons, with small children, old men, and an occasional housewife watching," chimed the Big Apple-based firm of Kenyon and Eckhardt, one of the nation's largest advertising agencies—and upon the social register of America the big leagues played mounting chords of disinterest. "The trouble, nearly half the nation's sports fans report," pollster Lou Harris, a lifelong baseball fan, said as early as April 1965, "is that baseball has become too dull." That year, 38 percent of American fans named baseball as their favorite sport; 25 percent chose football; the previous season, Dean and Allen's last of national primacy, baseball led the Harris survey by 45–23. By 1967, the pastime's edge had shrunk to 10 percentage points, 39–29—baseball was favored by those over fifty and making under $5,000, football by followers under thirty-five and clearing $10,000; "a sizeable 41 percent of all fans feel that the pace of games is too slow and they take too long to play," Harris said, adding, "there is a distinct ground swell for more televised games"—and as the sixties tumbled near their close, the unthinkable began to introduce itself: The American Game was no longer America's Sport.

In 1968, Harris respondents narrowly preferred baseball to football as their favorite sport, 39–32 percent, and the game they followed most, 39–37; for the first time, more people said they had less, not more, interest, in the bigs; in the South, West, and among the affluent (a thumping 52–22 percent), *football* was now the National Pastime. "Later that winter," Harris would write, "football passed baseball as the top favorite sport and has since held its front-runner position." In early 1969, football fronted, 31–28; in 1970, 30–27; in 1972, 28–23; and two years later, 23–19. "By 48 to 24 percent," the pollster reported, "fans agree that 'there are too many times during a baseball game when there is no action,' " and "by 44 percent to 31, a plurality of fans say that 'compared with football and basketball, baseball is not as interesting to watch on television.' " Then, in 1975, Harris released the majors' worst brush with agony. Only *16* percent of all fans named baseball as their favorite sport — far below football's 24 percent, and barely *one-third* the number who saluted The Game a decade earlier. Campaigning against Truman in 1948, a self-assured Tom Dewey strutted, "Just remember, when you're ahead, don't talk." Baseball responded in the mid-to-late sixties, "When you're ahead, don't act." Dewey lost a presidential election. Baseball lost a generation of fans.

"We forget it now, but that's how people were talking then, that baseball was a goner, that it was either dying or dead," Bowie Kuhn said in 1984, his game having reclaimed much of its lost popularity. "I took over in '69, and they were burying our corpse. When I left as commissioner [fifteen years later], we were more appealing than ever before. You ask me what my greatest satisfaction was? Precisely that." By the early seventies, however, the appellative *National Pastime* rivaled window dressing, figment — sport's answer to The Emperor Who Had No Clothes.

As baseball's network embodiment, was Gowdy responsible for the game's decline? Hardly. As its only national Voice, was he at least a tangential cause? Possibly. Did his public acceptance suffer from guilt by association, the sense that because baseball was more passive than it once was (or was perceived as such), its network telecasts must also be? Undoubtedly. Would the Message and the Messenger have benefited from a rise in network games/announcers — baseball so that fans could watch (and be attracted to) more than the niggardly amount of twenty-eight yearly telecasts; Gowdy so that he could avoid the risk of inevitable ennui? Undeniably.

There was, to begin with, the fact that literally millions of fans, accustomed, as they had been, even two years previously, to the 1964 network mouthpieces of Allen, Garagiola, Wolff, and Dean, found themselves suddenly limited to a *single* Voice. "I'm a friend of Curt's and I think he did, technically, a super job on 'Game of the Week.' But to sit him down with a microphone for ten whole years and have him as baseball's one and only network announcer — it was a terrible mistake," I remembered Bud Blattner saying. "You could have brought back the Good Shepherd to read the Twenty-Third Psalm and the rest of the Bible's poetry, and in this fast-paced society where everybody's attention span is so short and where people demand variety — if He was the only guy you heard, viewers would have even turned on *Him*." Comfortable and reassuring, a favorite uncle with his omnipresent cigar, Curt Gowdy wore well — but to broadcast an entire decade (every inning, every pitch, of a sport's entire coverage), no one wears *that* well.

There was also the truth that unlike baseball's past network announcers, Gowdy's identity blurred. For all his college bowls and other miscellany, Mel Allen meant Yankees; turning to The Voice, one thought, indelibly, of balls and strikes. Dean and Garagiola did only baseball; Barber may have been, as he wrote, a "professional broadcaster," but to the larger populace, he was a *baseball* broadcaster; even Nelson, despite NCAA football and related serials, was linked by outlanders to the Liberty "Game of the Day." But Gowdy had been the American Football League's network play-by-play man *before* becoming baseball's, and between that chronology and football's ratings lead (by 1970, NBC's pigskin audience beat baseball's by 1.1 Nielsen points), most viewers took Curt — ironically, given his fifteen years in Boston — as either *football's* man or, reliving McNamee and Husing, a diffuse, amorphous star; their allegiance leaned to network, not a single sport; their ties were multiple, indistinct. "Most announcers have always done more than one sport, and that was OK, because if you called baseball and football in the old days, the baseball was always more important — that's the game the broadcaster would be linked with," said Blattner. "Then comes the late sixties, and on the network level, football became the status thing. So you had guys like Gowdy doing both, a Ray Scott [CBS's Voice of the Green Bay Packers who doubled, locally, with the Twins], and the situation was reversed. When a guy did both sports, it's the NFL who won."

"And all during this decade when baseball most needed a distinct Voice, an announcer whom people would hear and say, 'Hey, there's that *baseball* guy,' a Prince or a Scully, if they'd gone national — this was the time baseball had no one," I said.

"It hurt badly," Bud said, "and the proof that it didn't work came a decade later, in the late seventies and early eighties, when realizing, finally, the game's need for its own announcers, the nets named *baseball* men to their play-by-play" — Vin Scully on NBC, Al Michaels on ABC.

Was it possible too, not a few critics asked in this age of baseball's press rivaling Richard Nixon's at the height of Watergate, that Gowdy was — if not, necessarily, the wrong *announcer* for "Game of the Week" — at least the wrong *kind* of announcer?

"It might be that baseball is the only sport which television does nothing for artistically. As a spectacle, baseball suffers on the tube," Harry Caray wrote in 1970. "It could be that the inability to create the same feeling for the viewer that is the case when he is at the ball park is the crux of the matter. The fan at the ball park rarely notices the time span between pitches and plays. At the park, he is busily engaged, buying a hot dog, ordering a beer, arguing with his company, disagreeing with the fan in front or behind him. At the park, there are myriad fillers, but that same fan at home can't do the various little things he does at the park. Therefore, he finds things dull, he becomes distracted." Only a Thespian, Caray concluded, able to distract these distractions, could squeeze that fan's attention.

By the late sixties and early seventies — with Bill Veeck bemoaning, "Baseball has become dull, not just slowed down, but dull. The owners recognize their failures and the loss in prestige to pro football. They're being murdered, but many won't admit it. They won't admit it because they don't know what to do about it"; *Forbes* magazine, the nation's foremost business periodical, featuring a battered baseball on its April 1, 1971, cover with the headline, "Baseball: The Beat-up National Sport," and text that read, "Baseball has been shoved aside by football as the most popular and profitable professional game. In growth it is [even] being thoroughly outclassed by formerly minor professional sports . . . Last year it really seemed to come apart at the seams"; and that clarion of authority, *The Wall Street Journal*, editorializing, "Not many years ago, baseball ranked with apple pie, the flag, and motherhood as an American Institution. If you weren't enthusiastic about it, you risked being considered un-patriotic. Not so anymore" — now, if ever, some observers claimed, baseball *needed* a network Thespian. Yet, deviating from Dean, who, quoting Blattner, "*was* the show," and The Voice, whose very presence, like Cosell's a decade later, often *became* the show, and Nelson, whose throb of a voice *adorned* the show, Gowdy subscribed to and capsulized — as literally as any sportscaster of post-World War II America — the maxim that the announcer was no worse/better than the game. Curt rarely summoned passion, or prompted a natural laugh, or brought a choke in the throat. "The one who remembers that the game is the important thing is the one who will make it," he said of young an-nouncers. "The guy doing play-by-play becomes almost incidental." The Cow-boy was no hypocrite; weekly, viewers heard what Curt, instinctively, believed. "In Gowdy, his philosophy led him to what his personality was already attuned to," said a former associate. "He adhered to the factual transmission of what was going on; in telling, as crisply as possible; in reporting, as a journalist. He wasn't a Barnum — he was more like a classy AP reporter. But what happens when, through no fault of Curt's, The Game itself, as opposed to its games, starts to seem boring? Then the question pops up: 'Is what Curt did all those years — his approach, his great talent — is that *enough?*' "

As Voice of the Red Sox, it *had* been; Gowdy gave his audience baseball with the bark off, as New England listeners wanted. "Because of a general attitude toward sports and listening habits developed from certain announcers, dif-ferent regions are receptive to varying styles," Jack Craig has written — or, as Lyndon Johnson, talking politics, once etched, graphically: "What's chicken salad to one part of the country is chicken shit to another." In Boston, as he would have been, I think, in such (purist, conventional?) dens as Philadelphia, Cincinnati, or Detroit, Gowdy was enormously popular; he presented the game as generations of fans were used to hearing it — straight, without frills. "A Fred Hoey, a Heilmann and Tyson," said Ernie Harwell, "they set the early pattern — low-key it, play it down the middle. And because listeners grew up on this style, woe to the broadcaster later on in these towns who departed from those guidelines." But what of St. Louis, Chicago, and Pittsburgh, where Caray, Wilson, and Rowswell vied as barbarously large extravagances? Here, guidelines decreed that neutrality bombed, that to low-key was to put to sleep, and that baseball happenings without drama — "without a red-hot style," said

Bob Prince—voided the essence of what Thomas Wolfe called "the million memories of America. Almost everything I know about spring is in it," he wrote. "The first leaf, the jonquil, the smell of grass upon your hands and knees, the coming into flower of April."

A Jack Brickhouse, I am convinced, would flounder at Fenway Park; a Lon Simmons, on the other hand, would drown at Wrigley Field. One approach was personal; the other, much less so. One's effect lingered; the other's ended, like *that*. Years after leaving play-by-play, Dean reaped louder ovations at the Hall of Fame ceremonies than those accorded the *inductees*; of Allen, Stan Isaacs said in 1978, "It was noted that of the two-dozen baseball personalities introduced from the floor [at a writers' dinner], he received the liveliest applause. This was not an unusual phenomenon." At the opposite extremity, when was the last time you heard someone say, "Gee, I miss Gene Elston on Mutual's 'Game of the Day'?" One school was reminiscent of Presidents Kennedy and Nixon, even now—across a thousand arguments—evoking torrents of admiration and disgust. The other celebrated the blandness of Presidents Ford and Carter; asked, "Now that they've left office, what did you think of them?" you were tempted to respond, "You mean their administrations are over? How can you *tell?*" Both brought to mind the analogy of 1984 candidates Mondale and Reagan. "Think of them as a violin," a discerning voter urged. "When one talks, it's like you hear every squeak of the box. When the other talks, you hear his soul." From 1951 to 1965, New England loved Curt Gowdy's squeaks; across the late sixties and early seventies, detractors jabbed, the nation wanted soul. If Milwaukee's Bob Uecker, debuting in 1972, rivaled a Johnny Carson monologue, Caray, a night of barroom joviality, and the Prince of Pittsburgh, something out of Lewis Carroll, the Cowboy, they said—spuriously, perhaps—resembled a mirror but not a magnet; their complaint, he neither attracted nor repelled.

"Sure, I might have chosen someone else to do 'Game of the Week,' " conceded Earl Gillespie, "mostly, I think, because Curt's style was such a departure after a decade of people like Barber and Dean and because during this time the majors maybe needed a different type of salesman. Then, again, I might not have—that's not the point. In the age you're talking about, you could have had Laurence Olivier do play-by-play, and baseball still would have stumbled." For more than Gowdy or Scully or "Hey, Harry!" as his revelers cried, it was *another* source that inflicted upon baseball its bitter, corrosive night. "Up until now, baseball had been sacrosanct, more American than Honest Abe, more Catholic than the Pope. No one had *dared* attack it," John Steadman of the *Baltimore News American* said. "So when, under Pete Rozelle, the NFL began to advertise itself as the new religion, baseball was totally unprepared to respond. They were like a punch-drunk fighter being belted around the ring. And everything the NFL did—either frontally or subliminally—was designed to disparage baseball, to get this message across: 'Hey, they're out of it. We're the ones who're relevant, the wave of the future, who have a sort of new culture sense of style.' "

Bursting from an early-fifties obscurity, professional football—promoting, merchandizing, always selling—touted itself as "Big-Game America," the very title of a 1969 prime-time documentary on CBS Television; it was, an NFL-produced book read with typical self-aggrandizement, "a game of varied but elemental excitements. . . . Football is a complex, patterned sport, a visual image well-suited to the changing flow of a television screen"; wedded to Norman Mailer's *Technologyland*, television was "the electronic core of the nation and football is the television sport."

Television, saw Rozelle, was not just the NFL's most lucrative commodity; it was its future. By 1969, over NBC and CBS, in a regular season one-half as long as baseball's, pro football televised more than *three* times as many network games. Unlike baseball, it used Sunday to *build* its TV audience—the day that families stay at home, friends and relatives drop by, and more men watch more television than at any other time. Then, having cemented its national sect, it welcomed a third network, ABC, and a novel notion, "Monday Night Football," which, in turn, reached women, pleased sponsors, and *expanded* that following. Pro football graced weekly syndicated programs, seized space on network newscasts, and became, *Newsweek* magazine ordained in a September 1969 cover story, "America's most popular sport, a wildly popular game."

The league even formed an in-house production company, the benchmark NFL Films, Inc., which, starting in 1962, produced more than twelve thousand separate pieces in the next twenty-five years—team highlight films, championship game and Super Bowl specials, and a litany of regular series for use on commercial television—and which, by the mid-eighties, was grossing about $10 million a year. Its long-time Voice was John Facenda, boasting a modulated baritone "that could make a laundry list sound dramatic. Someone once said he could make the coin toss sound like Armageddon. I called it his 'retreat from Dunkirk' voice," mused Steve Sabol, executive vice-president of the company, upon Facenda's 1984 death from cancer.

"How'd you happen upon Facenda as your Voice instead of, say, a Scott?" I said.

"When my father [Ed] started this all in the early sixties, he wanted to present the NFL on film the way Hollywood produces movies—lots of close-ups, pictures of faces and hands, great music. That meant it couldn't be done like other TV fare," Steve said. "It had to be different—so different that a guy watching a game on Sunday would watch the same highlights three days later to see how we treated it."

"Different," I said, "as in Facenda."

"He'd been the Walter Cronkite of Philadelphia anchormen in the late fifties and early sixties—tremendously impressive. But nationally and in football circles, he was a nobody. Well, to do our voice-overs we didn't want a sports announcer—a Gowdy or Summerall. That had been done before," he said. "On the other hand, we didn't want a big name like a Gregory Peck—he'd overwhelm the show. What we wanted was someone anonymous nationally who had a great voice. Presto, Facenda. And everybody in pro football fought us early on. 'Who the hell *is* this guy?' they said." Sabol paused. "They found out soon enough."

"And as he often said when a writer complimented him on reading a script, 'You gave me a good horse to ride.' "

"A spavined mule would have looked good with John on it," he gibed. "We knew from the beginning that our scripts were going to have fewer words than the average sports show, and the less we said, the more important it was that it be said right. John was so good we changed our entire writing style—shorter sentences, more staccato cadences. And his voice—it cut through music. Every year we give a sixty-five-piece Munich orchestra $200,000 to compose original music for our shows. With that kind of investment, you want a voice that's golden. His became one of the most twenty-four carat anywhere." Facenda became the NFL personified—"What he read," said Sabol, "seemed to be written on two tablets"; he often received fan mail addressed to "The Voice of God"—and his employer, sport's video leviathan. By the 1980s, the NFL Films Archives in Mount Laurel, New Jersey, had reached the size of a gymnasium. "It's pro football's Smithsonian," said Sabol. "The only thing better documented than the NFL is World War II."

As pro football spliced tape, won awards, and played the networks like a cello, major league baseball enjoyed a 1960s siesta. "Baseball's made some strides since then, and I'm glad, because I like the game. Even more, it keeps us on our toes," said an NFL Films official. "But I well remember how in the late sixties—before they finally woke up—whenever we wanted to feel good by comparison, we'd take a look at some of the few film efforts baseball was putting together—you know, we'd have a private screening—and we'd just sit there and roar. At first, we thought they were *trying* to be funny—sort of like a camp approach to baseball. Then we realized they were being serious. And my next sensation was in feeling sorry for them. I mean, the quality of what baseball was doing in films and for TV—it wasn't just bad, it was awful."

Annually, NFL Films crafted a thirty-minute highlight movie for each of its franchises; if the Yankees (or Red Sox or Cardinals) wanted a similar promotional tool, said the *bigs'* film division, let them produce it on their own. Pro football won hurrahs (and thirty-four Emmy Awards for everything from writing, directing, and cinematography to music and editing) for syndicated ventures like "Great Teams/Great Years" and "This Week in the NFL," "NFL Action" and "The Men Who Played the Game," "NFL Week in Review" and "NFL PRO! Magazine," "NFL Game of the Week" and "Inside the NFL," "NFL Yearbook," "NFL Films Presents," "Monday Night Match-up," and the "NFL's Greatest Moments," ad nauseam. In 1977, the majors introduced *their* first syndicated series, the estimable "This Week in Baseball"; the debut trailed football's by a decade.

"Sure, we were late bloomers. We were a long time getting off the ground with series like this," said the former Associated Press baseball editor, Joe Reichler, becoming Eckert's chief aide on February 4, 1966, and, ultimately, vice-president of the Major League Baseball Promotion Corporation. "Let's face it—baseball has only recently got started, and it has so much more to do. But we feel that this is the kind of program—a 'This Week in Baseball'—the sport ought to be involved in."

Absolutely, one wanted to cry. Yet, from 1965 to 1975, awash in pro football's flood tide of TV, baseball was content simply to father movies of the World Series and All-Star Game, and, occasionally, such cinematic forgettables as *Baseball's Incredible Year*, a twenty-four-minute review of the 1967 season "which seems to lack polish," *The Sporting News* said, charitably. I remember that flick vividly, for watching it in September of my 1969–70 freshman year at college, I became aware of laughter—directed not at its narrator, Gowdy, but rather (as I burned; mocking baseball was like renouncing Christmas), at the film's background music, uneven visuals and editing, and hackneyed, cliché-marred script.

Later that fall, during baseball's first Championship Series, I affronted another indignity. Nine years earlier, over radio and television, more than 250 *regular*-season baseball networkcasts had been carried to the public; now, failing to find, inconceivably, one station on my radio that covered the playoffs, I discovered that the majors couldn't/wouldn't arrange for even all *post*season games to be broadcast nationally. "The first year of the divisional format, I announced the American League playoffs [Orioles-Twins; the National's matched New York and Atlanta] which were broadcast over sort of an ad-hoc network [of less than one hundred stations, many weak and remote]," said Harwell. "The same was true of the other league." Through 1975, as the All-Star Game and World Series were aired over NBC Radio, the playoffs would continue in this suspended shape; several Championship Series—e.g., the 1973 Reds-Mets' tango called by Scully and color man Bob Gibson—were transmitted over a network packaged by the Robert Wold Company; in others, if one was removed from a television, it was next to impossible to hear baseball's new preamble to the Grand Event. "One of the things I'm proudest of," said Bowie Kuhn, "is that we finally got this straightened out." In 1976, baseball signed an exclusive contract with CBS Radio to broadcast the Autumn Occasion, Mid-Summer Classic, and both league playoffs. Each year, ratings rose, advertisers panted more heavily, and baseball blessed its fortune. Yes, congratulations for *everyone*. But still, I wondered, why so late—this expanding buzz saw of radio coverage? Why was the NFL always one step ahead?

What I recall most severely, though, was *television*—or the 1965–75 lack thereof.

Not, apocalyptically, gazing at NBC's superb handling of the All-Star Game, where Gowdy starred with Reese (1966–68), Blattner (1967), Sandy Koufax (1967–68), the Astros' Elston (in 1968, at Houston), Mickey Mantle (1969–70), Jim Simpson and Maury Wills (1973), Joe Garagiola (1974–75), and the ever-sidekick Kubek (1969–75). In 1967, the July Classic became a first-time evening program, "and we kept it right there, in prime time," said Kuhn, "where it could reach more people, where we'd get more exposure, and where it would help promote baseball the most."

Nor could one quibble, really, with The Sports Network's coverage of the World Series, which NBC promoted, quoting Gowdy, as "America's premier sports happening." Its director, Harry Coyle, proved himself a master— "Viewers will see what Coyle wants them to see," wrote one critic about camera shots, mid-action cuts, and replays, "which also usually is what they want to see." The Cowboy too, his reserve so assailed during the regular season, seemed ideally cast for Oktoberfests that, already satiated with drama, needed little verbal hyping. "Maybe some people got tired of Curt by June or August — maybe we should have had more announcing variety," said Lindemann. "I don't know — maybe that would have saved him later on from the vicious knives of writers like Gary Deeb of the *Chicago Tribune* who just kept slashing him. But how could you possibly knock Curt on the big events? God, he could rise to the occasions — so precise, accurate, knowing. He was the absolute best when it counted the most." Gowdy telecast the Classic with network colleagues Kubek (1969–75) and Garagiola (1975) and a medley of local announcers — in 1966, the Dodgers' Scully and Baltimore's Chuck Thompson; in 1967, Ken Coleman of the Red Sox and the Cardinals' Caray; the year afterward, Harry and Detroit's George Kell; in 1969–70, Nelson, Thompson (twice), and Jim McIntyre of the Big Red Machine. Enter 1971 and Prince and Thompson; 1972, and the Cincinnati-Oakland tandem of Al Michaels and Monte Moore; 1973, and a Monte-Nelson ticket; 1974, and Scully with the perennial Moore; and the final year's lineup (by now, Gowdy's decade-long October dominance was breaking up) of Cincinnati's Marty Brennaman and Boston's Martin and Dick Stockton.

Another television ten-strike was Kuhn's decision (or was it NBC's?) to make the Fall Classic nocturnal. On October 13, 1971, more than 60 million viewers watched Game Four of the Pirates-Orioles' convention, baseball's first Series outing scheduled in prime time; the numbers prompted the commissioner to schedule all nonweekend games at night beginning in 1972. "The writers hated the move, which I can understand," Kuhn said, dryly. "After all, the later starts gave them less time to put stories together before newspaper deadlines. But when they said television was now controlling the Series, that's where I got mad. *We* were the ones, not NBC, pushing for prime-time games [Lindemann: "Bowie's reversed what happened. It was *our* initiative — baseball just supported it"]. And we did it for a very simple reason. We're not here to please all baseball writers, or a given network. We were here to make baseball more popular, to expose it to as many people as possible. With day games during the week, you were shutting out millions of working Americans who couldn't see the games then. At night they could [since 1971, night games have about doubled the audience for weekday contests]. We wanted to make the Series a truly national community event. And I think we have." In 1975, more than 124 million Americans watched all or part of the madcap Reds-Red Sox' World Series. In 1975 and 1977–78–79, the Autumn Occasion pulled at least a 50 percent share of the TV audience; the '78 Dodgers-Yankees' festival earned a still-record rating of 32.8. On October 21, 1980, as 77.4 million viewed the ultimate act of the Royals-Phillies' pageant, Game Six became the then-most widely witnessed baseball contest; *in toto*, 130 million people saw the seventy-seventh Oktoberfest. Six years later, another Red Sox' calamity joined them with everyman's existence: Game Seven of the Boston-New York Fall Classic, an October 27, 1986, Yawkeys' hemorrhage seen in 34 million homes, lured an estimated 81 million of the devoted and the curious—easily, the most-watched baseball game of all time.

"Baseball's going to prime time in October was the overwhelming reason the game's network contracts became more and more valuable," said the *Boston Globe*'s Craig. In 1969–71, the majors pocketed $16.5 million annually from NBC; in 1984, baseball began a six-year contract with ABC and NBC worth $1.125 billion—or nearly *$188* million per year. "To have your network rights go up by that much in a little more than ten years is a whale of a coup—and, really, only the Series made it worthwhile."

"You had your regular season," I said.

"Yes, but their ratings have been mediocre for almost two decades now," he said.

"You had the All-Star Game."

"Sure, and the audience was large, but it was only a once-a-year deal."

"What about the playoffs?" I said. Under baseball's dual-network policy, starting in 1976, fans could see as many as five prime-time games during the Championship Series.

"Yes, but they were shorter than the Series, and their audiences were barely half as large. What made the Series so attractive to the sponsors and networks, and why it helped shove baseball's rights up, is that now you had a whole week of weekend day and weekday night games," Craig observed. "The Series became the perfect vehicle not only to get excellent ratings, and thus by itself push a network's entire Nielsen numbers up, but even more, to promote the heck out of your new prime-time lineup, since it was precisely at this time that the new TV season was getting under way."

"What about the years of Gowdy, 1966–75?"

"The Series was obviously a big deal then too," he said, "but baseball's whole relationship with the networks—and its need to promote the Series or the playoffs—was far less of a life-and-death arrangement than today. Everything was more low-key. Salaries were lower, teams depended more on attendance and local rights than network money to survive. Television didn't have the leverage then that it does now—how could it? Its cash wasn't subsidizing the game. Because only one network was involved with baseball and because, financially, it didn't have that much invested in the sport, NBC didn't have the incentive to go out and really shill."

"And baseball's attitude?"

"Because it wasn't wedded to TV as was the NFL and because it didn't get that much in dollars versus what it got locally, it didn't feel the necessity to push the network to promote the game."

In the late sixties and early seventies, such timidity cost.

The reality was, for instance, that baseball's packaging of the 1969–75 Championship Series virtually invited America to minimize the affair. The playoffs began the first Saturday after the regular season; NBC would televise, say, the American League contest at 1 P.M. [in 1973, with Gowdy and Kubek] and the National's [with Simpson and Wills] three hours later. Fine; it was the *next* day where insult rose. Because of Sunday pro football coverage, NBC

showed only one big-league playoff game; e.g., in 1969, the Peacock Network
telecast regional NFL action at 1 P.M. and both baseball sets, simultaneously,
at 4 o'clock. Attending college in western Pennsylvania, I saw the Mets and
Braves; viewers in Maryland watched the Orioles-Twins. "Jesus Christ, don't
those baseball people give a damn about what we get to see?" said a friend,
sitting, bleary-eyed, as the Steelers played the Eagles that Sunday afternoon.
"Here baseball has these new playoffs — the big deal, the doorway to the World
Series — and you can't even see all its fucking teams." His expletives softened
only slightly for the third games, on Tuesday, in New York and Minnesota;
one began at 1 P.M., the second at 2:30 (a pattern continuing for Games Four
and Five). If the Amazin's' drama consumed two-and-one-half hours, the
camera would switch at 3:30 to Minneapolis-St. Paul; with luck, you might
see the last four innings of the American League final. These overlaps (ending, finally, in 1976, ABC's first year of coverage) became the bane of baseball's early-October existence; unlike the NFL, demanding that each play of
a postseason tournament be televised in its entirety, the majors accepted tin-
pot treatment docilely, with a grateful and benignant smile.

Even worse, for those who recollected 1955–64, was baseball's *regular*-season
network diminution. It was not simply that "Game of the Week" promos
drowned beneath pro football's tri-network blizzard, or that syndicated newspaper critics, who move about in packs, largely ignored televised baseball in
their columns and reviews, or even that the pastime's meager TV coverage
comprised — for that slice of America limited only to network games; in 1966,
still nearly 50 percent of all households — what former umpire Jocko Conlan,
marooned in Phoenix, later dubbed "a sporting hell. Every week I turn on TV
and I see more football games than I know what to do with. How many baseball games can I see? *One*. This must be God's idea of athletic purgatory." It
was also, more pivotally, that the bigs abandoned Sunday afternoon, like the
French Army, Paris, in June 1940, to the National Football League.

"Over the years, there have been several times when baseball's contract came
up for bidding," a leading CBS sports executive told me in 1978, "and we've
gone to them and said, 'Let's broadcast a network series on Sunday. It's the
day more people watch the tube than any other — we'll get a lot of high-income
males. It'll get better ratings than Saturday.' And they've always turned us
down." Instead, its officials said, baseball meant to protect Sunday attendance
by barring network television (a misconception; there is no evidence that
"Game of the Week" has hurt Saturday gate receipts, or to suggest that *Sunday's*
would be hurt). Moreover, the major leagues intended to ensure Sabbath
exclusivity for their *local* television networks; national broadcasts, they said,
would divide the audience. "That's another fallacy," the CBS man affirmed.
"We told baseball, 'Even if each of your local teams televises at the same time
on Sunday — which never happens; most clubs don't televise each Sunday —
your networks still will reach barely half of America's population. There's a big
section of the country just begging for Sunday televised baseball — the Buf-
falos, the Denvers, the Miamis. As it is now, you're just writing them off.' But
they wouldn't listen. It was incredible."

Later, Lou Harris would show how baseball's popularity paralleled the degree of its television coverage. It was highest, understandably, said the pollster, where the bigs were already most heavily televised: the East, the Midwest, the cities like New York, Philadelphia, and Chicago, its denizens deluged by local telecasts. It was lowest where viewers were restricted solely to *network* exposure: stretches of the South and West; before SuperStations, a Conlan's Phoenix; even afterward, suburbs and provinces beyond the sweep of cable. "Interesting, isn't it?" a friend commented after reading several Harris surveys. "The linkage is unmistakable — you can't avoid seeing it. Those sections of the country which most sharply felt the void when NBC and CBS stopped doing Sunday baseball — the small towns, the rural areas away from big-league cities. Why wouldn't they feel it? It was about the only TV baseball they had — are *exactly* the same parts where baseball has lost the most popularity in the last twenty years." The NFL used Sunday networkcasts to engineer its rise; after the mid-sixties, baseball foolishly shunned them altogether. One reheard Dean saying, "Man, Sunday is the day to take it easy, when people are sitting around — they *want* to watch a game. Why don't them guys in baseball wake up?"; or Blattner, enouncing, "Because Saturday is your first day of the weekend, during the summer you're going to play golf. Or you've been in the office all week and now you're going to cut the lawn. Or take the kids out horseback riding. When it's gorgeous outside, you're not going to stay inside and watch baseball. But maybe you would the *next* day, after you've caught up with what you missed during the week. That's why baseball has constantly missed the boat by not switching to Sunday." One thought of Churchill's barb at a political opponent, defining, eerily, the caliber of baseball's 1965–75 TV design: "An empty car drove up," Sir Winston explained, "and Clement Attlee got out."

It was the absence of *ideas*, this late coming of awareness of the need to promote and enhance The Game, that became the prodigious cause of baseball's long, disturbing winter. What if, for example, the majors had used two networks to carry their games, thereby ballooning their publicity, and broadcast nationally on Sunday, thereby expanding their clientele, and aping the NFL, formed an aggressive production and marketing company, thereby courting fans on the periphery, and linked the Cowboy with a colorful color man (a Uecker, for instance) who offset, not reinforced, his broadcast milieu, and demanded that a Prince, Dean, or Caray air that Sunday telecast, thereby blunting Gowdy's overexposure, balancing Curt's studiousness with theatre and laughter, and galvanizing a generation — *mine* — weaned in our childhoods on the concept that baseball was not merely statistics, history, and the technicalities of the hit-and-run, but rather, that finest of three-letter words — *fun?* Would that not have made Gowdy's product more marketable, reduced Curt's burden of making baseball — by *himself* — a thriving network concern, and avoided the grotto from which, only recently, the pastime has returned: a period in which baseball plunged from a position, in the early sixties, as the Holy Father of American Sport, to its image, a decade later, as the game immersed in Last Rites? Looking back, it was not that Curt Gowdy failed baseball; it was that baseball failed itself.

All this, of course, lay in the future when, in 1966, Chet Simmons of a hopeful NBC pledged that five or six color cameras would cover each game. "That's never happened before," he said, "and our fans are going to see baseball like they've never seen before. They will have a variety of views"—from behind home plate, the outfield, first and third bases, and from high up in the stands. "We're going to show the instant replay, stop-action, and split screen, all the new techniques. But we're never going to forget, as Shakespeare might have said, that 'the play is the thing.' " The next season, NBC switched its three holiday games to night and inked the retired Koufax to a ten-year, $1-million contract; he would conduct a fifteen-minute pregame show and join Reese as Gowdy's sidekick. How would he prepare for television? "I don't know what I should do," Sandy confessed. "This is all so new to me." In 1969, Reese was quietly dismissed. Said Pee Wee after his release leaked to New York writers: "I just wonder what went wrong. Did I talk too much? Didn't I talk enough?" From the secondary contest, Kubek, a Lindemann favorite, vaulted to the primary "Game of the Week"; Simpson, now teamed with Koufax, survived as the backup play-by-play man.

Four years later, in the spring following Sandy's induction, at thirty-six, into the Hall of Fame, Koufax himself resigned ("I just never felt comfortable in front of the camera," he said in his soft-spoken way. "I'm just not suited to it. I never was"; "Koufax was one of the nicest guys I've ever known," Lindemann added, "and also one of NBC's worst mistakes"); the network hired Wills as his replacement ("Maury knows as much about journalism," Melvin Durslag prophesied, correctly, "as Edith Bunker knows about stealing second"); and NBC began a regular series of fifteen Monday-night telecasts—patterned, to some extent, after "Monday Night Football," and some, as we have seen, after Bob Wolff's machinations of 1955–61. Each week, the network vowed, a celebrity would occupy the Cowboy's booth—sharing reminiscences and airtime with Curt and Kubek; lending (it was hoped) an "extra dimension" to regular-season coverage.

On May 21, 1973, NBC invited Ol' Diz to grace the season's first prime-time outing. "Boy, it'll sure be nice to get back for one time," Dean declaimed. "When they told me I could go on network TV—just so I could say hello to all the fans we used to have—I was so tickled I almost shouted for joy"; for those whose imagination could retrace the workings of a decade earlier, it was a trip back, as ratings attested, to a warmer, more redeeming time.

There was the Great One mangling names and destroying syntax, singing "The Wabash Cannon Ball," bringing the game, as was his custom, *alive*; and as Ol' Diz rollicked, there was Gowdy too, perceptive and insightful, not striving, at least for these few bittersweet hours, to be an outcrier—freed to do what he did as well as anyone: *report*.

Where did Dean live? the Cowboy asked him.

"Why, in Bond, Mississippi."

Where was Bond? Curt said.

"Oh, 'bout three miles away from Wiggins."

Then, where was Wiggins?

"Oh," Diz replied, " 'bout three miles away from Bond."

Later that summer, Dean broadcast a second Monday "Game of the Week," then retreated to golf, outrageous barbecues, and, in July 1974, at sixty-three, a fatal heart attack; Gowdy returned to his final three years as the Voice of network baseball. But I like to remember them, frozen, from that May evening of good-bye songs and farewell pleasantries. They worked well together, these polar extremities — one, even as a play-by-play announcer, an analyst who disdained the catch-all phrase; the other, opinionated, a ham; Curt, the envy of his colleagues; Dean, the stuff of legend. They would have formed, I believe, an alluring, artful team.

"There'll never be another like me," Ol' Diz often said. In a more subtle, often unappreciated, and memorable way, the same was true of Gowdy.

*   *   *

Even apart from "Game of the Week," Gowdy would have found much in events of the mid- and late sixties to exhilarate his curiosity.

That first year of NBC coverage, Baltimore banners exhorted their heroes to "Bomb 'em, Birds!" — and in a season where the National League tossed garlands to pitcher Tony Cloninger, who lashed two grand-slam homers in one *game*; to Most Valuable Player Roberto Clemente; and to the Alou brothers, Matty and Felipe, placing one-two in its batting race, the Eastern Shore mercenaries complied.

Frank Robinson, stolen from Cincinnati in an off-season trade, smacked forty-nine home runs and 122 RBIs, hit .316 and won the Triple Crown, and became the first named MVP of both leagues. Brooks Robinson, saying of himself, "I could field as long as I can remember but hitting has been a struggle all of my life," and F. Robby, "Frank is not out to make friends, but to knock someone on his tail," showed why he was regarded — even then — as the standard against which all third basemen were compared. No. 5, Little Looie (Aparicio), Dave Johnson, and Boog Powell sparkled in/as the infield. At twenty, Jim Palmer won fifteen games. Having clipped their first pennant, the Orioles soared against the favored Dodgers of Koufax, 27–9 in his final season, and reliever Phil Regan, 14–1 with twenty saves, and the symphonic Scully, televising his first Fall Classic with Gowdy and eighth overall. Blanking Los Angeles for thirty-three straight innings, Baltimore swept the 1966 convention floor.

"We couldn't believe it — we had to slap ourselves to prove we were awake," was how Chuck Thompson, the Birds' principal announcer, tabbed their four-game Series victory. "It's like we were in a dream — that our reality was fiction."

Sadly, for the Republic, *its* reality was *real*.

While the Birds plundered, Americans learned of leech-infested tributaries and careening Southeast Asia hills, of casualty rates that, starting in early 1968, eclipsed five hundred a week; of costs exceeding $25 billion in 1967 alone; and of troop commitments that soared and multiplied, rising from twenty-six thousand in 1964 to five hundred and forty thousand. One remembered Adlai Stevenson, August 1953: "The ordeal of the twentieth century — the bloodiest, most turbulent era of the Christian Age — is far from over."

Two days after John F. Kennedy's assassination, Lyndon Johnson told a visiting diplomat, "I am not going to be the president who saw South Viet Nam go the way China went." Overtly patriotic, a devoted anti-Communist spawned on Texas pride and Alamo mythology, LBJ declined to leave Indo-China; the Saigon government must be saved. In August 1964, when two U.S. destroyers were attacked in the Gulf of Tonkin, Johnson ordered a retaliatory assault on North Viet Nam. Six months later, endowed with an electoral mandate after his pummeling of Goldwater, Johnson ordered a strike against the North, rebutting a Viet Cong mortar attack on an air base at Pleiku. March 1965 saw the first American combat troops disembark in Viet Nam, the inception of bombing raids up north without any pretense of retaliatory intent, and the debut of strategic sorties that caused more United States bombs to hit Viet Nam — North *and* South — than fell on all enemy targets in World War II.

To some Americans, such "gradual escalation" symbolized our weakness, not strength, the confusion of our president, not the courage of our people. U.S. policies, they said, invited even neutral powers to swagger; we ensured that every nation would treat us as a punching bag — and, ducking, we would stagger in response. "What we've got to do," George Wallace bellowed about the morass in Viet Nam, "is win. We've got to pour it on." But there were others who scoffed at the domino theory, and termed the North-South contest essentially a civil war. The United States, they believed, supported a corrupt government in Saigon against peace-loving forces in Hanoi. Roosing a three-syllable ultimatum — Get Out Now — they sought to oust the government their own president had helped install. To them, the war provoked mindless barbarism, a tragic diversion of resources that could better be used at home.

From Yale to Berkeley, violence, division, and terror assumed proportions undreamt of when the 1960s broke. "I think it would be difficult," sociologist Robert A. Nisbet has said, "to find a single decade in the history of Western culture when as much calculated onslaught against culture and convention in any form, as much sheer degradation of both culture and the individual passed into print, into music, into art, and onto the American stage [and into its streets] as the decade of the sixties." Increasingly, Americans spoke at cross-purposes. We thought at cross-world. We talked *at*, not to. What we understood was hate.

In 1966, Richard Speck murdered eight student nurses on the Second City's South Side; within three weeks a second madman shot and killed fourteen people at the University of Texas. The following year, Paris reported only twenty armed robberies; London, 205; Washington, D.C., 2,429. On college campuses, bombings, sit-ins, and vandalism harassed sites where beer blasts and panty raids had once been labeled daring. University buildings were burned and scholarly works destroyed; thousands marched on the Pentagon; teachers reaffirmed support for amnesty and Ché Guevara, demanded a curb on penalties for use of marijuana, mocked military budgets as bloated and obscene. Riots savaged not just Detroit but also Cleveland and Newark, Washington and Watts. In 1968, with labor unrest peaking, more man-hours were lost through strikes than any previous year. In August, watching the Democratic Convention on television, America saw trained antiwar protesters clash with club-swinging police — "the shock troops of the Establishment," radical Tom Hayden charged — in the blood-swept streets of Chicago. Between November 1968 and May 1969, according to the Center for Research and Education at Columbia University, nearly two thousand high schools endured severe disruption. "Violence," blustered militant H. Rap Brown, "is necessary. It's as American as cherry pie."

So, supposedly, was baseball; yet the sleepy summer game was ill-prepared by temperament for a decade in which only passions could prevail. Instead, it was the Rozelles who *celebrated* violence "to rise to dominance in the 1960s, at a time when the United States experienced a socio-political crisis unparalleled in its history," boasted an official NFL publication, *The First Fifty Years*. The field was "an arena for war," and on any football Sunday, "the field is occupied by two dedicated and disciplined armies." After all, pro football was "basically a physical assault by one team upon another in a desperate fight for land"; it was "America's vicarious warfare . . . an invitation for a man to express himself violently and powerfully while achieving the acclaim."

Football's acclaim, nurtured through such propaganda, meant that baseball and baseball broadcasting might shimmer, theoretically, as they had a decade earlier, but both would *seem* less all-important.

I recall, particularly, that intense, remarkable, and at times, quite wonderful year of 1967. The Orioles toppled to sixth. The Athletics said good-bye to Kansas City. Matty Alou hit .330 or over for the fourth consecutive season; Clemente won the batting championship at .357; Jim Lefebvre led the once-robust Dodgers with fifty-five runs batted in. Gowdy and Company stirred anecdotes and black coffee during the longest All-Star Game, an American's 2–1, fifteen-inning defeat. Behind such names as Lou Brock, Tim McCarver, and Orlando Cepeda, the Cardinals gripped the neologism "El Birdos" and an unexpected pennant, then subdued the improbable American League champions for whom even the World Series marked anticlimax: the 100-to-1 Red Sox, ninth the previous season, "ending one of baseball's great rags-to-riches stories," wrote the *Times'* Joseph Durso, by dueling three teams in a last two months of fury to win the flag on the final day, transport New England, and complete "The Impossible Dream." Said manager Dick Williams, years later: "Carl Yastrzemski in 1967 [.326, forty-four home runs and 121 RBIs, MVP and Triple Crown, and a season which almost dwarfed the heroic] was the greatest player I've ever seen." Gushed Tom Yawkey on the night of his ball club's triumph: "I haven't had a drink in four years, but I'll have one now." Wrote Roger Angell: "Even a restrained backward look at this season must appear hyperbolic."

The Red Sox' pennant waved, finally, in Set No. 162 of the regular season, a 5–3 victory over Minnesota, in the first "Game of the Week" — surprise — televised on a *Sunday* by NBC. "We knew that the American League championship was probably going to be won and lost in that one final game," said Scotty Connal, a former NBC executive producer who left in 1979 to become executive vice-president and chief operating officer of ESPN, the twenty-four-hour all-sports cable network. "So we decided to bump one game off our scheduled football double-header and broadcast from Fenway Park." The network's generosity was ill-rewarded; for this, the most crucial outing of the year, the Nielsen audience kept barely abreast of CBS's meaningless early-season telecast of the Lions-49ers; easily and thoughtlessly, baseball was seeing the consequences of its self-removal from the weekend TV psyche of America. "Football had become a drug, a Sunday habit," shrugged Carl Lindemann, "and even for a special baseball game like that one, once a habit's established, it's tough as nails to break."

By 1967, two other established habits had broken — Mel Allen, rebuffed in his campaign to announce the *Atlanta* Braves; and Red Barber, fired cynically by the Yankees one day late in the 1966 season.

"Mel and I had done those games from Milwaukee in '65," Ernie Johnson said, "and with the Braves coming south the next year it seemed for Allen like a perfect setup. He was the leading candidate, the obvious choice." But seeking to seize the loyalties of this entire region, the ex-Wisconsins sought a younger, less New York-buffed veneer, and when the team took the field at Atlanta Stadium on April 12, 1966, it was Milo Hamilton calling the first game of the hit-happy, error-prone Peach Street Braves. "It was a shock, his getting that job. It was a plum — everybody thought it would go to a bigger name," Lindsey Nelson observed of Bob Elson's 1961–65 sidekick. "But what had happened was that the White Sox' games in the early sixties had been pumped on their network throughout the South. So people in Atlanta had already *heard* Milo — to them, he *was* a name — and between his good voice, good looks, the easy-to-take manner, he won." He paused, briefly. "I'm sure of this: it was a jolt to Mel."

That year, Atlanta placed fifth. In the Bronx, Allen's Bombers peopled an unfamiliar cellar in what Barber termed, aptly, "the saddest season in their history." Something about the finish evidently disturbed the Yankees' electorate and their new president, the Ivy-educated Michael Burke — the fans so that only 413 spectators paid to attend a September 23, 1966, home game against the White Sox; Burke so that four days afterward, in the Edwardian Room of the Plaza Hotel, at a breakfast of hot coffee and ice blood, he stared across the table and informed the Redhead, "There is no reason to be talking about pleasantries. We have decided not to seek to renew your contract."

Almost two decades later, Walter Lanier Barber recollected that morning chill with a sharp-knifed edge that crept into his voice.

Who was responsible for his sacking? I asked him. His answer, succinct, as ever, took candor into account.

"When Mel was fired, Ralph Houk [then general manager] and Dan Topping brought in Joe Garagiola to replace him," the Redhead began. "With me, Phil Rizzuto, and Jerry Coleman, that made four announcers — one too many. And it made three ex-ballplayers, which was several too many. Late in 1964, the Yankees hired a fellow from NBC, Perry Smith, to be in charge of our radio and television — he'd been close to Joe. The next year they started to lose. And the *next* year CBS picked up its option to buy Topping's last 10 percent of the Yankees. He was a dead duck. CBS now owned every bit of the club."

"And the network brought over Burke to be the new president."

"Yes, and now we go to step two," he said. "We had two weeks to go in the '66 season and we were playing the White Sox on a wretched day at Yankee Stadium. When I got to the ball park, there weren't a hundred people in the stands. I knew right then that *this* was the big story—the smallest crowd *ever* to see a game there. And keep in mind also that this was Burke's first day at Yankee Stadium, and he was sitting, by himself, in a box seat."

"And you asked for a camera shot of the stands," I said.

"I was doing the game on television, and I was going to say this was the perfect place for Burke to begin—nowhere to go but up. Well, I didn't get the shot. I asked again. Again, I didn't get it. You see, Perry Smith was in the control room and told the director not to let the camera *show* the empty stands. The viewers at home were being kept from knowing the truth—that this was an historic day, the fewest number of people ever to attend a game."

Twice-refused by Smith (acting, almost certainly, at Burke's direction), Barber believed his credibility to be imperiled, and leaning toward the microphone, told his audience what it could not see: "I don't know what the paid attendance is today—but whatever it is," he said, "it is the smallest crowd in the history of Yankee Stadium, and this crowd is the story, not the game." By the time the paid attendance was released, Barber had switched to radio; he announced the crowd, informed WCBS listeners of its import, and after the game—leaving the September ghost palace—met a complete and stony still. "There were no cheering Yankee officials waiting for me. Nobody was saying, 'Say, that was a great job of reporting you did.' "

The following Monday, the Ol' Redhead traveled to the Plaza Hotel to agree upon, as he envisioned it, a new one- or two-year contract. "That morning, I had put on my blue suit and white shirt and went happily to breakfast," he later related to Associated Press. "I thought Burke was going to say that he had a bad ball club in trouble; that he was a green pea; that he was going to lean on me; that they needed me. I thought he was going to say that I could help the Yankees, as I had helped Cincinnati, as I had helped Brooklyn; that my great experience was surely one of the things the Yankees could depend upon. I thought he was going to say that I was a well-known figure; that I was a leader in civic organizations; that I was a personality that he could call upon time and time again to help this ball club. I thought he was going to, but he didn't." Instead, Mike Burke looked out a window onto 59th Street and informed Barber, tartly, that he was through.

Ironically, after being fired by his last ball club, the Redhead never made a farewell address (the Bombers' final three scheduled games, in Washington, were rained out). In its place, he made the next twenty years his valedictory. "I'm sure Mike Burke didn't have it in mind," said Barber. "If the decision had been left up to me, I'd have gone back for my thirty-fourth year of play-by-play and who knows how many more? After all those years, it got to be a habit. I was like a squirrel in a cage and didn't know it. But thanks to Michael Burke, I've been set free." Since 1967, Red noted, proudly, he had trimmed his flowers, raised his cats, and "kept house" with his wife, Lylah, written hundreds of newspaper columns and appeared regularly on National Public Radio's popular "Morning Edition," called isolated sports events, published six books, and was working now on a seventh tome, a group of essays on unrelated themes.

"Not bad for a 'retirement,' " I told him.

"I've loved it," he said in his crisp, professorial tones. "For so long I was somebody's servant — whoever, you name it. Now my time's my own. The Yankees did me the greatest service I can think of. They presented me with my life."

Meanwhile, The Voice tried to recapture his. "In the absence of any explanation [as to his 1964 Yankees' firing], Allen became a victim of rumors," *Sports Illustrated* would write in 1985. "He was supposed to be a drunkard, a drug user. Neither rumor was true, but he couldn't fight them. He worked briefly for the Braves and Indians. It was as if he had leprosy." After Atlanta, Mel began a decade of working at oddments: announcing the 1966 Little League World Series for station KRAK in Sacramento, making appearances for Canada Dry at store and restaurant openings, narrating a two-minute syndicated radio program, "Memories from the Sports Page," airing weekend sports for the NBC affiliate in New York. He called Miami University's football and playoff baseball games, hosted banquets, did voice-overs, and starred in thirty-second commercials for Ballantine beer. Typically, he took time to respond to "letters from youngsters in announcing," he said in 1975. "I answer the questions by mail or call the kids on the phone and talk to them." He did not forget (and was not forgotten by) his friends.

When, in 1968, Charles Finley moved the A's to Oakland, "Ol' Charlie O. asked me" to become their Voice. "We had a long talk, real long," The Voice said. "But I'd just bought a Canada Dry bottling dealership in Stamford [Connecticut, then his home], and I didn't want to walk away. So I told Charlie, 'I'll broadcast your games if I can live here during the off-season.' But he wanted me all year, you know, to do publicity stuff, to promote the team, and I just couldn't. Anyhow, who the hell wants to leave New York?" The Voice of the Yankees, in *Oakland?* Was Gertrude Stein a baseball fan?

Instead, The Voice spent much of The Year of the Pitcher flying from New York to Cleveland, where Tribe President Gabe Paul hired him to televise forty-six games. Looking back, one can be forgiven for grasping at pleasant abstractions — Pete Rose emerging as the first N.L. switch-hitter to win a twentieth-century batting crown; Willie Horton, Norm Cash, and Bill Freehan knocking eighty-six homers for the world champion Tigers; and baseball showing, belatedly, the good sense to dismiss the dismal Eckert. Yet on the whole, 1968 was a season of toting zeroes. The Indians' Luis Tiant compiled a 1.60 earned run average. The American League's .230 batting average was its worst ever, its 154 blankings the highest yet, and Jim (Catfish) Hunter's no-hitter against the Twins its first perfect game since 1922. Bob Gibson's 1.12 ERA was the lowest in the history of the Senior Circuit. Bert Campaneris was the only Junior Looper with more than 170 hits. Don Drysdale pitched a record six straight shutouts and 58⅔ consecutive scoreless innings. *For shame,* moaned the ghosts of Campy, the Duke of Snider, and other Dodgers' boppers from the past; Len Gabrielson led the '68 Angelenos with *ten* home runs. "Man," said The Voice, laughing, "hitting got so bad that year we wondered if somebody'd snuck out in the night and changed Abner Doubleday's dimensions."

As Harry Jones' TV partner, Allen watched the Tribe record a 2.65 ERA, club a lowly seventy-five home runs, and finish a grandiloquent third. More memorably, he also triggered what one Cleveland writer called "the single most bizarre sportscasting episode I've ever witnessed."

The curtain lifted during a tedious game, on an Indians' telecast out of Minnesota, where Jones sought to keep interest alive (or was it viewers awake?) by chattering about baseball. Allen, though, had other notions, launching a treatise on literature and geography—"This is the land of ten thousand lakes, Harry," he said. "They have these picturesque names"—after which he began *repeating* those names. When Jones tried to inject a bit of baseball into the discourse, The Voice paddled to the subject of Lake Superior, the setting for Henry Wadsworth Longfellow's poem, "The Song of Hiawatha." Was Harry familiar with the poem? Allen asked him. A weary Jones muttered that he was.

"Let's see now, how does it go?" Mel mused, rhetorically, and while the Twins and Indians dueled in peaceful slumber, The Voice recited, by *memory*, the poem's first thirty-seven lines.

As Allen concluded, Jones responded with a glare. Hearing the story eighteen years later, a friend responded with peals of laughter. "How could you *not* be addicted to an announcer like that?" he said. "Who the hell else could mix Longfellow and a ball game and make them sound like Siamese twins?" Nodding, I retrieved that 1968 night in Minnesota; it was the last time for a long time my mind would see Allen paint the colors of The Game.

With the Redhead retired and The Voice removed, it was left for other benefactors to preside over baseball's local-station empire. They almost needed a travel guide, for by TYOTP, the natural passing of the last four years had produced a quite different media-game.

In 1968, there were, for one thing, *fewer radio* outlets per team; the typical local network totaled thirty-five stations, down from thirty-seven in 1964 and more than *fifty* in 1955. The White Sox and Cardinals' networks each linked ninety stations; the Reds and Twins' had sixty-four and fifty; together, the Mets and Cubs' must content themselves with three. At the same time, *more telecasts* had joined the local parade—almost fifty-three per club, up from 1964's forty-seven and 1960's forty-three. Every team broadcast at least an assortment of matches (the last holdout, San Francisco, yielded in the mid-sixties); American League members averaged fifty-eight showings, the National's, forty-six; heading the charts were the Cubs and White Sox (144 games apiece), Mets (117), Yankees (112), Philadelphia (59), and Boston (56). As usual, the Giants and Dodgers were more parsimonious; in California's then-two largest cities, viewers could choose from only twenty-one games.

"What all the numbers show is that on the radio side, baseball was finding other sports and forms of entertainment hard to combat, especially the growing rival formats of all-news radio [appealing to upscale listeners] and rock 'n' roll [savored by the young]," said the former president of CBS, Tom Dawson. In 1970, he became baseball's media director, Tom Villante's predecessor twice removed. "It was being squeezed, its networks were being hurt, and they were also being clobbered by the simple fact that TV, more and more, was becoming *the* way to follow baseball. You could make more money; it was a more prestigious medium." By 1968, ten of the game's twenty teams were airing games in color. The Braves' TV Network, baseball's largest, fused twenty-two stations in Georgia, Alabama, Florida, Mississippi, Tennessee, and South Carolina. The Astros combed four states with sixteen stations; St. Louis and Minnesota recruited fifteen each. "It was in this very period, *after* the great network coverage of the late fifties and early sixties and *before* the cable explosion of the eighties, that the importance of these regional networks of the teams themselves became apparent," said Merle Harmon. "Through them, my club, the Twins, could hit all of North Dakota, for example, Iowa, Wisconsin — right on down the line. *Our* network games were really their primary vehicle to baseball — even more than Curt's 'Game of the Week.' And the thinking was this: 'If you come into Des Moines with fifty Twins' games a year, at least some of those folks are going to get into their car some weekend and hightail it up to *see* a game in person.' For teams that were in small cities and needed to become regional teams to prosper, TV was the most marvelous tool we had."

Since 1964, Bill O'Donnell had joined Thompson at Baltimore; the Orioles' Frank Messer would shortly travel to Yankee Stadium, replacing Garagiola, who joined NBC Television's "The Today Show"; Ken Coleman emerged as the new Voice of the Red Sox, succeeding the Cowboy; and Ol' Diz had returned for "special guest appearances" over Braves' television, lending song and banter to Hamilton's narrative. There were new stations in the majors' media texture (the Yankees switched to flagship WHN and the Mets to WJRZ and WGIL; "they were all weaker than their *former* originating stations," said an ex-Mets' official, "and that was typical of the whole late sixties and early seventies. Many powerful stations were going to talk or music. Their demographics were better than baseball's") and other new announcers (Red Rush as Hamilton's replacement at Comiskey Park, ex-pitchers Nellie King and Joe Nuxhall in Pittsburgh and Cincinnati, and the aging Al Helfer as Monte Moore's first-year Oakland sidekick) and frayed threads caused by the departure from the bigs of a superb baseball mouthpiece who was also the finest football broadcaster of our contemporaneous time.

"The very best of them was named Ray Scott. CBS's National Football League coverage didn't make a move to any big game without him in the late 1950s and early sixties," *TV Guide* wrote of the man who quit that network in 1974 because he refused to imitate a windbag. "Not all veteran fans remember [him]. Credit it to the fact that he was simply too good at what he did, which was use his voice with the range and subtlety of a concert violinist. When, in a mercilessly tight game, Scott intoned, slowly, profoundly, simply, 'First down, Green Bay,' a million spines would quiver."

Married, nationally, to the NFL, Ray Scott was the Twins' principal announcer from 1961 to 1966. In a way, his baseball facility was surprising. Calm, deliberative, he seldom abhorred the sport's "dead air," never believed that more talk was happy talk, refused to alter his doctrine that the less said, the better. "It's funny," said Bob Wolff, his 1961 colleague. "In baseball, you have little action, a lot of delays, dull stretches. To fill them, you've got to tell stories, be humorous, entertaining. And then you have Ray — sparse commentary, didn't go in for a lot of verbiage. He didn't mind a lot of silences. You'd think baseball, where the announcer, unlike football, has to carry the action, would have given him trouble. But somehow he pulled it off," and not with his approach, which would have crippled, I am sure, a lesser announcer, but rather, his *voice*, which underlined and even tingled.

Scott's home-town was Johnstown, Pennsylvania, and it was there, in 1937, that he took his first job in broadcasting — announcing, writing copy, selling advertising for 250-watt station WJAC, and earning $55 a month. After an Army stint in the Second World War, Scott joined, by turns, WCAE in Pittsburgh, the advertising agency of Ketchum, MacLeod, and Grove, and, in 1952, the then-conveyer of the NFL, the DuMont Television Network. "I went to work for DuMont's station in Pittsburgh, WDTV," he said, "and the next year I did the first pro football series ever shown on a weekly basis from coast-to-coast, their Saturday night 'Game of the Week.' Believe me, compared to the technology of today, it was like the Pony Express up against the Concorde."

On January 1, 1956, Scott aired ABC's play-by-play of the Sugar Bowl. "Bill Stern was that network's main guy and was supposed to do the game, assisted by Ray, but he was in the process of destroying himself with drugs," Tom Gallery recalled. "Just as the game started, Stern reached the broadcast booth, and everyone saw right away that he was doped out of his mind. There was no way he could go on. So Ray took over, did a beauty of a job, and his career took off." That fall, he was hired by CBS to cover the Green Bay Packers; three years later, Vince Lombardi became the Packers' coach. "CBS's first year of covering pro ball was '56 and they apologized when they made the original assignment," Scott said. "In those days, a given announcer did the same team each week — there was Chris Schenkel with the Giants, for example, and me with the Packers — and Green Bay had a small market and a terrible team. But then along came Vince, and the Packers exploded. I rode along on their coattails," calling nine NFL title games and four Super Bowls, thriving as the Packers won, evolving into one of sport's most recognized/recognizable Voices/voices.

"Maybe I'm old-fashioned or stubborn," said Scott, sixty-seven, at his home in Scottsdale, Arizona, "but I don't believe that radio or TV should take a bad game and try to make it better. That was my philosophy with the Packers, and it still is. I think the game is more important than the guy who describes it."

"No changing your style to hype an event," I said.

"No sir," he said, emphatically. "I never tried to draw all attention to myself. I never believed in trying to please the whims of a producer or director. I just considered myself a conduit to provide the fan with something he couldn't obtain himself. My primary concern was not making Ray Scott a household word," as he became exactly that.

One Saturday afternoon in 1960, Scott subbed for Lindsey Nelson on "Major League Baseball." "It was a game in Pittsburgh," he said, "and I can't even remember who the Pirates were playing or whether they won or lost. But that was about the extent of my pre-1961 baseball play-by-play—one game."

That (and his name) were apparently enough, for by the following spring, Scott had moved his wife and five children to a new residence in Edina, a Minneapolis suburb. "Whether I do football again is questionable because of the overlapping seasons," Ray said in April 1961. "But I wouldn't pull up stakes with my family in Pittsburgh if I wasn't sold on baseball for the future."

"How did a man with virtually no baseball background get such a prestigious job?" I asked Tom Mee, the Twins' director of public relations and the first person hired when the Senators moved west in late 1960.

"Ray had developed a great following in this area through the Packer games, and when Hamm's beer bought the rights to the Twins' games for our first season here, his name was the first to come up," Mee said. "The Hamm's account was handled by the Campbell-Mithun advertising agency in Minneapolis, and its radio/TV vice-president was a guy named Art Lund. Art was attracted to Ray's style and talent, and he asked Scott if the Twins would interest him. Ray said yes, and the parties then went to Mr. Griffith and said, 'Scott's a great favorite here. We'd like to have him.' "

"To join Wolff," I said.

"Mr. Griffith was adamant that Wolff stay with the club," Mee said, "and what made the timing right was that the Senators' other 1960 announcer, Chuck Thompson, had decided to stay around the Washington-Baltimore area. With that taken care of, the road lay open for Ray. And he's widely regarded, I suppose, as the finest play-by-play man we've ever had."

For six years, Scott exteriorized northlands' baseball—"not because he was a huckster or anything like that," said Wolff's successor, Herb Carneal, "but just through that drama in his vocal cords"—as the Twins stirred up undiluted enthusiasm to rival 1950s Milwaukee. "His effect was great—like the first ever, he was a teacher," added Mee, "and his reputation benefited enormously from his football work. When I said he was the finest at play-by-play, I think Herb is a better guy technically on baseball, but Ray was unmatched on football, and people said, 'Man, aren't we lucky to have this national celebrity as our local announcer.' "

"How," I asked Scott, "do you remember Minnesota?"

"Even through the worst of times up there, the response was fantastic, and as you may know, I'm not prone to overstatement," he said. "People don't always realize it, but that area has a tremendous baseball heritage. The minor-league Millers had been a huge hit, and when we came there in '61 it was like a flash flood—just a marvelous reception."

"You did Twins' radio and television," I said, "and it was football TV that made you big. With baseball, which grabbed you more?"

"With the exception of the playoffs and Series, which have a drama of their own and make the announcer almost unnecessary, I always found baseball on TV to be a really difficult assignment," Scott said. "The picture's there, so you can't say too much — but there's often not much happening, so you almost have to say *something*. There's that constant dilemma — it can be frustrating."

"And radio?"

"It's *the* medium for baseball," he pronounced, "and the reverse is also true — there's no sport as *good* on it as baseball. It's a game of lulls and a lovely tempo — you don't have to say things all the time, you can sort of take it at your own pace. And what made the Twins' radio setup so great was that we covered everything." At its height, the club's arrangement linked three 50,000-watt stations (flagship WCCO, the "Good Neighbor to the Northwest"; WHO in Des Moines; and WOW in Omaha) and a network of fifty-five stations in seven states and an additional fifteen in the Rocky Mountain area on weekends. "You'd go in the parking lot on Saturday or Sunday, and there'd be license plates from Colorado, Idaho, Montana, from Wyoming to Illinois. It was almost a family-kind of feeling."

By 1967, the celebrity had tired of the organized structure of daily coverage; leaving baseball, Scott joined CBS as its primary Voice of tournament golf. He returned to call the Senators' 1969-70 and Twins' 1973 and 1975 TV games; a year afterward, Ray handled the Brewers' thirty-game video package. There, he teamed adeptly with Harmon and Bob Uecker, talked of how the television networks had blackballed him from football "because I choose to speak out against the growing tendency to focus on the announcer, not event, and because I'm not afraid to deplore 'show biz broadcasting' and athletes-turned-announcers who have no talent whatsoever," denounced as "sheer vaudeville" the florid excesses of "Monday Night Football," and proclaimed himself a broadcast "traditionalist" and old-line reporter in a profession where, increasingly, only ex-jocks need apply.

In the late seventies and early eighties, deemed by the networks old-hat, he turned again to syndicated golf, college football, and Pirates' TV cablecasts, and heard Roone Arledge, now the president of ABC News as well as Sports, ridicule how Scott had "treated the NFL like a religion." Perhaps his tones *had* sounded like a cross between Alexander Scourby and Billy Graham, though Arledge was not impugning theology. But Ray Scott gave the NFL what he also brought to his craft — respect and presence, and a voice that seemed in bloom even in November, a springtime of magnificent possibility.

There are worse ways to be remembered.

* * *

After Scott's original peregrination to tournament golf, Herb Carneal became the radio/TV emblem of the Twins. Solid, literate, a *baseball* (as opposed to *sports*) announcer, he had worked with Harwell in 1957-59 at Memorial Stadium, became the Birds' Voice when Ernie traveled to Detroit, and in 1962 began the first of more than twenty-five seasons as Calvin Griffith's insignia.

"We were lucky to get him," Tom Mee said. "Herb worked for Hamm's, and after the '61 season they lost the Orioles' radio rights to National Bohemian. Thompson worked for them, and when National Boh said, 'We want Chuck to be the Orioles' main announcer,' Herb was out of a job. About the same time, Bob Wolff got the position as Lindsey Nelson's replacement on NBC's weekend baseball. So we're looking to replace *him*—and since Hamm's was our sponsor, the choice was Herb, and he's been there ever since"—holding forth for two decades from the homey platter of Metropolitan Stadium and post-1981 from the Cave also known as the Hubert H. Humphrey Metrodome; regaling Bismarck and Boise and Fargo with the magic feats of Rod Carew, stealing home seven times in 1969, and Ken Landreaux, hitting in thirty-one straight games eleven years later, and Cesar Tovar, playing all nine positions one day against the Athletics, and that gentle man named Killebrew, who was as strong as he was straightforward and whose quiet honor brightened our age.

Over two decades in which the Twins, senselessly, moved indoors and battled the fresh, lovely elements for the loyalty of the upper Midwest, Carneal was an enduring asset. He knew The Game and could explain it clearly. He tried not to impress but to analyze. Had his team remained in Washington, Herb would have broadcast from circular D.C. Stadium. Instead, it remained for WTOP's Dan Daniels and John MacLean, and after 1965, Shelby Whitfield and Ron Menchine over WWDC and its thirty-one-station network, and in the fading years of the Robert Short-owned franchise, Scott and the curious Warner Wolf, to filibuster for teams whose salvation lay in excuses and whose perpetuity rested in last place.

"It was a tightrope act," said Daniels, who began broadcasting at Barber's alma mater, the University of Florida, then moved to stations in Jacksonville, Orlando, Birmingham, and, in 1956, the capital. "Washington's unique—nowhere else are the broadcast conditions the same. What I had to remember is that there were government workers from every state in the broadcast audience—fans cheering for the teams that Washington was playing."

"Bye-bye, bias," I said.

"You couldn't be a rooter, and yet you had to recognize that there were a lot of fans pulling for Washington."

Usually, they pulled in vain. In their eleven years, the expansion Senators only once surpassed .500. This event—"by itself," canted columnist Morris Siegel, "a capital event"—came out of the season Theodore Samuel Williams returned to manage the Nationals and a sign, held aloft at Shea Stadium after the New York Mets won their first World Series, asked "What Next?" to which one responded, "Who Cares?"

Almost twenty years later, that 1969 screenplay invites mountains of unbelief. It was a season in which Kuhn, forty-two, became commissioner, the majors expanded to Montreal, San Diego, Seattle, and (back to) Kansas City, and baseball welcomed divisional play and the Championship Series; the Expos lost twenty games in a row, the Orioles—possibly the American League's finest club of the decade—won 109 games, beat second-place Detroit by nineteen, swept Minnesota in the playoff, and were virtually ignored by the populace of Baltimore; and Mickey Mantle retired, Teddy Ballgame was named Manager of the Year, the Junior Circuit witnessed the cannonading of Frank Howard, Reggie Jackson, and Killebrew, bashing, respectively, forty-eight, forty-seven, and forty-four home runs, and across both leagues, athletes—blessedly—(re)discovered how to hit the ball. Yet what about the '69 *Metropolitans*? Were they miracle or metaphysical? Phenomenon or inspiration? A recompense for Marvelous Marv? The Deity's reprisal against O'Malley? What next? Who cared?

In any year after the late fifties, how *could* one care in Cleveland? Since Herb Score became a broadcaster in 1963, only once has the Tribe cracked the first division; only five times have the Indians lured more than 1 million paid admissions; even the Cubs have known what almost three generations of northern Ohioans have not—the joy of a real, living *pennant* race; the wild, rarely sustaining hope that *this* year, at last, the baseball season would breathe past June.

A talented and exciting mid-fifties pitcher, Score was a twenty-game winner and almost incomparable Cleveland hero whose career plummeted, prematurely and tragically, after Gil McDougald's line drive glanced off his right eyeball on May 7, 1957. From 1963 to 1967, Herb did Indians' TV commentary before joining Bob Neal, Jimmy Dudley's successor as Voice of the Tribe, on WERE Radio. In 1973, the ball club's wireless rights were bought by WWWE, a 50,000-watt station whose reach penetrated far beyond Municipal Stadium; now the Voice himself, Score teamed for seven seasons with Joe Tait, then Cleveland-born Nev Chandler, and, since 1985, with ex-Met Steve LaMar, to earnestly embark on his crusade to stem the numbing form of pain which blew off Lake Erie like a monsoon full of Novocain.

Intelligent and knowledgeable, Score "would probably sound cheerful doing the play-by-play aboard a Kamikazee's final flight. He is the kind of guy you almost can't knock. An awful lot of listeners are going to be awfully angry with you if you do," columnist Bob Dolgan has written, noting, "I have a hunch I know why. In this nasty old world, filled with thugs, malcontents, and narcissists, gentlemen are finally beginning to be appreciated. And Score has always been a gentleman." Buddy Bell, the former Tribe third baseman, once called Herb "such a nice guy that I'll bet he makes the bed in his hotel when he wakes up in the morning." His style exuded kindliness, and his voice—if unpolished, rapid-syllabled, and burdened with the acute New York accent of which he said, "It's not as bad as it once was. I used to be a real deese-dem-dose guy"—at least bespoke sincerity, a posture that made listeners lean toward him. "So what if he's never been a Hall of Fame announcer?" a friend of mine and Indians' fan—after *all* these years—said one day, providing a logical perspective. "Look at it this way. Wouldn't the city of Cleveland have turned somersaults over the last twenty years just to have ball clubs as decent as their announcer?"

Presto. Like Waite Hoyt and his self-described often "bad news" Reds, Herb Score surpassed his product; by doing blahly, he did well. What if, from time to time, he was bloodless, leaden? Had the Tribe deserved better? Could Score have done more? "He was as good as he could be for teams that warranted much less," a former Indians' official said. For a franchise whose last world championship brightened Harry Truman's Fall, Herb Score was a natural.

So was Chuck Thompson, in an engagingly disparate sense. Slim and six feet tall and possessed of a jagged facial profile, the long-time Orioles' broadcaster fused informality, such irrelevancies as "Ain't the Beer Cold!" and "Go to War, Miss Agnes!" and a beguiling voice that went perfectly with the game into a niche as one of baseball's most sympathetic announcers, persuading without tension or strain.

"He has an excellent flow, a good understanding of the game, and he's extraordinarily easy to listen to," John Steadman said. "He's never tried to be controversial — you'll never hear anybody around Baltimore saying in amazement, 'Did you hear what Chuck said last night?' That might hurt him in a New York or L.A. — it's helped him here. He's just like the guy next door — pleasant, popular. He's been that way all during his career."

That career took root, ironically, in a Brookfield, Massachusetts, boarding house owned by Chuck's grandmother and boasting as a tenant one Cornelius McGillicuddy. "To the public, he was Connie Mack and he used to stay there back in the days when he was a semipro," related Thompson, born in nearby Palmer in 1921. "He'd tell stories about baseball, and my grandmother told them to me when I was young, and I guess she proved the old axiom that a man has to have some background that dedicates him to a life in sports. She gave me a love for baseball. She helped to set the stage."

It was a stage Thompson unwittingly stepped upon years later, as a high school student in Reading, Pennsylvania, after a friend kept daring him to ask the program director of the local radio station for a singing audition. "I'd always loved music," he said, "and this girl, knowing that, tried to get me started toward a career in a dance band."

"How'd your audition go?"

"I never *took* one," he said, "not in music, anyway. When I got to the station [WRAW], mainly because I'd played ball in high school, the audition developed into a sports broadcast. And I'm sure it turned out the right way because it gave me my start." Soon after, Thompson was hired to cover Albright College football games over a rival Reading station. "And not long after *that*, I got a great opportunity."

"With WIBG," I said, "in Philadelphia."

"I went there as a staff announcer in 1942," he said. "And that's where I returned to after the war [Thompson saw combat in three of the five major European campaigns]," and where he began calling balls and strikes with Byrum Saam and Claude Haring.

"When'd you begin doing baseball?"

"That break didn't involve my grandmother *or* an audition. Instead, it involved a balky elevator at Shibe Park. One day in 1946, they were having radio appreciation day at the park, and ceremonies on the field were being handled by Saam and Haring—I was alone in the radio booth," Thompson said. "There was a lot of confusion on the field, and they got delayed at the elevator, and as they were stuck the game began with no one to handle the mike. I just took over"—until, several minutes later, the harried regulars arrived.

At that point, Les Quailey, the veteran broadcast executive with the N.W. Ayer advertising agency in Philadelphia, found promise in tomorrow—"Claude, By, just listen a while," he submitted. "Chuck is doing all right. Let's keep him on for an inning or two"—and, at twenty-five, Thompson bathed in his first moment of more than four decades of baseball play-by-play. Through 1949, he covered the A's, Phillies, NFL Eagles, NBA Warriors, and then became, with Quailey's blessing, the Voice of the International League Baltimore Orioles. It was there that he patented his war-cry—"Ain't the Beer Cold!"—to describe an event of aerial drama; there too that he met a starched golfing partner who never swore, no matter how harsh the provocation.

"He was a great guy, very proper, and like any golfer, he had some real frustrations," Thompson said. "But instead of cussing, he'd come up with the phrase, 'Go to War, Miss Agnes!' I didn't know what it meant, but don't feel bad—*he* may not have known. What I did know was that it sounded so funny. I picked it up and used it to emphasize something big and exciting on the ball field, and it just caught on—with listeners, it snowballed." After three years of shoveling with the Orioles, Chuck was chosen as a principal announcer of DuMont's 1954 football "Game of the Week," succeeding Scott, and covered the American League Birds in 1955–56, the Senators in 1957–60, NBC's 1959–60 "Major League Baseball," and the transcendent football Colts.

On December 28, 1958, in the shivery twilight of Yankee Stadium, to more than 50 million NBC viewers, Thompson described the Colts' sudden-death triumph in the NFL title game. Two years later, co-anchoring, with Jack Quinlan, that network's radio coverage of the 1960 World Series, he called Bill Mazeroski's ninth-inning, seventh-set thunderclap that gave Pittsburgh the victory, 10–9, and a pulsating world championship.

"I was on the air for the last half of the game and when Maz blasted it to left, I was so excited I gave the wrong score," he confessed. "I said, 'The Pirates win it, ten to nothing.' "

"That was the same pitch," I said, "you had Art Ditmar throwing the ball when really it was Ralph Terry."

"Yes, but for some reason people didn't notice *that* error for a long time after the fact," Chuck said, and then, laughing, "Of course, the whole nation knows about it today." (On ABC's 1985 World Series coverage, the Anheuser-Busch Brewery used Thompson's play-by-play, including "Art Ditmar throws," as the voice-over for a warmly nostalgic TV spot; the error, now noticed, prompted hundreds of phone calls to its St. Louis brewery.)

"What about the other part—the wrong score?" I said. "At the time, back in 1960, did you get much of a reaction, people rubbing it in?"

"No, because everybody was going absolutely berserk—it was about the wildest crowd I've ever seen in my life," he said. "But later on, the Pirates put out a souvenir album, narrated by Bob Prince, and they asked if I wanted to make a voice-over correction on the score."

"You said no," I knew.

"I just told 'em, 'Hey, I said it, so keep it in.' The next year I came into Pittsburgh as one of the 'Game of the Week' announcers with Bill Veeck, and they were playing this record over and over as a special promotion offering to the fans. I kept hearing the wrong score, but somehow it seemed to fit into the confusion of the occasion."

In early 1962, Chuck Thompson became the major-league Voice of Baltimore baseball; he would perch there, uncontested, for the next twenty-one years. From Memorial Stadium and the Birds' enemy nests, carried over radio flagships WBAL (through 1978) and WFBR (1979–82), and aided by colleagues Bailey Goss, Jack Dunn, and Joe Croghan (1962–63), Frank Messer (1964–67), Jim Karvellas (1968–69), John Gordon (1970–72), and, moreover, the fluid Bill O'Donnell (1966–82), Thompson strove to avoid repetition ("In an ordinary game, pitchers on both sides will throw more than one hundred pitches each—that's the same situation to describe over two hundred times. Once in Philadelphia I listened to By Saam on a radio broadcast and he used eighty-six different ways of describing the pitcher throwing the ball to a batter—that, to me, is great broadcasting") and evoke gentle humor ("There was this game in 1965, and Lee Thomas of the Red Sox was batting at Fenway Park. He hit a ground ball to right field that bounced into the seats, then caromed out onto the field for a ground-rule double. Suddenly, out of the bull pen came a huge labrador retriever. The dog picked up the ball and raced away. I was astounded and so was everyone else. So I said spontaneously, 'Well, that was a doggoned double' ") and enjoy the fruits of what, by any standard, ranks as the most successful baseball team of post-Camelot America.

Thirteen times, the Orioles won championships in one fifteen-year (1966–80) interval—six divisional flags, five pennants, and two World Series. Five times, they took one hundred or more regular-season contests; their won-loss record, 1,417–990, was unequaled in either circuit; only in 1967 did the Birds swoop below .500; across 1969–71, placing six players a year on the American League All-Star team, Baltimore won 318 games. In his bemused, often quizzical way, Thompson lured listeners to hear Frank Robinson club a 1966 blast completely out of Memorial Stadium, Steve Barber and Stu Miller combine for a no-hitter the following April and *lose*, Dave McNally bomb a grand-slam homer in Game Three of the 1970 World Series, and F. Robby whack his five hundredth career home run on September 13, 1971. Orioles' pitchers copped six Cy Young Awards. Brooks Robinson hoarded sixteen Gold Gloves. On September 1, 1978, Sammy Stewart tied a record by fanning seven straight batters in his big-league inaugural. The season afterward, even cash registers jingled; long a box-office embarrassment, Baltimore caught Orioles' Magic and drew a record 1,681,009 customers. "After the '78 season, the Orioles went with a new station, 'FBR, which promoted the devil out of the team," Steadman said. "And suddenly, a year later, people began going to games. They'd always listened and watched on radio and TV—now, they were showing up. Finally, after all these years of great clubs and lousy attendance, seeing the Orioles became the thing to do. At last, Chuck had a supporting cast at the ball park, folks to make some noise—and that, in turn, made his broadcasts even better."

As a newspaper reporter for the Gannett Company, I recall listening with two friends to an Orioles' game in early 1975. A Baltimore hitter—Al Bumbry, I think—lashed a line drive up the left-center-field alley, and while the Bee roared around the bases, Chuck Thompson took full flight—recounting Bumbry's romp in sharp, rapid cadences; prompting a colleague to marvel, laughing, "Just *listen* to that guy. What *enthusiasm!*"

Airing the Orioles, naturally, Thompson had reason to enthuse. He became, in Hoyt's parlance, a "good news broadcaster," and was buoyed too by his friend and long-time sidekick—a New York City native, member of the same Fordham University class as Vin Scully, and a cordial, thoughtful man whose perceptions were as clear as his prose.

"Bill O'Donnell was an unflappable, impeccable kind of announcer—as calm on the air as he was shooting the bull off-stage," said Thompson. " 'If you're always excited, you will lose your credibility when it's time to *get* excited,' he'd say. And he was right."

"At the time, you two formed the league's longest-running announcing team," I said. "How'd you pull it off?"

"We couldn't have if Bill hadn't been who he was," Chuck observed. "Never, ever, did I hear him say a bad word about anyone. Never, ever, did I hear him utter one word of profanity. And, intellectually, he was as bright as any man I've known. Just a class act, and that's important. Understand that you're spending six, seven months, every day, with the same person. It's almost like marriage. And I know some broadcast teams who may work well on the air, but off it, they're totally incompatible—can't get along, are envious, jealous. And that can be hell."

"But you?"

"I would guess there were times when of maybe one hundred dinners I ate on the road, ninety-five were with Bill. You just can't overstate the importance of that—it makes the whole job so much easier, and because of that, it improves your broadcasts so much more."

O'Donnell was a tortoise, not hare; his rise to the majors was slow and studied, growing, as he rose, into a broadcaster of the essentials. He started on station WIBX in Utica, New York, covering basketball and football, and in 1951 moved to Pocatello, Idaho, home of the Class-C Cardinals of the Pioneer League. Two years later, Bill returned to upstate New York, where, for the next thirteen seasons, he did play-by-play of a Syracuse troika: the International League Chiefs and university basketball and football Orangemen. Once, he aired twenty-four high school basketball games over six nights at $5 a game; another year, he called twenty-seven boxing matches in two nights. Then, in early 1966, with Gowdy bound for NBC, O'Donnell applied for his job as Voice of the Red Sox. "Here fate intervened," he said once. "Because I

had done play-by-play the year before for the Colts, I asked for a recommendation for the Sox' slot from the agency that just happened to handle the
Orioles and Colts. Well, unbeknownst to me, that same *day* the Orioles' announcing job opened up. So the agency didn't recommend I go to Boston —
they offered me the Baltimore job." O'Donnell did TVS Network college
basketball, major college and professional football, and extensive televised
baseball — calling, with Thompson and, later, Brooks Robinson, more than
fifty games a season for WJZ, Baltimore; and from 1969 to 1976, ten backup
sets a year on NBC's "Game of the Week." He worked the 1969 and 1971 World
Series. He embodied, Orioles' general manager Hank Peters said, "the ultimate in professionalism." He also contracted cancer and died, at Johns Hop-
kins Hospital, on October 29, 1982, at the age of fifty-six.

The next year, pained by O'Donnell's absence and an intense dislike of
1979–82 colleague Tom Marr, Thompson left the wireless and switched, exclusively, to Orioles' television coverage; Jon Miller, arriving from Boston,
became Baltimore's radio *duce*. I would admit, even now, that I missed Chuck,
and there are moments when sitting by the receiver at home, I hear the crowd
roar and some voice proclaim a home run and I think out loud, " 'Go to War,
Miss Agnes!' Have a National Boh on me, the always-Voice of the Birds. My,
'Ain't the Beer Cold!' "

Since Monte Moore shunned liquor, the temperature of *his* beer was irrelevant. Germane, however, was Moore's apparent bent for masochism; for
sixteen often unreal and riveting years, he imperiled soul and spirit as the
Voice of the Athletics of Charlie O.

A native Sooner, with a twangy voice like Harmon's, Moore reached the
major leagues by way of Duncan and Lawton, Oklahoma; Hutchinson, Kansas; the University of Kansas, where he directed the state-wide radio network;
and, finally, WDAF Radio and TV in Kansas City. In 1961, Finley bought
the A's; the next year, Moore surfaced as his announcer. By the time Monte
resigned after the 1977 season, beating his dismissal to the door, the church-
going layman had teamed with sixteen different sidekicks (among them, Bruce
Rice, George Bryson, Red Rush, Lynn Faris, Helfer, Caray, and Jimmy
Piersall), survived several aborted axings, broadcast for three consecutive
world champions, and never missed a regular-season, exhibition, or postseason game — in all, nearly 2,900 — "or a chance," fumed one writer, "to praise
Charles Oscar Finley." He was dry, with energetic tones; he favored the excessive superlative; he was, above all, a homer.

"That's how Charlie O. demanded his announcers be," said Jim Woods, who
joined the A's in 1972, Moore's fifth associate in as many years. "He wanted —
he *insisted* — that you root and cheer."

Hearing, I flashed back to the 1972 World Series, over NBC, when Moore
termed "phenomenal" Joe Rudi's .305 batting average and dubbed "mirac-
ulous" Dick Green's survival of a Reds' block at second base. "Maybe that was
the secret of his staying power," I proposed. "Who else could curry Finley's
favor without panting to please?"

"We were entirely different," Woods said, "Monte and me, and that was true of a lot of his partners." In 1966-67, Moore and Faris barely tolerated each other; in 1968-69, Brother Al, "a huge man who drank triples without any apparent effect," wrote Ron Bergman, "and sometimes wore a cashmere cardigan that cost the lives of a herd of goats," mixed volatility and lapses. Once, Helfer forgot Cesar Tovar's first name in an interview that followed the game in which the Twin played all nine positions; on another occasion, when Reggie Jackson smashed a monstrous Oakland Coliseum home run with Ted Kubiak on third base, Al added, seriously, "and Kubiak will score easily on the play."

"Monte liked to stay at home, very quiet, didn't gamble — me, just point the way to the race track," the Possum said. "But he was nice enough — like an old shoe, and did what Master Finley told him to. I guess that's why he was there so long."

"But he got fired too," I said.

"Yeah, but not for a tremendous while," Woods laughed. "*I* only lasted two years. Monte sure as hell knew something that escaped dozens of Charlie's former employees all down through the years."

"Some said he was a mole, Finley's ear," I said, "that he'd go tell him what players were saying, who they were consorting with."

"Hell," Woods said, "Monte couldn't have done that if he'd *wanted* to — he didn't *know* what the players were doing, he was off by himself. Bert Campaneris, the Oakland shortstop, was really the guy who was Finley's stooge. *He'd* tell Finley everything. But Monte, for some reason, got blamed for everything."

"Even the firing of Caray," who joined Monte for the 1970 season and left after one year, returning to the Midwest.

"That wasn't Monte's fault — it was Caray's," Woods declaimed. "I remember interviewing with Finley before I came out there in '72 and I said, 'Charlie, why'd you fire Caray?' And Finley came back, 'Hell, that line of bull-shit Harry put out might have worked in St. Louis [it would later in Chicago too], but nobody was buying it here.' And to be honest, Harry wasn't buying Moore. The first time they started working together — Monte had been with Finley, remember, for a decade — Caray said, 'Listen, when I start doing my stuff, I don't want to hear a thing out of you. Just keep your mouth shut.' "

"What did Monte say?"

"He just sloughed it off," Woods said, "went on his merry way, outlasted Caray, and lived to broadcast another day."

His broadcasts were not deep but amicable, the product of a moral and middle-class mind, and when I thought of Moore, I recalled the Broadway musical, *The Most Happy Fella*; he did network baseball and college football and loved his family and invested well and praised the Swinging A's.

Over KCMO in Kansas City, Monte peddled a no-name, doleful team. Moving west, he engaged listeners over a variety of radio outlets — in the early seventies, a pathetic college station and several similar flagships; before and after, 50,000-watt KNBR. "At worst," said Woods, "it was awful — in the years they were winning the three World Series [1972-74], the station was so weak you could barely catch the games ten miles from the Oakland Coliseum." At best, Moore diverted "the entire West Coast from Alaska to Hawaii," read the 1976 Oakland media guide. "A's games can be heard in the following states: California, Washington, Oregon, Idaho, Utah, Colorado, New Mexico, Arizona, Nevada, and Wyoming." The Possum's voice sounded of mock contempt. "Yeah, but what they'd never tell you was that sometimes you could only hear the games *outside* the Bay Area. I remember how Monte would brag about Finley's network stretching to Hawaii. One day somebody called up and said, real bitterly, 'Hey, it's nice to know they can hear you in Hawaii, Monte—why the hell can't we hear you *here?*' "

In the Oakland-Alameda County Mausoleum, as the habitually deserted Coliseum was known, Monte was encased by ample outfield dimensions (330 feet down each line, 400 to dead center), vast foul territory (largest in either league), and heavy night air that seemed to puncture would-be homers. He was alternately defamed (what was "a solution to California's main source of pollution?" asked a letter in the *San Francisco Chronicle*; "install a catalytic converter in Monte Moore's mouth") and defended ("Homerism without truth is bad," declared another letter-writer. "Moore is a homer, but he tells me what's happening") and he revered the silver lining (when Texas touched Oakland for five runs in the first inning of a 1973 match, Monte supplied a wagon train of perspective. "Throw out the first inning," Moore bandied in inning seven, "and we'd have a great ball game here").

Less buoyant, spiffy, or blunt than, respectively, a Bert Wilson, Bob Wolff, or Ty Tyson, he brought to mind a long-ago writer's critique of Ford Frick as commissioner: "He's pure vanilla. I go to the typewriter to do a piece on him and the keys, they all stick." Moore was as digestible as custard, as dull as tapioca, and like a Chinese dinner; ten minutes after hearing him, you'd forgotten you ate. Except for Curt Gowdy, he broadcast more early-seventies World Series games than any play-by-play contemporary—somehow suitable, I thought, for this general microcosm of that pedestrian media age.

*   *   *

"I have to be careful about Scully," Red Barber has written. "He's my boy." I have to be careful about Bob Prince. Attending Allegheny College in western Pennsylvania in the early 1970s, I came to regard him as my undergraduate announcer. More than a decade later, I cannot shake the conviction: With the single (and singular) exception of Jay Hanna Jerome Dean, Bob Prince is the most entertaining baseball broadcaster I have ever heard.

"He *was* the Pirates, and they are different without him," a fan said of Roberto Clemente in March 1973, the spring following No. 21's death in a New Year's Eve plane crash on a mercy mission to help people left homeless by a Nicaraguan earthquake.

It would be hard, I think, for anyone to surpass my affection for what I consider the finest player of our post-Musial age—the Gunner describing

Clemente was like Roberta Peters nursing The Lord's Prayer — but to me and, I imagine, to millions of Buccos' listeners, *Bob Prince* was the Pirates, and they would be/have been incomplete without him.

In college, roaming the intimate shops and mist-shrouded streets of Meadville (population 18,500), ninety miles north of Pittsburgh, I drank coffee with hard-hats who cheered Spiro Agnew and excoriated the Chicago Seven. On campus, like other students, I challenged, queried, marched, protested, picketed and counter-picketed, above all, *cared*. In retrospect, my tenure at this small school "where the annual snowfall is 112 inches," wrote Jeanne Braham of Allegheny's English Department, "where Saturday tolls the class bell for Everyman, and where ten-month terms have the ballooning pressure of an inverted bell curve," was etched chiefly by work and study (work to best tuition; study to best one's peers) and by a voice whose vigor cut through the dreary sameness like a laser through dead cells.

His effect was everywhere; you could not escape it — in bars, where workingmen explored that evening's play-by-play; in early-morning breakfast klatsches, where the Buccos were a principal center of conversation; on mail routes and screened-in porches, where of an afternoon when the Pirates were scheduled, one radio after another was tuned to KDKA, Pittsburgh, and its forty-nine-station network; in back yards, traffic jams, and Allegheny dormitories, where students and commuters heard his ribbon of rococo commentary; in Tri-State hospital rooms, where patients fell asleep to the booming cry of "We had 'em all the way!"; on playgrounds, where budding Little Leaguers, copying the Gunner's nomenclature, called their sand lot the "alabaster plaster" and said, triumphantly, of a distant blast, "You can kiss it good-bye!" He was unfathomable and uninhibited, a baseball original, and his vast following was perhaps the most rabid in the nation.

"They were the craziest, most absolutely whacked-out years I've ever spent in broadcasting. Everybody told me, 'Don't go to Pittsburgh. Prince is out of control — you'll never get along,' but I did and I was never for a single moment bored. God, those years were fun," mused Jim Woods, his 1958–69 Pirates' sidekick.

"Because of Prince?" I said.

"Oh, yeah," argued the Possum, among the most talented No. 2 men in the maze of baseball broadcasting. "You have to understand there aren't really words to describe his impact in Pittsburgh. Christ, when KDKA fired him," in late 1975, a parting which hurt the Pirates more, perhaps, than even Allen's did the Yankees, "they had a parade for him in Pittsburgh and fifty thousand people turned up. The whole downtown was clogged. They lined up three and four deep on the streets — they were wild."

"Due to his play-by-play."

Woods whistled, quietly. "Not just that — after all, there were a lot of times when Bob did everything *but* play-by-play," he said. "He'd start talking about when he was with Perry Como or played golf with Bing Crosby and he'd go on and on, ignoring what was happening on the field. At last, he'd say, 'Oh, by the way, Clemente grounded out, Stargell flied out, and that's the inning.' "

"And he got away with it," I said.

"Because people there were used to it — it was like Rosey Rowswell before him; fans had come to *expect* that kind of treatment. It wasn't like some markets where you can ho-hum it, just the hits and errors. Here, people wanted more. Give 'em a song and dance, a soft-shoe, a few stories, a lot of jokes — what folks used to call the 'Rosey Ramble.' Anything to keep 'em listening," which for twenty-eight years the Gunner did. He was emotional, egotistical, and touched with unpredictability. He also made the muses dance with a beautiful appreciation of baseball.

The strange uproarity of Robert Prince, which seldom failed him even as a boy, had something to do, I suspect, with his vagabond of a childhood, as if a sense of belonging must rest in self, not place, and coming home was an impossibility.

He was a transient, the grandson of a United States Congressman and the son of an Army careerist, the late Colonel F. A. Prince, a one-time West Point halfback who scored five touchdowns in a game against Navy; by his own estimate, the future Gunner [christened by Woods after "Prince made a crack in a bar to a woman," wrote Phil Mushnick of the *New York Post*, "and her husband pulled a gun and pointed it at Prince"] attended fourteen or fifteen schools from Pittsburgh to Salt Lake City to Fort Lewis, Washington. "He raised me on about six Army posts," said Prince about his father, who later shepherded him through four universities. Finally, with a B.A. degree from the University of Oklahoma, Prince entered Harvard Law School, only to fail Procedure in his first semester. "I had three uncles and a brother who were Harvard lawyers, and I went there just so I wouldn't have to work. In those days, anybody could get in — it's not like it is now — and after flunking out, I probably could have gone back for the next term. Only one problem: One night in early 1940 my old man went to the movies in Montgomery, Alabama, looked up at the newsreel and suddenly started swearing."

"Bad movie?"

"No," he said, "because his son was up there competing in a jitterbugging contest."

"Who were you dancing with?" I said.

"A stripper," Bob pronounced.

"*What?*"

"You got it," he said in his familiar, invigorating rasp. "I've always said the title of my autobiography is gonna be, *I Should Have Never Danced With That Stripper*. See, I'd read in the law library that a famous jurist went to burlesque houses to relax and just let your subliminal thoughts flow. So I went to that joint and I entered this contest with the stripper in Boston, and not only did my dad see it in the movies, the picture of me dancing with the burlesque queen popped up in papers all over the country. My whole *family* saw it."

"What'd your father say?"

"Nothing about the stripper, and I can see why — she had a face like a ripped softball and walked like a knuckleball. But he blew his top at *me*. He phoned and he was furious. 'Is that what I'm spending my earnings for?' he said.

'You're just wasting my money at Harvard. I've had enough. You're dropping out — you're going to work. Here's $2,000 to get started. Go make a living.' "

The Gunner, of course, had something less high-class in mind. "Looking back, if I'd been my old man, I would have blown my head off. Talking about having to grow up — I was a mess. I just bummed around, even went to jail."

"For what?" I said.

"I was trying to hitch a ride on a train and got thrown in the slammer for vagrancy. That's why I say — anything short of murder or robbery, I've been there."

From Harvard, Bob retreated in 1940 to Zelienople, near Pittsburgh ("I'd been literally disinherited," he said, "so I went to the only town where I could find a place to live"), and met comfort and serenity in his grandmother's home. Soon, the telephone rang again. "Throw that bum out of the house," Colonel Prince ordered the landlord. "Go tell him to find a job."

More or less tossed in the street, the Gunner found little demand for a career playboy. He did, however, find a wife. "One day I see this lady walking along and she looked pretty nifty," he said. "So through a friend, I found out she was a school teacher at the Zelienople High School and, as Paul Harvey would say, 'the rest of the story' is that we got married in June of 1941."

By then, the native Californian (born July 1, 1916, in Los Angeles) had entered announcing — "What else was I going to do? The only thing I'd been trained to be was a loafer" — and, more specifically, sportscasting, a natural evolution for a man who had been a thwarted athlete all his life. "My old man had loved sports, and at all the Army posts I'd lived on, I got to play golf, polo, fencing. Then at college I was a swimmer," he said. "Hell, I was hooked on sports. How could I *not* become their broadcaster?" The Gunner pricked past reverie. "Once, when I was young and living in Cheyenne, I rode in a rodeo. I came out of the shoot on a big, black son of a bitch and rode him for about five seconds and, I tell you truly, then had the life kicked out of me. My old man couldn't believe it. 'You gotta be some kind of idiot,' he said. 'Why'd you do it?' I had to tell the truth. ' 'Cause some dope said I wouldn't dare try to.' "

There was a pattern here, worthy of a diffident respect, even then emerging; of challenges considered and promptly defied, and of an already flamboyant exhibitionist, often insufferable, who evoked a needling fascination. On various occasions, Prince fenced without a mask, had his upper lip scarred by a polo mallet, galloped a fox hunt trail — including jumps, to silence critics of his equestrian skill — at 3 A.M., and edging other show-business contestants, won a stock car race by forcing a frightened disc jockey off the track. It was a chain-letter not easily broken; early-1940s hecklers signed, carrying on a running feud with Prince over his WJAS program, "Case of Sports," and so did boxer Billy Conn.

"Let me address the sports show first, because that's where it all began, if I can remember back that far," Bob said. "I had to win an audition to get it and I did — and when I did I was flying high. Keep in mind that I was selling insurance during the day to support my family, not the most thrilling job, and going on the show at night — well, I thought I was at least Bill Stern. And I was probably as arrogant too. That's what I did for about six years, all the way through 1946, and I was disputatious as hell — by nature, I guess, and by design. I was building my name up."

"Then one day Conn tore it down."

"Not the name," he said, *"me.* This one night I had hit Billy's manager with some verbal knocks on the air — said he'd convinced Billy to duck tough fights. What I didn't say on the show was that I had a piece of a fighter, Harry Bobo, and Conn wouldn't fight him. A couple of days later I was in the Pittsburgh Arena when Billy saw me, grabbed me, and wanted to start a fight. So I whipped off my glasses and raised up my left arm — I'm a southpaw, you know — and Billy hit me, not hard, but he smacked me like a punching bag. He had me pinned between the staircase and the wall. I couldn't move — he could have hung me out to dry. So I told him, 'Billy, I can't fight, true, but I'll take you over to the Athletic Club and I'll *swim* you.' We laugh about it today, but back then, it was pretty tense. Billy still asks me, 'What would have happened if we'd fought in the pool?' I say, 'I'd have drowned you.' But if Les Biederman, the sportswriter for the *Pittsburgh Press*, hadn't intervened, we may have lost the Gunner right then and there."

Instead, through a coupling of Harvard and God, Prince took his flannel mouth and straw-framed body to the Pittsburgh Pirates' broadcast booth. "In law school," he said, "I'd become friendly with a guy named Tom Johnson," who now, in late 1946, with Bing Crosby, Frank McKinney, and John Galbreath, bought the Buccaneers. "When they got the club, obviously, I was delighted, and as I was congratulating Johnson, I said, 'You know, Tom, if the opportunity ever arose, I'd love the chance to announce for the Pirates.' " At about this time, Jack Craddock, Rowswell's assistant, began to seek salvation from Above, and determined to rescue himself and others, brandished a Bible and a bus ticket and set out for a more pure and Christian life. "For some reason, he got religion, he heard the Word," observed the Gunner, "and Jack literally packed his suitcase and pulled a Jerry Falwell — went all through the Bible Belt preaching repentance, appearing at revival meetings," forsaking bat and ball for absolution and, not incidentally, creating a Pirates' broadcast void.

"In 1948, Johnson in effect foisted Bob on Rosey, and I heard this personally in long talks with Rosey — he didn't like him, was afraid of him, he feared this incredibly brash kid," contended Ted Patterson, a Baltimore broadcaster and media critic. "As a result, Rosey shut him off — only let Bob read commercials and minutiae like that." At the end of the season, Prince, thoroughly ignored, accosted Rowswell and said, "What do you have against me?" Rallying his 112 pounds, Rosey sniffed, "You're nothing but a fresh punk." Replied the Gunner: "Look, all I want to do is succeed you when you retire or die. Even if it takes thirty-five years, all I want to be until then is your assistant."

His balm reassured the Pirates' Voice, and on April 9, 1948, via Western Union from Crosley Field, Bob Prince unveiled his first baseball play-by-play; his salary, the princely sum (one could hardly resist) of $50 a week.

From the start, he was incorrigible; he engaged in partisan crowing; he was unjaded and personal, "shaped so distinctly in his mold," *Sports Illustrated* wrote, "that every listener feels that for better or worse he knows him." He wore outrageous jackets ("I became controversial on purpose — controversial on the air and controversial in my dress to attract attention and establish myself") and committed felonies against the dictionary ("They don't mean a thing at this time of year," he explained of April batting averages, "so we *deign* to use them") and, dwarfing the players he chronicled, became "loved, hated, listened to," as a magazine headline blared; "a landmark," Willie Stargell said, "like United States Steel."

For seven years, the Gunner caddied for Rosey — telescoping the arc of fly balls as Rowswell's eyesight dimmed, enlivening dull games with prattle as the Pirates stumbled, dropping a dumb-waiter tray with bells and other artifacts as Rosey uncorked his dashing embellishment, "Open the window, Aunt Minnie! Here she comes!" At Forbes Field, the pair sat closeted in a tiny booth and looked out on a park heavy with vines, memories, and individuality; on the road, they remained at home, airing games by wire ticker from the WWSW studio. "The last couple of years, Rosey's health went downhill and when we'd do re-creations in the studio, he'd lie down on a cot and say, 'Wake me up if anything is going on.'" In early 1955, Rowswell died, "And that's the first year I traveled with the team to do actual road broadcasts," Prince relayed. "We were the last team in the majors to turn from re-creations to live away play-by-play."

"Why, because Rosey's health was too lousy to travel?" I asked.

"No," he said. "It was because of our sponsor, Atlantic Richfield. At this time, in the fifties, Atlantic owned the broadcast rights to the Yankees, Red Sox, Phillies, Orioles, and us, and their account was handled by N.W. Ayer advertising, whose main liaison to the sponsor was Les Quailey. He was a hell of a guy — the former spotter for Ted Husing, the guy who really invented the idea of side-line markers to tell people that the ball was at the twenty-yard line or wherever."

"What was Quailey's connection to re-creations?"

"Atlantic didn't want to spend money for all the line charges when the Pirates went to a Philadelphia or Cincinnati," he said. "But, gradually, Les gave up his opposition and one by one, the teams broke away — the Yankees started to do away games live, the Red Sox, the Phillies, and finally, we took the plunge."

Its depths were alluvial. From Ebbets Field, Wrigley Field, and Sportsman's Park, and when the Buccos returned home, to their suburban cabin that Prince called, incessantly, "The House of Thrills," the Gunner, now in his eighth season of Pirates' baseball — his first as its Voice — began a twenty-one-year reign in which he called Steelers, University of Pittsburgh, CBS, and Penn State football, Pitt and Duquesne basketball, ice hockey, boxing, wrestling, golf, polo, track, swimming, and even opera ("Not really play-by-play there," he whispered. "I just introduced Igor Gorin on the air for CBS"), the Gator Bowl, three National Invitational Tournament championships, the 1959 and 1965 All-Star Games from Forbes Field and Metropolitan Stadium, and the 1960,

1966, and 1971 World Series — an epoch, *Pittsburgh Post-Gazette* writer Charley Feeney confessed, which might "more easily be made into a movie entitled: 'Nobody Will Believe It.' "

Prince spread his palms outward and shrugged. "You know what they say — 'I don't care what they say about me as long as they spell my name right.' Well, that's how I felt, and it wasn't just ego. I knew that when people were interested in me, they were interested in the Pirates. That's the problem with broadcasters today — we're losing the radio characters, we don't have as much fun as we used to. Everybody's scared to say anything controversial, too afraid the general manager will fire 'em. So they play it safe — they statistic you to death. But you sure as hell can't statistic people to death when you're thirty games out of first."

"All the stats are bad."

"Not only that, those facts and figures — they just put people to sleep, if they're not snoring already. And we had some miserable teams when I took over, second division all the way. I had to stir things up — get after the umpires, root for the Buccos, be a showboat. You'd better believe people weren't listening 'cause they thought we'd win."

Ironically, in Prince's second season as Pittsburgh's conspicuous Voice, it was not the Gunner but rather a Pirates' journeyman who begged belief. After a career emblazened by twelve years, twelve leagues, and fifteen clubs, Dale Long uprooted himself from obscurity to homer in seven consecutive games — one short of the all-time major-league record. Jamming the yard at the foot of Schenley Park, 32,221 fans filed into Forbes Field to see Long try for No. 8 against the Dodgers' Carl Erskine on May 28, 1956. "The night before, a Sunday, 'The Ed Sullivan Show' had Dale go on," the Gunner said. A Philadelphia brewery signed him to praise its beer. Dale Long T-shirts besieged the market. Pittsburgh companies vied for his endorsement. "And all this for a guy who'd had a hard time getting his name in the box score — all of a sudden he was front-page news."

"Describe that Monday night," I said.

"It was electric, the most significant moment I've ever had in broadcasting," he said. "Think of how bad we were [in 1955, the Bucs had finished last] and suddenly we're the sports capital of America. In the first inning Erskine fanned him. Then came the fourth and the crowd is absolutely bonkers. Well, Dale bombed an Erskine overhand curve into the right-field seats, and Forbes Field about tumbled over. Long circled the bases and got such a standing ovation that he had to come out of the dugout for a curtain call."

"Commonplace today."

"Oh, but not in baseball then," Prince said, "and I look over in the adjacent box and there's Tom Johnson, John Galbreath, Ben Fairless, chairman of the board of U.S. Steel, David McDonald, the president of the Steel Workers Union, and Bishop Austin Pardue, Diocesan leader of the Episcopal Church — and *they're* going wild. That's what baseball and the Pirates meant back then. They brought the whole damn city together." They also brought the Gunner — or did, in part, the Gunner lift *them*? — to a position of influence unmatched by perhaps any institution in the Tri-State Area.

Even as Rowswell's assistant, Prince had a shrewd understanding of Pittsburgh's power structure. "It's a large city but really a small town," he was saying, "and unlike some announcers, who hire an agent to make contacts for them and so forth, I decided on another course. I began to join clubs" — a status symbol he cherished; Bob owned a life membership in the Pittsburgh Athletic Association and belonged to the St. Clair, Oakmont, Williams, and Bradenton Country Clubs, the University Club in Pittsburgh, and the Harvard-Yale-Princeton Club — "so that, for one thing, Betty and our children [two, born in 1942 and 1944] would grow up in a healthy, stable atmosphere, especially with their old man on the road all the time."

"So unlike your childhood," I said.

"Boy, you ain't just spitting past the gravestone."

"But there was a bigger reason for joining, wasn't there?"

"Pure self-interest," he said. "See, through these clubs I began to meet the most important people in Pittsburgh — *that's* how I made contacts, not through a résumé or agent. I'm privileged to be able to call the presidents of all the major corporations in Pittsburgh by their first names, and they'll do anything for me, within reason. And I'm not kidding when I say I can walk into any restaurant in Pittsburgh or even a meeting of any sort and one-half the people'll know me and think of me as a personal friend."

If they did not know before three o'clock one July afternoon in 1957 — two years after the bony-kneed Prince, on a wager from Giants' manager Leo Durocher, waltzed five hundred feet from the Polo Grounds clubhouse in deep center field to home plate carrying a brief case and clad in high stockings, pumps, a "dazzling jacket," formal bow tie, and screaming red satin bermuda shorts — it is safe to assume that all of Pittsburgh knew by sundown.

Sitting near the pool of the Chase Hotel in St. Louis, the Gunner was conversing with several Pirates. "I was kidding them," he recalled, "that baseball players are really lousy athletes. 'Christ,' I said, 'you take any ten sports. I'll beat you at polo, swimming, golf, riding a horse. OK, you got boxing — hell, anything else, I'll win.' " Amused, Gene Freese referred, not altogether unprofanely, to Prince's swimming background; betting $20, the Pirates' infielder dared Bob to dive into the pool. Without hesitation, the Gunner snapped up the gamble and, running to his hotel room, prepared to reactivate his collegiate form. He faced only one small handicap: To make the water, he must clear about twelve feet of concrete, for Bob Prince was about to dive from a third-story window. "It was strictly a blotter job," said Pirates' trainer Danny Whelan, staying, like the players, at the Chase. "It wasn't a question of whether he'd make the pool — it was a question of whether he'd keep his life." Marching to the windowsill, Prince coiled to dive, mumbled, possibly, "Blest Be the Tie That Binds," sprang from the ledge and descended straight as a Vernon Law fastball into the outer recesses of the pool. "I swear to God I wasn't drinking, and I *still* cleared the concrete by four or five feet," Prince insisted. "And it's a good thing I bet with Freese — he paid right up. If I'd bet with Dick Stuart, that son of a bitch never would have paid me."

In 1958, the Gunner hired Woods, left behind when the Giants left New York, and for the next twelve years their influence eclipsed, I believe, even the considerable sum of their parts. "When I got fired in '75, Milo Hamilton replaced me, and he carried the biggest brief case in baseball — facts, figures, averages, technicalities, that's what he loved," Prince said. "Well, that's exactly what Pittsburgh did *not* want. I remember how Possum and me would go into the broadcast booth every day with a pencil and scorecard — that was it. We'd do our tap dance routine if the game stunk, or we'd stick closer to play-by-play if it was exciting, and after the last pitch we'd throw the pencil away, ditch the scorecard, and we'd head for the door. 'OK, that's enough of that,' we'd say. 'Now let's go find a bar.' "

Among the most pictorial play-by-play men in the business, Prince and Woods were brisk, reasonably accurate, and when the Gunner managed to restrict himself to balls and strikes, surprisingly informative; their vocal quality was impossible to imitate; they were, more crucially, a splash of a riot to hear.

Once, thinking he was off the air, Prince leaned out of the booth and gazed at a well-endowed femme fatale strolling down the aisle. "Wow, check that one out in black," he admired. Later, Bob learned that his critique had reached listeners in Erie, Youngstown, and Ashtabula. "Jesus," he said, "it scares me when I think of what I *could* have said." Several years later, the Pirates were hosting the Astros when a No. 46 lumbered out of the dugout to pinch-hit for Houston. Looking at his scorecard, the Gunner saw no 46 listed; naturally, he turned to Woods for help. At that same moment, an announcement filled the Forbes Field press box: "Will Rab Mungee please report to the press gate?" Hearing the name of Mungee, the Gunner told his radio audience, "Rab Mungee is the Houston pinch-hitter" — the first time in history that a fan at a ball park became the designated pinch-hitter. Another time, the Possum asked Bob if he wanted a drink. No, replied the Gunner, he was on the wagon. "Then he laughed," Woods related, "and said, 'Don't worry — I'm just as crazy not drinking as when I am!' And the weird thing is — he was." In 1961, Woods told of how Prince won a bet — unfailingly, he got odds — by keeping totally quiet for an hour on a Los Angeles-to-Pittsburgh charter flight: "And you won't believe it," Poss informed his listeners, "but we got a bonus. The Gunner didn't say a word for another five hours." One spring training, both were returning to their Ft. Lauderdale hotel rooms when Woods, at four o'clock in the morning, pointed to a pool beneath their second-floor windows and said, " 'Gunner, how do you think your act would check out now?' and Bob said, without batting an eyelash, 'There's only one way to find out,' and he took his glasses off, jumped off the balcony and plunged, fully-clothed, into the pool."

All this complemented the circus of that sunny afternoon at Wrigley Field when, according to the Possum, "The worst-looking woman I've ever seen came into the press box and yelled, 'I want to see that fucking Brickhouse [Jack, the Cubs' TV Announcer].' Well, Jim Enright, the Chicago sportswriter, pointed to Prince and said, 'There, *there's* Brickhouse.' So she comes charging into our booth and said, 'Are you that fucking Brickhouse?' I mean, you could hear her over the air. Next, the ushers come rushing frantically into the booth and drag her away. As they're dragging, just out of curiosity's sake I followed this tub back to her box seat, and the woman she sat down next to was, if it's possible, even uglier than *she* was."

"Then you went back to the booth," I said.

"Yes, and I sat down, shook my head," and by now Woods was laughing, "and I said over the air, 'Bob, if you think *that* one was bad, you should have seen the broad she was sitting with.' About ten seconds later our telephone rang — it was Joe L. Brown, the Pirates' general manager. 'You can't be calling women "broads" on the air,' he said. I told him, 'Christ, Joe, if you'd seen how fat she was, "broad" is the only thing you *could* call her.' "

In 1968, amid the darkest pitch of the pastime's night, a letter in *The Sporting News* praised how "the enthusiasm Prince conveys during a game adds much-needed color and excitement to an increasingly dull and slow-moving sport."

Eight years earlier, to denizens of western Pennsylvania, eastern Ohio, and West Virginia, such rhetoric would have been labeled sacrilege — not about Prince, obviously, but rather, *baseball* — for the 1960 season oozed with an almost tropical density of cries of "Beat 'Em Bucs" and "The Bucs Are Going All the Way" and an all-time Pittsburgh attendance record of 1,705,828 and the Pirates' first pennant since 1927 and a World Series which confounded Ripley.

The 1960 Pirates never lost more than four straight games. Twenty-three times, they won games in their final time at bat. At 20–9, Law took the Cy Young Award. Hitting a major-league best .325, shortstop Dick Groat was the Most Valuable Player. At second base, Bill Mazeroski took vengeance on opposing hitters. First basemen Stuart and Rocky Nelson pounded thirty home runs and 118 runs batted in. Right fielder Clemente batted .314, drove in ninety-four runs, scored eighty-nine, and threw out nineteen base runners, highest in the league. Bob Friend posted an 18–12 record; Wilmer (Vinegar Bend) Mizell was 13–5; Elroy Face and Clem Labine anchored the bull pen. "The 1960 Pirates were something special," Biederman would write. "They blended hitting and defense and pitching into one of the most magnificent seasons I ever took part in as a writer." On September 25, the Buccos clinched the pennant. Ten days later, they opened a Fall Classic that boasted two big-league sanctums ("The House of Thrills" and "The House That Ruth Built") and story-surfeited managers, Casey Stengel and Danny Murtaugh, and almost mythic NBC Television messengers, the Gunner and The Voice, and a sequence of events, each cascading upon another, that crested at 3:36 P.M., Thursday, October 13, when Ralph Terry threw a chest-high slider, Mazeroski hit it, and the Pirates became champions of the world.

For Allen, the 1960 World Series marked a voyage in nihilism. Of Bill Skowron's fourth-game long foul ball, Mel malaproped, "That brought the crowd to its collective feet." In Game Seven, he called Yogi Berra's three-run homer at Forbes Field "foul, barely foul" — the greatest Classic miscue, *Sports*

Illustrated swaggered, "since Clem McCarthy's historic miscall of the 1947 Kentucky Derby [actually, to *SI*'s embarrassment, the Preakness]." Yet it was the same Voice whom Prince, a quarter-century later, credited "with saving me in the 1960 Series. If it hadn't been for Mel, I might have fallen apart on the air."

"The loosey-goosey Gunner?" I asked.

"Mel had been doing World Series, it seemed, forever by then. 'Mike fright' didn't bother him, but for me this was a big deal—my first ever. And as we were waiting to go on the air before the first game, some guy from the truck said in my earplug, 'All right, let's get 'em. We've got X number of people watching,' and when he said that, I got as white as a sheet," he said. "Two minutes go by—I haven't said a word. I'm practically tongue-tied. Mel saw how terrified I was, and tried everything to get me at ease."

"What worked?"

"Finally, he said, 'Bob, do you know who in our broadcasting team here is the most nervous of all right now?' I just mumbled. 'Well,' Mel said, 'we're now only twenty seconds to air time,' and then he pointed to the NBC-TV symbol and started talking the way a fag would, 'and can you imagine how long that dad-gum peacock has been waiting to spread his lovely feathers?' That did it—I nearly fell off my chair laughing. From then on, it was the old Gunner at work."

In Game Seven, it was a Gunner, typically, in turmoil, for even in the most celebrated moment in the entirety of Pittsburgh baseball, Prince—without *trying*—managed to upstage the World Series hero, dismissing Maz as Mickey Mantle would a visiting bat boy.

"Even when I set out *not* to be controversial, I fail miserably," Bob Prince said with a chuckle. "The backdrop was that NBC had a policy that the announcer for the winning team would conduct postgame interviews from the victorious clubhouse. After eight innings, we were ahead, nine to seven, and so I left Mel and headed for the locker room."

"Then, in the ninth, the Yankees scored twice to tie," I said.

"Yes, I learned that when I reached the clubhouse, so I immediately did a U-turn and headed back for the booth—maybe the Yankees were going to win, I thought, and Mel would do the postgame. Just as I reached the booth, Forbes Field shook with a great roar. Some network guy spun me around and said, 'Hurry up, get back downstairs! The Pirates won!' "

Breathless, and not knowing it was Maz's blast that won the Series, Prince maneuvered his way into the clubhouse and grabbed a microphone. "As I walked in," he said, "we were already on the air." Finding Mazeroski, an NBC aide pulled the protagonist to the Gunner's side; Maz was even holding his *bat*. "Well, Maz," Prince asked, automatically, as if No. 9 were a nameless reserve, "how does it feel to be a member of the world champions?"

"Great," Mazeroski answered.

"Congratulations," Prince said, and leading Bill off-camera, proceeded to interview everyone from Murtaugh to Warren Giles to the mayor of Pittsburgh; "everyone," Bob said ruefully, "except the one person in the world people wanted to see."

"When did you finally find out how the Pirates won?" I said.

"About two hours after the game ended, I was having dinner with my wife at the Pittsburgh Athletic Association," he said, "and downtown, people were going berserk. 'By the way, Betty,' I wondered, 'just how *did* we finally win?' She looked up and said, 'You must be kidding. Maz hit a home run.' And with that I looked down at my plate, and I wasn't very hungry any more. I had interviewed the toast of America for all of five seconds."

The memory of Maz's shot must sustain the Pirates' sixties, for after October 13, the Buccaneers entered upon a decade of shared reproof. From 1961 to 1969, Pittsburgh five times flunked the first division; only thrice did the Bucs' plank reach as high as third; increasingly, the Pirates relied on The Wonder That Was Clemente to grease their rusting turnstiles. Still, the KDKA Network radio and television ratings remained the highest of *any* big-league club; it was the Gunner, more than the team, that listeners and viewers responded to. "He was a legend when broadcasting Pirates' games," Jack Craig wrote in 1984, two years before Prince was inducted, posthumously, into the Hall of Fame, "and although I never heard him enough to really judge, folks I respect who did insist his popularity was earned, that his style was ideal for the time and place." Over stations from Jamestown, New York, to Cumberland, Maryland, to Charleston and Wheeling, West Virginia, and east to Johnstown, PA, baseball fans heard Prince dub Roberto "Arriba" or "the Great One," Bill Virdon "the Quail," Bob Skinner "Dog," Don Hoak "Tiger," Harvey Haddix "the Kitten," and later, Dave Parker "the Cobra" and Stargell "Willie the Starge," and call a disputed strike "close as fuzz on a tick's ear," implore Groat and Mazeroski to "Give me the Hoover," and salute the fragrance of a Pirates' victory with "How sweet it is!"

"With Clemente, I went to him and said, 'Bobby, what's Spanish for "Let's go, get going"?' He said, 'Arriba,' so whenever we needed him to rip one, I'd start chanting. But with the other guys, these names just popped into my head. If a guy reminded me of an animal, I'd call him that — after a while you didn't even have to say their names; folks knew them by the other."

"And the expressions?" I wondered.

"Same thing, they were ad-lib, you couldn't contrive 'em," he said, and after pausing, "I was raised by a black lady, a mammy, who lived with us from when I was about one year old. She'd come up with sayings like, 'It's as quiet as a gnat crawling' — actually, she said 'pissing' — 'on a bale of cotton,' and I'm sure that converted itself to my play-by-play."

"And people remembered 'em."

"Mailmen would tell me that they'd go around to houses and our games'd be on in the back yard, around the swimming pools, the front porch — even when we were *losing*," he avowed. "And the reason is because people were entertained — they liked those sayings, they repeated 'em, they'd stay tuned just for the laughs, to see what whackiness we'd get into next."

In 1963, Prince traveled to St. Louis to speak at a retirement dinner for Stan

Musial. "I think it is ridiculous," the Gunner told his audience, "that we are gathered here tonight to honor a man who made more than seven thousand outs." By 1965, *The Sporting News* could report, "He's known from coast to coast. Once you know Prince—and who in this business doesn't know him— and once you've heard him, you'd swear the man who invented the microphone had him in mind." A year later, reliving a party at which a hefty sportswriter lifted Bob off the floor and threatened to throw him out of a seventeenth-floor hotel room, *Sports Illustrated* quoted a Prince friend as saying, "I guess if you'd taken a vote, half the people in the room would have been for it and half against." That was the same season in which Prince, dining with a Pittsburgh drama critic, apologized, "I've got to leave now and get back to the booth. A million people are waiting to turn me off"; the Gunner, inviting black ballplayers to his house for dinner and a swim, warned, facetiously, "You'd better behave yourself, or I'll put lye in the pool"; Jack Berger, the Pirates' public-relations director, explained, "He's controversial, but he's one of the very best"; and the Tri-State Area worshiped at the Temple of the Green Weenie.

"Ah, yes, the Green Weenie," Bob Prince said, affecting his best W.C. Fields. "I remember it well."

"How'd it get started?" I said.

"It was in July of '66 and we had a good ball club, a great chance to win the pennant. We were playing in Houston, televising back to Pittsburgh, and it was a toughie—bases loaded for the Astros and Lee May at bat."

"And?"

"All of a sudden, out of the corner of my eye, I see Dan Whelan doing strange things on the Pirates' bench. So I pick up the dugout phone, call him, find out what the hell he's doing, and asked our director to point the camera at Dan. 'There, ladies and gentlemen,' I told our viewers, 'is a picture of a grown man pointing a Green Weenie at Lee May.'" When May popped up, Buccos' fans adopted as their hero this newest, weirdest hex—a rubber wiener painted green.

"And you milked it for all it was worth," I said.

Prince stared at me in undisguised triumph. "It was all camp, all in fun, but its effect was unbelievable—it literally went around the world. 'The Green Weenie, it's going to lead us to the pennant.' [It almost did; the Pirates finished three games back.] I mean, we had Green Weenie clubs around the league. Truck companies put the Weenie on their aerials—truckers would turn it upside down when we lost, right side up when we won. Rockwell Manufacturing sent me a power tool specifically made to rejuvenate the Weenie. The Certa Mattress Company made a mattress for the Weenie to sleep on between games of a double-header."

"And the players?"

"The Pirates thought it was great. The others hated it," he said. "I'll never forget one day in '66 at Forbes Field. It was packed, thirty-eight thousand people, and we were playing the Dodgers. Don Drysdale was pitching. The

Bucs get the bases loaded and Clemente comes up. So over the radio I say, 'Let's put the Green Weenie on Drysdale,' and because in those days so many people brought their transistors to the games the place went wild. A ball park full of people shaking their Weenies at Big D."

"Was he rattled?"

"Not usually, but this really got to him — he's just looking at the crowd going wild. Finally, umpire Ed Vargo comes out to the mound and said, 'Pitch.' Don glares at him and said, 'How the hell can I pitch with all these nuts going crazy and that skinny bastard up in the booth?' And Vargo said, 'I don't know, but pitch.' "

"Who won the battle?" I said.

"Drysdale finally threw to the plate, and Clemente bombed a triple and three runs scored. Alston [Walter, the Dodgers' manager] came out to relieve him and as Don goes toward the dugout, he shakes his fist at me. But that was the Weenie — indestructible. And it all began that crazy day in Houston."

From the Weenie's 1966 birthplace, Prince parted respectfully, boarding a plane to San Francisco via Dallas. "That's where the Pirates were next scheduled, and while I was getting on the aircraft I happened to mention the word 'bomb.' I wasn't even thinking about it when I said it. Well, before I know it, the stewardess told the captain, who told the FBI."

"Who told *you*," I said, "to bite your tongue."

"Oh, the FBI and police were real nice, but by the time they'd finished with me, the plane had left. I finally got to Frisco after about thirty hours without sleep." Ultimately, he returned to Pittsburgh and another bit of 1966 eccentricity: The Black Maxers — a select group of Pirates who doted on World War I flying gear — named Bob "official bombardier." Would the Gunner, at fifty, *ever* settle down? "I *am*," he said that contorted summer, "or at least my wife thinks it's *time* that I settled down."

By the Prince of Pittsburgh's standards, the next three seasons paled. The Buccos slumped, lethargy deflated home attendance, and in the fall of 1969, the Possum plunged overboard. "A few years before, KDKA had bought the rights to our games from Atlantic Richfield, and we'd begun to have problems," Prince said. "KDKA began to cut us up, saying we wandered too far from the action, that sort of thing. Then, in late '69, Poss got in this pissing contest with the station's owner, Westinghouse. They were about $1,200 apart on his salary; they couldn't get together." Woods' recollection is a tad more delicate. "I'd never got the money I should have," he said, "never, going back to '58. So when an offer for more dough came along, I grabbed it," and breaking up one of baseball's truly superb broadcast teams, the Possum moved to St. Louis; he was replaced at Forbes Field by Gene Osborn, joining Prince and Nellie King.

In the new triune's first year, the big leagues hailed the Big Red Machine (winning 102 games and the Western Division by 14½ games), the blooming of MVP Johnny Bench (the first catcher to lead his league in home runs and RBIs), the gross-grain fashionings of Bobby Bonds (striking out a record 189 times and *still* batting .302), the long-range enormity of Killebrew and Howard, tagging forty-four homers apiece, and not least among their joyances, a Mets' attendance of 2,697,479, the sport's then-second-largest figure. Atlanta's Rico Carty hit .366. Connie Mack Stadium and Crosley Field closed down. The concern referred to as the world champion Orioles declared dividends on three twenty-game winners, the American League's Most Valuable Player — the large and largely skilled Boog Powell — and a five-game October security alternately known as the 1970 World Series, the wrecking of Cincinnati's Machine, or, more enduringly, The Brooks Robinson Show. Off the field, old-liners found Jim Bouton's kiss-and-tell volume, *Ball Four*, the bizarre instability of Denny McLain (suspended three times in eight months by a busy Kuhn), and Curt Flood's antitrust suit against baseball's reserve clause more difficult to digest. The ex-Cardinal traded to Philadelphia lost his case, but by the mid-seventies, the Pandoras he unloosed taxed his ex-employers with a mortgage called free agency, whose interest revolutionized The Game.

The Buccos too found 1970 revolutionary, but in a different and more destructive sense. "The *good* side of the year is that we won the Eastern Division," the Gunner stated. At San Diego, Dock Ellis no-hit the Padres on June 12; on August 1, Pittsburgh scalped the Braves for forty-seven total bases and fourteen extra-base hits; on September 27, the Pirates beat New York, 2–1, to clinch the East. Matty Alou led the Pirates with 201 hits. Clemente, Manny Sanguillen, and Dave Cash batted over .300. Stargell, owner of a new Kentucky Fried Chicken franchise in Pittsburgh's Hill District — ergo, Prince's rallying cry, "Come on, Willie, let's spread some chicken on the Hill" — unlocked team highs of thirty-one homers and eighty-five RBIs. "It wasn't a great ball club," Bob said of the '70 Bucs, "but Murtaugh juggled a mediocre pitching staff, and, Jesus, could they *hit.*"

They did much of their whacking in the cavernous structure of Three Rivers Stadium, the Buccos' new Pennsylvania habitat; that was 1970's *bad* side. On June 28, the Pittsburgh National League Baseball Club played its final game at the site whose timeworn scoreboard in left field and double-decked pavilion in right, outrageous Siberia of a center garden, stone outfield wall, lush flowering environs, and seats so near the grass-draped soil that, observing No. 21, you could almost know what he was like, made this the most intimate and lovely of all big-league parks: Forbes Field, dead at sixty-one.

"Let me be perfectly clear," a friend said to me, aping the president of that time. "I think no baseball team in the modern era has suffered more by moving from one park to another" — even more, he gibed, in terms of warmth than attendance, in a sense of regional *identity*. Forbes Field, like Ebbets Field, was a baseball cynosure; to intrude other sports seemed heretical. Three Rivers was a different kind of church; with its football-oriented sight lines, Tartan turf, and upper-deck pews so distant from home plate they seemed rooted in West Virginia, it resembled as much a bull ring as a baseball park. "Why," I asked Prince, repeating the remark, "would the Pirates make such a move?"

"Its origins go back to 1958 [November 21] when the team disclosed it had sold Forbes Field to the University of Pittsburgh for $2 million," said the

Gunner. "The school wanted to expand its graduate facilities [building Forbes Quadrangle and the Graduate School of Business]. When the news came out, it was also added that the Pirates would be allowed to use Forbes Field until a proposed all-purpose new stadium was built." He paused. "And there was the fact too that the club wanted a bigger place to play than Forbes Field [capacity, 35,000]."

"Why didn't they expand it?"

"I think it goes back to the point that they wanted something new, jazzed-up—they didn't realize what they already had," he said. "When the Pirates left Forbes Field, they took the ballplayers away from the fans—you were near them, you had the real smell of grass, you could park five or six blocks from the park and have a walk through those great neighborhoods. It was easy to get to. Plus, you had the high wall in left, the right-field bleachers—it was so unique. So what if girders needed replacing or what else they had to fix? It could have been done—they could have put in more bleachers to get a bigger seating. But when they went downtown, gees, the park is hard as hell to get to, it takes forever to leave after a game." Prince stopped a moment. "After the team moved to Three Rivers—it's less colorful than Forbes Field, you know; less character—it was more important than *ever* to have broadcasters who *were* colorful, who practiced sort of a 'Let Me Entertain You.' "

At first, Three Rivers' attendance eclipsed the late-sixties bedragglement of Forbes Field. The 1969 Pirates drew only 769,369 spectators; a year later, paid admissions jumped to 1,341,947; and by 1971, 1.5 million customers flocked to the towering oval at the confluence of the Ohio, Allegheny, and Monongahela. "It was partly the novelty," Prince said. "People came to see what the place was all about." But by 1974, even with a divisional champion, that total slipped to 1,110,552; in 1978, the second-place Pirates fell below the million mark. "What really troubled us," said a team executive, "is that whereas in the late sixties, all playing in old parks and with the same kind of listless teams, the Phillies, Pirates, and Reds each drew about the same; now, a decade later—all in new parks and with contending teams—Philadelphia and Cincinnati were outdrawing us two and three to one." Pittsburgh became tarred as a "bad baseball town"; at Three Rivers, the Buccos knelt before their cotenants, the football Steelers, who went forth to dominate the city; devoid of both Forbes Field, their distinctive home, and after 1975, the Gunner, their unmistakable Voice, the Pirates, lacking a defined signet, receded into the blurry consciousness of the Tri-State Area. Returning to Erie, Oil City, and Meadville in the early 1980s, I was appalled by the sea-change in interest. Unlike even ten years earlier, western Pennsylvania for the most part had ceased to "love, hate, (*or*) listen to" the slashing Buccaneers. It was not merely that attendance had slumped; so had network radio and television ratings, and the outlands' portion of print exposure devoted to Pirates' baseball. Worse, and to a former Allegheny student, incredibly, talking to old friends in restaurants, classrooms, and stores, I found that almost no one seemed to *care* any more. Losing millions each year, you heard, the Bucs might soon leave Pittsburgh. Pittsburgh without its *Buccos*? Better Foster Brooks without his booze.

Such debility had looked implausible when, in 1971 — after, for the first time since 1920, a major-league team could flaunt four pitchers of twenty or more victories (the Orioles' quartet of Palmer, Mike Cuellar, Dave McNally, and Pat Dobson went 81–31); after the Birds streaked to a third consecutive division title and in October, against the youthful A's of Jackson's thirty-two homers, Hunter's first of five straight twenty-win campaigns, and the MVP comet of Vida Blue, Baltimore swept the Championship Series; and after obscuring even the season's most luminous footnotes (the Bengals' Mickey Lolich snared twenty-five victories, Tony Oliva won a third batting title, and Bill Melton became the first White Sox' player to lead his league in homers), the Orioles, by now an October fixture, seemed positioned to again cart away the Grand Event; after all of this — Nelson Briles shut out the favored Birds, Steve Blass threw a pair of one-run outings, and Clemente hit .414 and leaped into *Webster's* as a new definition of *dazzling* as the Buccos, prevailing in seven games while Gowdy, Thompson, and Prince swapped television play-by-play, prompted the Gunner to enunciate, "We had 'em alllll the way!"

"Joe Brown used to say of that '71 club, 'Most of the players were ones I had brought up to the team. I felt love for that team — it was my baby,'" Prince said. "He was right — it was a team hard *not* to love." Roberto batted .341 and had 178 hits. Sanguillen averaged .319. Stargell bombed a league-leading forty-eight homers and drove in 125 runs. Bob Robertson added twenty-six long balls. Blass tossed five shutouts and had a 2.85 ERA. Ellis won nineteen games, and Dave Giusti recorded thirty saves.

"Yes, and for a lot of these players, there was a common denominator that led to an ugly charge," I said.

"I know," replied the Gunner.

"People used to say the Pirates were so dominated by black and Latin players that whites in this area refused to pay to see them," I said, reciting how Woods once stated, "I told Brown, 'Joe, you got too many nonwhites, and Pittsburgh's one of the most segregated cities in the country. People just ain't going to go out and watch 'em,' to which Brown said, 'Jim, I just refuse to believe that about this town.' So he went on his merry way — more black stars, fewer whites, and you can see from the attendance figures where it got him."

Bob Prince nodded. "I've heard that a million times, and while I don't say it's totally true, it is a factor," he said. "This is a very union-oriented, lunch-bucket area; it's not a black city. If you go to a game and there are forty thousand people there, thirty-nine-and-a-half are white. But I don't think it's the whole reason for the attendance problems. In other blue-collar towns, there are black players, and the teams still draw. Most people don't care what color a guy is as long as he can hit. Besides, look at that '71 club — it was so good its quality had *no* pigment."

Neither, baseball discovered, did the 1972 Buccaneers, winning the East, as they did, by eleven games over second-place Chicago, and losing in the final inning of the playoff to Cincinnati's Machine. The Pirates batted .274 that year to lead the majors; a record-tying nine players compiled more than 100 hits; even the pitching staff sparkled, twirling a 2.81 ERA. "I've had a lot of seasons," confessed the Gunner, wryly, "but not many have affected me more emotionally than '72."

Not elegant but rather palpable, it began with a players' strike that lopped thirteen days and eighty-six games off the regular season, ended with a Series that was spirited and excruciating, and exhibited such entertainments as Gaylord Perry's 24-16 jubilee, Dick Allen's MVP certificate of thirty-seven homers and 113 RBIs, and the Padres' Nate Colbert's incendiary double-header against Atlanta: five home runs, seven runs scored, thirteen knocked across, and twenty-two total bases. In the National League, Billy Williams won the batting crown, Steve Carlton won an astounding *46* percent of the last-place Phillies' victories, and the Giants' Jim Barr retired a record forty-one straight batters. Mets' manager Gil Hodges died; Yogi Berra replaced him— "the easiest possible way," wrote Bill Veeck, "of bringing the Yankee fans into Shea Stadium." Clemente rapped a double for his three thousandth- and final regular-season hit; ninety-one days later, he was dead. In the American League, the Senators moved to Arlington, Texas; the batting champion— again, Carew—went homerless for the first time since 1918; and the Orioles dove to third. Lolich and Joe Coleman won forty-one games as Detroit won the East; with only Joe Rudi at or above .300 and a pitching staff of Hunter, Blue, Ken Holtzman, and Rollie Fingers, the Athletics took the West, the playoff, and a green-and-gold October Finleyfest. Vowed their manager, Dick Williams, of Oakland's owner/embarrassment: "Mr. Finley has been wonderful to me. I have nothing but the highest regard for him." Reminding Williams of that cheerfulness a brief twelve months later, you might have been warmly punched in the nose.

Since 1948, often inducing a similar reaction, the Gunner had been alternately jeered, cheered, booed, and assaulted by cries of "Shut up, Prince!" from nearby spectators whose expletives pricked his play-by-play. He had obtained virtually every credit card in captivity; "he's always flashing his money," said Bob Friend, "and he loves to show off those cards. But if a guy is down to his last ten bucks, Prince will always come through." He had also, quietly, at variance with his image, done more to help countless charities than any man in western Pennsylvania—turning over more than 90 percent of the fees he earned as a toastmaster; accepting no fee for any charitable event; cofounding the Allegheny Valley School for retarded children in 1960; helping, "without question, the underprivileged, the sick and the disadvantaged, more than any public entertainment figure in Pittsburgh," said its former mayor, Joe Barr; and "coming out here often and spending most of his time with the children, playing in the nursery or out on the lawn playing ball," said Regis Champ, the Allegheny School's executive director. "Every Christmas afternoon he is out here spending the day with children who cannot go home, who are severely retarded. And our kids feel his love—nothing more excites them than to hear Bob Prince is on our campus. He just believes very deeply that God has gifted him with a terrific voice and he, in turn, just wants to help others."

"And without publicity?"

"Bob's never even asked for an *award* for all the stuff he's done," Champ said. "He's raised millions of dollars for us. Whenever a legislative bill comes up concerning the handicapped, he's on the phone all the time — lobbying senators and congressmen. He'll call up companies asking them to donate wheelchairs, braces, that kind of thing. He even counsels parents of severely retarded children."

"Does he have a relative, a friend, enrolled here? Is that why he does it?" I said.

"No, and that's the amazing thing. There's absolutely no motive for him to do all this except for what he feels inside. I'll give you an example. Kraft Foods in Chicago has made slides for the school which illustrate stories like 'Little Red Riding Hood' or 'Snow White.' Well, when Bob was doing every game for the Pirates and he'd be in Chicago for a series or just passing through, he'd stop there and do the voice tape synchronization with the slides."

" 'Snow White'?" I repeated.

"Don't laugh," he said, "because it's really touching to hear Bob Prince doing 'The Night Before Christmas' for the kids. His dedication is overwhelming — literally hundreds of hours a year. And he was doing all this for us back in the early days when he wouldn't allow his name to be used, figuring people would think he just wanted P.R."

"Did you ever think of what *he* gets out of it?"

"I think it's buoyed him," Champ answered. "For instance, I know of times that when Bob was on radio and the Pirates weren't winning, he'd come into the nursery, picking up one of the children, play with him for a while, then leave. And on the way out, he'd say something like, 'That's what I needed.' They've touched him to the core."

It was *this* Prince — kind and sensitive, in a way observers seldom realized, and deeply moved by injury; "beneath all that bluster, a real softie," said Woods — whom Pittsburgh honored on July 28, 1972. "How sweet it was at Three Rivers Stadium," Bob Smizik wrote in the *Press* the morning after. "They honored a man who has become a baseball legend. . . . If there was any doubt that the Prince fans far outnumber the Prince detractors, it was proven last night." When "Bob Prince Night" was first suggested, the Gunner consented only if the Bucs would agree to donate all proceeds to the Allegheny Valley School; they had, and the charity received a check for more than $75,000. That same night, as nearly forty thousand Three Rivers patrons stood up to applaud, children from the school "presented Prince with two lamps — made by themselves out of Popsicle sticks," Smizik said. "The lamps are beautiful, but they couldn't compare with the gesture."

"I've witnessed many heroic feats on athletic fields," I heard the Gunner telling me, "but nobody hit me with such heroism as those kids did that night. Just to make the lamps — it took them weeks and weeks; they used about fifteen hundred sticks on each one — can you even begin to imagine the character, the *heart*, of those beautiful kids?"

"How'd you get involved with them?" I said.

"My connection to the Valley School goes back to 1960, when I got a phone call from Patricia Hillman Miller of the Hillman family — her family, I'm sure, is worth billions," he said. "She's a lovely lady who'd suffered polio late in life; she and her husband had no children, but they'd adopted four. Anyway, she said she wanted to do something for humanity and asked if I'd help. That's what I mean about belonging to clubs; you get to know people like this. So I said, 'If I do help, it's going to be full-throttle.' I went to see her and she had a retarded child. The kid came up to me, I hugged her, and I was hooked right there. And it just took off."

"How many kids in the school?"

"We've got about four hundred and they're on five campuses — sort of divided as to the degree of hardship that the youngsters have. We're involved with animal husbandry, that sort of thing. You know, I also helped found the Fred Hutchinson Cancer Foundation [named after the Reds' manager who died in 1964], and it's been a joy to help with that. To do what we can to stop that disease and to visit retarded kids, try and make their lives more fulfilling — they're the most worthwhile things I've ever done."

"And those kids got to you on your night."

"When the crowd went on clapping, and I saw those kids, it did something to me people said *couldn't* be done — they left me speechless," not at all a word I would ascribe to Pittsburgh in 1974, the year the Steel City unfurled its babushkas.

"What the hell does *babushka* mean anyway?" I said.

"Look it up in the dictionary. It's Slavic — it means handkerchief, a bandanna," he said, "but in baseball, it came to mean fans.

"We were in Atlanta," Prince began, "and we were coming home for a two-game series with the Cardinals before hitting the road again. We hadn't sold many tickets, and it shouldn't have surprised me when I got a call in the booth from Art Routzong [Pirates' treasurer], who said, 'Jesus, do something to spur sales.' So I went on the air and said, 'Ladies, we need your help. We got a Ladies Night coming up at Three Rivers when we get home. Why don't you bring out your . . . ?' and I couldn't think of the word handkerchief, so out of the blue came babushka. 'Why don't you bring your babushka out and wave it?' Then I got another call from Routzong. He says, 'Why'd you say *babushka*? They'll never know what you mean.' "

"The same week, you go home," I said.

"Yes, and when I got to the park, there are hundreds of women there waving — you got it — their babushkas. I go into the office and after a while I come out, look, and there are thousands of people waiting to get into the park. And most of 'em have babushkas! We had to hold up the game to get everybody into their seats. Forty-eight thousand people, total. Well, the Cardinals scored two runs in the first inning. We come up, get a couple of guys on, and I say over the radio, 'Come on, ladies, wave your babushkas.' And they start going wild. We get a run in, and I say, 'See, that's what Babushka Power is all about.' I can point out to you how in that year and the next we put in over a hundred thousand people just through playing up babushkas. All those extra fans, and it didn't cost the ball club a penny for promotions. It was something else."

There was something else too about Bob Prince's firing — something brutal and lacking even a semblance of sanity or courage.

After twenty-eight years of rooting for and hawking a baseball team — the then-longest unbroken skein of any Voice in major-league history; a breadth in which he opened and closed more big-league stadia and "saw more records set, I'm sure, than any other announcer. Like Caray, Allen, Chuck Thompson, I went from the ticker tape to the satellites" — the Gunner was gunned down, as if the Pirates' critical capacities had ceased to function, for, get this: telling stories at the expense of play-by-play. Yet, at the same time, there was something profoundly moving about the city of Pittsburgh's reaction, something which was, and remains, unbelievable, as if to reassert its love and express its outrage at what deteriorated, I think, into baseball's most self-destructive broadcast ouster.

For years, the Possum related, Prince had engaged in a running quarrel with Westinghouse Broadcasting officials — first, over money ("Once Bob and I were met by a Westinghouse lawyer, who told us, 'I want those contracts signed *now* so I can take them back to the offices,' " Woods said. "So Bob looked at me and said, 'Ready?' I said, 'Gunner, whenever you are,' and together, we ripped the contracts up at the exact same moment. 'There,' Prince snorted. 'Paste 'em together and take *those* back to your boss' "); then, the Pirates' pre- and postgame radio and TV programs ("Both with Nellie and me, Bob found himself jerked around — they were taking away these shows, cutting down on our air-time"); and, ultimately, even the tone and function of the Three Rivers broadcast booth ("Bob had been allowed to design his own booth, and I told him, 'You're making it too large' — it was the biggest in baseball; Bob made it that way so there'd be enough room in case they got into the World Series — 'you're going to have problems.' And that's exactly what happened — Westinghouse started bringing its guests, its clients, into Bob's own booth. Some of them could be heard over the air even rooting against the Pirates, and the whole situation got ugly"). Only in 1975, however, did the feuding become so intransigent and, it must be added, both parties so self-righteous that the diplomatic approach became bootless; and Westinghouse-owned KDKA encouraged to believe that to end the controversy, it must sack the Gunner — the public, The Game, and, in time, its own ratings be damned.

Edward Wallis, regional vice-president of Westinghouse Broadcasting — now, there was the rub; it was he, Prince said, who determined that the Gunner had turned *démodé* and overly digressive ("too big for his britches," a Westinghouse underling claimed) and that by sacrificing statistics to chitchat and levity, had converted Pirates' baseball into (God forbid) entertainment, not public education; show biz, not seminar.

Stop story-telling, he demanded, and (after three decades?) change your style — who cared that generations of Pennsylvanians *preferred* that style? "What we want," Wallis was overheard saying to a sponsor, "is an accurate, consistent, and exciting [?] description." I would say, naturally, with others, that it is accurate to say Prince was consistently exciting. Wallis responded that he knew better—if Prince wouldn't stick to hits, runs, and errors, he would find someone who *would*, and make Pittsburgh like it.

Wallis did.

Pittsburgh did not.

On October 30, 1975, after months of Wallis beseeching and Prince, fighting back, refusing, and Wallis insisting that the KDKA booth belonged to him ("Since Westinghouse owned the rights," Bob said, "he felt they could bring anybody into the booth") and Prince rebutting (" 'Hell,' I told him, 'how would you like it if I brought people into your office and started making a ruckus?' ") and a mutual refusal to accommodate ("Wallis completely misread this market—he didn't have the foggiest notion of what Prince meant to people," said one official; "Bob could have smoothed things over but he wouldn't," said another. "He felt he had the sponsors and the Pirates behind him") and one loud, climactic crash ("These two Westinghouse guests came into the booth," Prince said. "They were bombed, and they turned their radios on. Naturally, this teed me off—I mean, you could hear 'em over the air, and so I turned my mike off and told them, 'Shut the hell up.' Well, they wouldn't—and then one guy called me a mother-fucker and I slugged him. After that, I sat down at the mike, turned it back on, and said something that wasn't very smart—that Westinghouse was making it impossible for me to do my work properly"), the Gunner and, almost incidentally, Nellie King were fired.

The move, said Wallis, was "unanimous" on the part of KDKA, the Pirates, and Pittsburgh Brewery, the Bucs' primary sponsor. "For some people in Pittsburgh," wrote Charley Feeney the next day, "the baseball world yesterday came to an end."

There was no painful soul-searching involved in the Tri-State response—its partisans erupted; "the shock-wave," one columnist marveled, "was twenty megatons." Radio talk shows were beset and then inundated. Taverns stopped selling the brewery's Iron City beer. A variety-store chain ran newspaper advertisements proclaiming, "Prince-King: May They Reign Forever." The Pirates chose the fifth amendment; Pittsburgh Brewery began to second-guess its decision; even KDKA's Bill Currie, scoring his employer, told listeners, "The dismissal of Bob is no longer an internal company matter but a matter of supreme public interest. Prince's hundreds of acts for charity have elevated him to a place of public esteem where nobody can kiss him off with a terse announcement on one day's notice and expect public understanding."

On Wednesday, November 5, thousands jammed downtown Pittsburgh for a parade in the Gunner's honor. Many women spectators along the route waved babushkas; Prince carried a Green Weenie as he rode on the fire truck. Afterward, nearly ten thousand crowded into Point State Park to hear Bob rebuke Wallis as "totally insensitive"; a local politician say, "Two hundred years ago, I don't think there were this many people on this spot defending Fort Duquesne"; and Stargell, the team captain, lament, "Bob's a hero, a local institution. It's like the U.S. Steel Building falling down."

Weeks later, with Pittsburgh still obsessed with the tribulations of easily its most identifiable personality, Feeney wrote, "There are people in the Tri-State Area who think Prince is irreplaceable."

He was.

In December, the Buccos introduced as their new Voice the fact-reciting, scorebook-toting Hamilton, axed by Atlanta earlier that fall. He flopped. "It would have been hard for anybody to come in as Bob's replacement," a mutual friend explained. "How could you possibly do it? But it was especially unfair to Milo — matter-of-fact, not flamboyant, exactly the opposite of everything that smacked of Prince." After four years, Hamilton joined Brickhouse at Wrigley Field; his successor at Three Rivers was ex-sidekick Lanny Frattare. Meanwhile, traveling to Houston, Prince sustained a dismal 1976 as Gene Elston's colleague — "I hated it," he said now. "My wife couldn't come down for family reasons. I was there all by myself" — and dabbled, with similar futility, as that season's pioneering Voice of ABC Television's "Monday Night Baseball."

"It just didn't work — I never got a chance to be Bob Prince. But I'm not going to be too critical of ABC [for his release, in September]. I was just thrilled they chose me," he said in a way that suggested, somehow, resilience and what the Quakers call "peace at the center."

"Not quite like Pittsburgh," I said.

"I had too many people talking in my ear. 'Do this, do that,'" Prince said, "and all they wanted us to do [the Gunner, Warner Wolf, and Bob Uecker, ABC's short-lived first team] was talk, talk, talk — didn't matter what we said as long as we kept babbling. As you know, I *love* to talk, but these network guys had no conception of how even *I'll* allow a little dead air so you don't overwhelm your viewers. Again, this isn't to knock the hell out of ABC. It's just that I kind of felt I knew the game after thirty years in it."

From ABC, Prince came home to western Pennsylvania, took a job with station WEEP — "it *was* rather appropriately named" — and in the early 1980s, turning back to play-by-play, called Pirates' games on a Pittsburgh cable channel. "I enjoy it, I really do," he said, his voice soft but charged, "but we don't come into as many homes. And I have to be honest — it's not like daily radio, like the good old days. But you go on, you hang in there. What the hell, that's what it's all about."

He had *endured*, he was telling me that warm June day in 1983, endured late 1975 and ABC and the torrents of upheaval — endured so that after what had visited him, the trampling of an institution, he could know, even now, that no Voice and team, not Scully and the Dodgers, not Allen and the Bombers, had become so riotously married as the Gunner and his Buccaneers.

That same year, the city of Pittsburgh renovated Three Rivers Stadium; a season later, revisiting the Golden Triangle, I found the Pirates' hull a more scenic, less antiseptic, better baseball place. The following spring, righting a wrong done a decade earlier, "doing more to boost home attendance through one move," an Allegheny classmate said, "than they could through a thousand stupid mascots or promotions," the Pirates disclosed that Bob Prince would rejoin their broadcast team, calling three innings a game on KDKA Radio.

Said Harding (Pete) Peterson, the Buccos' then-general manager: "Bob is a fixture in this community, and he belongs in our broadcast booth. We welcome him back."

Opined Lanny Frattare: "This is a dream come true for me—I can't wait to work with him. I have never called myself the 'Voice of the Pirates' because Bob Prince always has been and always will be."

Remarked the Gunner, choking down tears at an April 18, 1985, Three Rivers press conference: "This is a very emotional thing for me. I'm just delighted to be returning. Other than my family, you're giving me back the only thing I love in the world."

As Pirates' fans envisioned it, Bob Prince would reignite the lure of their team. But strangely, even tragically, like a plot twist out of Thomas Hardy, it was at this very point—the *exact moment* when Prince, after a decade's passage, re-entered the daily broadcast booth—that reality showed lyricism the door.

In early April, the Gunner underwent extensive surgery to remove cancerous growths from his mouth. By Friday, May 3, he had left the hospital; that night, he aired his first KDKA Piratescast since 1975. Weak, exhausted, Prince called only three games and became ill during a two-and-one-half-hour rain delay on May 17. Three days later, he was readmitted to the hospital for dehydration and pneumonia in both lungs, and doctors decided to stop his radiation treatments.

The Gunner died, at sixty-eight, on June 10, 1985. "To many, he was more than just the Voice of the Pirates, he *was* the Pirates," said the Bucs' once-and-present general manager, Joe L. Brown, replacing Peterson in mid-May. "There is no doubt he was one of the great sports announcers of all time."

Bob Prince.

The Pittsburgh Pirates.

For a college student whose very air was pervaded by the histrionics of the Gunner's derring-do, their union—even now, in death—had survived, not submitted to, the years.

*   *   *

Had the big leagues possessed the luxury of a dozen Bob Princes—a statistical impossibility; as the Gunner would admit, a geneological nightmare—baseball might have avoided the quandary whereby excitement became from its late-sixties- and early-seventies broadcast realm what concord was from the Republic: *estranged*. Thinking back on that fitful time, what strikes me is the gap between the sleepy orb of baseball announcing and the larger world that was, if nothing else, *alive*.

On January 20, 1969, Richard Nixon was inaugurated as president. Violence darkened Northern Ireland, abetted by Americans who sold guns to contending forces, and tragedy lurked near Martha's Vineyard, where the names *Kennedy* and *Chappaquiddick* became insolubly linked. In New Haven, the president of Yale pronounced his doubt that "any black revolutionary could get a fair trial anywhere in the United States." In Philadelphia, the University of Pennsylvania—avoiding a confrontation with student war protesters—removed its American flags and placed them in storage. High above Cayuga's waters, one hundred black students, all armed with shotguns, captured Cornell University's student union and demanded that disciplinary reprimands to three black students be revoked (the Cornell faculty, not surprisingly, agreed). On November 13, with his superior's benediction, Vice-President Agnew lacerated network television for "its narrow and distorted picture of America." Said Julian Goodman, president of NBC: "Evidently, he would prefer a different kind of television reporting—one that would be subservient to whatever political group was in authority at the time." Five months later, vowing that America would never be "a pitiful, helpless giant," Nixon announced the invasion of Cambodia. In its wake, campuses exploded: four students were murdered at Kent State University and two more at Jackson State College; hundreds of colleges and universities closed or went on strike, their classes suspended and examinations canceled. Even the fall of 1969's peaceful moratoriums, when five hundred thousand protesters converged on Washington, and the Woodstock Music Festival, where four hundred thousand people sat in a rain-drenched field in upstate New York and listened to the amplified beat of rock, reinforced the disparity between rectitude and rebellion. It was a time of chaos; nothing made sense.

In Chicago, however, the Old Commander did.

By 1970, he was in his thirty-seventh year of play-by-play, and there were many to whom Bob Elson, at sixty-five, had become a camp figure/caricature. He was the Gunner's antithesis—slow, subdued, often monotonous—and his style resembled Jack Webb's; "just the facts, ma'am," TOC's mien seemed to say, its hits, runs, and errors interspersed with relentless promos and Elson's signatory "*He's* out!"

"We used to kid, not always kiddingly, that Elson *had* to be on the take. I've never heard *anybody* do as much shilling when he was on the air," Lindsey Nelson said. "Bob would be moseying along and he'd say, 'There's ball two, and speaking of ball, did we have one last night at Rosa Mesa's Restaurant,' or something like, 'Al Lopez is making a pitching change now, and I know you'll like the change at the bigger, the better, the new Don's Diner.' "

"These weren't White Sox' sponsors?" I asked.

"Oh, no," said Nelson. "Here's the difference. Allen used to mix commercials for White Owl and Ballantine and the rest with play-by-play—but they were regular Yankee sponsors. But with Elson, the White Sox never got a penny for Bob's barking for Don's or Rosa's. That's why announcers used to think Bob had to be getting a commission for these restaurants, bars, what have you—they got free publicity; he must have got money in return." The Tennessean yielded to a sigh. "You've got to give him credit—Bob raised shilling to a new plateau."

The Old Commander was a native Chicagoan who esteemed, among other things, accuracy, interviewing, and gin rummy. He was also a close friend of billiards champion Willie Hoppe, whom Elson visited one day in the late

1920s. It was there, in St. Louis, that Bob, on a whim, decided to tour radio station KWK. "I saw about forty young men outside the studio and when I got there," he said, "a young lady said to me, 'Well, you're the last one today — good luck and don't be nervous.' I was about to tell her, 'No, you're mistaken. I'm not here for a position,' when I figured, 'Hey, what the hell.' "

Ad-libbing a tryout, Elson, by vote of fans who phoned in, became one of three finalists and, ultimately, the victor — but having won the contest, TOC proceeded to lose the war, accused by a runner-up of stuffing the ballot box. The brouhaha soiled Elson's image — "I didn't want St. Louis anyway," he said years later, almost huffily — and, furious, Bob made ready to return to Chicago. At that point, pulling strings, KWK's now-apologetic owner, Thomas Patrick Convey, himself a play-by-play man as "Thomas Patrick," persuaded WGN to summon TOC to its quarters in the Drake Hotel. In 1928, Elson joined the station, helped Quin Ryan broadcast the Cubs and White Sox for a year, and when Ryan left play-by-play, replaced him as a Voice of Chicago baseball, lingering atop its ash heap for the next forty years.

He made it, quickly, and made his plain-spoken tones a shorthand for Midwest radio. TOC originated the on-field, pregame interview. He announced studio music shows, feuding with a vocal trio that set fire to a commercial he was trying to read (Bob's revenge; swinging a baseball bat within inches of the vocalists and forcing them, as with a turntable malfunction, to abort their song). He interviewed politicians, entertainers, and other nabobs on programs from the Pump Room in the Ambassador East Hotel and the "Twentieth Century Limited" at the LaSalle Street Station. He called his first World Series in 1929, and supplementing ambition ("To be the best," he said in 1969, "it's all I ever wanted") with FDR-era friendship ("I was very close to Kenesaw Mountain Landis when he was making all the big radio assignments — how could that not help?"), aired, all told, twelve World Series and nine All-Star Games.

Straitlaced and not above injecting the homer's "we" and "they," the Old Commander disdained Brickhouse's "Hey-Hey" and Caray's "Holy Cow!" and Bert Wilson's raucous cheering; by Chicago yardsticks, he was a paragon of objectivity. "I think it had a lot to do with Landis," Bob said two decades after the Judge's death in 1944. " 'Play it down the middle,' he'd bellow. 'Stick to baseball. I don't want you mentioning any movie stars attending the World Series even if they slide into second base.' " By late 1941, after covering three straight Series with Red Barber, Elson had already borne witness to a rider of unusual network things — Babe Ruth's called (?) shot against the Cubs in the 1932 Fall Classic ("He really did point to the spot before he hit the ball there"); the Sultan of Swat's home run a year later in the first All-Star Game ("For Babe to smash the first homer, how could it be otherwise?"); and Teddy Ballgame's ninth-inning wallop that sealed the 1941 Mid-Summer Affair ("It was the only time I ever saw Ted show emotion," Bob chimed. "He literally danced around the bases"). Paired, at times, with color men Ted Husing, Lowell Thomas, Gabriel Heatter, and Boake Carter, he spiraled, with his laconic bent and homely oratory, into a broadcaster of national reputation.

Enter Pearl Harbor, Elson's induction into the Navy, and Bob's leave — at FDR's request — to broadcast the 1943 World Series. "He was such an integral part of network baseball," mouthed Brickhouse, "that it was the only time ever that a president personally intervened so that someone in uniform could come home and announce a sports event."

Following the panorama of war, TOC reclaimed his niche as Voice of the White Sox — the Cubs having lumbered to Wilson's WIND — but as television superceded radio, Allen and Gowdy made Oktoberfests their preserve, and the late-sixties Pale Hose drooped paler yet, Elson retreated as a national fixture. Instead, trim and increasingly silver-haired, his rhythms beamed over WJJD, WCFL, and WMAQ, he watched the Eisenhower Sox regularly contend and, in 1959, win a pennant; players like Nellie Fox, Luis Aparicio, and Sherman Lollar develop into household words; and club officials gerrymander the yawning dimensions of Comiskey Park to encourage more offense and, hypothetically, attendance. Chicago found the "Go-Go" White Sox worth living by. Minnie Minoso became a synonym for *daring*. With a fine feel for drama, Bill Veeck unveiled an exploding scoreboard. The White Sox brandished such pitchers as Early Wynn, Billy Pierce, Tommy John, and Gary Peters. Between sponsor plugs for General Finance, Heileman Brewing Company, and General Cigar, Elson implored listeners to frequent the aging structure at 35th and Shields. He was only, in part, successful. The 1960 Pale Hose welcomed more than 1.6 million paid admissions; by 1966, finishing fourth, the Comiskeys had dropped below the million level; four years later, losing 106 games, Chicago averaged six thousand fans per opening.

With the Sox in decline, Elson deferred to other priorities — his family, for instance, or lunch at the downtown spots of Tommy O'Leary's, Café Bohemia, and the International Club, or off-air disparagements of colleagues he deemed a boor, or his most full-sized of avocations. "He was almost married to baseball, but his real love was gin rummy, and he was superb," said a longtime White Sox' companion, Jerome Holtzman of the *Chicago Tribune*. "He had pigeons in every town. Once, I asked him to teach me the game. Bob just looked at me, loftily, and said, 'That is like asking Jascha Heifetz to teach you how to play the fiddle. I give lessons, but they will cost you.' " How adept was he? So skilled, said TOC, smiling, that it was hard to find "a pigeon" who would play him; Bob could memorize discarded cards, Sox' manager Al Lopez added, better than anyone he had known. You had to judge gin rummy players by nationality, Elson insisted: "I'd rate the Jewish players the toughest — they've got minds like Univac machines. But all the rest, you can't bring 'em on fast enough for me. English, Italian, Swedish — it doesn't matter. Once, some people wanted to pit me in a gin rummy game against a Univac machine in New York. And, I'll tell you, if they had, I wouldn't have come out any worse for wear."

Neither had his voice, it seemed to many; his sense of relevancy, on the other hand, *had*.

In a thirties age of precise and economical verbiage, the Old Commander was hailed as reverberant; now, to a later generation, he was simply flayed as dull. "I grew up in Iowa and heard him as a kid," said Milo Hamilton, "and I was in awe of him when I joined the Sox. I learned from him that the game is the important thing. He never thought anyone tuned in just to hear him. They tuned in to hear the game. And because with the coming of Cosell and his merry men, that attitude became regarded as kind of quaint, Bob was, so unfairly, labeled square, out of it."

"Ever a question of ability?" I said.

"Hell, no," Hamilton struck back. "Even in his last years, Bob was a work-horse—he adored almost everything about the game. He'd get up at 8 A.M., study the box scores, talk to people, take a nap, then lunch with baseball people, take another nap, then go to the park. He was there seven or eight hours each day. There was never any doubt that he had the talent. It was just that in the sixties, with the world so damned frenetic, laid-back Bob and his slow, sedate style, well, to some he became a relic."

His sins, Elsonians saw as virtues. His virtues, critics saw as sins. His competence, they called mediocrity; his propriety, aloofness; his sentimentality, corn. Roving from clubhouse to dugout to broadcast booth, covering more than seven thousand games, he made it "a point never to criticize a player on the air, never second-guess a manager, never rap an owner. I hope people can say that as long as Bob Elson was on the air, he never hurt anybody"; he ran directly counter to the self-congratulatory ethos of "tell it like it is." He neither raged nor rhapsodized; he simply reported what happened. "I know there were idiots, no-nothings who said in the sixties that he was boring," dismissed Brickhouse, "but to me he was a pioneer, the most marvelous broadcaster who ever lived"; of TOC, the Cubs' Vince Lloyd proclaimed, "The first time I heard him, I thought he was the greatest I'd ever heard."

Distressed by a steady diet of losing, the White Sox dumped Elson in late 1970. The Old Commander took his civility to Oakland, replacing the more *au courant* Caray, who then gravitated to Comiskey Park. The Athletics' constituency, what there was of it, fell on Elson violently—"I didn't agree with them," professed Charlie Finley, "but fans used to say he talked too much about the old-timers, people like Rockne, Landis, Babe Ruth, and Connie Mack"—and it surprised no one when, at the end of a single year at baseball's then-dying seaside resort, Bob beat a hasty retreat to his home port of Chicago. There, he ridiculed retirement, hoped vainly for another campaign of play-by-play, and "remained behind the microphone and on the banquet circuit," wrote David Condon in the *Tribune*, "until a failing heart forced him to lighten his load."

On August 5, 1979, Bob Elson entered the Baseball Hall of Fame. Nineteen months later, he died at seventy-six; "one of the toughest losses," Condon said, "Chicago sports fans have had to suffer." For four decades, he had helped navigate the flow of Midwest baseball history—from Landis to Kuhn, from Ruth to Aaron, "from Jack Benny to Jack Benny," Elson mused, and from one pigeon to another. Playing gin rummy now, he must deal to One, in a strange twist of custom, who held all the Old Commander's cards.

* * *

In the early seventies, Bob Elson's career exuded reduction. Not so the country and world at large. As John Connally once expressed to me, Texas-style, "Everything about that period was *big*."

Abroad, despite Viet Nam, Richard Nixon engaged in diplomatic summitry, and helped end the postwar bipolar world.

In February 1972, five years after writing in *Foreign Affairs*, "Taking the long view, we simply cannot afford to have China forever outside the family of nations, there to nurture its fantasies, cherish its hates, and threaten its neighbors," and nine months after advising *TIME* magazine, "If there is anything I want to do before I die, it is to go to China. If I don't, I want my children to," he did what none of his predecessors could — visit the People's Republic of China. As more than two decades of enmity faded, millions watched via satellite-transmitted television, and housewives, shut-ins, and college students interrupted regular viewing to applaud the president's party, Chinese and American officials toured the Great Wall, traveled to Hangchow and Shanghai, were enraptured by the Forbidden City, toasted one another in Peking. Three months later, on a late-May odyssey to Moscow, détente was born in the dankness of the Kremlin. Nixon became the first postwar American president to visit the Soviet Union, and between bear hugs and vodka, joined Communist Party leader Leonid Brezhnev in signing the first agreement of the nuclear age to limit strategic nuclear arms.

At home, on August 15, 1971, Nixon froze wages and prices, devalued United States currency ("the most significant monetary agreement," he exulted, "in the history of the world"), and severed the dollar's link to gold — measures which acted as shock therapy and made the economy swell. Out went mid-length skirts, back came mini-skirts, and the Senate approved the Equal Rights Amendment. In New York City, the memoirs of Howard Hughes, written by Clifford Irving and thought to be authentic, were documented as a fraud. One beheld violence at Attica Penitentiary (forty-eight men died in the nation's worst insurrection) and the 1972 Munich Summer Olympics (Palestinian terrorists, seizing Israeli wrestling team members as hostages, caused seventeen deaths). One heard popular music shift from a public bent for Jimi Hendrix and Janis Joplin to tastes which could (and did) accept Gordon Lightfoot and Carly Simon, Rod Stewart and Creedence Clearwater Revival. Among movies, one might see *Cabaret, American Graffiti, The Exorcist*, and Diana Ross in *Lady Sings the Blues*. Marlon Brando starred in *Last Tango in Paris*, art that was discreet and elegant, and which posed a dilemma that plagued the decade: Was it sensitive cinema about sexuality, or pornography masquerading as art? The roots of America's singularly epochal scandal were planted. Thomas Eagleton became the first vice-presidential candidate to withdraw voluntarily. George McGovern lost the country's most one-sided presidential election. The Christmas bombing of North Viet Nam prompted invective. Seven weeks later, as the war in Viet Nam ended — its ceasefire, signed on January 27, 1973, was for Nixon a signal victory — returning prisoners of war met emotions nearer love.

With POWs leaving Southeast Asia, the stock market at its all-time high, and Nixon's public approval (as measured in the February 1973 Gallup Poll) even more extravagant than his November 1972 rout of McGovern, the president loomed — said *Newsweek*, published by The Washington Post Company — as "a stern, sure, and uncompromising man who disdained to conciliate his critics." He seemed invincible. Who could know that before the decade ended, America would lose a war, watch the resignation of a president, or bow before an oil cartel; that a loaf of bread, priced at 27¢ in 1972, would cost 60¢ two years later; or that by January 1975, more than 6.5 million Americans would be unemployed, the most since the Department of Labor first computed figures in 1948? Who could sense that fear of "another Viet Nam," so remote when peace in Indo-China appeared secure, would aid the Soviet Union's designs from Afghanistan to the Caribbean? Who envisioned that a "Decade of Entitlement," born of impatience with self-reliance, would imperil a dream as old as Ellis Island — the concept of the Melting Pot? Who could have dreamt that, in retrospect, the medium of David Brinkley, Eric Sevareid, and Walter Cronkite would be salvaged by John Dean, Sam Ervin, and Judge John Sirica?

Not the Old Commander, one supposed, nor Bob's ex-sidekick and twice-past Cubs' announcer who, sandwiched between those North Side stints, called games for the Pale Hose, Braves, and Pirates, and who heeded Elson's admonition to seek security in reserve.

"Bob'd talk about world events and how he called himself a 'reporter,' " Milo Hamilton noted, "but his whole life — he wouldn't admit this, of course — was really wrapped up in sportscasting. And he'd studied it — he had it down to an art. 'Save something,' he'd always say to me. 'Save something to reach back for if you have a thrilling finish. If you go pell-mell for eight innings, you've got no place to go with a thrilling ninth.' " He has rarely been thrilling, and it is ludicrous to think of him as remotely pell-mell. But you will find few to deny that across more than thirty years of play-by-play, Hamilton has been bright and studious and, oh, so smooth. Said TOC in 1965: "Milo is tremendous, caring, one of the best around." Said writer Bill James, diverging, two decades later: "Hamilton as a broadcaster is a model of professionalism, fluency, and deportment. He is, in short, as interesting as the weather channel, to which I would frequently dial when he was on."

Born in 1927 in Fairfield, Iowa, Milo was only eighteen when he got his first broadcasting job on the Armed Forces Radio Network ("I was stationed in Guam, and that's where the network was," he said. "The regular announcers were older than me, and when the war ended, they got discharged and went home. I stayed and got a year's experience"); twenty-two when he graduated from the University of Iowa and vaulted to station WQUA in Moline, Illinois ("In twelve months I did Three-I League baseball, pro basketball with the Tri-City Black Hawks, and University of Iowa football. Let the record show my first night on the job, I saw the first sixteen boxing fights of my life. What made it tough is that I had to *broadcast* 'em as well"); and twenty-five when he joined the St. Louis Browns for their final, tainted year ("I worked with Bud Blattner on Brownies' TV. Looking back, I'm not sure I was ready for the big leagues yet. 'Course, I had a lot of company—neither were the Browns"). It is not known how old Hamilton was when he purchased his first brief case. No matter; he has bought many since. "Nobody, I mean *nobody*, does more preparation, keeps more information around than Milo," said Lindsey Nelson. "The running joke is that he shouldn't have a file cabinet to keep his records in—he should have a truck."

A deliberator in an intuitive game, Hamilton "plays draftsman each winter," a Cubs' media guide once advised—commandeering a dozen legal pads to construct hitting, pitching, and related statistical charts; "just to prepare a book on home runs for the [upcoming] season took him more than ten hours." Following the Browns' 1953 exodus to Baltimore, such bookmanship led Milo to the rival Redbirds (for only one season; at the end of 1954, retiring as a player, Joe Garagiola took his .257 career average and clubbed Hamilton from his slot as Caray's colleague) and Wrigley Field (1955–57 on WIND, only to fall to another ex-athlete-turned-mouthpiece, Lou Boudreau) and at the start of 1961, joining Elson, to the cross-town Sox.

Maturing into a cheery, unflappable performer whose very presence seemed to speak of courtesies and hospitality, Hamilton called Stan Musial's five home runs in a 1954 double-header, Sam Jones' 1955 no-hitter against Pittsburgh, Ernie Banks' five grand slams the same year to tie a big-league record, and Early Wynn's sad, halting stab in September 1962 to win his three hundredth game. He even described Roger Maris' sixty-first homer on October 1, 1961. "That year the White Sox for some reason closed their season on a Saturday night rather than Sunday as they usually did," he said, "and it was our policy that when the Sox didn't play, we'd re-create another game from the Western Union ticker. So on that last day of the season, a Sunday, I did the Yankees and Boston, and when Maris belted Number Sixty-One, we had all the sound effects working—it was like it was live from Yankee Stadium. The ticker even told me that Roger tipped his hat to the crowd, and I passed that on to our listeners."

"You didn't get many thrills like that with your own club," I said.

"No, historically the Sox had always been sort of a Punch-and-Judy bunch," he said. "Dazzle 'em with pitching, drive 'em nuts with speed—that was the way we operated. But I enjoyed my years there."

"Did you think about succeeding Elson?"

"There was talk of that," he recollected, "but hell, what was I going to say, 'Why don't you drop dead, Bob, so I can have your job?' I just assumed early on that the Commander would outlast me in Chicago."

Then, in 1966, the Braves became Atlanta's, and to the bewilderment of many, it was Hamilton who became their Voice. "This was a whale of a position—whoever got it would be broadcasting to an entire region, and it's fair to say I was barely in the running," Milo said. "But in June of '65 the Sox and Braves, then of Milwaukee, came to Atlanta to play an exhibition game.

Bob and I went down there to do the broadcast — our General Finance Network covered even them — and keep in mind that the network could be heard through almost the entire South."

"Atlanta already knew you, or at least your voice," I said.

"Yeah, but what surprised me was how *much*. See, the Braves' Booster Club had arranged for a pregame luncheon at the Americana Hotel. Both clubs were there, and the emcee of the affair was the sports announcer of the Atlanta station which carried the Sox and who I'd met the year before and been, I guess, nice to," he said. "Well, now he gives me a Hall of Fame introduction at this luncheon — you'd have thought I was France Laux, Red Barber, and Mel Allen reincarnated into one. And when he finished and I stood up, the crowd just erupted."

"Which, in turn, woke up the Braves."

"Only then, I'm sure, did their officials begin to think in terms of me as a possible Number One," he said. "The night of the game, John McHale and Bill Bartholomay [Braves' general manager and chairman, respectively] came into the booth and said, 'That was some welcome you got today. You know, you ought to come down here next year,' and I said, 'I'd be interested in just that chance.' "

"Along with the fact that people knew your name, why else do you think the Braves wanted you?"

"I'm just glad they did," he chuckled. "My years there made me. I had a bigger area of the country on my network than any guy in America. I did a tremendous amount of free-lancing — eleven years as Voice of Delta Airlines, based in Atlanta. It shot me up to the big time. But, yes, I've studied on it. I was young [thirty-eight]. I was blessed with a fine voice. And I was a fresh face — I hadn't lived in the Southeast. Maybe, I believe the club hoped, I'd help create the image the Braves were looking for."

It seemed, on occasions, in Hamilton's decade at Atlanta, that the Braves had not the slightest concept of what that image was. A baseball team raiding the football South, they were treated as a curiosity, not an interloper; "there was a novelty about the whole thing. At a game in '66, there were about forty-five thousand people in the stands. You could hear a pin drop," said the Braves' Joe Torre. "Fans just didn't know what to do at a game — it was such a contrast to Milwaukee."

Deprived both of geographical continuity and — save their 1969 division championship — that condition called *winning*, the Braves must command interest through a dashing party of individual deeds. Phil Niekro threw a no-hitter in 1967 and led the league with a 1.87 ERA; at forty-six, Hoyt Wilhelm made his one thousandth pitching appearance. Ralph Garr and Felipe Alou compiled five seasons of two hundred or more hits. Felix Millan made six double plays in a single contest. In 1970, Rico Carty, Mike Lum, and Orlando Cepeda each hit three home runs in separate games. Flaunting more power, the Braves ripped four homers in one 1971 inning; the following year, they scored thirteen *runs* in an inning; Atlanta-Fulton County Stadium was dubbed "the Launching Pad."

In 1973, Dave Johnson bashed forty-three home runs, the all-time record for a second baseman—Johnson, Darrell Evans, and Hank Aaron each hit forty or more, the first time for three players on the same team—as even those whose attention wandered from Aaron's pursuit of "714" witnessed a season of at least discussible concern. On March 20, Clemente was named to the Hall of Fame. Two weeks later, the Junior Circuit ushered to its podium the designated hitter. In July, 27.6 million NBC viewers slumbered through the National's 7–1 All-Star victory; on September 28, whiffing sixteen Twins in his final start, the Angels' Nolan Ryan upped his '73 strikeout total to a record 383. The Mets (of a .509 winning percentage), Reds (for a third time in four years), Orioles (fourth in five), and Athletics captured division titles; surviving the playoff, Oakland won an eventful World Series. Detroit's John Hiller totaled thirty-eight saves, Hunter, Blue, and Holtzman each won twenty or more games, Jackson and Rose won MVP Awards, and Yogi Berra became the second manager to take pennants in both leagues. Said Luis Aparicio, to be released shortly by the Red Sox, of baseball's spitball king: "Once in my life, I'd like to play shortstop behind Gaylord Perry, to watch him pitch. It'd be an honor." Muttered Dick Williams, resigning, about his ex-employer: "He's a raving maniac. A man can take so much of Finley."

Welcome, shortly, a 1974 season of such liberality of achievement that, years later, one saluted its glow. A redemptive 22–16 for last-place California, Ryan struck out 367, threw a third no-hitter, and fanned nineteen Red Sox on August 12. The unconquerable Carew took his third straight batting crown; of Rod's 218 hits, 180 were singles. Mike Marshall became the first pitcher to appear in more than 100 games. At thirty-five, Lou Brock swiped a record 118 bases. At age five, the divisional format produced its closest demipennant races: Oakland staved off Texas, the Orioles won twenty-eight of their last thirty-four games to overcome the Yankees, the Dodgers beat Cincinnati by four lengths, and Pittsburgh cut the so-close Cards. The World Series confronted a wide gulf that severed it from its seventy predecessors; for the first time, its rivals were California teams. Devoid of any gulf was the Classic's outcome: another Oakland triumph, four games to one.

Plus, erasing the most memorized (and mesmerizing) landmark in all of professional sports, Henry Louis Aaron.

On the drizzly evening of April 8, 1974, in the fourth inning against the Dodgers' Al Downing, before a national television audience and 53,775 spectators at Atlanta Stadium, thirty-nine years after Babe Ruth (wearing the uniform of the Boston Braves) hit his last home run, No. 44 hoisted No. 715. "It had been on my mind a lot, what I should say when Henry broke the record," Hamilton recollected. "I thought about the obvious things, drawing the parallels between the two players, like both being forty when they hit 714. I wondered if I should say something as he touched each of the bases. I guess I might have been rehearsing in the back of my mind without even knowing it. But finally I decided that I wouldn't decide—that the crowd and the action of the moment would dictate your description."

Like the Wilderness Campaign after Gettysburg, the rest was anticlimax.

Their first season, the Georgia Braves attracted 1,539,801 people; nine years later, attendance slipped to 534,672 — even less than Milwaukee's lame-duck adieu. On July 6, 1975, after only 3,728 patrons watched a Braves' loss to Houston, Milo rapped Atlanta fans on his postgame show. "All I hear around town is negativism about the Braves' management, managers, players, all that business," he said. "But it is time somebody stood up and said something positive about this ball club. And it's time somebody supported it." In time, somebody would, but that blessing did little to comfort Hamilton; ninety-four days after indicting Atlanta's fealty, he was simultaneously praised (for his ability, by Braves' President Daniel Donahue) and fired (because "the Braves," Donahue explained, "are trying to change their image both on and off the field").

"You were popular in Atlanta," I said. "Why'd the Braves drop their bomb?"

"Understand, first, those last couple of years I was down there, we were terrible. We weren't drawing; we had some real bow-wows on the field. And we had absentee ownership who didn't realize how awful the team'd become — they didn't have to see them every day — and they started putting the heat on to shill," Hamilton said. "I came back and said, 'Look, I have credibility too. I can't make those oafs on the field out to be something they're not.'"

"They stunk."

"People could smell 'em all the way to *Chattanooga*," he said. "I wouldn't do what the Braves wanted me to, and it got messy. So I started to look around at about the same time in '75 that Jack Buck announced he was leaving to work for NBC Sports in New York. Well, that rang a bell — I'd worked in St. Louis, it's a hell of a city. I was very interested."

"Did you interview for the job?" I said.

"*Interview?* I was practically offered Buck's job — it was all set, we were even talking money. I had every confidence in the world that I'd be the Voice of the Cardinals in '76."

"What happened?"

"Buck and the Cardinals suddenly began to think of the box they'd be in if Jack's NBC program ["Grandstand"] were to bomb, which, of course, it did, through no fault of Jack's," Milo said. "So the Cardinals told him that if NBC didn't work out, he could come back and take over again in 1977. Well, no thanks — I wasn't going to St. Louis unless I had a firm multi-year guarantee as the top guy."

"Why not stay with the Braves?"

"'Cause I'd told them about the Cardinal situation, just out of common courtesy. They knew I was looking, and they said, 'Hey, why don't we simply end our relationship amicably?' And we did. I was free to roam."

He roamed four states and more than five hundred miles away, and was named that December 15 as the new Voice of the Buccaneers. "I'll be me. I have my own style," he told a news conference at Three Rivers Stadium. "It would be foolish on my part to try to be Bob Prince. You could be Mel Allen or Red Barber here, and they wouldn't be Bob Prince. I have to be myself." Hamilton was, and was ridiculed for his trouble. Pittsburgh found him antiseptic, and though he did his homework and carved what might be called a sense of grudging respect, Steel City locals treated Milo like a hangover after the Gunner's binge.

"It was like competing with a ghost," he remembered. "Everything was 'Prince did this, Prince did that.' I never tried to imitate him, but I couldn't *escape* him. And the problem really wasn't the average fan — it was the Pittsburgh press, the writers, the TV people. They were Prince's drinking buddies, and they just knifed me from the start. It was vicious. The Pirates could have brought Charlton Heston in to replace Prince, and the writers would have killed *him*."

"What did Bob say to you?" I said.

"We *had* been friends," Milo said. "That changed the day I was hired. Prince was incredibly bitter. If he hadn't shown such *hubris* in his fight against Westinghouse, if he'd shown a hint of humility, he'd have broadcast the Pirates till he died. But he hadn't, and it cost him the thing he loved the most. So he directed that bitterness at me — Bob had bad-mouthed me in every bar in Pittsburgh, and he set the entire media against me." Pause. "They thought *I*, supposedly, was dull. I thought *they* were blubbering idiots."

"Did you ever think you'd overcome it?"

"Oh, for fleeting moments, but not for long," he said. "When I came back in '79 for the final year of my contract, I knew that was it. No way was I going to extend that kind of living hell."

On October 29, 1979, following his four clammy Tri-State years, the beleaguered Hamilton leaped at the chance to rejoin the Cubs; he would assist, officials said, the long-time TV Voice of the Wrigleys, Jack Brickhouse, over the WGN Network. "Anybody in my place would jump at the opportunity," he told the *Chicago Tribune*'s Gary Deeb. "The Bob Prince thing may have affected my disposition on certain occasions, but the minute they played the National Anthem, I forgot about it and did my job." In late 1981, when Brickhouse retired and Hamilton, with ego exposed, stood ready to succeed Hey-Hey, the Cubs forgot *him*.

"*Promised?* I was practically guaranteed in blood that I'd be their Number One announcer for as long as I wanted," Milo sniffed of that dark November when the Cubs, stunning Chicago's baseball public, hired the Voice of the White Sox as Brickhouse's replacement. "I'd returned to Chicago from Pittsburgh to spend the rest of my life here. I was recruited — damn, the *Tribune* ran a headline about me coming back all the way across the top of the sports page — with the expressed understanding that when Jack left at the end of the '81 season, I'd succeed him as the top TV guy. Brickhouse had even been part of the group that selected me, and I'll never forget how on that afternoon in August 1981, when he announced how he'd be retiring in two months, Jack told his listeners, 'I'll be leaving soon, but we've all known that day was coming. And now let me introduce Milo Hamilton, who'll be the Voice of the Cubs for years to come.' "

"Three months later," I said, "the Cubs announce Caray as their Voice."

"It's a nightmare memory even now. I recall it so clearly: The station called me at seven-thirty one morning and said, 'Can you come down here to the office? We want to tell you face to face; we can't do it over the phone.' I get downtown and they say, 'We're announcing at ten that Harry Caray's coming over here.' My face must have dropped ten feet—I couldn't believe it."

It was like the fifties all over again—jilted, first, for Garagiola, then Boudreau, and now, for Holy Cow!—but Hamilton remained a broadcast warrior, and baseball was what he knew. Rebuffing pride, he was disposed to salary and self-discipline, and in his third decade of play-by-play, having fallen and risen and fallen again, Milo teamed with Boudreau on radio (for six innings each game) and Steve Stone on television (for three). "Looking back, I'm proud of what we did," he was saying. "I got more out of Steve than Harry ever did. I didn't treat him like a cigar store Indian, and Lou and I just respected the hell out of each other. I knew his role; he knew mine. I thought we were great."

In November 1984, Milo Hamilton was axed by the Chicago Cubs. The reason: "personality differences," WGN professed, with Caray.

"The station spent almost an hour telling me what nice work I'd done, and then they said, 'But the bottom line is that Harry doesn't like you, and he's more important to us than you are.' " He laughed derisively. "I guess I can't bitch about their honesty"; nor critics, with Hamilton's flair for symmetry. In early 1985, Milo replaced his Cubs' replacement, Dewayne Staats, in the Houston Astros' broadcast booth.

For Hamilton, Brickhouse, and a third Cubs' consequence, the 1981 baseball season translated into 1 B.C. (Before Caray), but with Harry's arrival, Vince Lloyd—like Jack, a native of Peoria; the Wrigleys' radio eminence, following Quinlan, since 1965; and with his throaty voice, a personal favorite—shifted from calling balls and strikes to a new role as color commentator.

Sixty-five at the time, Lloyd had been, I believe, his region's finest Voice of Big Ten football; the unseen link between the Friendly Confines and millions of Midwesterners for whom, fanatically and almost mystically, the Cubs were the sports center of the globe; and the first announcer to interview an American president at a baseball game: John F. Kennedy, on WGN's "Lead-Off Man Show," prior to throwing out the first ball at the White Sox' 1961 opener at Griffith Stadium. (Lloyd: "Mr. President, have you had an opportunity to do any warming up for this, sir?" The President: "Well, we've just been getting ready here today." V.L.: "Throwing nothing but strikes? Very good." JFK: "I feel it important that we get, ah, not be a nation just of spectators, even though that's what we are today, but also a nation of participants—particularly to make it possible for young men and women to participate actively in physical effort.")

In 1982, breaking with his past seventeen years by leaving play-by-play, Lloyd was eager, nonetheless, to expand the Cubs' broadcast empire. He conducted the "Lead-Off Man Show" on television, hosted the postgame radio highlights show, and was named cogeneral manager, with WGN sports editor Jack Rosenberg, of The Tribune Company's radio syndication, ballooning the North Siders' network from only one station in 1970 to more than sixty by

1986. "It used to be that the team depended on WGN alone to get their games across to folks," Lloyd said. "It was so strong we figured, 'Hell, anybody that wants to hear us, they can get us there.' Its power [50,000 watts] also discouraged other stations in Illinois from carrying our games — they were afraid to compete. But now we're reaching states *way* beyond what WGN can reach in the daytime. We've gone into southern Indiana and Illinois, Iowa, Wisconsin, Michigan. And it's growing every year."

"Do you miss play-by-play?" I said, knowing that his listeners did.

"Oh, the old war-horse in me feels an ache," he said. "After all, I'd been doing radio for so long and TV even longer [with Brickhouse, airing the White Sox and Cubs, from 1950]. And I think that first year ['82] was the worst — to break away gradually, I still made all the road trips, sort of a phased withdrawal. Now that I mention it, one thing I *don't* miss is the road trips. In any event, I'm so engrossed in what I'm doing now that I don't have much chance to miss anything."

"How'd you get into the syndication?"

"When Harry came over to do TV, that meant Milo would do more radio, and that created a surplus there," he said. "Plus, I'd reached quitting age. So when The Tribune Company [having bought out the Wrigley family in June 1981] came to me with this syndication idea, I said, 'Sure, why not?' After all, there's a little bit of Cub in all of us — that feeling of a good deal of hope and lots of trepidation and excruciating loyalty — and I thought there'd be a market in expanding our exposure."

"Anyway," I said, "you're not totally removed from the booth."

"Hey, I'm still doing color [until, retiring, Lloyd left radio in October 1986], and with Lou beside me, you know our fans are in good hands."

Aping Allstate, Boudreau must have found it difficult to forget how, as a fine figure of an athlete with the forties Indians, he played shortstop well enough to enter the Hall of Fame. He was born on July 17, 1917, only forty-six days after Lloyd, starred in basketball at the University of Illinois, and joined the Tribe in 1938; four years later, Lou became Cleveland's player-manager.

The ghost of his MVP 1948 season, among the most celebratory in sports history, still stalks a forest of northern Ohio suburbias, and there are those who claim that Cleveland baseball died the 1950 day that Boudreau, released in November, signed with the Boston Red Sox. Lou retired the next year, managed the Sox in 1952–54 and the Athletics in 1955–57, succeeded Hamilton as Quinlan's 1958 sidekick, and brought to WGN a high-pitched voice and terse analysis. "Lou is my cup of tea," Caray, usually preferring *other* beverages, exhaled in the early eighties. "I'm of his vintage and I know who he was and how good he was. And I know how to get him to open up and talk about all those memories up in the booth. The fan loves it," especially when in 1984 (the Second City's answer to Boudreau's 1948) the now-Tribunes became America's Cubs, the sadder but wiser losers who hadn't quit, winning a division title, erecting a bandwagon, and touching chords that no mere winner could: a marvelous anachronism, a match striking rampant good will. "It was a fairy tale year," Lou observed of his twenty-seventh season as a Chicago broadcaster. Like Boudreau in the year George Orwell wrote *1984*, the Cubs left the nation's baseball fans singing, dancing, and enshrining The Game.

That, of course, was exactly what *another* team had done in 1969 — interpreted, primarily, by Lindsey Nelson but also by two personalities for whom 1986 (their twenty-fifth straight season of Metropolitans' play-by-play, the bigs' longest-running broadcast team east of Vin Scully and Jerry Doggett) marked a special anniversary.

With Bob Murphy, Ralph Kiner called the Mets' first-ever game in April 1962; who could know they would outlast three baseball commissioners, five U.S. presidents, more than *two hundred* major-league managers, and those two Bastilles of devotion to college football: Paul (Bear) Bryant and Wayne Woodrow Hayes?

A Tri-State totem for the better half of a decade, Kiner belted 369 home runs in a ten-year career; seven times, he led the National League in roundtrippers; in 1947 and 1949, he lofted more than fifty. After retiring in 1955, Kiner moved to San Diego as general manager of the Pacific Coast League Padres, then to Chicago as the Old Commander's 1961 sidekick. Early on, he was tentative, parochial, and his rhetoric sputtered. But by the late sixties, Barber would write, "Ralph Kiner . . . a good man . . . steadily improving . . . in my judgment anchors that three-man crew at Shea Stadium." One could differ (after all, Nelson was a Hall of Famer, in the best and deepest way) yet still acknowledge, freely, that the Mets' broadcasters ranked among the two or three best triumvirates in baseball.

Kiner advanced the ex-ballplayer's legitimate point of view. Murphy provided intelligence and sharp-edged imagery, etching word portraits whose eloquence countervailed the stumbling of many non-Mets' contemporaries. A World War II Marine and University of Tulsa graduate, he attained the major leagues, like Gowdy, by way of University of Oklahoma football and Oklahoma A&M basketball; in 1954, Bob shuffled east to Boston, joining the Cowboy for six T. Ballgame years; then it was on to Memorial Stadium and, in early 1962, the Polo Grounds for the expansion Stengels. It was that season too that the National League's other embryo, the Houston Colt .45s, announced *their* play-by-play men: gregarious Loel Passe (whose "Hot ziggety dog and good ol' sassafras tea," "Now you're chunkin'," and "He breezed him one more time" would, in time, become part of his region's nomenclature) and the veteran Elston, reaching Texas after layovers in Fort Dodge, Iowa (in 1941, he won his first broadcasting job), and nearby Waterloo (five years later, he made his baseball debut in the Three-I League) and Wrigley Field (with Bert Wilson, airing games in 1954) and Mutual's "Game of the Day."

Until 1976, when the Gunner, teaming with Elston on Astros' radio, relegated Passe exclusively to television, The Gene and Loel Roundup evoked an unbroken cattle drive; in fourteen years, neither man missed a single game; over a thirty-plus-station radio network and a fifteen-outlet TV arrangement linking markets in Texas and Louisiana, they brought baseball's sounds and actors to the lonely little towns and growing cities of the ambiguous, flamboyant Southwest. Their commentary carried out into the Gulf and Panhandle and eastward toward New Orleans. They told of names like Don Wilson, Jimmy Wynn, Cesar Cedeno, and Mike Scott, of moments like the Astro-dome's 1965 opening, the Astros' 1972 vault into second place, and Houston's ascension to the 1980 and '86 Western Division titles, and of football-weaned home patrons, so quiet at first, who came, finally, to grasp the pastime's élan. Before Elston's December 1986 firing, they were scout and teacher; they de-scribed mostly second-division teams; and had they broadcast nearer the com-munications centers of America, their fluency would have been labeled, as it too often was not, among the National League's most obvious.

In Cincinnati, it was enthusiasm, not glibness, that draped Joe Nuxhall's language. In 1944, with the Redlegs stripped of wartime talent, Nuxie had crashed into the majors as a fifteen-year-old pitcher from Hamilton, Ohio; he was the youngest ever to grace a big-league game. "I pitched two-thirds of an inning and got bombed," he recalled of his June 10 debut against St. Louis. "They beat us something like eighteen to nothing or eighteen to one." He would go back to high school, suffer one long bus ride after another during seven seasons in the minors, and, in 1952, returning to the Reds, begin a Cincinnati voyage that occupied all but one of the next fifteen years. "In total," he said, "my baseball career spanned twenty-three years, and my biggest regret is that the only year I was out of the organization [1961, traded to Kansas City], the Reds won the pennant." At thirty-eight, Nuxhall retired after the 1966 season (his record, 135–117) and grabbed another full-time job. His new employer was the primary sponsor of Reds' radiocasts, the George Wiedemann Brewing Company; he would work in sales and promotions and supply color over WCKY. That first year, Joe assisted the play-by-play of Claude Sullivan and Jim McIntyre; in 1971, Al Michaels became the Reds' silken-toned Voice, and three years later, Marty Brennaman succeeded him.

What Bud Blattner said of Dizzy Dean was also true of Nuxhall; he was "not a linguist," which is not to condemn his following, for he *was* a fan, and he brought a clarity and droll exuberance — if also, one must concede, erratic syn-tax, an unhewn voice, and his inevitable hallo (while Joe's partner described a Reds' ball socked into the darkness, Nuxie could be heard in the background, screaming, "Get up, get up, get outa here!") — to fans in Louisville and Zanes-ville and Muncie and Marietta over what became, by 1975, baseball's second-largest radio network: 110 stations in seven states, originating from WLW, Cincinnati. "It's like being a player," Joe remarked in his twentieth season as a Reds' announcer. "If you don't have a great interest in what you're doing, you've lost your competitive spirit. The same holds true in the booth."

Winning two pennants and another division championship, the early-seven-ties Reds were glorious on the field; Nuxhall was not their equal above it. He was, however, a tangible influence who closed each broadcast by saying, "This is the Ol' Left-Hander rounding third now and heading for home." He spoke for his own people. To baseball-loving Rhinelanders, he was as reassuring as the Ohio.

Unlike TOL, Jerry Coleman's voice was almost dapper. As a 1963–69 Yankees' broadcaster and the 1972–79 and post-1980 Voice of the expansion

Padres, this former Bombers' infielder evinced conviction and industry, and his handling of a baseball game deserved more praise than it received — in part because of the Padres' dismal condition; in part due to the location of his base, at the edge of the Mission Valley, in San Diego, a place far removed from big-league publicity. Across two decades, Jerry was one of baseball's most resourceful play-by-play announcers. He was also, as we shall see, the master of the malapropism.

Coleman broke into professional baseball in 1942 with the Yankees' organization, but had his career interrupted by the Second World War. He made the majors in 1949 and was named Associated Press Rookie of the Year, won the Babe Ruth Award as the Most Valuable Player of the 1950 World Series, went to war again in 1952–53 (between Korea and WW II, flying 120 missions, receiving two distinguished Flying Crosses, thirteen Air Medals, and three Navy citations, and earning the rank of lieutenant colonel in the Marine Corps), and returned for four final big-league seasons (his last hurrah, a .375 batting average in the 1957 Oktoberfest). Lifetime, he hit .263; in his nine years at Yankee Stadium, the Bombers won eight pennants and six World Series; and it jarred few insiders that upon retiring, Jerry moved into the New York front office (as Yankees' personnel director, he oversaw the signing of such then-anonymities as Tom Tresh, Jim Bouton, and Joe Pepitone). In 1960, Coleman joined the CBS "Game of the Week," conducting a ten-minute pregame show for Dean and Pee Wee Reese, and three years later meandered to the Yankees' broadcast booth. There, for the next seven seasons, he announced with Allen, Barber, Garagiola, Rizzuto, and Frank Messer, and tried, if futilely, to revive public interest in a pinstriped series of increasingly talent-less teams.

Coleman left the Yankees in 1970, replaced for a year by the comic Bob Gamere, whom one could count on to utter *ad infinitum*, "Here it comes, there it goes" — his description of a pitch thrown homeward and batted *anywhere*. Moving to Los Angeles, the ex-Marine aired postgame Angels' television shows, called boxing, golf, and UCLA sports, hosted the evening news sportscasts of KTLA-TV, part of Gene Autry's Golden West Broadcasting System, and on November 8, 1971, was named the Voice of the Padres.

Born three years earlier at the cost of a $10 million franchise fee to owner C. Arnholt Smith, the Pads had tabbed Jerry Gross and Frank Sims to handle radio, and Bob Chandler, television; initially, Duke Snider would migrate between both mediums. But as the ball club bombed (the 1969–71 Padres finished 133 games below .500) and attendance flummoxed (in 1971, San Diego averaged fewer than seven thousand people per date), its ratings acquired an endangered blush; perhaps, concluded Buzzie Bavasi, the Padres' president, a native Californian could clog the bleeding. "I couldn't be more enthusiastic," said Bavasi, disclosing Coleman (born, September 14, 1924, in San Jose) and Chandler as San Diego's 1972 radio/television team. "I believe they will complement each other quite nicely. Both have earned excellent reputations."

For Coleman, describing the birth of the San Diego Chicken and the team's

1974 purchase by McDonald's founder Ray A. Kroc, Randy Jones' twenty-victory seasons of 1975–76 and the thirty-four home runs and 118 runs batted in of Dave Winfield's 1979, San Diego's twenty-four-hit splurge against the Giants on April 19, 1982, Alan Wiggins' sixty-six stolen bases and Tony Gwynn's twenty-five-game hitting streak of a year afterward, and the sunlit fall of 1984 in which the Padres bushwhacked Chicago to win the Championship Series, that reputation deepened as the franchise took root—not among distant fans, necessarily, who seldom knew of him; rather, it was colleagues who recognized his basic decency and resolve.

In 1976–83 and 1985, Jerry called CBS Radio's coverage of the National League playoffs, and it was here that I heard him regularly for the first time since the late sixties. His play-by-play was rich and intimate; he was the bearer of a clean, meticulous story line. Sadly, for baseball's second-biggest event, Coleman had solemnized his act, omitting the hilarious misstatements that freckled his career; still, listening, I thought of Danny Ozark: Surely, the two had bloodlines reminiscent of Ol' Diz.

As the 1973–79 Phillies' manager, Ozark became infamous for a remarkable bevy of malapropisms. Once, during a losing streak, Danny said, long-faced, "Oh, I know we're having troubles, but that's nothing new. Even Napoleon had his *Watergate*." Several weeks later, as Phillies' losses crested, Ozark was asked about team morale. "*Morality*," he huffed, "is not a problem here." Of a Philadelphia second baseman, Danny noted, "His limitations are *limitless*." Of a quarreling shortstop, he said, "He and I have our *indifferences*." Of a surprising three-game sweep by Atlanta, he mourned, "Those games were beyond my *apprehension*." Of his players, Ozark stated, "Contrary to popular belief, I've always had a wonderful *repertoire* with them." Blistered for his devotion to the incomprehensible, the Phils' skipper snapped, "What do you mean? You reporters got it all wrong. Don't you know I'm being a *Fascist?* You know, a guy who says one thing and means another."

Perhaps not facetious, memorable Danny was; and so was the Voice of the Padres, unearthing a wooded hill of Colemanisms.

• "On the mound is Randy Jones," Jerry related, "the left-hander with the Karl Marx hairdo."

• "There's a fly ball deep to center field—Winfield is going back, back . . . he hits his head against the wall. It's rolling toward second base."

• "He slides into second with a stand-up double."

• "Rich Folkers is throwing up in the bull pen."

• "Whenever you get an inflamed tendon, you got a problem. OK, here's the pitch to Gene Tendon."

• "Pete Rose has three thousand hits and 3,014 overall."

• "Redfern won't be twenty-two until October. Hey, he's only twenty-one." Then, more.

• "It's swung on and Gamble sends a long fly to right, but Gamble goes back to the wall and makes the catch."

• "They throw Winfield out at second, and he's safe."

- "Swung on and fouled to the backstop. No, wait a minute, that was a wild pitch and the runner moved over to second."
- "Reggie Smith of the Dodgers and Gary Matthews of the homers hit Braves in that game."
- "[John] Grubb goes back, back. He's under the warning track, and he makes the play."
- "Young Frank Pastore may have just pitched the biggest victory of 1979, maybe the biggest victory of the year."
- "Gaylord Perry and McCovey should know each other like a book. They've been ex-teammates for years now."
- "There's a hard shot to LeMaster — and he throws Madlock in the dugout."
- "Urrea had Owchinko in a hole, O-two, but now the count is even, three-two."
- "Thomas draws a throw but it went nowhere."
Time, now, for the seventh-inning stretch. . . .
- "Jesus Alou is in the on-deck circus."
- "Over the course of a season, a miscue will cost you more games than a good play."
- "Ron Guidry is not very big, maybe 140 pounds, but he has an arm like a lion."
- "From the way Denny's shaking his head, he's either got an injured shoulder or a gnat in his eye."
- "There's a shot up the alley . . . oh, it's just foul."
- "Royster has gone six-for-seven against Shirley this year . . . and there's a single that makes him five-for-eight."
- "Winfield is on first base, and he's always a threat to grow."
- "The way he's swinging the bat, he won't get a hit until the twentieth century."
- "Hi, folks, I'm Jerry Gross."
. . . and for a slam-bang, rock 'n' roll windup.
- "[Al] Hrabosky looks fierce in that Fu Manchu haircut."
- "Bob Davis is wearing his hair differently this year, short and with curls like Randy [Jones] wears. I think you call it a Frisbee."
- "Next up for the Cardinals is Barry Carry Garry Templeton."
- "[George] Hendrick simply lost that sun-blown pop-up."
- "Sometimes big trees grow out of acorns. I think I heard that from a squirrel."
- "The Padres need one run to tie and two to win. So, going into the ninth, the score is San Francisco one, the Yankees nothing."
- "This is the only afternoon day game in the National League."
- "Shortstop Ozzie Smith was so stunned with the news, he lost his appetite right over the dinner plate."
- "We're all sad to see Glenn Beckert leave. Before he goes, though, I hope he stops by so we can kiss him good-bye. He's that kind of guy."

As far as one could tell, Coleman's humor, unlike Dean's, was largely inadvertent. That fact itself stood in apposition to another early-seventies National League announcer, Jack Buck of St. Louis, whose speaking style was satirical and whose Midwest popularity was immense.

One August day in 1970, Buck addressed the then-raging controversy of the lively ball. "You know who I'd like to see in the outfield?" he said during an 11-8 Cardinals' victory over Los Angeles. "Chub Feeney [president of the National League], Joe Cronin [same, American], and Bowie Kuhn."

The next year, Buck defined "what a racket" his business was. "You golf, swim, or shoot pool during the day, go to the park and b.s. with the manager and players a little before the game, do the game, b.s. some more, and go home. It's tough, real tough."

On an early 1971 occasion, accompanying the St. Louis Symphony Orchestra and the St. Louis Civic Ballet in a classical music program, he narrated Benjamin Britten's "Young Person's Guide to the Orchestra." It was as close to culture, he said with a courtly gesture of self-disparagement, as he was likely (or would choose) to get.

Spearing, bantering, already a skeptic at the core, Buck sprang forcibly from his Holyoke, Massachusetts, childhood to Buckeye puberty ("He moved to Cleveland when he was fifteen," said Bob Broeg of the *St. Louis Post-Dispatch*. "His father was dying, his family was poor, and God knows the jobs Jack had as a kid — on river boats, assembly lines, selling things on corners, working with cranes — just to support everyone") to World War II service in Europe ("Lindsey Nelson and I got to talking one day, and we found some incredible parallels," Buck said. "Not only did we both do baseball for a National League team and pro football for CBS, but we both got wounded at the exact same spot at the Remagen Bridge, crossing into Germany in March 1945, and we both got hit in the same place — the left shoulder. And we never even knew each other until years later") to school at Ohio State University ("After the war, I came home, worked for over a year, and was talked by a friend into going to college. I graduated in three years, majored in radio speech, and took a football course from Woody Hayes. Didn't get any credit for it; just attended classes to learn about the game. You don't think I had the sportscasting itch, do you?").

In 1950, Buck grasped his first baseball radio job with the Columbus Redbirds of the American Association; three years later, at Red Wing Stadium in Rochester, New York, he became the Voice of the Cardinals' other Triple-A affiliate. "One night the Wings' regular announcer, Ed Edwards, got up at a dinner and told a dirty story," Jack said. "He got fired and that's how I got his job. I don't know if it was destiny, maybe, or just bad taste on Ed's part, but I'm grateful for his lapse. Even as a kid, growing up in Cleveland, I knew I wanted to be a baseball announcer. I remember listening to Bob Elson, Ty Tyson, Mel Allen, and Red Barber on the national games — at night, I'd even listen to games in Spanish from Havana. Now, Rochester put me one step closer to the bigs — it was really the Cardinals' top farm club — and to reach the bigs was really all I ever wanted."

After one year in Rochester, what Buck wanted, he got — bounding to Busch

Stadium, where, until late 1959 (when Jack was fired to make room for Blattner), he warbled with Caray, Hamilton (1954), and Garagiola (post-1954) over the Redbirds' enormous KMOX Network.

"It was Harry's show, lock, stock, and barrel," he said, casually. "Garagiola and I were both under Caray's control—he ran it all; absolute, total reign."

"How'd you like that?"

"Nobody would," Buck said, "but you accept things as they are. And about Harry, I'll say this: He was the first, the very first [forgetting Dean] to tell it like it was, to editorialize. Sometimes he went too far, trying to create and stir up controversy, but he was talented as hell. And people anywhere, they liked his honesty."

"Did you get along?" I said.

"Hell, some people criticize him—I never do. I learned a lot from Harry—style, pacing, the need to stick to your guns when you thought you were right."

In 1960-61, the gunsel hit ambivalence—the disaster of ABC Television's 1960 baseball "Game of the Week," the distinction of calling the first American Football League telecast that fall, the 1961 decision to rejoin Holy Cow! when Joe G. fled part-time to NBC and, later, Blattner to the Angels—followed by nine more campaigns as Caray's colleague: a time frame marked by three Cardinals' pennants, two Series championships, and vessels of mail and attendance that stamped St. Louis as, "with the possible exception of Detroit," the *Boston Globe*'s Peter Gammons wrote in 1985, "the best baseball town in the world."

Jack Buck chuckled to himself as he remembered. "When I think of where I *could* have ended up," he said, "a Houston, where people don't know baseball, or San Francisco, with that miserable park."

"Instead, home run."

"Well, you know our network reaches into fourteen states. We've got more than a hundred stations. With those kinds of numbers, how can you *not* have some kind of interest? I tell you, I'm constantly amazed at the reaction. If I say anything remotely controversial, I get tons of letters from Oklahoma, Arkansas, Tennessee. On weekends here, you'll see people in the parking lots and hotels from Mississippi, Alabama—don't forget, before Kansas City and Houston came into baseball, we had practically the whole middle of the country to ourselves."

Unorthodox and nonchalant, Buck made baseball whimsically come to life; "he is low-key, extremely witty," spiced Broeg, "not nearly as heavy-handed as some announcers"; he was a biting toastmaster and anecdotist, and "I always tried to make the broadcasts attractive, not just ho-hum report, to get excited but still not to lose control, and to have a style."

"Like most broadcasters had two, three decades ago—Dudley, Bob Wolff," I said.

"See, the difference between today and when I first broke in," Buck said, "is, of course, the training. The guys you mention—I'd include myself in there—we knew baseball, and because we broke in and came up through the minors, we learned how to articulate our knowledge—Gene Elston, for instance."

"And today?"

The Voice of the Cardinals paused. "There's no question the caliber of big-league broadcasting has dropped a peg in the last twenty-five or thirty years," he said. "Too many guys today have poor grammar, don't finish sentences, don't have the vocational background to excel. They just have a lack of imagination."

"Baseball doesn't seem to excite them."

"No," he disagreed. "It's just that these ex-players, the jocks and so forth, they don't know how to *express* their excitement. And the problem lies with the listening public — they're too willing to put up with inferior broadcasting."

Who can recall when that contretemps last perplexed St. Louisans — serenaded since 1941 by Dean, Caray, Garagiola, and Buck, and touched by a quality of announcing surpassed, perhaps, only by New York City in the early fifties?

In October 1969, that prosperity clanged somewhat as Caray was sacked by owner August Busch and banished to Oakland. Succeeding him, Buck suffered an uncommon tinge of embarrassment. "I don't usually feel awkward about things," he said, "but how could you not in a situation like this? The guy'd been broadcasting for a quarter-century. In St. Louis, he could get away with anything. Over KMOX, you could hear him in half the country. His impact was unbelievable, and then, boom, like that, he's gone. I already had a following in St. Louis, so it wasn't as tough for me to replace Harry as it would have been for an outsider, but still — it had its moments. I had to cross picket lines, things like that."

Presently, Jim Woods disembarked from Pittsburgh and became Buck's partner; two years later, after "coming to hate the Cardinals' front office, the city, the whole tight-lipped atmosphere, where you were afraid even to smile," the Possum left to imbue the Finleys. His replacement was ex-Cardinals' third baseman Mike Shannon, working on the team's promotions and sales staff since his 1970 retirement, and who, in turn, joined the phlegmatic Bob Starr in 1976. *That* arrival, through St. Louis' revolving seventies door, arose from Buck's short-lived and painful hiatus at NBC Sports, New York.

"I am leaving what undoubtedly is the best baseball broadcasting job in the United States, but the opportunity to join NBC is immensely attractive," Buck said on August 8, 1975. "Sometimes you have to take chances." He left to host the network's new fall "Grandstand" program; ensconced in a studio each weekend, he was to link five hours of live sports programming, mostly professional football; his intake would far exceed Jack's $100,000-plus Cardinals' salary. "I gave up some security," he admitted, "but one of the beauties of this offer is that I didn't go after competition where I had to sell myself. They came after me." They also soon shepherded him away.

Curiously ill-at-ease in the studio format, Buck was dropped from "Grandstand" in early March 1976 and replaced by Lee Leonard, cohost of a local New York sports program, and the unknown Bryant Gumbel. Returning to St. Louis, his ego refurbished by an undisguised local affection, Jack occupied his followers' leisure time with tales of Bob Forsch's 1978 no-hitter; the 1979 cavalcade of Lou Brock, whacking his three thousandth base hit, and Keith

Hernandez, named the league's co-Most Valuable Player; the Redbirds' sashay to the 1982 world championship; and, finally, the magical 1985 of Vince Coleman (110 stolen bases), Tom Herr (110 runs batted in), John Tudor (21 victories, 1.93 ERA), MVP and batting titleist (.353) Willie McGee, and a fourteenth Cardinals' pennant.

Over CBS Radio, Buck called the play-by-play of the 1976 All-Star Game, 1979–82 National League playoffs, and 1983–86 Oktoberfests, and became that network's Voice of the National Football League; in 1987, he was inducted at Cooperstown. "Now the whole country heard what we already knew," Bob Broeg observed. "The guy's incredibly versatile—he's done everything from bowling to jazz. Sure, he goes through enough antacid pills every day to sustain that company, but the beauty is you'd never know it."

"His assets?"

"He's laid-back, he's biting, and he wears so very well. I don't say this just because Jack loves the horses—that's one hell of a trifecta."

He was home, and the low- and middle-South loved it. He was theatrical, in an oblique, often caustic way, in a baseball age of pure vanilla. Listening to the broadcasts out of Busch Stadium, Cardinals' fans were reassured that with Buck, at least, they would never taste of bland.

*   *   *

Jack Buck gave his first "Grandstand" performance on September 21, 1975, six days before Boston clinched the American League East title. The Sox had last won a championship in 1967, the year of "The Impossible Dream," and their victory now not only roused Connecticut, Maine, Massachusetts, New Hampshire, Rhode Island, Vermont, and other assorted provinces, but also began the tumbleweed of events that, in the minds of many, brought baseball back from its Decade of the Media Dead.

The 1975 Red Sox so enthralled New England, one critic wrote, that if the light were to appear in the Old North Church again, its signal would likely transmit: one if by Jim Rice, two if by Fred Lynn. Yet popular as their broadcasts were, they did not, *could* not, match the sheer inconceivability—the sense that even after pinching yourself, you *still* did not believe it—of the Bosox' rise, eight years earlier, to a plane so apostolic that on the evening of the final day of the regular season—at the exact hour Boston seized its first pennant since 1946—one of baseball's most able reporters toweled champagne from his hair and, speaking from the home clubhouse at Fenway Park, said on behalf of millions: "This is, if I might add a personal note, the greatest thrill of my life."

His name was Ken Coleman, and his voice was familiar to a nation of baseball and football fans. As a boy, he had idolized slugger Jimmy Foxx, but at age twelve, losing an eye when it was stung by a bee, Coleman traded one icon (Old Double X) for another, Sox- and Braves' announcer Fred Hoey, and began to dream of broadcasting.

After his 1943 graduation from a Boston-area high school, Ken served in Burma during The Good War, returned to major in oratory at Curry College, a school for prospective announcers, then took his first broadcast position covering Vermont's old Northern Baseball League. From there, he moved back to Boston — doing Quincy and Weymouth high school football; climbing to a college berth as play-by-play man for Boston University; and "being written up" and coming under the scrutiny of Paul Brown, owner and head coach of the Cleveland Browns' football club.

"Bob Neal had been doing the Browns' games for Schaefer beer, but now Carling got the rights, and they began to look around for their own broadcaster," Coleman recounted. "They didn't want a Cleveland sportscaster — they wanted a new face, somebody from *outside* Cleveland. I heard about the opening, and two guys who knew Brown and had come to know me — Tom Dowd, the Red Sox' late traveling secretary who was also an NFL official; and Buff Donelli, the coach at B.U. — wrote letters to Paul plugging my credentials."

"They obviously worked," I said.

"In the end, it came down to two finalists," he said. "I went on to whatever it is I've done. The other guy went to NBC that same year and eventually handled everything you can think of. Ever heard of Lindsey Nelson?"

In early 1952, Coleman was tapped to call Browns' games over one of the most far-flung radio networks in the land. He was only twenty-seven; his Athens of America accent was pronounced; and there were some who wondered how well and long, in that age of an older regionalism, Midwesterners would accept him. "I'll admit I went with some trepidation. In '51, I'd gone to work for a 250-watt station in Worcester, Massachusetts. Now it was on to a 125-station Browns' network. They had stations in St. Louis, Texas, San Francisco — all around the country," said the current Voice of the Red Sox. "So it was a great opportunity, but even so, Ohio, Middle America, it was all foreign terrain to me."

It was home country soon enough. By 1954, Coleman had become the Indians' *television* Voice (that season, also, the Browns'), and for the next eleven years, focusing on luminaries from Herb Score and Rocky Colavito to Otto Graham and Jim Brown, he described the deeds of Cleveland's two professional dominances, worked at various times as nightly sportscaster for the city's three network TV stations, and moved one columnist to advise his readers, "He is one of those fellows who proceeds through the jungle of sports broadcasting without making an enemy."

The native of North Quincy laughed, easily. "From the minute I started in broadcasting, I had to try and not imitate someone else, to just be myself," Coleman said. "When I was growing up, Sundays my dad and I would go to Fenway Park or Braves Field. I can remember looking at the radio booth, seeing Fred Hoey, and thinking, 'Some day I'd like to be up there.' My generation grew up on radio and in our region Hoey was the pioneer. Believe me, I had to fight not to talk like him."

"What else did you learn early on?" I asked.

"This lesson came slowly, because as a young announcer you can be so totally ambitious, single-minded, so desperate to succeed. I'm talking about the ability in broadcasting, as in anything else, to make fun of yourself—not to think the sun sets and rises with the fate of one individual."

"Examples?"

"Even all the preparation in the world can't guard against mistakes," he said. "I was broadcasting an Indians' game in Kansas City in the fifties and describing a catch about to be made by Rocky Colavito. What I intended to say was, 'There goes Rocky back against the wall,' but instead it came out, 'There goes Wally back against the rock.' Fortunately, I caught the error and, hoping to redeem myself, said, 'For those of you interested in statistics, that was my twelfth fluff of the year. It puts me in third place in the American League.' "

"But that wasn't your biggest laugh," I said.

"Boy, that's the truth," he said. "That came a long time later [1983]. The Red Sox were playing, ironically, in Cleveland. They were ahead by one run but the Indians had runners on second and third, and Ralph Houk [the Boston manager] brought in Bob Stanley to pitch. Mike Hargrove came to bat for Cleveland and lined a single to left scoring two runs. So I said, 'Here comes the tying run and the winning run, and the Indians win, three to two.' "

"And?"

"Well, as the second run crossed the plate, I looked out toward the mound and Stanley was still standing there. I thought, 'Why isn't he walking off the field? The game's over.' I looked at my partner, Joe Castiglione, who returned an equally puzzling look. And then it hit both of us—we were only in the *eighth* inning. I didn't have much recourse, so I said, 'Ladies and gentlemen, I'm sitting in the broadcasting booth in Cleveland, Ohio, and I have a very red face. It's red because the game isn't over—we're only in the eighth inning.' And fans wrote letters to me saying not to worry—that they made mistakes too. When you make fun of yourself, people relate."

I first related (and listened) to Coleman in 1960, over the CBS Network, on Browns' videocasts piped each Sunday into western New York. Televised pro football was still a bantling, and I remember thinking how wonderful it was to sit there, in my parents' living room—or often, in my grandparents', thirty-five miles away—and watch black-and-white figures on a shadowy, sixteen-inch screen hurl themselves at one another while, outside, snowflakes dappled the upstate taiga and, sitting next to me, my father read his newspaper and smoked a cigar (it too was terrific; the scent, not the Browns). By 1966, I was hearing Ken more frequently, for it was that spring that Gowdy abandoned Fenway Park for NBC, and Coleman, parachuting in from Cleveland, became the Voice of the Sox. "God, it was like a dream, going back to my roots, replacing a giant like Curt, taking the same job Hoey had," he said. "To come back to my friends, to Tom Yawkey, to the wonderful park."

"And to a terrible team," I reminded him; the 1966 Red Sox would finish ninth, twenty-six games behind the Orioles. "That had to dim your spirits some."

"Nah, I was too high for anything to get me down," Ken retorted. "Anyway, what happened next made any preliminary stumbles all the more worthwhile."

What happened was what Red Sox' fans refused to *concede* was happening—

their team in *contention*, in an honest to goodness, praise be, hallelujah *pennant chase*.

In Coleman's second Fenway season, he described — at times, not grasping it himself — how the Boston American League Club buffeted its historical amalgam of bad luck and clawed past the Tigers, Twins, and White Sox to win The Great Race and brighten one of baseball's most floodlit ventures. Over the WHDH Radio-TV Network, New England's lodge of oft-denieds became caught up — many, given past Sox' debacles, against their will — in the chronicles of Carl Yastrzemski, climaxing what Ken later called "the greatest season I've ever seen a professional athlete have," and "Gentleman Jim" Lonborg, Boston's stylish twenty-two-victory pitcher, and power-hitting shortstop Rico Petrocelli, assaulting the Wall in left, and outfielders Reggie Smith and Tony Conigliaro, among the league's emerging stars, and the cat-like first baseman, George (Boomer) Scott, and, moreover, backup casting so weak that, analyzing the rosters of the four contending clubs, one said, sadly, of the Bosox, "*no way*."

"When I was going to school and starting my broadcasting career," Coleman noted, "the Sox had been one of baseball's truly great franchises. Then they started to fall apart, and by the early sixties, the fabric just ripped — they were boring, almost no one came to Fenway. There were even rumors the club might leave Boston."

"Then '67," I said, recalling how the *Globe* explained, "Ken Coleman always has been a lucky coin as a broadcaster. Wherever he has gone, success has existed or followed immediately for the team he has covered."

"Many baseball fans have told me they followed the progress of the '67 race by listening to Ned Martin and me on transistor radios at the beach," Coleman said. "I remember that year for a lot of things — how we came home from a July road trip where we'd won ten games in a row and there were ten thousand fans waiting at the airport for us, or the final day of the season, when we beat the Twins to win the pennant and the players were practically torn to shreds by fans on the field."

"And New England as a whole?" I said.

"I'll give you an example of how it was," he said. "There was one game in which there was no score going into the tenth inning. Reggie Smith led off with a triple, and he eventually scored, the Sox won, and a traffic jam resulted. It seems that a man refused to drive through the Sumner Tunnel in Boston until he heard the outcome of the inning — they had hundreds of cars backed up; he just wouldn't move. Those last two months were just wild — fans, nonfans, the whole region got swept up."

"And it's never wholly subsided."

"That's what the Sox *really* accomplished. They just didn't win a pennant; the year was so electric that it recharged interest all throughout New England" — their home park, the most Arthurian in baseball; their playing surface, God's real grass, not the obscenity of artificial turf; their inducement, Red Sox' baseball, not gaudy giveaways and high-tech scoreboards; their philosophy, eschew the game's finer points (the hit-and-run, the stolen base, an art form called *pitching*) and, bombarding the Green Monster, blitzkrieg opponents into submission. "Starting that year, folks began to realize again that especially when they win, the Sox are sort of like the Brooklyn Dodgers in the fifties," Coleman said. "They play in a small, homey park — great atmosphere. They have fans around the country. When you go to a game, you *get* the game, not a lot of extraneous distractions. Both stack their lineup with right-hand sluggers."

"Both seemed afflicted by clouds of self-doubt," I said. Brooklyn lost eight World Series; the Sox had not been a team triumphant in nearly seventy years.

"Yes, 'Wait Till Next Year,' " he said. "I know this: If every big-league team was like the Red Sox, you'd never hear anybody questioning which sport was the real National Pastime."

Over CBS, Coleman had telecast the 1964–65 NFL championship games, a Browns' 27–0 shellacking of Baltimore and 23–12 loss to Green Bay. With Gowdy and Harry Caray, he did NBC Television's play-by-play of the 1967 World Series, then moved back to radio for the next four summers — calling balls and strikes, like the Cowboy before him, in a manner that was at once effective and understated; alternately cheering and despairing as the club drew nearly 2 million spectators in 1968, Petrocelli smacked a league-record forty homers by a shortstop the following year, Yaz lost the 1970 batting title in his final at-bat to Alex Johnson of the Angels, and Luis Aparicio went zero-for-forty-four in 1971. After that season, WHDH-TV lost its license; leaving radio, Ken jumped to the team's new flagship outlet, WBZ. "Since 'HDH was now only going to cover the Red Sox on one medium [radio], not two, they only needed one main announcer, Ned," he said, "and I was notified that I was 'free' to negotiate my own services. So WBZ picked up John Pesky and me, and we went over there for three more TV years." But when WSBK, Channel 38, took over the Sox' television contract in 1975, quickening the sequence of musical chairs, Coleman found himself without a job. "I went in to see Bill Flynn [Channel 38's general manager], and he simply stated he was going with a new cast [ultimately, Dick Stockton and ex-Yawkey Ken "Hawk" Harrelson]." Six weeks before Opening Day, the Reds hired the adopted Buckeye as their television Voice, and, alluding to the *Globe*, "success . . . followed immediately." The 1975 Cincinnati won their first world championship in thirty-five years.

In the spring of Coleman's first year at Riverfront Stadium, it was no trick to find Red Sox' TV fans who admitted they missed him; on radio, however, the complex waves of loyalty had ebbed. The reason was that by early 1975, the road show of Martin and Woods had spiraled into a New England tandem rivaling Orr and Esposito, Cousy to Sharman, or Teddy Ballgame by himself — "surely, one of the finest in the country," enthused *Sports Illustrated*, "one of the most articulate and delightful teams not simply in their own league, or in baseball, either — but rather, in any sport, anywhere." They were knowing and inquisitive — the Possum, baseball's peripatetic "second" announcer, with his booming voice and stronghold of enthusiasm; Martin, the poet who, quoting Hamlet, said once of Red Sox' ineptitude, "When sorrows come they come not [as] single spies, but in battalions" — and they enjoyed, for five too-brief seasons, the most devoted regional clientage of any seventies broadcast co-op.

Jim Woods grew up in Kansas City, was a bat boy for the minor-league Blues, and later studied journalism at the University of Missouri. In his freshman year, he quit school to cover local sports on 100-watt KGLO in Mason City, Iowa, the mythical River City of Meredith Wilson's *The Music Man*. Two years later, a young man named "Dutch" Reagan left his job as the University of Iowa football announcer to sign a Hollywood contract; the future Poss replaced him. By 1948, at thirty-one, he offered a proven appeal, and when Ernie Harwell flew Atlanta for the promise of Ebbets Field, Jim was named play-by-play Voice of the Southern Association Crackers. "Talk about a tough act to follow," Woods exclaimed. "Here I go into Atlanta, where Harwell was a southerner and exorbitantly popular—there were a lot of people who told me, 'Don't even try it.' But it was too good an advancement not to. I figured, 'The worst that can happen is I bomb.' " Instead, he won Georgia's radio allegiance—"The finest thing that's ever happened to me was when Ernie's mother called me one day and said, 'You know, Ernie's broadcasts were our life, and we didn't know if we'd survive his leaving Atlanta [Harwell's father was an invalid], but you've made us forget all our worries' "—and in 1949, after the Crackers sold their TV rights for $100,000, Woods became the first announcer to do an entire home season of video balls and strikes.

Four years later, more awed than terrified, Jim joined the Voice of the Yankees at the Big Ball Park in the Bronx. "Being a tremendous pro, Mel helped me more than any broadcaster I've ever worked with. He kept pointing out little things—he had that great eye for detail. If I said, 'A foul ball back,' he'd whisper, 'Back where?' "

"Anything else?" I said.

"I'll never forget one day walking into Allen's suite. There was Mel on the phone talking to Joe DiMaggio about Marilyn Monroe. And it shook me up. I knew then," he affirmed, "I was in the big leagues. But the one thing about doing Yankee games was that George Weiss, our general manager, had a hot line into the booth. He would monitor the broadcasts, and he had an opinion on everything. A light would go on, you'd pick up the phone, and there was George—he didn't miss a trick. 'You guys are laughing too much,' he'd say, or, 'We got a big series with the Tigers coming up. Damn it, promote it more.' "

In late 1956, when shortstop Phil Rizzuto was released by the Yankees and kicked upstairs to the broadcast booth, it was Woods himself who needed promoting.

"Tell me how Rizzuto got you fired," I said.

The Possum laughed. "He didn't directly, but the effect was the same," he said. "The first step in the circus was that after all these years of starring for the Yankees, Rizzuto reached the end of the line. Weiss let him go on the club's annual Old-Timers' Day [August 25] and, bang, Phil is out of a job. Ballantine beer was our major sponsor, and its head guy [Carl Badenhausen] just loved to pal around with Phil. They played golf. And apparently they got to talking."

"And Ballantine told Weiss to have Phil replace you."

"That's the rumor," he said. "I'll never forget how it happened. In fact, later that day I was standing at the bar at Toots Shor's Restaurant when Barber walked in. I told him the same story."

"How Weiss unloaded."

"George had called me earlier that day and asked me to drop by in the afternoon. I thought it was just a routine extension of my contract for '57 with Red and Mel," Woods said. "George seemed nervous when I came into his office, looking at the ground, real unhappy — not at all like the Weiss I knew. He asked me to sit down, and he was halting, trying to find his thoughts. 'Jim, you've done a wonderful job for the Yankees,' he said. 'You, Mel, and Red have been a magnificent team. And I'll always appreciate it. But, Jim, I have to do something I hate doing, something I've never done before — fire somebody without a reason, a guy who's been a solid pro. Jim, Ballantine has ordered that we take Rizzuto on as a broadcaster. You're out.' "

Stunned, the Possum was also free. After working the Giants' last season in New York, he joined the Gunner at Forbes Field. "They were an incredible pair," said Coleman. "When Jim came to the Red Sox later on, we became very close, and he'd almost always talk about Prince. We were in different leagues back then, and I hadn't heard Bob that much, but when I did, I could see his point. I remember going into Pittsburgh for a 'Game of the Week' broadcast once — I was substituting for Garagiola — and I turned on the radio Friday night in the hotel. It was raining and Prince said, 'Poss, I wish they'd call the game so I could beat it home and turn on the John Wayne western that's playing.' It was just so *different* from anything we did in Boston."

Often during Woods' tenure in Pittsburgh, Betty Prince would introduce Jim's wife as "Mrs. Possum." But in late 1969, Jim traded friendship, longevity, and title for a two-year layover in St. Louis. Finley was Woods' next way-stop, and they peacefully coexisted until the Athletics' potentate telephoned the Possum in November 1973 and handed down an unconditional sentence. "He said he liked me personally," Woods said, "but that I wasn't his type of announcer. Charlie lived in Indiana, and he liked the midwestern style of announcing — a Brickhouse or Wilson — where the announcer screams on a foul pop fly. 'Jim,' he told me, 'you're one of the best announcers when something is happening, but when nothing is going on you don't make it very exciting.' " Poss had been Finley's thirteenth announcer since 1961.

Five weeks into the new year, Woods signed with the once-and-always Jersey Street Jesters; presently, the telephone rang. "Jim," the caller said, "I've thought this over and I'd like you to come back."

"Charlie," said Woods, "I've obligated myself to do the Red Sox' games for the next two years."

"Shit, Jim," Finley riposted, "everybody knows those contracts aren't worth the paper they're written on."

"Charlie," Jim said, "I told you, I'm tied up with the Red Sox. I'm not coming back to Oakland."

Instead, employed by his sixth big-league club in the last nineteen years, Poss joined an announcer whose adolescence in the Delaware Valley had stirred with the cadences of Byrum Fred Saam. "I grew up in Wayne, about eighteen miles from Center City in Philadelphia, and the first announcer I remember is Bill Dyer," Ned Martin mused. "But the one who succeeded him and who everybody lived with so long was Saamie, and his voice alone would have been enough to inspire me into broadcasting."

"Describe it," I said.

"His voice was a cross between Stern and Husing, one of the best I've ever heard. It had a resonance, a timber, it was heavy, and it was the kind of tool that just cried out to do the big games."

"When did you start listening to By?"

"He got there in 1938, when I was fifteen, and I listened to him for the next four years. With the A's and Phillies, he had some terrible teams—but you tuned in anyway," Ned said. "After all, in those days there weren't many places you could go and *not* hear Saam boom through the action. Cars, homes, stores—radio was really emerging then as a tremendous plus for baseball."

Following high school, Martin's road led in 1941 to Duke University ("I was there only a little while before something called a world conflagration happened on the scene") and, a year later, the Marine Corps ("I enlisted, got shipped to San Diego, and was on Iwo Jima the day we captured the island. Sad to say, however, I'm *not* one of the guys who raised the flag that you see in the monument") and, at war's end, back to Duke and an English concentration. After graduating, Ned took his theatre of expression to, successively, a New York advertising agency, the Dell Publishing Company, and station WINX in the Washington, D.C., suburb of Rockville, Maryland. "Once my fabulously unsuccessful career in advertising and publishing ended, I figured that maybe I should re-enter radio, which I'd done in college and enjoyed," Martin said. "So I went to Rockville and did it all on the ground floor—news, commercials, afternoon shows, playing hillbilly music. And the interesting thing was that Bob Wolff was a big hit in Washington by then—and this was the same guy who'd been a senior at Duke when I was a freshman and who'd helped me so much on my delivery, listening to tapes and all the rest."

By May 1954, it was on to sportscasting at WRFC in Athens, Georgia, where Martin called a no-hitter by that town's schoolboy Jupiter, Fran Tarkenton, and in April 1956, to Charleston, West Virginia, and Detroit's Triple-A affiliate, the American Association Senators. His big-league hope was real, but mainly clouded. "I just believed in some vague way that I'd make the majors some day," he said, "and for the next four years I kept bothering people, sending tapes to the clubs in both major leagues, trying to show that I belonged." He could not know that Red Sox' announcer Bill Crowley would agree in 1960 to become the club's publicity director, or that Martin would be asked to audition for the upcoming broadcast vacancy, or that, joining the Cowboy, he would enter the bigs on the same Opening Day as Carl Yastrzemski: April 11, 1961. At/from the top, Ned was wryly descriptive, bringing subtlety to play-by-play, and he developed into "a huge favorite of Boston's vast New England audience," reported the *Washington Star*. "He seems so perfectly matched for Red Sox' fans that if the low-key Martin did not exist, New England would have to invent him."

In springtime 1972, Coleman left Red Sox' radio, and Martin became its Voice; for part of that season, he paired with John MacLean; its last three months and all of 1973, Ned aided Dave (no relative) Martin. When Finley ousted Woods, the Sox (having dumped the hapless Dave) bagged the bulky Possum. It was, New England soon discerned, quite a catch.

"It wasn't very far into '74 that I could see Ned and I were going to click," Woods said. "The letters, the columns, you name it—they were so positive it was like we wrote them ourselves."

"But you didn't announce like you did with Prince," I said.

"Hell, no," he roared. "First of all, Ned's quieter, a lot different from Bob. Then, again, who's not? But the big thing is that you had to tone down your dramatics, the kind of Ringling Brothers deal Mr. Prince and I had. Fans all over this area had grown up with a certain kind of announcer—Gowdy, Coleman, Ned. I didn't try to imitate them, but I had to complement their style. Hell, if I'd pulled a Gunner revisited or a Caray, I'd have been run out of town."

His first Fenway season, Woods saw the Red Sox fly to a seven-and-one-half-game lead in late August before, like the *Hindenburg*, collapsing. Batting catatonia lit their pyre, and few Boston fans expected a more tolerable 1975. Yet the Yawkeys, surprisingly, broke to a wide division lead, and watched ratings on WHDH Radio (its thirtieth straight year of carrying the Sox) and WSBK (paying $1.6 million for television rights) leap from merely high to extravagant. Rarely had the Bostons enjoyed a wider audience; never had their fans enjoyed more telecasts. Under the Channel 38 arrangement, Stockton and Harrelson—less glowingly received than Ned and Poss; one critic barbed, "Harrelson is doing for instant replays what the Boston Strangler did for door-to-door salesmen"—beamed a record eighty-six games over the Bosox' six-state network. Only the Cubs (148 games), White Sox (125), and Mets (120) commandeered more videocasts; also-rans ranged from the Phillies and Yankees (sixty-eight each; the Bombers' total barely half of their early-sixties high) to the Bay Area's co-inhabitants, televising a sum of forty games, to, hitting bedrock, fainéant, unattractive San Diego, unable to secure even a flagship station.

All told, showing 1,039 games, 239 stations engaged in local and regional big-league coverage (seventy-two in the American League and 167 in the National; the Astros, Braves, and Cardinals' networks led with twenty-two, twenty-one, and eighteen affiliates; through sixty English- and French-speaking stations of the Canadian Broadcasting Corporation, the Expos captured turf from Newfoundland to the Yukon), and it was the Senior Circuit, reversing a two-decade-old pattern, which televised more heavily—fifty-three sets per club, minus Padres, v. the American's fifty-one. Over radio, the Nationals also fronted—by 1975, their average network totaled forty-five affiliates; the Junior Loop's, thirty. Turning to the "bottom line," a favorite wordmark of the era, the separate realities widened—in 1973, the National's teams garnered $13,560,000 from radio/television rights; the American's mustered only $10,825,000; the Dodgers led everyone with revenue of $1.8 million.

These facts, among many, helped to spur a smugness in the National

League's behavior to outsiders and to itself. They also suggested, however, I came to feel, as did scattered returns from the "other league" — the Tigers' TV Network exploding to sixteen outlets and the White Sox' to ten, or the Angels' Don Drysdale, Dick Enberg, and Dave Niehaus sparkling over flagship radio station KMPC, or Bud Blattner and Denny Matthews proselytizing ten states for the expansion Royals — that grappling with the need to promote itself, baseball was slowly, even self-awaredly, recovering from its broadcast interregnum of mirages and parched earth. "I think a lot of the pro football boom was strictly imagery, P.R.," said Bob Wirz, the baseball commissioner's superb then-director of information. "They had wonderful promotion. They were willing to exploit and be exploited by television. But two can play at that game, and though we started late, we won't be long in catching up. I think you'll see the press reviews about this game turn out much different over the next few years than perhaps over the last few."

When Wirz foretold, accurately, baseball's revival — a decade later, Bill Lyon of the *Philadelphia Inquirer* would write, "Baseball's hold on the American public is [again] narcotically powerful. No matter what it does, no matter how it misbehaves, it is granted absolution. It cannot fall from grace" — it was February 1975, and the sport was trying to shake the shadow of its flashier, more telegenic rival. It was only four years since *Forbes* magazine had ridiculed the pastime as "on a long road downward in popularity, especially among the young," an interlude in which local broadcast rights had climbed from $21.55 million to $26.5 million. The rise was central enough to a game, pre-free agency, already anxious about financial solvency; it was even more of a tactual reminder that just as radio and television had escorted the majors into their 1965–75 wilderness, they could just as easily retrieve them. "After it went bigtime, the NFL never had to worry about local contracts," Tom Dawson related. "Just look at this year [1973]. Through its three network systems, football brings in more than $42 million, right? Except for preseason games, their contracts forbid teams from having any TV but network, right? So all that's left is regular-season radio, right? You know how much the teams get from that? A lousy $3 million. The NFL's *soul* belongs to network television."

The Game's did not. "We sort of like it that way," said Kuhn's then-media director, making a virtue of necessity. "It gives us more independence." Offered such liberty, most of America's baseball public might have yearned for ball and chain.

There loomed, as a first hindrance to NFL-type exposure, the fact of baseball's historic marriage to local broadcast coverage; because of that entwining, network exclusivity was foolstuff. Then too, baseball was a less palatable national TV commodity: From 1970 to 1974, Saturday "Game of the Week" ratings fell from 8.1 to 7.3 (and, by 1975, to 7.1); while "Monday Night Football" demolished the notion that sports could not successfully invade prime time — in the series' first four years, Nielsen numbers rose from 18.5 to 21.2 — baseball's other network vehicle, the Monday evening "Game," bathed in a bay of viewer indifference.

In 1970, NBC's three night broadcasts commanded a 10.6 national rating.

The following year, the audience for five evening games jumped to 12.0, then dropped in 1972 to a middling 11.3 for ten assorted prime timers. "It was already apparent that prime-time baseball, while not a bomb, exactly, wasn't going to be the biggest thing on TV since Milton Berle," said an official of *Broadcasting Magazine*. "Just take a look at the totals for a year, say, like '72." That season, viewers watched "Monday Night Football" in 12 million homes, the Saturday "Game" in between four and five, and Monday baseball in 7.2 million. "Some of baseball's trouble was explainable—fewer folks watch TV in the spring and summer, they're outside, the weather is better, so the entire industry suffers from fewer sets in use. But the fact also was unavoidable that network baseball hadn't clicked yet in prime time. Maybe it was too slow, the game itself. Maybe it was the lack of regularity—you couldn't know from one Monday to the next whether there'd be a game on. Who knew? What we *did* know was that baseball and NBC were scurrying around, trying to find some answers."

Enter 1973, the second of baseball's four-year, $72-million television pact with NBC, and a determined stab at a sustaining niche in prime-time programming. For the first time, Dawson announced in February, NBC would televise fifteen consecutive Monday games—May 21 to September 15; broadcast by Gowdy, Kubek, and their "celebrity guest." "There's no question that continuity will help," claimed the former CBS president, "the fact that people will know in advance there will be a game each Monday night."

To hype its audience and, therefore, obtain top dollar for its commercial time, NBC demanded—and received—a ban on competing local telecasts; if the network aired the Reds and Dodgers, say, the same evening that Boston played New York, Sox and Yankees' fans could follow their favorites only via radio. On the other hand, baseball *refused* to lift its blackout rule forbidding a network contest from invading the home market or the territory of a visiting club—"even," marveled Jack Craig, "when the latter's station is not bringing the game back on TV." It was this rule, to cite an instance, which created the comic absurdity whereby if NBC featured the Mets and Dodgers, teams from the nation's two largest markets, viewers in New York and Los Angeles must watch a *backup* game. The reason? To protect home attendance and, furthermore, the exclusivity of local media—here, Mets and Dodgers' radio. "It was a relic, a rating-killer, this blackout," Tom Villante sniffed in 1982. "It meant that we could never fully realize the big markets to boost our audience. We could never, for example, televise the Yankees or Mets—either at home or on the road—and show them in New York. The same with the White Sox and Cubs in Chicago. We were losing millions of bucks we could have got by higher ratings. And all for what? Largely, to protect the local radio audience—meager, by comparison—of the individual clubs."

Even so, *Broadcasting* insisted, "No one is more confident than NBC that 1973 will be a banner year for baseball. In particular, its people feel the ban on rival local telecasts will lift nightly ratings." For its sixty-second World Series commercials, the network was charging $70,000 and a baseball-record $110,000, respectively, for day and prime-time contests; for the All-Star Game,

$90,000 a minute; for Monday night set-tos, $35–45,000; for Saturday after-noons, the only continuum whose sales were lagging, $15–20,000.

Surely, the pastime's gentry felt, *this* would be the year baseball kicked apathy aside and crashed through, like the NFL a decade earlier, into a kind of splendid network arcadia.

It never happened; in 1973–74, as Spiro Agnew resigned as vice-president, Arab oil-producing nations slapped a total ban on oil exports to the U.S., Washington gaped at the "Saturday Night Massacre," and Nixon resigned, was pardoned, and nearly died, the Monday Night "Game of the Week" drew a network rating of exactly 12.0 each year — disappointing; insufficient to mush-room the majors' television rights.

"Baseball's media problem was very simple," explained John Lazarus, the former ABC Sports salesman who succeeded Dawson on June 1, 1974. [Carl Lindemann: "Tom was a talented guy who didn't take his baseball job that seriously — which, of course, was part of baseball's trouble back then. After all, Dawson had headed a CBS empire, and baseball was a comedown for him. Worse, he believed that his employer, Bowie Kuhn, was a jerk. Worse yet, he was indiscreet enough to go telling everybody at cocktail parties and so forth how much of a jerk he thought Bowie was. Bowie heard about it. So when in '74, Dawson got the brilliant idea of moving to California and still holding his baseball job by commuting to New York, Bowie had the excuse and — I'm sure — the pleasure of saying, 'You're fired.' And Lazarus replaced him."]

"Simple?" I said, now, to Lazarus. "Back then, baseball's media problems were diverse."

"Maybe, but they all boiled down to the same set of facts," he said. "Even before the free-agent rule sent salaries through the roof, baseball's costs were expanding. You couldn't keep up with them through giant increases in rights for local radio and television. Sure, the money for these rights was going up some, but the rise was minor; the potential wasn't there. At the same time, the ratings for regular-season national games were flat — baseball wasn't going to get a huge increase from whatever network had the entire package." In 1969–71, each big-league team received $668,000, annually, from NBC; in 1972–75, $750,000. "As we approached negotiations for our network pact which began in '76," Lazarus continued, "there were indications that if we stayed with only one network, we'd get only the same kind of minor boost. Even worse, with only one network, baseball was getting killed in promotion — the other two nets would ignore us while pro football was getting P.R.'d to the sky on NBC, ABC, and CBS." The solution fairly smacked baseball in the face: like Soviet and American troops piercing the German Reich in April 1945, divide and em-brace the spoils.

After months that turned into a Byzantine durance of conjecture and comic intrigue — of reports that baseball had lured three networks into its TV fold, or rumors that Mutual Radio would commence a "Game of the Week," or gossip intimating that the bigs had consented to a Sunday television series — The Game unfurled its less-brave-than-new broadcast world in March 1975.

During the next four years, the baseball assembly learned, NBC and ABC would alternate coverage of the World Series, League Championship Series, and All-Star Game. In 1976 and 1978, NBC was to telecast the Oktoberfest; ABC, the playoffs and Mid-Summer Classic. In 1977 and 1979, they would reverse events.

"The spring that this was arrived at and announced must not have been very pleasant," I reminded Lindemann. "After a decade of having baseball to yourself, boom—ABC grabs half the package."

"I felt all along that baseball would divide its package, and I couldn't blame them," he said. "They'd seen the blizzards of publicity the NFL got from three networks. Baseball wanted at least a degree of that. What bugged me—what still infuriates me today—is how unethical Lazarus was about it."

"Take it from the start," I said.

"In early 1975, we began negotiations for our new TV deal, and we started off with a lunch one day—Lazarus, me, and Sandy Hadden, Kuhn's chief aide. I told them we wanted to reduce somewhat our number of Monday night games—not cut them out, but slice the number. Baseball knew their ratings hadn't been that great," observed the former NBC Sports head. "Shortly afterward, we had another meeting about a new contract. We wanted to keep exclusivity, and we were looking for ways to accommodate baseball's wishes for more P.R. Lazarus assured us baseball wasn't thinking of leaving us in the lurch."

"How'd you find out otherwise?"

"One Friday I got a phone call from a friend of mine at BBD&O [the advertising agency of Batten, Barton, Durstine, and Osborn], and he said, 'Look, you ought to know this—I've heard baseball is about to split its package with ABC.' I didn't believe it—if it was true, it meant baseball was lying to us. So I called Herb Schlosser [NBC's president] and said, 'I don't know how accurate this is, but here's what I just heard,' and Herb, who'd gone to school with Bowie Kuhn and knew him, said, 'I'll have a drink with Bowie and find out.'"

"Which he did."

"Yes, and at a party at Pete Rozelle's home that weekend, Herb came up to me and said, 'Talked to Bowie. No problem. We've still got the package.'"

"When did you find out you didn't?"

"We already had a meeting with Lazarus scheduled for the following Monday at two-thirty. An hour later, he still hadn't showed up. Finally, he comes into NBC, and we go into the office. Lazarus says, 'We just sold half of the package to ABC.' And I said to him, 'You cock-sucker.' I never blamed Bowie—it wasn't his fault. It was Lazarus who was the double-dealer." A short, derisive grunt. "The next year he went back to ABC as a vice-president. Does that sound like a little conflict of interest to you?"

Soon after ABC's thunderclap, baseball also inked CBS Radio to an exclusive 1976-79 contract—in effect, giving the sport two-and-one-half networks—to beam its All-Star Game and postseason schedule over more than two hundred affiliates. "The addition of ABC Television and CBS Radio should result in considerably more publicity as each network promotes its own package," *The Sporting News* recognized. "Baseball's gray heads have never quite appreciated the worth of this, and it is probably one reason it has taken so long to move on dividing the action." Buried, blissfully, was NBC's policy, pursued since 1969, of overlapping some playoff games and ignoring others; under the new contract, each set would be televised in its entirety; many would be seen at night. Gone too were the makeshift radio networks that kept many Americans ignorant of each playoff's happenings; no longer must transistors turn cartwheels to grasp static-clinged play-by-play from weak and faraway stations. CBS Radio had a deep and honest identity and a considerable ability to promote; its exposure blanketed the nation, and made baseball's post-1975 postseason a *community* peregrination. "I don't see how any fair-minded fan could criticize how we've arranged our postseason coverage," said Kuhn, understandably, in 1979. "You can be anywhere in the country and not miss a single pitch on either radio or TV."

It was, rather, across the *regular* season where baseball's new pact stumbled, for its progressivity benefited the *networks*, not fans, and did nothing to increase TV coverage. In 1976, NBC would again endow viewers with twenty-six Saturday games. But ABC had agreed to a mere sixteen Monday telecasts, only one above baseball's then-current sum, and while ratings, putatively, should improve—"Under our new deal, baseball said it would help us with scheduling flexibility, giving us better games," said producer Don Ohlmeyer of ABC, "and, most important, they've lifted the blackout in the visiting team's market"; e.g., a Yankees' away game could be televised back to New York— many fans, still reduced to exposure deemed miserly by the NFL, found themselves, depending on the moment, revulsed with futility or anger. Yet up in the counting house, their forearms weary from back-slapping, baseball's well-to-dos surveyed the dual-network contract and blessed the nearly $1 million each franchise would receive, annually, through 1979. "In reality, the deal wasn't *quite* the great financial breakthrough we made it out to be," conceded Lazarus. The entire package totaled $92,800,000, or $23.2 million per year—at the time, impressive; in retrospect, given the tornado of late-seventies inflation, a small-fry leap over the $18 million of 1975. "But keep in mind that this was before the last-decade explosion in network rights fees, and anyway, it wasn't just the money I was concerned with—even though many owners were. It was the extra P.R., the needed publicity, that made the deal so good." A decade later, seeking not merely P.R. but greater profiteering, baseball would adopt a more hard-line stance; for now, to a team like the 1975 Indians, cash-poor and floundering, and whose local broadcast rights netted barely $800,000, the infusion of *any* extra network revenue must have seemed scented with Shangri-La.

NBC Television's last regular season of exclusivity began on April 6, 1975, with a sixty-minute special, "Next Year Is Here," hosted by Joe Garagiola, and ended on September 27, the Saturday of the Red Sox' clinching. Nonplussed by baseball's decision to split its TV package—"There was some disillusionment at NBC over losing the Monday series. Its ratings weren't great, but they *did* top Saturday's," a Lazarus aide said later. "But what really bugged 'em was losing the big events every other year. Losing the Series, especially, that's what hurt" — the network ditched its Monday night "celebrity concept," restricted Kubek to Saturday, and in a move ripe with portents, unveiled a new broadcast paradigm. Every other Saturday, Garagiola and the Cowboy would alternate as "Game's" play-by-play men; Kubek would do color. Turning to Monday, Joe G. and Gowdy would appear together; while one called balls and strikes for four-and-one-half innings, the other handled commentary.

"This was really the first move in what I can only call a campaign to get Curt off baseball altogether," Lindemann remarked. "Maybe it was a case of a pair of talents too big for the same booth — I don't know."

"When did you know Gowdy and Joe had troubles?" I said.

"Curt and Joe did the 1974 All-Star Game from Pittsburgh, and the next day Garagiola came up to me and said, 'I've had it. I can't work with him. He kept cutting me off last night — I couldn't get a word in edgewise.' So I went to Curt, and he said he hadn't realized he'd been so dominant."

"What was the NBC position?"

"Joe wanted to be the Number One baseball guy at NBC, and he had a lot of support. Kuhn was in Garagiola's corner, and his big ace was Chrysler, which as you know was our major baseball sponsor," he said. "Joe was their boy. He was under contract to them; he did their commercials. They had one hell of a lot of money invested in him, and they put the heat on NBC to give Joe half of the '75 play-by-play."

"How'd Gowdy take the demotion?"

"He didn't like it one bit." Lindemann paused. "But then, there were other things to come later in the year that he liked even less."

For Curt Gowdy, unknowingly, 1975 became a kind of *The Last Picture Show* — his final chance to share in The Game's springtime of fresh endeavor, its annual tide of reawakening. In early April, he could not grasp — nor did Woods and Martin, staking out Fenway Park — that this tenebrous age would end, joltingly, with a sunburst of such surprise and light that the entire year seemed a panacea for the media slights and lost prestige of the pastime's last decade.

The fun commenced with the New Year's Eve signing of Jim Hunter, nabbed by the Yankees after Finley, breaching the right-hander's contract, prompted arbitration to declare the Catfish a free agent. There followed the debut of the majors' first black manager, Frank Robinson, the fourth no-hitter by Nolan Ryan, matching Koufax, and Carew's fourth straight batting title, the retirement of Bob Gibson (his record: 251–174) and San Diego's belated vault from the cellar (in its seventh year), the debilitation (of opposing pitchers) by Boston's gold dust twins, rookies Rice and Lynn, and, moreover, a World Series which became a genuflection: the seven-set celebration where the Red Sox bowed, no one lost, and after which one felt like shouting, "Take that, you pompous asses and NFL Films and 'Big-Game America.' Let's hear it for the good old days. Baseball *lives!*"

Martin's voice softened. "Nobody had picked the Red Sox to go anywhere that year," observed the man whose "Mercy!" dotted moments of Sox' excitement. "Baltimore was supposed to win it all." But Rice hit .309, whacked twenty-two home runs, and drove in 102 runs; Lynn, a gifted center fielder, batted .331 with twenty-one homers and 105 RBIs, and became the first rookie to win the MVP Award; and the Bosox parlayed the skills of Carlton Fisk (.331), Cecil Cooper (.311), Dwight Evans (.274), Captain Carl (.269), and pitchers Rick Wise (19–12), Bill Lee (17–9), and the florid "El Tianté" (Luis Tiant, at 18–14) to win the East by four-and-one-half games, sweep the playoff from the A's, and stage, with Coleman's Reds, a Grand Event that regained much of the old game's grip on the American sensibility. "The Sox had always been a folk team throughout New England," Martin said. "The key, though, is that in the '75 playoff and, especially, the Series, the country saw what we saw every day—the small park, the fanatic fans, the depth of their knowledge of the game. In other words, baseball like at Ebbets Field or Shibe Park. Baseball like it was *meant* to be."

During the late summer and fall of 1975, the heart of the Yawkeys' appeal as a regional institution—the transfer of allegiance from parent to child; the certitude that in *rooting* for, in passionately *caring* about, this team that every year broke our hearts, lay a continuity binding generations on Long Island Sound and northern Vermont and the easternmost tip of New Brunswick— expanded until a goodly portion of the nation too cared whether *this* was the year the Red Sox, without a world championship since the Twenty-Sixth (Yankee) Division was in France, would strike down their vengeful deity and christen a state of exultation.

It was; they did—almost.

For its last World Series (on radio) and twenty-ninth in a row (on TV), NBC chose a jigsaw of announcers—Gowdy, Garagiola, and Kubek, Cincinnati's Marty Brennaman, and the Red Sox' Voices of Stockton and Ned. "I sort of snuck under the wire," said Martin. "Under baseball's new TV contract, they yielded to the networks from 1976 on the total right to choose their announcers. And the nets began to go with their *own* people."

"So from then on, ABC and NBC wouldn't be obligated to pick Brickhouse, say, if the Cubs were in the Series, or Herb Carneal from Minnesota?" I said.

"I preferred it the old way," he replied. "That way, you got a flavor of the competing clubs—and besides, who'd know the teams better than their regular announcer? But anyway, I was glad to make just '75—all of us alternated between radio and television, and as you'll recall, we saw one hell of a show."

It opened at Fenway Park on October 11–12, traveled to Cincinnati for Sets #3–5, and returned to the Red Sox' misshapen plot of land for an electric sixth affair that ended at 12:34 in the morning, tied the seventy-second World Series at three games apiece, and as it postponed the bedtime of 62 million NBC viewers, stunned the imagination of a people rediscovering that "when there is a game that means something," wrote Dave Anderson in the *New York Times*, "baseball is the best game of all." As long as we have a baseball memory, we will freeze in time Carlton Fisk silhouetted against the New England night—swinging and arcing a twelfth-inning pitch toward the Wall in left, and employing hand signals and body English to push or force or (was it?) pray the ball fair, and when it was and the Red Sox had won this sensational, spectacular, unanswerable game, seven to six, leaping high into the air as Fenway exploded with an intensity that mocked cries of the pastime's supposed demise. The next night, a Series-record 75,890,000 Americans watched Cincinnati win the seventh game, 4-3, and its first Fall Classic since 1940. But it was Game Six and Fisk's gyrations that almost everyone would recall — of one show-stopping play after another, and of the Red Sox' catcher waving wildly and twisting like Arnold Palmer on a green, a moment reminding all of us of baseball's essential beauty.

"That shot of Fisk waving, waving, waving the ball fair gripped the nation," said the man who made it possible, NBC-TV director Harry Coyle, "and it really came about through a booklet of procedures I started to put together about twenty years ago for our cameramen to follow — it's sort of our Bible. By '75, one rule in it said that when a ball is hit to left field, the left-field camera [at Fenway, peering toward home plate through a hole in the Wall] should follow the ball if possible and, if not, then should focus on the hitter."

"Couldn't your cameraman see the ball? Is that why he stayed with Fisk?" I said.

"His name was Lou Gerard, and it was a misty night in Boston, so Lou's choice was clear — keep the viewfinder on Fisk," Coyle reminisced. "But because Fisk didn't start to motion until a little bit after he hit the ball, I edited the rule book. Now it says that instead of cutting away from a play when it ends, you stay with it for an extra five seconds to make *sure* you get the possible reaction."

"You won an Emmy for coverage of the Series [officially, as the "Outstanding Live Sports Special"]. And yet the shot that clinched it for you," I knew, "you almost missed."

Briefly, the four-decade veteran fell silent. "It was an historic picture, and people don't realize how close it came to the trash can," Coyle said, finally. "Fisk was up to bat, and Lou was focusing the camera on him when, all of a sudden, he noticed something about four feet away from him — a rat."

"Sitting inside the Wall?"

"Yep, right there next to him," he confided. "But that's OK — the rat helped make the shot. See, Lou had one eye on the rat and one on the camera — he was preoccupied, you can imagine — so when Fisk hit the ball, Gerard didn't dare go through the movements needed to shift the viewfinder and follow the ball. He played it nice and safe and stationary — he kept the lens on Fisk. Who knows, if the rat hadn't showed up for a guest appearance, it's possible Lou would have switched to the ball, even with the mist. And we'd have missed the shot which really changed TV sports coverage around."

"Up till then, it was almost exclusively action shots," I said.

"Yeah, and since then we've had a ton of *re*action shots," he said. "We have too many, in fact, and they all stem from that."

For Ned Martin, calling Fisk's poke over NBC Radio, what stemmed from the Reds-Red Sox' fandango was further distinction as an announcer of creativity; extravagant praise from such disparities as Craig, hailing his reputation "as a quality announcer of pure gold," and Anderson's fellow *Times*man, critic John Leonard, lauding Ned's depiction of Gowdy, Kubek, and Martin as "Winkin, Blinkin, and Nod"; and, ultimately, assignments to co-anchor, with Ernie Harwell, CBS's coverage of the 1976–78 American League playoffs.

Somehow, however, the word never seeped down to Dizzy Dean's old caddy, Gene Kirby, now the Red Sox' vice-president.

In late 1975, Kirby negotiated a club-record $450,000 rights deal with radio station WMEX (later, renamed WITS), the Bosox' new originating outlet. To reclaim its investment, the tiny station opted for an advertising binge — marrying play-by-play with sponsor pitches not just between but *during* each inning; forcing Ned and the Possum to inject drop-in spots and wrap-around commercials; demeaning once orderly broadcasts with what became, to many listeners, baseball's rendition of The Flim-Flam Hour.

Martin and Woods took unkindly to such relentless vending; Kirby and the station's owner, Mariner Communications, chafed at the pair's candor and refusal to massage sponsors on and off the air; and it was less unexpected than deplorable when, in November 1978, misjudging its market as Westinghouse had western Pennsylvania, WITS released the duo "for marketing reasons. We need the right kind of attitude on pre- and postgame shows, for dealing with clients in the VIP lounge, for the constant marketing exposure," general manager Joe Scallan pronounced. "I just don't think [they] were comfortable in all that." That New England was entirely comfortable with both of them, needless to say, was a truth entirely ignored.

From WITS, Martin moved to the ball club's television booth, replacing the CBS-destined Stockton; Woods retired to the race tracks of Florida; and Coleman returned from Cincinnati to again become the Red Sox' radio Voice.

It was far better than nothing — Pirates' fans, stripped totally of Prince, could attest to that — but considerably less poetic than the alive, aware, and independent magic that burnished the core of the Possum and Ned. In the majors' arid season of 1965–75, broken by such wellsprings as The Impossible Dream, the Miracle Mets, and the Phantasmagoric Series of '75, there were few radio teams whose work I more admired. Had Martin and Woods survived into the 1980s, their appeal would have corkscrewed, I believe, during what evolved for baseball into a Jacob's Ladder of popularity and cash.

10
The Hungry Years

"The heavenly rhetoric of thine eye."
—William Shakespeare,
Love's Labour's Lost

ANOTHER ENCORE FOR SANDY

It is 9:46 P.M. Two and two to Harvey Kuenn. One strike away. Sandy into his wind-up. Here's the pitch. Swung on and missed! A perfect game! . . . On the scoreboard in right field, it is 9:46 in the City of the Angels, Los Angeles, California . . . and a crowd of 29,139 just sitting in to see the only pitcher in baseball history to hurl four no-hit, no-run games. He has done it four straight years. And now, he capped it—on his fourth no-hitter, he made it a perfect game! And Sandy Koufax, whose name will always remind you of strikeouts, did it with a flourish. He struck out the last six consecutive batters.

—VIN SCULLY, September 9, 1965.

Dodger Stadium, Los Angeles, CA. Was there ever a more spectral pitcher than Sanford Braun Koufax? From 1961 to 1966, he won 129 games and lost forty-seven; he won the Most Valuable Player Award once and the Cy Young Award in 1963, 1965, and 1966; he struck out a then-record 382 batters in a single season and three times led his league in victories. In 1972, Sandy's first year of eligibility, he was elected to the Hall of Fame.

A TWINS' KILLING

The Twins have won ninety-eight games. Number ninety-nine means the pennant. Here's the windup—and the pitch! Strike three! He struck him out! The Twins win! . . . Final score: the Twins 2, the Senators 1. The Twins have won the American League pennant!

—RAY SCOTT, September 26, 1965.

District of Columbia Stadium, Washington, D.C. Four years earlier, in their first year west of the Potomac River, the erstwhile Washington Senators staggered to a seventh-place residence, thirty-eight games behind the Yankees. Now the Twins themselves were champions, ending the greatest dynasty (in sixteen years, fourteen pennants and nine world titles) in the history of professional sports. With New York convalescing in the bowels of sixth place, Minnesota finished seven games ahead of the Chicago White Sox—the Twins' first and, thus far, only flag.

393

STARBURST OF THE BIRDS

The outfield way around to the left on Frank Robinson, a right-hand hitter. Long drive to left field! Way back, way back! Kiss it good-bye! Home run!

— BOB PRINCE, October 9, 1966.

Memorial Stadium, Baltimore, MD. Acquired from Cincinnati after Reds' owner Bill DeWitt termed him an "old thirty," Frank Robinson joined the Orioles in 1966—winning the Triple Crown and Most Valuable Player Award and, for Baltimore, its first pennant. The Birds then plucked Los Angeles in the World Series; Robinson—its MVP—thrashed two home runs, including a fourth-game *touché* (above) off Don Drysdale. By October 1971, the Orioles' six-year record read: 603 games won, 393 lost, four pennants, and two world championships. "We were a good ball club," said teammate Brooks Robinson, "until we got Frank. He made us a winner."

"THERE SHE GOES!"

Three balls, two strikes. Mantle waits. Stu Miller is ready. Here's the payoff pitch by Miller to Mantle. Swung on! There she goes! There she goes! . . . Mickey Mantle has hit the five hundredth home run [of his career], and the score at the end of seven complete innings: New York 6, Baltimore 4.

— JOE GARAGIOLA, May 14, 1967.

Yankee Stadium, New York, NY. "I wish I was half the ballplayer he is," said Al Kaline, himself a future Hall of Famer, of the firmament who won the 1956 Triple Crown and also led the league in slugging, runs, and total bases; won the Most Valuable Player Award in 1956, 1957, and 1962; and was, related Casey Stengel, "a better ballplayer on one leg than anybody else was on two."

THE IMPOSSIBLE DREAM

Billy Rohr on the threshold with a tremendous performance today. Eight hits in the game— all of them belong to Boston. Rohr winds—here it comes. Fly ball to deep left. Yastrzemski is going hard, way back, way back! And he dives . . . and makes a tremendous catch! One of the greatest catches you've ever seen by Yastrzemski in left field! Everybody in Yankee Stadium on their feet roaring as Yastrzemski went back and came down with that ball!

— KEN COLEMAN, April 14, 1967.

Yankee Stadium, New York, NY. After Yaz's ninth-inning thievery, the next batter singled. Even so, when Billy Rohr one-hit the Yankees, 3–0, in his major-league debut, "The fans began to sense it," a Bosox' announcer said. "This year was not quite the same."

Trailing, 8–0, Reggie Smith homered in the fourth to make it 8 to 1. Yaz had a three-run homer in the fifth, and they got four runs on three hits in the sixth and tied it . . . Fly ball hit deep into left-center field and it is . . . a home run! . . . Jerry Adair has hit his second home run of the 1967 season and the Red Sox, who trailed, 8–0, are now leading in the eighth inning, 9 to 8!

— K.C., 8/20/67.

Fenway Park, Boston, MA. From Brunswick, Maine, to Mystic, Connecticut, during their utterly stouthearted rise from ninth place in 1966 to a possible championship, the '67 Red Sox engrossed New England.

The check by Merritt, the three-one delivery. Hit deep toward right field! This may be gone! It's outa here! Home run! . . . [ten seconds later] . . . If you've just turned your radio on, it's happened again. Yastrzemski's hit a three-run homer, and it's now 6 to 2, Red Sox!

— NED MARTIN, 9/30/67.

Fenway Park. Of Carl Yastrzemski's 452 home runs, the single stroke embodying his career occurred against the Twins, in the first set of a crucial weekend series, on the next-to-last day of Yaz's Triple Crown, Most Valuable Player year. The Red Sox won this game, 6–4, and tied Minnesota for first place.

Lonborg is within one out of his biggest victory ever . . . his twenty-second of the year . . . and his first over the Twins. The pitch . . . is looped towards shortstop. Petrocelli's back, he's got it! The Red Sox win! And there's pandemonium on the field! Listen!

— N.M., 10/1/67.

Fenway Park. In the entire history of baseball, no race had equaled its theatre and transpontine unlikelihood. With one week remaining, four teams virtually shared the American League lead; on the final day, three clubs were separated by one-half game. Amid noise that was insupportable, the Red Sox beat the Twins, 5–3, to ensure a tie for the pennant; when Detroit, needing a double-header victory over California to force a playoff, could only manage a split, Fenway Park welcomed its first World Series in twenty-one years.

THE MAESTRO

Here's the set by Segui, the pitch. Swung on, a drive to left — that'll be the ball game! It's over the head of Gosger! McLain wins his thirtieth! Here comes Stanley in to score. Willie Horton hits a single and the ball game is over, and the Tigers win, 5 to 4! Denny McLain is one of the first out of the dugout, racing out, and Horton is mobbed as the Tigers come from behind and McLain . . . has his thirtieth victory of the 1968 season!

— ERNIE HARWELL, September 14, 1968.

Tiger Stadium, Detroit, MI. Later suspended three times for erratic behavior, termed "not mentally ill" by Bowie Kuhn, and, ultimately, sentenced to prison for racketeering, he was a free spirit, aspiring organist, and self-proclaimed "character"—and in 1968, his gold rush before the crash, Denny McLain became the first pitcher since Dizzy Dean (30–7 in 1934) to win thirty games in a single season. "In his own wild way," wrote Joe Falls, "[he] created every bit of an impact as Cobb or Cochrane did in their greatest years."

"Let's Listen to the Bedlam"

This big crowd here ready to break loose. Three men on, two men out. Game tied, 1–1, in the ninth inning . . . McDaniel checkin' his sign with Jake Gibbs. The tall right-hander ready to go to work again . . . and the windup . . . and the pitch. He swings—a line shot, base hit, right field, the Tigers win it! Here comes Kaline to score and it's all over! Don Wert singles. The Tigers mob Don. Kaline has scored. The fans are streaming on the field. And the Tigers have won their first pennant since 1945! Let's listen to the bedlam here at Tiger Stadium!

—Ernie Harwell, September 17, 1968.

Tiger Stadium, Detroit, MI. "In story-book style, the Tigers won it," a Detroit columnist declaimed. "Then the fans poured from the stands; they caved in the left-field screen and overran the field, starting a celebration that lasted almost until dawn." After an interregnum of twenty-three years, who could denigrate these true believers or begrudge them such resolute joy?

Gibbie Does October

Gibson has tied the record of Sandy Koufax—fifteen strikeouts in a single World Series game. Trying for number sixteen right now against Cash to break the record. He takes his set position, he delivers, here's the pitch. Swing and a miss! He did it!

—Ernie Harwell, October 2, 1968.

Busch Stadium, St. Louis, MO. Five years earlier to the day, Sandy Koufax had set a World Series record, striking out fifteen Yankees in a single game. Now, Bob Gibson went him two better—fanning seventeen batters, besting Denny McLain in baseball's "pitching duel of the century," and destroying the Tigers, 4–0, his sixth complete-game Classic triumph in a row. Said Detroit infielder Dick McAuliffe: Gibson "didn't remind me of anybody; he's all by himself." Added Tigers' manager Mayo Smith: "He threw the greatest pitching performance I've ever seen." Said the principal, penning a more imperious response: "I'm never surprised at anything I do."

TIGER RAG

Lolich fires. Ball is hit high in the air. This should be the Series! Freehan waving everybody away in foul territory. Detroit wins! . . . Lolich is being mobbed at home plate . . . The Detroit Tigers, down, three games to one, came back and have won it, something only two other teams have ever done — Pittsburgh over Washington in 1925, and the Yankees over the Braves in 1958. And now the Tigers have done it over the defending world champion St. Louis Cardinals. Down, three games to one, they have taken three in a row with Lolich today winning his third. Denny McLain won the fourth [actually, sixth] game yesterday.

—JIM SIMPSON, October 10, 1968.

Busch Stadium, St. Louis, MO. For minute after minute, nothing happened. Then, in the sixth inning of a scoreless seventh game, two Cardinals were picked off base. One inning later, with two out, Curt Flood — the best center fielder in the National League — misjudged Jim Northrup's line drive and two Tigers' runs scored. For St. Louis, disaster. For Detroit, in two innings, the championship of the world. For Bob Gibson, the hard-luck victim, unaccustomed grieving. For motorcyclist Mickey Lolich, he of the curveball and paunch, champagne and vindication: the first lefty to pitch three complete-game victories in a World Series.

AMAZIN'

And the pitch back, a curve, chopped out to third. Garrett has the ball! The throw to first! And the Mets are the National League champions!

—RALPH KINER, October 6, 1969.

Shea Stadium, New York, NY. Conceived in 1962, a hybrid of endearment and revolt, the New York Mets — in their first seven seasons — finished ninth twice and last five times. Then, in the year men first walked on the moon, the Amazin's walked on air. They ousted Chicago and St. Louis to take the National League East, swept Atlanta (above) in the first-ever Championship Series, and traveled to Baltimore to open the sixty-sixth World Series: the Miracle (née Wilderness) Mets seeking their Promised Land.

Gentry throws a fastball! Hit high and deep to center field! Agee, who was pulled around to right, goes over with his speed. And watches it — he's got it!

—JIM SIMPSON, 10/14/69.

Shea Stadium. Preserving New York's 3–0 lead, Tommie Agee made a diving catch in the fourth inning of the Series' third game.

Ryan's windup. Two-strike delivery. Here's a fly ball to right-center field. Deep in right-center! Shamsky with Agee. Agee dives — and he makes the catch! Agee made a diving catch at the warning track in right-center field!

— BILL O'DONNELL.

Three innings later, a Game-Three encore.

Two-two from McNally. A curve. Fly ball, deep left field. To the warning track. It is in and up for a home run! . . . Donn Clendenon has just smacked his third home run of the 1969 World Series on a belt-high McNally pitch!

—B.O., 10/16/69.

Shea Stadium. With New York ahead, three games to one, but losing the fifth contest, 3–0, Donn Clendenon blistered a two-run homer off the auxiliary scoreboard of the left-field stands.

McNally ahead 0 and one. Fastball. Here's a fly ball out to left-center field. Buford going back! Buford at the warning track! It is over the fence for a home run! . . . Well, the Mets have played long-ball now in the last two innings and they've locked up this fifth game at three runs apiece.

—B.O.

Let the Force be with you. Al Weis' home run tied Game Five in the seventh inning. Improbably, the slender reserve infielder — homerless in two seasons at Shea Stadium — received the Babe Ruth Award as the outstanding batter of the Series.

Swoboda waiting. Watt working. Slider — here's a fly ball, deep left field. And it's on the warning track! Picked up by Buford. On comes Jones to the plate! The throw is late!

—B.O.

In the eighth inning, doubles by Cleon Jones and Ron Swoboda, and a double Orioles' error at first base, doubled the Mets' fun. The score: 5–3, New York.

Two-one pitch. Fly ball, deep left field. Jones is back to the fence! Jones is on the warning track! The World Series is over! Jones makes the catch! Jones made the catch on Johnson's deep fly ball. The Mets have won it by a score of 5 to 3. Met fans are pouring on the field — trying to steal home plate, trying to take the rubber at the mound!

—B.O.

When Ezio Pinza warbled, "Who can explain it? Who can tell you why? Fools give you reasons. Wise men never try," he was not simply mouthing Oscar Hammerstein II's lyrics in *South Pacific*, circa 1949; he was presaging the ineluctable providence of the '69 Mets.

MR. CUB

One-one pitch. He swings and a drive — a liner, left field! It is — there it is! Mr. Banks has just hit his five hundredth career homer! He is getting a standing ovation! He is trotting to third base! A handshake from Peanuts Lowrey. He hit a low liner — a fastball. Doffs his cap as he steps on home plate! . . . Waves to the fans as he jogs into that dugout! They are standing here at Wrigley Field and giving Ernie an ovation!

—JACK BRICKHOUSE, May 12, 1970.

Wrigley Field, Chicago, IL. He was the Franchise, the player who added "Let's play two" to baseball's lexicon, and, of course, Mr. Cub. For nineteen seasons, he personified the Chicago club, National League: a slugging shortstop/first baseman, captain/inspiration, two-time Most Valuable Player, and man without an enemy (and without a pennant too). Ernie Banks retired in 1971; his 512 home runs, 290 whacked in "the friendly confines" of Wrigley Field, rank eleventh on the all-time list.

THE INCOMPARABLE H. AARON

Hank Aaron at the plate with Felix Millan on second base, one down. First inning, game number two of today's twin-bill. And a swing and a high bouncer over the mound. Charging over, Woodward in front of the bag, up with it. Here's his throw to first! Not in time! Millan is coming around third, he's headed home. Here's the throw from May to the plate. Not in time! There, he slides in safe. And Aaron is safe at first! And there's that three thousandth hit! Time is called — they're holding up the game. And there's Hank Aaron at first base. And the crowd is standing to applaud as Aaron doffs his cap. Time called. He walks over and . . . here's Stan Musial coming out to congratulate him and hand him that ball that he just got his three thousandth hit with.

—JIM MCINTYRE, May 17, 1970.

Crosley Field, Cincinnati, OH. Sixteen years after his first big-league safety, Baseball's Man in the Gray Flannel Suit stood a single away from becoming only the ninth player in the game's 101-year history to collect three thousand hits. Still only thirty-six, he had batted .298 the previous season; he was a centurion of durability; "I came to the Braves on business," he said, "and I intended to see that business was good as long as I could." In the second game of a double-header, off rookie Wayne Simpson, Henry Aaron beat out an infield grounder, then made hit No. 3,001 a celebratory deed: In the Hammer's next time at bat, he bombed an elongated home run.

Auf Wiedersehen, Good-bye

Johnny Bench's home run has just tied it at 4–4, and Mr. Marichal has now allowed the Reds nine hits, and we've got a brand-new ball game here in the eighth inning. Two and two to May. On deck, Bernie Carbo. The outfield around to the left and deep. Now the pitch. Swung on, a high drive, deep center field! . . . [in background, partner Joe Nuxhall shouting, 'Get outa here, outa here, babe, get outa here! I tell ya, out, out, outa here!'] . . . That ball is up, it's up, it's over the center-field fence! A home run for Lee May! And the Reds have taken the lead, 5 to 4!

—Jim McIntyre, June 24, 1970.

Crosley Field, Cincinnati, OH. Sterile and imitative, multi-purpose coliseums benumb the game of baseball. They are not *ball parks*; they are *stadia*, bereft of charm, idiosyncrasies, and soul. Hello, Riverfront, Three Rivers, and you other gleaming ovals. Good-bye, Ebbets Field and the Polo Grounds, Forbes Field and Sportsman's Park, and sainted Crosley Field. In this, the birth-year of the Big Red Machine, Lee May's home run marked the final run of the final game at the park where, on May 24, 1935, the major leagues' first night game was played. Long live the waves of progress; Americana, *R.I.P.*

A Pitcher's Best Friend

McNally hit a home run in the 1969 World Series at Shea Stadium in the fifth game against Jerry Koosman. Two balls, two strikes, three on, two out, sixth inning. Here's the pitch. Swing and a fly ball to deep left! It might be! A grand-slam home run!

—Jim McIntyre, October 13, 1970.

Memorial Stadium, Baltimore, MD. Eight hundred and twenty days before American League owners approved the "designated pinch-hitter"—the DH—Dave McNally struck a dissenting chord. Batting right-handed, the southpaw hurler became the first pitcher (and twelfth player) in World Series history to smash a home run with the bases full. The third-game blow helped the Birds spank Cincinnati, 9–3.

Our Mr. Brooks

The two-two to May. Swing, ground ball, third-base side. Brooks Robinson's got it, throwing from foul ground toward first base! It is . . . in time! And the Golden Glove artistry of Brooks Robinson was never more apparent than on that last play!

—Chuck Thompson, October 10, 1970.

Riverfront Stadium, Cincinnati, OH. He was, said rivals, Baltimore's human vacuum cleaner—a "Hoover" in Orioles' orange-and-black—and his sixth-inning, Game-One robbery of Lee May (what Reds' manager Sparky Anderson later called "an impossible play") helped preserve a World Series victory, 4–3.

Three-one pitch to Bench. Drilled — a stab by Brooks Robinson at third! He caught the ball! A line shot that Brooks Robinson dived and grabbed in his glove for the third out to retire the side! What a play! Wow! Boy, that Robinson is something!

— JIM MCINTYRE, 10/13/70.

Memorial Stadium, Baltimore, MD. By the sixth inning of Game Three, Baltimore owned the Reds, and Brooks Robinson, the Series. Mourned Pete Rose, glumly pointing to the sky: "That guy belongs in a higher league."

It's a ground ball to third. Brooks Robinson throws to Powell. The Orioles win!

— J.M., 10/16/70.

Memorial Stadium. Poetically, in Game Five, No. 5 made the engagement's final out, then received an automobile as the Classic's *nonpareil*. Marveled Johnny Bench: "If we'd known he wanted a car so badly, we'd have chipped in and bought him one."

OFF THE CANVAS (THREE TIMES)

Score tied, 3–3, in the bottom of the seventeenth. One ball and one strike. Coombs into the windup and the one-one pitch. Swung on — driven deep to right field! You can kiss it good-bye! Oh, baby, did he hit that baby outa sight! He cremated it! And the Buccos — we had 'em allll the way!

— BOB PRINCE, July 15, 1971.

Three Rivers Stadium, Pittsburgh, PA. One of baseball's most wizened axioms — "On the road, play to win; at home, play to tie" — flowered this evening in the Gateway to the West. Three times, the Padres tallied to lead the game; three times, the Pirates, reduced to their last at-bats, countered with a tying run. In the seventeenth inning, Roberto Clemente, who once said, "All season, every season, I gave everything I had to this game," gave tonight as well. Off relief pitcher Dan Coombs, the Pirates' outfielder lined a fastball into the right-field seats to untie the score, end the game, and (incidentally) prove again the maxim.

THE GREAT ONE

Now here is Bobby Clemente, who has had — if there has ever been a vendetta — this might be it. Pitch to him from Palmer. And there's a ball hit very deep to right field! Going back for it is Frank Robinson. He's at the wall. He can't get it! It's gone for a home run! Bobby Clemente continues to totally annihilate Baltimore pitching!

— BOB PRINCE, October 16, 1971.

Memorial Stadium, Baltimore, MD. He shone with grace and a burning will, and with a zeal that was astonishing. By illuminating the World Series (e.g., his third-inning home run in Game Six), Roberto Clemente showed America what Pittsburgh already knew: "He had about him," said Bowie Kuhn, "the touch of royalty."

————————

The Pirates, now one out away from a clubhouse celebration. The Orioles, picked by most to win the World Series, still are within a run. One swing of the bat can tie it up . . . One-strike pitch to Rettenmund. Right up the middle, Hernandez in back of second base, throws from there! And that's the Series! Pittsburgh wins!

—Jim Simpson, 10/17/71.

Memorial Stadium. Of Clemente, Roger Angell wrote: He played "a kind of baseball that none of us had ever seen before—throwing and running and hitting at something close to the level of absolute perfection, playing to win but also playing the game as if it were a form of punishment for everyone else on the field." He flung throws like an arrow, attacked the ball with insolence, and made basket-catches at his knees; and was named Most Valuable Player as the Pirates triumphed, four games to three.

REDEMPTION FOR THE LCS

One and two. The wind and the pitch to Bench. Change—hit in the air to deep right field! Back goes Clemente! At the fence—she's gone! Johnny Bench—who hits almost every home run to left field—hits one to right! The game is tied!

—Al Michaels, October 11, 1972.

Riverfront Stadium, Cincinnati, OH. Born in 1969 and christened the "League Championship Series," these best-of-five festivals had prematurely aborted; in five of the first six playoffs, the losing team was swept. This year, though, one saw spectacle, not diversion, as the Reds and Pirates engaged in combative toil. In Game Five, with Pittsburgh three outs away from a 3-2 victory, Johnny Bench banked a Dave Giusti pitch into the right-field pavilion. Said Big John: "It's my most memorable homer ever."

————————

The stretch and the one-one pitch to McRae. In the dirt—it's a wild pitch! Here comes Foster! The Reds win the pennant! Bob Moose throws a wild pitch, and the Reds have won the National League pennant!

—A.M.

With two out in the ninth inning, the pennant led off third base. Facing pinch-hitter Hal McRae, reliever Bob Moose thrust his third pitch wildly. When the ball eluded catcher Manny Sanguillen, George Foster scored the winning run, the Reds went to the World Series, and the Pirates went home — Roberto Clemente to Puerto Rico, where he died December 31.

FIRST STIRRINGS

Fryman is set. Here's the pitch to Tenace. Line drive into left field — this may be tough to score on. Here's Hendrick around third. Here's the throw coming on into the plate. He's safe! The ball is dropped — ball is dropped by Freehan! And Oakland moves into the lead, 2 to 1, on Gene Tenace's first hit of the playoffs!

— JIM WOODS, October 12, 1972.

Tiger Stadium, Detroit, MI. In the American League playoff, the Tigers and A's collided — twice opting for extra innings; dividing the first four games. One day earlier, scoring three runs in the tenth inning, Detroit had trimmed the Mustachios, 4–3. This afternoon, breaking an 0-for-fifteen spell, Gene Tenace gave the A's a fourth-inning, Game-Five lead.

Tony Taylor moves up to the plate. The count is two balls, two strikes. There are two down, there's a runner at first base. Vida gets set. He kicks high, he throws. There's a drive into center field. Back goes Hendrick. He is under it! The Swinging A's have won the American League championship! The Oakland A's are champions!

— MONTE MOORE.

Not since 1931, before deserting Philadelphia for Kansas City and, then, the Bay, had the Athletics outflanked the American League. Now, in the year of the springtime strike, the extravagance of Steve Carlton (who won twenty-seven of the last-place Phillies' fifty-nine victories), and, less splendidly, the roily complexities of owner Charles O. Finley, they ruled. The final score, final game: A's 2, Tigers 1.

DYNASTY (INCEPTION)

One out in the scoreless Oakland fifth. Hits this one a long way to left field down the line! Rose looking up! It is — gone! Home run, Tenace!

— JIM SIMPSON, October 19, 1972.

Oakland Coliseum, Oakland, CA. Reserve catcher Gene Tenace, whose two home runs in the World Series opener had quelled Cincinnati, tagged fourth-game pitcher Don Gullett for yet another souvenir. Ultimately, the A's scored twice in the ninth inning to win, 3–2.

McGlothlin is ready, throws. Long drive — left field! Back goes Rose, looks up. Home run! His fourth of the Series! It's 3 to 1, Oakland!

—J.S., 10/20/72.

Oakland Coliseum. "There you go again." Erasing an early deficit, Tenace launched a three-run stiletto in the second inning of Game Five, only to see the Reds prevail, 5–4, and thwart elimination. With Oakland leading, three games to two, the road show returned to Cincinnati.

Rose steps in. He is two-for-four today and has made great contact all four times. The other two were driven deep to the center-field wall . . . Fly ball, deep left field! Rudi goes back near the warning track, is there. The World Series is over! And on one pitch, Rose is out and the underdog Oakland Athletics win their first championship since they were in Philadelphia in 1930! The A's win it, 3 to 2!

—J.S., 10/22/72.

Riverfront Stadium, Cincinnati, OH. A Series to shout about. Of its seven acts, six were one-run decisions; Gino Tenacci had nine runs batted in and Joe Rudi made a game-saving catch; the Reds lost their first two games at home and still almost triumphed; both clubs batted .209 against effulgent pitching; and their evocative imagery — clean-shaven v. hirsute, Kiwanis v. camp, gray/white conventional garb v. green-and-gold habiliments — announced a classic Fall Classic.

DYNASTY (CONTINUED)

There's a little looper out to Campaneris. The A's are the world champs! Oakland has won it again!

—CURT GOWDY, October 21, 1973.

Oakland Coliseum, Oakland, CA. Three days earlier, in Willie Mays' last Oktoberfest, Oakland left New York, trailing, three games to two. Back home, the A's tied the drama with a 3–1 conquest of Tom Seaver; then, banishing Mets' pretensions, 5–2, they became the first team since the 1961–62 Yankees to win back-to-back World Series.

Von Joshua is up. If the A's win, we'll go immediately to the Oakland A's locker room and the presentation. Here, it could be — he [Gene Tenace] caught it — and the A's are world champions! Rollie Fingers put 'em down one-two-three! The Oakland A's are the first team since the New York Yankees to win three world championships in a row!

—C.G., 10/17/74.

Oakland Coliseum. In a chronicle replete with contentious baseball (four games ended 3–2), the A's closed out Los Angeles in five installments. By winning the first all-California World Series, this band of quarrelsome athletes (united only by ambition, ability, and aversion to their owner) completed a trilogy of Series adventures as arrestive as the personae themselves.

THE OLD ORDER PASSETH

Now here is Henry Aaron. This crowd is up all around. The pitch to him . . . bounced it up there, ball one. Henry Aaron in the second inning walked and scored. He's sitting on 714. Here's the pitch by Downing . . . swinging . . . There's a drive into left-center field! That ball is gonna be . . . outa here! It's gone! It's 715! There's a new home-run champion of all time! And it's Henry Aaron! The fireworks are going! Henry Aaron's coming around third! His teammates are at home plate! Listen to this crowd!

— MILO HAMILTON, April 8, 1974.

Atlanta-Fulton County Stadium, Atlanta, GA. What was Joe Friday's badge number on the television program "Dragnet"? The show's star, Jack Webb, was a baseball zealot; his badge read "714." At 9:07 P.M., in his second time at bat, in the Braves' first home game, Henry Aaron — of whom Stan Musial said, "He thinks there's nothing he can't hit" — lofted a fly ball toward the sullen Georgia sky. When the ball descended, it cleared the fence, and Aaron had eclipsed a hero, breaking the unbreakable: the career home-run record of the Sultan of Swat.

A CADILLAC CAMPAIGN

And there goes a shot deep to right field! High in the air, and we watch this one go into the upper deck! His third home run of the night as he goes five-for-six with three home runs and ten runs batted in!

— NED MARTIN, June 19, 1975.

Tiger Stadium, Detroit, MI. Perhaps not since Joe DiMaggio (with whom he was often, if impulsively, compared) had a rookie so riveted the American League. In a hostile Tigers' den, Fred Lynn evoked the Evening of the Year.

Lee getting the sign from Blackwell. Pitch to Graig Nettles. Swings, drive to left-center field. May be a gapper! Lynn is running, Lynn is going! He's got it in a great catch! A great catch by Freddie Lynn! Oh, mercy, what a catch by Lynn! He outran that ball in the alley in left-center and Red Sox' fans are going ape out here . . . This is World Series time!

— N.M., 7/27/75.

Shea Stadium, New York, NY. Touring the American League, its future Most Valuable Player helped New England's pride/problem thrive. In 1974, Boston had endured a September catalepsy; now, after "what a catch by Lynn!" the Red Sox led the Yankees by a season-high ten lengths.

TWILIGHT OF THE GODS

Fly ball, deep left-center field. Way back! Toward the wall! Toward the screen! It is up into the screen! Home run — Yastrzemski!

— NED MARTIN, October 5, 1975.

Fenway Park, Boston, MA. The three-time champion A's, having bowed to El Tianté in the opening match of the A.L. playoff ("Luis Tiant," said Reggie Jackson, "is the Fred Astaire of baseball"), renewed command in Game Two. Oakland led, 3-0, when Carl Yastrzemski, batting in the fourth inning, launched a netfinder to the opposite field. His drive struck high above the Green Monster and brought Boston within a run.

———————

Fingers with a full count of three and two. Here's the delivery. Fly ball, left field. Don't know whether it's deep enough or not. And Rudi will watch it go into the screen for a home run! Rico Petrocelli has homered into the screen! Boston leads, 5 to 3, and Fenway Park is an absolute madhouse!

— JIM WOODS.

Yaz's poke, in any park but Fenway, would perhaps have been an out. Ditto, three innings later, for Rico Petrocelli, another veteran to whom the Wall gave life. Final score: 6-3, Red Sox; now leading, two games to zero.

———————

Bando at third, Jackson on at first. Drago is set. Here's the pitch. Ground ball hit down to Burleson, on to Doyle for one, on to first. They've got two!

— J.W., 10/7/75.

Oakland Coliseum, Oakland, CA. They fell valiantly, these Finleys of legend and song, not with a win but with a rally. Down, 5-1, six outs from elimination, the A's scored twice in the eighth inning, Game Three, and brought the lead run to the plate. Joe Rudi then hit a sharp bouncer to shortstop Rick Burleson, who began a double play — the noble 6-4-3 — that ended the Oakland dynasty. Boston won, 5-3, and, incredibly, swept the Championship Series.

THE GREATEST WORLD SERIES GAME EVER PLAYED

Swung on, a fly ball deep into right-center field. Griffey is back to the bull pen and it is gone, a home run! Freddie Lynn has hit one out of here to deep right-center field with two men on base and the Red Sox have bolted out in front at 3 to 0.

— MARTY BRENNAMAN, October 21, 1975.

Fenway Park, Boston, MA. After trying for three days, unsuccessfully, to play Game Six of the Reds-Red Sox' World Series, an easterly vanished, the weather cleared, and in the first inning — plating Carl Yastrzemski and Carlton Fisk — Fred Lynn lost a baseball in the bleachers beyond the Boston bull pen.

There goes Morgan. There's a fly ball to deep center. That ball is off the wall! It'll score two runs. And Foster has doubled off the top of the center-field wall and nearly had a home run.

— CURT GOWDY.

In the seventh inning, one victory from a world title, the Reds went ahead, 5-3.

Geronimo hits a high drive down the right-field line. That one's deep and it is a . . . home run for Cesar Geronimo! Right down the line it went and dropped into the right-field grandstand. And the Reds now lead, 6 to 3.

— C.G.

In inning eight, insurance.

Two balls, two strikes. The pitch. Carbo hits a high drive! Deep center! Home run! . . . [bedlam for fifteen seconds] . . . Bernie Carbo has hit his second pinch-hit home run of this Series. That was a blast up in the center-field bleachers. It came with two out and the count two and two. And the Red Sox have tied it, 6 to 6!

— C.G.

Barely fouling off the previous pitch, thereby avoiding an eighth-inning strikeout, pinch-hitter Bernardo Carbo arced a memorable, epochal, unfathomable drive.

The Reds have the infield in, the outfield very shallow. And the pitch. There's a high fly ball down the left-field line. It's going to be close. It is . . . caught by Foster. Here's the tag! Here's the throw! He's out! A double play! A double play — Foster throws him out!

— C.G.

Quintessentially, the Sox. In the ninth inning, with the bases loaded and none out, Denny Doyle — ignoring the entreaties of his third-base coach — tried to score on a short pop fly. He was doubled at the plate; the game remained 6-6.

The pitch. There's a long shot! Back goes Evans — back, back! And . . . what a grab! Evans made a grab and saved a home run on that one!

—C.G.

Two innings later, the Reds. With one out and one on, Joe Morgan pulled a curveball toward right field — good for two bases, surely, and possibly a triple or home run. But Dwight Evans, sprinting wildly toward the bleachers, intercepted the ball and threw to first base, completing a double play.

Game tied, 6-6, Darcy pitching. Fisk takes high and inside, ball one. Freddie Lynn on deck. There have been numerous heroics tonight, both sides. The one-0 delivery to Fisk. He swings. Long drive, left field! If it stays fair, it's gone! Home run! The Red Sox win! And the Series is tied, three games apiece! . . . [Curt Gowdy]: Carlton Fisk has hit a one-nothing pitch. They're jamming out on the field . . . His teammates are waiting for him. And the Red Sox have sent the World Series into Game Seven with a dramatic 7 to 6 victory. What a game! This is one of the greatest World Series games of all time!

—NED MARTIN, 10/22/75.

A snapshot for the ages. Leading off the bottom of the twelfth, the game now four hours old, Carlton Fisk lanced a blow that was far enough, but was the baseball fair or foul? It caromed off the left-field foul pole; it was a game-winning, Series-tying, Falstaffian home run; the Fens were alive with music; the Red Sox lived.

11

Free Again

(1976–88)

"It is easier to go down a hill than up, but
the view is from the top."
— Arnold Bennett

THEY PASSED *Go* WITH A HOPE, THESE NEXT THIRTEEN SEASONS OF BIG-LEAGUE broadcasting — the hope that radio and, particularly, network television would reclaim baseball's foothold as the Everest of Sports U.S.A. It was a hope not easily or totally fulfilled, and I would find it hard to say, today, that in these years baseball again turned all-consuming, as it was in my early-sixties childhood, or reassumed its shape as the athletic Holy Land, the kindly light that led. What I do believe, however, is that baseball mattered to tens of millions of Americans to a remarkable, even passionate, degree lacking in the early 1970s; mattered because it was still exquisitely second-guessable and composed of sudden, dramatic starts and because, unlike the pastime's pre-October 1975 Dead Sea of a Decade, people could again *see* and *hear* the damned game. Given what came before, that was a considerable achievement.

"It'll take something different for baseball in prime time to work," Roone Arledge proclaimed in March 1976 as American Broadcasting Company colleagues applauded in the background. "A different approach, a different twist." To its credit, ABC knew what the vulnerabilities were — the yawning lull between pitches, the sport's often dawdling tempo, the screen's inability to encase the field — and its twist *was* different. It employed the Gunner, briefly, tossed in Warner Wolf, sprinkled heavily with Bob Uecker's humor, leavened with Busby Berkeley, and prescribed increasing doses of Howard Cosell. "It won't be easy," Arledge, then ABC Sports president, said about "Monday Night Baseball," "but it can succeed." It wasn't, of course (as ratings verified), and it didn't (not entirely, as Arledge hoped), and by mid-season ABC accosted the same reality to which NBC had already deferred: Seeking *fashionability*, baseball after dark, as seen through the regular-season prism of network television, must content itself with *respectability*.

It was a philosophy of limits — of baseball caught between the brilliance of Ol' Diz and his "Game of the Week" and the mortuary summoning of 1965–75; its radio and television coming not all but most of the way back — and somehow in keeping with the age. For 1976 was a disenchanting year of *purlieu*, of adapting to the actuality of things running out — a time, also, in which Jimmy Carter was elected the thirty-ninth president of the United

409

States. Triumphant Israeli commandos rescued 104 hostages at Uganda's
Entebbe Airport; twenty-nine persons attending an American Legion convention in Philadelphia died of a mysterious ailment called "Legionnaires'
Disease"; with a glorious burst of fireworks, 6 million people celebrated the nation's two hundredth birthday by watching a grand flotilla of tall ships in
New York Harbor. Americans found passing fancy in discomania and citizens-
band radio. On screen, *Taxi Driver* and *Rocky* buoyed movie theatres. Chicago
authored "If You Leave Me Now," a lambent ode to lost faith and the pain and
joy of relationships. Said Elizabeth Ray: "I can't type, I can't file, I can't even
answer the phone." Said the president-elect: "I'll never lie to you." Said almost
everyone: "Have a nice day."

In early 1976, Bob Prince, publicly, intended to. "I'll be rooting for the game
when we go on national television," said "Monday Night Baseball's" play-by-
play announcer. "We're going to humanize the game, go after younger viewers
local baseball attracts, and convert people who claim they're not interested in
baseball or don't know anything about the game." Yet there was an insecurity
beneath his usual *sang-froid*, a small grain of self-doubt, so telling in retrospect,
that what had played in Pittsburgh would wash in Washington, D.C.; doubt
too that an expansive local announcer, at fifty-nine, could adjust his style and
habits to the corporate standards of 1330 Avenue of the Americas, New York.

"I remember having dinner with Bob in spring training '76, and afterward
I was driving him back to the hotel," Jim Woods reminisced, "and all of a sudden he said, 'Poss, pull the car over for a minute.' I did, he sat there, and finally
said, 'You know, I wouldn't say this to anyone else, but I'm worried as hell about
this ABC thing.' "

"Looking back," I said, "he had reason to be."

"He knew he'd never done anything regularly on a network level, and that
ABC had picked him because they wanted the entertainment, the songs-and-
trumpets approach," Woods said. "Whatever else he is, Bob ain't dull, and ABC
thought he'd give the game a lift on the tube it hadn't had with Gowdy."

"So why the anxiety?"

" 'Cause it was all so *new*," he said. "I told him, 'Look, Bob, I know it's not
going to be easy, but you gotta make some changes. You can't *do* what you've
done in Pittsburgh. You can't go doing a "Rosey Ramble," talking about playing golf with Bing Crosby last night — nobody'll give a damn.' I think he knew,
even then, he was going to have problems converting his zaniness to the con-
strictions of network TV — promo this, say that, the producer always carping
in your ear. He tried to make the transition, he really did," and grew increasingly unhappy: The broadcast life around him was different from what
he knew.

Originally, the Gunner was assigned all of "MNB's" balls and strikes. "They
hired me to do 100 percent of the play-by-play," he said. "That was my clear
understanding." He was its Voice but not its anchor, for in March 1976, Arledge
blazoned Warner Wolf as the host of the ABC-christened "A" team.

A Washingtonian, Wolf had left that city's Channel 9 the previous year to be
"a kind of [series] interlocutor," wrote Kay Gardella in the *New York Daily News.*

"He'll supply the snappy patter and keep the show on the road." By then, Warner's road had zigged from his 1937 Armistice Day hatching (his father and mother were born on the Fourth of July and Labor Day and were married on Thanksgiving) to hot, glazy afternoons at Griffith Stadium (his boyhood announcer, Arch McDonald) to college at American University (he had a weekly radio show) and, eventually, stations in Pikeville, Kentucky, Martinsburg, West Virginia, and Silver Spring, Maryland. At twenty-seven, he moved to Washington's WTOP, about to launch a new concept called "Talk Radio," and then to the same-lettered TV affiliate. Wolf was aggressive, gee-whiz, and impertinent, "the bushy-haired interrogator," teased columnist Morris Siegel; he begot such catchwords as "Boom!," "Swish," "Boo of the week," and "Hey, gimme a break!"; as an evening sportscaster and the color or play-by-play man for the Senators, Redskins, Bullets, and Capitals, he became a capit(a)(o)l VIP.

Warner, it was hoped, would balance the Gunner's calculated lunacy with slick and spirited chatter. Meanwhile, Roone explained, "color commentary" would revert to the "A" team's other member—a flip and imaginative ex-receiver who despaired of mediocrity as a player and flaunted it thereafter, and who outlasted Prince and Wolf and, ultimately, outshone the series: "The man famous chiefly for being locked out of a tavern in a beer commercial, a television personality who made his debut on 'The Superstars' by swimming out of the Atlantic Ocean in a double-breasted jacket and slacks," read the erudite *People* magazine, "a guy who has parlayed a .200 lifetime batting average into a six-figure career as an after-dinner speaker, night club comedian, 'The Tonight Show' regular and author of an autobiography entitled [with no apologies to J.D. Salinger] *Catcher In the Wry*."

Let me admit it: I was (and remain) a Bob Uecker habitué. A native Milwaukean and self-made clown, he prepped for broadcasting as the 1962–67 backup backstop of the Braves, Cardinals, and Phillies. "I used to sit in the bull pen talking into a beer cup," he said in his dead-pan way. "Of course, a lot of the stuff you couldn't say on the radio." Not content with expletives undeleted, he shagged fly balls with a tuba, fielded as adeptly as he hit (his "specialty" was handling the knuckleball), and envisioned himself, in that afterlife beyond the playing field, as a Will Rogers with a jockstrap, a Joe Garagiola with hair. In 1968, Uecker retired and joined the Braves' public-relations staff; he would evangelize the South on the rubber-chicken circuit; at banquets in Savannah and Jackson and Tallahassee, his gelastic delivery was a smash. "I did stand-up, weird and ignorant stuff about my career—anything for a laugh. Believe me, even back when I was bumbling around, just getting started, anyone who ever saw me play knows I had plenty of material."

Then, one night Uke performed at friend Al Hirt's *Atlanta* night club, and Bob's power of humor transformed the audience into surprised and vigorous supporters. His success led to the early-seventies Merv Griffin and Mike Douglas Shows, the podium of the celebrious Friars Club, and in 1970, to the first of more than seventy-five appearances on Johnny Carson's "The Tonight Show."

"How do you catch a knuckleball?" Uke asked his NBC viewers. "You just wait till it stops rolling and pick it up." How harsh are fans in Philadelphia? "So bad that when there's no game scheduled they go out to the airport and boo good landings." As a player, when did he know it was time to quit? "When the manager looked at me and said, 'No visitors in the clubhouse.' " Who held the big-league record for passed balls? Uke did. "But it had a good side too. I got to meet a lot of people in the box seats." He was not simply an ex-jock turned mikeward; he was a comic and, increasingly, a professional. Through his ardor and faculty, even scripted monologues seemed cheerfully offhand. Which manager best understood him? "Gene Mauch," he'd chime. "When I was with the Phillies, he used to say to me, 'Get a bat, and stop this rally.' Or, 'Forget the bat, and try for a walk.' " Which teams respected him? "None of 'em," he said. "I wouldn't say the other clubs regarded me lightly, but it never was reassuring to go up in the ninth inning, look into the visitors' dugout, and see everybody in street clothes against us." But his parents, surely *they* had been exponents. "Nah, my mom was always critical of my play. She was always saying, 'Why don't you get a job?' " And his father? "There was a *real* fan. He booed me too."

Ah, those fans, flashing ahead to Miller Lite beer, he loved 'em, and as early as December 1971, when Uke returned to the Braves' ex-haunt, joining Merle Harmon and Tom Collins over the Milwaukee Brewers' Radio/Television Network, and began the career that spurred him to a mid-eighties niche, wrote *Sports Illustrated*, as "the funniest man — Joe Garagiola included — in sports broadcasting," the reverse was also valid.

At first, subdued and aimless, Uecker practiced deficit broadcasting, stumbling, oddly, over extempore material. "It's amazing to think of now, given his great ability, but Bob's problem then was in finding stuff to ad-lib," Collins said. "He'd constantly repeat the count and the score, and swing his legs like a pendulum, and smoke cigarette after cigarette." But he worked and improved and "didn't try to wisecrack my way through," Uke noted, and welding an identity separate from that which, one day, would charm Madison Avenue — "Uecker," radio/TV critic William Taaffe observed, "[is] the man who made mediocrity famous" — he surfaced as the Voice of the Brewers in 1980, the Wisconsin Sportcaster of the Year two years later, and a full course of seamless facts, stories, and asides. "People who know him through his comedy expect him to be like that on the air and they're surprised when he's not," said Bill Haig, the Brewers' vice-president of broadcasting. "When he's up on stage, he's a comedian. When he's on the radio, he's one of the best four or five play-by-play men in the business."

Actor or announcer? Fad figure or baseball man? Self-parody or flesh and bones? One recalled the repartee of Henry Cabot Lodge, then U.S. ambassador to the United Nations, after his Soviet counterpart objected to being called a *gentleman* (but not to the moniker *delegate*). "I had hoped," Lodge said, icily, "the two were not mutually exclusive." Was it a question, then, of cognomens, guises, or both? "Uecker," Taaffe wrote in 1984, "has always worn two faces. The one less known is that of the real Bob Uecker . . . the catcher-turned-broadcaster who has been the Voice of the Brewers for thirteen years. The other is the make-believe Bob Uecker, the poor knucklehead who keeps getting locked out of bars and dumped on by fans in Lite Beer from Miller commercials . . . that gave him something of a cult following on campuses. Outside the booth . . . Uecker's schtick is basically this: He's so dense and such a blowhard, yet so completely out of it—after all, he doesn't even *know* that people are on to him—that he's lovable. He's self-effacing and eternally optimistic. What a wonderful jerk!"

Two faces, both attractive, and in early 1976, seeking to uprear the style and content of "MNB," Roone Arledge *purchased* both. "I thought we'd be great," Uke conceded. "I'd heard good things about Warner, the Gunner was a legend, and I knew what I could do. In my own mind there was no doubt—the series would be a hit." Somehow, it was more miss and error; failing to arouse the attention of Bicentennial America, the sum of its parts proved greater than the whole.

Why ABC's "A" team failed—"Let me say this," Warner wrote in his autobiography, "Uecker, Prince, and I were not the greatest on-the-air combination"—remains open to conjecture, even now.

Most glaringly, perhaps, the network's camera work was atrocious; game-action shots blew fly balls, the simple 4–6–3, and routine run-down plays; the Network of the Olympics found baseball a Chinese puzzle. "I felt sorry for them," said NBC's Harry Coyle, generously. "Baseball is a terrifically difficult game to televise well—the action's not all in one spot like football, it's scattered around the field. You have to anticipate, to know what's wrapped up in a double steal, where the shortstop is on a relay throw, who's backing up, for example, and that means you have to know the game."

"And you're saying they didn't," I said.

"We'd been doing baseball for so long. They hadn't been doing it for years," he said. "It showed."

Then too, Wolf's role was ill-defined; he would sign on and off, read promos, serve as Uke's straight man, and host—but what? This was baseball, not Phil Donahue. Worse, Prince himself seemed confused and often tentative— "It was one tough son-of-a-bitch transition to the network," he said. "Plus, to be honest, I didn't know the American League teams that well"—and Uke, burdened by the clutter of on-air voices, found *each* of his faces defaced. With the Gunner on play-by-play, balls and strikes were out of bounds. On the other hand, the concept of three-in-the-booth made Uke's stream-of-consciousness humor impossible. "Looking back, if I'd just done play-by-play, or if I'd been the humorist with just one other guy in the booth, not two," he said once, "we'd have been better off. But ABC, I think, having seen how three guys [Cosell, Don Meredith, and Frank Gifford] had been perfect for 'Monday Night Football,' now thought they would transfer that to baseball [Prince, to rival Frank; Uke, to ape Dandy Don; Wolf, one guesses, to imitate Humble Howard], not realizing they're different kinds of sports and need a different treatment."

There was also the fact, quickly evidenced through its producer, Don

Ohlmeyer, that ABC was a network which neither much liked nor understood The Game.

"It wasn't just the camera work, though that was bad enough," the Gunner was saying. "The lousiest part, as far as I was concerned, was that none of the ABC people had any affinity — emotionally, culturally — with the kind of game baseball was or what it took to cover it. All they knew was college football and the NFL — *that's* what they thought was important."

"How do you mean?"

"The guy who ran the show was Ohlmeyer," a mercurial presence who later became the executive producer of NBC Sports. "He was a pain in the ass, and he didn't know a damn thing about baseball. Worse, he didn't care. Uke, Warner, me — we all felt that way."

Their feelings toward Ohlmeyer, warmed by ABC's first-year coals of hope for "MNB," turned into a collective chill as ratings, after an early-season upward flutter, began, though not as sharply as pre-1976, to slide.

Typical of the network's desire to avoid just that outcome, Arledge had featured New York teams at the center of his first two broadcasts — the Yankees v. Baltimore on April 12, the Mets at St. Louis the following week, each beamed back to the Apple. "As part of our new contract, remember, ABC had insisted upon lifting the blackout rule," baseball's then-media director, John Lazarus, remarked, "so that, beginning in '76, any game of a club from the biggest markets *could* be piped back to its viewers. We knew early on that ABC would link baseball and New York teams as often as they could. The reason was obvious enough — to maximize the audience." It made little difference; by June 8, reviewing the Gunner's night-before return to Pittsburgh (during the televised Reds-Pirates' game, the message board welcomed Prince back to Three Rivers Stadium, the crowd spewed out a two-minute ovation, and after bowing several times and triumphantly waving a babushka, Prince, struggling to speak, said, "I have to apologize to Warner and Uke and turn over my mike." Added Wolf: "That applause, for a broadcaster, I've never seen anything like it"), even the home-town *Post-Gazette* noted rumors of ABC's proximate decision to jettison the crew. " 'Monday Night Baseball,' " it read, "has not been an overwhelming success. Ratings are low, negative reviews rampant."

Three weeks later, having misgauged the chemistry of its trio of personalities, ABC managed to flaunt insensitivity to baseball as a sport. "We were in Detroit for a Yankees-Tigers' game," Prince said, "and we found out that Mark Fidrych was going to pitch that night." A near-anonymity at season's start, Fidrych — named "the Bird" after the "Sesame Street" TV character — had now become a sacrament: talking to the ball, cavorting on the mound, and packing big-league stadia on his rookie stage. He was refreshing and unaffected, so *different*; his appeal spun far beyond baseball's boundaries. "We were just delighted — we could showcase the kid before a national audience." What a break for ABC, what *timing*. This chickabiddy against the big, bad (again, at last, first-place) Yankees. What a Frank Capra, G-rated, Made-in-USA storyline.

Don Ohlmeyer took one look at the Fidrych manuscript and promptly threw it out.

"He didn't know Mark Fidrych from Mark Twain, even with all the publicity the kid had already gotten," the Gunner huffed. "We go in the morning of the game for a meeting to determine the opening of the show, right? Well, obviously, Fidrych is the guy you want to spotlight. So Ohlmeyer says, 'Kenny Holtzman is pitching for the Yankees. We gotta open the show with Holtzman.' "

"How'd you guys handle it?" I said.

"We couldn't believe it. Warner was there and he said, 'Look, how can we not go with Fidrych? The game is sold out tonight because of him. People are lining up to buy tickets when he pitches. And the guy, the way he acts — having conversations with the ball between pitches, talking with his infielders, patting the pitching mound like a gardener.' And Ohlmeyer says, 'You just don't understand. We only open with the big names here. A Reggie Jackson, an O. J. Simpson. Nobody knows who this guy is.' "

"Did he budge?"

"We said, 'Don, they may not know who he is now — of course, a lot of people do — but *everyone* will after tonight. We can open with shots of him warming up, tell how he behaves, why he's getting bigger every day,' " Prince said. "But it was no go with Ohlmeyer. 'We need a name,' he said. The baseball — it was totally incidental."

That night, June 28, Mark Fidrych became a name. The Bird beat the Yankees, 5-1; afterward, shook hands with Tigers' regulars as they neared the dugout; and minutes later, returning to the field when the crowd refused to leave, acknowledged what is believed to be the first nationally televised sports curtain call. "Folks," Wolf exulted over ABC, "they're not going to stop clapping until the Bird comes back from the dugout. . . . This is fantastic! Mark Fidrych is born tonight on coast-to-coast television."

Yet, even then, ABC's top broadcast team was afflicted by the physical inevitability of death. For Prince, the end came in phases, like alcoholism or the gout. He was reduced, first, to six innings of play-by-play each Monday, then three, and in September 1976 was relieved of his contract. "We greatly appreciate the time and effort involved in 'Monday Night Baseball,' " a network flack said of Bob and ex-Tiger Norm Cash, a member, like Al Michaels and Bob Gibson, of the ABC backup, or "B," team, "but they do not fit into our playoff plans." Wolf did, barely, and covered the National League series; the next year, sliced to three "B" and "C" (backwater backup) games, he drifted slowly from the scene. Gibson's demise was more abrupt, dating from an August 9 broadcast out of western Pennsylvania. That night, John Candelaria threw the first Pirates' no-hitter in Pittsburgh since 1907, then was interviewed by the ex-Cardinals' pitcher. Gibson was halting and unprepared; his expression appeared almost stricken; and to an audience deserving of at least *au fait* questioning, he asked everything, it seemed, you never wanted to know. Was the Candy Man nervous? Was his family at the game? How much extra money and what kind of bonuses might the hero reap from his display? "There's really no excuse," Ohlmeyer would concede. "He's a professional, and he's paid to do a job. We threw Bobby into something he wasn't quite ready for." Watching at home, one cringed for Bullet Bob.

After its burst of April optimism, "Monday Night Baseball" tumbled to a final regular-season rating of 12.6—unimpressive against the NFL's 1976 prime-time average of 21.1; a thumbed nose at those, predicting, as we had, success by ABC where NBC had failed. Scrambling to rearrange that figure, Arledge unveiled his lineup for the playoffs: to broadcast the Cincinnati-Philadelphia final, Wolf, Tom Seaver, and Michaels; starting for the Royals and Yankees, Uecker, Keith Jackson, and Howard Cosell.

Jackson had called play-by-play, one will recollect, for ABC's 1965 baseball "Game of the Week." Returning, presently, to a form of big-league *Anschluss*, the son of Georgia and tall ex-Marine handled the assignment with the same dignity and professionalism that accented his network treatment of college football, the NBA, the first year of "Monday Night Football," boxing, auto racing, and other vignettes on "Wide World of Sports," and, at the time, two Olympiads. In 1972, he distinguished himself as the Voice of Mark Spitz' seven gold medals at the Munich Games; eight years later, he would showcase the unprecedented five gold-medal victories of speed skater Eric Heiden. Jackson was a bubbling corn-pone type of mouthpiece. He was good, in a way Vichy baseball announcers seldom are, and fertilized ABC's coverage of the '76 Championship Series (also, that network's airing of the 1977–82 regular season, 1978, 1980, and 1982 League Championship Series, and 1977, 1979, and 1981 World Series). But his heart was never really in it. After all, Jackson was of the deep South and a good ol' boy, and his rich, lyric voice was of a piece with his region's wild devotion to the weekly beat and wholesome vespers of college football. His style was down-home, and his homes were Auburn, LSU, and the University of Alabama, not Fenway Park or Wrigley Field. In late 1982, ripping his "embarrassing lack of baseball knowledge," *Sports Illustrated* advised Keith's network: "[In the future] don't have your play-by-play man moan about a) his travel schedule or b) how he's missing his first college football Saturday in twenty years, which was Jackson's lament. He may not want to watch baseball, but presumably, his viewers do." By and by, ABC dropped the five-time national Sportscaster of the Year from baseball, pleasing Jackson and, presumably, *SI*. Did he miss it? a reporter asked in early 1984. "Baseball?" Jackson asked, rhetorically. "You know, someone put the same question to me at a function Howard Cosell and I were at together." By then, Cosell had removed *his* voice from much of ABC's big-league coverage. "He looked at me and I looked at Him, and we both came up with the same answer. We laughed."

Laughter, roused even more than experienced, was not unindigenous to Cosell—that is, along with ridicule, hate, respect, exasperation, disparagement, hypocrisy, and not a little envy.

There is no need, here, to recount the folk story of Humble Howard. He, Himself, has said it all, and had others say it for Him. They have told of his Brooklyn boyhood, passion for the Dodgers, schooling at New York University

(He was an English major and Phi Beta Kappa), and service in the Army; of Cosell's subsequent return from war to Wall Street, a $30,000 salary, and respectability as a lawyer; and of his first 1950s brush with broadcasting (a Sunday morning Little League show over ABC Radio), followed by regular radio sports commentary, an ABC-TV program called "Sports Focus," boxing coverage for that network, and his 1962–63 Metropolitans' pregame show, teaming with Ralph Branca, Bobby Thomson's foil. They have, strangely, minimized Cosell's first network TV entanglement with a major-league sport—his role as host of the 1965 baseball pregame program. "At the time, Howard had been blackballed for five years from ABC for reasons [anti-Semitism? unbearability? Cosell's contrivance of a voice?] I never fully understood," Arledge pronounced in 1982. "[But] I was very impressed with the fact that, at a time when ABC didn't have the major events on the scale of CBS or NBC, Howard had more access to athletes than just about anybody. So I was determined to break down the blackball against Him. In 1965, I kind of snuck Howard onto the network by letting Him interview ballplayers. He did a helluva job. This was still a time . . . when nobody criticized anything, nobody *ever* asked an athlete a difficult question. Howard stood all that on its head."

Thereafter, in an unbelievable and, to many, inexplicable ascension to pop-celebrity status faithfully chronicled by Himself and his Boswells, it was on to heavyweight boxing fights, "Wide World of Sports," his heretical (to the country) and critical (to Cosell's career) alliance with Muhammad Ali, and, finally, in September 1970, to the series that became an institution: the frenzied and still-running "MNF." He has been brilliant and militant, obnoxious and egomaniacal, capable of abrasion and sentiment, and an extraordinary broadcast influence—a critic, gadfly, and caricature, by shifts journalist and whore. He has not been mistaken for a *baseball* announcer—not like Allen, Uke, or Michaels, or the Phillies' Harry Kalas—nor has his place been large within the game. But He *has* been, if for no reason but sheer opportunism, an unerring barometer of baseball's gut health and prestige; if you want to know how obsessive or receding its appeal, just listen to Cosell.

In the baseball of pre-1958, which is to say before the Dodgers moved west, Howard succumbed to its transcendent magic; even in the early sixties, as a fan and reporter, his knowledge of the game was extensive. But as the decade unfolded, pro football exploded, and Cosell's two baseball marriages ended—the Mets because of a mutual animus between Himself and Casey Stengel; the '65 "Game" because of frigid ratings—Howard progressively found the pastime more static and impersonal. By 1970, He was terming the big leagues "boring, a dying art—it won't outlive our grandchildren." Among the trendies and beautiful people with whom The Mouth now broke bread, it was the NFL, not baseball, that fulfilled a hunger for viscera and on-screen gore; baseball was like patriotism—an irrelevancy, antique. In 1973, anointed as a "celebrity guest," Cosell invaded the NBC booth for a Monday night "Game of the Week." He was flanked by Gowdy and Kubek; He was there, allegedly, to enliven a Red Sox-Tigers' match from Fenway Park; and while Tony acclaimed baseball's arc-lit grace, Cosell mauled the bigs—in prime time, on the *sport's own series* — as "tedious, outworn. . . . No amount of description," He counseled viewers, "can disguise the fact that this game is *lagging insufferably*." Gowdy smiled. Kubek smirked. Contented, Humble Howard chewed on his cigar. Listening to the fusillade, Bowie Kenton Kuhn set his lips and fumed.

The Mouth's distaste for baseball, in fact, became so pervasive and widely known that it shocked no one when Kuhn asked Arledge, vainly, in 1976, to bar Cosell from ABC's coverage of the Championship Series; nor was it surprising that Arledge refused (under the new contract, ABC, not baseball, could dictate announcers; whatever his foibles, Roone thought, Cosell was perfectly cast to infuse the playoff with Olympian drama) or that upon renewing his link with baseball, after a decade's absence, Howard rediscovered of a sudden its vividry and lore. He more or less ceased slamming The American Game, declared a seeming truce with Kuhn, and suppressed that part of Him which still found baseball loathsome — at bottom, I think, his genuine feeling, inclined to "Tell [in this case, "Damn"] it like it is" — under the façade of the corporate soldier who recognized this inescapable force of nature: Baseball was now a property of ABC and, as such, worthy of at least an elemental legitimacy.

To Arledge, baseball itself was nothing special. Well into the two-network pact, a columnist observed, "ABC is peerless on football, bowling, and spanning the wide world for whatever it can scrounge up for weekend afternoons. But baseball? Sorry, Keith. Sorry, Howard. Unlike . . . NBC, [which] understands the magic of baseball, [on] ABC, baseball — even the playoffs or the Series — seems to be just another sporting event." Ratings, on the other hand, *were* important, and to his mid-to-late-seventies honor, Roone promoted the pastime (as part of ABC's larger video dance, not as a separate dancer) as NBC Sports rarely had.

Baseball appeared on ABC's "World News Tonight" (during the network's first World Series, the 1977 Dodgers-Yankees' tarantella, a story about the Classic *led* one newscast); received liberal blurbs on prime-time programs (to some avail; in 1976, the "Monday Night" series averaged a 24 percent share of the total audience, surpassing NBC's previous-year share of 19 percent); saw the network imbue its October coverage with household names (e.g., Seaver, Lou Brock, Reggie Jackson, Tim McCarver, and Jim Palmer), mirroring Arledge's intent, expressed in an in-house 1960 memo, to "In short . . . ADD SHOW BUSINESS TO SPORTS"; and sent forth a hearty (more or less) *well-done* as ABC's ratings, clear into the mid-eighties, remained comparable to or higher than its rival's for the same body of events.

Of "Monday's" totals, ABC spokesman Irv Brodsky has said, "It's true our ratings aren't as good as they are for pro football, but they're higher than what the game had seen on a regular-season basis. So we're relatively [yawn] satisfied." But it was postseason where cleavage tore a blouse. For the 1976, 1978, 1980, 1982, 1984, and 1986 Autumn Occasions, NBC's Nielsen statistics were 27.5, 32.8, 32.6, 27.9, 22.9, and 28.6; in 1977, 1979, 1981, 1983, and 1985, ABC commanded figures of 29.8, 28.5, 30.0, 23.3, and 25.3 — marginally, a

Peacock edge, 28.7 to 27.4. The Championship Series ledger read: ABC, 16.3, 18.4, 20.5, 18.5, 16.2, and 15.3 (average 17.5); NBC, 18.1, 16.1, 14.4, 14.4, and 15.6 (15.7). Turning to the All-Star Game, the gap was most emphatic. Where across its first six Mid-Summer Classics, the Arledges averaged a national rating of 24.2, there was a flattened quality to NBC's post-1975 landscape; its numbers of 24.5, 24.4, 20.1, 21.5, and 20.5 (avg. 22.1) suggested that the network that loved baseball less had, ironically, profited from it more.

It was not numbers, however, but impressions that concerned viewers of televised baseball in its regular- or postseason form, and after my dismay at the Gunner's dispatching, I came to value, like daisies in a badland, the redeeming vestments of ABC's major-league coverage.

Had "Monday Night Baseball" toppled Arledge, temporarily, from the carousel of wonder that carried him through "Wide World," "Monday Night Football," and five Olympiads? Who cared? At least baseball now boasted two networks, not one. Did ABC's camera work more befit an Afghanistan camel race than The American Game? Big deal. At least their announcers formed a checkerboard of curiosa. In time, I grew fond of Jackson, ill-suited though he was to baseball, and accustomed to Cosell; there was Uke, of course, and Don Drysdale, sweeping from the Angels in the late seventies to handle commentary, and the Brooklyn-born Michaels, joining ABC at thirty-one: an intriguing variety of mouthpieces; a pasticcio of styles.

In 1983, replacing Jackson, Michaels secured the mike as "Monday's" primary play-by-play announcer—the Arledges' first *true* baseball Voice. He teamed with Cosell and Earl Weaver, the ex-Orioles' manager, but not with Drysdale, airing balls and strikes on the backup game, or Uecker, intent, as Bob was, on fulfilling fantasies far beyond the big-league orbit. By then, Uke had left ABC baseball to engage, one must call it, in the gilding of his image: sport's rejoinder to that great Gleason character, the Poor Soul, the comedic sap who "comes across like we all have sometimes in our lives, as a schnook," observed talent coordinator Marty Blackman, a representative of the Miller Lite All-Stars. "We all have memories of being rejected, of someone stomping on us."

Actually, it was Uke himself who stomped upon the limits of possibility. "The man's bigger than the game, he's bigger than the team, he's bigger than the league, he's bigger than the sport," roared Humble Howard, greasing his penchant for overstatement, in early 1983. "They talk about a new commissioner. If I had my pick, it would be you, Bob Uecker." Recalling that mini-monologue (or Uke's riposte: "Howie, I wish I had time"), I thought of Uecker at his most maverick and timeous—mimicking self and self-awareness on "Midnight Special" or "Hee Haw" or "Late Night With David Letterman"; starring in the ABC comedy series, "Mr. Belvedere," hosting ABC's "Battle of the Network Stars" and NBC's "Saturday Night Live," punctuating the movie *O.C. and Stiggs*, and releasing what passed (as in ball) for his autobiography; earning the nameplate "Mr. Baseball," saying of his career, "It was a little discouraging to me as a hitter when I'd look at the third-base coach and he'd turn his back. And the other catcher, instead of giving a signal to his pitcher, would just yell out what he wanted," and filling viewers with cheerful anticipation whenever any of his germinal Miller Lite commercials took to the air.

Even now, from a faraway space, which of these sentences beggar depiction?

"Wow! They're having a good time in there!" said Uke, staring with beagle-eyed sadness and clad in a patchwork coat which "cures hangovers [he later said] just by looking at it," of boisterous fans who locked him out of their downtown saloon.

Or . . .

"So I lied," Uecker said of his next-commercial vehicle to get *into* the saloon: impersonating Whitey Ford.

Or . . .

"You know, one of the best things about being an ex-big leaguer is getting freebies to the game. Call the front office — *bingo!*" Uke said in yet *another* spot, heading for his seat at Dodger Stadium.

Or . . .

"Oh! I must be in the front rooow!" ("No, you deluded fool, your ticket's not down there by the field," one was tempted to say when that same-commercial usher tossed Uke out of a lower-level seat.)

Or . . .

"Good seats, eh, buddy?" (See, *that's* where your ticket is: the Himalayan extremities of the upper deck.)

Using the word *truculent* one faceless Monday night, Cosell allowed that since Uke was a mere product of the jockocracy, he couldn't possibly know its meaning. "Sure, I do, Howie," Uke said. "If you had a truck and I borrowed it, that would be a truck-you-lent."

On a different occasion, turning to Uecker, Michaels asked about his father. "Oh, my pop came from the old country," was Bob's reply. "He was on the soccer team." Did his dad play goalie? Brother Al inquired. "Oh, he didn't play anything," Uke said. "He just blew up the balls. There's where I get a lot of my talent."

Had Uke, Michaels wondered, ever been thrown out of a game? "No, but I got thrown into a couple without notice." When a reporter raised the subject of orange or yellow baseballs, Uke dismissed it with a sigh. "It'd be tough. The problem is finding enough jaundiced horses to keep up with the supply of baseballs." Once, he said of his fourteen-year-old son, striking out three times in a Little League game, "I loved it. The biggest thrill a ballplayer can have is when your son takes after you." What were his five biggest thrills as a big-league athlete? Getting out of a rundown; driving home the winning run by walking with the bases loaded; watching a fan in the upper deck; showing up for most games; and catching the games on radio that he *didn't* show up for.

He became an airwaves personality in a way not even the Gunner had; self-invented, perhaps, but farcical and unique. Amid the balky, erratic, and often football-tinged beginnings of "Monday Night Baseball," Bob Uecker remains my most memorable avatar: a parody who seemed authentic, a network archetype of Everyman.

*   *   *

For baseball, its two-network era began with three yeasty and turbulent seasons, blending, as they did, stark removal from the game's plantation order (under free agency, athletes could play out an option year and sell their services to the highest bidder), old familiarity (the Yankees and Dodgers won five of the frame's six pennants), acute domination (in 1976–78, only five clubs won division titles), and the Junior Circuit's first playoff game in thirty years (October 2, 1978, Boston v. New York, the American League East).

It was an age of Mafian characters (the Bird; The Billy and Reggie Show, at once amusing and bizarre; and virtually the entire lineup of the 1976 Cincinnati Reds) and mythic moments (Chris Chambliss' blast in the ninth inning, Game Five, to give New York the '76 Championship Series; R. Jackson's long-ball parade in the next year's World Series; and Bucky Dent's soul-crushing playoff poke that delivered unto the Red Sox yet another one that got away) and prodigious deeds (the 1976 Oaklands stealing a record 341 bases; a year later, Rod Carew building a .388 average on 239 hits; and Ron Guidry going 25–3 for the 1978 Bombers while Boston's Jim Rice wafted forty-six home runs) and the bulky, bellowing two-time world champion who succeeded Charlie Finley as baseball's Bad Boy: G.M. Steinbrenner, Boss George. Five Reds started in the 1976 All-Star Game; that November, Joe Morgan won his second straight MVP Award. The next season, George Foster banged fifty-two homers (the Red Sox hit 213), the Americans expanded to Toronto and (back to) Seattle, and the Finleys fell to last. Said a National League scout the following year: "Dave Parker [its Most Valuable Player] is the closest thing to perfection." Said Billy Martin: "One [Reg-gie! Reg-gie!] is a confirmed liar and the other [Steinbrenner] is convicted." Did Dodgers' owner Peter O'Malley, echoing the Gunner, *really* say, "How sweet it is"? He *should* have; the 1978 ex-Bums became the first ball club to draw more than 3 million spectators.

It was, by any plausible reckoning, a clamorous time, and condemned by NBC Television to a post-Red Sox v. Reds' niche as a "Game of the Week" nonperson, Curt Gowdy watched from his condominium in Florida, summer home in New Hampshire, and estate in the Boston suburbs.

His baseball end had clanged suddenly, which is not to say easily, in November 1975, when Carl Lindemann boarded a plane in New York City, flew to Bangor, Maine, and informed Curt that his crisp, illuminative line of rhetoric was no longer enough. He was the Voice of network baseball; he had burned brightly for a decade, airing more than four hundred regular- and postseason games; and now this — dismissed from baseball altogether, at age fifty-six, in favor of Joe Garagiola.

"What it came down to was leverage, to the fact that money talks," said Lindemann. "Both Chrysler and baseball wanted Garagiola. And not for any one-half the play-by-play, like in '75 — they wanted the regular season, the Series, everything. And because of my position as the head of NBC Sports, I was selected to present one of my very dearest friends with his head on a platter—me, the one guy who'd kept arguing with Kuhn and our sports people, who'd tried to keep Gowdy on the 'Game.' "

"How'd you tell him?" I said.

"I'd known it was coming—the decision to put Joe on as Number One. That's what made the '75 World Series so poignant—it was so great, it involved Gowdy's Red Sox, and I watched it knowing, as Curt didn't, that this was going to be his last baseball for NBC," he said.

"Then you dropped the bomb."

"I flew up to Bangor, where Curt was doing an 'American Sportsman' show with Brooks Robinson. We go back to the hotel room afterward and I tell him, 'Curt, it's all over, you're out.' And he was shocked. Then I had to fly down to their winter home in Palm Beach and tell his wife. The whole thing—I hated doing it."

After Gowdy's Peacock "Game" lifework slid headlong into memory, Curt returned to college basketball and the NFL, was invited by the network to serve as a "roving reporter" on the 1978 World Series—"It was embarrassing," said a past NBC director, "to stick a guy of that caliber with such a minor assignment. For Curt, it was the final straw"—and the next April, consigning NBC to yesterday, he inked a three-year contract with CBS Television.

For two years, teaming with former coach Hank Stram, he handled pro football play-by-play, then left "with no hard feelings. There's no big unhappiness on my part that I'm not going back." His new destination was an old friend, and over CBS Radio Gowdy called five eighties baseball playoffs and the 1985–86 "Game of the Week." In this way, he never entirely left the network broadcast field; the critics were kinder than during those final taunting years at NBC; and though Curt would have preferred to complete his career on national television, the technical demands of the wireless refocused for a new generation of listeners the generous dimensions of Gowdy's reportorial skill.

The Cowboy, I knew, had always loved baseball's siren song on radio; yet as opposed to television, the medium stashed exposure in the closet. Two blocks away, at 30 Rockefeller Plaza, Curt's successor as NBC's principal baseball announcer embroidered his reputation as a Man of the People, a pastiche of gags and darts and recollections: as reliable as a Univac punch-line machine and earthy as his boyhood in the Dago Hill section of St. Louis. Publicly, at least, the prototypal (forgive me) Average Joe.

Two decades earlier, *Variety* had christened Mel Allen's as one of the twenty-five "most recognizable voices in the world." By the time Joe Garagiola aired his first "Game of the Week" as its undivided Voice—April 10, 1976; Cincinnati 13, Houston 7—he rivaled Yul Brynner for the most recognizable bald pate in America. He was splashy—far more than Gowdy—and more complicated than his image. A vivid storyteller, his sense of humor could bring an audience to tears. When the Cowboy toppled, Garagiola had already been a baseball broadcaster for more than twenty years. Less intense as a stylist than in the 1950s, he was still outspoken and, above all, proud—proud of his roots, of his career, of his place on the network scene.

According to official records, Garagiola was born on February 12, 1926, the son of a father who worked in a brickyard and a mother, "a dear, loving, simple woman," Joe said, "who could not speak English." *De facto*, though, he evolved in the evolutionary chain from Jay Hanna Jerome Dean.

It was Ol' Diz who preceded Joe as a Cardinals' ballplayer, then Redbirds' announcer, then the quintessence of the ex-jock behind the mike; Dean who evinced that laughter and personality could soar above bare hits, runs, and errors; Diz who showed how the public would enfold rhetoric that lightened, not solemnized, The Game. Dean, of course, apotheosized Middle America; he was homespun and heartland. Joe's ethnicity colored his being; "if you tie an Italian's arms," he often said, "you render him mute." Dean's humor was broader, more biting, and forever grammatically errant; Joe was more reliant on patterned ad-libs. A performer, the Great One was incidentally a broadcaster; a broadcaster, Joe was secondarily a performer. Successful, Diz was enormously popular; popular, Joe has been enormously successful. But the parallels are real. Both were aggressive, self-confident individuals. Each understood the import of his ripening on-air persona. Each flowed from the same stream of athletes yearning for television credibility. Both are not easily dismissed.

By 1976, Garagiola's life of influence and wealth had already become a distant dream, impossible almost to conceive of, for a young bravado whose childhood experiences revolved around Dago Hill, baseball, and his friend Lawrence Peter (Yogi) Berra. He lived "a pickoff throw away" from Yogi, and the two became inseparable; energetic and dispossessed, they owned one glove between them and played on the same sandlot team, the Stags; to one day break through into the major leagues — they thought of little else.

In 1940, Joe and Yogi played in a WPA (Works Progress Administration) summer league and served as bat boys, or errand boys, at the Cardinals' tryout camp. "Mostly," Garagiola said, "we just hung around hustling cracked bats." It was not long before Joe *himself* was hustled — signing a 1942 contract for a $500 bonus with St. Louis and moving, in quick succession, from the Cardinals' Class-C affiliate at Springfield, Missouri, to Columbus of the American Association to overseas service in the Army. "It was in Manila in 1944, and this one day I was listening to the radio when I heard the announcer say the Cardinals got a young catcher coming up who could run the bases like a deer, could hit home runs like crazy, and was gonna be another Walker Cooper," he recollected. "So I turned to my closest buddy in the Army, Joe Ginsberg [later, playing with seven big-league teams], and said, 'Gee, if the guy's that good, I'm in trouble.' And then I hear the same announcer say the guy's name is Joe Garagiola. What a shock. When I got out of the Army they told me I was gonna fill Walker Cooper's shoes but didn't say with what. Hell, I couldn't hit thirty home runs battin' from second base."

Back from the clap of war, Joe made the Cardinals in 1946, led St. Louis past the Dodgers in the National League's first-ever playoff, and batted .316 against the Red Sox in his first and (as a player) only World Series. He had made it, this cocky, high-spirited rookie. Or had he? The next season, he appeared in only seventy-seven games; he spent most of 1948 in the minors; in 1950, convalescing from a shoulder separation, he followed baseball through the broadside bursts of the brassy Harry Caray. "My wife [Audrie] was pregnant then, and it made me start thinking," Joe said. "All I used to think about was going to the Hall of Fame, but then I had to start thinking who wants an old ballplayer." Shrewdly, at twenty-four, Garagiola began to pursue the radio ideal whereby, one day, he might exchange mitt and mask for a tape recorder and a scorecard. For a downhill-tumbling receiver, it was a possibility as hearty as Caray's voice.

There first played out, of course, what remained of Joe G.'s playing career, which, had it been a play, would have closed *before* New Haven.

On June 15, 1951, Garagiola was traded to Pittsburgh. He hit .239 that year and .273 the next, and graced a team so abominable (the '52 Pirates compiled a 42-112 record) they tested one's fill of tolerance. "Branch Rickey was then in the ninth year of his five-year plan," he said, "when one day after I'd just joined the Pirates, he called me into his office and gives me that look with his big, bushy eyebrows. 'By Judas Priest, Joe,' he tells me, 'we're turning the corner here. We're coming out of the wilderness. And you, my boy, figure in my plans.' Three days later, he traded me"—to the Chicago Cubs; from there, Joe fell to the Giants in September 1954. Later that year, the Cardinals dumped Milo Hamilton, and without an inning of play-by-play experience, the already-Funny Man joined the KMOX broadcast team. "Man, I was ready," Joe said. "I used to sit in the bull pen and say, 'Why the hell doesn't he throw the curveball?' Well, all I had to do to become an announcer was to take out the 'hell.' "

Cleansing the netherworld, Garagiola teamed with Caray for the next eight seasons. His 1955–62 Redbirds were attractive, but mostly mediocre—their record was 624–616; only in 1957 did the Cardinals vigorously contend; in places far away from Busch Stadium, fans set their interest upon Ernie Broglio, 21–9 in 1960, or Ken Boyer, batting safely in twenty-nine straight games the previous year, or Sam Jones, leading the league in 1958 strikeouts, or Stan Musial, collecting his three thousandth hit that very season, winning his seventh- and last batting title in 1957, and vying with T. Ballgame as the pastime's most arresting force.

Joe G. would talk about these exploits to anyone who would listen, and when a game grew boring, he extemporized to make the time pass—mocking his baseball talent ("You can't imagine the thrill," he told colleague Jack Buck, "to walk into a clubhouse and wonder if your uniform would still be hanging there") and parodying his background ("When I reached the big leagues, the word got around my neighborhood. I guess the compliment about me my mother will never forget she got from one of those door-to-door peddlers. This man told my mom I was 'the first boy from the neighborhood with a name ending in *a, e, i, o,* or *u* that gets his name in the papers and he no kill anybody' "); gabbing and cutting through the tension and saying of baseball, "I don't think it's like going to church"; defaming statistics ("I couldn't care less about them") and extolling simplicity ("The big intrigue in baseball is laughable. The signs and signals the manager gives — an idiot could pick 'em up") and traveling a Burma Road of Berraisms.

"I'll ask him, 'What time is it?' Yogi'll think for a moment and then say, 'Now?' "

"I was going to Yogi's home and got lost. So I phoned him from the library-museum of that town. 'Where are you?' he asked. I told him. And he answered me: 'You're not so far away. You come this way. Don't go that way.' "

Looking back, "We had this soccer game scheduled when we were kids. Yogi looked awful. I said, 'You look terrible. Why don't you go home if you're feeling so lousy?' He gave me a funny look and said, 'If a guy can't get sick on a cold, miserable day like this he ain't healthy.' That Yogi — what a card!"

To Redbirds' listeners, Joe G. seemed sincere and amiable; his delivery matured until it was quick and practiced; like Buck and Holy Cow! he was an irreverence, not apologist; and his brattle of witticisms moved over twelve hundred Cardinals' games, caustically, not unpleasantly, and making him a regional celebrity.

He also broke, in time, after all of this — the waggeries, his folktelling on the banquet circuit for his employer, Anheuser-Busch, the union with Lindsey Nelson and Bob Wolff on the 1961–64 NBC "Major League Baseball," his exit from St. Louis in December 1962 to join the network full-time, Joe's resourceful and even brilliant appearances on "The Tonight Show," and the extraordinary triumph of his collection of anecdotes, *Baseball Is a Funny Game*, the largest-selling baseball book ever — with the whiskey-voiced Odysseus of St. Louis.

"I'd got him his start — even as a player, Joe had talked to me about what he'd do in the future, and I always told him I thought he'd be terrific on radio, which back then was still the thing, much more than TV," Harry Caray, his sonancy not dissimilar to sandpaper seering a veneer, remarked to me in 1979. "So we bumped Milo, got Joe on the air, and I poured my heart into making him an announcer."

"But he had a lot to start with, agreed? And he worked like hell."

"Work, yes," Caray said, "but he still had a lot of problems — a lousy voice which he has to this day. I used to take him out to night clubs and show him how singers, tiny little gals, could sing up a storm. I was trying to teach him that it came from your belly, from your diaphragm. I've always said that I treated Joe Garagiola better than I did my own son [Skip, since 1976 a Braves' announcer]."

"And yet," I said, "today you're not even on speaking terms."

"And I'll tell you why," he said. "About a year after Joe left St. Louis, I was doing a World Series [1964, Yankees-Cardinals], Joe was working with NBC, and I hadn't seen him in a while. He's around the batting cage, and I walked toward him to say hello — my old buddy. He starts walking toward me — I figure for the same reason — and he walks right on by me and says, 'Hi, how are you, nice to see you.' I called him every name in the world, and I'm half-Italian myself! But that's Joe — as long as you can help him, you're his friend, but if you can't help him any more he doesn't have time for you."

Whether Caray's anger lay rooted in Joe's perceived ingratitude, or a clash of egos unavoidable between two strong-willed men, or the fact that Harry's reputation, so stratospheric in St. Louis, shrank nationally until the early 1980s beside Garagiola's and even Buck's, or, possibly, all of the above — who can say? Neither totem's humanity allowed for a dull-elbowed naïveté. But leaving the hinterlands in early 1963 for NBC, New York, Joe's makeup *did* allow for a clutch of useful qualities — perseverance, surely ("I didn't have any choice," he said. "I got a tape of my first play-by-play. Wow, I wouldn't have hired myself"); a phobia of stale, shopworn parlance ("Look at that guy smiling on third base," began one Joe G. line. "He looks like he swallowed a banana sideways"); a Jessel-like gift for timing; and a fashionable unsophistication.

"I'm not Joe Show biz," he would insist in 1965. "I'm not jet set or the country-club type. Those guys on the bubble gum cards, those are my guys." It was a parcel that carted Joe to the 1963 World Series (with Ernie Harwell) over NBC Radio, and second 1961, first 1962 and 1963, and 1965 All-Star Games (with Gowdy, Allen, Scully, and Buck) and 1964 Grand Event (with Phil Rizzuto) on NBC Television; that network's radio program, "Monitor," where he became a regular, and the daily "Joe Garagiola Sports Show" ("His sports strip," read a Sindlinger Report, "has the distinction of being the highest-rated program on the NBC Radio Network and the highest-rated of all sports programs on any network"); and on December 17, 1964, to the Bronx as the new Voice of the New York Yankees.

"I wished Joe nothing but the best," Mel Allen said of his Ghost of Seasons Yet-to-Come. "Hell, it wasn't his fault. The Yankees just decided to make a change. In fact, Joe said later that the first wire he got when the Yankees hired him was from me. It read: 'Hope you stay on the job as long as I did.' I remember Joe telling me, 'Christ, Mel, I didn't know there were nice people like you still around.' "

There was no way Garagiola could *replace* The Voice. But he did *succeed* him, and for four bathetic years, up against more than he had bargained for, Joe unearthed warmth and a freewheeling geniality to mask what was happening on the field: the utter, total, and stunning collapse of baseball's Teutonic Knights. Joe's first season, the Yankees fell below .500 for the first time since 1925; the next year, hitting bottom, they were atrocious, and in 1967, rising to ninth, merely awful; in a weak American League, the 1968 Yankees hit .214 and climbed to fifth. From a removal of almost two decades, Bombers' fans still wince at such remarkabilities as Horace Clarke, leading the 1967 Houkmen with a .272 batting average, and the infield of Joe Pepitone, Clarke, Ruben Amaro, and Charley Smith, or Fred Talbot and Dooley Womack, torching the Yankees' pitching staff with joylessness and walks. Where were the *Yankees?* one wanted to (and often did) lament; to children weaned on Richardson, Skowron, Mantle, and Ford, how could Joe explain *Thad Tillotson?*

Understandably, Garagiola avoided, whenever possible, anything related to the day's scores, standings, and batting averages. "With the kind of team we had," he once jested, "it was easy to let your attention drift to subjects outside the ball park." On NBC's "The Today Show," which Joe joined in early 1969, fleeing the Yankees' bunker, he proved himself, to the surprise of many, "a guy who can indulge knowingly [not only] in diamond talk with Frank Robinson and Yogi Berra," wrote Ben Gross in the *New York Daily News*, but also "boxing with Muhammad Ali, poetry with Marianne Moore, and politics with Hubert H. Humphrey. And yet, his formal education has not gone beyond the high school level." Rising at 4:30 A.M. in his Scarsdale, New York, home, Joe worked "Today" five days a week, from 7 to 9, until 1973; at the early hour, his puckish humor went down well. He also hosted the TV "Joe Garagiola Memory Game" and "Sale of the Century," spread like jam over the network's radio programs, starred in a fifteen-minute Monday night pre-"Game of the Week" show ("The Baseball World of Joe Garagiola," winning a 1973 Peabody Award for broadcasting excellence), and became, literatim, a one-man agglomerate. By the early seventies, a columnist noted, he was "one of the most likeable and well-heeled stars of broadcasting. His words hit home runs."

In late 1975, as Lindemann observed, Garagiola hit a tape-measure shot that rustled the Cowboy from the mound. "You gotta hand it to him, it's why he's such a great success," Carl said. "Joe knew what he wanted — and what he wanted, he got."

Except, of course, for the ratings; those, Joe could not command.

Originally, it had been the fondest hope of NBC management that the gold-plated Garagiola, through his charm and unorthodox dwelling on the personal and quaint, could stop the decade-long audience hemorrhage of Saturday's "Game of the Week." But it did not happen that way. Instead, the "Game" smelled less of Canaan or Cockaigne than of So-So on Parade; it was not that viewers, leaving Joe G., deliberately turned him off — rather, conditioned to regard network baseball, post-Dean, as a kind of lukewarm attraction, they were never there to begin with. From 1976 through 1982, Joe's last act as the Peacocks' Voice, NBC's baseball numbers resembled a speedometer on semi-cruise control — dropping slightly (to 1977's 6.7 national rating), then climbing (to 7.5 in 1978), then falling, advancing, and finally tumbling to the 6.3 plane of 1981–82. "The reason they didn't vary that much was that there was a solid constituency each Saturday, *regardless*, but one we found hard to expand," explained ESPN's Scotty Connal. "And that's too bad, because we'd hoped for more."

"Why didn't you get it?" I asked.

"Baseball hadn't been smart enough yet to ban competing Saturday telecasts by the teams," he said. "And we weren't paying enough to force them to do it. Cable was now coming on the scene — in addition to these local networks — and that was even more dividing the audience."

"What about Garagiola? Any fingers pointed there?"

"I don't see how," Connal said. "He knew the game, he kept it simple and light, he had a great rapport with the players. I always thought that between him and Kubek, we had as good a baseball team as any sport on the networks."

In his most colorful moments, and they were often, Garagiola evoked a baseball world that was rich in its informality. He laughed, barbed, canvassed; his sense of expansiveness lent itself to backchat.

Listening of a Saturday, one heard him reminisce about his good friend Yogi (Though less frequently than earlier; "this is a particularly sore point with Garagiola, and for good reason," Jack Craig wrote in 1983. "The charge of endless Yogi stories was so widespread that he went cold turkey on them years ago") and the piteous 1952 Pirates ("It was the most courageous team in baseball," Joe began one weekend. "We had 154 games scheduled, and we showed up for every one. We lost eight of our first nine games and then we had a slump. That was probably the only team that clinched last place on the opening day of spring training").

He needled his ancestry. "I remember once, I was on Johnny Carson with Kaye Ballard and June Valli, and I said, 'This is the first time a group of Italians have gotten together when there wasn't a Senator present.' "

He razzed his diction. "A few years ago, I got inducted into the Missouri Hall of Fame the same day as Yogi and Dizzy Dean," he said on a Yankees-Orioles' telecast. "Dizzy, Yogi, and Garagiola in the Hall of Fame! Think of it! Do you wonder why when I got up to address the crowd at the celebration, I asked, 'What do you want? Good grammar or good taste?' "

He breathed pertness into the abbreviated phrase. How do you know, Joe was asked, that a pitch of Cubs' reliever Bruce Sutter was a spitball, not sinkerball? "Because the pitch created its own rainbow."

He was also aided by what the viewer saw on the screen — "The undeniable fact is that when it comes to baseball coverage," one critic said of the network's skill at camera angles, restraint with instant replays, and voluminous tub of statistics, "there's NBC and then there's everybody else" — and by his sidekick, whose syntax, discipline, and stream of analysis forged across greater expanse in a comparable period, I am inclined to say, than any announcer I can think of.

When Tony Kubek joined NBC in 1966, he was gangling, inarticulate, and he talked too fast. By the time, a decade later, he linked up with Garagiola for the first of their seven years together, he had self-liberated into a color commentator and part-time play-by-play man who was less colorful than insightful, less insightful than stubborn, and less stubborn than direct.

"I have a confession. Tony Kubek is my favorite TV sports analyst," Craig said in the March 22, 1980, *The Sporting News*. "The NBC baseball broadcaster has an untrained voice, really no sense of humor, speaks a little too often, and may be too much in love with his sport. But regardless of how often Kubek speaks, one listens, because we hear his unvarnished, shrewd judgment formulated on the basis of more than two decades in and close to the game. Yet there is more than that. In a line of work so insecure that it provides too much praise and too few unhedged opinions, it would be unfair to call him the last honest network broadcaster. But he may be the most honest."

Who would have "thunk it?" to burlesque Ol' Diz, when, as an All-Star infielder, Yankees' utility man, and natural resource of Casey Stengel, Kubek was so unaccountably shy that he resisted countless orisons to grace the club's pre- and postgame programs. "I was the last guy you'd ever think of going into broadcasting," Kubek recalled. "I'll never forget how Red Barber and Mel Allen would kid me. 'Come on, Tony,' Red'd say at the beginning of each season, 'do one of our shows this year.' " To the chary Milwaukean, such petitions were intimidating; he was insecure and twittery on the air. "And then all of a sudden I'm in this business. Thank God for baseball. You look over the stops of my life. You know what made each of them possible? This silly little game."

In the end, shorn of frivolity, The Game impelled Kubek from Yankee Stadium to broadcast respectability and, some would argue, semistardom. It ferried him, first, in 1954, at the age of seventeen, to a station where every major-league club wanted his signature. "That was in the era of the big bonus babies, and it was a question of which team could outbid the others — they all came after me," Tony said. "But my dad had been a pretty good hitter in Triple-A, and he took the long view. He thought it best that I didn't sign a big bonus deal, since I wouldn't have been able to go to the minors under the rules back then. And that's where he wanted me to go — to the minors to learn the game." Spurning larger offers, the crew-cut string bean boarded the Yankees' train, for a $3,000 bonus; his initial station stop was Owensboro, Kentucky, in the Kitty League, then Quincy, Illinois, in the Three-I League; at his next stop, Denver, he hit .296 and .331 for the 1955–56 American Association Bears; then it was on to the bigs, where Tony won the 1957 American League Rookie of the Year Award, smacked two home runs in a World Series game that fall in his own home-town, and anchored a club of larger, almost mythical names with seasons that were splendid and overpassed.

Under Stengel, Kubek shuttled between as many as seven positions each season. "In one World Series game, Casey had me at short, third base, and all three places in the outfield," said Tony. "He liked to be cute that way." But replacing the Ol' Perfessor, Ralph Houk declared on February 10, 1961, that "Tony and I have talked, and he will be my shortstop, period."

For the Major, the accord's benefits ballooned. In Houk's first year as Yankees' manager, Kubek hit .276, fielded widely (leading all shortstops in average chances per game) and well ("With Berra, Mantle, Maris, Ford around, the people don't notice him, but ballplayers do," Luis Aparicio said. "You talk about Zorro Versalles and Dick Howser at shortstop. Forget it. Kubek's the best"), and helped The Greatest Team Since Murderers Row leave opponents at a loss. At twenty-five, predating George Allen's saw, Tony's future was now. Natural and unaffected, his play seemed a metaphor for his personality, and he ranked, say, among the dozen most valuable players in either league. "Don't write about me — write about *Kubek*," Roger Maris scolded a reporter that glorious August of 1961. "I just hit home runs. He plays great every day, and he *never* gets his name in the newspapers." He was as reliant as a Ford (the company, not pitcher) and as quiet as its engine. He escorted the Yankees to seven pennants in his first eight years. Like Thomas Wolfe, who often thought he would never die, Kubek could not imagine that his career would ever end.

And then it did, suddenly, in the fall of 1965 — Wolfe had died before the age of forty; Kubek retired at twenty-nine. "I hadn't been playing that well [hitting .229 and .218 in 1964–65], and so I went to the Mayo Clinic for a checkup," he said. "For quite a while, I'd had a bad back — I thought it went back to the time I'd spent in the Army [1962]. I'd played touch football, hurt it, and it had gotten worse. When I got to Mayo, the doctors asked me when my neck was broken. They took some tests and said the closest they could detect was that it happened five years before [In the final game of the 1960 World Series, a ground ball hit a pebble or spike mark at Forbes Field, jumped up and smashed Kubek in his throat, planting him in the hospital]." Whether from the Army mishap, Game Seven of the Yankees-Pirates' convention, or any of the hundreds of jolts inflicted by enemy base runners, three vertebrae had fused together; if Tony remained in baseball, doctors warned, a jarring collision might paralyze him.

As a player, Kubek, improbably, was through. "I came to New York to announce my retirement," he said, "and the day before I was to leave to go home to Milwaukee, I was sitting in Phil Linz' club, 'Mr. Laffs,' when Dave Kennedy, an NBC executive, sat down and asked me to try out for the weekly baseball telecasts the network had acquired." *Network television*, for *Kubek?* It seemed preposterous. Yet he auditioned, won the job as color commentator for the backup "Game," and spent 1966–68 with play-by-play man Jim Simpson, the civil and humane Washingtonian who advanced from radio and television work in the capital to ABC, joining Jim McKay on "Wide World of Sports," and from there to NBC. Calling balls and strikes, Simpson was terrific at football and hoops; he was a reporter and sparse anecdotist, and his formal style suffered before The Game's television need for flowing rhetoric. Baseball, he often admitted, gave him trouble. "You do basketball and football, and their action carries you along. You tell what's happening; you don't have to hype," he said. "Golf is tougher — so many dead spots. But baseball! It's even harder. You have a whole season of dead time between pitches — what do you do with it? It takes a real artist to fill in, to sort of ride the game's stream along." A baseball artist Simpson was not. What he was, in an enduring way, revolved around the watchword *mentor* — coaching and challenging the TV novitiate; prodding Kubek, after much tribulation, into chiseling some sense of broadcast identity.

"It wasn't easy," Kubek would later (under)state. "I'll never forget how that first season of broadcasting began. It was in early April of '66 and I was attending a meeting with fifty baseball, network, and advertising executives. Someone got up and said they had a report there was a 90 percent chance it would rain in the primary city the next day — the day of the game. Then someone stood up and said Jim Simpson had laryngitis and couldn't talk above a whisper." As someone sat down, Tony continued, the room shook with a still. "While everybody else was stone quiet, I held up my hand and said, 'If Simpson's got laryngitis and can't talk and somebody thinks I'm gonna do that game by myself, you'd better look for me in the back room 'cause I'm going to be throwing up.'"

Thankfully, it never came to that — Simpson reclaimed his voice; Kubek stumbled through his first game as an announcer—and by the 1968 Fall Classic, watching the ex-Yankee, steadily maturing, conduct player and fan-in-the-stand interviews, what struck one was not Tony's inexperience but his *enthusiasm;* not Tony's polish (there was none) but his deepening baseball education and devotion to the sport.

Hidden for three years on the backup "Game," Kubek's improvement—illumined, as it was, on the World Series—startled many NBC officials. It especially pleased Scotty Connal.

"I'd seen almost from the time that we hired him that Tony was a diamond in the rough, and Simpson—he gets a lot of the credit—brought him along as he later did Len Dawson in football," Connal said. "That '68 Series was Tony's first real national exposure, and he was absolutely superb."

"So you dump Pee Wee [Reese, Gowdy's partner since 1966] and put Kubek on the primary 'Game,' " I said.

"We were looking for someone who'd be outspoken, who'd be a maverick, and, God, Tony didn't disappoint," and here Scotty started laughing. "When Tony thinks he's right, that's all there is to it. He's not terribly political, and he doesn't like to tread lightly. He's also a perfect gentleman, and best of all, he has that keen appreciation of what you should talk about, how to use the wealth of material you accumulate over the week to make the Saturday 'Game' come alive."

"Rate him as an analyst."

"I'm the guy who brought in Billy Packer and Al McGuire on basketball and Merlin Olsen on football, and I think Tony was every bit as good as they were. He's by far the best analyst in baseball," Connal said. "He has been for years."

I cannot now pretend, even in retrospect, that I much admired the Gowdy-Kubek brace. Individually, each man was lucid—the Cowboy from the start; Tony more across the 1970s—but their modes were too analogous. Neither was a humorist; neither was given to extravagant claims or stabs at gaiety. Both resisted any urge to treat the "Game" as floor show; each deserves respect for his earnest, logical approach. Both directed their faculties and energies at the game itself, and at its notables and gradations; they were more informative than entertaining, and one came away from a typical Saturday split by polar sentiments—usually pleased with what was told; often tepid from the telling. Gowdy would have profited from a Uecker or Dizzy Dean as his color commentator; likewise, Kubek would have complemented an Allen or Lindsey Nelson, his bright analysis a tonic to those rhetoricians' gin. Ernie Harwell is no comedian, but Gowdy paired brilliantly with the Georgian on CBS Radio's 1980–81 and 1983–85–86 playoff coverage; as the Voice of NBC's backup "Game," Kubek and Bob Costas formed a splendid network coupling. But Curt and Tony, as a *team?* They were cogent, spirited, and uncommonly perceptive. They were also too damned dull.

It must be said that Kubek worked better with Garagiola—or, at least, for whatever reason, it merely seemed that way. For one thing, more than Gowdy, Joe G. added to his broadcasts the quality of laughter. He milked his punch-lines as well as Don Meredith, and I waited for Garagiola to do his bits as one expected Barbra Streisand to sing "Happy Days Are Here Again." For another, like Kubek, Joe was an ex-jock; his background, I felt, put Kubek at ease, and summoned an on-air chemistry to rival Dean and Bud Blattner's 1955–59 arabesque. "I can get a better answer from a player than a professional announcer can," Tony boasted. "Remember, I once smelled the same sweat. It's important for the players to like me. I think they do. They feel freer with me. The players feel an empathy with me." There was also the simple fact of Kubek *himself*; he had blossomed, in a way few had portended, becoming by the late seventies facile and poised. Was Tony more opinionated? No; as a broadcaster as opposed to player, he had invariably been blunt. It was, rather, his style and manner of speaking, it was *that* which had changed: "It was Curt who suggested in the early seventies that I start working in the off-season on my delivery — he should get the praise. I began reading out loud and listening to myself on a tape recorder. I think only you can help yourself in this business." Involving and even piquing his audience because, at last, he could articulate his feelings, Kubek emerged as a superb interviewer and analyst; "quick and bold," wrote *TSN*, "with limitless anecdotes about the players" — perhaps the finest color commentator, outside of Packer, assigned to any big-time sport. "I thought he and Garagiola were the best example in sport of black and white," Scotty Connal was saying. "The viewer doesn't want to hear one guy echoing the other, agreeing all the time. That's boring. He wants opinions, arguments, and here is where Tony and Joe were great. It's like Packer and McGuire. There'd be an error at second base on a throw from home, and Joe would say, 'It's the second baseman's fault.' Tony would come back, 'No, you're dead wrong. It's the catcher's fault.' It was their honesty, that clash — that's what the guy at home liked. That's why Tony was so good."

He was not a firebrand, exactly, but instead, like Blattner, one of broadcasting's last honorable, old-fashioned men; leaving the ex-Quiet Man, I would remember how James Fenimore Cooper rhapsodized, "Truth was the Deerslayer's polar star. He ever kept it in view, and it was nearly impossible for him to avoid uttering it, even when prudence demanded silence."

• Did he like the between-innings World Series interviews Kubek helped to foist on the late-1960s public? "I hate it now," Kubek said in 1972, "and I hated it then. If the World Series can't carry on by itself without gimmicks, then there's something wrong with the game."

• What was Tony's view of the "celebrity guest" his network attached to the 1973–74 Monday "Game of the Week"? "It bugs me," he said at an NBC luncheon held to *promote* the concept. "Our staff of broadcasters, directors, statisticians, and announcers works for hours preparing for the game, and then some guy comes on and spends the time shilling for a book or a movie or himself."

• How did Tony (dis)regard the designated hitter? "I'm very liberal in most areas, except where baseball is concerned," he pronounced in 1977. "I'm a purist. I hope we never go to inter-league play. And I don't like the DH. I've said it over and over again — it's a dumb rule."

• Could the ex-Yankee have played for George Steinbrenner? "Never," he remarked over the air in 1978. "I couldn't feel comfortable on the Yankees now. Baseball's tough enough to play without an owner constantly harassing you, intruding upon the team." Shortly, reaching NBC, Steinbrenner tried to extract his prickly thorn. Would the network accede to Boss George's hectoring and drop Kubek from the "Game"? Almost; only Don Ohlmeyer's intervention saved Tony's job. "There were a lot of executives who—I couldn't believe this—were ready to cave in to Steinbrenner's bullying," Tony said in 1980. "I was just surprised I didn't receive more support."

As early as 1972, covering the A's-Tigers' playoff, Tony had enraged Detroit (and its Chrysler Corporation) by defending Bert Campaneris after the Oakland shortstop, retaliating to a knockdown pitch by Lerrin LaGrow, threw his bat at the Bengals' pitcher. "It's justified," he told his NBC audience. "Any pitch like that—it was aimed right at Bert's legs—endangers his career. Campaneris' whole livelihood involves his legs." Chrysler contacted Bowie Kuhn, demanding Kubek's apology. Kuhn called the Peacocks' Chet Simmons, "who finally called me," Tony said. "He wanted to know what I was going to do. I told him I was going on the air and say it all over again." (On his next broadcast, he did.) Now, post-Steinbrenner, almost a decade later, Kubek went contrarily on his way. Would he partake in NBC's coverage of the 1980 Summer Olympics, a role for which most announcers would kill? "I don't *want* to," he said. "Before I signed another four-year contract [through 1983], I insisted on getting a letter from Arthur Watson [president, NBC Sports] pledging I wouldn't have to go. In the eyes of most fans, a guy who does one sport loses credibility when he goes to another. What would I have *done* in Moscow?" (After the U.S. boycott, it turned out, nothing.) Would he consent to make off-season speeches for up to $2,000 a whirl? "I've never done one. Some guys would write a few jokes for you, you'd read them. It wouldn't be me." Or appear in national commercials? "Nope. I do one for a Wisconsin-based insurance firm, that's all. I don't need the money." Or fill November through March with football and basketball commentary? "I've had a lot of offers, but why would I spoil my off-season? I spend time with my family, go hunting—I coach a junior high basketball team. Besides, to broadcast anything after you've done baseball—it'd all be downhill."

A dauntless and unordinary presence.

A very (sorry) untoni Tony.

As the turns of the Kubek-Joe G. axis proceeded, I grew equivocal about its sense of place. It was a feeling, strangely, not unlike my late-1970s view of America, for we lived now in a nation with leaders who spoke of malaise; with voters, regardless of party or ideology, who agreed only that things would get worse; with a growing fear that problems were too unmalleable to solve.

Carter himself, *TIME*'s Roger Rosenblatt has written, oversaw "a presidency characterized by small people, small talk, and small matters. He made Americans feel two things they are not used to feeling, and will not abide. He made them feel puny and he made them feel insecure." Inflation flew the cage. Rising interest rates screamed *no* to the American Dream. A form of self-centered giddiness seized the country; who among us was not *Looking Out for #1*? Carter pardoned most Viet Nam War draft evaders, handed the Canal to

Panama, and unveiled a $1.5 billion loan guarantee plan to rescue Garagiola's guarantor. Hubert Humphrey died. The Trans-Alaska Pipeline opened. Polish Cardinal Karol Wojtyla became the first non-Italian Pope in 455 years. Triumphs: by Anwar Sadat (shattering precedent with a trip to Israel), Carter (engineering the Camp David Accords), and Margaret Thatcher (elected Britain's first woman prime minister). Disasters: the Boat People, Three Mile Island (almost), and the 1979 crash of an American Airlines DC-10 jetliner, killing 275 people. Humiliation: day No. ____ of the Iranian hostage crisis. Entertainments: *Star Wars* and *Saturday Night Fever* and *Apocalypse Now*. Disgrace: this country's role in deposing the Shah of Iran. Blessing: the decade's end.

By then, the "Game of the Week" had settled somewhere closer to blessing than disgrace. Each Saturday, I enjoyed Garagiola's solidity and Kubek's intellectual courage; splitting color and play-by-play, they supplied a humanity and depth of knowledge that one could hardly fail to marvel at. Yet I was struck too by what I subjectively missed—the necromantic rhythms of a Ray Scott, or the kind of sublime poetry that Vin Scully fashioned ("It was so hot today," he mused once, "the moon got sunburned"), or the trenchant speaking style of a Jim Woods or Ernie Harwell, or the almost astonishing pleasure evoked by one "How about that!" Even with Joe G.'s quips, his tandem's "Game" resembled meat and potatoes more than a banana split or Bloody Mary; it was hearty, stable, and orthodox. It presented baseball, I supposed, as Kubek's "purists" wanted—unvarnished, often humorous, but bereft of theatrics—and through the eyes of two ex-players for whom The Game, quite literally, had been a job, not faraway ritual, livelihood, not romance, and whose boyhoods bumped against the baseball of pressure, dimly lit ball parks, insects, potholed infields, and long, meandering bus rides—baseball, in short, leaving nothing to the imagination. In a sense, Garagiola and Kubek were typical, I think, of most ex-athletes-turned-announcers. Up close, straining to make the major leagues, how could they—how would it have been *possible* to—perceive baseball (or, ultimately, as broadcasters, translate their perceptions) in the same idealized and often wondrous way as a generation of young souls, less athletically deft, who spent a thousand nights lying in bed and supposedly asleep, their radios picking up Barber, Byrum Saam, and background noise, and who, later, took their alchemy of sound to adulthood? For them—for me—baseball was diversion/obsession, not profession, and more mysterious than real. It was not absence, but *distance*, that often made one's heart grow fonder; over radio, usually, and even television, the baseball abstract became imaginable, even utopian, and better than it was.

"When you're involved with something—baseball, a business, even war—it's always less attractive than when seen from far away," Lindsey Nelson would tell me. "When you think of it, it would have been implausible to expect most ex-athletes to think of baseball in the same warm, romanticized way as a child, or in college, that I did, or you did, or Mel Allen or Russ Hodges did. Sure, all of us played baseball when we were young, but casually—we weren't good enough to think of it as a career. Our connection to the game was more, I

His nickname was "the Gunner"; his following ranked among the most fervent in The Game; he *was* the Pirates, and they have been a sorry sight without him. For twenty-eight (1948-75) tumultuous seasons, Bob Prince regaled Tri-State listeners with a Byzantine mix of theatricality and prose. Of a Pirates' home run, Bob screamed, "Kiss it good-bye!" and "How sweet it is!"; of a Pittsburgh victory, it was, "We had 'em allll the way!" He gave players animal monikers, treated baseball more as show biz than seminar, and in 1986 was elected, posthumously, to the Hall of Fame. (Photo: NBL)

LEFT – Baseball has known no better No. 2 announcer than the gravel-voiced, crew cut Jim Woods – "the Possum." Woods got his radio start in the 1930s, replacing the Hollywood-bound Dutch Reagan as the University of Iowa's football Voice. In 1948, he succeeded Ernie Harwell at Atlanta, and, in 1953, joining Mel Allen, formed the first of Poss's superior broadcast teams. Through 1956, Jim worked with Mel and Red Barber; in 1957, Russ Hodges; 1958-69, Bob Prince; 1970-71, the Cardinals' Jack Buck; and from 1974 to 1978, Boston's Ned Martin. (Photo: NBL)

RIGHT – A marvelous mid-fifties Cleveland pitcher, Herb Score plummeted after his face was struck by Gil McDougald's May 1957 line drive. In the early sixties, retiring as a player, Herb turned to broadcasting. He has been the Indians' radio Voice since 1973. (Photo: NBL)

LEFT – Chuck Thompson began as a part-time 1940s Voice of the Phillies and A's, later went to Baltimore and Washington, and returned to Memorial Stadium in 1962. Since then, Chuck has parlayed warmth, knowledge, and soothing tones into radio and television Orioles' Magic. (Photo: NBL)

ABOVE — Throughout baseball broadcasting, have there been more polar opposites than Al Helfer (left) and Monte Moore? A college football running back, World War II hero, the only man to announce for all three pre-1958 New York City teams, and early-1950s domo of Mutual's "Game of the Day," Helfer was huge (6-4, 275 lbs.) and boozy, egotistical and profane, and an unforgettable Voice. In 1968-69, Brother Al joined the Oakland A's, where he teamed with the Finleys' veteran mouthpiece, the conciliatory, church-going Moore. Monte enlisted with the 1962 Kansas City Athletics, transferred west in '68, did three World Series over NBC, outlasted sixteen different sidekicks, and resigned in late 1977. (Photo: KNBR-San Francisco)

BELOW — For nearly half-a-century, Mel Allen (right, waving to the Yankee Stadium crowd on "Mel Allen Day," 1950; former postmaster general James Farley presides) has called balls and strikes — the most prominent and, quite probably, finest play-by-play man in baseball's tide of times. Allen described more World Series and All-Star Games than any contemporary; as the Yankees' 1939-64 embodiment, he owned perhaps the largest allegiance of any sports announcer.

In 1985, *Sports Illustrated* said: "If baseball is back, Mel Allen must be too. Salaries and cities and even grass may change, but Allen remains forever the same. Like the game itself, Allen is timeless." In 1978, unable to choose between Allen (right) and Red Barber as its first broadcast inductee, the Hall of Fame named them jointly. The selection was fortuitous, since, together, The Voice and Ol' Redhead fostered, in a rich and even magical way, a golden age of broadcasting.

LEFT – As a 1950s and sixties pro football announcer, Ken Coleman was a Cleveland institution; in early 1966, replacing Curt Gowdy on Yawkeys' radio and video, he returned in triumph to his Boston roots. Already, Ken had covered seven NFL title games over network radio/television; now, in his second Hub season, he narrated the Red Sox' "Impossible Dream" and called the 1967 World Series. Born eight miles from Fenway Park, Coleman has spent most of the past two decades reporting, applauding, and despairing of the Sox. (Photo: *TSN*)

RIGHT – "When sorrows come," said Ned Martin, quoting Shakespeare over WHDH Radio, "they come not [as] single spies, but in battalions." At once classicist and Red Sox' fan, Martin has broadcast Boston baseball since Don Buddin and Pumpsie Green gave new meaning to Ned's exclamation, "Mercy!" Sorrows? Hearing Martin, not among Red Sox' fans. Mercy! What a career. (Photo: *TSN*)

LEFT – As a baseball speaker, Jon Miller became a modern master of the ancient art of rhetoric; his repertoire included sarcasm and mimicry, irony and allusion, and graced the A's, Rangers, Red Sox, and, ultimately, Memorial Stadium. The Birds' post-1982 radio Voice, replacing Chuck Thompson, Miller detailed Baltimore's '83 world championship and helped enlarge the Orioles' wireless network. (Photo: Baltimore Orioles)

ABOVE – Jim Piersall (right, interviewing Jackie Robinson) and tranquility were *Perfect Strangers*. A talented 1950s and sixties outfielder, Piersall was the subject of the 1957 film, *Fear Strikes Out;* in 1977, tumbling into White Sox' broadcasting, he joined Harry Caray as baseball's rejoinder to *Butch Cassidy and the Sundance Kid.* Jim was acidic, emotional, suspended (once, by the club), and a hit (with Sox' fans). In 1981, he was fired for comments on Chicago television. (Photo: NBL)

BELOW LEFT – In 1987, Brooklyn-born Phil Rizzuto began his thirty-first season as a Yankees' announcer, sparkling as one of baseball's last broadcast *characters* – an irrepressible throwback to the era of Ol' Diz, Bert Wilson, and Earl Gillespie. Rizzuto has been a Bronx Bomber since 1941. (Photo: NBL)

BELOW RIGHT – For nearly forty years, Bob Elson (with Mickey Mantle) presided over the slings and errors of Chicago baseball. He was the originator of the on-field, pregame interview; his style was laconic, reserved; he loomed among radio's brightest stars of pre-World War II America. Known as the Old Commander, he was inducted into Baseball's Hall of Fame in 1979. (Photo: NBL)

LEFT – Since 1953, covering seven teams, Milo Hamilton has been a peripatetic and baseball academician. "Nobody, I mean *nobody*, does more preparation, keeps more information around than Milo," said Lindsey Nelson. "The running joke is that he shouldn't have a file cabinet to keep his records in – he should have a truck." (Photo: NBL)

RIGHT – In 1965, Vince Lloyd became the Cubs' radio bigwig, and with his throaty voice, presided over Wrigleys' play-by-play through 1981. A Big Ten football Voice, native Illinoisan, and WGN color commentator, Lloyd was the first announcer to interview an American president at a baseball game: John F. Kennedy, April 10, 1961. (Photo: WGN-Chicago)

For the past quarter-century, often disbelieving it themselves, Ralph Kiner and Bob Murphy have espied that maze of myth (to baseball historians) and magic (to their fans) otherwise known as the New York Metropolitans. A seven-time home run champion, Kiner (above right, with Bob Hope, center) joined the White Sox as Bob Elson's 1961 sidekick; in '62, he baptized the Mets. There, he teamed with Murphy (left), moving to the Polo Grounds after stints in Boston and Baltimore, and Lindsey Nelson to form a three-star radio/TV triumvirate. In 1979, the act disbanded as Nelson left for San Francisco; later, when Ralph shifted solely to Mets' television, Murphy emerged as their radio Voice. (Photos: NBL)

ABOVE LEFT – In the very season of the Mets' inception, the National League welcomed its other expansion team, the Houston Colt .45s. Their Voice was the veteran Gene Elston, reaching the Lone Star State after broadcast stops in Iowa, Chicago, and Mutual's "Game of the Day." Elston was fired by the Astros in December 1986. (Photo: NBL)

ABOVE RIGHT – When the Giants moved west in 1958, Lon Simmons became their local link, aiding the transplanted Russ Hodges, to a baseball-crazed Bay Area public. In 1971, Lon succeeded Hodges as the Stonehams' mouthpiece, and jumped to the cross-bay Athletics a decade later. (Photo: Oakland A's)

BELOW LEFT – Few play-by-play men toiled longer or more arduously to reach the majors than the Missouri-born Jerry Doggett, broadcasting eighteen years in the minor leagues before arriving at Ebbets Field. A Dodgers' announcer since 1956, Doggett has been unsung but seldom unappreciated. (Photo: NBL)

BELOW RIGHT – At fifteen, the youngest ever to grace a major-league game, Joe Nuxhall became a Rhineland favorite in 1944. Four decades later, he was still a Cincinnati fixture, having retired as a player in 1966, shuffled quickly into radio, and assisted such mouthpieces as Claude Sullivan, Jim McIntyre, Al Michaels, and, later, Marty Brennaman. (Photo: NBL)

ABOVE LEFT – Jerry Coleman was a 1940s and fifties Yankees' infielder, WW II and Korean War intrepid, Most Valuable Player of the 1950 World Series, and 1963-69 Bombers' announcer. He is now in his second decade as Voice of the San Diego Padres. His listeners revere Coleman's amazing affinity for malapropisms. (Photo: *TSN*)

ABOVE RIGHT – His speaking style is barbed and satirical; his Midwest popularity is immense. Jack Buck came to Busch Stadium in 1954, aiding Harry Caray, and, eventually, earned his niche as the post-1969 Redbirds' Voice. In 1987, Jack was inducted at Cooperstown. (Photo: ABC-Television)

BELOW – By the 1980s, the Phillies packaged baseball more nimbly than perhaps any radio/TV troupe in the National League. One reason was the broadcasting caliber of Richie Ashburn (left), the former two-time batting champion, and Harry Kalas (right). After a fifteen-year career with three N.L. teams, Ashburn retired in 1963 and became a Phillies' announcer; in 1971, fleeing Houston, Kalas arrived at Veterans Stadium. Four years later, Byrum Saam retired, and Harry replaced him as the Quakers' Voice. Today, among America's leading play-by-play men, his "It's outa here!" emblematic of Philly's baseball life, Kalas is also the chief mouthpiece of NFL Films. (Photo at left: NBL; at right: Philadelphia Phillies)

In the 1980s, via cable technology that linked the bigs with remote and faraway burgs, TV SuperStations (an Atlanta's WTBS, the Mets' WOR, and WGN-Chicago) raised America's baseball consciousness. The most visible was WTBS, entering more than 40 million homes by 1987, and its leading play-by-play men were Skip Caray (above) and Ernie Johnson (below). Caray, Harry's oldest son and a biting, colorful force, "grew up," he said, "with and around baseball," and joined the Braves in 1976. By then, covering the team since 1962, Johnson had evolved into the Wigwam's Voice. With Caray, John Sterling, and Pete Van Wieren, the Vermonter helped make Atlanta the eighties self-proclaimed "America's Team." (Photo above: *TSN;* below: NBL)

In 1976, after a decade's hiatus, ABC-TV renewed its ties with The American Game. For the next seven years, the network's big-league Voice was football-leaning Keith Jackson, but in 1983, awaking, the then-Arledges replaced the Georgian with Al Michaels (above). Born in New York, raised in Los Angeles, and weaned on Vin Scully, Al richened the 1970-73 Reds and 1974-76 Giants, and ABC's 1976-82 backup coverage; ultimately, as that network's baseball strong man and the 1986 National Sportscaster of the Year, Michaels brought to the pastime literacy, understanding, and love. (Photo: *TSN*)

ABOVE LEFT – At once personality and ex-player, video star and play-by-play announcer, Bob Uecker has been a stand-up comedian, network series regular, commercial cult figure, Milwaukee Brewers' Voice, and, moreover, wrote William Taaffe, "the funniest man – Joe Garagiola included – in sports broadcasting." (Photo: *TSN*)

ABOVE RIGHT – A Hall of Fame pitcher with the Los Angeles (née Brooklyn) Dodgers, Don Drysdale moved smoothly into radio and television – airing the Expos, Rangers, and, in 1973, the California Angels. Later that decade, Drysdale took his act, part-time, to ABC. Since then, Don has speckled the network's treatment of the playoffs, Mid-Summer and Fall Classics, and "Monday Night Baseball." In the early 1980s, he left Anaheim for the wind and success-starved fans of Comiskey Park, Chicago. (Photo: *TSN*)

BELOW – From 1959 to 1980, Tim McCarver became one of seven modern-day players to span four big-league decades. After retiring, he turned to Phillies' broadcasting; in 1983, he leaped to Mets' TV. At Shea Stadium, McCarver was megapopular, wiling critics with informality and wit. Said *Sports Illustrated* in 1986: "McCarver is the very *best* at what he does." (Photo: *TSN*)

"Peerless . . . a joy to listen to . . . intelligent, the consummate reporter . . . a tremendous repository of baseball knowledge and lore," rank among Vin Scully's more modest plaudits. A graduate of Fordham University, Scully, at twenty-two, became a Brooklyn announcer, succeeded Red Barber as the Dodgers' Voice in 1954, and spiraled into a radio phenomenon when the O'Malleys fled Ebbets Field for the lush real estate of Southern California. By late 1982, Scully had entered Baseball's Hall of Fame; three times, been named National Sportscaster of the Year; and received the George Foster Peabody Award for excellence in broadcasting. The best, however, was yet to come. The next season, joining NBC, Vin became *the* Voice of network baseball. (Photos: NBL)

ABOVE LEFT – When, in 1966, after nine years as a Yankees' shortstop, Tony Kubek became NBC's backup "Game of the Week" color man, he was erratic, untrained, and he talked too fast. But over the next two decades – climbing to the primary "Game" in 1969 as Curt Gowdy's sidekick; in 1976-82, helping Joe Garagiola; and, since 1983, with Bob Costas, forming a splendid network mix – Kubek has worked, improved, and evolved into perhaps the best analyst in baseball. (Photo: *TSN*)

ABOVE RIGHT – Like Curt Gowdy in the 1960s and seventies, Dick Enberg is NBC's Renaissance Man – calling, at one time or another, the World Series, Rose and Super Bowls, and NCAA basketball tournament; winning over viewers with honesty and style. Although replaced by Vin Scully on "Game of the Week," Enberg continues covering other sports for NBC. In 1985, he also rejoined his old team, the California Angels, as a part-time Voice. (Photo: NBL)

LEFT — It was in 1982 that "Game of the Week" viewers first glimpsed Bob Costas' whimsical irreverence. Born in New York City, Costas graduated from Syracuse, aired pro basketball and football, and landed at NBC in 1980. When the "Game's" backup Voice, Merle Harmon, was bounced two years later, Costas succeeded him, and went on to drape the pastime with a warmth and insight that eclipsed the bare and statistical. Costas was named the 1985-87-88 National Sportscaster of the Year. (Photo: *TSN*)

LEFT – As a baseball Voice, Joe Garagiola vaulted higher, more quickly, than any former athlete. He began as a 1950s Cardinals' announcer. Then, it was on to NBC's "Major League Baseball," the Yankees' broadcast booth, and back to NBC as a "Today Show" regular. In late 1975, Curt Gowdy was dropped as NBC's baseball Voice, and Garagiola became its play-by-play man. Through 1982, Joe evoked a baseball world that was rich in its informality. He laughed, barbed, canvassed; his sense of expansiveness lent itself to backchat. In 1983, with Vin Scully's arrival, the Funny Man returned to NBC analysis. (Photo: *TSN*)

BELOW LEFT – Wandering Chicago's Rush Street, waving a fish net from the booth, or bellowing "Take Me Out to the Ball Game," Harry Caray has defied credulity, convention, and fatigue. Exceedingly controversial, he has been enormously popular – first, as a 1945-69 Cardinals' announcer (Caray, left, with fifties colleagues Stretch Miller, center, and Gus Mancuso), where his regional following domineered the Midwest; then, as the White Sox' 1971-81 embodiment, in all likelihood saving the South Side team; and, finally, as the 1980s Voice of America's Cubs, "Holy Cow!"ing viewers over cable television and attaining, in his sixties, an almost Falstaffian renown. (Photo: NBL)

BELOW RIGHT – Exuberant and unafraid, Caray (here, broadcasting from the bleachers at Comiskey Park) has aired three World Series; won "The Announcer of the Year" Award, formerly presented by *The Sporting News*, seven times; made "It could be . . . It might be . . . It is!" his home run signet; and, delighting listeners – "my people," said Harry, "the little man" – enraged players, owners, and colleagues. To quote the late Bill Veeck, he made of baseball a carnival, every day a Mardi Gras, and every fan a king. (Photo: Associated Press)

guess you'd say, elevated; certainly, more removed — listening to Graham McNamee do the Series, or reading Granny Rice's great columns on big-league players as they were supposed to be and as Granny assured us they were. A ballplayer's exposure to baseball was warts and all — there's not much magic in the travel, the sweat, the clash of personalities, the gnawing fear that your career could end tomorrow. It's not, necessarily, that ex-jocks couldn't articulate this magic — it's more that many never felt it as *fans*. But for me, Prince, or Harry Caray, our baseball upbringing was magical. It's a feeling we never lost even as announcers, and I like to think that's the world we conveyed to the audience."

Of this ability, Kubek and Garagiola possessed little. They also blanched before a bugaboo not of their making — NBC's mid-to-late seventies inability to decide whether baseball was a spectacle worth honoring.

"Its publicity for 'Game of the Week' has been — and remains — atrocious," I wrote, at twenty-four, of the Peacock Network. "Football, basketball, tennis, and golf, even boxing receive more fanfare. In fact, with each latest slap in the face, NBC never appears to weary of rebuffing the diamond game."

It was not alone, of course (my primitive 1976 sputterings, sadly, failed to appreciate that fact); coming late to baseball, ABC Television seemed uncertain too of how to merchandise the pastime. Was baseball, like "Monday Night Football," to be exalted drama? Could Cosell imbue a *second* series with his weird self-confidence and pride? Football was made-for-TV narcissism, a prime-time pageant; baseball was religion, all mythy and sweetly rural. How, Roone Arledge wondered, could his coverage make the leap? Understandably, for the moment, ABC stumbled. But the big leagues' television *père?* — network lynchpin, for a quarter-century, of the red, white, and blue. What was *its* excuse?

In 1976, NBC used its baseball pregame "Grandstand" segment to highlight golf, tennis, and professional football; according to several studies, aired a weekly average of five times more promotions for the NFL than the "Game"; and in a November program marking the network's "First Fifty Years," virtually ignored baseball while dubbing pro football the "perfect electronic sport." The year afterward, Simmons, succeeding Lindemann as head of NBC Sports, publicly derided the majors' TV drawing power; late that summer, Til Ferdenzi, the NBC Sports publicist, declined to repeat his catchword of twelve months earlier ("Baseball," he muttered then, "is one of our prize properties"). On October 15, 1978, the network televised the two-hour "Bob Hope's Salute to the World Series," that week's fifth-highest rated show and baseball's first prime-time network special, revealingly, in nearly fifteen years (three months later, NBC aired two nightly tributes to the 1979 Super Bowl). "Starring Danny Kaye, Glen Campbell, Charo, and a host of other figures, the program was a salute to the Series and the game it represents," I wrote for a baseball publication. "Especially memorable were Kaye's rendition of 'Take Me Out to the Ball Game,' an old clip of three Dodgers singing, 'We're in the Money,' and a biblical interpretation by none other than Howard Cosell [who, now that ABC also televises baseball, has belatedly discovered the game's virtues]." The special hinted at baseball's limitless TV possibility, but it was one-shot and isolated, and disappeared as quickly as it came.

That same year, NBC scrapped baseball's customary sixty-minute preseason program ("We decided to abandon it," said a network spokesman. "It was as simple as that"); refused to televise any game on Saturday, July 9, three days before the All-Star Game, in the heart of the big-league season, opting instead for day-long Wimbledon tennis coverage ("We asked NBC to put our weekly game on," explained Tom Villante of the first baseball Saturday *sans* "Game" since 1953, "but they had televised a double-header the first week of the season, so in the end they'd fulfilled their contract and televised their scheduled twenty-six games. That gave NBC their out. They wouldn't listen to us"); interrupted numerous "Games" for live feeds from golf and tennis tournaments; missed a Willie Stargell home run because NBC was transmitting an update segment on women's golfer Nancy Lopez; and balked at sparing ten seconds on July 2 to show Willie McCovey's five hundredth homer hit two nights before (that very Saturday, it found ample time for Garagiola to make at least *fifteen* references to *tennis*, by my count, as the *baseball* game progressed). It was awful.

In these strange, imperfect seasons, at mid-passage between the prior ten years of Spenglerian gloom and an eighties cheer where, as Ralph Waldo Emerson wrote, "The only sin is limitation," with both baseball networks still skeptical of its relevance and appeal, NBC was not prepared to tell The American Game, as Emerson had the American people: "Nothing great was ever achieved without enthusiasm."

Not yet, anyway.

"A lot of the problem was Don Ohlmeyer—he'd just come over from ABC, was setting himself up to be the network's strong man, he was edging out people like Connal and Lindemann, and he couldn't care less about the game," observed an NBC director. "He didn't appreciate how you do baseball, what it had meant to the network. Football, taped sports—they excited him more. And it was too bad. NBC had always been so proud of baseball—Scotty loved it, and Lindemann [who left in 1978 for a slightly less senior position at CBS]—and now this. Thank God it all got straightened out." The gift was not cavalier.

Reawakening a light not seen since the early-sixties eminence of Allen, Nelson, and Bob Wolff, NBC strutted out of the darkness, its neons blinking, in the early- and mid-1980s—after Kubek, airing the 1978 Oktoberfest with Garagiola, Gowdy, and Tom Seaver, the 1980 Classic with Joe G., T. Terrific, Merle Harmon, and Ron Luciano, and the 1982 World Series (drop Ron and Merle; add Dick Enberg), had burnished his reputation for unapologetic bluff —as the Peacock Network broadcast the bigs as well as any network ever has, or is ever likely to.

By then, Ohlmeyer had fled NBC to found his own production company; in early 1983, Kubek too left the primary "Game." He was victimized not by a housecleaning spree but by overcrowding. That spring, Vin Scully, the most

Herculean and possibly popular play-by-play man in baseball, arrived from CBS to call balls and strikes; Garagiola shifted back to color commentary; Tony tumbled to the backup series.

To squelch Kubek's hurt, NBC doubled his salary, to a reported $350,000. To please the public, it made an inspired choice: the thoughtful analyst to handle — surprise — only analysis; a newcomer who was not a neophyte, Bob Costas, to chaperone play-by-play.

"I'm sure they didn't have that in mind when they made the change [NBC, of course, maintained it had], but the way it worked out, everyone won," a friend of mine remarked after a round of beer-drinking and both games of a 1985 NBC double-header.

"You kidding?" I said, thinking of the first game. "The Red Sox got killed."

"No, I mean the announcing," he said. "You take Garagiola and Kubek, right, the way it used to be. Both great on analysis, not quite so fantastic calling the play. Put 'em together and what you got? A decent, middlin' team. But then you put Joe on with Scully, and they're tops — they complement each other. Same with Costas and Kubek — Bob'll give you the high-flown rhetoric; Tony, the inside dope."

Pausing, he littered the floor with yet another empty beer can. "Instead of one team that's OK, like it *was*," he said, "now you got two that are great." Stone-drunk or sober, I could not help admitting to myself, this NBC convert was right.

                              *   *   *

While network television staged a dance marathon on the majors' late-seventies floor of ratings mediocrity, the pastime's older electronic medium jitterbugged through its greatest baseball programming achievement since the Mutual "Game of the Day."

The triumphal performer was CBS Radio, and beginning in 1976 it reminded listeners — as Mutual had, and Liberty — of the wireless' pervasive force. It also showed ABC- and NBC Television, not entirely by intimation, how one could present and retail The Game, if one were so inclined, so that its treatment exhibited an *attitude* about baseball — prideful and, by extension, futuristic. Its product was masterful. Better yet, it is still on the air.

There was never any doubt, even at the start, of how CBS intended to fortify the baseball legs of its tripod coverage.

It would promote the All-Star Game, playoffs, and World Series more aggressively than their television outlets dreamt of. It would choose professional baseball announcers, not oafish tenderfoots or football-leaning clones. It would regard the sport as worthy of respect, as Mutual had two decades earlier, and as CBS Television did — Gadzooks — even with the National Basketball Association. "From our first year of covering baseball," said Dick Brescia, then-senior vice-president of CBS Radio, "we didn't view it as a stepchild or orphan or something that had to be forced on our affiliates. We put premium prices on our advertising spots, we embraced it, plugged the hell out of it. We treated it — even in its earliest stages — in a very special way."

In 1961, Brescia had been at Mutual when that network's baseball house came tumbling down. "We were in terrible financial shape and looking anywhere to cut costs," he related. "The last couple of years, the baseball revenues hadn't been matching our expenditures — local networks were cutting into our number of affiliates, interest in the 'Game' overall didn't seem to be as high, and to end the series was a relatively simple call."

The decision meant that for more than a decade, the big leagues' national radio exposure consisted, solely, of NBC's dispirited/dispiriting coverage of the World Series and All-Star Game. But by late 1975, Brescia had become vice-president of sales for CBS, and it was there, in a reverse twist of chance, that he helped rebuild the game's network domicile. "It all began with a move NBC made," he said. "They had gone to a new format on their radio network, all news, and in '75 they decided that sports were interruptive, that it didn't fit in with what they were trying to do."

"So NBC kissed off the Series?" I said.

"After all these years [airing the Classic, continuously, since 1957], they literally abandoned baseball," Brescia replied, "and, I might add, they told Bowie Kuhn about it very late in the game — he had almost no time to put together coverage of the '76 jewels. I wouldn't say he was desperate, just extremely concerned, and so he called Sam Digges [then-president of CBS Radio] and asked if we'd take on baseball. They wouldn't charge us much for the fees, but would we please do it?"

"How soon did you decide?"

"Digges called me in and we talked. We knew that NBC's track record had been mixed. We knew also that there was a mind-set at this time that sports on radio were great locally and regionally — an easy sponsor sell, good ratings — but nationally? Would people listen? Would advertisers buy? We didn't know — it would be a gamble. In the end, we decided it would work if we handled it right and considered baseball a big thing."

"In '76, your first season, how was it?"

"The All-Star Game, the playoffs, even the Series — they weren't automatic sells. There was a sort of 'show-me' attitude, you know," he said. "We had to build slowly — persuade our affiliates in stages. But I'd seen how baseball had worked once before on network radio. I thought, 'If we do our job and hustle, promote, get the affiliates enthused, it can work again.' " By October 1976, CBS gleefully imparted the obvious: It had.

That first year, the network bought full-page ads in *TIME*, *Sports Illustrated*, and *The Sporting News* to banner its triune of events. "The day NBC or ABC does that," said a friend, "is the day George Steinbrenner becomes Queen of the May." CBS broadcast late-season baseball features, flooded its airwaves with promos for the games, and, inversing television's propensity, placed *baseball* spots on its *NFL* schedule. How much did the blizzard help? "There's no doubt in my mind," Brescia said, "that the evident fact that *we* thought a lot about baseball gave our stations confidence to carry the games, and that our

PR helped build the numbers." Huckstering, CBS meant to steer listeners into the network's baseball den; once there, its Voices, meticulously chosen, would gratify their senses.

Jack Buck, calling play-by-play, and color man Brent Musburger broadcast CBS's first baseball milepost — the 1976 All-Star Game. The American League final listed Ernie Harwell and Ned Martin; the National's, Ralph Kiner and Jerry Coleman: Two Bills, White and Sorrell, handled the Grand Event. The next two years, only the playoff lineup endured intact; while the Dodgers' Vin Scully, recently hired by CBS, aired All-Star balls and strikes, his colleague, Ross Porter, joined White, the Gold Glove infielder-turned-Yankees' voice, on the 1977–78 Oktoberfests. Then, in 1979, Scully was named to *both* Classics, mid-summer and fall, and doubling up through 1982, dwarfed his network analysts: Musburger, Win Elliot, Herb Score, and Tigers' manager Sparky Anderson. After even a brief wisp of Scully, my first thought was that hearing him exceeded being at the game, but when, in early 1983, Vin took his tenor to NBC Television, his CBS position was occupied, if not entirely filled, by Musburger, elevated to All-Star play-by-play, and Buck, coming full circle on the 1983–86 World Series.

"Looking back over the first ten years," said Brescia, who left CBS in November 1986, "you'd have to say Scully was our most *prominent* announcer. But he was also a *typical* CBS announcer."

"A contradiction?" I said.

"Not really," he said. "I'll never forget talking to Vin when he was first preparing to do our All-Star Game and, ultimately, the Series. I said to him: 'Tell me what you see in the booth.' He said, 'What do you mean?' I said, 'What's in there? What's in the booth?' He still didn't get me. So finally I said, 'I see one guy — you, the Voice — who is our producer, cameraman, director, announcer, all rolled into one. That's how important your job is.' It's much more important than a baseball announcer on TV — or a football announcer on radio. In our medium, the announcer is the show, and because baseball allows the announcer to really let his personality blossom — the slow pace is perfect — if you've got a great announcer on radio, you can't lose. No matter how good or bad the game is — it helps, naturally, to have a good one — you have it made."

"But Scully, typical?"

"In a way, yes, because Vin represents everything we tried to get in our announcers. We didn't just look for names who *happened* to broadcast baseball. We exerted tremendous care, and we went for guys who had great baseball credentials, who we felt could help our broadcasts — guys who know *baseball*, have a sensitivity and love for it, and could transmit that love so that listeners feel it, share it."

"And who have the national name."

"Some had, like a Scully — he'd built up a national reputation," he said. "Same with Curt Gowdy covering the playoffs — you didn't have to be a brain surgeon to know he'd help. But we also tapped the not so well-known. An Ernie Harwell from Detroit wasn't that famous, but I knew he'd be superb. A

Buck with the Cardinals. A Coleman with the Padres, same thing, or Harry Kalas with the Phillies." Harwell starred on the 1976–83 and 1985–86 American League playoffs; Gowdy worked in 1980–81 and 1983–85–86; Boston's Martin, the Yankees' White, and Denny Matthews of the Royals graced the 1976–78, 1979 and 1984, and 1982 affairs, respectively. The National's chronology listed: Kiner (1976–78), Coleman (1976–83 and 1985), Buck (1979–82), the Expos' Duke Snider (1983), Kalas and Porter (1984), and Musburger (1985–86). "So it wasn't just Scully's name, though that helped. It's what he meant — a knowledge, an appreciation, what he could do for baseball. It came down to quality."

Yet was it quality, alone, that lifted CBS's World Series audience from 41 million listeners in 1976 to more than 56 million nine years later; or boosted its 1976–86 All-Star ratings to an average of 21.5 million adults age eighteen or older; or induced CBS to begin a Saturday "Game of the Week" in 1985, baseball's regular-season return to network radio after an interregnum of twenty-four years? Was it Scully's éclat that prompted 58 million Americans to tune in all or part of the 1982 Grand Event, Harwell's sustained narration that caused Brescia to term the bigs' success "greater than we could have ever hoped for a decade ago," or Buck's tart humor that led Dick to say, now, after the final 1986 radio "Game": "The key has been treating it just like our post-season coverage, as something invaluable. When we first decided to do this series, we sent personally engraved baseball bats to each of our station managers, playing it up. I've been absolutely amazed how quickly our advertisers have accepted the 'Game of the Week' — not only the car companies, breweries, the traditional baseball sponsors, but we've also attracted new and youth-oriented summer advertisers."

"Describe the series," I said.

"Baseball and CBS agreed on the concept of the 'Game' as part of our new deal [$32 million from 1985 to 1989]. Our first two years, we began our broadcasts on Memorial Day weekend — late enough in the season to give the local clubs a chance to consolidate their coverage — and went on through the rest of the year. But beginning in 1987, because the response to the series has been so tremendous, we're going to start the very *first* week of the season and be on every Saturday from there. And as before, we'll even carry some important weekday contests in September."

"Through early October, then, one game a week?"

"No, it's more complicated," Brescia said. "Every Saturday, we offer our CBS affiliates an afternoon and evening game [each blacked out in the home team's market]. If the Orioles are playing that afternoon, our Baltimore outlet can air the night game. If the Cardinals are scheduled at night, KMOX can cover us in the daytime. If it wants, a station can broadcast 'em both. We know our production costs are going to be higher with two games than one, but this way we avoid local conflicts in the big-league markets. And it's worth it to our ratings. We didn't get into this to do a shoestring job."

Did such solicitude arise only *from* the announcers? Would Columbia have enthused over Scully describing soccer, or Buck airing bocceball, or Kalas doting on croquet? The answer is self-evident: The Voices helped, and they were often transporting, but the network's announcers were more a *vehicle* than cause of its baseball prosperity. The real star — the surpassing personality on all of CBS's coverage — was the sport itself, and, more specifically, baseball on radio.

Hearing Brescia, I recalled how Harwell told me, "Radio is the best medium for baseball — sitting at home, you can imagine it all. The game is linear. The bags, the positions, the batter, the pitcher — they're all definite designations. You start with the bare bones, and your creativity fills in the rest." It was true, I thought — Ernie's keen-edged phrasing; unlike football, baseball *did* play better over a bitsy portable than on the pre-eminent agent of television. "What is baseball on television? A pitcher staring in for a sign? A batter tugging at his jersey? A game that should be poetry in motion becomes only a still life," columnist Art Spander has written in the *San Francisco Examiner*. "Baseball is a game of numbers and nuance in which time is subordinate to circumstance. TV has never quite been able to respond properly. Dancing bears do well on the tube. Lifeless statistics do not." But on radio, Spander said, "Sounds fall on the ear, and a world rises in the mind. The game drones on, hypnotic tedium, filling the minutes with glories of the past and possibilities of the present. Baseball exists unto itself, with its own boundaries and timelessness. So does radio. The message and the medium were designed for each other."

Unraveling baseball, television left almost nothing to the imagination; TV made the game more inert, somehow dinkier than it was. Radio, on the other hand, spurred by a Martin, Lindsey Nelson, or Jimmy Dudley, left almost everything, and ingrained baseball with a springy charm. Television shows all, like a *Penthouse* centerfold. Radio insists on a veil of concealment, like a stripper enticing the glands. Locally and, in time, over cable, video baseball thrived because of rooting interest; New Yorkers would always watch their Amazin's, no matter how interminable the telecasts ("I know the game's dragging, Mom," one might hear around dinner time, "but can't the meat loaf wait a while? *Throneberry's* coming up to bat"). But as a rule, baseball has conquered *network* television only when its Voice has been outrageous enough (e.g., Dizzy Dean) to distract the viewer from the game's stolid countenance, or when the event itself has been so crucial or rousing that each pitch is freighted with importance (a Fall Classic or All-Star Game), or, most favorably, when those two tracks cojoined (The Voice's Oktoberfests, 1951–63).

It was not, I believe, that the announcer necessarily *mattered* more on radio; it was that, inevitably, he had more to work *with*. A Scully could animate TV baseball; on radio, he was magical. "We felt baseball could thrive on network radio, as it hadn't always on network TV, because this was the medium created by God for the game," Brescia was saying. Or, as Harwell explained: "If you take a competent football announcer, you'll almost never have a boring TV game — football is just packaged better for the screen. Likewise, if you've got an average baseball announcer, you'll almost never have a boring radio game — baseball is packaged better for the mind. At the other end, it takes a great football announcer or game to make his sport as exciting as even a mediocre baseball radiocast. And it takes a tremendous baseball voice to make his game, even a good one, as attractive as humdrum TV football."

Had all its post-1975 television announcers *been* tremendous, baseball might have reclaimed its niche, lost somewhere in the mid-sixties, as America's sports sovereign. Yet even as it was, The Game journeyed back to the good old days, *de novo* contending for the crown.

From 31,318,331 in 1976, the two leagues' attendance jumped two years later to a then-record 40,636,886, and for the first time, six teams, three in each league, attracted more than 2 million fans at home. "This is baseball's Golden Age," *Sports Illustrated*, favoring slight floridity, said in its April 9, 1979, issue. "Indeed, there is impressive evidence to suggest that the old game . . . is now enjoying unsurpassed popularity and prosperity. . . . Pro football is still very much in the picture, but the latest polls show baseball to be *the* sport these days. And statistics suggest that the upward curve has been steep and is almost surely still climbing." It is true that sports editors in a 1979 study named football over baseball, 267–118, as the game most important to their readers; undeniable that in an Associated Press–NBC telephone survey that year which asked, "Which would you say you are the most interested in . . . that is, which sport do you follow most closely?" the cathode sport led decisively, 47–33 percent; unbogus to say that the old disparities clung fast—baseball was favored by respondents making less than $8,000, by high school graduates, and by fans over sixty-five; elsewhere, football trumped the field. But at least baseball was *competitive* again—its future brightened by low ticket prices, mass promoting by individual clubs, and the free-agent rule, so despised by the game's ruling barons, which kept the pastime before its off-season public—and has *remained* competitive; the once-Promethean champion, decked by the NFL's rise to prominence, itself rising from the floor.

In September 1977, Lou Harris reported, "For the first time since 1968, more sports fans in the country follow baseball than football. The margin may be only one percentage point [61–60], but the trend is unmistakably in baseball's favor, and quite significant for the fortunes of both games. When fans are asked to name their favorite sport, they still opt for football by [only] a slim 22–21 percent. It is clear that baseball has made a real comeback." The season afterward, football retrieved an edge, 30–19 percent, and galloped to a fifteen-point margin in May 1981. "In recent times," Harris now wrote, "baseball has had trouble attracting the younger, more affluent fans who are more likely to attend games in person and who form the kind of audience that is attractive to television sponsors. Baseball has yet to solve that problem." Yet eighteen months later, as the football players' strike darkened Sunday afternoons, there was baseball taking "a clear lead [23–20]," according to the pollster, "as the nation's favorite spectator sport"; and even when Harris disclosed in November 1984 that pro football had resumed its season of triumph—the Rozelles now led by the same three percentage points—it was clear that baseball had achieved a rough equivalency with the NFL. In 1983, big-league admissions topped 45 million, and that spring baseball managed to extract the stupefying figure of $1.125 billion from ABC and NBC for its 1984–89 television contract. The next year, Peter Ueberroth, hero of the 1984 Los Angeles Summer Olympics, became Kuhn's successor as commissioner; he knew quite a lot about setting and imagery, and he did not hesitate to apply it. Driven, street-smart, and steely tough, Ueberroth embodied baseball's new self-confidence, a turning away from the game's late-sixties- and early-seventies inferiority complex of stricture and passivity. He was can-do, and baseball did—draping its marketing with artful technique; spawning such baubles as the CBS "Game"; "looking for new ways," Ueberroth said, "to PR ourselves in every-thing from baseball cards to television"—a baseball driving, renewing, *coming back*.

Not surprisingly, the pastime's new vigor paralleled and, no doubt, was partly forged by more refreshing national TV coverage; after baseball's decade of one network, one Voice, and scant exposure, the chords of Scully, Garagiola, and Al Michaels projected an aria of orotund delight.

Not quite so obvious was the role of other late-seventies- and early-eighties announcers, less nationally prominent than a Vin, Joe, or the newest Brother Al—announcers who shone, *locally*, on radio and television, and who were bolstered by the belief, caressed by the 1975 World Series, that baseball had been born again. Because their commodity was deemed to be more attractive, it became more saleable; because it was suddenly more vendible, they occupied a wider platform.

In 1976, with radio/TV revenue nearing $51 million—of the $27.2 million from local rights, the Red Sox and Dodgers led with $2.05- and $1.75 million; on baseball's shadowed side, the Brewers, Rangers, and Padres inhaled, collec-tively, only $2.1 million—the bigs hit a new local peak of televised games and radio affiliates. That year, American League clubs showed 613 TV sets and the National's, 505, for a record 1,118 broadcasts. At the same time, local radio struck up a theme of self-celebration—audibly in the Junior Circuit, where 367 affiliates transmitted its coverage; with brass and cymbals in the Senior Circuit, whose 524 outlets were acrawl with three teams (St. Louis, Cincin-nati, and Atlanta) of seventy-five or more. "Because baseball was seen as hav-ing regained popularity, it was easier for its teams to expand radio networks," Nelson stated. "That was especially true in the National League, which had greater areas in which to build those networks—after all, it had always had the great regional teams, the Braves in the South, the Cardinals in the Midwest. So what you had was an imbalance—National League teams, on both radio and TV, reached a greater portion of the country."

By 1981, that imbalance extended to (North) America's old talent for mak-ing a buck—coalescing territory through the French- and English-speaking arms of the Canadian Broadcasting Corporation, the Expos copped $6 mil-lion from TV alone; the Phillies mustered that total from radio and television; the Yankees led the A.L. with a $4 million video heist; from both mediums, the Royals and Brewers hauled only $1.3 million combined—and by mid-decade, it blanketed every index of the pastime's broadcast coverage. In 1987, fourteen American League teams aired 774 games over free and cable, as op-posed to per-view-cable, television: The Red Sox carried seventy-five games; Twins' fans could fetch sixty-eight; six clubs allowed fewer than fifty. Mean-while, the twelve N.L. franchises flaunted 847 games, or almost seventy-one

per team. In large part, the inequity resulted, as we will see, from the extraordinary 1980s growth of cable technology. In 1977, fewer than 13 million subscribers imported cable programming; five years later, the figure topped 24
million, nearly 35 percent of all U.S. households owning televisions, and Atlanta owner Ted Turner—beaming the signal of his so-called SuperStation,
WTBS, into cable homes throughout America—brought Braves' baseball to
more than 21 million subscribers. By 1985, five teams had joined the Super-
Station invasion, and only the WPIX Yankees and KVTV Rangers played
outside the National League. The Braves transmitted 145 games, the Cubs,
150, and the Metropolitans, 87, and not only did their *exposure* outstrip any
American's team, their *audience* dwarfed it; the previous season, Atlanta, the
Mets, and Chicago reached a cumulative total of 60 million cable homes against
the Bombers and Rangers' less than 6 million—a disparity which, in turn,
justified such inclusive coverage.

"It's a delightful situation where everybody wins," said Braves' announcer
Skip Caray, whose narcissism was understandable. "We get a lot of viewers
because we have a lot of games on. But we have a lot of games on because the
viewers watch. Our team's marketing and attendance jump because interest
is up. But interest is up largely because of the coverage. Everything is interde-
pendent—it's the positive side of Catch-22." The explosion of cable television
ushered baseball into remote communities ill-served by the game's network
packaging, and created an enormous viewer interest. But to those teams buffeted by the cable tycoons, it was cold-blooded and cyclical, and powerfully
emblematic of baseball as Darwinian theatre. "One of our biggest problems is
the imbalance between those teams who have the SuperStation capability and
those who don't," Bowie Kuhn said in one of his last interviews as commissioner. "Those who have it will get viewers and advertising, and they'll make
more—much more [the Braves, an estimated $250,000 in advertising per
game]—than those who don't. They'll be able to buy more free agents. They'll
corner the talent. We'll have winners and losers, and never the twain shall
meet."

If Kuhn's pronouncement had its touch of hyperbole (the record of the
free-agent era shows, categorically, how local television income does *not* guarantee on-field success), it also showed respect for common sense. In 1987,
National franchises welled up with an average of $6 million from local radio
and TV rights; the other league checked out with receipts of $5.8 million per
team; only the Yankees ($17.5 million) surpassed the Mets and Phillies' win-
nings of $16.5- and $9.5 million; the Giants and Mariners struck bottom with
$2.9- and $2.2 million. "And that's just the local rights," Kuhn said. "It doesn't
begin to get into how much exposure or money the Braves or Cubs, for instance, collect from sponsors or spin-off merchandising sales as a result of
the SuperStation saturation." On mid-eighties *radio*, National League networks
averaged fifty-nine affiliates to the American's fifty-five; of four teams enlisting
more than 100 affiliates, three belonged to the Senior Circuit; Kansas City was
the only Junior member to boast more than eighty-four stations; the Padres,
Giants, and Dodgers even transcended language with a Spanish-speaking

network. Across baseball's media terra firma, local congruity had endured a fall.

National broadcasts, of course, could correct that imbalance — precisely the point of CBS Radio's "Game of the Week," bringing, as it did, the same degree of coverage to New York City, the Republic's most populous market, as to Glendive, Montana, No. 205. Listening, one heard Musburger, the former *Chicago American* sportswriter who now aired "The NFL Today" and college basketball and football for Columbia — there he was, teaming with tyros John Rooney and Ted Robinson; and Dick Stockton, the Syracuse University graduate, pro football and basketball ubiquity, and ex-TV Voice of the Red Sox who joined CBS in 1979 — there *he* was, calling balls and strikes; and White, the ex-Giants, Cardinals, and Phillies' first baseman who, joining the Bombers' broadcast team in 1971, became the first black man to handle big-league play-by-play — there *he* was, showing a national audience the same resonance Yankees' fans heard over radio and TV; and Lindsey Nelson, shedding retirement to enhance the "Game," his voice more durable than a cocker spaniel's undercoat — there *he* was, working with ex-Redleg Johnny Bench. The series glowed with other play-by-play men like Gowdy, Bob Murphy, Gene Elston, and Jerry Coleman, preached the baseball of renaissance and mood, attracted an average audience of more than 6 million adults, and seemed to tell the pastime's followers, as Goethe had, once, a larger body: "America, you have it better."

By design, CBS utilized announcers who broadcast regularly for American and National League teams. "Long before our first 'Game of the Week,' we'd written to all of the twenty-six clubs asking if we could use their daily announcers," Brescia was telling me. "We asked the Tigers, for instance, that if we happened to be doing a Tigers' game with Kansas City, could we use Ernie Harwell as one of our broadcasters."

"You mean, to simulcast [Harwell's rhetoric carried out at the same time over WJR, Detroit, and the CBS Network]?" I asked.

"That or, more preferably, from our point of view, if Ernie would do his innings on the Tigers' station, then come over to do an inning on our network," Brescia said. "Our intent, from the beginning, was to have a number of regulars — a Gowdy, Lindsey — and then complement them with local announcers most fans had never been able to hear before."

"Why, to guard against overexposure?"

"We just figured that since so many of baseball's best announcers already worked, understandably, for teams, that this way we'd get quality," he said. "We'd drape the 'Game' with a variety of announcers — nobody'd get bored. It would be like the golden days of radio, when local-team broadcasters dominated the network show — sort of a radio kaleidoscope."

It was terrific, the CBS "Game of the Week" — its exposure, its linkage with distant cities and backwater terrain, its Voices whose tones and self-assertion invested baseball with pervasive color.

Would the network present Dewayne Staats, a graduate of Southern Illinois University who became, by stages, the sports director of KPLR-TV in St. Louis, Elston's 1977–84 partner in Houston, and the Cubs' post-1984 radio mouthpiece, or Hank Greenwald, succeeding Nelson in 1982 as KNBR's Voice of the Giants before moving ultimately to Yankee Stadium, or Porter, who took his first broadcasting job with the Dodgers' Shawnee, Oklahoma, farm team and joined the big club in 1976, twenty-three years later, or that ex-jock-turned-wireless conduit, the Angels- and, later, Giants' slick-tongued Ron Fairly? Would the Athletics' Bill King, normally reporting over KSFO, San Francisco, or George Kell, Tigers' TV deputy and Hall of Fame infielder, or the talented Dave Van Horne, touching Oshawa, Ontario, and Brandon, Manitoba, and Saskatoon, Saskatchewan, over the Expos' radio and CBC Television networks — would *they* command this week's Columbia microphone? Would listeners in Dallas and Dubuque hear the Blue Jays' television entity, Don Chevrier, or that club's radio signature, Tom Cheek, or the ex-CBS employee, Andy Musser, a Phillies' announcer since 1976, or the vivid nuances of Denny Matthews, replacing Bud Blattner in late 1975 as the Voice of the Royals and stroking an eleven-state network from New Mexico to Tennessee?

From Saturday afternoon to night and one weekend to another, you never knew. "Coming into the first season for the 'Game,' we realized that as the year went along, there'd be a lot of weeks we wouldn't have much advance notice of what clubs would be on," Brescia said. "We might decide to do the Red Sox-Yankees four days before they played, and *then* we'd arrange our broadcast team — not the other way around. One of our two regulars assigned to the game would handle the first four innings, then the local-team announcers — a Ned Martin from Boston, a Phil Rizzuto from New York — would divide the fifth, and the other CBS regular would do innings six through nine." Not every bigs' announcer — not even a majority — dotted the "Game of the Week," but hinging on their reputation and availability ("A few clubs wouldn't let their guys broadcast for us. Mainly, it was the clubs who themselves had far-flung networks, going way beyond their home market. In those towns, fans could hear that team's broadcasters and our 'Game,' and the teams didn't want their own announcers taking listeners away from them and bringing them to CBS") and, moreover, their club's position in the standings, they, conceivably, *could* have.

In March 1938, CBS Radio's Edward R. Murrow and William S. Shirer sired the first "World News Roundup"; on a national and less elevated scale, this was baseball's response, and I enjoyed the 1980s chance to hear the verbal mix of capacities and styles.

Turning the dial that decade, I also nibbled on another treat: favorites, often long-time, broadcasting for their *local* teams — a Buck or Ken Coleman, a Murphy in New York.

Over WLW, for instance, there was Marty Brennaman, the Reds' radio Voice since his 1974 junket from Virginia, where he was its Sportscaster of the Year three years in a row, to Riverfront Stadium, where, bright and effortless, his scrubbed urbanity a complement to Joe Nuxhall's gab, Marty succeeded the popular Michaels and soon fathered a trademark call. "A couple weeks into that '74 season, we won a game at home in the bottom of the ninth inning and out came a phrase. Basically, I'm very unoriginal," Brennaman said, "but I liked that phrase and it caught on, and now after I'm long gone people will remember Marty Brennaman as the announcer who always said, 'This one belongs to the Reds.'"

Because the eighties Reds were less robust than a decade earlier, Marty's catch phrase was heard less often. But in Washington state, "My, oh, my" and "It will fly away" fashioned an ongoing supremacy; those lines, after all, referred to home runs, not victories, and how could they *not* endure in the natty, matchbox Kingdome?

Out West on vacation, I heard their inventor describe a series of Mariners' blasts, and was reminded, as on previous visitations, of Dave Niehaus' ingenuity. A lively repast, Niehaus had reached Seattle by way of Indiana University, Armed Forces radio and television, Madison Square Garden, Chavez Ravine, and, finally, Anaheim Stadium. After eight years of Angels' play-by-play, he aired the expansion Mariners' regular-season baptism—an April 6, 1977, rout, 7-0, by California—and went on to navigate, as of 1987, more than nine hundred Seattle defeats. Capable, far more than his teams, Niehaus broadcast nearly three thousand miles from mid-Manhattan and was tristely underrated. In the mid-1980s, that condition also plagued another mouthpiece, Baltimore's Jon Miller—to myopic New Yorkers, Maryland might as well *be* Seattle—but, one suspected, not for long. As the columnist, Orioles' cable television analyst, and Cable News Network TV- and Mutual Radio talk-show host, Larry King, has written, "He is the best young announcer in major league baseball today."

Miller was born in Northern California and, at twenty-two, covering the home-town A's, broadcast his first big-league game. In 1978-79, he handled Rangers' play-by-play, then toured Fenway Park for three years as Coleman's sidekick, then replaced Chuck Thompson as radio's Voice of the Orioles. At the time, Jon was thirty-one years old; that first Baltimore season, he was also preternaturally lucky. The 1983 Orioles won the pennant, beat Philadelphia in the World Series, and drew more than 2 million spectators for the first time; Miller inherited a huge following over WFBR's seven-state network. Quickly, listeners discovered that Jon was a mimic, parodying Michaels, Vin Scully, and Mel Allen during dull stretches and rain delays; that he avoided the clinical morass that Brother Al condemned as "boring, absolutely boring. I've got a satellite dish at my home in Menlo Park, California, and I've been able to watch eight or nine games a night. In every game, it seems, the local announcer always has the same conversation—should they send the man over to second. It's a baseball seminar—it's really starting to bug me"; and that he was a roundish, impious, and regaling resource who understood, viscerally, humor's ability to renew and outdo the game.

Locally, Jon Miller set a mid-eighties standard for play-by-play excellence. He had many compatriots but few peers, and his blue-chip consortium allowed grudging entry.

One who *did* ingress was an ex-athlete-turned-sportscaster who glittered on *analysis*, and who "has rekindled hope," observed columnist Phil Mushnick, "that sophisticated baseball commentary has a place in New York." He had been a catcher, 1959–80, with the Cardinals, Phillies, Montreal, and Red Sox, a two-time All-Star and world champion, and one of only seven modern-day players to decorate four big-league decades. His last season, he moved to the Phillies' broadcast booth, and in 1983 to a forum which ensured that, unlike Miller or Niehaus, Tim McCarver would not be underrated.

"He has received much praise for his . . . work as a broadcaster for the New York Mets," Jack Craig wrote the following year. "This is much better than being lauded in Kansas City or Houston because the networks are in New York, and so are the decision-makers." In a way, McCarver, droll and incisive, *made* their decision; he was a natural personality, with a casual, blue-collar appeal, and reaped a tumbleweed of certified assignments. In 1984, ABC named him to its All-Star team; three months later, he graced the network's Cubs-Padres' playoff series; that same season, baseball chose McCarver to host its new highlight series, the syndicated "The Greats of the Game." Then, in 1985, Tim joined the Arledges' Fall Classic coverage, saying of St. Louis pitcher John Tudor, "He's just like a surgeon. The only difference is that when he takes the heart out of a team, he doesn't replace it"; striking *USA Today*'s radio/TV critic, Rudy Martzke, as "clever, witty, an undeniable plus"; and prompting *Sports Illustrated* to scribble, "Nobody explicates the game with as much patience and with such good humor as McCarver." Added Michaels, his Oktoberfest play-by-play colleague: "I have a certain way of doing a ball game, and I was able to manifest it during the Series. And one reason was Tim. He doesn't always agree with what I say, but he has the remarkable ability to hear where you're going and get in the flow. I just felt the 'fit' was there. It was like working a jigsaw puzzle and finding all the pieces."

By now, the Yankees were rumored to be calling (one can almost see the *Daily News* headline: "Steinbrenner steals Mac: Mets to Yankees — 'Drop Dead' "), and so too the Red Sox and Phils. Would the Tennessean flee the forest and concrete of Flushing Meadow? "Don't think so," he said. "You know, I sort of like it where I am." Small wonder; in the mid-1980s, like Kubek (the color man, helping Chevrier, on thirty-five Blue Jays' CTV games a year) and Don Drysdale (the White Sox' TV Voice and ABC's backup play-by-play man), McCarver had achieved what he called "the best of three worlds" — local luminance, network prestige, and sprouting mushrooms of wealth.

That did not mean, by inverse, that Drysdale was not *already* comfortable when the Dodgers' hurler retired in 1969. After a fourteen-year career of 209 victories, a 2.95 ERA, five World Series, and nine All-Star Games, a big-league record of 58⅔ straight scoreless innings, and beanballs, spitballs, and confounded speed, he *was*.

The owner of a ranch in Hidden Hills, near Los Angeles, Big D could easily have returned there; by that point, he was raising thoroughbreds; a number had raced competitively. Instead, Don broke through into broadcasting with the 1970–71 Expos, went to Arlington Stadium for a year, and returned in 1973 to Southern California, joining Gene Autry's KMPC Radio and KTLA-TV. "I've always been interested in announcing," he affirmed as early as 1967. "I've listened for years to the deliveries of different announcers, their styles, the way they enunciate, and so forth. Of course, you've got to work at it like anything else. I realize it's not like summertime and the living is easy. Baseball ain't just all *Porgy and Bess*."

From 1973 to 1976, the Angels' troika of Niehaus, Drysdale, and Dick Enberg broadcast the pastime with honesty and understanding. Dave was excitable; Dick, conversational; Big D, as soothing as Perry Como's pitch. "Here on the West Coast, there's a tradition of being more reserved in our description of a game," Drysdale said. "I think Vinnie Scully is the backbone of that attitude. We don't cheerlead, and we don't make excuses. We just call the game down the middle." When Niehaus set out for Seattle, The Don & Dick Show began a triumphal tour as one of baseball's hottest series. Said Gene Mauch, the Minnesota manager, playfully: "Enberg—we know he's tops. And Drysdale? Don talks great—particularly great for a guy who spent most of his life with two fingers in his mouth." In 1979, the tour ended as Enberg went full-time to NBC; by then, signing a part-time contract with ABC, the ex-Dodger and future Hall of Famer (inducted, belatedly, at Cooperstown, on August 12, 1984) himself had scaled the network wall.

At The House of Howard, Drysdale broadcast "Monday Night Baseball," the playoffs, All-Star Game, and World Series, and assorted hopscotch: att., the "Superstars" competition. He was polished if not ennobling; his style was gently persuasive; and yet I felt, somehow, that his detached sense of *California*, so ideal for local-team coverage, lacked the celebrated hype and gymnastics one expected from ABC. "It's funny," said a former sidekick. "Don always struck me as an NBC-kind of announcer—a Gowdy, Scully—where they give you baseball, not Barnum. At ABC, they have the three rings in the circus. I've never thought Big D fit in."

At their broadcast cores, Drysdale and Cosell were antipodean. Howard was never *easy* to take, but he was *easier* on the Big Events. At a Super Bowl or XXIII Olympiad, his voice, idioms, and even unclipped ego added a natural drama that struck one as appropriate; The Mouth, *daily*, on the other hand, would seem hilariously inane. Big D inverted that balance sheet. On a World Series or All-Star Game, Don was effective but cool, too reserved for a schoolboy raised on Allen and Dean, and I found myself, at times, sharing this October 1984 critique in *The Sporting News*: "Drysdale was articulate, assertive, knowledgeable, and experienced, but those qualities are offset by the clichés that tumble from his tongue. Drysdale was competent—but not outstanding—during the baseball playoffs." Daily, locally, however, or even on "Monday Night Baseball," it was that very familiarity, contempt for melodrama, and sense of not trying too hard, that made Drysdale so easy to take. He was neighborly, and his manner showed it—"Hey, he's one of us" (though taller, tanner, more handsome, and possessed of a better grasp of the game), the mythical fan might state—talented but not surpassing, impressive but not intimidating, and, thus, approachable. If you *really* want to appreciate Don Drysdale, one felt like saying, catch his act over KMPC (until late 1981, when Big D left the Angels) or, starting the season afterward, seduced by bucks, from Comiskey Park, Chicago.

As a Dodger, Drysdale won eight games and lost twelve at Connie Mack Stadium, and it was there that he pitched against and, later, played before the local Valiant to whom Philadelphians gave their hearts: Richie Ashburn, retiring in early 1963, after a fifteen-year career with the Phillies, Cubs, and Mets, to become, like Don, an ex-jock behind the mike.

A two-time batting champion, hitting .338 in 1955 and .350 three years later, Ashburn had steered the 1950 Whiz Kids to a pennant, three times led his league in hits, and in his final season, amazed the expansion Amazin's by hitting a team-high .306.

"They lost one hundred and twenty times," George Vecsey wrote of those 1962 Metropolitans, "and Ashburn went down kicking and screaming one hundred and twenty times." At thirty-five, he was still lithe and a pugnacious competitor; he could have played for several years. But "I had to quit sometime," Richie said of his decision to become a Phillies' radio and TV commentator, "and this gives me security. If it was any other job in any other city, I don't think I would have taken it. But Philadelphia has always been like a second home [his first: Tilden, Nebraska]. And this is a really good job. I could be carrying a lunch pail."

From 1948 even beyond his 1960 trade to the Wrigleys, Ashburn was "one of the most popular men," Ray Kelly noted in the *Philadelphia Bulletin*, "ever to play here." Joining Byrum Saam over radio and television station WFIL, he became equally popular as an announcer. Not a Redhead or Barrymore — "Those first few years," he was saying now, "I thought at the time I was all right; looking back, I know I was awful" — he was, at bottom, a reassuring figure; Richie furnished continuity, back to Granny Hamner and Del Ennis and the Golden Year of 1950; his boyish enthusiasm was seen as engaging, not sophomoric, and because people liked him (Re: H. Cosell), they also liked his broadcasts.

One month after Ashburn's hiring, the Phillies named Bill Campbell, longtime WCAU sports director, as their No. 3 announcer. Eight years later, Campbell was assigned to antiquity, and from Houston, having aired Astros' games in 1965–70, sprang his replacement and son of a minister — the gifted Harry Kalas, whose angelic face belonged in the Vienna Boys Choir and whose voice was sharp and voluble, like a wrecker demolishing cars.

"Harry had worked at Houston under Bill Giles, and when Bill came up here [in 1970, as the Phillies' vice-president, business operations], he shortly brought Kalas with him," explained the team's vice-president for public relations, Larry Shenk, "and instantly you were hit by two things. First, Harry's baby face — he'll look ten years old when he's sixty [in March 1987, he turned fifty-one]. Second, when he opened his mouth, boom — a deep, rich baritone, like a bottomless volcano, almost like he'd had years of opera training. It's like when I grew up around here with Saamie — no one could call a home run like him. An inimitable voice, and Harry's cultivated it."

By 1965, Kalas had already employed it to leap from the University of Iowa, where he majored in speech, radio, and television, and moonlit in drama and debate, to a two-year hitch in the Army, serving as public-information specialist, to the Hawaii Islanders of the Pacific Coast League, whom he broadcast for in 1961–64, and, finally, to Texas. Arriving in Philadelphia, he proceeded to form, with Saam and Ashburn, a triad rivaling the Mets' concern of Nelson, Kiner, and Murphy. "Yes, and for just the caliber of their voices, the excitement they could cause, I think only Pittsburgh's Prince and Woods [and, I would add, St. Louis' Buck and Caray]," a relative and Phillies' fan suggested, "could exceed the sum of By and Kalas."

Then, in late 1975, Saam retired, was replaced by Andy Musser, and Kalas became the Phillies' Voice. "As Saamie's successor, it was a great platform for him," Shenk said, "and between that visibility and his popularity, which he's well aware of, Harry has nationally taken off." Spurning hundreds of candidates, NFL Films chose Kalas to cohost the nationally syndicated "NFL Films Presents" and "NFL PRO! Magazine" and to do the voice-over narrations of the "NFL Game of the Week," "NFL Week in Review," and "Inside the NFL." He was invited, like Nelson, years earlier, to call the televised games of Notre Dame football; for Metro-Sports, he handled the play-by-play of Fighting Irish, DePaul, and Marquette basketball. When, in 1980, the Phillies won their first pennant since the Golden Year, fans in the Delaware Valley, collecting petitions, urged NBC to graft Kalas onto its World Series coverage. They failed, but not the Phillies, and, plainly, not Kalas' career.

By the 1980s, with Woods retired, Nelson exodused from Shea Stadium, and the Caray-Buck union severed, the Phillies packaged baseball more nimbly, I felt, than any radio/TV troupe in the National League. Amid the American's teams, how could one say that about the *Yankees?* and yet, there was always the Scooter.

"Housewives love him. The kids all think he's terrific. And the only man of the house, who normally likes his baseball straight and spiked more with statistics than levity, wouldn't swap the one hundred and fifty-pound pundit for a ton of those data-sprouting encyclopedias often found behind the mike," Will Grimsley wrote for Associated Press. "Too bad the Scooter's act is confined to the upper East Coast. He is a refreshing departure from the norm. He ought to be a national commodity."

I can hear Phil Rizzuto now, even from my boyhood—unleashing "Holy Cow!" upon moments of Bombers' theatricality; dotting air-time with references to "my bride," Cora, his wife since June 1943; terming a ballplayer or colleague a "huckleberry," i.e., an object of whim or disagreement; acknowledging birthdays and sending messages, praising pasta and reading notes from listeners, twitting his compulsion to beat postgame traffic by leaving in the seventh or eighth inning; diverting, entertaining, inevitably *amusing.*

Born on September 25, 1918, in Brooklyn, he had been the exciting and often marvelous Yankees' shortstop on nine 1940s and fifties world championship teams, deserving of induction into the Hall of Fame, but I never knew it. The Scooter, after all, retired in August 1956, when I was five. A year later, he replaced Jim Woods behind the Home of Champions microphone, joining Allen and Red Barber, but I never thought of him as a sportscaster, not even as a child. He touched me, rather, as a playactor bristling with a special pungency; he was his own best subject matter, and veering far from play-by-play to discourse on allergies (which he had) and lightning, plane trips, and crumb cakes (which he, respectively, feared, disliked, and delighted in), the Scooter seemed utterly at home.

In *The Broadcasters*, the Ol' Redhead remarked that "Phil had the quickest reflexes, next to Jackie Robinson, I ever saw. He has a sparkling charm when he wishes to turn it on, and no matter the jam he gets in, he gets out of it by assuming a childlike innocence he can call upon instantly. But Phil has not become the professional broadcaster he should be because he won't do the professional preparation." Woods, in his ringing, unabashed way, would tell me, "Allen and Barber were never that close — there was a coolness there, but after '56 their common hostility to Rizzuto drew them together. They were professionals and he wasn't, and they resented him. Phil'd go down to the dugout and get stories about players, write down the stuff on a scrap of paper, come up to the booth, and he'd hide the paper so they couldn't share in it. To them, it was immature."

As a Yankees' fan growing up in the early sixties, even in the very different baseball age of the 1980s, I didn't care. The Scooter was no Allen, naturally, or Barber, but he *did* own a flair and certain exhilaration — "Bad game or good," observed a one-time college roommate, "he always gives you a show" — and like every bodacious mouthpiece I can think of, his identity and mannerisms were instantly recognizable.

There's that Rizzuto, I knew at the very moment, turning the dial, I heard Phil's first sharp-brimmed syllables; over the Yankees' flagship outlets, WABC Radio (post-1980) and WPIX-Television (continuously, since 1951), his airwave voice flaunted especiality, and as the Scooter "reached over and grabbed a broader spectrum of the viewing audience," Grimsley noted in late 1982, "nonbaseball people who might otherwise be watching Carol Burnett, Merv Griffin, or a movie," it impressed me that Rizzuto, perhaps without realizing it, had emerged as one of baseball's last broadcast *characters* — an enlivening, irrepressible throwback to the era of Ol' Diz, Bert Wilson, and Earl Gillespie — announcers who, if not always bigger than the game, at least made The Game seem bigger than it was. He was not Ralph Ellison's nameless, faceless *Invisible Man*; if one was bored by baseball, one might still dote upon the Scooter; he knew, like Dudley, Waite Hoyt, and Rosey Rowswell, that "almost any idiot can handle balls and strikes of a game that's great on its own," the Cubs' Jack Quinlan once mused. "But it takes a different approach — tell a joke, begin a story, explain how to make moonshine in a still, anything but hits and runs — to keep you listening when the game's so lethargic even shock treatment couldn't save it."

That had been, of course, exactly the Scooter's approach, lethargic game or not, and I was happy to find, listening now to Rizzuto's thirty-first year as a Yankees' announcer, that I enjoyed it more than even a decade or two earlier — in part, I'm sure, because of its uncommonality.

"Television has changed everything — that's why there's not much color left in baseball broadcasting," I recalled Lindsey Nelson saying. "You've got a generation of announcers today who've been brought up to think of TV as pictures with cut lines. You don't say as much; you downplay personality in favor of fewer words that complement the camera. It's the visuals, not announcer's style, that count. If you want to make it big as a broadcaster today, you have to make it on television, and to make it, you have to really minimize your language."

"But when they go back to radio, can't they be more expressive than a robot?" I asked.

"They don't know *how* to, that's the problem," he said. "Most broadcasters today weren't brought up on radio. From the very first of their training, TV was the story. For announcers of my era, it was a different story. We put *radio* first. Even after we changed our style to fit, we could always revert to opening up, to paint pictures the listeners couldn't see. Because we had the great training in radio, we could go from points A to B, and we'd always bring, instinctively, some of that radio color along. But now, it's the other way around. It's much harder to go from points B to A, to go from TV to radio. By then, your color has already been bleached out by the tube."

"So the wireless is almost incidental."

"No, no," he countered, quickly. "If you do it right, radio makes baseball soar. But what hurts the game now is that when announcers switch from TV to radio, they use the same dry, mechanical style that works on television. They feel they have to be cool on TV, and their style laps over to radio. Well, that's all wrong. If you don't change, get warmer, excited, you're left with no pizzazz." Lindsey Nelson was no *paison*, but the Scooter had *pizzazz*.

Were many 1980s local, in contrast to network, announcers duller than greasepocked pans? — a Frank Messer and Wayne Walker with the White Sox and Athletics, a Joe Angel at Minnesota.

Did some consider it, apparently, their martial call to reshape baseball in a cast of boredom? — a Fran Healy with the New York Mets, a Jim Rooker in Pittsburgh.

One could hardly blame Rizzuto, whose color would have survived, I believe, a hundred full-cycle bleachings.

Or Kalas, or McCarver, or the Orioles' Jon Miller.

Or the outlaw dominance whose outrageous career defied the laws of probability, longevity, and cirrhosis of the liver.

His name was Harry Caray, and he had a passion for appetites and fame.

* * *

There has always been, with Caray, the urge to engage in caricature — the boozy philanderer whom Chicagoans dubbed the Mayor of Rush Street; the unapologist who, almost effortlessly, crafted a jaunty, inescapable image; the effervescence who broadcast from the bleachers, waved his fish net to trap foul balls, and led fans in his rendition of "Take Me Out to the Ball Game"; the unorthodox stylist whose jarring cadence, delicious sarcasm, and evident love of The Game made him, some said, the finest baseball broadcaster of all time.

A weighty and exceedingly cocksure figure, he seemed, even now, quasi-fictional and certainly unquenchable. *Caricature* or reality? Listening to or observing Harry Caray, could one tell any difference between his real-life and on-air personae? By the 1980s, was there anything to tell? Did it really matter? The caricature was his message, and his message was gold.

He had mined it, looking back, almost from the start—in a childhood where, orphaned at an early age, he was raised by friends of his mother, and later, as a teenager who followed the Cardinals through the eyes and irenic oratory of France Laux; in his early-1940s radio investiture, working, first, in Joliet, Illinois, and then Kalamazoo, Michigan, and later, as a big-league mouthpiece who aired his initial Redbirds' game in 1945; in his twenty-five-year reign as a St. Louis preoccupation, where he parented a regional cult one must term enormous, and later, as the rasp-voiced fixation of both Chicago clubs—broadcasting glibly, brazenly, more often right than wrong, and with astonishing zeal.

When Caray first captured my imagination, in the early sixties, from a thousand miles away, over the gargantuan signal of KMOX, St. Louis, I discovered him to be, outside of Bob Prince, the most engrossing announcer in the National League. He was a fan, the Redbirds' prosopopeia, and he called the action clearly—discharging the Carayism, "Holy Cow!" (Harry says Rizzuto stole it; the Scooter claims the opposite); mixing bite with home-town cheer ("He'd get on a Cardinal—Kenny Boyer, for instance—and he was merciless," said Bob Broeg of the *Post-Dispatch*. "Boyer'd come up in the ninth inning, the game on the line, and you could just tell from his voice, he expected, he was *certain*, Boyer'd make an out"); and absorbing baseball's largest network with his jubilant home-run call ("It might be . . . it could be . . . it is!").

A generation later, reaching millions of households over cable television, he had molded a *national* following, and despite (because of?) the fact that, increasingly, during boring set-tos, Harry left the action to dwell on anything *but* the game—"I'm a long-time friend of Harry's, and I watch the cable in Knoxville all the time," said Lindsey Nelson, warmly. "I'll sit there in front of the TV and talk back to him. He'll be telling stories and this or that, and I'll scream, 'Get back to the game,' or he'll call a pitch low and outside, and I'll say, 'Like hell it is. It was right over the plate' "—the startling thing, even phenomenal, was that as the 1980s Voice of America's Cubs, he had become larger than in St. Louis, almost larger than the team, and the only daily play-by-play man, thriving, now, over four decades, to bridge the chasmal gulf between precommercial television and the Good God VCR. Caray was "Holy Cow!"ing audiences before the sunburst of V-E Day. In an age of Yuppies, heavy metal, and Arnold Schwarzenegger, he was somehow still a star.

"One is tempted to call Harry Caray a throwback, but a throwback to *what?* He's unique. He charges through his professional and personal lives with the throttle wide open. He's a ham. He's colorful, controversial, complicated, compulsive, impulsive, flamboyant, opinionated, and outspoken," *Inside Sports* columnist Bob Rubin wrote in May 1984. "All of these qualities account for

Caray's extraordinary popularity. [During games] he exults, he mourns, he rips, he praises, he questions, he agonizes . . . After games, his drinking, romancing, back-slapping . . . exploits into the wee hours are the stuff of legend. . . . It has been suggested he is the most popular man in Chicago, a thought that makes him beam. He is probably the only broadcaster ever to consistently overshadow the players whose action he describes." Unless one flung Allen, Prince, and Dean into a sort of electronic lethe, Caray was *not,* of course, "the only broadcaster." But he *was* "unique," he *did* command attention, and his career, to parrot Rubin, *had* been "legendary"—the last, perhaps, of baseball's red-hot play-by-play men, a media dinosaur who defied the years.

The legend took root in 1942, when Harry, arguably, twenty-two ("Who knows what date he was born on?" said Nelson. "His son Skip says that whenever Harry takes on a new job, he automatically lops four years off his age"), suddenly unlocked a puzzlement.

Caray frequently visited Sportsman's Park, and the games there were *alive.* But at home, via radio, they seemed interminable, and gradually Harry began to ask himself, "Was I that lucky—happening to only go to games that were great—or were the broadcasters that bad?"

It was the announcing, Harry decided—that France Laux and his plodding style. Without experience, he was sure he could do better, if only he got the chance, and mailing a letter to Merle Jones, the KMOX general manager, Caray petitioned for the job. Shrewdly, he sent the missive to Jones' home; he marked it personal; "something about my freshness and brashness must have appealed to him," Caray related forty years later, "because he had me come down and audition." The audition fell flatter than a barren Holy Cow. "I must have been terrible, and the guy giving me the audition kissed me off. I was ready to leave, but then I remembered Mr. Jones had said he'd listen to me personally. I made an issue of it and got another chance."

This chance, he seized.

In 1943–44, Caray went to work for stations WJOL in Joliet and Kalamazoo's WKZO; then it was back to St. Louis, where Harry expected to join the service. But bad eyesight defrocked him—"I've always needed thick glasses," he said, "and it kept me out of the Army"—and instead of touring Munich, Bastogne, and Nuremberg, Caray was soon jousting with names like Musial, Slaughter, and Moore.

"Once I found out the service wouldn't take me, I hit the pavement looking for a job," he said, "and finally, I got a nightly radio sports talk show. Hell, people today talk about controversy—they should have been there when *I* took over. I just didn't read scores—I went wild. I editorialized. I 'Walter Winchelled' like crazy."

"And St. Louis sat up and took notice," I said.

"How couldn't they?" he said, emphatically, his tones even hoarser than usual. "Everything I did was to *get* noticed. And it all paid dividends when in early '45 one of the two stations carrying Cardinal games developed an opening for play-by-play. I went in and pleaded with the president of the brewery who sponsored the games—Griesedieck Brothers. Well, he was very nice and praised my work, and then promptly said, 'Sorry, you got a great future ahead, but right now we're looking for a big name.' "

"What'd you say?"

"We were sitting there, and this guy mentions one candidate he's got in mind. 'I can listen to him,' he said, 'and read the paper at the same time.' Well, then I sat up. 'That's your problem!' I told him. 'You're paying hundreds of thousands of dollars and what are you getting for it? People are reading the damn paper while your commercials are on!' "

"That convinced him?"

"He just stared at me for a minute, frowned, paused, picked up the phone, and got his guy from the advertising agency on the other end and said, 'Get over here. I want you to meet our new play-by-play man.' "

On April 17, 1945, having never called a baseball game, Caray aired the Redbirds' Opening Day tussle, a 3–2 loss to Chicago. He broadcast over tiny WTMV, East St. Louis; his Cardinals were defending world champions; and his sidekick was gabby Gabby Street, one of twenty former Redbirds to enter broadcasting, the most of any big-league team (the rest: Dizzy Dean, Jim Bottomley, Frank Frisch, Leo Durocher, Joe Garagiola, Bud Blattner, Mike Shannon, Bob Uecker, Tim McCarver, Bill White, Harry Walker, Ron Fairly, Larry Dierker, Cookie Rojas, Dave Campbell, Gus Mancuso, Nelson Briles, Jim Kaat, and Al Hrabosky).

An ex-Senators' receiver, Walter Johnson's battery mate, and the original manager of the Gas House Gang, Street was also the first man to catch a baseball dropped from the top of the Washington Monument (on August 21, 1908, on his thirteenth try, of a ball released 555 feet from the ground and traveling 290 miles an hour, according to the Army ballistics department, when it hammered Street's glove). In 1945, Caray transplanted the routine to St. Louis, and of three baseballs falling from the roof of the Civil Court Building, 387 feet away, Gabby snagged two. "It was quite a sight — they had a rope tied around me when I threw the balls so I wouldn't fall off the roof," Harry said by way of explanation. "But Gabby took it all in stride — like he did everything, even that day at the Washington Monument. He always said it wasn't that big a deal that he caught a ball dropped *from* the top. The trick, he said, would have been to throw a ball from the ground *to* the top." Added Street: "Harry dropped the balls for the benefit of a War Loan Drive. I autographed both that I caught and together they sold for a million bucks in bonds. And it was my greatest catch — better than the Monument. Back then, I was young [twenty-six], keen-eyed, I had great reflexes. But with Harry, it was almost forty years later, and any man who thinks he is as good at sixty-three as he is at twenty-six better have his head examined."

For two years, forced to choose between Caray, Laux, and Dean's simultaneous play-by-play, it was St. Louisans who scratched their heads. Then, in early 1947, Cardinals' owner Sam Breadon — wanting more money for his radio rights and more followers for his coverage — awarded Griesedieck Brothers, the Caray-Street sponsor, an exclusive contract. "The Cardinals had won the '46 Series [over Boston, in seven games], their third in five years, and

Breadon thought this was the time to strike for more dough. He felt that even though I was on a weaker station than Diz or Laux, I could sell the Cardinals — we'd already built that kind of audience. So Breadon figured, 'Hey, if only Caray's doing the games, people'll have to tune in the games, and once they hear him, they'll stay,' " Harry said. "And I have to say that Gabby and I were a hell of a team. He was such a great influence on me — I was just a kid when I started out, and he guided me along. He was born forty years too soon — today he'd be a national figure. Gabby was perfect — he'd always have a humorous story to fit a situation on the field and, to go along with it, he was a great base-ball analyst."

The Caray-Street ticket was blithe, even captivating — the professional and anecdotist, the Thespian and ex-jock — and prophetic of future bell ringers: Jack Quinlan and Lou Boudreau, Nelson and Garagiola, Dick Enberg and Don Drysdale, the mid-eighties offering of Vin Scully and Joe G. "We showed how to put your broadcast team together — the main guy, me, aided by the former athlete — we did it the way you should," Caray was recalling. "I'd served my apprenticeship in the sticks, I'd improved my vocabulary, perfected my style, learned the game, so that when I got the opportunity, boom! I was a success right away, and I ran the show. That's why I hate the thought of so many fine young announcers being out in the boonies like I was. I got the chance — they don't. And the reason they don't is because as soon as a ball-player finishes, they move him into a broadcast booth — he's never even been before a microphone. Hey, if it's that easy, some of us wasted a hell of a lot of time."

"But Street was an ex-ballplayer. What about him?" I said.

"First of all, he was a great talent — so charming, colorful, he didn't *need* the training. He could just go on the air, be himself, be a hit — he didn't have to improve. Not many jocks can do that," he said. "But the key is that as good as Gabby was, he did only analysis. *I* did balls and strikes. Today, Jesus, they've got boobs who can barely speak trying to call play-by-play. And they aren't capable. I don't resent the ballplayer's success. But it deprives so many deserving young talents around the nation of the opportunity they should have somewhere along the line."

After Street's death, at sixty-eight, on February 6, 1951, a second former catcher, Gus Mancuso, prattled as Caray's partner, and *his* end of the line arrived when, in 1954, Jack Buck and Milo Hamilton became the Cardinals' announcers. By that time, the Redbirds had dumped flagship WIL for Amer-ica's most profitable CBS affiliate, the spiring KMOX. It was an apropos transition, for the Cardinals now had new broadcast sidekicks, a new originat-ing outlet, and a new owner: August A. Busch, Jr., the Anheuser-Busch Brewery mogul. "In '47, Breadon had sold out to Fred Saigh and Bob Hanne-gan, and by the early fifties, they were in real bad shape financially," said Caray. "There were rumors the Cardinals were in trouble, were going to move, and to literally save the club for St. Louis, Gussie Busch bought the team." He refurbished Sportsman's Park, renaming it Busch Stadium. He also named Anheuser-Busch as the Redbirds' radio/television sponsor.

"You were Griesedieck's guy, selling the beer on the air for eight years, and now a competitor not only buys the rights, he buys the team," I said. "How'd you survive?"

"I almost didn't," he gibed. "Gussie was afraid every time I said 'Budweiser,' people would think 'Griesedieck.' But fans started a hell of a lot of petitions, telling Gussie to bring me back. The brewery's beer distributors in the whole Cardinal listening area said they wanted me — unanimously. So I went to Gussie and said, 'Look, just give me six months to show what I can do — that's all.' By the end of '53, without once even mentioning Griesedieck, I'd put them out of business in Missouri and southern Illinois." He was full of himself and of redemption, and his legend was on its way.

"You have to understand what Harry was to the Midwest in my childhood," author Bill James has written. "In the years when baseball stopped at the Mississippi, KMOX Radio built a network of stations across the Midwest and into the Far West that brought major league baseball into every little urb across the landscape. Harry's remarkable talents and energies and enthusiasm were the spearhead of their efforts, and forged a link between the Cardinals and the Midwest that remains to this day; even now, some of my [Kansas] neighbors are Cardinal fans." Or, as Peter Gammons explained in the *Boston Globe*: "For more than the first half of this century, as the western and southernmost team, they were the club of the heartland from Raleigh to Memphis, Mobile to Little Rock, Omaha to Dallas, because the games on KMOX grew to become baseball's first, foremost, and most powerful. From any of the eight states that border Missouri — all the way down through Mississippi — the Cardinals draw weekend trippers. The Cardinals are the *real* America's Team."

As KMOX's 1953–69 baseball Voice, Caray evolved into the mirror and magnet of the Redbirds' huge discipleship. He glazed a reputation for sharp, curt commentary, rooted zealously for the Cardinals while yet drubbing parish heroes, and reaching as many as 124 stations in fourteen states, became almost a magical property in Webster City, Iowa, and Cleveland, Tennessee, and Lawton, Oklahoma; his rhetoric dominated the place.

"In St. Louis itself, opinion was divided on Caray, say fifty-fifty. They compared him to France, or Diz, and opinion was split," said Bob Broeg, of whom Gammons observed, "There isn't a finer or more captivating baseball historian writing in a newspaper today."

"What about the hinterlands?" I asked.

"That's the difference," Broeg said. "There, it was like ninety-five to five — Harry was a god. One reason is that the club's network had been nothing before Harry took over — now Cardinal games were being boomed all over, and Caray was the first guy they'd heard, and they had no frame of reference. My predecessor as the *Post-Dispatch* sports editor, Roy Stockton, used to say, 'You could have put Mother Goose on as the Cardinal Voice, and the sticks would have loved her' — they were that starved for baseball." He stopped a moment. "This isn't to demean Harry. It's just that he had a couple things going for him. First, for the outlying network fans, he was the first. Second, he knew how to entertain."

Years before Howard Cosell, surfeited with self-importance, professed to "tell it like it is," Harry Caray did.

When Don Blasingame made an error, Caray wouldn't merely say of the 1955-59 Cardinals' infielder, "a tough chance, he almost had it"; or "ball four, barely missed," of a walk by 1962-64 pitcher Bobby Shantz; or "Ken Boyer — he hits a pop-up to second base," of his favorite local victim. Instead, his voice rich with ridicule, each inflection dripping with despair, Caray might mourn, "Right at him — *muffs* it! *Shouuuld* have made the play," or mutter, "Ball four — *Holy Cow! What* a time to lose your control," or be moved to swashbuckle, "Let's see if Boyer can come through *this* time . . . Oh, no! *Paaaaahhpped it up! Another* chance goes by the board!" Years later, Jack Craig would write, "As if to flex his muscles, Caray on occasion will turn against one of his own team's players, a reverse rooting. Getting away with this is the personification of power."

Was Caray prejudicial, as detractors charged, another Brickhouse, Rizzuto, or Prince? Asking, I recalled how Plato said, "Before we talk, let us first define our terms." Unlike every "homer" I can think of, Harry never minimized criticism, hesitated to second-guess, or was afraid to step on toes. Because he lived and died, outlandishly, with the St. Louis Cardinals, his put-downs gained credibility. Because, to idolaters in Stoutsville, Missouri, and Jerusalem, Arkansas, Caray *was* the Redbirds personified, he could be, and was, their severest Zoilus.

"My whole philosophy has always been to broadcast the way a fan would broadcast. I'm so tough on my guys because I want them to win so much," he was telling me. "I've often thought that if you gave the microphone to a fan, he'd sound a lot like me. The disappointment, the hurt, the anger, the bitterness, the love, the ecstasy — they'd all be there."

"And players' anger toward you," I said, "that's there too," and not only in St. Louis but, later, on Chicago's South and North Sides.

"I have to inform the fan, even if it means hurting the player," Harry said. "Look, I'm not being noble. I'm just being smart. If you've got 150 games on the screen like the Cubs do now — or even forty TV games a year like we had with the Cardinals — how the hell are you going to fool the people? If a guy strikes out four times with the bases loaded, what the hell are you going to tell them? That he had a real good hard swing? Who cares about that? They care that he choked. I don't criticize the ballplayers, I just report what they do, and if they do badly, then they get a bad report."

"Seriously, don't you love to blast?"

"Hell, no," he said. "I hate to rip players, to say they puke. But baseball isn't like football, where a lineman's goofs can be hidden in a big pile of players. In baseball, everything's out in the open. If it's a great game, I'll say it — even if my guys lose. And if my guys win, I can't tell you it's terrific when there are fifteen errors and the crowd is jeering the players who're stinking up the joint."

"How many players think you tell the truth?"

"Most of 'em," he said, quickly. "Listen, nobody likes to be criticized and that goes for me or you or anybody else. That's the most overdone thing in the world. I don't go to the ball park with the idea of criticizing anybody. What I say is what they do. If they're horseshit, there's nothing I can do about it. The way I broadcast — I sound the way I do because I'm just an inveterate fan who happens to be behind the mike."

He was that, of course, but more than that; raw fans, no matter how inveterate, do not call the 1964, 1967, and 1968 World Series for NBC Television, as Caray did, or win the "Announcer of the Year" Award, formerly presented by *The Sporting News,* a near-record seven times. "It was an award the newspaper presented from the thirties into the fifties, and every year they had two plaques — an Announcer of the Year in both leagues," he said. "Mel Allen won it about ten times, and it finally got to the point where we were so dominating the voting that other clubs began to gripe to J. G. Taylor Spink. We were making a mockery of it, I guess. In the end, they got to him and the award was discontinued."

He relished the Redbirds' "glorious history in a city uniquely tied with its past," the *Globe* ordained, "which creates a perfect marriage between the traditional game and a traditional city," and brought a body of knowledge to ad-lib orations about Grover Cleveland Alexander and Rogers Hornsby and the Gas House Gang.

He knew his baseball and could explain the niceties of the infield fly or hit-and-run. "Hell," Harry retorted, "that's nothing. It's an easy game to know; your own grandmother could learn it."

He was tenacious and would boast in 1984, three years before suffering a mild stroke, that "Here I am in my fortieth year as a play-by-play man and have never missed a week, a day, an inning, a batter. I've worked with guys who have never drank or smoked in their life, and, Christ, they're sick every other day. To them I say, 'Live it up, boys. It's later than you think.'"

Under the extraversion, there lurked too, surprisingly, a reporter — "I never thought that to be correct about the facts meant you had to be dull," he said, "or that you couldn't avoid mistakes *and* be entertaining at the same time" — and fairly, precisely, with an unexpected grasp of particulars, Caray etched the goings-on of Red Schoendienst and Joe Cunningham, hitting .342 in 1953 and .345 six years later, respectively, and Wally Moon and Bill Virdon, the National League's 1954–55 Rookies of the Year, and Curt Flood and Lou Brock, twice whacking two hundred or more hits in a season, and the infield of Bill White, Julian Javier, Dick Groat, and Boyer, starting the 1963 All-Star Game in its entirety, and Stan Musial — his coiled stance frozen like a diamondback — playing in a then-league-record 895 consecutive games, averaging .330 at forty-two, and retiring, with two singles, on September 29, 1963. "There stands baseball's perfect warrior," Ford Frick declared of the Polish Cardinal. "There stands baseball's perfect knight."

In 1964, Boyer knocked in 119 runs and won the MVP Award, Brock, heisted from the Cubs, hit .315, and the Cardinals caught Philadelphia in the last week of the season to snare their first pennant since 1946; in the Series, Bob Gibson won twice and Tim McCarver, the fifth game with a tenth-inning homer. Three years later, Orlando Cepeda became the Most Valuable Player and Gibson, three times beating the Red Sox, the Oktoberfest; the following season, Gibbie *was* the season, hurling thirteen shutouts and twenty-eight complete games and yielding only thirty-eight earned runs. At third base, Boyer grabbed five Gold Gloves; ranging across center field, Flood nabbed seven; by the end of 1969, Gibson owned five of his eventual nine. In 1966, the Redbirds closed one Busch Stadium and opened another; three straight years, they broke their all-time attendance record; twice, the Cardinals lured more than 2 million spectators. During 1953–69, St. Louis and, therefore, Caray published much of baseball's ribbon of news. "All people thought of him as was a great actor, a showman," Jack Brickhouse complained. "They never acknowledged — never stopped to notice — that he could also do a damned clean and honest job of play-by-play."

But, above all, he *was* a showman, and I know outlanders who, even now, reliving a Cardinals' baseball game as told by Caray, are suffused with a nostalgic feeling of regret. "The games haven't been the same since Harry left," said my high school political science teacher, Gerald Cox, a Redbirds' fan since childhood. "I used to listen to him all the time [over KMOX, in upstate New York], and there wasn't anybody like him. He was more immediate than the Cardinals, he made a ten to nothing game come alive. As the years went by, you began to take it for granted — the excitement, the color. He was to the Cardinals what Allen was to the Yankees ["the Babe Ruth of broadcasting," said Bob Hyland, regional vice-president, CBS]. You never stopped to think for a moment that someday Caray might be gone."

At the time, it scarcely seemed possible. There was Caray, series after homestand after season, leaning outside the booth to snag a foul ball in his fish net, or serenading some schlep in St. Joseph on the occasion of a seventieth birthday, or saying, as he did in the fifth inning of a 1958 Cardinals' shellacking, "Well, we've really blown this one. Let's hurry up and get this one over with and get me out of here — *fast*." I have heard people recite, verbatim, long-ago Caray calls. Once, he invaded the top row of the left-field bleachers at old Busch Stadium to get a fan's-eye view. When Flood, moments later, caught a long fly ball, Caray's account made the fact seem more actual than actuality; listeners could not know that Flood's grab, made at the base of the wall, lay out of Harry's sight. Another year, making a belated rush at first-place Los Angeles, St. Louis led, 5–4, in the ninth inning of a crucial September set. "Here it comes," Harry cried of the pitch to Dodgers' rookie Dick Nen. There followed a soul-wracking silence. "Oh my God," he said, finally. "It's over the roof." The next season, on April 17, 1964, in the Cardinals' fourth game, a St. Louis pitcher drove in two runs with a double. "I can't believe it! I can't believe it!" the Redbirds' Voice rejoiced. "Roger Craig has hit the left-center-field wall! The Cardinals are going to win the pennant!" One hundred and seventy days later, in Game No. 162 they did. Surely, it would last forever — the wrangling, the chortling, the "Holy Cows!" "There was no doubt in my mind," Caray said, "I'd be doing Cardinal games until my dying day, that with my last gasp I'd say, 'Cardinals win!' "

On November 3, 1968, early in the morning, on a rain-splashed street, nine hours after Caray ended his broadcast of the Missouri-Oklahoma State football game, that gasp almost proclaimed, "It might be . . . it could be . . . it is!"

From the football match in Columbia, Caray mused, he returned to St. Louis that evening, stopped at a Blues' hockey game, and "was on my way to the Chase-Park Plaza Hotel to eat." Arriving there, he parked his car and began to cross the street, "then turned to see if anything was coming from my left. The next thing I remember was, 'Am I okay out here?' "

Barely.

He had been hit, doctors later told him, at 1:15 A.M., by a car driven by a young Viet Nam veteran, recently returned from the war. The man was not driving his own car, owned neither insurance nor a driver's license, and "had been engaged the day before," Harry chuckled. "Maybe that's what caused him to drive so wild." According to witnesses, the accident knocked Caray forty feet in the air; his shoes were found twenty-five feet south of the hotel; he landed forty feet to its *north*. He suffered a broken nose, shoulder separation, and multiple fractures of both legs below the knees. "It was close, real close, closer than any Cardinal game," he said that December, assisted by a wheelchair, casts encasing both his legs, and recovering in a cottage at St. Petersburg Beach. "You know, it's funny. Here you are, filled with the love for life one minute, and the next minute you can be dead. I'd always thought when you died, you knew about it—that you died in stages, knowing each stage as it came along. But no, death can be an instantaneous thing." Actually, so was Harry's dismissal, stunning, as it did, the greater Cardinals' public. However, its rumored explanation was not, having supposedly bloomed in stages until, on October 9, 1969, Caray was told that his contract with Anheuser-Busch, Inc., would not be renewed.

"While Harry was still convalescing, some members of the Busch family began to notice there were a lot of telephone charges on the bill linking Harry's room to one of the Busch residences," a former sidekick claimed. "This rang a bell, and after some checking around, some following by a detective of Harry, it was discovered that Caray was apparently having an affair with the wife of young August Busch [III], Gussie's son. Naturally, this isn't the greatest way to keep your job—breaking up the marriage of your boss' son, and as it got more involved, it wasn't long before the situation became impossible. Why the hell else would Harry have been fired? He was tremendously popular, the greatest salesman Anheuser-Busch'd ever had." Replied Caray, bemusedly, in that May 1984 *Inside Sports*: "Hell, at forty-seven, I preferred to have people believe the rumor than keep my job. I mean, think of it. I was so irresistible that a beautiful young starlet-type would go for me over the twenty-five-year-old billionaire heir to the crown. . . . At the time, all I said was that I never raped anyone in my life."

It was this effrontery, this disdain for circumspection, that so offended Caray's more decorous/envious confreres. "When I read that in the magazine, it made me sick," Milo Hamilton told me. "It was as plain as Harry's face that he was admitting to having an affair—'never raped anyone,' he said. Saying on the air, 'Well, today I mailed alimony checks to all my ex-wives,' practically bragging about it—no wonder we never got along." Retorted Nelson: "All I can say is that he was a warm kind of guy, fun to be around. And I'll tell you— his impact was enormous. People love him or they hate him, but they always listen. We [the Mets] used to train at St. Petersburg in the spring with the Cardinals, and I'd go to dinner with Harry. *I'd* be ignored—*he'd* be mobbed by people from the Midwest. People'd crowd around, 'Hey, Harry. Hey, Har-ry! Sign this, autograph that!' I was absolutely amazed. I'd never seen anything like it. Nobody had, I think, the kind of following Harry did when he was with the Cardinals—they totally idolized him. In so many ways, he was like Bob Prince, and yet he was still Harry Caray—the norm against which all exciting baseball broadcasters are measured. There was only one of him—there could only *be* one of him. Nobody ever broadcast like he has. Nobody could if they *wanted* to."

Unlike the Pirates, crippled by Prince's firing, the Cardinals thrived beyond Caray's ouster. "Yeah, people were upset," Bob Broeg recollected, "but his successor, Jack Buck, was already well-known and liked, especially in St. Louis. Plus, much more than Pittsburgh, this is a superior baseball town ["There isn't a kid in St. Louis," read the *Philadelphia Daily News* in 1984, "who can't tell you the starting lineup of the Cardinals—the 1934, 1944, or 1964 Cardinals"], and its rooting interest goes deeper than any one announcer or player, no matter how popular." Still, the dispatching stung. During 1970–71, Buck and Woods strove, at best, to peacefully coexist; in the hinterlands, stripped of Caray's gaiety, network ratings tumbled; and Gussie's action even shook the principal, though Harry dismissed it publicly with the breezy throwaway, "After twenty-five years, I was expecting a gold watch. Instead, I got a pink slip."

That fall, rumors had Caray bound for Cincinnati, replacing Jim McIntyre, or Comiskey Park, sinking the Old Commander, or, less probably, Atlanta, axing Hamilton. Instead, those cities awoke in early 1970 to a peculiar bond between baseball's oddest couple. Caray, it was announced, would become the Voice of the Oakland A's, serving at the pleasure and endless whims of Charles Oscar Finley.

"Baseball needs color, and I don't mean just green shirts and white shoes," Charlie O. remarked at the time. "Any time people in baseball can put color into the game, we should do it. I'm doing it with Harry Caray, whom I consider to be the finest baseball announcer in the country." Contemplating self-effacement, Harry could not help himself. "Yes, people have always liked my style," he said. "I've criticized the Cards and got into hot situations with the management, and I'll tell the truth here too. The biggest thing I have as an announcer is believability. If people don't believe me, what can I sell?"

With Monte Moore, the Finleys' long-time holdover, Caray sold valiantly, incessantly, and to little effect. In 1969, their second year in Oakland, the Athletics had drawn only 778,232 customers; this season, Harry hoped to drag them past the million mark. The Bay Area, he bragged, was *his* kind of place—"good eating, good drinking, good fun, good company, good music"— and carousing over KNBR's six-station network, Holy Cow! played the Bee

Gees to Monte's Fred Waring and the Pennsylvanians. He was novel, vibrant, and the radio audience grew; one Midwest transplant wrote, "Listening to you makes me think I'm back in Kansas. I can feel the hot sun and almost see the corn growing"; a newspaper critic noted, "Harry gives a new dimension to the game. Why, he even makes baseball sound as exciting as football. Trouble is, he may be just too good. It seems a lot of citizens would rather listen to Harry than go to the games."

At fifty, Caray watched the Swinging A's develop.

For the first time, Catfish Hunter made the All-Star team; Bert Campaneris led the club in five offensive categories; the Finleys ripped 171 homers and won eighty-nine games, more than *any* Athletics' aggregate since 1932. "I learned a great lesson out there in Oakland," Harry said. "As enthused as I'd been over seeing Musial, Boyer, and Slaughter, I felt myself getting caught up in the development of the young players on the A's — Reggie Jackson, Sal Bando, Hunter, Campaneris. You know what it taught me? That it wasn't as much that I was a great fan of the *Cardinals*, but that I was a tremendous *baseball* fan. I'd never have known that if Gussie hadn't kissed me off."

After a quarter-century of play-by-play, Caray watched his salary swell.

"Lesson number two," he said. "With Charlie and the A's, I learned what a stupid businessman I'd been. When I was with the Cardinals, I'd never even bargained about my pay. I was just so in love with the Cardinals and my job that I took whatever they offered. Then Mr. Finley came along and offered me $30,000 more than I'd ever made. I didn't know that kind of money existed [Holy Cow! hyperbole: By 1969, Caray owned some $500,000 worth of Anheuser-Busch stock]."

He did not, however, much enjoy the Master.

"Oh, nobody could have treated me nicer than Charlie — he disproved this old story that you have to be in baseball fifty years before you know the game," Caray said, "but he was always too damn cruel to the little people in the organization. I used to say to him, 'Charlie, why do you have to hurt them?' He'd say, 'If you ever own a business you'll find out that if people don't fear you, they won't work for you.' He's a funny guy. If you needed him, Charlie could be terrible, but if you didn't, he could be the sweetest guy."

Nor the city's locus.

Once, Caray observed on the air that April nights in Oakland "must be like living in Siberia." Another time, he told a columnist, "I've got a bachelor's apartment here. It's great. But it's just too damn far away from St. Louis." Now, he explained that in July of 1970, "Charlie and I sat down to talk about my future. He said I was doing a great job for the A's, but that he didn't think I could continue being effective unless I moved there. Well, my roots were too strong in St. Louis for me to break up my home and move to the West Coast. I had a beautiful home there and two little girls in school."

Nor, it must be said, the 1970 season's ledger board.

For all of Caray's dramaturgy, his Athletics lured exactly 123 more patrons than they had in 1969. "He'd been brought here specifically to boost attendance," an Oakland writer said, "and whatever excitement he'd produced was irrelevant. The bottom line was that he hadn't." Was Oakland too reserved and cold? Was Harry too risque and hot? More pivotally, was the Bay Area too much a football fortress for even this magniloquence to sunder? Yes[3], I suspect, and few shook their heads when the A's confirmed on October 15, 1970, that Caray had gotten the hell out of California. Three months later, I was reading a newspaper when, at the bottom of the page, I spotted a story announcing Harry's next job. The article implied that the hiring caught many Midwesterners by surprise. I wondered why. Caray was merely returning, it seemed to me, to his following and his roots.

I doubted that he had really left.

As the 1971 radio Voice, succeeding Bob Elson, of the Chicago White Sox, Caray inherited a hemophiliac. Worse, he was asked—and expected, taking account of his $50,000 salary and escalating attendance clauses—virtually, by *himself*, to clot it.

"When I'd been with the Cardinals, I had three different offers through the years to go to New York," Caray said. "Usually, the ad agencies wanted to link me up with Mel Allen—now there's a turn in the road to ponder on. But I always said, if I had to consider working anyplace else, it would be Chicago." Pausing, he laughed. "I never dreamed the day would come when I'd have to really consider it." Another laugh. "Of course, I never considered that when I did, things would be as bad as they were."

A year earlier, the Pale Hose had lost 106 games, attracted fewer than half-a-million spectators, and been canceled by their flagship station, WMAQ. "There was no talent, fans were afraid to come to the ball park because of crime, little coverage in the Chicago newspapers, practically no interest in the team," Harry said. "That's how it was when I joined the Sox in January— absolutely awful. The silver lining was that I thought to myself, 'You're starting at the bottom. It can't get any worse.' " Shortly afterward, on January 23, 1971, *The Sporting News* reported that because no major Chicago station would deign to *carry* the Sox, "Executive vice-president Stu Holcomb has signed a suburban network on three small stations, two of which are FM. They will include WEAM-FM of Evanston, WTAQ in LaGrange, and WJOL-FM in Joliet."

Congratulations, Harry twitted himself; what a draconian way to revisit the Midwest. Even in Oakland, he had fathomed the sheer repugnance of his new commodity—the losing, drudging White Sox, "the most unexciting team in baseball," declaimed the *New York Times;* obscured by the Cubs, deserted by all but a small circle of fans—*that* Harry had bargained for, even *before* taking the job. It would be difficult, but doable; selling, after all, was Caray's strength. But to sell without a Second City station, on three clunkers barely audible in northern Illinois—that Caray had *not* expected. Minus display counter, how could one vend even discount Hose, or persuade consumers to frequent the Sox' South Side store?

How could you do it?

(But if you could.)

Looking back, whatever shadow Caray cast from 1945 through 1969, I believe, was matched by his eleven-year run at Comiskey Park. It was not, by any summing up, that the White Sox flourished — 1971–81 were wobbly and erratic years — but rather, lacking family capital, television and radio revenue, and the other accoutrements of contemporary baseball, that they survived the seventies, indeed, survived at all — *that* was the miracle.

On September 21, 1970, 672 spectators paid to see the Pale Hose fumble. In late 1975, the Sox nearly flew to Seattle until Bill Veeck, mortgaging his dog, car, and house, improvised a syndicate that rescued the franchise. His first season, the old warrior lost $670,000. The next year, strapped by free agency and budget financing, Veeck unveiled the "Rent-A-Player" scheme. On July 12, 1979, the field at Comiskey Park was trampled by crazies on "Disco Demolition Night." Twice in the next five weeks, Veeck, desperate for cash to augment his club's income, booked rock concerts into the Chisox' yard; by September, the hilly, rain-soaked outfield resembled the battlefield at Verdun. "What was needed was someone who flew around in Lear jets and operated under the protection of a tax shelter," Richard Lindberg wrote in his book, *Who's on 3rd? The Chicago White Sox Story.* "Someone who was ready to turn the old candy store into a streamlined, thinking corporation. Sensing the inevitability of it all, Veeck began looking around for such a person." In early 1981, fueled by a desire to fill that void, the American League approved the sale of the White Sox to a limited partnership headed by Jerry Reinsdorf, a Chicago real estate syndicator, and Eddie Einhorn, founder of the TVS Television Network. What Chicago fans will tell you, though, is that without Harry Caray, even more than the Hustler, Veeck, the White Sox might have crumbled into the Atlantis of the major leagues.

"Harry was ready for Chicago, and Chicago was ready to be wild about Harry," Lindberg said. "Only in Chicago could the announcer become bigger than the team." Or, as Veeck expounded in 1979, "There were years when Harry was the only performer we had. They say guys in his business don't put people in the ball park. Well, he draws more people than any player on our club or the opposition. And I've had front office people of other teams tell me that Harry even draws people to *their* parks."

Amid a briar patch of mediocrity — in Harry's tenure, the White Sox won 820 games, lost 889, five times finished fifth and only twice contended for a demipennant — those who came witnessed flashes of schizophrenia. They saw, on the one hand, the despairing indifference of pitchers Ken Brett, leading the 1976 Hose with ten victories, and Ken Kravec and Francisco Barrios, best among the 1977–78 White Sox with earned run averages of over *four;* and on the other, the surpassing tenacity of Jim Kaat, winning forty-one games in 1974–75, and baldpated, fleshy Wilbur Wood, whose knuckleball danced to four twenty-victory seasons in a row. They watched, lips pursed, as 1976–80 prosaism doomed the Sox to one player, annually, on the All-Star team. They felt gurgles of pride as 1972's Dick Allen smacked a franchise-record thirty-seven home runs, became the fourth player to belt a ball into Comiskey Park's center-field bleachers (and the first White Sox to smash two inside-the-park shots in the same game), skipped batting practice, posed for a *Sports Illustrated* cover with a cigarette in his mouth, and won the American League MVP Award. The season afterward, Wood and Stan Bahnsen lost forty-one matches. On July 28, 1976, Blue Moon Odom and Barrios no-hit the Athletics. That same year, the Hose lost ninety-seven games. "We were abominable, atrocious, awful—we were even bad," said Barnum Bill of the Bicentennial Hose. "No one could have believed—even imagined—that the next year we'd come up like we did."

Jolting baseball, the 1977 Sox bombed 192 homers (Oscar Gamble and Richie Zisk hit thirty-one and thirty), popularized the curtain call (where players acknowledged applause by emerging from the dugout), embraced a forgotten rock anthem as their rallying cry (by the mid-eighties, "Na na, hey hey hey, kiss them good-bye" had draped uncounted high school, college, and professional games), acquired a signet, the "South Side Hit Men," raced to a wide lead in late July before fading to third, and broke their all-time attendance record, drawing 1,657,135 patrons. "An incredible year, really," Veeck remarked. "So much better than everything before and everything that was to come." The next three seasons, the Sox fell back to fifth. "But that's how it was all during the seventies—never quite enough money, the team good one year, down the next, a Zisk or Gamble to cheer one year and, then, poof, they're gone the next. But hey, on a shoestring, what could you expect? And it wasn't all bad; I'd do it over again—just knock on my wooden leg. There was fun, laughs. There were some great games, some thrills, all those fantastic fans."

But mostly, there was Caray—bantering with fans, hurling volleys at ballplayers, hitting bars to and from the ball park, and saying of his clientele, "There's a lot of people who hate me. Personally, I know a lot of them who love me"—never allowing *interest* to die, even when the White Sox *had*.

By late April 1971, he was welcomed by the first banner reading, "Holy Cow!"; by May, he was broadcasting from the center-field bleachers, encircled by hundreds of fans, and "not even the rain stopped him," noted *TSN*. "He just raised a beach umbrella"; by early October, the Sox had lured 833,891 paid admissions (338,000 over 1970) and Caray, attendance bonuses of $30,000. "When I was considering going with the White Sox, Rollie Hemond, their general manager, said to me, 'Look, we can't afford to pay you more than fifty grand, but I know you've got a hell of a reputation for putting fannies in the seats. So here's the acid test. I'm ready if you are. Beyond your base salary, we'll give you ten thousand bucks for every hundred thousand fans we draw over last year's total.' So I agreed, came over to the Sox, and went on to break the bank." The next year, attendance rose again, to 1,186,018, and then again, with a *fifth-place* club, to 1,316,527, and not only that; on Sox' trips to the West Coast, over stations almost no one could *hear*, "Caray's ratings were so astounding that they far outdid several major Chicago stations combined. 'I couldn't get to them,'" Harry told Associated Press in 1972. "'My job was to generate interest and excitement so they would try to find me.'"

Unsurprisingly, he did.

Improbably, they had.

"It's Wednesday afternoon at White Sox Park [in 1976, under Veeck, renamed Comiskey], and Harry Caray grabs his satchel and a cooler full of beer and heads for the bleachers," that AP story began. "He winds his way through the crowd saying 'hello' and signing autographs. When he finally reaches the bleachers, there's a loud roar. 'Holy Cow, it's Harry Caray,' with the fans emphasizing the 'Holy Cow,' Caray's favorite phrase of astonishment. In makeshift fashion, he sets up to broadcast the game from the bleachers as he does every Wednesday afternoon when the Sox are at home. But first, he does his pregame show, which is devoted entirely to the fans. They ask questions. They answer questions. Harry kisses the girls, hands out free passes and every now and then spots an old-timer and slips him a beer saying, 'Have a cold one on me.' The crowd cheers his every gesture. His boyish enthusiasm, before the packed crowd, is epidemic. They love him and let him know it. He loves the adulation and responds accordingly. Harry Caray has done his part in bring-ing back the fans to the White Sox. 'It used to be,' says ticket manager Tommy Maloney, 'that the fans wanted seats on the third-base or first-base lines. Now the tickets that go first are in the upper deck in front of Harry's broadcasting booth.' "

In baseball's broadcast culture, I can think of no parallel — not Allen and the Yankees, or Prince and his Pirates, or even Scully in Los Angeles — to fasten upon Caray's White Sox' Odyssey. "There have been great announcers who've brought people to the park to watch good teams, or when their teams have gone bad, who've kept people listening to the radio and TV even when atten-dance slipped," said Veeck, as if envisioning The Voice, the Gunner, or a Mar-tin and Woods. "But Caray had mostly lousy teams, had especially lousy sta-tions for a while, and not only were the ratings great — far better than the clubs deserved — but attendance was far higher than the standings warranted. Whether we won or lost, folks followed the White Sox — even when they shouldn't have. Why? With rare, brief exceptions, the Sox didn't have stars people could iden-tify with — it wasn't the players. It wasn't the marketing — God knows, we didn't have dough to market. It was Caray," and knowing that, he turned increas-ingly self-indulgent and indefatigable; recalling *Inside Sports*, "Harry owned the town."

In 1973, buoyed by Caray's audiences, the White Sox reacquired a decent flagship station, WMAQ, and also moved to WSNS-TV. It was that year that Caray began handling both mediums; that year too that he enraged manager Chuck Tanner by repeatedly telling viewers, "Look at that guy — he just loafed down the first-base line. What do you bet after the game Tanner will tell the writers he was hustling? Let's look at the replay, and you can make up your own mind."

Reaching more Chicagoans than before, Harry became more unterrified than ever. In April 1974, when Rick Reichardt was released by the Pale Hose, the journeyman blasted Caray's "abuse." Replied the Mayor of Rush Street: "Rick's too intelligent to be a crybaby — at least I thought he was." In early 1975, several regulars scored "Harry's giving us hell." The old Democrat laughed and quoted another Harry: "I just tell the truth and they *think* it's hell." That same season, upon learning of Caray's on-air shaft, "Why, the way he [Bill

Melton] was swinging, even if he did hit the ball, it wouldn't have gone as far as the pitcher's mound," Melton threatened to deck the Voice in Milwaukee's Marc Plaza Hotel. Were the '75 White Sox near-last on merit, to paraphrase Branch Rickey, or merely bad because of Caray's say-so? On October 1, John Allyn blamed Harry; his fault-finding, the then-Sox' owner said, had wrecked the Hose; if he, Allyn, owned the Sox in 1976, Holy Cow! would be led away. One day later, Caray released a statement from his suite at the Ambassador East Hotel: "I can't believe any man can own a ball club and be as dumb as John Allyn," the text read. "Did he make enough money to own it or did he inherit it?" Its content apparently impressed the newspapers, who backed the would-be victim, and, more crucially, WMAQ—no Caray, it calmly told the White Sox, no coverage—and when, on December 16, Veeck purchased the ball club, it was he who inherited Harry.

Thereafter, six more years of unflagging exuberance and leverage—"every minute," Caray clattered, "caused by the God-fearing, wholesome, upright life I lead."

Entering 1976, Caray had teamed with four broadcast banalities in as many seasons. "One year I had an assistant named Bob Waller—no great shakes there," he said. "Another year they put a former catcher, J. C. Martin, on the air with me, along with some guy named Bill Mercer. Their job was to protect Tanner. I would rap him, and they'd say something good about him. Tanner, Mercer, and Martin had a real cozy little group. Anything to shut me up." But Veeck had not hired Caray to shut him up, and having once employed Blattner, Dean, and Jimmy Dudley, the Hustler disdained what Lindberg titled Harry's "past series of happy-talk, dull-as-paint sidekicks." The new Sox' owner got to mulling: If "dull-as-paint" dampened Caray's energies, as far as that was possible, could a mercurial sidekick, tapping Harry's creativity, bring him even more alive? The ex-outfielder, Jim Piersall, was at least mercurial, and in 1977, the same year Veeck briefly engaged the bigs' first woman broadcaster, shrill-voiced Mary Shane, he began a madcap and ultimately self-destructive reign as Holy Cow!'s accomplice. Like the Hose's chief shaman, Piersall was unreticent—acidic in his White Sox' analyses, he became almost as fashionable as Caray—but as Gerald Ford gave way to Jimmy Carter, and Carter to Ronald Reagan, as Miss Vicki yielded to Miss Piggy, as Jay Silverheels died and Bert Parks was fired, it all got out of hand.

One day, "gesturing" at umpire Joe Brinkman from the broadcast booth, Piersall nearly caused a forfeiture. In June 1980, spinning out jokes over WSNS, he savaged Sox' players so unmercifully that they demanded (and got) his removal as part-time outfield coach. Shortly afterward, Piersall appeared on a local talk show and called Veeck's wife "a colossal bore," and on July 2, angered by a column in a suburban Chicago paper, he stormed into the Pale Hose clubhouse and grabbed the story's author by the neck. He was suspended for two weeks; received, Lindberg noted, "an outpouring of support from Sox' fans, who paraded banners in Comiskey Park"; and was reinstated on July 15, "after Veeck and the radio station determined that he was fit for duty." The reprieve was illusory. On September 6, 1981, sharing the WLS-TV dais with, among others, Shelley Winters, the Sox' announcers were asked by the program's host, *Sun-Times* columnist Mike Royko, how they braved baseball wives' criticism of their on-air commentary. Smiling, Caray answered, "You know what, Mike. I would love to call all the wives together some day and tell them what their husbands say about them across the hall." Even to themselves, viewers could not imagine how Piersall proceeded now to dynamite his own career. "First of all, they were horny broads who wanted to get married," Jim began as the group sat, widemouthed, "and they wanted a little money, a little security, and a big strong ballplayer. I traveled, I played. I got a load of those broads too." More comical than Caray, he was obviously less restrained.

That same week, suspended again, Piersall tumbled, permanently, into White Sox' memory. It was a material but not inconsolable loss, for the Hose yet owned what Veeck styled "the best baseball announcer in the country." There he was, what *The Arizona Republic* termed "the hottest act in Chicago and has been for a decade," a man now in his sixties, foraying up and down Rush Street and, *literally*, stopping traffic. There he was, on evening newscasts, in the gossip blurbs, in letters to the editor, jamming bars with groupies who exchanged the obligatory "Hey, Har-ry!" for a glad-hand and a drink. There he was at Comiskey Park, grabbing the public address microphone between halves of the seventh inning, shouting, "All right, lemme hear ya, everybody!" leading the hordes in a roughhewed rendering of "Take Me Out to the Ball Game," and presiding over what the Hustler dubbed "the world's largest outdoor saloon." Caray — except for church, garden parties, and afternoon tea, he was *everywhere*. "I came to Chicago in 1977, no rooting interest in either Chicago team, and, right away, he made me a White Sox' fan," a *Chicago Tribune* reporter and ex-colleague of mine, Bill Parker, declaimed. "I used to think — still do — that for almost all his years on the South Side, Caray wasn't the best thing the White Sox had going for them — he was the only thing."

And then he was gone, to the North Side, suddenly, and a different, even Noachian baseball world.

The events may be stated briefly. On November 16, 1981, The Tribune Company broke the exceptional news that Caray would become the new Voice of its recently acquired subsidiary, the Chicago National League Baseball Club. The city's newspapers and radio and television stations carried the story with the same fervor and detail normally reserved for presidential inaugurations or prostitution exposés. For a long time, Caray shocked people at Wrigley Field by the simple fact of his presence. He *was*, after all, the working-class, beer-guzzling White Sox, and slightly *déclassé;* the Cubs were genteel, more prim and respectable, sort of an Ozzie and Harriet behind ivied walls. It was like Lindsey Nelson, circa 1964, jumping to the hated Yankees, or a 1950s Allen, at the pinnacle of "How about that!" absconding for Fenway Park. Jack Brickhouse, retiring as the Cubs' principal announcer, was surprised. Milo Hamilton was embittered. "The news made front-page headlines," Caray said, proudly. "I don't know why, but every year I just seem to get bigger in the media. It was something — people tell me the move hit Chicago with the force of the famous fire [of October 1871]."

The kindling dated back to early 1981, when Reinsdorf and Einhorn bought the White Sox. If Caray was headstrong, so were they, and almost from the beginning, I believe, he sensed the possibility of a torch being passed, of a time — *his* — running out. They intended to renovate Comiskey Park, cleanse its interior and its image, and make Chisox-going, again, a family concern. "We're going to restore class to the White Sox, make it so that every kind of person wants to come to our games," Reinsdorf said that February, jabbing Veeck and, by inference, his mouthpiece. "Baseball is more than one guy, more than a park full of drunks" — more, perhaps, than even "Holy Cow!" "It might be . . . ," or an a cappella seventh-inning stretch.

"When did you know things weren't going to work out?" I said.

"From the very start I didn't like the owners," Harry said. "They're too slick. They talked about 'class' — hell, they're just snake oil salesmen. They wouldn't know what it was. When I first met Reinsdorf and Einhorn, I didn't know them well and I didn't respect them very much. Now, five years later, I know them a lot better and I respect and like them a lot less. What it really came down to was they were jealous of me 'cause my picture was in the paper more than theirs. They didn't give a damn about the fans, and they were trying all year to fire Jim Piersall, whom I trust and who is my friend."

Piersall, in turn, mistrusted not his colleague but, rather, Pale Hose officials; the two-time Gold Glove recipient considered himself Harry's dear friend. Caray, on the other hand, should have felt only equanimity toward his new employers. They had matched his 1980 salary, a reported $225,000; they had not asked Caray to curb his darts and salvos. Still, his picture *was* in the papers more than either Reinsdorf's or Einhorn's; he *did* belong to a previous regime; and in October, talking contract, the Sox' hierarchy reduced the Mayor to a one-year extension. That was bad enough. Worse, Caray now faced the daunting unknown of pay-cable television, a new technology which, even from a distance, imperiled his place in Chicago's consciousness.

"Einhorn's background was television," Harry began, "and he came to the team with this great idea of how he was going to make himself a TV fortune, or so he thought." In 1980, the White Sox broadcast 125 games over WSNS; if you had a television, you watched for free. Einhorn's "great idea" would change all that. It was known as SportsVision, a pay-per-view cable system whereby viewers must pay a fixed amount for the right to see the Hose, and it meant to yank Sox' games off the conventional (free) airwaves, implant them on Eddie's wired screens, and make Einhorn "a TV fortune [or so he thought]."

By the mid-eighties, eighteen major-league teams had fashioned some type of local or regional pay-per-view coverage; the other eight either flaunted SuperStations or abstained from cable altogether. "First, a primer," read *The Sporting News*. "Pay television is a separate channel for which a monthly fee usually is charged but with the capacity for a one-time fee. It began and still exists where there is no cable. It flowered in New York, Los Angeles, and Philadelphia, among other places, because those huge population areas were not wired for cable. But as the metropolitan outlets obtain cable, pay television is fading, down to about 500,000 subscribers and sinking. The future, if there is one for super payoffs, is with pay cable. But only 7 million of the 35 million cable households [as of 1985] now have the capacity to deliver a pay channel via addressable converters. Even so," it said, "more and more pay channels are operating too, showing local or regional sports for a monthly fee."

In 1984, for instance, Dick Bramer and Harmon Killebrew televised forty-five Twins' games over Spectrum, a local pay channel; the Mets' Ralph Kiner, Tim McCarver, and Fran Healy offered sixty sets to Tri-State viewers over the prosperous SportsChannel; by subscribing to Sports Time, a fifteen-state regional outlet cofounded by Anheuser-Busch, one could see 154 outings of the Cardinals, Royals, and Reds; the Tigers carried eighty games to two hundred cable systems throughout Michigan, Ohio, and Indiana over the Pro Am Sports System. Even so, most front offices maneuvered warily; pay-cable was suspect, unproven; baseball still relied on *free* television for the bulk of its broadcast interest, exposure, and revenue. "We've encouraged our clubs, even as they try to expand cable growth, not to severely cut back on conventional exposure," warned Bryan Burns, Tom Villante's talented successor as baseball's director of broadcasting. "We're acutely aware of the danger of out-of-sight, out-of-mind. We don't want our cable systems to supplant free coverage — that would limit the game to a wealthy few, deprive the general public of baseball, and, let's face it, cost us fans. We want them, where they can, to complement the regular TV. That way, Joe Fan'll still get his X-number of games each year, and the real die-hard, the guy who wants to see, say, every Tiger game — he can pay to watch the rest on cable." In 1965, the Orioles presented fifty-one free telecasts; two decades later, allowing fifty freebies, they carried eighty sets on their pay channel, the enterprising Home Team Sports. During that same interval, while the Dodgers, Phillies, and Astros' combined pay-cable showings leaped from zero to 123, their number of free games *also* rose, respectively, by thirty-seven, ten, and fifty-nine. "Most clubs have approached it right, with a 'show-me' attitude toward cable," Burns maintained. "Some clubs' pay-cable deals have been accepted; some have bombed. Until its potential is decided one way or another, we'd be stupid to put all our eggs in cable's basket."

Most ball clubs, I believe, would second the 1982 analysis by a leading firm of consulting economists, the National Economic Research Associates, Inc.: "Pay TV seems to be a method of extracting more profit from the television audience — which, as a form of price discrimination, it could be expected to." They would recognize too that because barely half of all mid-eighties households were wired for cable; because, of that total, a far smaller percentage would unfurl cash to see forty San Diego or fifty-two St. Louis cablecasts; because, while attractive to cable *operators* who needed live programming to snare subscribers, baseball's large volume of games "cuts another way with *viewers*," Jack Craig wrote, "by diminishing the value of each particular game"; because "the specter of SuperStations [has] hung over the baseball telecasts from the outset," perceived *TSN*. "Why pay $10 a month to see two hundred baseball games (on pay-per-view) when up to five hundred were available to some cable subscribers from the SuperStations at cheaper prices?"; and because of viewers' natural resistance to paying for a TV product [major league baseball] they had come to regard as a *gratis* right — because of these and other truisms, the growth of baseball's local and regional, as opposed to network or SuperStation, pay cable, has been excruciatingly slow. One could point to Pittsburgh, where the Pirates' pay channel collapsed, or Sports Time, which died in 1985, or Texas, where would-be subscribers were too smitten, apparently, with the football Cowboys to bother with the Rangers, or the post-1983 Red Sox, convinced of pay television's potential, who sliced their free coverage by thirty games, put eighty-seven contests on the struggling New England Sports Network, and watched New England fans respond with a yawn. "Pay-per-view hasn't been nearly the gold mine so many had predicted. The clubs that best understand television," said Tom Villante, obviously not alluding to Boston, "have thought of free coverage as the cake — the base, the foundation you build upon — and local cable as the icing, nice but not essential, and not to be depended upon."

It was Caray's (mis)fortune to be the White Sox' announcer when his new employers, like the Red Sox, turned that recipe upside down.

In 1968, the Comiskeys had televised 144 games over their UHF channel, WFLD; since then, no White Sox' team, no matter how appalling, had graced fewer than sixty-four TV games a year. "Sox' games went into every home," Caray said. "It was like with the Cubs — every day they were in your living room. How could you *not* get interested? They were like a next-door neighbor — you knew them, they were part of your lives." Now, with SportsVision, Reinsdorf and, more to the point, the blunt and explosive Einhorn — graduate of Northwestern University's School of Law; later, executive producer of CBS Sports; his moniker, "Fast Eddie" — proposed the unthinkable: to slash the White Sox' schedule of free TV games and make pay-cable, available to a far smaller audience, the *cornerstone* of their coverage.

For the most visible of all White Sox, whose ego required daily tending and for whom applause, like liquor, was almost a psychic need, it was the end.

"All that fall [of 1981] I kept thinking about what the Sox were doing," Caray said, "and the more I thought, the less I liked. The money they were offering was fine, but they wanted to cut me to just one year, through '82. It's funny — when Reinsdorf and Einhorn first came there, they wanted to ink me to a three-year contract. I told them, 'No, we don't know each other that well. Let's just go for one, and see how it works out.' Now, a year later, they wanted me for just one. I'm sure they thought I'd bring some credibility to SportsVision, and then after I'd done that, they wouldn't need me any more — I figured they'd drop me. Even worse, if I went to cable, I'd be doing a flip-flop. Always before, I'd gone into every corner of Chicago, and that's what made it worthwhile — my people. The bartenders, the taxi drivers, the post office guys."

"And if you stayed with the Sox, with pay-cable in '82 they'd never hear you," I said.

"They were talking about SportsVision having the capacity to go into around fifty thousand homes in the entire city of Chicago — that's all that were wired.

And that was an *optimistic* figure. Hell, I can piss on fifty thousand homes. I figured at the end of '82 I might have been Harry Who?"

"So you started thinking, 'Cubs.' "

"See, what Einhorn never understood is that the White Sox weren't operating in a vacuum — they aren't today," he said. "Chicago's always been a Cubs' town, even when the Sox were up — it's tough enough to fight 'em when you're on TV *all* the time. But the new owners didn't get that. They thought you could just wipe out the free TV [in 1982, the Hose permitted forty-five free telecasts; in 1983, thirty-seven] and still stay competitive."

"You disagreed."

"I knew that while the White Sox were screwing around, the Cubs would be on WGN every day, reaching every home in Chicago. Hell, no — I couldn't see it working. That's when I called the Cubs and asked if they'd be interested in having me come over."

In retrospect, Caray was uncannily prescient. In Harry's first season at Wrigley Field, SportsVision encroached upon fewer than fifteen thousand of Chicago's three million households; even by 1984, the year after the White Sox' first title in a quarter-century, the number had climbed only marginally, to 102,000. "I thought what we did was visionary at the time, but I've got to re-think the whole thing now," Einhorn told the *Tribune* in early 1985. "Even in the oldest profession, it's a cardinal rule: You can't charge for something people are getting for free." Added Chuck Schriver, the former White Sox and Cubs' publicist: "SportsVision was an unmitigated disaster. The White Sox are finding out too late that there's no substitute for that daily TV exposure."

But the Cubs! WGN, Channel 9, scattered the Wrigleys' TV image into every corner of the city.

Touting itself as "America's No. 1 Sports Station," the outlet had broadcast baseball since 1948; "we've covered it longer than any station in America," said Jack Rosenberg, the WGN sports editor. "We know and love the game." In certain ways, the Cubs were not "so much a baseball team as a [television] series," the trade paper *Electronic Media* observed, and, locally, that "series" was a smash.

In the very bleakest of the team's funereal years, the Cubs still drew a twenty-five-plus share of Chicago's TV audience; even in 1980, airing a sorry last-place club, "WGN — the TV, radio, and network operations," the *Tribune* reported, "earned $4 million from the Cubs' connection." What's more, WGN corkscrewed in the early eighties into a *SuperStation*, beaming almost the entire Cubs' schedule *nationally* by satellite. "The station's signals are picked up — pirated, in essence — by an organization called United Video, which pays nothing for them," said the *Trib*. The pirating, it was true, did not *directly* enrich the Cubs — a cable subscriber paid his local operator, not the Wrigleys, for the daily privilege of hearing Harry — but "the free broadcasts are a boon to the Cubs themselves, in that they build fan interest and boost ticket sales." In 1981, WGN telecasts reached 8 million cable households; five years later, the figure topped 20 million; and as viewers in Albuquerque, Portland, and Buffalo caught the contagion of Cubs' baseball, soaring ratings enabled WGN (an acronym for "World's Greatest Newspaper," which is what the *Tribune* once called itself) to charge higher advertising rates—here, the spin-off *was* direct.

All of this, naturally, pleased The Tribune Company, having bought the Wrigleys on June 16, 1981, for $20.5 million, at a time when the Cubs, in the words of columnist Bob Verdi, were "a joke, the most ridiculed, least imitated sports franchise of your lifetime, and your parents' lifetime, and their parents' lifetime."

By 1984, the Cubs were no joke, though they often seemed chimerical, for it was that season that this ineffectual munchkin of a team—fifth the previous two years, a spell in which Caray himself, at first, had been resisted by many fans who distrusted his screaming *bonhomie* and White Sox' leanings—was transformed overnight from a paradigm of folksy bungling, a *local* story, into sport's most chic object of cult devotion, an *American* story. It was a year of concourse, of wonders dovetailing: of the lovables winning the National League East, their first championship in thirty-nine years, and almost making the World Series ("Part of the Cubs' charm," noted *USA Today*, "is how bad they have been for so long"); of Cubs' fans flocking to away games ("Everywhere we go," said coach Don Zimmer, "the ball parks are full of Cubs' T-shirts and Cubs' hats") and jamming the marvelous anachronism of Wrigley Field (the final count: 2,108,055, an all-time attendance record); of cable television, unavailable even a few years earlier, in one breadth reporting the phenomenon, packing the Cubs' bandwagon, and marketing its product with understandable exuberance ("Once the Chicago Cubs belonged to the city's North Side," a columnist wrote. "Now even North America isn't big enough. Cable television has made the Cubbies more than a home-town team"); and, finally, their Voice, who knew of, reveled in, and expanded this following, and who found himself, incredibly, bigger than ever—at last, a national, not merely regional, name.

God, how the old war-horse loved 1984.

At Wrigley Field, forget about his Pale Hose past; he was now a bona fide institution. In Chicago, wherever he went, one heard shouts of "Hey, Har-ry!" or "Har-ry Caray!" or "Har-ry! Are the Cubs gonna do it?" On the road, Caray was mobbed by autograph-seekers in hotel lobbies. At enemy stadiums, hangers-on beseeched him to sing "Take Me Out to the Ball Game." In Cincinnati, Atlanta, and Houston, newspaper, radio, and television reviewers eulogized his career. "What a happening the Chicago Cubs are!" he said that September. "A little ball park where they play day baseball will draw 2 million people this year. That's like drawing 4 million in Yankee Stadium. And everywhere, people are *seeing* all of this. I know we can reach 28 million [viewers] with the cable. And you should see the mail!" Seven months later, he told me, "Over the winter, a bunch of the players, their wives, and I went on an ocean liner cruise down through the Caribbean. And then it struck me, everywhere we stopped on the tour—the sheer power of cable. You had all these great players there, and it was *me* people were flocking to. And the reason was they saw us every day on TV."

In Kodiak, Alaska (pop. 4,756), carpenter John Ferrentino mused that "availability made me a Cub fan. I like baseball and they're the team I could get." At a New Orleans lounge, bartender Janet Alexander told of how "we got cable in here two years ago, and since New Orleans didn't have a team, we just naturally adopted the Cubs. We could have watched the Atlanta Braves [over SuperStation WTBS], but the Cubs were losers and that appealed to us. Why not? We were already New Orleans Saints' football fans." In Boise, Idaho, Cubs' Power fan clubs took root like potatoes. At Costa Rica's Key Largo bar, the flagpole flew the Cubs' and city of Chicago pennants. In his Knoxville condominium, Lindsey Nelson roared as his long-time friend, exuding cheek and disbelief, called the game-ending double play of a late-season triumph: "Cubs win! Cubs win!" Caray bellowed. "The Good Lord wants the Cubs to win!" You could, as *USA Today* said, "watch the newly-crowned champions of the National League East in much of the Western Hemisphere — anywhere television stations can pick up SuperStation WGN-TV." In wired households or via satellite dish, a signal-filching device, you heard Harry, his play-by-play falling to lengthy reminiscences, his voice thicker by the day, stroll through tales of friends, sycophants, and ballplayers; or delight long-sufferers with such names as Leon Durham (driving in ninety-six runs), Rick Sutcliffe (an astonishing 16–1), Lee Smith (thirty-three saves), and MVP Ryne Sandberg; or entertain the lyrics, "I don't care if I never get back . . . so we'll root, root, root for the home team ["Cubbies," Harry sang], if they don't win it's a shame"; or describe the division-clinching victory over Pittsburgh, on September 24, at 8:49 P.M., Chicago Time, the exact moment when intercession slew four decades of defeat. It was striking, really — not only the Cubs' return from their wilderness march, but withal, their emergence as the eighties most popular baseball team, the persevering naif buoyed by hope and natural greenery, like America itself.

As the Voice of the Cubs, Harry was a beneficiary of their 1984 fantasyland. As Harry Caray, he was also a cause. "The man is *really* good," said Bill James. "His humor, his affection for language, and his vibrant images are the tools of a craftsman. He is the most objective announcer I've ever witnessed. His unflagging enthusiasm, his love of the game, and his intense focus and involvement in every detail of the contest make every inning enjoyable, no matter what the score or the pace of the game." Yet he was not the first baseball broadcaster to prosper from cable's macropenetration; nor did his SuperStation rank at the head of its line. Caray was simply the most flamboyant and original of cable's baseball mouthpieces. The Cubs' success, which, of course, was largely his, brandished how "cable has been good for baseball by drawing a wider audience," said National Cable Association spokesman Ed Dooley. "And baseball has been good for cable by drawing new subscribers."

Some subscribers, as we have seen, paid fees to watch baseball over local or regional channels — the Phillies' PRISM, for example; the O'Malleys' Dodgervision. But their numbers were limited, and the channels, piddling, at a time when America's *basic* cable services — offering coverage to cable systems from

Hoboken to Honolulu and, therefore, unlike a PRISM, capable of *national* exposure—were becoming more entwined in sports programming.

ESPN was launched in 1979; eight years later, it had dilated into cable's largest "network," reaching 41 million households, which represented nearly 47 percent of the total U.S. households owning televisions. There was Cable News Network, entering 38 million homes, and USA and Home Box Office, TIME Inc.'s cable system, available, respectively, in nearly 37- and 15 million homes. "These are the biggest, the ones crucial to baseball and cable's future," said Tom Villante. "They hit the whole country through the local cable systems, they command higher ad rates. They're cable's answer to CBS and NBC."

In 1977, major league baseball inked a contract with USA, its only pay-TV cable network, for a series of Thursday night telecasts. The games were blacked out in the home team's market area (protecting attendance), commonly proffered a double-header (the first match at 7:30 P.M., Eastern Time, from a Tiger Stadium; the second, three hours later, at an Oakland or San Francisco), and cast as announcers somebodies like Jim Woods and Monte Moore. For seven years the series complemented ABC and NBC's meager coverage; its popularity strengthened The Game. But in 1983, the bigs' two free-TV carriers demanded a renewed claim on network exclusivity, and as a precondition to the six-year, $1.125-billion contract with ABC and NBC, baseball and USA filed a no-fault divorce. "They were afraid of overexposure, the two conventional networks," a USA producer stated, "afraid that somebody watching two cable games on Thursday night might have his appetite dulled for NBC's Saturday coverage or ABC on Monday night. The way to guard against that was obviously to eliminate the competition. Sure, baseball would have liked to have continued with us. But it liked the network cash even more."

I had enjoyed the series. I was sad to see it end. Still, there was WGN, seen over many of the same local systems that offered USA, and three smaller SuperStations—the Mets' WOR, available in nearly 13 million cable households; the Rangers' KVTV; and the Yankees' WPIX, shown in more than 5 million homes—"which make this country a whole lot smaller," said Thad Mumford, an ex-Yankees' bat boy who grew up to write "M*A*S*H" scripts. "There was something missing before I could get Yankee games here in Los Angeles. Now I'm able to watch the team I was weaned on."

Eagerly inhaled by baseball fans, these station forays helped fill the vacuum left by USA's departure. At the same time, however, they bowed before baseball's first and *largest* SuperStation, Atlanta's WTBS—the brain child of a roguish iconoclast who tripled as the Braves' owner, three-time Yachtsman of the Year, and cable television's Don Vito Corleone, saying of each local system operator, "I'll make him an offer he can't refuse." It was Ted Turner who, by energetically selling sports and other WTBS programming to cable systems nationwide, proved that a single station, beaming its signal via satellite, could command a respectable audience; Turner who built a cable service which became the nation's second-largest by the mid-1980s, penetrating more than 40 million homes; Turner who showed how a baseball team, previously unable even to develop a *regional* identity, could convert itself, spectacularly, through cable, into "America's Team."

For the Braves and, therefore, baseball, cable's breakthrough year was 1982. Six years earlier, Atlanta telecasts had been picked up in 694,746 households over station WTCG; now, they were available to *thirty times* that number. "Available, yes, but not always watched," said Ernie Johnson, the effective, soft-spoken Vermonter who has called every Braves' game since their arrival from Milwaukee. "We were still just one offering among many. We were fighting the regular networks for viewers. We were fighting other cable programs. People still weren't aware of the importance cable could have on baseball, how the daily coverage could make a die-hard Brave fan out of someone, say, in Nevada who'd never been closer than a thousand miles to the state of Georgia." In 1982, Atlanta won its first thirteen games, a major-league record, and suddenly, almost overnight, people were aware. "One man put it best," Johnson said. "He said that streak was the 'two-by-four which hit America between the eyes,' which woke the country up to the SuperStation." It was not simply what cable was *doing* — that an average of 1 million viewers watched each game, or that in Valdez, Alaska, the Nanook Chapter of the Braves Fan Club renamed the local saloon the "Braves Lounge" and, pooling cash, bought a giant television screen, or that a coterie of fans in Kailua-Kona, Hawaii, formally adopted the Georgia Braves as their "home" club, or that fans in Storm Lake, Iowa (pop. 8,814), erected a billboard reading, "The Atlanta Braves: Iowa's Team," or even that Braves' ratings, rising steadily, leaped 86 percent over 1981. It was, more vitally, what cable *might* do — swell into "the greatest thing to happen [to baseball] since Bat Day," as *Philadelphia Inquirer* sportswriter Frank Dolson, tongue in cheek, put it; or sell the bigs on a scale smaller than, but similar to, CBS's late-1950s- and early-sixties marketing of the NFL as a video religion.

By 1987, the game's pentagon of SuperStations broadcast more than five hundred games over local cable systems to, literally, increasing numbers of subscribers each week. The influx has troubled many in baseball's official family; they blame it for everything from lower minor-league attendance ("If you can sit in your warm living room in Helena, Montana, and every day see a Cub game," Peter Ueberroth said in 1984, "how many times are you going to venture out into the cold to see baseball live? Cable's exposure hurts us at every level of the gate") to lower local TV ratings ("In 1983, for example, the ratings in Tulsa, which is in the Texas Rangers' territory, were higher for Braves' games than for the Rangers when the two went head-to-head," he added. "Now that's a violation of another team's territory. It's blatantly unfair") to the fear, expressed by the new commissioner, that "the SuperStations will so oversaturate the baseball market that when our network contract is due," the networks would never again pay anything like $1.125 billion.

I agree, up to a point. Unfairness, it seems to me, *has* been a problem. "If the Cubs, to cite an instance, beam a game into San Diego's territory, then they should have to pay for their penetration into someone else's market," Ueberroth reasoned. "Otherwise, if they won't, I'm going to take action to reduce what they can show." There you have it, Ueberroth, flexing his muscles, told the SuperStations in November 1984: Pay other clubs for the privilege of invading their terrain, or slash your number of cable telecasts. The demolition of "America's Team," of course, was the last thing a Turner would allow; and in early 1985, the Braves' owner — followed, shortly, by the other SuperStations — surrendered: Over the next five years, they would make annual payments to every club under a television revenue-sharing plan.

How much would the SuperStations yield? According to their penetration — the more households you reached, the more cash you forked over. "Under this formula, the Braves [will] pay a total of $30 million over a five-year period, which works out to about 20¢ a head for each of the Braves' cable households and $230,000 a year for each of the twenty-six major-league clubs," the *New York Times* announced. "The payments will be made to the Major League Central Fund for equal distribution to each of the clubs, including the Braves." In return, said the newspaper, Ueberroth agreed "to drop lobbying efforts for federal legislation that would restrict cable telecasts beyond a station's local market."

This alternative, I thought, was creative, fair, and far preferable to fewer cablecasts. For there is no discernible evidence — on this, I disagree totally with Ueberroth — that SuperStations have been anything *but* an impressive baseball selling tool. "Baseball owners do not have clear-cut evidence of the [possible] damage to out-of-town broadcasts, despite Ueberroth's alarm. Major-league attendance and local TV revenues are at record levels, and there supposedly is no measurable pattern of decreasing minor-league attendance when big-league telecasts are imported," Craig has commented. "Even now, the Cubs and Braves can point out that they are giving exposure to the sport — and that the fans love it."

What *is* overexposure, anyway? Subjective, discriminating. To most Americans, one network soccer match a year is *too* much; at times, four pro football games each Sunday, not enough. SuperStations show what the market will bear; or, as two fans from Springfield, North Carolina, and Bay Springs, Mississippi, wrote to *TSN* in February 1985, "SuperStations promote baseball the entire year and create fans in areas in which there are no professional teams. Making baseball accessible to millions of viewers can only add to the popularity of the game," and "Thanks to Ted Turner for getting baseball *back* in the hearts of many people in rural America."

In part, viewers have flocked to SuperStations because network TV has failed them; if The Game's national coverage were better — that is, if the bigs were not *under-* rather than *over*exposed — the need for cable would decrease. [It is difficult to forget August-September 1985. During the month preceding its regular season, the NFL aired *twelve exhibition* — alias, preseason — networkcasts; in that interval, despite three electric division races and Pete Rose's pursuit of Ty Cobb as the all-time hitmaster, baseball boasted *four regular-season* network games. Even worse, from September 8 to 13 — with Rose whacking his historic Ty-breaker, the first- and second-place teams in each division colliding head-on, and the Mets and Yankees, before SRO crowds, playing crucial series in "the first time in the twenty-three-year history of the Mets," read the *Times*, "that both New York teams have been in pennant races this late in the season"—baseball was virtually blacked out on network television; in the season's penultimate innings, its viewing public was reduced to periodic NBC and ABC updates on Charlie Hustle. Yet at the same time, the Rozelles flaunted *five* early-season network telecasts in as many days, and on Thursday, September 12—"Baseball Thursday," the *Times'* George Vecsey said, "that rarest of baseball days in New York, with two teams at home on the same day, both entertaining their closest rivals in excruciating pennant races": the Yankees v. Toronto at the Stadium; the Mets v. St. Louis at Shea—baseball fans, turning to the national tube, must content themselves with the Los Angeles Raiders at Kansas City.] Also, cable has grown because baseball is, as Bob Prince once told me, addictive, like a drug; the more you inhale and know of it, the more you want and need. "How can you get overexposed on the greatest game ever invented?" he asked. "It's not like pro basketball—you see one game a month, it's enough. But with baseball, every day you need your fix."

Ernie Johnson laughed. "That's the great thing about cable—it hooks you," he said. "Another great thing, and we learned this only in that 1982 season, is that we reached thousands of people who weren't within the viewing area of local clubs' telecasts. Cable filled their void. We'd go into New Mexico, and their closest team was the Astros, but they didn't get Astros' TV games—their network didn't stretch that far. Or maybe, in Oregon, they didn't get the A's, Giants, or Mariners; they were caught in between. These people were dying for baseball—all they got was the network 'Game of the Week'. And we freed them, and they learned, I think, how wonderful this sport can be." Once captured by the *Braves*, Johnson said, they became, at least theoretically, more receptive to *baseball*: its network telecasts, its pennants, yearbooks, and related merchandise, its names, inner workings, and history. "The beauty of cable is that we just didn't attract viewers in '82 who were already avid fans. We also began to appeal to the peripheral or nonbaseball fan who became, first, an Atlanta fan—we broadcast almost daily and that coverage becomes a habit; you begin to watch every day—and then, ultimately, after he began to get the swing of things, he turned into a baseball fan who couldn't get enough."

Looking back past the 1984 Cubs, one spots heavy parallels to those 1982 Braves. Like the Wrigleys, Atlanta won its division (on the final day) and lost the playoff (to St. Louis). Each rose from the bowels of the second division. Both rode cable TV as a portent and pioneer—a portent of television's future; a pioneer ostending, for the first time, how this technology could energize baseball. Each carved out a considerable national retinue. Both led the league in road attendance. Each starred a Caray in its broadcast booth.

Atlanta's Caray was named Harry Jr., or Skip, and he was the senior's oldest son. The most colorful and conspicuous of Braves' announcers, he "grew up with and around baseball," started in radio at age fifteen with a weekly high school sports show, majored in journalism at the University of Missouri, worked summers at KMOX as a writer, director, and producer, and made his play-by-play debut in the state high school basketball tournament. In 1963, now twenty-three, Caray joined the Tulsa Oilers of the Texas League. The opportunity led quickly to a mid-season switch to the International League, where Skip called Atlanta Crackers' contests through 1965. On May 30 of that year, he subbed for Mel Allen on the broadcast of a Braves' game out of Houston. "That was the year station WSB, with Allen as one of the voices, was televising some of the Milwaukee games back to Atlanta," he said. "This one day I got a call telling me that Mel's mother had just died, that he was flying back to New York, that WSB needed a guy to air the telecasts and could I, I guess because of my Atlanta experience, fill in for him on short notice. *Could I?* It was my first big-league broadcast." It was also believed to be a precedent: the first time, either on radio or television, that a son of an American- or National League announcer broadcast major-league play-by-play.

"Having a famous father in the business has been a help and a hindrance — mostly, it's been a hindrance," Skip would later say. "At first, it bothered me — people saying, 'Ah, he got this or that job because he's Harry's kid.' I even thought of changing my name, but I dropped the idea. I finally looked at it this way — chances are I wouldn't have gotten a job to begin with if I hadn't been Harry's son. I accept that. But I also realize that I'd worked hard — I wasn't an overnight success, I paid my dues. And I always knew that if I did become a major-league announcer, it would have to be because I'm good." Large ("I'm not that good-looking or a threat to Twiggy") and tart (an Atlanta disc jockey termed his squelches "brutal") and versatile (at different times, he aired Falcons football, Hawks basketball, and Flames hockey), Caray *fils* became a Braves' announcer in 1976, replacing Milo Hamilton (another correlate with Harry Sr., who had Milo fired in 1954), at which point Southeast baseball fans discovered how "good" he was. Caray was both the butt (his weight) and source of comedy — with Rick Camp, a weak-hitting pitcher at the plate, Skip advised, "Parents, if there are any young children in the room, please beware. This is not going to be pretty" — and, like his father, direct. "Ed Vargo's a good guy," Skip once told his listeners, and then, "but he may have just made the worst call in baseball history."

By 1986, Caray seven times had been named Georgia Broadcaster of the Year. He consolidated interest with *Anschauung* and a sassy twist, and enhanced the Braves' other mouthpieces on the SuperStation and a hundred-plus-station radio network — Johnson, the ex-Marine and big-league pitcher; the boyishly winning John Sterling, who succeeded Darrel Chaney three years earlier as the No. 4 announcer; and Pete Van Wieren, nicknamed "the Professor."

Van Wieren spent his boyhood, as I did, in Rochester, New York, listening to Allen and Barber, then graduated from Cornell University, joined the *Washington Post*, and took his first broadcasting job at a daytime-only station in Warrenton, Virginia. "I did everything at that station," Pete said. "D.J. jobs, news, sports, high school football on a tape-delay basis. It was a real education." From that 500-watt outlet, higher learning took him to Tidewater, where Van Wieren aired baseball for the Mets' Triple-A affiliate, and in 1976 to

Atlanta-Fulton County Stadium. "That year was a double whammy in two ways," he said. "First, we had two rookies in the booth—Skip and me. And second, I also doubled as the club's traveling secretary—planes, buses, equipment, trunks, hotels, meal money, tickets—you name it, I did it." But with cable's boomlet, WTBS began televising 145 games a year; the Braves needed four full-time voices to handle radio and TV; and lopping off his job as travel guide, Pete reverted solely to the broadcast booth.

A reserved and studious man, Van Wieren brought sensitivity to baseball and an appreciation that "we're on the air for so long and talk about a player four or five times a game and a pitcher all game long. If you don't constantly do your homework, you can run out of things to say." Less glib than Caray or volatile than Sterling (a native New Yorker who hosted sports-talk shows, called play-by-play for the Yankees, Astros, basketball Knicks and Nets, and hockey Islanders, and hopped from WMCA, New York, to the Enterprise Radio Network to WSB before landing at the SuperStation in 1982 as color analyst for the NBA Hawks), Pete seldom struck one as bereft of things to say. His brief case bulged, like Hamilton's; each telecast was a big-league walking tour. Hearing him, in fact, my first thought was how closely he resembled his remaining colleague, the club's director of broadcasting, Ernest Thorwald Johnson, also low-key, who struck me, above all, as *nice.*

"With a down-to-earth, on-air delivery, Ernie accurately shows his real self during his broadcasts," an Atlanta free-lance writer said. "He isn't a controversial broadcaster because he isn't a controversial person. Easy-going and folksy, his is a style that rarely intrudes, and his manner is such that the listener can sense he's that way off the air as on." Wholly without self-puffery, the son of Swedes who emigrated at the turn of the century and met in America, Ernie went back a far piece, as I often heard him say, with the Boston-turned-Milwaukee-turned-Atlanta Braves—back to 1942, when, at eighteen, tall and angular, he signed a playing contract, pitched briefly for Hartford of the Eastern League, and entered the Marines; back to his 1950s career in the bigs, relieving and spot-starting, winning forty games, losing twenty-three, and recording a 1.29 ERA in the 1957 World Series; back to 1961, the year Johnson broke into television by moderating a Milwaukee talk show, and the season afterward, his debut as a Braves' color man, and 1966, joining Hamilton after the ball club left Wisconsin, and a decade later, replacing Milo as Atlanta's media *padrone.*

Skip Caray tells of how, doing his first game that spring as Johnson's sidekick, he announced the lineups and said, " 'And now, here with the play-by-play, the Voice of the Braves, Ernie Johnson.' Well, when the half-inning was over, Ernie leaned over during the commercial break and said, quietly, 'If you don't mind, we're all the Voice of the Braves. I don't need all that ego stuff—we're all in this together.' That impressed me right away." He was respected for his honesty, his lack of cynicism and charade, and his humanity clashed with much of the frivolity and conceit one encountered in his profession. "I guess," Johnson said once, "I'm sort of an optimistic, straight, happily married, religious sort of guy." He was both substantive and traditional, a SuperStation fixture who merited synchronal praise as an emblem of the South's courtesies and codes.

Among all the broadcasters I knew or knew of, Ernie Johnson, with his quiet, receding voice falling lightly on the local and national ear, was as halcyon as any—the counterpole of Harry Caray, who was neither quiet nor receding. Yet, sitting before a television set, listening to a radio, or wherever I heard baseball announcers vent their more or less moving melodies, I understood—as *away* from their voices, one could not—how comparison was unfair.

Caray, like Ol' Diz, Cosell, Ethel Merman, and Ali, had no "off" button. His life was theatre; he was monumentally public; he could only be assayed as such, by his influence and reach. He loved baseball as deeply as any broadcaster I can think of. He called it for as long as any Voice, and served it more grandly than most. Parts-barker and magnifico, he was now the minstrel of the Cubs, and hailing this—yes—Living Legend, I recalled the Merm musing, in those tones more shattering than sham, "Yes, Broadway's been very good to me—but then, I've been very good to Broadway."

Once, surveying announcers, Harry passed judgment on Baseball's Disciples of the Dead. "Lots of guys doing the game today—you have to kick 'em to see if they're still breathing. There's no heart and soul there," he said. "They're automatons. They want the big paychecks, so they prostitute themselves. They don't rock the boat, don't say anything negative, and it comes out bland. Who can't say, 'Strike one. Ball one. There's a pop-up to short'? Man, baseball can be dull enough without having dull announcers. Make it fun, that's what I say. It's not life or death. It's a game, and it's like I say [all together, now], 'You can't beat fun at the ol' ball park.' "

Holy Cow! Mr. Mayor, this one's for you.

It might be! The shameless extrovert who became a regional superstar.

It could be! The recipient of happenstance who, later, in his mid-sixties, became a cable household word.

It is! The raw personality who evolved, in essence, into a patch of folklore on SuperStation television.

Harry Caray! The possessor of an almost mystic sense of timing, saving—who among us can boast of this?—the very *best* for *last*.

*   *   *

"By the last weeks of the campaign, those forty or fifty national correspondents who had followed Kennedy since the beginning of his electoral exertions into the November days had become more than a press corps—they had become his friends and, some of them, his most devoted admirers," Theodore H. White wrote in *The Making of the President 1960*. "When the bus or the plane rolled or flew through the night, they sang songs in chorus with the Kennedy staff and felt that they, too, were marching like soldiers of the Lord to the New Frontier."

He was everything, White later claimed, that reporters, wishing to be,

were not — handsome, humorous, impeccably garbed, and Ivy-educated, almost elegant — and it seemed somehow inevitable that as president, chronicled
by newsmen-turned-awestruck flacks, John F. Kennedy basked in the most
adulatory press coverage of our time.

Vin Scully was Fordham-, not Harvard-, glossed, and his politics leaned by
nature, I suspect, closer to those of his former neighbor, Ronald Reagan of
Pacific Palisades. Like JFK, however, he too was restless and inquisitive, with
a mind that was quick and self-confident, and he had a passion for slicing
through clichés. Am I equating, then, this son of the Bronx with what Massachusetts Governor Paul Dever called the "first Irish Brahmin"? No, except to
say: Vin Scully, in his stylish, melodic, and understated way, has reaped the
most extraordinary praise of any baseball broadcaster in post-World War II
America.

Exempli gratia (in school, Scully took Latin):

• "[He] always manages to live up to his reputation as a peerless baseball
play-by-play man," *The Sporting News* proclaimed in a typical bow to Scully's
sleight. "There is no announcer who so combines baseball depth and the
ability to express it."

• "Scully played the game at Fordham and has been announcing it, it seems,
since about '02," added a long-time apostle, the *Los Angeles Times*. "[He is] a
tremendous repository of baseball knowledge and lore."

• "Scully has the best voice in baseball," enthused the *Washington Post*, a more
new-sprung admirer. "He gives immediate perspective. He is a joy to listen to."

• "A pro is a pro is a pro," said Dick Young, the superb *New York Post*
columnist, playing Gertrude Stein; or, "Scully has elevated the business of
broadcasting to an art," contended Cooperstown's Ed Stack; or, "Vin is intelligent, literate, well-prepared, concise, the consummate reporter," raved *Post*
writer Henry Hecht. "He's been announcing Dodger baseball for [now, thirty-
eight] years, and he's still the very best."

The first crude, overwhelming impression was that few announcers could
have differed more from Harry Christopher Caray.

One rainy weekend, listening to Harry on the SuperStation and Scully over
NBC, I found myself juxtaposing them with The Voice and Ol' Redhead,
which seemed only natural since Vin has titled Barber "the most influential
person in my life." Like Mel, Harry favored showmanship. Like Barber, Vin
sanctioned mellowspeak. Caray was a homer who laced his rhetoric with "we"
and "come on" and "let's score a run." Scully was a middleman who boasted,
"I never say 'we,' never, *ever*. It's always been a point with me." Blatant and
exaggerated, Caray was as subtle as a Joe Louis jab. He was a polemicist;
controversy clung to him like August fleas on a Mississippi hound. Scully, on
the other hand, was resonant and metaphysical. He was an artist, baseball's
man of letters, and would no sooner have screamed "Holy Cow!" than dub Los
Angeles "Bridgeport, West."

Yet, ultimately, their likenesses were far more trenchant. Entering the big
leagues, each was a broadcast neophyte. Each became a student of baseball's
glamour boys and afterthoughts; other sports were something to take or leave.

Both enriched the pastime by invoking *individuality*—Scully's manner treated you like a guest, made you part of the game's hospitality; where would you find another *Caray?* Both thrived, exorbitantly, in two major markets—Harry in St. Louis and Chicago; Scully in New York and Los Angeles. Each, for all of that, lay curiously hidden from America until the mid-1980s; even Scully, *TSN* perceived, "despite his fame, is an unknown entity to many fans who have heard only snatches of his radio work in postseason baseball and with the Dodgers. Not everyone lives in Los Angeles." When, at last, through network- and SuperStation television, both blossomed into, arguably, baseball's most popular play-by-play men, stories they had told a thousand times before tasted, to this new, broader audience, fresher than a Caray martini.

Like his broadcast voice, rich with dramatic restraint, the early facts of Scully's life spoke neatly and clearly: born, November 29, 1927, the child of a silk salesman and a mother he termed, "Irish, red-haired, and, like me, unemotional—I was taught not to show my emotions. She was not the type to put her arms around me"; a Giants' bug whose family "had an old radio, one of those four-legged monsters that sat high enough off the ground that I was able to put a pillow directly under it and crawl up under it, actually *under* it. I'd sit under there for hours with a box of saltines and a carton of milk and listen to guys like Ted Husing and Bill Stern do college football. Games like Georgia Tech-Navy, Mississippi State, which I should not have cared the least about, but was enthralled with. It didn't matter to me. I used to just love to hear the roar of the crowd wash over me—I'd get goose bumps hearing them"; a fan, strangely, of the *Dodgers'* Redhead who "always wanted to be a sportscaster, even when the good nuns asked us what we wanted to be when we grew up. I remember back to when I was a kid. Everybody wanted to be a nurse, doctor, lawyer—not me. I wanted to be a sportscaster." On to Fordham Preparatory, graduating in 1944, and the Navy, putting in two years, and then Fordham University, where Vin worked on the school paper, ran the college radio station, majored in communications, was a center fielder on the baseball team, played against Yalie George Bush, and obtained his degree in 1949.

It was that spring that Scully, at twenty-one, passed into broadcasting— "They were looking for someone to do anything, and I ended up doing everything"—when station WTOP, the Washington CBS affiliate, hired him as a news, weather, sports, and disc jockey replacement. "The first couple of weeks I was in town," he said, "I stayed with some guys in an old place in Georgetown. You talk about the movie *Animal House*, we had it. I slept in the basement in a storm coat."

Scully's doldrums were short-lived. Vin soon had his own place, a growing sense of his potential—he was a natural; he knew it—and, not surprisingly, an offer to join WTOP full-time in February 1950.

He intended to accept.

Until Scully's archetype of radio arete fashioned Vin's first break in a splendid broadcast career.

Along the way, Vin had interviewed—"sort of as a token, a courtesy to me," he said—with the CBS Sports director, the Ol' Redhead himself. "I'd gone up to New York to talk with some CBS officials, and after I'd finished with the news director, I got shuffled over to Red. He didn't have much time for me — his wife was in the car, circling around the block, and Red was about ready to leave — but he did ask me to leave my address." Now, in the fall of 1949, Barber, recalling the encounter, asked an aide to phone "that red-haired fellow."

Each weekend, Vin said by way of remembrance, CBS Radio "staged its 'College Football Roundup,' with different games being aired from around the country, and Red chose the announcers. This particular Saturday, because of an illness to an announcer, Ernie Harwell was elevated to the headline game," Notre Dame v. North Carolina. "But that left a vacancy for the backup game — Maryland against Boston University." To fill it, Barber's aide called the Scully residence. "He got my mother," Vin said, "who took the message, but told me it was from Red Skelton."

By Saturday, the foul-up had been forgotten; Scully's valiance would not. The game, Vin's first network assignment, was in Boston, and Scully left his coat at the hotel "because I assumed I'd be working in a broadcast booth. But I get to Fenway Park and there's no booth — nothing. I don't have any coat, and I go up on the roof to broadcast and, I mean, it's *freezing* up there." He had a microphone, fifty yards of cable, a sixty-watt bulb for his only source of light and heat, and two eyes fixed on "the Golden Greek," B.U.'s Harry Agganis.

"Agganis was the big story, and every time he threw a pass, I'd run down the roof trying to see what happened. It was just wild." While Scully fought frostbite, the Ol' Redhead, directing the "Roundup" from the CBS studio, switched network coverage from Notre Dame's rout of North Carolina to Fenway Park. "Our game was close, and so starting in the second half, the entire country heard me," Vin said. "It was a great forum, and even though I probably did just an ordinary job, Red got a letter from the authorities at Fenway Park apologizing for not having a broadcast booth. I guess that impressed him."

The newcomer's intuitions were in tune. Barber *was* impressed — perhaps it was the voice alone; perhaps Vin's combination of maturity and zest; perhaps that "not once did that boy complain about how cold he was or how he couldn't see," Red told the *Los Angeles Times*. "He didn't even tell me about the lousy conditions when I saw him the following Monday. I had to find out from other people"; perhaps Barber's desire to mold a virtuoso — and despite the fact that, at twenty-two, Scully had never broadcast an inning of play-by-play, when Harwell fled Brooklyn in early 1950 to join Russ Hodges at the Polo Grounds, it was, in a real sense, the Redhead's future Telemachus that he called.

"Where are you going to be tomorrow morning?" barked Barber.

"In your office," Vin said.

The next day, Scully found not only Barber but also Branch Rickey, the Dodgers' president, waiting for him. Later, Rickey told his ball club's mouthpiece: "I don't want to trespass on your territory, Walter, but you have found your man."

On Opening Day 1950, flanked by the Redhead and Connie Desmond, his other play-by-play colleague, Vin began the first of eight seasons with the thwarted, passionate, and, ultimately, most beloved of all baseball teams — the Dodgers of Ebbets Field.

In time, over four decades, eight American chief executives, and starting that October, two O'Malley presidents, Scully would set a big-league record, clipping the Cubs' Jack Brickhouse, for the longest broadcast tenure with a single team. But at first, he cautioned, there were no thoughts of a rendezvous with destiny, which, after all, can be remarkably accidental, or even the Baseball Hall of Fame, which he entered on August 1, 1982. For the anxious rookie, untested, still living with his parents, the war whoop of humility, not history, was in the air. "It was on-the-job training," he said of the early fifties. "I would bring the lineup to the booth and Red would say, 'This man batted seventh yesterday. Why is he fifth today?' "

"The next time you brought the lineup," I guessed, "you knew the answer."

"Red was a stickler that way. He knew my youthful enthusiasm had to be tempered, and he knew how to do it. If I used a superlative about a player, he'd say, 'How dare you say that?' "

"To Red, still wet behind the ears?"

Scully laughed, softly. "Nobody was going to get a big head working for Red Barber," he said. "He was like my father, and Connie was my older brother. For whatever reason, we all took to one another, and what made it great — Red, in particular — was that they really cared. We had a wonderful relationship, and I still practice two pieces of advice Red gave me. One was not to get too close to the players — and he was right. Very early I found that it was easier for me to be objective, to remain unemotional. Then I saw things with my eyes instead of with my heart, and I cut down on a lot of mistakes."

"The other piece?"

"Red taught me that dead air wasn't the worst thing, that people liked to hear the crowd once in a while. And he told me not to listen to other broadcasters — not that I couldn't learn from them, because I could, but Red's point was that I would bring into the booth one precious ingredient that no one else could bring there — me, and whatever personal qualities made me a human being."

It was peculiarly telling, I thought — Scully's choice of adjectives. Not "grandiose . . . suave . . . opulent"; rather, "precious . . . personal . . . human" — the very qualities that explained why "no other baseball team," columnist Leonard Koppett has written, "generated a richer collection of memories, more closely held by so many people," than the 1950s Brooklyn Dodgers.

One marveled at, first of all, the players — the huge and modest Gil Hodges, and the captain, Pee Wee Reese; Jackie Robinson, fierce and truly unconquerable, and Billy Cox, an acrobat with a glove; Roy Campanella, the finest catcher in baseball, and outfielders Duke Snider and Carl Furillo, graceful and at war within themselves; pitchers like Carl Erskine, Don Newcombe, Preacher Roe, and Ralph Branca — a veritable squad of household names, more gifted individually than the Yankees.

You remembered, then, the team, and its glorious cross-hatchings of victory and defeat. In Scully's first two years, Brooklyn lost the pennant on the last day of the season. In 1952–53, the Bums won twice by a combined 17½ games, only to drop both World Series to the Yankees — the first in seven sets, the next in six. For the 1955–56 Dodgers, two more titles and a daguerrotype: Their four pennants in five years neared the most triumphal streak in National League history — the New York Giants' four in a 1921–24 row. On October 8, 1956, the O'Malleys' fortunes were of a different nature; Don Larsen fixed the Dodgers in his crosshairs with the first Oktoberfest no-hitter. It had been a headier time just twelve months earlier — the closest, in fact, that Brooklyn came to nirvana. After losing seven straight Fall Classics, five against the Bombers, the Dodgers won Game Seven, 2–0, at Yankee Stadium — believing, as few others did, that even in baseball's fifty-second World Series, a borough could run into luck.

"That was the happiest point of my career — that '55 championship," Scully stated, "because it meant everything. It was the only one the people of Brooklyn would ever experience. That was a great emotional thing, because I felt the frustrations of players, fans, and management. They had lost so many times, and almost always to the Yankees. And then finally to win — I was just so very thrilled." (Said Scully, simply, upon the final-game final out: "Ladies and gentlemen," he told his NBC audience, "the Brooklyn Dodgers are the champions of the world." Later, people would ask how he remained so calm. "If I'd said another word at that very instant," he averred, "I'd have broken down crying.")

At the moment, it seemed vaguely Messianic — an act of grace, the tie that bound — and a portent, surely, of Series' masterworks to come. But there were none, at least not in Brooklyn, and looking back at the Eisenhower Dodgers, one grew ruddy, in sentimental bloom, by recollecting Ebbets Field, tiny and grimy and wonderful, termed by the Ol' Redhead, "the Rhubarb Patch"; and the Faithful, more raucous than a cockfight, more Byzantine even than the park; and Barber himself, leaving Walter O'Malley in late 1953 to join Allen at Yankee Stadium, after "Connie and I trained him [Scully], loved him, teased him," he wrote, "and rejoiced in his remarkable development"; and the object of Barber's affection, the public speaker who talked with, not at or to, his listeners, seemed constitutionally unable to utter a prejudicial word, and within months of his teacher's leaving, beaming ebullience over the Dodgers' WMGM Radio and WOR-TV networks, became the Voice of Flatbush baseball.

"Desmond had been there for a longer time and by seniority should have been the Dodgers' top guy when Barber left, but he was an alcoholic, terribly unreliable — he ruined his family," said Harold Rosenthal of the *Herald Tribune*. "I covered the Dodgers all through those years, and O'Malley had taken an instant liking to Vin — he was an outgoing kind of guy, a friend of everybody, bartenders, the clubhouse guy. So there was no question that Scully would get the top job, even though he was just a kid."

At twenty-six, Vin Scully embodied a vision of boundlessness. He was happy, in his home-town, doing what he loved, and reaching and suiting his public. "He wasn't as big as Barber, who'd been very, very popular in Brooklyn, and not as big as he'd get later in L.A., and there wasn't the attention paid to Vin that Allen got, who overshadowed everybody," Rosenthal continued. "But he was already a professional, he was getting better all the time, and he had the great fortune to cover what, outside of the Yankees, was baseball's most controversial team. I think if he'd stayed in New York, he would have grown, matured, become one of the giants in broadcasting." Eventually, he did, three time zones and a baseball world away.

Of the Dodgers' Brooklyn apostasy, formally disclosed on October 8, 1957, but anticipated, like a prison sentence, with fear and inevitability, it must be said: To his credit, Scully saw no reason to leave. He knew and reveled in New York. He was pleasant, reliable, and already a success—a figure one took to the heart. "A very religious kind of guy," Rosenthal said. "We'd go on the road to Chicago where you played in the daytime, and later, when the game was over, Vin'd inevitably go to a movie. Didn't matter what it was—he'd be at the theatre, and he'd ask me to go along. And one day, he confided in me. 'You know why I go to so many movies at night, Harold?' Vin said. 'It keeps me out of trouble'—women, I guess." He smiled, faintly. "We should have that kind of behavior today." Moreover, why *would* the Dodgers leave? Had they not passed the million mark in home attendance a big-league record *thirteen* straight years? Did Flatbush fans not revere their players to an unprecedented extent? Had O'Malley himself not chortled, "My roots are in Brooklyn"? How could one trade all of this—loyalty, love, the Bums' earthy allure—for the corporate-zombie future of upward mobility and wealth?

Quite easily, as it happened.

"Historically, we shall be proven right," said the Dodgers' owner when he moved the team to Los Angeles. The mathematics of the past thirty years make it hard to argue with his cussed upheaval, and there are many, perhaps a majority in The Game, who insist that Walter O'Malley has been vindicated.

Their first four California seasons, the Dodgers played in a stadium designed for track and field and college football, the pythonic Memorial Coliseum. Converted to baseball, it flaunted a left-field foul pole 250 feet from home plate (to forestall a home-run siege, O'Malley erected a forty-foot-high screen, alternately called the Great Wall of China and the Bamboo Curtain), a seating capacity of 94,600 ("It's the only place," began a favorite *bon mot* of the time, "that can hold almost a hundred thousand people and two outfielders"), and center-field seats more than six hundred feet from the pitcher's mound (flaming, in part, Scully's coming glory as a celebrity). In 1958, the club placed seventh, rivaled Sominex, and drew 1,854,556 home patrons, a gain of more than eight hundred thousand over its final year at Ebbets Field. The following May 9, baseball's largest crowd ever, 93,103, attended a Yankees-Dodgers' exhibition match on Roy Campanella Night; that October, having startled even themselves by winning the pennant, the Angelenos hosted more than ninety-two thousand spectators at each of three Series games; by the end of 1961, the O'Malleys had lured 8,400,676 paid customers. *Vindication?* It was absolution. *Prosperity?* It was a gold mine, a strike. "They just took to us, right from the start, and that was so important because we hadn't known what to expect out here," Scully was saying now. "The move had been such a jolt; it was like starting all over again. I'd established myself for eight years in New York; everything I cherished was there. But there wasn't any real decision involved because I loved broadcasting, I loved being with the team, and I was in love with my job." He was, said Vin, like the bride whose husband had been transferred. "She might not want to go, but she goes."

There was something almost surrealistic about the New World Dodgers, sort of a California dream both trailblazing and unforgettable—the clamor and diversity of the Coliseum hordes; Wally Moon's wrong-field homers ("Moon Shots," naturally) which fell, like chip shots onto a green, over the Bamboo Curtain; the eerie beauty of Campanella Night, when the stadium lights were turned off and, at a signal, thousands of people lit matches ("a blizzard of fireflies," one writer said, "dancing in the night") to honor the crippled ex-Dodger; the dimming of Snider and Hodges, retirement of Erskine, Furillo, and Reese, and the rise of a preacher's son, Maurice Morning Wills, whom Scully styled "the Mouse That Roared"; the parade of Hollywood toadies and notables, the advent of the trumpet blare, "CHA-A-A-R-GE!" sport's ongoing call to arms, and the distant fan who said of baseball-watching in this freakish yard, "It was like observing a game in pantomime. My seat was in another time zone."

It was Scully who, through the transistor radio, reached that fan and, more inclusively, a goodly portion of the entire West Coast, and made them aware of baseball and, more to the point, the game before their eyes.

"Don't forget that until '58 the closest big-league baseball we'd ever had here was sixteen hundred miles away, in St. Louis. Contrary to popular impression, there were a lot of baseball fans around here, but not all of them understood the Dodger mystique," recounted the marvelous *Los Angeles Times* columnist, Jim Murray. "So the Dodgers had a selling job to do, and it was Vinnie more than anybody who did it. Baseball is a game of long, lagging periods, and Vinnie distracts you from them. He paints clear word-pictures, he'll segueway into a story about Duke Snider that happened thirty years ago, and he'll do it so smoothly you'd swear Duke was playing now. He's almost like a Celtic poet—he keeps your attention. I think it's almost impossible to overstate his importance when the Dodgers first came out here. He was their greatest link to the public," beguiling, calmly explaining, his voice regressing at the right moment, letting the Coliseum crowds take sway, and winning over by intimacy the devotion of his listeners.

Within months of Vin's arrival, Southern California found him extraordinary; he became, literally, emblematically, more popular than his team, the heart of O'Malley's marketing. In 1976, Dodgers' fans chose Scully—not Sandy Koufax, not Don Drysdale, not the Mouse That Roared—as the "Most Memorable Personality" in the franchise's history. A decade later, the *Times'* Rick Reilly wrote: "The Vin Scully Show . . . the most transfixing, regaling, entertaining show in baseball, carries elegantly on. Scully appeals to the truck driver and the English lit professor alike. He knows his way around homers and Homer, Shakespeare and stickball. If Scully says an errant shortstop is like 'the

Ancient Mariner—he stoppeth one in three,' one minute, then the next he's describing a change-up that 'squirts out like a wet bar of soap.' Los Angeles has lapped it up since the Dodgers came to town with Scully running interference." Except for Dizzy Dean, no broadcaster, I feel safe in saying, not even Bob Prince in western Pennsylvania or Caray, the Midwest—their congregations, one must realize, enjoyed a longer major-league heritage—has sold more people, more quickly and enduringly, on the game of baseball. "Does Los Angeles love Vinnie?" Reilly asked, rhetorically. "Vinnie doesn't *do* the Dodgers. Vinnie *is* the Dodgers."

Why?

To begin with, he was the Scout; except for Dean and Lindsey Nelson, whose network telecasts impregnated Los Angeles from 1953 to 1957, Southern Californians had no big-league frame of reference. "Vin may have been a smash no matter when he came along, but we'll never know—because to be a pioneer was a tremendous advantage," said Prince, whose cries of "Come on, Buccos, let's play Screeno!" dotted every Pirates' broadcast from the Coliseum. "There's no question that he's tremendously talented, but I suspect L.A. would have loved anybody when the Dodgers came West. It was his good fortune to *be* that body, and now Vinnie's style is what the area expects. That's the great imponderable—could another style have clicked back then? Who knows? Who can say? I was born in Southern California, and I've often wondered how they would have reacted to some Gunner's razz-ma-tazz," and chuckling, he seemed reflective, not plaintive or sore. "This isn't to take away from Vinnie—he's baseball's poet laureate. It's just that to be the First—it helped Rosey Rowswell in Pittsburgh, Ty Tyson in Detroit. It also helped Scully."

It was not "the First," alone, however, that accounted for Scully's popularity.

In Brooklyn, the Dodgers had televised each home and many road games; now, airing only the team's rare late-fifties visits to San Francisco, O'Malley—panting for the riches of pay-TV—banned *all* free home television. The reversal, disdained by Angelenos, filled Vin with a deep and abiding leverage. It boosted home attendance ("To see the club," Tommy Holmes wrote, "the new Dodger fan had to advance cash in hand"), which, in turn, presumably heightened local interest; forced fans to follow the Dodgers almost exclusively by radio, of which Scully was a wizard; and blanketed Southern California, already bulging with transistors, with the names and central chords of Dodgers' baseball. "Here, as in so many other ways, Walter O'Malley was brilliant. He knew that there were probably more radios in this area than anywhere in the world," Scully would later say, "and he knew that for every guy listening on the beach at Laguna or at his home in Apple Valley, some would eventually find their way to the Coliseum." Appended the *Times* in 1985: "He turned Los Angeles into a transistor town, first and foremost. Forget video, from April to October for twenty-seven years, Scully's mellifluous musings have drifted up from every traffic jam and outdoor café, every limousine and ice cream truck. The portable Vinnie. Scully may be the single-largest influence on transistor radio sales in Los Angeles. In fact, so many people pack a radio to Dodger games that KABC engineers often have to adjust for the noise of Vinnie's voice cascading up from the stands into the booth."

Looking back, there was the Coliseum—in many locations, you *needed* a radio simply to tag along. "People were so far removed from the playing field," Vin said, "that my voice, I guess, gave them some feeling of connection with the game"—and its hungry, naive fandom. "Although people were aware of some of the superstars, they weren't aware of the rank-and-file ballplayers. So they brought their radios to hear me tell them about the players. Then it became a habit, even after we moved out of the Coliseum to a park where you could follow the action. I've always thought it was strange knowing that thousands of people are listening to *you* describe a play *they* are watching."

There was Scully's baseball knowledge—"When he was at Brooklyn, Vin was the only broadcaster I knew to use the same detailed scorebook the writers did," Rosenthal said. "He'd played the game in college and wouldn't give you fluff; he'd go inside the game and explore its guts"—and his mastery of language. "They say radio is like skywriting," allowed a Los Angeles columnist. "The words, once spoken, merely float away to the winds, lost forever. But only Scully can still the sky."

Then too, there was Scully's affable, dispassionate manner, a kind of soft-shoe informality that, as I was to learn, is among the dominant attributes of Southern Californians; he was one of them, if by adoption, with his anecdotes, objective tones, and geniality of spirit, and belonged in a way that might have proved impossible in such hardened dens of roaring as St. Louis and Chicago. "Fans respect Vinnie because Vinnie respects the fans," Reilly said. "Vinnie does not scream at you. Vinnie does not numb you with numbers. Vinnie does not try to impress you. Nor will Vinnie rail at umpires, root for the home team [Cubs' fans, shudder here], or rag the visitor. He is as comfortable as your favorite college sweat shirt. Flip on the car radio, and you can almost see him riding shotgun, swapping stories, affecting no pretensions or style except for the simple feel of himself."

Above all, there was "the City," as Jack Webb, himself a Dodgers' fan, apprised a generation. In the late fifties and early sixties, Los Angeles was diffuse and sprawling, bereft of a defined focal point, and stocked with transient emigrants devoid of new-town ties. "When you talk about Los Angeles, you're talking about the drifter. Fundamentally, Californians aren't in contact with their neighbors," Teddy White, quoting a perceptive local politico, wrote in *The Making of the President 1964*. "Out here, people are lost. They have no one to talk to. And the doorbell-ringer has an importance far beyond his normal pictorial quality. These guys who win elections [or baseball audiences]—they've reached out and touched." In Southern California, I believe, *this* was the nub of Scully's magic. Over radio, he was a doorbell-ringer; echoing Ma Bell, he reached out and touched, and touched because he sounded, well, like a friend, like someone you would trust, someone you would want to know. In time, you felt you *knew* him, and his ball park became a home; the *Dodgers* became your focal point, and their Voice your new-town tie. You might not know your next-door neighbor, but who needed local belonging when Vin Scully, as was his custom, invited you to "pull up a chair"?

As the 1962 O'Malleys opened their palatial sanctum, Dodger Stadium — "It will be," Sir Walter told his son, Peter, "a permanent monument to our family" — with its five levels, broad flowering lawn, surpassing beauty, and 56,000 capacity, and that fall, collapsing in the final week, managed to blow the pennant; as the Dodgers won World Series in 1963 and 1965, beating the Yankees and Twins, and the pennant a season afterward; as Wills stole 104 bases in a year, Tommy Davis won two batting titles, Big D clasped a Cy Young Award, and Walter Alston — baseball's Gary Cooper — managed with dignity and deftness; as Koufax, maturing into a kind of pitcher no one had ever seen before, threw four no-hitters, captured three Cy Youngs, five times led the league in earned run average, and won ninety-seven games in 1963–66 and twenty-seven that final season; as the ex-Brooklyns broke the bank, drawing a record 2,755,184 customers in 1962 and more than 2 million each of the next four years; and as transistor-hugging spectators, at Scully's provocation, serenaded umpire Frank Secory in 1960 — "It was a particularly dull game," Vin said, "and so I got to looking through the press guide and noticed that it was Frank's birthday. So I said over the radio, 'I'll count to three and everybody yell, "Happy birthday, Frank!" ' " Scully: "One, two, three." The Coliseum cast of thousands: "HAPPY BIRTHDAY, FRANK!" — the terrain seemed grown over, lush with Scully's rhetoric, with a prolific pulling-up of chairs.

"When the Dodgers moved West, O'Malley negotiated the broadcast rights with the sponsor, Union Oil, and he insisted — demanded — that Scully be the Number One announcer," said Rosenthal. "He believed in him — so much, in fact, that in '57, at a time when O'Malley desperately needed up-front cash to build Dodger Stadium — in effect, Union Oil had him over a barrel [ouch!] and he could have jeopardized everything by his insistence on Vin — he got Union to pay for the first ten years of rights in advance and *still* take Scully." Noted Jim Murray: "Vin is the only guy I know of in any field who started off as a phenomenon and then every year got even more popular."

By 1969, he had broadcast eight World Series (five with Allen, one apiece with Brickhouse, Ray Scott, and Curt Gowdy), three All-Star Games (in 1959, 1962, and 1963 with Allen, Gowdy, and Garagiola), received the *Look* magazine Award for his coverage of the 1959 Oktoberfest, won the 1966 National Sportscaster of the Year Award, missed exactly two Dodgers' games since 1950 (taking off once for his sister's marriage and a second time for the birth of his third child), and plunged into the nonbaseball bailiwick of game-show television. "I am forty-two. How much more time do I have for trying something new? It's now or never," Scully said of his '69 debut as the host of NBC's quiz series, "It Takes Two." "I would hate to wake up, say, at sixty and wonder what I could have done if I had taken a chance outside baseball. Could I have become a moderator? An actor? A singer? A newscaster? A fellow never knows what he can do unless he tries."

Inevitably, Scully tried. (He said, once, of his avidity for homework, "I'm always secretly afraid of going out and sounding like a horse's fanny, which is one reason why I prepare. I prepare out of fear. Sir Laurence Olivier was asked what makes a great actor and he said, 'The humility to prepare and the confidence to bring it off.' Believe me, I'm loaded with the humility to prepare.") In 1969, he aired 190 baseball games and 165 network shows, taping "It Takes Two" in Burbank when the Dodgers played at home. One day, he recorded three programs and called a twelve-inning ball game; the next morning, he taped four shows, then headed out to Dodger Stadium for a twi-night double-header. Could the Dodgers take the pennant? Vin might ask his radio fanciers. (Between 1966 and 1974, no.) Back at "It Takes Two," could you tell me, miss, how many feet of nylon thread one needed for a pair of stockings? (Miss didn't know. Did Scully really care?) Was the aging Wills, reacquired after a December 1966 trade to Pittsburgh, more has-been or panacea? (Has-been.) How many pair of shoes came from a male adult alligator? (There once was a girl in Nantucket . . . oops, wrong card.) What was today, anyway, and where the hell were we? NBC? Dodger Stadium? A time for taping? A time at bat?

"It was a point in my life where I was looking to express myself in ways other than I'd known before. After all, I'd done baseball — nothing else, *nothing* — for two decades. And I'm glad I did it. It's just that with that crazy scheduling, I'd hate to have to do it again," Vin said a decade after "It Takes Two" passed, quietly, from the 1971 air (and his other network effort, CBS's afternoon "Vin Scully Show," was canceled after thirteen weeks. "It was a talk show and really something. I was sandwiched around the soap operas and actually nobody knew it was on and nobody really knew when it went off"). Yet one cannot flee this stretch of Scully's life without reciting, as *TV Guide* did on February 28, 1970, the Voice of the Dodgers' maddest brush with hilarity. "As a novice around NBC, Scully [was] a prime target of studio practical jokers, who carry their levity to the show," the magazine said. "On [one] occasion a black sedan, once used for a rub-out in a George Raft movie, was driven on-stage. Scully was to open the trunk to find the answer to a question on bootlegging. Unknown to him, crews, actors, and administrative staffs, including the whole company of 'Laugh-In,' had left their work in other parts of the building to slip quietly onto the set of 'It Takes Two.' Unsuspectingly, Scully opened the trunk. His jaw fell. Reclining within, unseen by the audience, was a delicious redhead, who had starred in *Playboy*. She leaned on an elbow, staring soulfully at Scully. She was as naked as a jaybird." Fordham had not prepared him for ladies who had on not a stitch. "Vin was speechless. His first impulse was to remove his coat and cover the lady, which, you must admit, is a knightly thought; but he realized this would stir suspicion among the audience. Nervously, he lifted the answer from the trunk and closed it. The plotters watching from the wings roared."

In early 1971, the Irish Catholics' son left such sensual wonders to revert — O bore — to baseball. The Angelenos were getting good again — in 1973, they contended for the title; the next year, Steve Garvey won the MVP Award, Cy Young reliever Mike Marshall graced a record 106 games, Jim (the Toy

Cannon) Wynn hit thirty-two homers, and the Dodgers snared their four-teenth pennant — and Scully found himself, to his listeners' delight, still intox-icated by the crowd. "That's the secret why I've never had to work to maintain my enthusiasm," he said. "The crowd always gets my adrenaline going. I still get goose bumps when the crowd sings the National Anthem or when I hear the roar before the first pitch. Maybe it means I haven't grown." But he had, of course, and so had his family, and when Vin's wife, Joan, only thirty-five, died in January 1972 of an accidental overdose of medication she was taking for a bronchial condition, Scully, his life suddenly beset by grief and disarray, became the sole parent of three children ages twelve, eight, and three.

The tragedy helped sharpen Vin's dislike of baseball's lonely, rootless road — "I was on a routine trip with the Dodgers," I recalled Scully saying in 1970, "and when we got to Atlanta, I phoned home. My oldest son, Mike, said to me, 'Why don't you come home, Dad?' I answered, 'I'll be there in only twelve more days.' I felt like a louse. It isn't right to ask my kids to understand road trips" — for now, far more than with his wife alive, his children would need him, miss him, curse the physical distances. "The whole uncertainty, plus my loyalty to the Dodgers, was one reason I turned down opportunities, many tempting, to do more network assignments [In 1970, he was offered the play-by-play on ABC's "Monday Night Football"; three years later, it was rumored that Vin would call Monday's "Game of the Week"]. I just chose to stay home with the family as much as I could — that was especially true once I became all they had." Then, in September 1973, the Dodgers' Voice announced his engagement to Sandra Schaefer, the secretary of Los Angeles Rams' owner Carroll Rosenbloom, and a new element took the floor: For the first time in a long time, Vin Scully might need the fresh capital network television could bestow.

"For so many years, just working baseball was enough," he said in January 1975. "But when I got remarried, I had three kids, my wife also had several, and we're expecting another one next month. So I thought maybe I ought to work a little harder." That month, solidifying his financial structure, Vin signed a three-year contract with CBS Television, which assigned him to tennis, golf, and the NFL. "Let's just say the money is good," he quoted an unnamed sportswriter as saying, "and there is no heavy lifting." There also was no baseball, since Columbia, believing it untelegenic, "made no great, serious effort," chimed NBC's Carl Lindemann, "to steal away part of our coverage and start broadcasting the sport."

Ironically, the new CBSer's only network sports coverage of the past decade involved those two now-empty chairs — baseball *and* NBC.

The previous fall, Scully had richened the Peacock Network's treatment of the Dodgers-Athletics' Oktoberfest. "Remember the 1974 World Series?" the *New York Post*'s Hecht would ask. "Curt Cowdy, Tony Kubek, and Oakland's Monte Moore sounded like rejects from a college radio station compared to Scully." Inured, by now, to commendations, the recipient turned back-patting away. "Someone told me afterward that I had done a good job on the Series. I figured," Vin said, dryly, "after eight years, I had to." He was referring to the

1966 Fall Classic, improbably the Voice of the Dodgers' last prior network sportscast. There too Vin had performed superbly, with a wealth of banter and sophistication. Yet Scully's joy was not unspoiled, for unlike past years, when each *team's* principal announcer aired half of every Seriescast, this season, for the first time, that honor fell to the network's big-league Voice—here, the Wyoming Cowboy. "It was just a bad situation back in '66—one might say there was an overriding nippiness in the air," Lindemann said. "Keep in mind that Scully may have been baseball's finest announcer. In addition, he was hugely beloved in Los Angeles. Always before, when appearing on the Series, Vin had done the play-by-play of four-and-a-half innings each day. If the Yankees were in the Series, in New York Mel Allen would do the first half of a game, Scully the second—then they'd go to L.A. and reverse the order. But in '66, we were in the first year of our new contract with baseball, and, naturally, we intended for *our* chief announcer, Gowdy, to have the most exposure, to carry the load—that's what we were paying him for. So we had a meeting before the Series began and explained the ground rules. 'In L.A. [for the first two games],' I said, 'Curt and Vin will split the TV play-by-play. Chuck [Thompson, of the Orioles] and Bob Prince'll do radio. Then we go back to Baltimore [for Games Three, Four, and possibly Five] and Curt and Chuck'll do TV, Vin and Bob the radio.' "

"How'd Vin accept the change?" I said.

"Slowly," Carl chuckled. " 'My fans [in Southern California], they won't be able to hear me,' he said. In effect, Vin thought he should be on TV every day, just like in the past. So we broadcast Game One and Vin goes first. He does his four-and-a-half innings and is, as usual, tremendous, with Curt supplying the color. Then we go to the bottom of the fifth inning, and Curt takes over play-by-play, and Scully shuts up. He, literally, sat there and didn't say a word. I guess it was Vin's way of getting back at us. There was a chill between him and Gowdy that started right there." Four years later, Lindemann added, baseball hosted a December 3, 1970, late-night awards dinner "that was televised nationally out of Los Angeles, and Curt and Scully were chosen to be the emcees. We kept them totally apart, practically had to do handstands to make sure they got exactly the same amount of TV exposure."

By the mid-1970s, with Gowdy driven from NBC baseball, Garagiola consolidated as his successor, and Scully ensconced as a CBS reporter, the Big Chill seemed obsolete, irrelevant. Adept at football, Vin was rousing on tennis and golf, and he enjoyed the chance, having sliced his Dodgers' schedule to all home games (on radio) and selected road shows (via TV), to donate time and money to his expanding brood.

In 1977, for instance, Scully's baseball commitment totaled barely 100 games; between Dodgers' and network salaries, he was reputed to be the highest-paid sportscaster in America; and he could watch his children grow up, his ball club win the division and then its playoff against the Phillies, and the O'Malleys draw the astonishing sum of 2,955,087 paid admissions, the most copious harvest in baseball history. It was a bounty, sadly, which benefited few fans of the pastime in Nashville, Newark, or New Orleans, deprived, as they were, of play-by-play's most rarefied Voice. "I used to get it from fans in New York, where they remembered me, or other places where they were aware of my work, and they'd say to me, 'Gee, why aren't you on network baseball? Why can't we hear you?' " Scully told the Associated Press in 1983. "And, of course, I was flattered — who wouldn't be? But I was enjoying those years. I was doing a full schedule on CBS. At the same time, I could do what I loved most — the Dodgers, whom I knew I would never leave. And, anyway, to work network baseball — it was just never that big a deal for me. I was happy as it was."

Enter the 1977 Oktoberfest and "a deal," it must be said, that fetched Scully's happiness, briefly, to the graveyard.

Its plot was dug, in retrospect, by baseball's 1975 decision, as part of the 1976–79 dual-network TV pact, to grant ABC and NBC autonomy in their choice of correspondents. No longer could the commissioner demand, as Happy Chandler, Ford Frick, William Eckert, and Kuhn had since the 1940s, that the World Series showcase announcers from the participating clubs; if it wished, the Classic network could tap only in-house mouthpieces, foregoing, eschewing, the Cardinals' Buck, Tigers' Harwell, or even California's Scully.

Massaging custom, NBC, the 1976 Series carrier, chose compromise; in Cincinnati and New York, respectively, Marty Brennaman and Phil Rizzuto, the Voices of the Reds and Yankees, would handle three innings of each set's play-by-play. ABC was less agreeable, muffling, in effect, any announcer marked *not invented here*. "There are two things drastically wrong with ABC's coverage of the Series," Larry Stewart of the *Los Angeles Herald Examiner* wrote on October 13, 1977. "A) Vin Scully is not involved. B) Howard Cosell is. Scully will not be seen or heard at any time during the Series, going against the wishes of the baseball Commissioner's Office. ·. . . ABC chose to go with its own announcers. Scully was offered a few crumbs. He could have had a bit part in the pregame shows and could have done play-by-play for two innings of the games in Los Angeles. CBS, which has Scully under contract, had given indications it would allow Scully to work with ABC on the Series. But Scully never had to ask for final approval from CBS. Scully's lawyer and business advisor, Ed Hookstratten, insisted Scully turn down ABC's offer, reasoning it was an insult. . . . [On the other hand,] ABC went to great lengths to use Cosell, who admittedly does not like baseball and obviously doesn't know much about it, on the Series. . . . Roone Arledge, are you listening? The public is outraged that you have forced Cosell down its throat and, particularly here in Los Angeles, is outraged Vin Scully is not behind the mike with the Dodgers in the Series." The incident rankled — Vin Scully, ditched for two football trucklers, Cosell and Keith Jackson, and Tom Seaver, with his giggling, untrained voice? — but was also, in its way, strangely instructive. This was not 1957, when local announcers ruled baseball, or even 1966, when Scully, after his triumphs of the previous decade, reviewed NBC's bid of half of each home Seriescast and found half-a-loaf unfit. It was another time — for baseball, almost another cosmos — and network television, with its huge contracts and national coverage, was transforming American sports. If Scully intended to broadcast another World Series, his tenth, or an All-Star Game or Super Bowl, he must venture forth as a network-, not local-team, employee. Blighting October 1977, it was a lesson he did not forget.

The next season, Los Angeles won a seventh pennant; NBC, copying its rival, studded the Autumn Occasion with network TV hirelings Garagiola, Kubek, Seaver, and Gowdy; and Scully, decreasingly content with network baseball anonymity, aired CBS Radio's coverage of the All-Star Game.

"Ah, but for the World Series, I took it easy," he said, lightly. "It was strange to be relaxing and in the stands, not the press box, and expensive too — seventeen dollars a seat. My wife was uptight, but I wasn't. It was just a case of understanding the situation — baseball sold the rights to the network, and the network wanted to use its own announcers. I got to the point where it didn't bother me. When fans said, too kindly, 'Gee, you should be on the Series — you're an All-Star behind the mike,' I'd tell them, 'You only think that way because I didn't have to fight the curveball.' "

From 1976 to 1978, swatting curveballs, fastballs, and balls of doctored substance, the Phillies, Dodgers, Yankees, and Royals won eleven of twelve demipennants; in 1979, as Scully covered the Fall- and Mid-Summer Classics for Columbia, it was the old order fighting change.

For Baltimore, Ken Singleton bombed thirty-five homers and Mike Flanagan went 23-9; the Angels' Don Baylor plated 139 runs, Kent Tekulve recorded thirty-one Pirates' saves, and Willie Stargell was named the league's co-Most Valuable Player; the Birds, California, Cincinnati, and Pittsburgh won divisions, and the Buccos, on October 17, the Series. Yet that year's bananas shrank beside the overstuffed cantaloupe of 1980. George Brett batted .390 (highest since the Splinter's .406), Milwaukee's Cecil Cooper wound up at .352, the Royals' Willie Wilson averaged .322 with 230 hits, and Reggie Jackson had his best year, batting .300 with forty-one homers and 111 runs batted in. Steve Stone of the Orioles won twenty-five games, the Brewers belted 203 home runs, and Oakland's Ricky Henderson, under the watch of Billy Martin, stole 100 bases to erase Ty Cobb's old league mark of ninety-six. For the fourth time in five years, the playoff linked Kansas City and New York; departing from form and memory, the Royals swept the pinstriped Hessians. In the National League, the Phillies' autumn was equally redoubtable. After a regular season of MVP Mike Schmidt's forty-eight long balls, Steve Carlton's twenty-four victories, Bake McBride's speed and elan, and Manny Trillo's unarguable grace, Philadelphia zonked the Astros in a brilliant semifinal; the World Series was no less rewarding, a Quakers' triumph, four games to two. Thereafter, injury (a fifty-day players' strike), insult (the idiocy of the Split Season), and disgust (the poststrike network television audience, reflecting fans' revulsion, dropped by more than 20 percent) — in other words, the miserable 1981 season, which silenced and humiliated The Game. "Look only at the facts," Bertrand Russell said. The facts appalled in The Year That Baseball Stopped.

Finally — after the Voice of the Dodgers' estrangement from network TV baseball; his franchise's strike-tainted 1981 world championship; and Scully's radio handling of the 1978–82 All-Star Games and 1979–82 Oktoberfests, pleasing listeners with exhaustive, roving commentary — broke a junction of reawakenings.

By NBC, offering Scully its chief baseball play-by-play job.

By Scully, accepting.

And by the viewing politic, alerted, to a degree not matched since the 1975 World Series (when the event transcended) and Dean and Allen's early-sixties monarchy (when the announcers did), to how riveting televised baseball could be.

The stirring began, indirectly, with another transplanted Southern Californian to whom Scully had been a self-proclaimed "idol": Dick Enberg, long-time Voice of the Angels.

From my first encounter of the television kind, Enberg had been a favorite. He was attentive and outgoing; his enthusiasm was infectious; he conveyed the game's titillation and core.

A Wolverine who attended Central Michigan University (working his way through school as a $1-an-hour janitor at the local radio station) and received his master's and doctor's degrees in health sciences from Indiana University (where he defrayed expenses through sportscasting), Enberg reminded me of the profile sketched by Lindemann's predecessor, Tom Gallery, of his friend and ex-colleague, Lindsey Nelson: "He's not simply a *professional* broadcaster — he's a *professor* of broadcasting."

This was really quite natural, since Enberg wanted to *be* an educator. "In 1961, I got my doctorate and landed a teaching and coaching job in what is now Northridge State in Southern California," he said. "So I headed out there. Not to be a sportscaster — that was just a sideline, a way to supplement what I knew would be a meager teaching salary. I had so little money, and I needed the work."

"But your main ambition?" I said.

"To be the best professor around," Dick said. "I never gave the same test twice. I wanted my students to get something from their time in my classroom."

As ennobling as academia was, Enberg soon found that broadcasting was more rewarding. "Often, creatively," he joked, "and inevitably, *always*, financially."

Those first years, looking for work between semesters, Dr. Dick took tapes to local radio and television stations — "thirty-five of them" — and latched on to some disc jockey jobs in the summer. This wax led Enberg swiftly to Saturday football reports, Western Hockey League play-by-play, coverage of Los Angeles State's 1964 small-college football championship, and weekly boxing from the Olympic Auditorium. "Boxing was a great experience for me, and it underlined a nice lesson I learned from teaching: honesty," he said. "I never attempted to say any more or less than what was happening. If it was a lousy fight, I said so. After three years, that show was one of KTLA's highest-rated programs."

Next came the local prestige assignments and, leaving the classroom *in toto*, a sad farewell to seminars, sabbaticals, and blue books. By 1967, at thirty-two,

Enberg teamed with Bob Kelley on Rams' radio, and relished huge success as the television announcer of UCLA basketball; that same season, he joined the Angels as Bud Blattner's colleague. Four years later, Dick took to the airwaves as host of the syndicated TV nostalgia series, "Sports Challenge," which featured athletes as panelists, entered more than 120 markets, and "played to almost 10 million viewers every week," *The Sporting News* reported.

"The people on these shows," Enberg was saying, "were all idols to me as a kid. Suddenly, on 'Sports Challenge,' I was asking them questions." From there, he trouped to "The Way It Was," the Emmy-winning sports retrospective that he helped produce; another nationally televised game show, "Baffle"; and his signing by NBC in 1975, the same year Enberg was divorced—"the only crisis of my life," he said now—from his wife, Jeri, a playwright and mother of three who critiqued Dick's every broadcast and of whom he observed, "I'll be forever grateful for her part in my development." He became, one columnist wrote, "a conglomerate"; in the early seventies, his salary rivaled Scully's; and by later that decade, working Wimbledon, boxing, segments of "SportsWorld," pro football with Merlin Olsen, and college basketball with Billy Packer and Al McGuire ("Dick's the only guy in sports," Al mused, "who could work with Billy and me at the same time and still keep everything sane"), he had emerged, Craig wrote, "as the coming star of stars at NBC."

Enberg's rise delighted viewers, who appreciated not only his consonant style but his manifest niceness. Unintendedly, it also decimated another of broadcasting's decent and modest men, Curt Gowdy, then plummeting at the network, for it was he whom Enberg replaced as NBC's Voice of the Super Bowl, the NCAA basketball tournament, and on January 1, 1980, "The Granddaddy of them all." Airing more than fifty network events a year, Dick left the Angels after the 1978 season. "I'm just too busy with everything else to broadcast the club every day," Enberg said at the time, "and it just breaks my heart. I owe so much to this club, the fans, my partners, and even worse, baseball is the sport I like best." Turning elsewhere, he was named to anchor NBC's coverage of what decayed into a phantom venture: America's nonparticipation in the 1980 Summer Olympics. Between football, basketball, and related treats, his voice was heard, it is possible, more than any network sportscaster's of the early 1980s. Weekly, he pricked Craig's 1978 prediction: "The era of the man for all seasons is fading."

Ironically, since Dick loved the sport, if understandably, given Chrysler's allegiance to Garagiola, baseball remained the one major network ware eluding Enberg's tentacles. It was not, of course, a *total* blackout—he *did* announce numerous backup "Games," grace NBC preseason baseball specials, and, insisting on a contract clause which spun him onto the 1982 World Series, share air-time with Seaver and Kubek and play-by-play with Garagiola—and listening to Enberg that autumn, I recall thinking how closely he reminded me of Scully. Like Vin, he was precise, warm, and well-prepared, and armed with a literacy so alien to rough-edged members of the jockocracy. Yet, lucklessly, Dick became more symbol than beneficiary, for it was that season too that NBC discovered *another* mouthpiece in the Voice of the Dodgers' mold. *His* name was Bob Costas, and he was full of stories and light badinage; he had an inventive mind, an abiding passion for The Game — "I believe," he said of a battered Mickey Mantle card which, until lost in 1987, bedecked his wallet, "that you should carry a religious artifact with you at all times" — and he could have given an hour lecture, I believe, on every regular of the 1961 Yankees. In short, relaxed and knowledgeable, like Enberg — only younger, less certi- fied, and, therefore, easier to afford.

By the time of Enberg's 1982 Oktoberfest, Costas had already led an intensely charmed existence. Born in Queens, he graduated in 1974 from Syracuse University with a degree in broadcasting, quickly landed a position at Bill O'Donnell's old station, WSYR-TV and Radio, vaulted late that season to KMOX, where he handled play-by-play for the American Basketball Associa- tion Spirits of St. Louis, and called his first NFL telecast, at twenty-four, two years later. He did weekend CBS Network jobs into 1980, then switched to NBC, which, with fewer quality pro football voices, was more receptive to his talent. Joining color man Bob Trumpy, former tight end of the Cincinnati Bengals, Costas deciphered, embellished, and invariably opined; he gave listeners a whimsical, self-deprecating twist of humor straight out of George Burns by way of David Letterman.

In that first Peacock season, the critics unleashed effusion; Costas was praised for his charm, his prose, for the fullness of his hair. Still, Bob met un- fulfillment; football, as *The New Republic* discerned, was "too complex, too simultaneous for anything other than analysis. Baseball, with . . . its delicate sequentialism, lends itself to abstraction and poetry." As a broadcaster, Costas meant to be a poet. "There's no hanging around in football. You go into town on Saturday, check into the hotel, wake up Sunday morning and go to the stadium," he said. "But baseball is the greatest hanging-around game ever in- vented. You hang around the batting cage, in hotel lounges or bars after the game, talking to baseball people. There's a romance and mystique to baseball that nothing else can match." When, in early 1982, Merle Harmon — NBC's 1980–81 backup "Game of the Week" announcer — was "not renewed by the net- work," Craig noted, "because his contract calls for too much money compared to the events available for him to work," Costas, whose salary was then a frac- tion of Harmon's, received a thirtieth birthday present that nothing else *did* match: He became a play-by-play Voice of NBC's backup "Game," going on that year to drape the pastime with a warmth and insight that eclipsed the bare and statistical.

Costas. Enberg. Kubek. Garagiola. Each, if asked, would choose baseball as his favorite sport; each was capable of expressing, through different strengths, some sense of its personalities and lineage. Bob and Joe could even make you laugh. For a viewer who had recoiled, like millions of others, a mere decade earlier, from NBC's degrading backup tandem of Jim Simpson and Maury Wills — one announcer chillingly indifferent to the game; the other, basely incompetent — the network's 1980s baseball roster of riches seemed almost unbelievable. And then, in December 1982, as Arthur Watson, the

president of NBC Sports, announced with undisguised elation that Vin Scully
had become the Voice of NBC baseball, the getting that was good got even
better.

Starting in 1983, Scully would call the play-by-play of each primary (or "A")
"Game of the Week," the All-Star Game, more prominent league playoff, and
World Series; shifting to analysis, Garagiola would be his colleague. At the
same time, the secondary ("B") coupling would consist of Costas, the future
host of NBC's pro football coverage, 1985 National Sportscaster of the Year,
and a rising star, and Kubek, not a falling star, precisely, but neither a happy
one. "I must admit I'm not crazy about possibly being assigned to the backup
game," Tony said after learning of Scully's hiring, "but still, it's not a big ego
thing. I understand this type of deal. Vin is a star, Joe is a name, and they're
both getting more money than I am. Paying them as much as they are [be-
tween his Dodgers' and Peacock salaries, Scully would earn an estimated $1.5
million a year], they have to justify it by giving them top billing."

Demoted after fourteen years on the primary set, the ex-Yankees' shortstop
at least survived NBC's spree of musical chairs. Less fortunate was Enberg,
dispatched from network baseball altogether. "There was just no room for
me—they had the guys they needed for their two teams a week," he said in
1985, the year he returned to baseball as a part-time Angels' broadcaster.
"People ask me, 'Why do you want to come back now to local baseball after
you've done it on the *network* level and you're still doing network everything
else?' and I give them the simplest and most honest answer I can—'I love the
game. I miss it.' "

The shakeup cost—I, for one, missed Enberg—but its consequences could
not help but sell. This was how it should have been all along, in the two
decades reaching back to The Voice's Oktoberfests and the CBS Television
"Game of the Week": for the first time since Nikita Khrushchev domineered
the Kremlin, baseball's Best Announcers calling its Celebrity Events. It was
so *obvious;* its common sense had removed the scales from NBC's and baseball's
eyes.

Garagiola was to blend anecdotes, sapience, and a player's perspective; "Joe
would say the batter wiggled," NBC director Harry Coyle said after the 1984
World Series, "so we'd place the replay on the guy, he'd talk about the catcher's
positioning, and we'd put the camera there. He'd be right and we'd all look
smart. With Joe, you'd be surprised how many times that happens during a
year."

Kubek and Costas were both traditionalists—"Going to Wrigley Field is not
just a trip to the ball park; that would be downplaying it," Bob pronounced.
"I equate it with a pilgrimage to Mecca"—and it was hoped, the network said,
that as they worked together ("meshed" was the term you heard), they would
feel affinity, exchange ideas and clashing views, and nurture Tony's knowledge
of inside baseball with Costas' appreciation of its mythology.

And Scully? In 1982, he had entered the Hall of Fame, been named Sportscaster of the Year, savored Vin Scully Night at Dodger Stadium, received, like
Gowdy, the George Foster Peabody Award for excellence in broadcasting, and

unloosed for Dodgers' fans and CBS Radio the craft that prompted Jim Murray to call him "the Fordham Thrush with a .400 larynx." Now, NBC expected, Americans would learn—would see and hear, not mostly hear *of*—why Southern California, regarding Scully as a media Secretariat, dismissed competitors as a stable of Mr. Eds. Belatedly, he was where he belonged. Reliving Wills, I assumed God had become a baseball fan.

For that, I was grateful, or as Watson said upon Scully's arrival, "We are proud that we will be the network that brings to America this superlative announcer. He reflects the importance we place on baseball." Yet there was no explanation, either formal or informal, as to why—after the bland voices and canceled "Games" and inferior publicity; after the shivery disinterest NBC once heaped upon the pastime—the network had decided to lavish, first, money, and, as it turned out, affection on what became—I could hardly grasp it—perhaps its most valued sports property of the 1980s.

Scully's hiring *was* emblematic, the shield of NBC's design to treat baseball with esteem and—even—enthusiasm, not as a regular-season afterword to be tolerated for its entree to the All-Star Game and World Series.

Still, why *now?* Why Vin, *after all these years?*

For one thing, I believe, the Peacock Network approached Scully because it sensed receptivity, not rejection. Vin's posture had changed from a decade earlier; he welcomed an NBC entanglement. "My schedule was more flexible, I was doing fewer Dodger games—it was easier for me to broadcast nationally every week," he said. *Un*said was the fact that a niche as baseball's network spokesman—as Coyle sallied, "its national Olivier"—would be a natural evolution, the perfect capstone for Vin's career.

For another, *baseball* had changed. The Game was more popular than, say, in 1973 and, potentially, more marketable; it might, now, more than then, *warrant* Scully's salary. By late 1982, NBC had already begun bargaining a new network pact that eventually cost the company $550 million from 1984 through 1989, a 407 percent increase over its previous fee. Against that backdrop, Watson needed a Voice capable of insuring his network's investment; the numbers were too colossal to rely upon a Gowdy, Simpson, or even, as a team, Garagiola and Kubek.

There was also the reality that *NBC* had changed since the late sixties and early seventies. Its new president was a Fordham graduate and admirer of Scully's whose taste ran to announcers like Enberg and Costas—wry, fluent, almost lyric. "Arthur was going to hire Vin anyway, regardless of what happened in 1982—he felt Scully was the one who could maximize the sport on TV, enliven it. He knew Vin was a stylist, a poet, something NBC baseball hadn't had before," a friend of Watson's related. "But it also happened that this was the year that Dick and, to a less evident degree, Costas came on the network scene and were greeted with hosannahs by the press. Well, that was just more icing on the cake for Vin—as if there'd been any doubt about whether he'd be a TV hit; he *was*, after all, the guy after whom they'd been patterned. But it was also the end for Dick, even though, ironically, he had shown how successful a Scully-type could be. Logistics dictated that he be dumped for his trouble."

Lastly and most crucially, I suspect, there entered into the network's thinking an element of simple pride, the cry of *Why Not the Best?*, to echo the
massively ironic title of Jimmy Carter's autobiography.

Scully *was* the best.

If NBC intended to mold, as its higher-ups insisted, baseball coverage that
was seminal, it could hardly consent to less.

* * *

"Skeptics could wonder how well [Scully] will do on TV [v. radio] at a network
level [v. his diadem in the West], and how well he will work with Garagiola,"
a columnist wrote in early 1983. "It will require two large egos, talkative ones,
to share one microphone."

As the Voice of the Dodgers recovered from a middling start to — what
else? — "mesh" with his colleague ("A team either grows or it stagnates," Vin
said, "and I feel we grew as the season progressed. It's like a dance team. You
have to work together to learn each other's style"); as Joe G., strangely quiet
at first, grew more at ease as an analyst; and as NBC's El Dorado of a TV co-
operative, armed with more than six decades of experience, bobbed its way
through a year mined with critics eager to condemn — viewers considered those
questions and, ultimately, dismissed them.

By late in the 1983 season, climaxing in the National League playoff between Philadelphia and Los Angeles, Scully and Garagiola formed baseball's
most complementary network broadcast team since Dizzy Dean and Bud Blattner. Opined the *New York Times*: "That the duo of Scully and Garagiola is very
good, and often even great, is no longer in dispute."

Observing, critiquing, leading the camera, Joe had adapted artfully — speaking less, he was saying more — and his routines and one-line usage seemed re-
endowed with bright cheer. But it was Scully who emerged as the apotheosis
of the sport's national coverage, the latest in a line of magnificent network announcers from Graham McNamee to Red Barber to Lindsey Nelson to Melvin
Allen Israel. For an entire generation of baseball viewers, too young to recall
Nelson, The Voice, Bob Wolff, and Diz, he was the first extended network
Voice to make the pastime breathe, dance, *sing*. He prodded, luring comebacks
by Garagiola and raised eyebrows at home; he had a genius for the ringing
phrase ("Gil Hodges' big hands made his glove about as handy as Michael
Jackson's"); in a McLuhan age bent on video worship, he helped the "Game"
seem as exalted and contemporary as the star-helmeted Dallas Cowboys.

Oddly, Vin was most proud of how he and Joe G. had tripped consensus.
"People couldn't wait for us to be the odd couple, always sniping at each
other," he mused. "But they forget that Joe and I are two pros. There never
was a problem. We drove in from the airport together, dined together, and
went to the ball park together. Both of us have been in the business long
enough that we weren't reaching any more. So what we tried to do is emphasize
the 'we' and not the 'I.' " It was not redemption but diversion, though, that
weekly garnered 8–10 million viewers around their televisions, and each

Saturday Camp Scully sprang forth as a rare and remarkable habitat, its broadcasts a magical mystery tour that swept from this team ("The first-place Bengals are clawing up a storm") to that player ("So Rice hits a long out and Tony Armas hits one out long") to some occurrence a decade earlier (one, perhaps, of the thirteen no-hitters Vin had broadcast by 1987) and which, as it traveled, endued this old and often sullied game with an almost neoteric character.

In 1983, "Game of the Week's" national rating actually dropped by 0.4 percent to 5.9; the next year, the series' first of exclusivity, it rose to 6.4; in 1985, moving Bill Carter of the *Baltimore Sun* to write, "If there is [a] message in [this year's] ratings information, it is that baseball has come back with a vengeance as a TV sport," the "Game" trounced the Masters golf tournament, professional bowling, and the made-for-TV, springtime United States Football League; in 1986, bereft of even lukewarm pennant races, its Nielsen rating fell to 6.3. Even so/more, the retreat *itself*, gussied up by weeknight promotions, splendid camera coverage, and, of course, its Voice(s), was so much *classier*, more of a broadcast Ritz. "It's going to take some time," Tom Merritt of NBC Sports publicity, borrowing from Carole King and the Carpenters, said in late 1983, "to get our regular-season ratings up to where, exactly, we want them. Over the years, some people got out of the habit of watching a 'Game' each Saturday. But we're coming back strong. We've got exclusivity now"—under the bigs' 1984–89 contract, no team could broadcast locally before 4 P.M., Eastern Time, on Saturday; until then, it was hoped, the total baseball audience would swing en masse to NBC—"so we're picking up a lot of local viewers who previously watched, say, a Yankee game in New York instead of NBC's featuring the Pirates and Reds. We're publicizing the 'Game' more. And we have marvelous broadcasters—Bob, Tony, Joe, naturally Vin. We think as more people are exposed to them on the big events—the All-Star Game, the Series, the playoffs—they'll hear baseball as they've never heard it before, they'll be wowed, they'll also start watching on Saturday, and our 'Game' ratings will be higher in the future than they've been in the past."

For the moment, Merritt's theory seemed plausible (if, still, unverifiable). At its center lay a sort of trickle-down belief in announcing's salience—that a decent portion of America, hearing Vin, for instance, on a Fall Classic, would turn the next year, seeing baseball in a better light, to the Voice of the Dodgers and the "Game." Regardless, Scully's tour reached Athena in October 1984, when he and Garagiola—the Classic's only two mouthpieces; that month, ABC assigned three to each playoff; NBC had blitzed the 1980 Grand Event with a five-voice band—aided by the technocracy of producer George Finkel and director Harry Coyle, broadcast baseball as raptly, facilely, and with as much respect for the viewer, as any TV tandem I have ever heard.

Later, Jack Craig declared, "NBC's coverage of the [Tigers-Padres'] World Series was a pinnacle for televised sport. Never before has an ongoing story been told so well, not only in pictures, but commentary as well." Using fourteen cameras, the network offered vivid replays, graphic close-ups (an eyeball-to-eyeball view of runners leading off from first base), an extra slow-motion camera (the "Super Duper") that allowed fans to see the ball's seam and rotation, and mercifully few in-stand shots (that ABC staple) of players' wives primping their hair.

In his eighth Oktoberfest, seven on TV, Garagiola provided background subtleties for "the casual guy," he said on the air, "the ones who don't see us every week"; compared the batting stance of Detroit's Ruppert Jones to a hula dancer during a Don Ho record; and innerved his audience by prophesying a Padres' pitchout seconds *before* it punctuated Game Two. "How did you know that?" Scully asked on behalf of 50 million viewers. "The fist," Joe replied; the sign for a 1984 pitchout hadn't changed since 1944; as a former receiver, Garagiola picked it up. Yet it was his straight man, calling play-by-play with nerve and journalistic instinct, who was "the star broadcaster of the Series," *TSN* reported. "When five games are congested into six days and nights, Scully's standards can be taken for granted. That does not lessen them." Padres' pitcher Tim Lollar, Scully said, "is trying to keep San Diego from disappearing without leaving an oil slick." After Lance Parrish touched fast-balling Goose Gossage for a home run, he noted, "With the clocking of the [speed] gun, the Goose has been clocked." Of stadium lights speckling the TV screen, it was, "There you see a spider web of light"; the Padres' Game-Two revival meant the Tigers' lead had "gone a-glimmering"; a ground ball by San Diego's Terry Kennedy "knocked the letters off [Lou Whitaker's shirt]."

When Vin heard that Mickey Lolich, hero of the 1968 World Series, had been consigned to the upper deck of Tiger Stadium, debatably the worst seat in the house, the old Latinist crystallized the ex-Bengal's fall. "*Sic transit gloria*," Scully advised his viewers. ("Thus goes the glory.")

When Kurt Bevacqua smacked a three-run homer, tipping the second game, "as soon as the ball dropped into the seats, Scully . . . fell silent," and shrewdly, heightened drama with restraint. "For one minute, as the replay showed Bevacqua turning around in a circle and jumping for joy, [Vin] didn't say a word. The San Diego celebration melted into a commercial. With absolutely nothing said," divined the *Washington Post*.

When viewers learned that Detroit manager Sparky Anderson had told pitching coach Roger Craig, "We've got to get these guys early [or face the Padres' bull pen]," we discovered that Scully even read lips. "Yes, I really do," he conceded later. "I taught myself a lot by reading them. Tom Lasorda [the Dodgers' manager and outrageous combination of pasta and theatricality] is the easiest guy in baseball to read."

Talking baseball, leaving such irrelevancies as the state of the NFL, upcoming "Battles(s) of the Network Stars," and Humble Howard's weekends in the Hamptons to "Monday Night Baseball's" fun gang at ABC, Vin had become the easiest guy in baseball to *listen to*. Hearing Scully dress his 1980s network product, I wondered if even a 1950s Allen could have better spun its fabric.

By now, the dust was also settling at Cosell & Co. After a late-seventies- and early-eighties network revolving door more crowded than NBC's, Bob Uecker was back mixing wealth and caricature at Miller Brewery and County Stadium;

Steve Stone, a "MNB" backup analyst, had been banished to Wrigley Field as Caray's cohort; and in 1983, his eighth season at ABC, Al Michaels was finally named the primary baseball announcer of the network, Gary Deeb had observed in the *Chicago Tribune*, "that neither admires nor comprehends the Great American Pastime." Perhaps it was this inscience and animosity—the poorly concealed disdain for baseball by Roone Arledge and kindred ABC avatars, genuflecting at the affected Shrine of Rozelle—that caused the Network of the Olympics to slight Brother Al: first, by sticking this self-professed "baseball freak" on "Monday's" "B" game in 1976–79; next, by forcing him, obviously the superior baseball announcer, to alternate primary game assignments with Keith Jackson in 1980–82. Whatever, Michaels and "Monday" viewers deserved better, long before they got it.

"It bugged me, there's no question," Michaels would say. "I felt I should have had the chance to be Number One for years." Yet in a strict sense, Al's late coming to network primacy seemed appropriate, if not Calvinistic, for it looked to be merely the latest in a series of eerie likenesses with his NBC counterpart.

Like Scully, Michaels was born in New York City, pierced baseball broadcasting in his early twenties (in 1968, with the Hawaii Islanders of the Pacific Coast League; he was voted Hawaii Sportscaster of the Year two of the next three seasons), and promptly was named the Voice of a defending National League champion (Scully, in late 1953, at twenty-six; Michaels, on November 24, 1970, at the same age, of the Cincinnati Reds). Two years later, both called a World Series on NBC Television—Vin, in 1955, with Allen; Al, in 1972, with Curt Gowdy. At twenty-nine, each shifted to California—Scully, in October 1957, to the Coliseum; Michaels, fleeing Cincinnati in late 1973, to the cold and isolation of Candlestick Park.

Brother Al, it was true, graduated from Arizona State University, not Fordham, and matured in markets far from Scully's Big Apple and L.A. But the analogies were extraordinary; his tones even *echoed* the Voice of the Dodgers'. "Nature gave him a voice that sounds exactly like Vin Scully's. It is nothing Al Michaels cultivates or puts on. When he is sitting in your living room talking about the rising price of oil in Saudi Arabia, he still is the exact duplicate of the nation's best-known baseball broadcaster," wrote Wells Twombly, the late columnist of the *San Francisco Chronicle*. "I honestly don't know about the similarity," Michaels vowed. "I grew up in Brooklyn and Los Angeles, when Vinnie was just rising to greatness. So I copied his technique. When I discovered I sounded like him, I stopped listening to him. It wasn't because I don't admire him. That would be ridiculous. I just didn't want to sound *that* much alike." At one time, Michaels said, he feared the similitude would harm his career. I never knew why; to me, it showed good taste. What if he had imitated Herb Score?

From 1971 to 1973, Score's peril was that he would be compared *to* Michaels, not copied *by* him. While Herb mimed the banal, bungling Indians, there was Al, barely two hundred miles to the southwest, riding the Big Red Machine. Over the WLW Network, Reds' fans followed their heroes in a devoted and bracing way. With players like Bench, Rose, Perez, and Morgan, they had cause to follow; the team won its division in 1972–73, drew 5,130,182 customers in Michaels' three years, and spiraled into baseball's transcendent regional franchise. But Michaels was more than a passive conveyer of future Hall of Famers' folklore; he was also a stimulant. "He was more exciting, more keyed-up, than Waite Hoyt or Jim McIntyre [his two predecessors] and Cincinnati liked that — Al was a refreshing change of pace. At the same time, he was more of a homer than he'd be later on, and the town liked *that*," a former colleague said. "He was already very good. Naturally, he *knew* that he was. Added to the fact that Al had a tendency to be exceedingly blunt — in person, on the air — and you had the potential for a collision."

Cincinnati had adopted Michaels immediately; Dick Wagner, the Reds' starchy, Prussian then-vice-president, had not. Unfortunately for Rhinelanders, it was Wagner who negotiated his Voice's contract — "He asked for a salary of $119,150, a figure quite high for a baseball announcer with three years of major-league experience. At thirty, perhaps [Michaels] needs some maturing," Wagner wrote in a bitter 1975 exchange of letters in *The Sporting News*. Retorted Al: "I have known Dick Wagner for five years and have come to the conclusion that his definition of maturity is total subservience" — and in November 1973, four weeks after the Reds, losing the playoff to New York, nearly made their second World Series in a row, Michaels moved to San Francisco and the Scavenger Giants; or, as columnist Art Spander termed them, "baseball's version of The Impossible Scheme."

Less quodlibetic than Scully (the only *transit* Michaels had confronted was the NYC Authority), Brother Al was more acerbic. In catholic San Francisco, already disposed to announcers — unlike Monte Moore, shilling across the Bay — who told it like it was, Michaels entered a villa greased for his sarcasm. In the second-division Giants, he inherited much to be sarcastic about.

Milking his material, Michaels defied indifference. "This team doesn't care if it wins or loses," he scolded the Giants in June of 1974. "It has a lethargic, apathetic attitude. The players show a complete, a total lack of respect for the manager." Early the next season, he disclosed one night's attendance. "That's 1967," he told KSFO listeners. "There are 1967 people here tonight. Don't worry, folks . . . that's a great year . . . 1967 . . . a great year for Ingelnook Wine. Not so good for the Giants, however." Another evening, with a Giants' runner perched on third base, Al spotted Pirates' catcher Manny Sanguillen calling for a pitchout. "Oh, look at that," Michaels crowed. "I guess Manny doesn't read the scouting reports. The San Francisco Giants haven't called a squeeze play in more than twenty years. I thought everybody knew that."

Journalists glowed — that Michaels, his temerity!

The Giants lost.

Listeners slapped their thighs. "The Giants have something to be proud of," read a September 7, 1974, letter to *TSN*. "They have in Al Michaels and [sidekick] Art Eckman a fantastic broadcasting team that really puts excitement into a game."

The Giants lost.

"Considering the way the Giants have been playing," the publication replied, "Michaels and Eckman must be truly fantastic to put excitement into the game."

Ratings rose.

The Giants lost.

Deliberately provocative, Michaels turned hugely popular. "It has been said — not altogether humorously — that the reason the Giants are last in home attendance in the major leagues," Twombly wrote in 1975, "is because everybody stays home and listens to Michaels." In April 1976, he took a job with ABC as its "Monday Night Baseball" backup Voice. That season, the Giants finished last. The following February, Michaels left the Stonehams to join the network full-time. The Giants' harlequinade survived his exit.

At ABC, Michaels was smooth, less acidic, and mega-affluent. Variously paired with Norm Cash, Bob Gibson, Bill White, Don Drysdale, Stone, Uke, Tim McCarver, and Cosell, the latter materializing, when he chose, like the Loch Ness leviathan, Al broadcast "Monday" backup games for seven years and buoyed that network's All-Star Game, playoff, and World Series coverage. He aired college football and "Wide World of Sports," and as the play-by-play hockey Voice of the 1980 Winter Olympics, sealing the American team's stunning conquest with the inscription, "Do you believe in miracles? *Yes!*" became recognized, for the first time, as a major ABC personality. Wasn't it odd, then, that at this very moment, the early 1980s, he seemed somehow stifled by resentment? Actually, it wasn't odd at all. Characteristically, Michaels wanted *baseball*, the sport of his childhood, and, more specifically, *all* of the primary "Monday" game, and as he tried and failed to dislodge Jackson from his position as ABC's baseball mouthpiece, it "was no secret he was miffed that network execs took their sweet time making him the No. 1 announcer on 'Monday Night Baseball,' " *TV Guide* related in November 1984. "That was frustrating for me," Al told the magazine, "but I don't hold grudges."

On June 6, 1983, calling his first game, with Cosell and the recently-retired Baltimore manager, Earl Weaver, as ABC's undiluted deputy, Michaels had no need to. That season, the trilium aired twelve Monday and three Sunday telecasts. The year afterward, as Weaver proved sharp, accurate, but surprisingly bland, Jim Palmer, the Valentino who was released as an Orioles' pitcher on May 16 and whom "ABC finds an irresistible prospect," Craig said, was hired by Arledge as an "A" team analyst. "In addition to possessing a superior voice and sound knowledge of the game, he projects as almost a matinee idol thanks to his superior looks and to his popularity attained from underwear commercials. Palmer has star appeal."

It was ABC's hope that the Birds' ex-manager and star, legendary for past rows on the field, would transfer that excitement to the broadcast booth — "Here it is, only the third inning," Al exclaimed on a June 1984 telecast, "and we've already had our first Weaver-Palmer shot" — but too often, their exchanges, falling flat, seemed torpid, forced. In December, the Earl of Baltimore was bounced, unconditionally; and deep into 1985, ABC's lineup flaunted Michaels, Humble Howard, and the "matinee idol," with Drysdale and McCarver in "B" game reserve. If less adroit than NBC's crooners at expressing a feel for drama—only McCarver and Brother Al, who were excellent, could have cracked, I believe, the quartette of Scully, Garagiola, Costas, and Kubek—they at least were competent; save Cosell, their baseball roots were palpable. If they stirred little fantasy and eschewed sentimentality, so be it; this was, after all, a hard, unmawkish age. If no Allen or Ted Husing dotted the Arledge speakers' list, so what?; at least Cash and Gibson were missing too.

Then, in early October 1985, on the eve of the eighty-second World Series, Cosell released his bitter, paranoic, and backbiting book, *I Never Played the Game*, and suddenly, deliciously, The Mouth *Himself* was missing.

"The best managerial move of the '85 Series was made by Roone Arledge," William Taaffe wrote after the Cardinals-Royals' Oktoberfest. "It was Arledge, ABC's president of news and sports, who effectively blocked Howard Cosell out of the Series broadcast booth, which Howard had traditionally used as a pulpit from which to discuss his views on . . . sundry subjects having nothing to do with baseball. Good riddance. It was a pleasure to listen to the games for a change.

"The reason for Cosell's fall [and, by and by, his 1986 departure from ABC] was not his commentary, which on baseball grew more and more deplorable, but his . . . recent book . . . and his cold-war relationship with Al Michaels, the play-by-play announcer for the Series. In the book, Cosell snipes at almost everyone who has worked with him on and off the air at ABC, including Arledge. ABC was afraid of an on-the-air scene between Cosell and Michaels. Cosell baited Michaels during their telecast of Game 3 of the AL playoffs last year, and the two had a bad argument after the game. 'Howard has become a cruel, evil, vicious man,' says Michaels. 'He always had some of these traits, but they've now manifested themselves in spades. As far as his booth colleagues are concerned, Howard loves you if you kiss his rear end. But the minute you take your lips off his buttocks, you go on his demolition list.' "

Replacing Cosell on the 1985 Classic, McCarver wiled critics with his unpatterned humor. Palmer brandished thought and intuition; Brother Al, dash and an ability to summate ("Dick Howser," Michaels said of the Kansas City manager, "is to Billy Martin what the Salvation Army is to the SWAT team"). Even ABC, oft-maligned, "won critical raves for its coverage," read the *New York Daily News*. "For a change, the network's technical prowess was also singled out for praise." Added *Sports Illustrated*: "[Among] ABC's entry of Michaels, Palmer, and McCarver . . . individually, each announcer is superb." There followed, naturally, the predictable tut-tutting from the Peacock Network: "Why *shouldn't* ABC finally get its act together?" barbed an NBC producer. "After all, they've had baseball for a decade now—what the hell took them so long? It's about time they did it right." No matter. Turning the era's big-league dial, what I knew and was thankful for—what made the eighties so set apart, so vastly superior to a decade or two before—was that unlike baseball *then* (recalling a Wills, a Sandy Koufax struggling merely to survive) or, in fact, another major sport *today* (how do viewers even tolerate a Terry Bradshaw or O.J. Simpson?),

I could watch any network baseball game (even when, in 1986, Jackson briefly resurfaced as a backup play-by-play man) and hear its Voices treat the spoken word with fondness, familiarity, and a certain fluency.

This was where The Game had been born anew, in an age when after the apprehension of the seventies, doubters asked whether baseball's revival was truth or merely catchword — not *locally* as much as *nationally*, on a wider kinescope, over NBC, ABC, and cable's Harry and Skip Caray Show.

Locally, though one glimpsed a Harry Kalas in Philadelphia, a Chuck Thompson and Jon Miller at Memorial Stadium, Boston's Ned Martin and Ken Coleman, Hank Greenwald and Jerry Coleman, an Ernie Harwell and the Uke, *overall*, one looked vainly for the parade of boisterous regionalisms, the umbrella of concentrated brilliance, which characterized baseball's broadcasting theatre of the early 1960s.

"It's such a mystery, it's so objective — this unpredictable business of talking into a microphone and describing players throw, hit, and run around the bases. And everybody's style is so different, even now — a Rizzuto, a Gene Elston in Houston, me, Bob Murphy," chimed the Cardinals' Jack Buck, whose style was different, unpredictable, and whose appeal was not a mystery. "The good ones are the broadcasters who never change and who value knowledge of the game above everything else — above show biz, flair, the one-liners. I remember growing up in New England and listening to Fred Hoey, then moving to Cleveland and lying in bed at night. I'd hear Jack Graney there, Ty Tyson and Harry Heilmann out of Detroit, By Saam from Philadelphia, Rosey Rowswell and Bob Prince. They knew the game — they were baseball people, and they had the great fortune to come along at a time when those stations *hired* for baseball. You'd get a Graney — he'd do baseball, period. He got to know the game before he did anything else in broadcasting. Now, there's the stereotype that's evolved — that the guy has got to be able to do talk shows, football, do a beauty pageant. They're more homogenized, their personality gets watered down. Are they blander? Sure. They're not baseball broadcasters who bring a sense of themselves and their approach to other events. They're generalists who bring a duller approach to baseball. That's why, as a rule, you don't see the color with local broadcasters, the affinity with the game, you used to."

But on a 1980s *network* screen — with a Scully and Michaels, a Holy Cow! — one could indulge oneself by etching them, correctly, as the lineal descendants of the Redhead, The Voice, and the Great One. They *were* baseball announcers. They *did* bring something of themselves to their clientele and their work.

Think of baseball broadcasting as a river, I said once to a colleague, twisting down through the years. Underneath flowed the local Voices; while some carved their own identities, spurting like a hidden rivulet in the pastime's ground, most came at you less extravagantly than two decades earlier; as a whole, the current was less rambunctious. Next, think of baseball's network galoots as the river's surface. Once, even from a distance, its territorial waters seemed murky; now, up close or as far as the eye could see, they appeared clear and lovely — like baseball itself, the river's face set one's senses churning.

Finally, the sunlight dancing off the waves—that was Scully, making the river a sudden, magic place. In a nation transfixed on conventional and, increasingly, cable programming, for a public whose eighties sports signals, tastes, and valuations arose, more than ever, from the images traipsing across a TV screen, the ability of baseball's contemporary network announcers was a prodigal bequest.

There remained, then—in this time of baseball Thanksgiving—only for the networks and the sport itself to catch up with their Voices.

I am not referring to the SuperStations, WTBS and WGN, with their upward ratings and exposure, or NBC Television, airing, as it would in 1987, a pre-season special, baseball features on "Nightly News," and thirty-two regular-season games (two prime-time outings and thirty Saturday sets, including four afternoon double-headers; all told, six more games than in 1979). Instead, baseball's major 1980s video *bête noire* lay squarely at the door of the same entity, ABC, which I admit to having believed, a decade previously, in a fit of zany optimism, would uplift and publicize the bigs.

" 'Monday Night Baseball' can become a hit—we feel strongly that it will," Roone Arledge was quoted as telling *Playboy* magazine in 1976, his network's first year of baseball since the woebegone 1965 "Game." "This will entail that we depart greatly from what's been tried before [ergo, the Gunner and Uke], but we're confident we can bring it off."

Given "Monday Night Football," Arledge's college football pioneering in ambience and camera shots, and the industry's then-article of faith—"fast attaining the status of a folk myth," Ron Powers noted in *Supertube*—"that ABC was unmatchable in sports coverage," I was confident the network would. Hah! *They* would show that boring NBC, I smugly said (I was not alone; many baseball people shared this view), how to wrap baseball in a self-congratulatory glow. I could not have been more wrong, of course; the joke was to be on me. Contrary to my every word, it was *NBC* that moved from an uneven mid-1970s truce with baseball to a decade-later smothering. At the same time, after a burst of activity in its primordial "Monday" years—personality profiles on the evening news, prime-time plugs for crucial telecasts, a litany of Oktoberfest pronouncements—ABC came, first, to lose interest in The American Game and then, ultimately, to demean it. In retrospect, Arledge misread baseball's prime-time outlook. Looking back, baseball misread ABC's commitment.

While NFL exposure soared on all three networks, climbing to more than ninety national telecasts by 1986.

While ABC allotted 180 hours in seventeen days to its coverage of the 1984 Summer Olympics.

While Arledge bought rights to the USFL because, as Roone said in early 1983, infuriating Bowie Kuhn, "There really is no other attractive sports programming available *at that time of year.*"

While rallying from The Strike, the bigs piqued an interest and a curiosity. Never—not even in the 1940s—had the game enjoyed such parity: From 1982 to 1984, as Pete Rose got his four thousandth hit and Gaylord Perry and Steve Carlton won their three hundredth games and Kuhn, exhausting his ninth life, resigned as commissioner, the major leagues experienced three different world champions, six different pennant winners, and an optimum twelve division titlists. Ricky Henderson stole 130 bases in a single year. Steve Garvey passed Billy Williams' National League consecutive-games-played streak. Dave Righetti threw the first Yankees' no-hitter since Don Larsen joined a select aristocracy. Seen (but not believed): the Tigers' 1984 beginnings, a 35–5 astonishment. Welcomed (with expectation and a mandate): the sport's new commissioner, *TIME* magazine's 1984 "Man of the Year." Gladdened: the Royals, Blue Jays, Cardinals, and Dodgers, copping 1985 division pennants, and Missouri, hosting the "Show-Me" World Series; Tom Seaver and Phil Niekro, pitching their same-year three hundredth victories, and Rod Carew, getting his three thousandth hit; Charlie Hustle, at forty-four, collecting hit No. 4,192, and the Mets' Dwight Gooden, twenty, winning twenty-four games. Delighted: the 1986 Red Sox, Angels, Mets, and Astros, winning their divisions by runaway margins; the pastime itself, by a national opinion survey conducted by Lieberman Research Inc., for *Sports Illustrated* and released that June—a 3 percentage point lead over the NFL as the sport "Americans said they had watched on television in the past twelve months"; and, ultimately, the Republic, by a glorious '86 autumn of taut playoffs (the Mets in six sets; the Yawkeys in seven) and a seven-game World Series (true to form and the sins of their forebears, another almost unbelievable Sox' loss) and baseball over an extended stretch as it has rarely been played before—a lyric mix of poetry, low comedy, and a Ferris wheel of drama—"baseball at its summit," wrote *Newsweek*'s Pete Axthelm. "Even [now], millions . . . are still savoring their rendezvous with baseball at its pinnacle. It leaves you breathless." Rewarded: Fans of the Minnesota Twins, overcoming 150 to 1 preseason odds to win the 1987 World Series; Paul Molitor, hitting safely in thirty-nine straight games; and Tony Gwynn, whose .370 average was the National League's highest since Stan Musial. Stunned: 1988 N. L. batters, by the Dodgers' Orel Hershiser, pitching a record fifty-nine consecutive scoreless innings; A. L. pitchers, by the A's' Jose Canseco, the first big-league player to hit forty home runs and steal forty bases in a season; and The Game itself, by Hershiser's teammate, Kirk Gibson, whose '88 World Series ninth-inning Game One home run evoked memories of *The Natural*.

While Carter was ousted, overwhelmingly. The Ayatollah Khomeini released fifty-two U.S. hostages moments after Ronald Reagan was inaugurated. "We have every right to dream heroic dreams," declaimed the new president; by the mid-1980s, few Americans believed that the Oval Office was too big for one man. Congress passed the largest tax cut in the nation's history, the fires of inflation cooled, and the worst post–World War II recession (followed by the loudest recovery) gripped the economy. Britain won the Falklands War. An amphibious force invaded Grenada. Washington said *yes* to tax reform. As many as twenty thousand people perished in a Mexican earthquake. The space shuttle *Challenger* exploded; its crew of seven

died. Signed: By the Gipper and Mikhail Gorbachev, the first agreement by
the two major powers to reduce the size of their nuclear arsenals. Disproved:
The claim of Jim Bakker and Gary Hart, "Never the twain shall meet." Said
rock historian Dave Marsh of the Boss: "In his generation, there's no one
who can touch Bruce Springsteen as a live performer." Said Bishop Desmond
Tutu, recipient of the Nobel Peace Prize: "As long as some of God's children
are not free, none of God's children will be free." Margaret Thatcher won a
third term as prime minister. The *Exxon Valdez* raped Alaska. Could Mondale
or Dukakis seize the presidency? Could democracy be denied in Eastern
Europe? Will the Three Stooges ever be passé?

While all of *this* was transpiring, baseball fans gaped at the American
Broadcasting Company's diminution of The Game.

Its first year of coverage, ABC telecast sixteen games on Monday night;
in 1978, the figure jumped to eighteen. Two years later, "rendering 'Monday
Night Baseball,' " wrote Gary Deeb, "nearly invisible," Arledge slashed the
number of Monday sets to *five,* all televised in June (to fulfill its contract,
the network aired eight August and September games on Sunday afternoon).
In 1981, the coverage leaped (or would have, had The Strike not intervened)
back to eighteen games. The next season, it was down to sixteen; in 1983,
to fifteen; and in 1984 and 1985, the first third of ABC's new six-year baseball
contract, to eight prime-time and three Sunday matches. It was unbelievable,
the more you thought about it: eleven games over each twenty-six-week
season (barely half of ABC's 1985 pro football total in a sixteen-week schedule; less than 23 percent of CBS's 1964 baseball exposure) tendered by what
the bigs presumed to call, in a spirit of generosity, one of their two network
"partners." More improbably, baseball *accepted* such insulting treatment.
"In effect, it's gotten to the point where ABC pays baseball *not* to make it
televise regular-season games," Jack Craig told me. "The network only wants
the sport for October, anyway."

From the start, ABC's baseball stumbling block was ratings; dashing
Arledge's *Playboy* fantasies, they simply weren't there. In 1976–81, "Monday
Night Baseball" commanded a national rating between 12.0 and 12.7; the
numbers were flat and mediocre. "That has always been our regular-season
baseball rub. The prime-time viewers are loyal, constant. There just aren't
enough of them," said an ABC publicist. "As a result, the network could
either push its ad rates up each year and put off sponsors, who didn't want
to pay more and still reach the same number of people, or they could keep
the rates down, sell the 'Monday' spots, and make less money. Either way,
night baseball became a problem." The "problem" explained why ABC
banned prime-time baseball in May, the so-called "Sweeps" month which,
by gauging audiences, dictates the commercial rates to be charged that fall;
why the network, increasingly, sliced the number of prime-time games; and
why, in a year when conflicts with political conventions and the Summer
Olympics furnished an excuse to limit coverage, as in 1984, the sighs were
almost audible.

ABC's baseball languor, then, was not entirely causeless. But neither was the network blameless. After all, NBC confronted slowpoke ratings by hiring Scully, increasing baseball's air-time, and fostering cohesion; irrespective of month, year, and the division standings, you *knew* there was a TV game each Saturday, a reason to "pull up a chair." In the 1980s, with baseball's April-through-September audience walking a nearly straight line, the Peacocks could have weakened their commitment to the "Game"; instead, they strengthened it.

ABC chose a different course; more often than not, it gave up, not built up.

Unlike NBC, the Arledges promoted less, not more, as their baseball tie-in lengthened. Even worse was the fact that as opposed to the "Game" or "Monday Night Football," ABC's regular-season baseball schedule dissuaded viewers from adopting it as habit; untouched by continuity or, for that matter, common sense, it was a grab bag, a random toss, to be witnessed almost by accident. Starting in 1979, Arledge ceded baseball's first two months to other sports programming (picture Pete Rozelle enduring a similar affront); ended its "Monday Night Baseball" telecasts in mid-August (you can't; September tumbled, naturally, to "MNF"); and after Tom Villante complained, bitterly, about Roone yielding "all of our most decisive month — September — to pro football, which happens to be their *least* important month," threw the big leagues a bone: their series of late-year (and as it happened, meagerly watched) Sunday broadcasts (again, lack of continuity; after a full network season without Sabbath baseball, few fans, now engrossed in the NFL, were even *aware* of the games) meant to placate the baseball squirearchy and bolster the pretense, however flimsy, that Arledge, Inc., actually cared whether viewers in Montpelier, Wheeling, and Miami ever saw — had the *opportunity* to see — baseball's "most decisive month" unravel. By 1984–85, the retreat was wholesale; there were eight mid-summer games each year, then a two-month lull, then three September sets to complete what passed for coverage.

After the 1984 All-Star Game, *TSN* observed: "It was a TV treat because it presented a rare chance for those without cable to see ballplayers known ordinarily only via box scores. There will be about forty regular-season games televised by NBC and ABC combined this season, and ten or so teams will be seen in a disproportionate number of these games. If a fan misses a rare telecast involving one of the lesser teams, he may not see the team at all in 1984." Can you name the last NFL team you did *not* see on television? On the other hand, can you recall the last time the Seattle Mariners *did* invade a network series? "It's not just that ABC's schedule is all over the place — that's always been true. The last couple of years, the even bigger problem is that ABC has cut way down on their coverage — there aren't any games *to* schedule," a former Gannett colleague, replying to a letter, wrote. "Baseball talks about its 'two-network policy.' Let's be honest: Today, what it really has, at best, is a one-and-a-half network policy." In 1984–85–87, baseball offered a mere forty-three network outings, the same number, *exactly,* as ten years earlier: an average of barely one-and-one-half games per week, far behind the NFL's four (always), five (often), and six (four times each year); a televised identity so marginal that in nearly two of every three weeks, if one missed the Saturday "Game of the Week," one missed network baseball. Looking back, it was, and is, pathetic.

The solution to the bigs' sparse network air-time was, of course, so obvious as to fairly bellow, "Play Ball." Baseball would simply approach ABC and say, "If you intend to keep the Series, playoffs, and All-Star Game, you'll have to telecast one game a week during the regular season—like the NBC 'Game'; like the NFL's three networks. We want to be fair. You won't have to televise every Monday—we know the ratings don't warrant it. In fact, if you like, you can skip Mondays entirely and televise each Sunday [starting, say, at 3 P.M., Eastern Time, avoiding most overlaps with local-team coverage and profitable early-evening local news]. You want the World Series? [Who wouldn't? e.g. On October 27, 1986, for the first time, Fall Classic coverage (Game Seven, NBC) collided with ABC's "Monday Night Football"; in audience share (55- to 14 percent) and Nielsen ratings (an astonishing 38.9 to 8.8), baseball obliterated the Rozelles; in Los Angeles, New York, and Boston, the Series swaggered, 4-, 7-, and 19-to-1]. We want more exposure and April-through-September continuity: at least twenty-six games in as many weeks. Otherwise, we'll go to NBC and CBS and see if they'll broadcast the games we want." And, in fact, the time arose for just such a proposal: in late 1982 and early 1983, in the negotiations with the three networks over the sport's new TV pact. But I doubt that the notion seriously crossed the minds of baseball's negotiating principals—Bowie Kuhn, leaving shortly as commissioner, and Eddie Einhorn and Bill Giles, owners of the White Sox and Phillies—for other priorities lay heavy on their consciousness.

Graphically, almost regally, unconcerned about what the regular-season fan, vulnerable and unimportant, saw at home, the triune was obsessed—in large part, given rising players' salaries and other expenses, understandably—with fleecing the networks of more money.

It was Einhorn's plan, in particular, to hold the All-Star Game, league playoffs, and Autumn Occasion as ransom, play one network against another, feed on NBC and ABC's fear of losing the Series, and force whomever won the rights to fork over an historic increase in fees. Fast Eddie succeeded, brilliantly. From baseball's two past-and-future networks, the industry learned in April 1983, Einhorn and his fellow owners would be extracting nearly $188 million annually, or $7.2 million per team, more than a *quadruple* rise over baseball's present contract. Given baseball's 1980–82 network ratings dip—while NFL audiences fell by 10 percent, the bigs' slumped by 22—it was a stunning, even numbing, feat.

It especially impressed Carl Lindemann.

Lindemann, NBC Sports' head for more than a decade, had sauntered over to CBS in 1978; among his goals, to pluck off part of baseball's coverage. "That's a major reason I came," he was saying. "CBS was aware that I knew the baseball people from my days at NBC, knew how they worked, and could be of some help in bringing the network into baseball." He was also a friend of Einhorn's. "I knew he'd be a tough negotiator, but I hoped we'd be able to work something out. And I knew what baseball wanted — all three networks to carry the games. Not for more exposure for the fans. All they wanted was more money for the owners."

"Explain how the bidding went," I said.

"Right at the beginning, NBC threw a bomb. They came in and made an unbelievably high bid [$500 million over five years for one-half the package] with a *guarantee* that they'd pick up the other half, ABC's [for another $400 million]. It was way, *way* above anything baseball had ever gotten before, and it shocked the hell out of us. NBC had made a conscious decision to go big on baseball, and once they'd thrown their wad, one of two things would happen. One, CBS or ABC would have to spend a ton matching their offer — that way, Watson [Arthur, of NBC Sports] would bleed us dry. The other possibility was that if we couldn't match the bucks, NBC figured they'd get back exclusivity and wrap the Series and playoffs up for every year, which would have been a ratings-killer."

With NBC in tow, Einhorn came to Arledge, who bit hard on two options, each distasteful. ABC could equal the Peacocks' offer and preserve its alternate-year coverage of the playoffs, World Series, and All-Star Game — spending what one official styled "an exorbitant amount because NBC had blackmailed us into doing it, throwing money out the window just to save our postseason coverage, swallowing baseball's deal." At the other end, if Arledge wished, it could throw baseball *off* the air — allowing NBC to spend $900 million for October exclusivity through 1988.

Arledge threw.

Next, Fast Eddie — "He did all the negotiating," said Lindemann. "He had the TV background — Bill and Bowie were just there to back him up" — went to CBS, whose totems considered Sunday programming ("We talked it over and decided we couldn't make enough money from sponsors on Sunday games to justify the kind of money baseball wanted") and a Thursday night inter-league series ("Baseball was ready to sponsor a limited number of games between, say, the Mets and Yankees, the Cubs and White Sox. It would have been great — Neal [Pilson, the head of CBS Sports], Einhorn, Kuhn, and I agreed on it. But after we'd come to an understanding — we would have been baseball's other network with NBC — our own entertainment programming people came back to us and said, 'No go. Baseball can't be shown on Thursday night.' CBS already had a strong prime-time lineup, and they weren't going to disrupt it") before deciding, finally, that baseball would not gouge them.

"I was out of the country at the time," Lindemann said, "but as I heard it, Eddie called Neal one night and said, 'OK, here's the dough we want. X number of dollars. Match it and you're in. Yes or no.' And Neal said no — he thought NBC was bluffing, that they'd never really pay what reports were saying they would, and that in the end, baseball'd get back to him. Besides, we'd looked at it carefully — for what baseball was asking, our ad bucks just weren't there."

Twice-rebuffed, hoping to avoid exclusivity, Einhorn shifted back to ABC;

this time, Arledge swallowed. He proposed a compromise: a six-year pact, not five (that way, ABC could recoup more money from rising ad rates), with each network to air three World Series, three All-Star Games, and six league playoffs; ABC would pay $575 million through 1989, NBC $550 million. Watson agreed. Einhorn rejoiced. Kuhn breathed deeply; the bounty, he hoped, vainly, would save his job. ("It's safe to assume," one owner said of several anti-Kuhn colleagues, "that a billion dollars buys a lot of goodwill.")

The new contract, admittedly, bulged like a Christmas tree with provisions to enlarge the audience. ABC could require West Coast teams—read, the Dodgers—to change the starting times of as many as four games a year; for each club, it could lift three home blackouts a season (showing the White Sox in Chicago, the Tigers in Detroit), and beam up to seven road sets into each home market (the Yankees, New York). Like NBC, it also benefited from the pact's ban on playoff and World Series telecasts by local-team stations—a WPIX in New York, the Dodgers' KTTV. The Peacock Network reaped even more: It could switch, for example, four Saturday Red Sox' games from night to day; lift the home blackout four times and televise the same number of away games back to Boston; and ban Saturday local coverage, as we have seen, making *its* telecasts the only game in town. In 1985, NBC programming director Rich Hussey related: "The new contract has already helped to boost our ratings. We're maximizing the appearances of the major-market teams. [This year] we'll have the Yanks, Mets, Cubs, White Sox, Tigers, Dodgers, Angels, and Braves each on a Saturday maximum eight times. [In 1986, the Bombers graced an NBC-high nine games; six teams—the Indians, Giants, Pirates, Mariners, A's, and Rangers—were not scheduled to appear at all.] Whenever possible, we're moving our starting times of games to get fully into the exclusive 1–4 P.M., EST period for our Saturday games. And without local-team TV games to compete against, instead of sending our backup games to 10 percent of the country like we used to, we're sending it to 30–40 percent. In all, the new deal with baseball has been a winner for us."

Even so, *après l'astonishment,* the initial sorting out, submitting, in time, to general consensus, was that Einhorn's deal had thrown the networks (i.e., ABC) a curve. In 1986, the Arledges' baseball coverage lost a reported $30 million. "Sure, NBC did fine under the new contract—they had all those regular-season afternoon games from which to recover advertising dollars. ABC's situation was different," Craig said. "See, under their six-year baseball deal, ABC bought the rights to televise prime-time games. But, eventually, because of lackluster ad sales, they wound up not airing many of these night games, which made it impossible for the network to get enough advertising dollars back to reduce their red ink. Under their 1984–89 contract, ABC could never win with baseball [nor could Arledge, dumped in January 1986 as ABC Sports president by the network's new owner, Capital Cities Communications; observed Roone's successor, Dennis Swanson, three months later: "I can hardly wait for it (the contract) to end"]." Instead, it was the pastime that *really* won — the contract consisted of escalating rights fees; each team would get $9.2 million in 1989, a 484 percent vault over 1983; it was a Golconda, a Klondike rush — or had it? Lost in baseball's exultation was one sustaining fact: Across the 1980s, the new pact did virtually *nothing* to increase The Game's network exposure and, inevitably, its popularity.

"What would have happened if baseball had gone the way Pete Rozelle has — insisted on X number of TV games as well as dollars?" I asked Carl Lindemann. "What if the bigs had approached NBC and said, 'We want you to keep doing the "Game." We want this much dough,' then moved to CBS and said, 'You can have the Series, playoffs, and All-Star Game every other year if you'll televise a weekly Sunday afternoon series,' or maybe even construct a deal whereby you'd have all three networks rotating the big events?"

"It would have been real tough to involve all three, a lot harder than the NFL, and it goes back to the two sports' regular-season games. In pro football, their ratings are excellent — each network *wants* to televise games every week. That's not as true in baseball," said Lindemann, whom *Washington Post* reporter John Carmody called "a delightful man who managed to convey the sheer fun he had every day, without front, rubbing shoulders with sports legends while doing a variety of just plain behind-the-scenes chores that affected, eventually, every golf, baseball, football, and basketball fan who ever watched a game on network television and came to share his enthusiasm for what he or she saw on the box," and who died on June 3, 1985, at sixty-two, of an inoperable brain tumor.

"Still," I said, "baseball *had* entertained the hope, originally, of landing ABC, NBC, and CBS."

"There was a chance," he conceded, "but the only way that would have happened was if . . . *if* . . . baseball had been willing to take less money overall. The reason is that with all three networks doing baseball, you wouldn't have the threat which otherwise drives the price up: two networks trying to keep the third out. Anyway, you don't really need all three, not if baseball wakes up."

"How so?" I said.

"See, in the past baseball has usually left it to the networks to decide upon the amount of coverage. Baseball's been passive, and let circumstances, not their own game plan, call the shots. In the future, baseball must be much more aggressive. Too often, they've been content to say, 'To hell with how much and what kind of coverage. We just want the bucks.' Well, as I see it, that's just not good enough."

As a matter of fact, baseball needed those bucks. But it also needed a degree of television exposure not enjoyed since 1964: to alter a 1981 Gallup Poll which listed five football players, to baseball's one, among teenage boys' ten most admired athletes, and reverse the November 1984 Lou Harris survey, which found "baseball [to be] followed by 55 percent of [all] fans, in second place [behind pro football's 59 percent], down sharply from 62 percent the year before"; to stem the ludicrous imbalance whereby ABC televised two fewer *baseball games* in 1984 than NBC did that fall on one *football team,* the Raiders, and transpose the outcome of a 1985 CBS/*New York Times* poll, a Rozelles' 53–18 percent advantage over baseball as the "sport fans said they most enjoy watching"; to reclaim a generation of fans—*this* generation, weaned on prep ties and BMWs and video hardware—and instill, to the fullest extent possible, the same rooting interest I had in baseball as a child, or the affection that my father felt, or the loyalty and love of a nation growing up in the forties and fifties that must seem now, to a son of Woodstock, positively quaint.

Instead, in the next fortnight—negotiating the 1990–93 network television pact—the pastime's hierarchy, in a mad exercise of stupidity and greed, effected the single greatest calamity in baseball's seven-decade broadcast history. The blunder orphaned millions of Americans, shattered The Game's most fabled TV series, and troubled those who run baseball less than a windblown pop fly.

12
Day by Day

"The public is wiser than the wisest critic."
— GEORGE BANCROFT

THE BIG RED MACHINE

There's a looper, may drop. It's in there for a hit! Here comes the throw to third. Rose hits the dirt. He's safe! And there goes Morgan on to second. And the Reds have the lead, 4 to 3!

— CURT GOWDY, October 22, 1975.

Fenway Park, Boston, MA. After Game Six of the World Series reached its resounding coda, "I went home," said Reds' manager Sparky Anderson, "and I was stunned." Yet, like 76 million other viewers, he returned for the finale of this elegant struggle; Boston vaulted to a 3–0 lead, then squandered its advantage, and in the top half of the ninth inning, Joe Morgan lobbed a hit to center field.

Here's a high fly ball. It should be all over. Geronimo is under it. And Cincinnati wins the world championship, beating the Boston Red Sox, 4 to 3!

— C.G.

Who really won? Baseball did. Months later, *The New Yorker* reflected: "The Series, of course, was replayed everywhere in memory and conversation through the ensuing winter, and even now its colors still light up the sky."

Swung on. High fly ball to left-center should do it! There's Foster! And the 1976 world championship belongs to the Cincinnati Reds!

— MARTY BRENNAMAN, October 21, 1976.

Yankee Stadium, New York, NY. This Fall Classic was languid, but this ball club absorbed. Not since 1922 had a National League team won two consecutive World Series; the Reds won 102 games in the regular season, swept Philadelphia

521

in the playoff, and bludgeoned the Yankees in the World Series with a clamorous array of skills. Cincinnati led both leagues in eleven separate categories; five regulars hit more than .300; four won Gold Gloves. Among all teams in post-World War II baseball, these '76 Redlegs, arguably, hold sway.

His Way

Here's a drive to right field and deep! Smith going back! It's gone! Home run, Reggie Jackson!

— Ross Porter, October 18, 1977.

Yankee Stadium, New York, NY. The Yankees' epicenter, who homered in the Series' two previous matches, came to bat in the fourth inning, Game Six. With Thurman Munson at first base, No. 44 pulled Burt Hooton's first pitch into the right-field stands.

Sosa set. The pitch. Drive to right field and deep! Way back! Going, going, gone! Another home run for Reggie Jackson! And the Yankees lead, 7 to 3!

— R.P.

In inning five, Mickey Rivers singled. On his third swing in two games, "Reggie! Reg-gie!" again delivered—lining a fastball, amid baying in the Bronx, into the "Ruthville" section of the lower deck.

Jackson with four runs batted in, sends a fly ball to center field and deep! That's going to be way back! And that's going to be gone! Reggie Jackson has hit his third home run of the game!

— R.P.

Batting against Dodgers' pitcher Charlie Hough, "If I played in New York, they'd name a candy bar after me" bombed a knuckleball into Yankee Stadium's most distant expanse. For the gifted and perplexing Jackson, four home runs on four straight swings in two games, and, on this night, Civitas Dei.

For New York, Like Old Times

Torrez, who's pitched a nine-hitter, stretches, deals. Bunt—popped up. Torrez has got it! And the Yankees are the world champions for the twenty-first time—and for the first time in fifteen years!

— Ross Porter, October 18, 1977.

Yankee Stadium, New York, NY. When the Yankees last won a World Series, John F. Kennedy was president, Milwaukee still loved its Braves, and the pregame Voice of the lowly Mets was Howard Cosell. Now, after streaking, hot-tubs, and est, baseball's once-perennial titlists again reigned as rounders champions of North America. Kudos: Mike Torrez, who threw two complete-game victories; Thurman Munson, hitting .320 and throwing expertly; and Reginald Martinez Jackson, he of the .450 average and Series-record five home runs.

Popped up behind the plate! Coming back, Munson! Throws the mask away! He's there. It's all over! It's all over — the Yankees charge out on the field! They mob Goose Gossage. The Yankees have won their second straight world championship!

—Bill White, October 17, 1978.

Dodger Stadium, Los Angeles, CA. Once more, with feeling. Having warped the Boston Red Sox (after July 19, trailing by fourteen games in the A.L. East, they finished 62–28 and won a one-game playoff) and torn Kansas City (in the Championship Series, for the third straight year), the Yankees secured the bolt. Against the Dodgers, the Steinbrenners prevailed, four games to two — the first Oktoberfest team to lose the first two decisions and still oust its rival in six.

Bucky Dents the Red Sox

Deep to left! Yastrzemski will not get it! It's a home run! A three-run homer by Bucky Dent! And the Yankees now lead by a score of 3 to 2!

—Bill White, October 2, 1978.

Fenway Park, Boston, MA. On a crisp, sunlit New England day, "The Red Sox-Yankee competition reached a peak of intensity rare even in that legendary rivalry," the *Boston Globe*'s Peter Gammons wrote of their playoff for the Eastern Division title. Entering the seventh inning, the Bosox led, 2–0. But on a two-out, 0–2 pitch, Bucky Dent hoisted a wind-blown fly ball into the Screen to score three Yankees' runs and prepare ye the way for a Bombers' triumph, 5–4. Said Gammons: "Few so ballyhooed sporting events ever match the anticipation; this one did."

"Pops Has Hit It Out!"

Willie Stargell. And, of course, he always makes the opposition uneasy, especially in this kind of situation. One-nothing, Baltimore, and a man aboard and Stargell at the plate. McGregor comes to him. And there's a high fly ball into deep right-center field! Back goes Singleton, away back, to the wall! It's gone! He's done it! Pops has hit it out!

—Vin Scully, October 17, 1979.

Memorial Stadium, Baltimore, MD. Eight years earlier, in a rousing assembly, the Pirates had edged Baltimore, four games to three. Does World Series history repeat itself? Ask Earl Weaver and his '79 Birds. Within a single victory of their third world championship, the Orioles were whacked by scores of 7–1, 4–0, and, finally, 4–1, only the fourth team to lose a Classic after leading, three games to one. The villain, predictably, was Pirates' captain Willie Stargell, who stilled the multitudes with a first-pitch, sixth-inning, final-game home run. Said teammate Dave Parker: "Why shouldn't Pops win it for us? The man is a legend. Right now, to me, he's a god."

After Ninety-seven Years, Jerusalem

The pitch to Schmidt. Long drive to left field. He buried it! He buried it! Way back! Outa here, home run! Mike Schmidt puts the Phillies up, 6 to 4! Oh, what a drive by Schmidt! Unbelievable! He hit that thing deep to the seats in left field! And the Phillies greet Schmidt at the plate! What a wild scene in Montreal!

— Andy Musser, October 4, 1980.

Olympic Stadium, Montreal, QU. Three times, Destiny's Orphans had won the National League East, only to crumble in the League Championship Series. Today, in the next-to-last game of the regular season, Mike Schmidt racked a tenth-inning wallop against the pursuing Expos — eliminating the Canadians to clinch the division; affording the Phillies a chance (again) to upbraid the ghosts of 1976–77–78.

The windup by Ruthven, the three-two pitch. Here's a punch-shot to center field. Maddox racing over. He catches the ball! Phillies win the pennant! The Phillies have won the pennant! The Phillies have won the ball game, 8 to 7! They go to the World Series for the first time in thirty years!

— A.M., 10/12/80.

The Astrodome, Houston, TX. In 1950, in its 154th- and final game, the Whiz Kids downed Brooklyn; their prize, the National League pennant. Three decades later, in a tense and rewarding playoff, with four of five games going extra innings (and, in the final contest, the lead vanishing or changing hands five times), the Phillies clipped the Astros; their sensation, *déjà vu.*

Sixty-five thousand-plus on their feet at Veterans Stadium. The Tugger needs one more — one more out. Willie Wilson standing in, bases loaded. One-two pitch. Swing and a miss! Yes, he struck him out! Yes, they did it! The Phillies are world champions! World champions of baseball! . . . It's pandemonium at Veterans Stadium! All of the fans are on their feet! This city has come together behind a baseball team! The Philadelphia Phillies!

Tug McGraw being mobbed by his teammates — who better than the Tugger to finish the 1980 World Series. Phillies are world champions. This city knows it! This city loves it!

— HARRY KALAS, 10/21/80.

Veterans Stadium, Philadelphia, PA. "We prayed our heads off," confessed a seventy-eight-year-old nun (and lifelong Phillies' fan). Aided, perhaps, by supplication, this squabbling, perturbing, oft-analyzed team climaxed a stirring six-game conquest of Kansas City: the first world championship for the Phillies' franchise, now ninety-seven years old.

A HOLIDAY MAGNIFICO

Will he do it? This crowd is standing! This crowd is wild! The Yankees are leading, 4 to 0, and Wade Boggs, one of the top hitters in the American League, standing between Dave Righetti and a pitcher's dream. Outside — ball one. Three sixty-one is what he was batting going into this game. Wade Boggs — Dave Righetti trying to get him out. Two out. And there's a strike, and it's one and one, and this crowd is roaring! There's Billy Martin, nervous. Everybody on the bench is nervous. Even on the Red Sox' bench, they're trying to break it up. Dave Righetti, under the toughest pressure. Will he get it? Wade Boggs swings and misses! Strike two! . . . One strike away for Dave Righetti. This crowd is going nuts! And there's Ralph Houk looking on. Everybody at Yankee Stadium is standing and roaring. The Red Sox, trailing, 4 to 0, a runner at second. A foul ball out of play beyond third. . . . Dave Righetti, who has permitted only three Sox to reach base, all on walks, has got just about as tough a man to get out as the Red Sox could put up at the plate. It's the ninth inning, one ball, two strikes, two out, Hoffman on second. Boggs takes just outside, ball two. . . . The deuces are wild! Two balls, two strikes, two out. Billy Martin, anxious. The crowd is standing, forty-thousand-plus people standing and roaring, and Righetti trying to get Boggs. . . . And he gets him! A no-hitter, a no-hitter, a no-hitter for Dave Righetti! How about that! He got the no-hitter! Dave Righetti pitches the first Yankee no-hitter since 1956! . . . And former President Nixon standing . . . This is the first no-hitter by a Yankee pitcher since Don Larsen in 1956 in the World Series! The perfect game! How about that!

— MEL ALLEN, July 4, 1983.

Yankee Stadium, New York, NY. On America's most star-spangled occasion, in the land's pre-eminent arena, before the age's surpassing figure, and with baseball's most notable broadcaster doing play-by-play, the game's most celebrated rivals observed a Yankee Doodle afternoon. Quoth Ethel Merman: "Who could ask for anything more?"

THE (PINE) TAR BABY

U.L. Washington at first represents the tying run with two out. The stretch by Gossage, the pitch. There's a drive to deep right field. Back goes Kemp at the wall. Home run!

George Brett has done it again, and the Royals have a 5 to 4 lead in the ninth! . . . The Yankees have picked up George Brett's bat and they're going to claim that Brett's bat is illegal. Billy Martin is out of the dugout. Now the umpires are all huddled off by themselves — the four of them looking at George Brett's bat. They may be talking about how much pine tar is on the bat, and they are now measuring the pine tar with home plate. They're using home plate as a measuring stick to measure the pine tar on the bat! Now they've called George Brett out, and here comes an argument! Here comes an argument! George Brett at the plate — oh, and he is furious! He's trying to get to an umpire! George Brett may have already been suspended. Dick Howser is out arguing. George Brett came charging out of the dugout. The Royals have lost the home run and the ball game!

— FRED WHITE, July 24, 1983.

Yankee Stadium, New York, NY. For decades, Uncle Remus had marked America's closest brush with tar. No more. In an imbroglio that intrigued the nation, George Brett 1) wafted a ninth-inning home run to give the Royals an apparent 5–4 victory, 2) was called out by umpire Joe Brinkman because pine tar on his bat exceeded eighteen inches, violating Rule 1.10 (b), and 3) paraphrased the biblical injunction, "Once it was lost, now it is found." When Lee MacPhail, president of the American League, ruled that Brett's home run was valid (the game was completed on August 18 before 1,245 fans), he wrote *finis* to one of the most convoluted chapters in the Book of Baseball. Even George Steinbrenner was nonplussed. "There are no words to describe all this," mourned Boss George. "No words at all."

THE DA(R)(M)NING OF THE SOX

Two-O delivery. Swing. There's a high fly ball to deep right-center field! And, baby, way back! It's long gone! Upper deck! Right-center field! Kiss it good-bye! Three-nothing, Orioles! And Eddie Murray's first hit is a monster shot at Comiskey Park. And the fans here, who were chanting, 'Let's Go, Sox,' just moments ago, are in stunned, muted silence right now.

— JON MILLER, October 7, 1983.

Comiskey Park, Chicago, IL. They were, the cliché kept telling us (and as the Phillies, in the eightieth World Series, so skulkingly proved), the two best teams in baseball. The Orioles (their last world championship, 1970) had won ninety-eight games in the regular season; the White Sox — devoid, since 1959, of even a pennant — won ninety-nine; no National League club broke the ninety-one-victory plane. In Game Three of the A.L. playoff, with the series tied, Eddie Murray reached the farthest extremity of the Pale Hose yard. Baltimore romped, 11-1.

———————

They've given Landrum the left-field line. He's a right-handed batter. The one-nothing is on the way. A high fly ball to left field. It could be, it might be! And it's an upper-deck home run for Tito Landrum! Oh, my goodness! What a shot by Landrum! Into the teeth of a heavy wind! Tito, with an upper-deck shot, and it is 1 to 0, Baltimore, in the tenth!

—TOM MARR, 10/8/83.

Comiskey Park. The following afternoon, execution came abruptly for the long-suffering Sox. With his handsome blow, reserve outfielder Tito Landrum propelled the Orioles to an ALCS victory, three games to one, and into their sixth World Series.

"NOW OUR LIVES ARE COMPLETE!"

One more and it's over! The Chicago Cubs will be the new Eastern Division champs! They're getting security on the field. These Cubs' fans are going to explode . . . Who's excited? Listen to this crowd! Might as well join 'em . . . Hey, it's in there! Cubs are the champions! The Cubs are the champions! The Cubs win! Orsulak down on strikes! Rick Sutcliffe—his thirteenth in a row, sixteen-and-one for the year! He faced only twenty-eight men! He pitched a two-hitter! Let's just watch it. The fans are getting on the field! And they [the players] come into the clubhouse . . . The expressions—that's what made them a team! Genuine affection. Now our lives are complete! The Cubs are Number One! The Cubs have clinched the Eastern Division title!

—HARRY CARAY, September 24, 1984.

Three Rivers Stadium, Pittsburgh, PA. How substantial a part do the Cubbies play in Chicago's diurnal life? "This is the biggest story in Chicago since Mayor Daley died," *Chicago Tribune* columnist Steve Daley said of the Wrigleys' frenetic rise to the apex of the Eastern Division. Had he been alive, Jack Benny, himself a baseball fan, would quickly have approved; the Cubs' last championship brightened 1945, thirty-nine years earlier.

SWEET SIXTEEN

Steve Garvey, who has been a hero tonight with three base hits and three RBIs, steps in . . . One ball, no strikes. One away. Five-five ball game . . . Padres have pushed ten hits on the board, the Cubs eight. Pitch is on the way to Garvey. Hit high to right-center field! Way back! Going! Going! It is gone! The Padres win it! . . . In a game that absolutely defies description, Steve Garvey, in the ninth inning, hit one over the 370-mark, and the Padres beat the Cubs, 7 to 5! Oh, Doctor, you can hang a star on that baby!

—JERRY COLEMAN, October 6, 1984.

San Diego/Jack Murphy Stadium, San Diego, CA. Alternately disparaged and ignored, the San Diego Padres seemed forever cast as baseball's Rodney Dangerfield. But in the franchise's sixteenth year, the Pads won the West—their first title of any kind — and, in a rousing playoff against the Cubs, the National League pennant. To many, the Championship Series turned on Steve Garvey's poke, which downed Chicago, 7–5, and tied the preliminary at two games each.

WIRE TO WIRE

One ball, two strikes. Tug of the cap by Morris. Kittle waits. Here it comes. He struck him out, and Morris has a no-hitter! Lance Parrish goes out to grab him! And the Tigers get a no-hit performance for the first time since 1958 when Jim Bunning did it! Jack Morris, the no-hit hero, surrounded by his teammates. In the ninth for Chicago, no runs, no hits, no errors, one man left! And the final score: Detroit 4, Chicago 0!

— ERNIE HARWELL, April 7, 1984.

Comiskey Park, Chicago, IL. After airing nearly four thousand Tigers' games, Ernie Harwell finally called a Detroit no-hitter. It came in the Bengals' fourth game of the regular season, on a bright and chilling day, and was the first of Jack Morris' nineteen victories. It was also, as they say, a premonition of things to come.

Ball one on Kirk. Here's the pitch. He swings, and there's a long drive to right! And it is a home run for Gibson! A three-run homer! The Tigers lead it, 8 to 4, in the eighth inning!

— E.H., 10/14/84.

Tiger Stadium, Detroit, MI. In a season when "Bless You Boys" swept Detroit like courage, London, during the Blitz, the Tigers became only the third big-league team to lead its league (here, division) every day of the year. The Bengals won the A.L. East by fifteen games, swept Kansas City in the playoff, then crushed San Diego — Kirk Gibson's Game-Five, eighth-inning shot was the clinching blow — in a pentagon of sets to win their fourth World Series. A concomitant benefit: Detroit smashed its all-time attendance record, drawing 2,704,794 patrons.

TOM TERRIFIC

Two outs! Fans come to their feet! . . . The biggest media representation in Yankee Stadium in years! So it'll be two veterans — Seaver and Don Baylor, who represents the tying run. Baylor hitting at .240, 18 homers, 67 RBIs. High to left, playable! Reid Nichols camps underneath it! History!

— KEN HARRELSON, August 4, 1985.

Yankee Stadium, New York, NY. Before a throng of 54,032, nearly three thousand miles from Rod Carew's same-day *touché,* in the city where he began his career, in a game White Sox' second baseman Bryan Little termed "so intense it was like a World Series. I could hardly breathe," Tom Seaver beat the Yankees, 4–1, for his three hundredth major-league victory. Said Seaver: "I was so nervous today I felt like I was levitating out there. This is truly a day I'll always remember."

CHARLIE HUSTLE

A standing-room-only crowd at Cincinnati on its feet. First inning. Pete Rose against Eric Show. Ball one . . . Rose looking for hit 4,192 . . . and it's one ball, one strike . . . If you have a lump in your throat, you're only human . . . it's two balls, one strike on Rose. Everybody on their feet here in Cincinnati, and a world-wide television audience watching these moments tonight here at Riverfront Stadium. Two-one pitch from Show. It's into left-center! There it is! Rose has eclipsed Cobb! That's hit 4,192! . . . [more than one minute later] . . . For Pete Rose, this certainly his crowning achievement. And for baseball, a game that grows with its past, that combines warmth and statistics, this is one of the all-time great moments. Well, there is love aplenty here in Cincinnati, and Eric Show becomes a spectator as this city mobs their native son. The moment we've all waited for — hit number 4,192 that makes Pete Rose the all-time baseball hit leader!

— KEN WILSON, September 11, 1985.

Riverfront Stadium, Cincinnati, OH. "He is forty-four years old, but seems both younger and older, sort of timeless too, and he is still thriving at the major-league level," read the August 19, 1985, *TIME* magazine cover story. "It took Pete Rose two decades and more, just a blink and a nod on the eternal baseball schedule, but he has come to both a paramount moment in his game [eclipsing Ty Cobb's all-time hit record on the fifty-seventh anniversary of the Georgia Peach's final at-bat] and a place of moment in any enterprise. By the numbers and beyond them, he is what he does. Rose *is* baseball."

OZZIE AND CLARK

Smith rips one into right! Down the line! It may go! Go crazy, folks, go crazy! It's a home run! And the Cardinals have won the game by the score of 3 to 2 on a home run by the Wizard!

— JACK BUCK, October 14, 1985.

Busch Stadium, St. Louis, MO. In 2,967 major-league at-bats, Ozzie Smith, the Cardinals' $2 million gemstone of a shortstop, had never — as in, well, *never* — hit a home run from the left side of the plate. But in Game Five of the National League playoff, with the score (and series) tied, 2–2, Smith launched a ninth-inning, game-winning drive off Dodgers' pitcher Tom Niedenfuer, and as "the baseball flew out toward the right-field fence, seemingly pushed by the roar from the crowd," wrote Bob Rubin in the *Miami Herald,* "a mystical, magical transformation took place in Busch Stadium. The ballyard by the Mississippi became the land of Oz."

Swing and a long one into left field! Adios! Good-bye! It may be that's the winner! A three-run homer by Clark and the Cardinals lead by the score of 7 to 5!

—J.B., 10/16/85.

Dodger Stadium, Los Angeles, CA. Two days after Ozzie Smith shocked everyone, including himself, Jack Clark made a Hades of the City of the Angels. In the ninth inning of Game Six, with St. Louis trailing, 5–4, and down to its final out, the Cardinals' first baseman smashed a three-run thunderclap to crush the Dodgers, 7–5, win the first best-of-seven Championship Series, and thrust the Redbirds into an all-Missouri, "Show-Me" World Series v. Kansas City.

A Royals' Flush

And there's a looper to right field for a base hit! Concepcion scores! Here comes Sundberg! Here comes the throw! He scores! And we go to the seventh!

— Al Michaels, October 26, 1985.

Royals Stadium, Kansas City, MO. After trailing the California Angels for most of the season (before rallying to win the Western Division in Game No. 161) and, then, after trailing the Toronto Blue Jays, three games to one, in the American League playoff (before rallying to win three straight sets and its second pennant), Kansas City opted for instant replay. Behind, three to one, in the eighty-second World Series, the Royals claimed the fifth match, 6–1, and stunned St. Louis in the ninth inning of Game Six, tying the Fall Classic on a one-out, two-run, broken-bat, pinch-hit single by sudden-death hero Dane Iorg.

One out to go in the ninth inning. Eleven to nothing. The one-0 pitch. High fly ball! Motley going back to the track! No outs to go! The Royals have won the 1985 World Series! And they converge on the mound in celebration!

— Denny Matthews, 10/27/85.

Royals Stadium. The night after Iorg's stiletto, Kansas City unsheathed the knife. Until now, the Cardinals had won the seventh game in seven of eight previous Oktoberfests. But as Darryl Motley bashed a two-run homer in the second inning, the Royals scored three third-inning runs and six in the fifth, pitcher Bret Saberhagen scattered five hits and teammate George Brett reaped four, and the Redbirds slunk to a worst-ever .185 Series batting average, the plucky, unsung, and marvelous Royals a) repelled tradition, winning an 11–0 laugher, b) avenged the loss of the 1976–77–78–84 league playoffs, '81 divisional series, and 1980 Fall Classic, c) became only the fifth World Series team to overcome a 3–1 games deficit (and first to lose Games One and Two at home and still prevail), and d) clasped their first world title in the franchise's seventeenth year. Of the Cinderella champions, Randy Galloway of the *Dallas Morning News* wrote, "Move it on over, you Mets of '69. Way over. Go to the history board and rip out a page about the Miracle Braves of '14. And don't let anyone tell you about the Giants' Miracle of Coogan's Bluff in '51. The Royals of '85 are in an upset class of their own."

THE JOLLY ROGER

And here they come up at Fenway! . . . A new record! Clemens has set a major-league record for strikeouts in a game! Twenty! . . . What a performance by the kid from the University of Texas!

— NED MARTIN, April 29, 1986.

Fenway Park, Boston, MA. A young Tom Seaver pitch-alike, former college All-American, and Boston's best mound prospect in the past thirty years, Roger Clemens underwent shoulder surgery in 1985, imperiling his career. The next season, No. 21 punctuated his comeback in unanswerable style — striking out a nine-inning record twenty batters (Phil Bradley [above] endured the final K) to break the big-league mark of nineteen shared by Steve Carlton, Nolan Ryan, and Tom Terrific. Observed Clemens, a 3–1 victor over the Seattle Mariners: "The strikeouts just kept coming." Quoth Red Sox' fans, unaccustomed to lambent pitching, of Roger's tour de force: "*C'est pas possible.*"

REG-GIE!

The one-one pitch on its way to Reggie Jackson. Swung on, and there's a high drive to deep center field! Armas going back — away back! It is gone! Reggie Jackson has homered, and the Angels have a 2 to 0 lead on Roger Clemens in the first inning! Number 537!

— AL CONIN, May 14, 1986.

Anaheim Stadium, Anaheim, CA. "When I was growing up, we had to root for the black players like Mays, but I always admired Mantle," Reggie Jackson confessed. "You had to root against the Yankees, because they were so good, but Mantle was it." In his twentieth big-league season, four days shy of his fortieth birthday, off the Red Sox' Roger Clemens, Jackson bombed his 537th career home run, passing the Mick for sixth place on the all-time list. "What a thrill, just to be mentioned in the same breath," he said. "When you say 'Mickey Mantle,' the name does something to you." So too the sobriquet *Mr. October.*

GREAT SCOTT!

Now the hitter is Will Clark. He's O for three. Swing and a bouncer! This could be it! Davis runs to the bag! A no-hitter! Astros win the championship! Mike Scott throws a no-hitter and the Astros are the champions of the National League West!

—MILO HAMILTON, September 25, 1986.

The Astrodome, Houston, TX. Stealing from Hollywood, the Astros won their first championship since 1980 in truly storybook script. Before what the *New York Times* dubbed "a delirious sellout crowd," with many fans waving Lone Star flags, right-hander Mike Scott struck out thirteen batters, allowed only two base runners, and pitched a no-hitter as Houston downed San Francisco, 2–0, to clinch a National League demipennant, spread-eagling its Western Division. "Shakespeare," chimed Houston reliever Charlie Kerfeld, "couldn't have written it any better."

SOXSATIONAL

Donnie Moore out of the bull pen to face Dave Henderson. One and 0. In there—two strikes away. One and one . . . one and two . . . two and two . . . And Boone to the mound now . . . The two-two pitch—he stays alive . . . The pitch . . . Deep to left and Downing goes back! And it's gone! Unbelievable! You're looking at one for the ages here! Astonishing! Anaheim Stadium was one strike away from turning into Fantasyland! And now the Red Sox lead, 6 to 5! The Red Sox get four runs in the ninth on a pair of two-run homers by Don Baylor and Dave Henderson!

—AL MICHAELS, 10/12/86.

Anaheim Stadium, Anaheim, CA. The previous night, California had scored three ninth- and one eleventh-inning runs to shock the Red Sox, 4–3, in kaleidoscopic Game Four of the American League playoff. Next afternoon, with the Angels leading, three games to one, the Sox one strike removed from elimination, Angels' fans poised to assault the infield, and champagne chilling in the California clubhouse, Dave Henderson walloped a two-out, two-run, ninth-inning thunderbolt to complete a four-run rally, still Anaheim Stadium, and electrify the Republic's baseball body. Two innings later, Henderson's sacrifice fly gave Boston a 7–6 victory. "I've been in over two thousand games," the Bosox' Don Baylor said afterward, "and this is the best I've ever seen or been a part of. I'll probably watch it on videotape this winter, and I *still* won't believe it."

Three and two with two down. Four-nothing, Boston, in the fourth . . . Now the set, Rice waits—the pitch. He swings—there's a fly ball to left! It's deep! Going back is Downing—looking—it is long gone! A home run for Rice! A three-run homer, and a 7 to 0 lead for the Boston Red Sox in the fourth inning!

—ERNIE HARWELL, 10/15/86.

Fenway Park. It became — this A. L. Championship Series, wrote columnist Mark Shields — an exception to the Red Sox' rule that "to be born a Boston fan is to learn early that life is not going to work out." In stunning role reversal, the Yawkeys — cursed, historically, by ineptitude, ill fortune, and ghosts, deflations, and pratfalls of the past — turned tradition on its head, pummeling California, 8–1, to win the American League pennant — their first victory in a winner-take-all game with a division flag, pennant, or World Series at stake since 1912, the year Fenway Park was built, and their first seventh-game postseason triumph in eighty-three years. "What can you say?" Boston manager John McNamara asked of the Red Sox' revival — due, partly, to Jim Rice's Game-Seven, *coup de grâce* homer (above) — from a near-terminal playoff condition. "After all, you know what the poets say: 'hope springs eternal in the human breast.' " Verily, even for the ill-starred, oft-scarred, beloved Sox.

LET'S GO METS!

Hit to right! Bass going back! Going back! It's gone! The Mets win!

— KEITH JACKSON, October 11, 1986.

Shea Stadium, New York, NY. "Their MTV video has more stars than Hands Across America," *Washington Post* reporter Richard Justice wrote of such bigwigs as Dwight Gooden, Darryl Strawberry, Keith Hernandez, and Gary Carter, "which is perfect for the New York Mets and another reason they present opponents with special problems." Mets' "stars" helped the 1986 Flushings orbit the National League, thumping the Eastern Division by 21½ games. But in Game Three of the Championship Series, it was a relatively minor meteor — outfielder Len Dykstra — who propelled a two-run, ninth-inning homer to ambush Houston, 6–5, and give New York the playoff lead, two sets to one.

We're tied at one in the twelfth inning. Here's the pitch to Carter. Base hit to center! That's it! Wally Backman scores, and the Mets go to Houston leading, three games to two!

— BRENT MUSBURGER, 10/14/86.

Shea Stadium. Awaking from a one-for-twenty-one playoff slumber, Gary Carter slapped an extra-inning single to score Wally Backman from second base, deal the Astros another sudden-death fatality, and push the Mets within a single victory of their first Oktoberfest since 1973.

The tying run, Denny Walling, on second base. The winning run on first base. Three-two to Bass. Struck him out! Kevin Bass swings and strikes out on three breaking balls! The New York Mets have won the 1986 National League pennant! And Jesse Orosco becomes the first pitcher to win three games in relief in Championship Series history!

— K.J., 10/15/86.

The Astrodome, Houston, TX. "The most tiring ball game I have ever been part of, either as a spectator or as a player," ABC announcer Tim McCarver remarked of the Mets' 7–6, 16-inning, 282-minute, Game-Six, pennant-winning victory — the longest and, it must be said, among most riveting games in post-season history. Behind, 3–0, New York scored thrice in the ninth inning, traded runs with Houston five innings hence, and outscored the Astros, 3–2, in the final, decisive frame. "After the game," wrote *USA Today*, "players and fans on both sides shook their heads in disbelief and appreciation." Said the *New York Daily News:* "It was about as lovely as the most lovely sport in the world can be. Rapture! Congratulations to all!"

THE HEARTBREAK KIDS

Hurst has struck out five, walked one, scattered ten hits. And Dykstra waits on an 0-two count. And a swing and a miss! And that's the way it ends! He chased a bad ball high! And Boston has won it to take the lead, three games to two — the final game they'll play in their home park this year! Here's the final score: Boston 4, New York Mets 2.

—Jack Buck, October 23, 1986.

Fenway Park, Boston, MA. When Bruce Hurst fanned the Mets' Len Dykstra to end Game Five, the Red Sox, leading the Autumn Occasion, three games to two, moved twenty-seven outs from their first world championship since 1918. "Is this the threshold of a dream or the eve of destruction?" Dan Shaughnessy wondered in the next day's *Boston Globe*. "Are baseball's heartbreak kids finally going to keep a promise, or are they just setting you up for one final apocalyptic, cataclysmic fall?" Hoping for the best, expecting the worst, its open veins bleeding, and carting history's baggage, the region of Cotton Mather, Jonathan Edwards, and hope receding into Calvinistic tragedy once more approached the abyss.

So the winning run is at second base with two out! Three and two to Mookie Wilson! . . . A little roller up along first . . . behind the bag . . . It gets through Buckner! Here comes Knight! And the Mets win it!

—Vin Scully, 10/26/86.

Shea Stadium, New York, NY. Just when Boston fans thought — naively, as it happened — they had seen every collapse imaginable, the Red Sox unveiled the Lourdes of baseball catastrophes. With two out, no Mets on base, Game Six past midnight, and the Sox ahead, 5–3, in the bottom of the tenth inning; with the Yawkeys on their feet in the dugout, the Shea Stadium message board prematurely flashing, "Congratulations Red Sox," and Boston twice a single strike away from victory; with Bruce Hurst already chosen the Classic's Most Valuable Player and the World Series trophy gracing the Red Sox' clubhouse, ready for the historic celebration — New York bunched three hits, reliever Bob

Stanley's game-tying wild pitch, and Bill Buckner's immemorial error to score three runs, stun New England, and tie the Series; and as the Mets rallied, a friend of *Sports Illustrated* columnist Peter Gammons prophesied, correctly, "They're [the Sox] going to do it. Just when we thought that we had been freed at last, they're going to create a way to again break our hearts that goes beyond our wildest imagination"; and as the ball went through Buckner's legs, giving the Mets a 6–5 triumph, Gammons wrote, "Forty-one years of Red Sox baseball flashed in front of my eyes. In that one moment, Johnny Pesky held the ball, Joe McCarthy lifted Ellis Kinder in Yankee Stadium, Luis Aparicio fell down rounding third, Bill Lee delivered his Leephus pitch to Tony Perez, Darrell Johnson hit for Jim Willoughby, Don Zimmer chose Bobby Sprowl over Luis Tiant and Bucky (Bleeping) Dent hit the home run"; and as the final act of this heart-lifting, heart-wrenching, unforgettable game reached its surrealistic denouement, a nation, exhausted and disbelieving, shook its collective head.

Schiraldi pitching to the lead-off batter here in the seventh inning — he's behind on the count to Ray Knight. The pitch — swing and a fly ball, left-center field, well-hit! May not be caught! It's gone! It's gone! Over the fence in left-center! A home run by Ray Knight to give the Mets their first lead of the evening, 4–3! That ball just squeaked over the top of the wall — it kept going and going and going!

—J.B. 10/27/86.

Shea Stadium. Even when Boston's Dwight Evans and Rich Gedman bombed consecutive Game-Seven home runs; even when Bruce Hurst allowed only one hit in the first five innings; even when the Yawkeys carried a three-run lead into the bottom of the sixth — even then, wrote *Baltimore Sun* columnist Larry Littwin, "You knew the ending. You just didn't know how. They are the Red Sox. You change the ending and there's no more mystique. Just as Hamlet dies every night, the Red Sox die every time they take the stage." As Sid Fernandez sparkled in relief, Keith Hernandez bashed a two-run single, and Ray Knight broke a 3–3 tie (above) with his seventh-inning homer, the inevitable began to disclose itself: the New York Mets would win the 1986 World Series. "Pity the Mets," the October 29, 1986, *Washington Post* declaimed, perhaps a tad unfairly. "They win 108 games in the regular season, pull off a string of late-season victories, take the World Series in seven games [the final game, 8–5], and how will they be remembered? They will be remembered years hence as the other team in the Series the Red Sox blew. That is the triumph of enduring notoriety over fleeting fame; the Red Sox always lose in the end, but in ways that are so imaginative and heart-rending as to be more memorable than victory." Ultimately, observers hailed a more catholic *Weltanschauung*. "The 1986 World Series seized the nation like no other in recent years," mused Shirley Povich. "It was baseball as Americans know and love it — a throbbing, good-God-what's next World Series that had Americans' hearts pumping in every time zone — the kind of theatre that no other sport can generate." Wrote Dick Young of baseball's dreamstuff autumn: "The four divisional races were a drag. Not one hot finish. Then, two breath-holding playoffs and one excruciating see-saw World Series. Always, it seems, the game has something to redeem it. As The Natural said, contemplating the end of his career: 'God, I love baseball.' "

THE BREW CREW

The pitch to Murray — a swing and a drive to center! Robin is chasing — a long run — he's got it with a diving catch! And Nieves has made history here in Baltimore! A diving, diving, sensational catch by Robin Yount to preserve the no-hitter! Nieves is being mobbed! What a play by Robin — the final out of the game!

— Bob Uecker, April 15, 1987.

Memorial Stadium, Baltimore, MD. *Sans* pennant since 1982, the Milwaukee Brewers — a consensus choice to finish last; their lineup awanting noted names — stunned rivals, critics, and, presumably, themselves, by winning their first thirteen games of the 1987 season. The skein tied Atlanta's season-opening record of April 1982, and its Mona Lisa was Juan Nieves' masterwork v. Baltimore. "This is incredible," the Puerto Rican southpaw said of the first no-hitter in Brewers' history. "I wish my mother were here tonight. I'd squeeze her to death."

MICHAEL JACK

Here's the pitch. . . . He takes a shot at it! There it goes! It is out of here! Michael Jack Schmidt has hit his five hundredth home run! What a spot! What a spot! And the entire team comes out to greet Schmitty! He puts the Phillies in front, 8 to 6! For Mike Schmidt, his five hundredth homer!

— Andy Musser, April 18, 1987.

Three Rivers Stadium, Pittsburgh, PA. He was a leviathan at bat, palatine in the field, eight-time home-run titlist, and three-time Most Valuable Player, and in his sixteenth major-league season, off the Pirates' Don Robinson, before 21,537 lookers-on, perhaps The Game's finest-ever third baseman became the fourteenth eminence to whack five hundred home runs. "You couldn't write a more perfect script," said Michael Jack Schmidt of his two-out, three-run, ninth-inning blast which gave Philadelphia an 8–6 victory. "When you're a little kid playing ball each day, this is the kind of thrill you only *dream* about."

CIRCUIT BREAKER

So Ozzie Virgil at second base, and of course he's the big man. Hubie Brooks at first. Two and 0 — line drive into left-center field. That's a base hit and it will go to the wall! In comes Virgil, in comes Brooks, Raines to third, and he's in there with a triple!

— Vin Scully, July 14, 1987.

Oakland Coliseum, Oakland, CA. In the Season of the Lively Ball, pitchers turned the tables in the fifty-eighth All-Star Game. Ending the longest scoreless streak in All-Star history, Tim Raines drilled a two-run triple in the thirteenth inning to help the Nationals win, 2–0.

INSTANT/DISTANT REPLAY

Cardinals lost Game Six and Game Seven to Kansas City in '85. Lost here last night
[Game Six] after leading, 5 to 2. Led it here, 2 to 0, tonight. Trailing now, 4–2, in the
ninth with two out. The pitch to Willie McGee. Swing and a ground ball to third!
Gaetti has it! Minnesota wins it! It is a joyous celebration on the field by these Twins!

—JACK BUCK, October 25, 1987.

Hubert Humphrey Metrodome, Minneapolis, MN. Twenty-two years earlier,
the Minnesota Twins won their first American League pennant. Now, at last,
the ex-Griffiths sojourned further—taking the World Series over the favored
bridesmaid-again Cardinals. Minnesota's (not-so-secret) weapons: the Metrodome (nurturing baseball's best home record) and its homer hanky-waving
fans—achieving "decibel levels," a writer said, "normally associated with jet
aircraft takeoffs."

BROWNING GIVES DODGERS BLUES

In the history of this franchise, there has never been a perfect game thrown by a Reds'
pitcher. . . . They are all up and on their feet . . . Browning is ready for the 2–2 to
Woodson. And here it comes! And it is swung on and missed! And Tom Browning has
pitched a perfect game! . . . Twenty-seven outs in a row! And he is being mobbed by his
teammates just to the third-base side of the mound! Boy, what a memorable scene! And
this one belongs to the Reds!

—MARTY BRENNAMAN, September 16, 1988.

Riverfront Stadium, Cincinnati, OH. Not once did Tom Browning go to a
three-ball count. The game took less than two hours—but seemed an eternity
to the O'Malleys. On a drizzly Rhineland eve, Browning became only the fourteenth pitcher to hurl a perfect game, beating Los Angeles, 1–0. Afterward he
was asked if President Reagan had called. "No, but he's from the West
Coast," Browning said. "I guess he's a Dodger fan."

JOSE

Canseco on the threshold now of major league baseball history. . . . There he goes! The
pitch inside. The throw by Suerhoff. Not in time! And Canseco is a forty-forty man! And
the fans at County Stadium give him a standing ovation. Boy, that is something!

—PAT HUGHES, September 23, 1988.

County Stadium, Milwaukee, WI. If "30" is journalism's way of writing finis,
"40-40" is baseball shorthand for demolishing opponents. When Jose Canseco
stole two bases against the Brewers, he became the first player to hit forty home

runs and swipe as many bases in a single season. Said Oakland's Bunyan, "I got nervous [only] when I was going for the fortieth steal. My legs locked. I almost had to laugh." Not so, the American League.

OREL SURGERY

Orel Hershiser is looking upstairs and saying, "Lookit, You guide me. I don't know what to do." It gets to the point in these situations where . . . the best thing is just to put your hands in the Guy Above and let 'er go. Here's Morehead waiting. Runners moving off second and third. Two down — bottom of the tenth. Hershiser winds again — the righthander — the one-two pitch. And there's a drive to right field — he's going to put it away! Gonzalez is under it! And Hershiser sets a new all-time consecutive scoreless innings pitched record at fifty-nine! Oh, doctor! History was born right here at San Diego!

— JERRY COLEMAN, September 28, 1988.

Jack Murphy Stadium, San Diego, CA. On August 30, Orel Hershiser gave up a run. In the next four weeks, he turned thirty, became a new father, helped the Dodgers win the N. L. West, and made history. Hershiser threw fifty-nine straight scoreless innings — including ten against San Diego — to break Don Drysdale's 1968 mark of fifty-eight. Holding batters to a .155 average, hurling five shutouts in the streak, and letting only five runners reach third base — he set the stage for L.A. miracles to come.

ROY HOBBS REDUX

Three and two . . . Sax waiting on deck, but the game right now is at the plate. High fly ball into right field! She is . . . gone! . . . In the year of the implausible, the impossible has happened!

— VIN SCULLY, October 15, 1988.

Dodger Stadium, Los Angeles, CA. Orel Hershiser beat the A's twice in the World Series, was named MVP, and helped the Dodgers stun favored Oakland, four games to one. Yet all pales beside a screenplay even Hollywood would spurn. With two out in the ninth inning, Kirk Gibson — injured, barely able to walk — limped to the plate like Walter Brennan, fouled off several pitches like Hank Aguirre, then stunned America with a pinch-hit thunderbolt that gave the Dodgers a celluloid 5-4 Game One victory. Exulted Dodgers' manager Tommy Lasorda: "Whoever the good Lord has for a scriptwriter, I'm giving him a raise. You'll never see a finish like this in a hundred years."

13
Where's That Rainbow
(1989-)

"When I make a mistake, it's a beaut."
— Fiorello La Guardia

FOR MUCH OF AMERICA, THE "GAME OF THE WEEK" WAS—WITHOUT hyperbole—an institution without peer, a televised Main Street linking provinces hundreds of miles from the nearest major-league city. Born in 1953, it became network TV's longest-running sports series—preserving the big leagues' identity through a ribbon of narrative. If baseball is our national myth, the "Game" was the stage on which the myth transpired—familiar and intimate; the pastime at its purest. As long as baseball lived, it was unthinkable that the "Game of the Week" would ever die.

Yet in the spring of 1990, tuning in to see their old Saturday friend— seeking, Americans did not find. R.I.P. the 1980s most widely watched April–August sports series. Dead, at thirty-eight, of self-inflicted wounds— its viewers betrayed by a sport swayed less by decency than greed.

The "Game's" end stemmed from baseball's decision to grant CBS exclusive network broadcast rights for 1990–93 and limit regular-season coverage to a minute 12 games aired haphazardly over 26 weeks. It struck, especially, at the Idaho farmer, the Mississippi laborer, and the retiree in rural Ohio— anyone who lacked access to local team and/or cable television. Herbert George Wells said, "Human history becomes more and more a race between education and catastrophe." The CBS catastrophe mocked Bart Giamatti's words—"Of all sports, baseball's regular season matters most"—treating the estimated 60 million people who rely solely on network TV for baseball like untouchables at a bazaar.

It is impossible to conceive of now, but Giamatti's predecessor as commissioner, Peter Ueberroth, was jubilant when in December 1988, he announced what ultimately became sportscasting's *Exxon Valdez*. (He was not alone: While Ubie appeared at CBS's Fifty-second Street headquarters, "bearing a host of white baseball caps, emblazoned with the majors' red and blue logo," the *New York Times* said, CBS president Lawrence Tisch had his own supply of victory caps, "emblazoned with the CBS logo.")

Baseball gave CBS the whole package for the simplest reason: bucks. Only

CBS so desperately needed the playoffs and World Series (to lift October ratings and promote its wretched prime-time schedule) that it would pay anything to gain exclusivity. That CBS couldn't (due to prior programming) or wouldn't (unlike NBC, it has almost no interest in the regular season) air a Saturday "Game" didn't trouble major league baseball's powers-that-be. It *did* trouble those who knew that baseball needed healthy regular-season exposure for its post-season to thrive—and that the "Game of the Week" was its April–September umbilical cord.

The day of the CBS bombshell, *Boston Globe* columnist Jack Craig asked baseball's broadcast director, Bryan Burns, how many *sans* local team/cable viewers would be hurt by the new format. "He had no idea," Craig recollected. "He hadn't even bothered to check." Three weeks later, the *New York Post*'s Phil Mushnick met a triumphant Burns at the Waldorf-Astoria Hotel's Starlight Roof Room. "He freely admitted that millions would be deprived of baseball," Mushnick said. "To him, Big deal."

Four weeks later, Ueberroth announced baseball's first-ever arrangement with a national cable network—for four hundred million dollars over the years 1990–93, ESPN would air 175 games a year: doubleheaders on Tuesday and Friday evenings, a single game on Wednesday and Sunday nights, and tripleheaders Memorial Day and Labor Day.

Following on the heels of the CBS deal, the cable package led many to marvel at baseball's gold rush. Compared to other sports, though, the numbers were less impressive. Through 1993, CBS would give baseball $265 million annually, only 7 percent over ABC/NBC's 1989 rights fees; later, the hike proved minuscule in light of the NFL's 1990–93 $2.71 billion heist from NBC, ABC, and CBS—a 93 percent increase—and the NBA's 1991–94 pact, which amounted to a *300* percent rise. Financially, Ueberroth's deal had a sub-Midas touch.

Yet it was outside the countinghouse where, almost immediately, the CBS package evoked rancor. The deals incensed anyone who knew that even baseball risked becoming out of sight, out of mind.

• The CBS pact made baseball the first sport to *voluntarily* slash its number of network carriers. From 1961–70, the NFL mushroomed from one to three nets; post-1975, baseball boomed by adopting two. CBS's exclusivity gave ABC and NBC no incentive to publicize baseball—which became, in effect, a rival property—on newscasts, prime-time specials, and "Good Morning America" and "Today." In 1990, while baseball would have only CBS and ESPN to spread its message, the NFL had CBS, ABC, NBC, ESPN, and Ted Turner's TNT to carry games.

• Negotiating its new contracts, pro football considered two criteria— money, for the owners; coverage, for the fans. Disdaining the latter, Ueberroth's arrangement made baseball a regular-season nonentity. CBS's schedule was dubbed *The Dirty Dozen* or *The Twelve Days of Baseball*. It included no coverage of Opening Saturday, only two games before late June, and none after August 25—the major leagues' most decisive time. CBS aired three times as many college basketball games on one January 1990 weekend as it would baseball games during the baseball season's first ten *weeks*. Put another way: Football had more 1990 *pre*-season games than baseball had *regular*-season games on TV.

• The pact abandoned NBC, baseball's ambassador from 1947–89. Said then-NBC president Arthur Watson, who is such a baseball fan that, in 1990, he invested in a group seeking an expansion franchise for northern Virginia: "To us, baseball was like Hope and Carson—a jewel that *means* NBC." Watson's network wanted to air a 1990–93 "Game."

In contrast, CBS Sports president Neal Pilson—a self-avowed hockey and football fanatic—flaunted his disdain for the regular season. "Our emphasis," he said, "will be on the post-season"—the sport was to be used, not loved. One recalled CBS's then-Number 1 baseball man, Brent Musburger, saying of the August 1985 players' strike, "If they don't settle it, who'll miss baseball? Pro football's *exhibition* season begins in a couple of weeks."

At ABC, the tears were crocodilian; baseball had cost it an estimated one hundred million dollars between 1984 and 1989. Few were surprised when, after Roone Arledge was dumped in 1986 as ABC sports president, his successor, Dennis Swanson, sniped, "Baseball is one of the biggest losers our network has."

The loss at NBC, though, was obvious. " 'Game's' demise cuts baseball out of the lives of many people," Bob Costas said in 1989, still reeling from the blow.

Costas' early 1980s role on the backup "Game" had led to a panoply of broadcasting plums. He was named 1985-87-88 "Sportscaster of the Year" by the National Sportscasters and Sportswriters Association, and won two Emmy Awards as outstanding sports personality/host. He graced his network's late-night 1988 Olympics coverage, as well as the weekly sports talk show, "Costas Coast to Coast." He was an NBA and NFL studio host, and anchors NBC's "Later With Bob Costas." Yet Bob's Everest was still baseball—it meant more to him, he says, than all other sports. "It would have been so easy for this contract to satisfy the fans and owners," he said, "if only baseball had been more patient. They could have kept the two-network format—us and CBS—and we could have kept the 'Game.' "

To many, the weaknesses of the "trade" were glaring. Musburger for NBC's Costas/Vin Scully and ABC's Al Michaels. Twelve games for NBC/ABC's forty in 1989. A network with little feel for the pastime for one which revered it. That's some trade.

• History teaches that network television is a sport's best salesman. It enters every living room and shapes the viewing habits of America. George Vecsey has written, "The 'Game of the Week' was baseball's way of saying, 'We're the national sport. We go everywhere.' " By moving regular-season reliance to local team/ESPN coverage, the CBS deal turned history on its ear. "Localcasts" were nonexistent in much of America. Worse, cable reaches barely 6 in 10 households—creating a ludicrous imbalance: 187 games for cabled America; only 12 for the rest.

• Most cruelly, the CBS arrangement disenfranchised those without cable access, or the funds to afford it: the poor and elderly, the habitants of inner cities, farms, and small towns. To the nearly one of two homes *sans* ESPN, baseball coverage was as remote as a Sunday school in Hades.

The end of the "Game" is a sordid tale, unprecedented in the history of baseball broadcasting. So let us detail how baseball tried to defend the deal; how, later, Giamatti hoped to save it; and how his successor as commissioner told millions of fans to—in effect—get lost.

*　　*　　*

One month after CBS's December 1988 announcement, Phil Mushnick began his column by saying, "Peter Ueberroth and Curt Smith have a lot in common. Mr. Smith works in Washington, where he's a devout Republican, and a senior speechwriter in the Reagan Administration. Ueberroth's a strong Republican and a Reagan man, too. Smith worked hard [in the last election] to elect a President of the United States. So did Ueberroth. It seems that the only element of their lives Smith and the outgoing Commissioner differ on is baseball. Smith loves baseball."

Thus commenced a season in which I became perhaps the most vocal critic of baseball's television deal—leading *The Sporting News* to say, in late 1989, after public outcry forced CBS to increase regular-season coverage, "If there is a hero among the fans, it is Curt Smith. He may be a villain at CBS," and the *New York Daily News* to write, "Smith hasn't forgotten fans without cable. He has been a thorn in the side of the Lords of Baseball. Smith has hammered the suits in major league baseball's Office who were a party to Ubie's great sellout." Did I enjoy my clash with baseball and CBS? No—it took time, cost friends, and burned bridges. Would I again lead the fight to preserve baseball's TV access? Faster than a Feller fastball. The "Game's" end hurt a sport I love, and the people who love *it*.

The collision began in April 1989. *Sports Illustrated* asked me to do a "Point After" column, which noted that the CBS pact violated the axiom "exposure begets promotion begets national appeal," and that CBS and baseball had "a stake in the 'Game's' reprieve." CBS had gambled everything on baseball, I wrote; baseball needed the network's window on the land. The solution: Have CBS air its 12 scheduled Saturday games, then explore other time-slot options.

For instance, CBS could present Saturday/Sunday 10:30 morning games, bridging from Pee Wee Herman and Charles Kuralt to its afternoon programming. In the East/Midwest, the "Game" might follow grocery shopping; in California, one could sample "Breakfast With Baseball." Alternately, CBS could air games at 8:00 P.M. EDT on Saturdays, bumping TV's lowest-rated menu (according to the 1988–89 Nielsen ratings, CBS's three Saturday night programs finished fifty-fourth, sixty-fourth, and sixty-seventh out of seventy prime-time network series). CBS could also cover late-night Saturday games from the West Coast, preempting its existing Rubik's Cube of old movies, talk-show repeats, and related lemons. The design would give CBS more games to sell its ad spots, recouping greater rights fees; serve its fans who, already, felt abandoned; and ensure a "Game" each weekend—if not each Saturday afternoon. Good stuff? Responded CBS and baseball, tartly: Fella, good luck.

The afternoon the *SI* piece appeared, CBS's Neal Pilson and I talked by phone. He is a Hamilton College graduate, and as that school's public relations spokesman I had met him in the late 1970s. Now, a decade later, our conversation was frigid and polite.

"You should have checked with me," he said, "before writing stuff like this."

"Why?" I said. "The facts are right."

"We know how to run our business," he countered. "We don't need help from you." (One year later, estimates put CBS's 1990 baseball losses at $100–160 million.)

"Not from me," I said, "but I think you'll need help before all of this is over."

As we spoke, CBS's baby was already being scored—in print and protests to the Commissioner's Office—as what the *Post* later called "nothing short of an abomination." Yet Pilson would not admit it (later, he blamed baseball for demanding only twelve games)—nor, at first, would Ubie, "explaining" the network abandonment by saying no one would air a "Game" (which was untrue; NBC bid, and yearns, for its return). Ueberroth, though, had a preternatural feel for public relations—he could smell a debacle a continent away. Resigning as commissioner, he told George Vecsey in May 1989, "You have a point" about the pact's inadequacy; denying parentage, he left others to justify his sport's near-suicidal contract.

Bryan Burns' first line of defense was to release a "White Paper" called "Television: A Look Ahead."

"Most sports are proud of their network pacts," said Larry Stewart of the *Los Angeles Times*. "This 'White Paper' was a historic first—the first time a sport was so defensive about a network contract they felt forced to defend it in writing." Added *Daily News* columnist Bob Raissman, "Since we've been working this beat, we have never seen a sports organization try to justify a TV deal the way baseball has." Sadly for baseball, its linen didn't wash.

Burns began by citing falling Nielsen ratings—"We were responding to the marketplace"—to defend stripping millions of baseball coverage. His tack was novel: By saying baseball had little national allure, he trashed the product he had just sold for over a billion dollars. Unfortunately, a month later, the A. C. Nielsen Company contradicted him—calling "Game" *the* decade's most popular April–August weekly sports series, its ratings more stable than any save the NFL and NBA. (A Nielsen official quipped that since World Series, League Championship Series, and All-Star Nielsens from 1980 to 1989 had plunged by greater percentages than "Game's"—1989 Star ratings were the lowest since '69—by "White Paper's" rationale, they, too, should be banned from network TV.)

Burns next touted the pact by saying CBS's exclusivity would help viewers "locate" the playoffs/Series (who missed either because of ABC/NBC's coverage?), and that baseball had received "complaints" about "big-market teams" — e.g., New York and Los Angeles — dominating network coverage. As paradoxical as it seems to argue that the way to address this problem is to lower the number of network games, baseball's CBS deal made things *worse*. In 1989 all of the twenty-six teams graced network TV, against only sixteen in 1990. More specifically: The '89 Pirates — hardly a "big-market" team — appeared seven times, compared to three appearances in 1990. The 1989 White Sox, Cubs, Mets, Tigers, Dodgers, Angels, and Braves each had eight NBC games; the Yankees, nine. No 1990 or '91 team appeared more than five times.

"Even now, when I reexamine this ridiculous 'White Paper,' I think of the Flying Dutchman," Mushnick recalled. "He sailed from port to port. Baseball went from one rationalization to another — failing to find one remotely believable. The two most remote were its *final* ports" — cable and local-team coverage.

The cable (ir)rationalization was etched by Burns, "We will [replace 'Game'] by display[ing] the bulk of our regular season in a way never before possible via cable." According to Paul Kagan Associates, 41.3 of America's 90.4 million households lack cable. Nearly 11 million homes don't even have wiring. Millions of others lack access — shut-ins, the retired, inner-city, small-town and rural, low- and middle-class viewers — the very heart of baseball's constituency. Cable also has some inherent disadvantages. Coverage is grossly uneven — from New York to San Francisco, one block has it, the next does not. Moreover, to view cable you must be in a wired room. Unlike the nets, cable isn't portable — you can't watch it at the beach. Reading the "White Paper," you asked whether we should wire ourselves.

Finally, Burns' document claimed that local-team broadcasts could replace the "Game" as baseball's prime TV carrier. This idea, too, ignored truths more powerful than Murderers Row. The CBS pact repeated — precisely — an earlier colossal miscalculation. In the 1960s, baseball slashed network exposure and shifted its focus to local TV. The result was baseball's most ruinous decade. Other truths: Individual clubcasts do nothing for fans who live outside major-league team networks; worse, varying wildly by franchise, the balkanized coverage burlesques the term "national pastime." As Bowie Kuhn wrote in his autobiography, *Hardball*, localcasts cannot sell baseball against the NFL: They create Braves' or Indians' fans, while networkcasts bore *baseball* fans. Nothing, he said, rivals the nets' "promotional, marketing, and prestige potential."

Burns and Ueberroth also knew that few clubs play games every Saturday afternoon (thus, the need for the "Game of the Week"); that, increasingly, teams were switching local broadcasts from free to pay TV (in New England, there is now no "Game of the Week," no Saturday afternoon local free TV, only New England Sports Network pay TV — and if the Sox play on Saturday night, no afternoon baseball *period*); and that the CBS schedule virtually invited football to steal baseball's regular-season cachet. With no September games, cableless America would be blacked out during the season-ending pennant races.

Said *Insight* magazine: "The network deprivation prompts serious speculation over whether the reduced visibility during the long regular season will undercut the sport's claim as the national pastime."

Countered the Commissioner's Office as the summer of '89 came and fled: Problem? What problem? We've got ours. The hell with you.

*   *   *

While Bryan Burns strove to defend the CBS contract, one of the finest public servants of any age succeeded Ueberroth as commissioner.

Many public men are weak, uncivil. A. Bartlett Giamatti was strong and gentle. His career was a metaphor for decency; he ennobled public service. And if not judged — even now — the greatest commissioner in baseball history, it is only because the insanity of the moment never gave him a chance.

I first met Bart Giamatti in Manhattan on December 1, 1988, shortly before I left the Reagan administration. Giamatti was then president of the National League, shortly to become commissioner. We talked of baseball, and literature. We spoke of love of country, and The Game. We also agreed, laughing, that the two could be synonymous.

"Our backgrounds are more than a little similar," he began, more than a little charitably. Giamatti had been a Renaissance scholar, professor of literature, and at thirty-nine president of Yale University; I had served "Little Ivy" Hamilton College. Giamatti had written articles for academic journals; I ran the *Saturday Evening Post.* Both of us loved politics and were intrigued by the canon of Catholicism; for all of that, we were *Bull Durham* members of Susan Sarandon's Church of Baseball. Our families came from Massachusetts; and I recall telling him that I was a Red Sox fan and a Nixon Republican, and asking whether that denoted masochism or loyalty. Giamatti sat back and roared his teddy bear of a laugh. "Undoubtedly both," he replied.

That meeting is frozen in memory — it struck me then, and afterward, that Giamatti was a unique mix of intellect, integrity, and whimsied vulnerability "whose life," quoting the movie *Body Heat,* "was based on trying to do the right thing."

Later, as commissioner, he would agonize over *l'affaire Pete Rose,* inherited from his predecessor; he was determined to be fair — to do the right thing. Yet it was another issue that concerned us that afternoon: Ueberroth's imminent decision to exile baseball from network TV. Ueberroth had frozen him out of the negotiations, and Giamatti said he was ignorant of their consequences. Hearing them, he grew alarmed; by August 1989, said the *Daily News,* he "was preparing to meet with CBS officials in an effort to alter the national TV deal by increasing its number of games. 'He was very upset by that arrangement,' a source close to Giamatti said." By preserving "Game of the Week," he sought the right thing for the pastime that was his passion.

Not once as commissioner did Giamatti publicly defend "Game's" demise, nor mouth absurdities about "responding to the marketplace." In letters to me, he observed, correctly, that "contracts have been signed, and I have no power to undo them"; unsaid was the idea that he wanted to change them, and would.

"Whatever you decide, I want you to keep in touch," he told me. "We think alike on the big things." Chief among them was the belief that baseball must be protected for every American. To Giamatti, football was a mastiff—hulking, imperious. Baseball was a cocker spaniel—precious and unaffected and worthy of love.

When Giamatti died, suddenly and stunningly, of a heart attack on September 1, 1989, Brewers' owner Bud Selig said that except for his father's death it marked the darkest day of his life. My father is alive—but I know what Selig meant.

Giamatti had the soul of a poet, the mind of a scholar, and a heart as big as Yankee Stadium. His loss robbed baseball, and America, of a leader and a friend. It also left the fate of baseball's television exposure to less selfless men.

*   *   *

By autumn 1989 more and more fans were beginning to realize how the CBS deal had sold baseball down the river, and, like Ueberroth, Bryan Burns went underground—leaving Giamatti's close friend and successor as commissioner, Fay Vincent, "to take the heat for a contract," said the *Washington Post,* "that a Peter Ueberroth protégé negotiated."

Able and self-effacing, Vincent had molded a magnificent career: Yale University law graduate, prominent Washington attorney, later, president of Columbia Pictures. He first met Giamatti at a 1970s cocktail party, and Vincent became Giamatti's deputy when the latter became commissioner. Now, Fay hinted that he would cleanse Ubie's wreckage. "I am searching for a solution," he wrote me in a letter. "Bart was very troubled by this contract, and so am I. We are trying to change it—it will not be easy."

As the new commissioner, Vincent watched ABC's baseball marriage end in a no-grief divorce. Trivial pursuits: The net aired its eight '89 ex–"Monday Night Baseball" games on eight straight Thursday nights, ending July 27. ABC again took a bath (paying $125 million for rights fees, and recouping less than $100 million; 30-second spot ads lured $40,000–45,000, less than half "Monday Night Football"'s rate). In its 1984–89 baseball pact, ABC never once made a profit.

More poignantly, on Saturday, September 30, 1989, NBC aired its 981st and final "Game of the Week." The place: Toronto's new Skydome. The score: Blue Jays 4, Orioles 3, a riveting contest that clinched the American League East. The announcers: Bob Costas and Tony Kubek, preceded by a thirty-minute pre-game show that chronicled "Game" as baseball's national grandstand. Related memorabilia: Lindsey Nelson and Jim Woods aired NBC's first "Game" — an exhibition match, April 6, 1957, Brooklyn versus Milwaukee. First game televised in color: June 11, 1960: Pale Hose at Fenway Park. First year of split screen, instant replay, and stop-action pictures: 1966. First night "Game": Also '66, Memorial Day evening.

At Camp David, George Bush watched "Game" expire; later, he told reporters, "It's not a decision for the White House — but the more games on free television, the better." In New York, the *Times* observed, "Only CBS can help Vincent preserve TV's oldest sports institution. And must." From Portland, Maine, to Portland, Oregon, viewers thought of "Game's" first star — CBS's Falstaffian Dizzy Dean — and his partners, Bud Blattner, a consummate professional, and Pee Wee Reese, to Diz almost kin. Or NBC's Nelson and Garagiola and Kubek, Costas, and Scully — men who loved their sport, and who helped the pastime thrive.

In the end, perhaps *USA Today*'s Rachel Shuster said best why "Game" transcended networks, and announcers: "The passing of 'Game' is one of those moments in a sports fan's life that gets marked with an asterisk. *Never the same since.* What are we going to do on Saturday afternoons next year when CBS isn't showing a game? Mow the lawn? Balance the checkbook? The options are limitless, none of them fulfilling." She noted how Saturdays revolved around getting to the TV in time, and the peerless Scully would invite us to pull up a chair. "Nothing will compare with the special homey feeling of watching the 'Game of the Week.' "

Shuster realized — like anyone who understood the "Game" — how we would all feel older without what Scully termed "a Saturday afternoon at the ballpark with a couple of old friends."

By and by, most sympathized as Fay Vincent endured a hellish autumn. First, Vincent braved calumny to help ban Pete Rose for life for gambling. Next, Giamatti's death. Then, two drab 1989 playoffs (Blue Jays-A's and Cubs-Giants — Costas, Scully, and Kubek's network farewell; miffed that some NBC officials judged him old-timey, Garagiola had resigned the previous November and been replaced by Tom Seaver) lured the event's all-time worst ratings. Finally, in his first World Series as commissioner, Al Michaels' *au revoir*, Vincent brooked an earthquake that delayed the Autumn Occasion through October 28 — a four-game, "California only" (A's-Giants) mismatch that tranquilized America and shrunk the Series' audience to another all-time low: 16.4 rating and 29 share (versus the 24/41 and 23.9/39, respectively, of 1987–88).

From the Bay Area, Vincent retreated to New York, where he confronted his remaining flash point. "It's moving forward," he said in November of undoing Ubie's folly. "We've had discussions with CBS to revise the present arrangement." His talks — like Burns' June "White Paper" — marked another historic first: The only time that public opinion had forced a sport to renegotiate its network pact. The revision, however, smelt of window dressing: A token 1990 increase from 12 to 16 regular-season games — still no weekly presence; only two games in baseball's last six weeks; and the bigs' rendition of the Great American Blackout—*no* coverage from April 21 through mid-June.

Undaunted, Vincent moved, literally, to put the "Game" behind him—traveling to Washington to testify before a Senate Judiciary Subcommittee. "Beginning next year," he said, "baseball's exposure on local and national TV will be *expanded* and *deepened* by our new telecasting arrangements. . . . The combination of local and national telecasts will provide broader coverage of the game than *ever before*."

Perhaps Vincent should have thought of those baseball fans in areas without cable and/or local coverage, like a friend of mine who lived in a small town in upstate New York.

At Christmas 1989, my ninety-year-old grandfather observed that, "Each week I've looked forward to the 'Game of the Week.' It's been a pastime of mine for as long as I can remember." Under the new arrangement, and with no local or cable games available, he was, for the first time in decades, without baseball. The sport had left behind millions for whom TV baseball *was* the "Game of the Week."

Recalling my grandfather, I wondered about the 1990 season. When would baseball—striving to explain the inexplicable—remember Joe Louis' counsel, "You can run, but you can't hide"? Of only this was I certain: We were about to enter a self-defeating and ultimately cruel regular-season black hole.

*   *   *

Since 1989, baseball's black hole has hurt the network side more than local broadcasts. In 1991, *Broadcasting* magazine would say, "For now, home team ball remains a moneymaker"—luring a record $253 million from local radio, broadcast television, and cable TV rightsholders. That year, 230 U.S. TV stations—118 in the American League—broadcast the majors locally (Canada's English- and French-speaking networks carried the Blue Jays and Expos). Baseball's largest network, the Cardinals, fused 27 stations in eight states; the Reds added 23 in seven. The Blue Jays combed eight provinces with 22 affiliates; at the other end, California and Cleveland had none. Years earlier, Merle Harmon explained of individual teamcasts, "For clubs in less populous areas—the non–New Yorks and L.A.s—local TV was a great device to help regional teams prosper." But the device was uneven, varying in effect by franchise. The 1991 imbalance cloaked every index of big-league baseball's exposure.

For instance: Rights fees ranged from four clubs earning under four million dollars each to the Yankees' forty-million-dollars-plus, annually, through the year 2000. Ditto, network size: Ten teams had twelve or more affiliates; eleven, eight or less. Games broadcast deepened the schism: The fourteen American League clubs aired 814 games over free and cable television. The Red Sox and Rangers boasted 75; the Tigers, just 45. At the same time, the twelve National League teams covered 779 games, or nearly 65 apiece (compared to the American's 58). The Cubs led with 142 games; three teams had only 50.

The gulf recalled what Vincent had said of Yankees' telecasts: "Local baseball was all I had to live for [after a serious accident in 1956]—it helped me recover. If it was an off-day or rainout, I was very sad." Three decades later, it never seemed to occur to him that other Americans who lacked localcast access might simply *need* network coverage.

By 1991, other media carriers were just as disparate. Six teams eschewed pay-per-view TV. Yet the Orioles' Home Team Sports and Yankees' Madison Square Garden network aired (respectively) 85 and 103 games to nearly 2 million and 4.4 million homes; the Astros carried 50 games over the 2.4 million-subscriber Home Sports Entertainment; and the Expos' Sports Network reached 5.4 million viewers. On radio, 1,229 outlets—topping 1975's 871 but down from 1990's 1,320—proselytized the pastime; "baseball," said San Diego broadcast director Jim Winters, "is the salvation of AM radio today." To prove his point, the Reds, Royals, and Cardinals flaunted (respectively) 98, 130, and baseball's all-time high of 135 affiliates; nine eclipsed 48. At the other end, the Padres had only 4; the Giants and Angels, 14 and 18.

Such crazy-quilt coverage was partly broadcast by sixty-five former players-turned-announcers. Among them: the Blue Jays' Buck Martinez, the Padres' Rick Monday, and the White Sox' Ken Harrelson, Tom Paciorek, and Chico Carrasquel. In all, ten Hall-of-Fame players doubled as broadcasters: From Baltimore's Brooks Robinson and Jim Palmer to Don Drysdale, returning to Dodger Stadium in 1988, to Detroit's Al Kaline and George Kell.

Since 1988, CBS's John Rooney had become a fixture on Pale Hose radio; Sean McDonough and Bob Starr now shone on Red Sox radio and TV; two men who began with the Hawaii Islanders, Al Conin and Ken Wilson, anchored the Angels' wireless and video; and ex–Columbus Clippers' Voice Tom Hamilton joined Herb Score on Cleveland's WWWE. At Tiger Stadium, Ernie Harwell and Paul Caray staged their nineteenth and, as it turned out, final season—the league's longest-running radio team. In Kansas City, Paul Splittorf began his fourth TV season. In Minnesota, Jim Kaat and Dick Bremer observed their third on WCCO. At the Oakland Coliseum, Monte Moore again reigned as mouthpiece of the ex-Finleys—and the Yankees had welcomed Kubek, Bobby Murcer, Tom Seaver, John Sterling, Al Trautwig, Dewayne Staats, and arriving from Memorial Stadium, Joe Angel, into their crammed-crushed-squeezed booth. (In 1992, the year Seaver entered the Hall of Fame, Angel returned to Baltimore.)

Turning to the National, hello to the Braves' Don Sutton, speaking with Skip Caray and Pete Van Wieren to TBS's fifty-two-million-plus homes. Skip's father, Harry—who with his son and grandson aired a 1991 Atlanta-Cubs' game—was now flanked by three ex-players: Steve Stone on TV and radio's Ron Santo and Bob Brenly. Vin Scully started his forty-second season with the Dodgers, Dave Van Horne his twenty-third at Montreal, and George

Grande his first at Busch Stadium. Bill Brown was aiding Milo Hamilton and Larry Dierker at the Astrodome. "This Bud's for you" was being pitched by the Wrigleys' new radio mikeman, Thom Brennaman, Marty's son. Hank Greenwald had returned from Yankee Stadium as Voice of the future San Jose Giants.

Claude Pepper, the populist United States Senator, once said, "One has the right to be wrong in a democracy." There was much of each in local late-1980s and early-nineties broadcasting.

Wrong was breaking up that old Red Sox gang of mine. Ned Martin moved from free TV to the Sox cable outlet, the New England Sports Network. His once-radio partner, Jim Woods, died in 1988. A year later, Boston's wireless Voice, Ken Coleman, retired after nearly a half-century of play-by-play. Wrong, too, were the absence of Vince Lloyd and Lou Boudreau, retiring at Wrigley Field; the 1988 retirement of Jerry Doggett and semiretirement of Ernie Johnson after the 1989 season, returning to air assorted 1990–91 Braves' games; the presence of the Orioles' Jim Palmer, perhaps the worst TV play-by-play man I have ever heard; and Ralph Kiner's mangling of the English language. In 1990, the Metsman began a game by saying, "Live from Pittsburgh, New York." At other times, he identified Howard Johnson as Walter Johnson, Darryl Strawberry as Darryl Thornberry, Marv Throneberry as Marv Strawberry, Gary Carter as Gary Cooper, and Milt May as Mel Ott.

Worst of all was a dismissal that mocked common sense.

In December 1990, a week before Christmas, the Tigers fired Ernie Harwell for no apparent reason. Ernie had broadcast the Tigers' 1987 division championship; in the 1988–89 season, he aired CBS's American League playoffs. He was, and is, an institution — the Bengals' signature — leading the *New York Times* to say, "Bumper stickers, T-shirts, and billboards ('Say it ain't so, Bo') appeared, denouncing Bo Schembechler, the team president. At a Red Wings' hockey game in Joe Louis Arena, fans began to chant, 'We Want Ernie! We want Ernie!' " Talk-show phone lines and newspaper headlines "sizzled with threats of boycotts against the team, the radio station, and the pizza marketed by the team owner, Tom Monaghan. The furor wasn't just local. Nationally, it [was] like losing a good friend and wondering why."

Harwell's firing, the *Times* opined, was radio's "equivalent of a killing freeze." *Detroit News* columnist Mitch Albom added, "What the Tigers did . . . was one of the most shameful acts I have ever witnessed from a sports franchise. They took a man who is a national treasure and told him to start packing. They took a man who literally has taught baseball to hundreds of thousands of fans, summer after summer, and they told him he's too old, his time is up."

Ultimately, Schembechler and the Tigers' flagship station, WJR, settled, *ex post facto,* on a defense: They were afraid Ernie would retire and leave them without a replacement. Since Harwell, at seventy-two, had no intention of retiring, their allegation seemed ludicrous. So did the club's and station's claims that the other greased Harwell's good-bye. (Either could have prevented the dismissal.)

Ernie fulfilled the final year of his contract while the Tigers conducted a search for his successor. (In November 1991, Detroit named the Mariners' No. 2 man, Rick Rizzs.) It was one long glorious farewell — a triumphal tour of American League cities.

He was given a day at Tiger Stadium; the club presented a lithograph of the shrine at Michigan and Trumbull. He reveled in a standing ovation at his final home game — the fans chanting his name after the sixth inning. "It seemed like forever," Ernie said of the applause. "They were paying this tribute to me. What really touched me was that it was so spontaneous. It's something I'll never forget." During Detroit's final series, Harwell even met George Bush in the Oval Office before going to Capitol Hill for a tear-streaked luncheon. "Someone said I was lucky," he laughed. "They pointed out usually you have to die before people say nice things about you."

From Belding, Michigan, Tony Hanley, thirteen, captured the public's tangle of outrage and love. "If you need anything," he wrote Harwell, "a job, or money, or you need a place to stay, or even a new organ, just call on me." Typically, Ernie responded, and the two became pals — much like America's relationship with Harwell. One writer had called Harwell, "the voice of baseball." There was something right — so *proper* — about the adoration which now punctuated his career.

Between 1988 and 1990, also rightly, Lindsey Nelson, Harry Caray, and Byrum Saam were elected to the Hall of Fame; Joe Garagiola, elected in '91, had returned in 1990 to NBC's "Today" program. In 1991, Red Barber received a Peabody Award for six decades of excellence as a broadcaster and one as a commentator on National Public Radio's "Morning Edition"; eight Spanish-speaking radio networks beamed the game to a growing constituency; and in Baltimore Chuck Thompson, having retired in 1987, returned to air more than eighty radiocasts. At year's end, he got roaring applause at the final-ever night game in Memorial Stadium, then traveled in 1992 to the Orioles' new park. There was much to enjoy about Chuck and the Birds' Voice, Jon Miller. That was not true of every big-league booth.

*   *   *

"Look at this local broadcasting coverage — effective in places, often a boon for baseball. But it is totally irregular. Anyone who believes it can ever replace network TV that goes into every home," Phil Mushnick predicted in 1989, "probably thinks Leona Helmsley is Mother Theresa in disguise."

No one likes a person who says, "I told you so." So be it: I told you so. What baseball said *would* happen, didn't. What I, Mushnick, and others said would happen, *did.* Local 1990–91 broadcasts did not, magically, replace "Game of the Week." Nor did cable: ESPN's ratings were a disaster. At CBS, baseball's other net was mocked or ignored altogether — playing Harold Stassen to NBC's pre-'90 FDR. For millions of Americans, baseball disappeared from TV consciousness as Poland disappeared from the map of Europe in September 1939. Yet who should be surprised? Never was a sport so *wrong* about so *much*.

Baseball engaged reality April 28, 1990 — the first baseball Saturday *sans* "Game" in thirty-eight years. Instead of that afternoon's A's–Red Sox, Cubs-Dodgers, or Angels-Yankees games, CBS presented an NBA doubleheader. For the next two months, until resuming coverage June 16, it proffered events from the NBA playoffs to Kemper and Western Opens to the Heritage Classic. *Anything* but baseball.

By early May, Vincent's office was bombarded by hundreds of letters and phone calls. Bryan Burns, resurfacing, claimed that "we've received, maybe, a dozen letters from around the nation regarding the 'Game.' " (At that point, *I* had copies of more than fifty unsolicited letters.) In particular, the uproar focused on cable's unavailability. Responding, Burns told *USA Today,* "In those areas that can't get cable, people can buy a dish, and ESPN will sell them the service." This moved the *Daily News* to write: "Screw the fan who struggles to pay his food bill. The hell with those who have no access — technically or financially — to cable. Does Burns *really* think a guy struggling to support his family can plunk down that much money [as much as $2,000] for a dish? If he does, he's lost it — totally."

That same month, the NBA — whose regular season, unlike baseball's, matters not at all — announced a deal which ensured up to twenty-six games on NBC, annually, during 1991–94. "We were determined," said basketball commissioner David Stern, pouring salt on baseball's wounds, "to have as many games as possible reach one hundred percent of America." (Unlike baseball's pact, pro hoops' also cared about kids — demanding, as part of its package, a half-hour series, "NBA Inside Stuff," which ran each Saturday morning on NBC). Trying to change the venue, Burns' aide, Leslie Lawrence, wrote a letter to those who scored "Game's" end. "Baseball's national and local telecast activity," it read, "have resulted in a larger number of local telecasts than ever before."

Spying this misrepresentation, reporters blasted the Commissioner's Office, and forced Vincent to admit to the House Subcommittee on Cable in May 1990 that, aping *Porgy and Bess,* his November 1989 testimony "[hadn't] necessarily been so." Two months earlier, *Broadcasting* magazine reported the number of '90 localcasts had actually *dropped* to 1,639 from 1989's 1,653. (In 1991, it plunged further to 1,593.) The reason was that clubs were moving to pay-per-view cable — up from 1989's 1,061 games to 1,172 (and in 1991, 1,235). Chastened, Vincent heard other sports heads — Stern, hockey's John Ziegler, and the NFL's Paul Tagliabue — discuss their television game-plans for the 1990s. Fay could not partake: Seventeen *months* after the CBS announcement, baseball's commissioner spent his time besieged by hostile questions from congressmen: Why had the majors cut off millions of loyal fans?

Like Lady Macbeth's, Baseball's damn spot would not out — and as its stonewalling hardened, the discord spread: Major newspapers condemned the "Game"'s death. So did columnists from Bill Madden to Bob Rubin. During 1990, it became clear who was right, and who was wrong.

The Mets showed only three games in the eleven "Game"-less Saturdays; the Yankees, one; the Red Sox, zero: The twenty-six clubs averaged a near invisible 1.9 Saturday afternoon telecasts. (On Saturday, May 12, exactly *one* local game was shown in the entire country in the 1:00–4:00 P.M. EDT formerly reserved for "Game.") In almost every community, every Saturday afternoon, free-TV baseball simply ceased to exist.

Nor did cable fill the vacuum. Originally, Burns and Ueberroth promised ESPN coverage that would revolutionize the pastime — coast to coast, April– October, anywhere there was a cable hookup and a TV. But far fewer viewers than expected tuned in, and ESPN lost an estimated fifty-three million dollars on baseball. By August *Sports Illustrated* was writing, "If you think George Steinbrenner had it tough this summer [Vincent ousted him from the Yankees], consider what has happened at ESPN. In its first major league season, the total sports network has racked up losses faster than a ski shop in Miami." Baseball, said the network's president and C. E. O., Roger Werner, "is a substantial loss leader for us. With luck, maybe by the fourth year we will break even." (If so, Werner would miss it; he was fired two weeks after the *SI* story.)

ESPN had predicted an average 3.8 Nielsen rating (or 2.2 million homes) overall and 5.0 (2.8 million homes) for "Sunday Night Baseball." *Ex-cuuuuse* me. Baseball averaged a 2.1 rating — trailing even the Winston Cup auto racing series' 3.1; Sunday telecasts averaged 3.0, a shortfall of 1.1 million homes. Ratings were 75 percent higher than programs for the same '89 time slots, and the net's ad sales rose 70 percent. Still, advertisers received slashed rates for thirty-second spot ads, and buyers guaranteed certain ratings were compensated with free ad time. "So far," said Werner in June, "we've given away nine million dollars worth of inventory." Months later, his successor, Steve Bornstein, said of ratings 70 percent of what ESPN projected: "We suffered some big losses."

ESPN's camera coverage was adequate, often relying on local feeds. (The Unimmaculate Exception: The already legendary bungle of Red Sox outfielder Tom Brunansky's last-out, ninth-inning October 3, 1990, catch which clinched the A. L. East on the final night of the season. The *what:* Both Bruno and the baseball disappeared from camera view in Fenway Park's right-field corner, behind the part of the grandstand that juts out. Worse, no replay showed whether or not he caught the ball — "not from any angle," said the *New York Times,* "not even a slow-motion version of the original view." The *why:* Instead of keeping its eye on the ball, ESPN's six replay cameras focused on possible in-stand reaction shots. The *outcome:* "Murphy's law struck," said Bornstein. "What used to happen to the Red Sox, happened to us.") Nor could one deride the net's baseball commitment: ESPN captured moments like Dave Righetti's ninth-inning bases-loaded May 1990 strikeout of Ken Griffey, Jr., to preserve a Yankees victory; the dramatic June twin-bill where fans, watching from 7:30 P.M. to 1:20 A.M.,

EDT, saw Dave Stewart and Fernando Valenzuela hurl no-hitters on the same night—a first in baseball history; and a mad set of late-season games between the Red Sox and Blue Jays. (In autumn 1991, it featured the contending Dodgers and Braves.) As pledged, ESPN switched from one game to another, and kept viewers abreast of personalities and trends.

ESPN's announcers were also capable—though, as *The National* columnist Norman Chad said, some of its pairings resembled "folks who ought to be announcing blue-light specials at your local department store." Bluest was the twice-weekly team of Gary Thorne and Norm Hitzges: "It threatens the very core of the game," he wrote, "if not the nation at large." Banal and utterly humorless, Thorne achieved the impossible—making one yearn for Bob Gamere. (Calling Brunansky's catch, Thorne at first said, "The Red Sox win!" Then, "the tone of his voice changed," the *Times* reported. "No! He dropped the ball! He dropped the ball!") Trying to echo basketball's Dick Vitale, Hitzges sounded like a grating Tom, Dick, and Harry. (Like Dave Marash, host of ESPN's "Baseball Tonight," Norm was fired in early 1991.) Mediocre, too, was the coupling of Chris Berman and Tommy Hutton; Berman, the grand host of "SportsCenter," should have stayed in the studio. Yet Sean McDonough sparkled as ESPN's Tuesday-night announcer, as did analyst Dave Campbell and former Met Steve Zabriskie—"a low-key professional," as Chad noted, "devoid of hype or hysteria"—on Fridays. Best of all was the Voice of the network's Sunday showcase game, dubbed by writer Larry Littwin the "Rich Little of the baseball world."

Even as a child, Jon Miller had embraced the airwaves. "I grew up just outside Oakland," he said, "and I remember when I was nine. Did you ever hear of Strat-O-Matic, the baseball board game? I would broadcast the games as I played them, in the voices of Russ Hodges, Vin Scully, and Chuck Thompson. I did crowd noise, the P.A., big crowd, small crowd."

"A tad out of the ordinary," I said.

"Yes, I guess you could say I had an odd childhood. My friends were out surfing, and I was home playing the Giants against the Dodgers"—and recording them, too.

At fifteen, Miller became the Voice of Haywood High School. At basketball games, he sat at a table, with call letters KMIL draped over the side. The next morning, he was heard on the school's intercom, playing the highlights of the game he had announced into his reel-to-reel tape recorder.

A year later, Miller vaulted to Candlestick Park and the Oakland Coliseum, broadcasting for himself on the recorder. Fast-forward to Jon's sophomore year in college, when he became a sportscaster at a new TV station in Santa Rosa. "The pay was awful, the hours were worse, and it was incredible fun," he said. After another year, he leapfrogged again—this time, improbably, to the National Hockey League California Seals.

"How'd that happen?" I said.

"It was a lark," he recalled, laughing his Ed McMahon–style laugh. "Charley Finley owned the team, and I sent him a letter applying for the TV job." The actor's pause. "Only one problem. They didn't have a TV affiliate." Soon that changed, and Miller, a ripe twenty, did hockey play-by-play until the Seals folded in 1973. Out of work, he heard from Monte Moore. "He was, of course, the A's' Voice, and asked if I'd be interested. I was unemployed. What was I going to say — 'no'?"

Across 1978–83, Miller said *yes* to moves to Texas, Fenway Park, and Memorial Stadium. He became a frequent guest on national talk shows, especially ESPN cable's "SportsLook," spurned job offers from Wrigley Field and Yankee Stadium, and did backup "Games" during 1986–89 for NBC. Then, in 1990, he evolved into what Cole Porter called "the top" — appointed the Number One announcer on ESPN's "Sunday Night Baseball" (in '91, becoming, too, the Orioles' TV as well as radio domo). Miller welcomed the ESPN assignment: "It's a very exciting opportunity," he said in February 1990, "if you consider standing on the edge of a cliff exciting." Two years later he still stood there, having elevated his listeners.

He is "The Franchise," *The National* observed, "intelligent and funny, with great broadcast instincts and sensibilities. His is a voice that sounds just right for baseball." Jon Miller was superb, and brought elegance to his craft; his bass was deep and resonant, and his knowledge spanned both leagues. On occasion, he left play-by-play to imitate public address announcers Bob Shepherd and Sherm Feller; he showed the gift for mimicry which "has made him a staple on the banquet circuit, as his well-fed body will attest." A friend mused, "He does a better Scully than Scully." Baseball entertains you, Miller said, and amazes you and you care about it. "What I love is the company of baseball."

In the end, ESPN's ratings Titanic flowed from a problem as clear as it was avoidable: Who in their right mind would watch six "network" games each week? "With so much coverage, there was no novelty," said Bob Costas, "no way you could point to a game and say, 'This is a big event.' Baseball is such a special game. Yet with its cable overkill, no game was special. If you missed Tuesday night, big deal — you could always watch on X or Y or Z night."

ESPN loaded too much coverage onto too small a part of America. Which brings us to the greatest fact baseball would prefer to, but could not, ignore: CBS's virtual *non*coverage of the 1990–91 regular seasons.

*   *   *

Many had predicted that — given its twenty-five-year baseball absence, and slipshod schedule — CBS's return to the big leagues would be difficult. We were wrong. It was worse. "CBS not carrying baseball every week has had more of an impact than I thought it would," NBC's Marv Albert said in September 1990. "You need to be on every week to develop a rhythm of presentation with viewers." In April, CBS talked, grandly, of baseball's "dream season"; months later, it had become a nightmare.

Sans continuity, the net's aimless coverage gave no one — announcers, cameramen, or technicians — the chance to master this most difficult of TV sports:

The network missed ground balls, butchered relay plays, and bannered insipid visuals. (For example, CBS's graphic announcing that the Mets' Kevin McReynolds was, "Two for twenty-four in late-inning pressure situations.") Unlike NBC, CBS also ran few in-house commercials to promote its telecasts—making it even harder for fans to find the games that *were* on TV.

All of this surely hurt a CBS announcing team, which had such trouble meshing, that *USA Today* columnist Rudy Martzke wrote in July 1991, after a month-long network hiatus, "Jack Buck and Tim McCarver might have to hold a reunion before CBS's [upcoming] telecast of the Pirates-Dodgers game."

Buck replaced Brent Musburger—fired partly because of atrocious pre-season ad sales—as CBS's Number 1 baseball man ten days before the 1990 opener. Critics expected the Hall of Fame announcer and McCarver to form a duo rivaling Scully and Garagiola. Instead, the two talked past one another, ignored each other's lines, and forged a chemistry which would have flunked Introductory 101. That October, the executive producer of CBS Sports, Ted Shaker, said, "I wish we'd had more regular-season games with which to practice. But we played with the hand we were dealt."

In place of a "Game of the Week," CBS scattered sixteen regular-season games among its basketball playoffs, football games, and tennis matches. To wit: On Saturday, September 1, 1990, it *could* have aired any of the then-division leaders: Red Sox (versus the Yankees), Reds (against the Cubs), Mets (playing the Giants), or A's (against the Rangers). Instead, CBS televised six and a half hours of early rounds of the U.S. Tennis Open, completing baseball's snub with an Eagles-Steelers pre-season football game. The next Saturday, no baseball—eight hours of tennis. Ditto, September 15—two college football games.

Even when CBS resumed coverage, it still made baseball fans its lowest priority. To protect cable's exclusivity, decisive late-season CBScasts—among them, September 22's Red Sox-Yankees—were blacked out in the markets that cared most—Boston and New York. "Incredible," said *Boston Herald* TV columnist Jim Baker. "Here you had the year's most important stretch, and baseball *still* was protecting local pay-TV. Screw non-cable viewers. Forget the general public." The October 6–12 *TV Guide* observed, "CBS approaches its World Series broadcast having received plenty of flak from viewers for slowing down its baseball coverage during September, just when the pennant races were heating up." The pattern renewed itself in 1991: From August 4 to mid-September, the sport was showcased twice. When CBS finally deigned to air September 14's Braves-Dodgers game—two teams battling for the pennant, in what *Sports Illustrated* called the net's "first compelling game of the season"—it pulled the plug in mid-game after rain delayed its coverage. CBS's refusal to preempt local news for baseball caused CBS affiliate switchboards to light up like a nova. Said *SI:* "CBS seems to stand for Covers Baseball Sporadically. The general impression among baseball fans is that CBS just doesn't care."

With no weekly "Game" to ritualize viewing habits, fans didn't know when games were scheduled. "Baseball has gone underground," read the *New York Times,* "almost disappearing from free television." It was bad enough that CBS flaunted its distaste for weekly baseball. On July 12, 1990 – during a seventy-three-minute rain delay in which the network showed not player interviews, nor highlights of past All-Star Games, but leaving baseball in the lurch, a repeat of the show "Rescue 911" – it even demeaned the All-Star Game.

"It was an amazingly revealing moment," Mushnick said, "because it showed how little CBS thought of baseball. When the rain came, the network had such little faith in the sport's ability to hold viewers that it snubbed a chance to talk with its stars." He shook his head. "This was CBS's first year in baseball – and given a chance to promote the game, it said, 'Hey, we're outa' here.' "

"How did baseball react?" I said.

"Hell, they took it like the little lambs they are. They'd already gotten their bucks from CBS – they didn't care whether CBS showed *Rebecca of Sunnybrook Farm.* Placed in the same situation, the NFL would have blown its stack. That night showed how little passion CBS and, by his acquiescence, Fay Vincent had for the game. To them, baseball only counted as a prop."

At CBS Radio, baseball was anything *but.* In 1985, the network began a five-year, thirty-two-million-dollar contract. Voices like Harwell, Dick Stockton, Jerry Coleman, and John Rooney aired the All-Star Game and league playoffs; Buck did play-by-play of the 1983–89 World Series; CBS Radio blanketed listeners from Bangor to Anchorage. Between 1990 and 1993, as part of a fifty-million-dollar pact, the network added twenty new Sunday night and four holiday games to its Saturday schedule – all told, 52 games over 26 weeks – as well as special programming that included live coverage of the Hall of Fame induction ceremonies, special broadcasts preceding the All-Star Game and World Series in both English and Spanish, and a fifteen-part pre-season preview, anchored by Rooney. Best of all, it hired Harwell to air its 1992 Saturday afternoon games.

The contrast to CBS-TV was antipodal. "Look at America's television sports columnists all during this time," said Jack Craig. "None of us were writing about the sport. Why? Only network coverage reaches every reader, and baseball wasn't a network player"; at the same time, other sports were examined ad nauseum. In July and August (1990), once considered baseball season, *TV Guide* ran a four-part series on the NFL's new video pact; later, in its fall preview issue, America's largest-selling magazine devoted a page to pro football – and not one word to baseball 1990 and/or '91. The *Washington Post* TV columnist Mark Asher spoke for many when he said, "I've watched less baseball in 1990 than any year I remember." Larry Stewart focused on the trickle-down effect. "Baseball being off the nets' radar screen didn't just hurt it nationally – it harmed it locally. Take the '90 Dodgers – an interesting, contending team, but their TV audience plunged. Without a network TV foundation to bolster interest, many clubs' local ratings fell off of a cliff. The lack of a weekly national presence hurt baseball at every possible level."

Ultimately, baseball's TV deal spawned *Poseidon Adventure* ratings. It is true that the bigs led Nielsen's 1990 chart for 10 of baseball's 15 TV weekends — so much for "White Paper's" claim that the games didn't appeal to audiences when compared to sports like golf and auto racing. Yet CBS's schedule averaged a 4.7 Nielsen rating versus NBC's 5.4 in 1989, showing — what? a) Viewers, correctly, knew CBS's baseball treatment to be substandard to the Peacocks', and b) just as likely, "Because this schedule forgot the baseball fan," Mel Allen said as we celebrated the first communications scholarship in his name at my alma mater, the State University of New York at Geneseo, "the fan found it easy to forget baseball." In 1991, *The Sporting News* reported, "baseball on television hit rock bottom." CBS's May 5 coverage lured an all-time low 3.1 rating for a network telecast not shown against an NFL game; its September 21 game pulled only 2.8. Two months earlier, the All-Star Game reaped the second-lowest numbers (17.4/32 percent share) since 1968's move to prime-time — and far behind 1970's All-Star record of 28.5/54 percent.

Lisa McWalters is director of national broadcasting for Vitt Media International. In 1991, she observed, in shades of the 1960s, "Baseball is becoming less and less popular."

Perhaps she was thinking of how Game One of the 1990 LCS had the lowest prime-time rating in playoffs history; crowed Don Criqui on NBC's *News at Sunrise,* "The first four prime-time games of the 1990 playoffs are the lowest-rated ever." (This dubious record lasted only until Games One and Two of the '91 American League playoff.) Perhaps she meant the '90 World Series, which was also a disaster: Originally asking $300,000 per thirty-second commercial, CBS sold some for $240,000; Classic ratings were second-lowest (20.6/36 percent) since the move to prime time in 1971. (The seven-game 1991 Twins-Braves' classic jump-started ratings: 24.0/39 percent.) Perhaps Lisa remembered how two months later, CBS sought a *refund* from baseball because of its losses. "I assume CBS's baseball strategy has to be a big disappointment to them," gloated NBC Sports president Dick Ebersol. "This proves that baseball needs to be on two networks, not one." More probably, she recalled how CBS eliminated thirty-minute pre-game shows in favor of regular programming for its weeknight 1991 LCS games — jibed *Times* columnist Bill Carter, "Just two years into the contract with CBS, baseball's value as prime-time entertainment has been drastically diminished. Baseball was supposed to entice viewers to watch CBS programs, not the other way around" — and another event which proved that just when you thought CBS's baseball disdain couldn't multiply, it did.

In 1990, Vincent and Pilson announced a Championship Series schedule the *Daily News* headlined, "Fay ball: CBS caters to pigskin." Unlike NBC/ABC's playoffs coverage, with games aired back-to-back on successive days and blanketing the weekend, CBS's seemed designed by Paul Tagliabue: Like baseball's regular season, the playoff slate was disjointed, and staggered to accommodate pro and college football. The National League series began Thursday and Friday, then took the entire weekend off; the American's didn't commence until Saturday; even if each series went seven games, stretched over eleven days (prior playoffs had taken no more than nine), they would only grace the *same* day three times. The schedule reeked of off days, no Saturday or Sunday afternoon games, and a checkerboard of odd starting times. The *Chicago Tribune*'s Bob Verdi asked, "Have any Chicago teams been confused" by the chaos? His answer: "Well, the Blackhawks hired a goalies' coach, Vladislav Tretiak, from the Soviet Union even though he can't speak English. Then they sent a Czech goalie, Dominik Hasek, to the minor leagues because he can't speak English. That doesn't have much to do with baseball, but neither does CBS."

"Remember that unforgettable statement Ueberroth made when he announced the CBS deal?," the *Daily News'* Bob Raissman said, and at that moment he was one of God's irate men with a sense of humor.

I nodded. "The one where he said that with only CBS carrying games, fans wouldn't have to worry about not being aware where the playoffs were?"

"Look at the '90 playoff schedule. One network, and you needed a computer just to *find* the games." He thought back to better days. "With NBC and ABC, it ran like clockwork. The National would be on in the afternoon, the American at night. Next day, reverse it. The moron of the year could keep it straight. With CBS, Einstein couldn't have figured it out."

Like the rest of Columbia's coverage, its playoffs were a fiasco, and moved writer Peter Pascarelli to score "CBS's novel approach to promoting its showing of baseball—namely, keep it a secret." Who, I asked Raissman, arranged the '90 schedule—Vincent or CBS?

"Both did, but you have to blame Vincent," he said. "I understand CBS—they have a business agenda. To them, unlike NBC, college football and the NFL are more important than baseball's second-biggest event. What's unbelievable is that Vincent didn't fight. A playoff of fits and starts—what kind of commissioner is that?

"What kind of message, too?"

"The whole deal sends a message a deaf man could hear. It's more important to pacify CBS than to serve a loyal baseball fan base. And the thing is, every time baseball turns the other cheek, it encourages CBS to treat baseball like a tramp."

In 1991, Raissman noted, the NBA playoffs would end in early June; at the other extreme of baseball's year, the NFL—starting its season one week earlier—was now stretching 16 games over 17 weeks. "Baseball's getting squeezed, and it has no network or commissioner to defend it. Look at what CBS is doing with tennis. They won't televise 'Game' in September because of prior U.S. Open programming. But starting in 1991, it dropped coverage of the first Sunday of the Open. Why? To accommodate the expanded NFL schedule."

"What it declines to do for baseball, it does for the NFL."

"Bingo," he said, "at the drop of a hat. And the result is less popularity."

An October 18, 1990, *New York Times* poll showed baseball interest falling since 1985: Less than one in five Americans (19 percent) were "very interested" in baseball; 43 percent had "no interest at all." From other sources came similar alarum. A 1990 *U.S. News* survey showed the percentage of Americans for whom baseball was their favorite sport to watch had plunged to 17 from 39 in 1948. A 1991 *Sports Illustrated for Kids* survey answered by 4,478 subscribers (ages nine to twelve) revealed that "boys and girls preferred reading about pro basketball (57 percent) to reading about . . . baseball (17 percent)."

That same year, in an *SI* nationwide poll, conducted by Lieberman Research of New York, 60 percent of respondents said they were most interested in pro football, paralleling results from an *SI* poll five years earlier. Baseball was a distant second with 52 percent — down 7 per cent from 1986. Pro hoops was third at 34 percent — up 4. Wrote columnist Tony Kornheiser: "Football is still king. Baseball is slipping. Basketball is rising. The *SI* poll says that the average football fan is younger and better educated than the average baseball fan. Baseball's thickest fan base — the only category where it beats football — is among people 65 and older, the same group that still listens to AM radio."

The decline's cause was as clear as its extent. According to Nielsen Media Research, only 16 of the 637 sporting events televised in 1991 by the three networks, were baseball games. College and pro football accounted for 22 percent of the events; college and pro basketball, 20 percent; golf, 18 percent; and multisports programming, 11 percent. Baseball tallied a pathetic 5 percent — out of sight, out of mind.

Much of this sprang from Fay Vincent's refusal to simply concede a mistake, then correct it. As 1990 ebbed, the *Washington Post* said, "Vincent could create unbelievable good will by reinstating a Saturday Game of the Week. With the advertising market flat, CBS could be happy to have 11 more games for which to sell commercial spots. And Vincent would be relieved of defending a contract many fans find indefensible. To two entities that need positive publicity, maybe that solution is too simple."

It was. As commissioner, Fay Vincent began as the victim of Ubie's sellout; in 1990–91, he became its accomplice.

*   *   *

In December of 1991, CBS replaced Jack Buck with Sean McDonough. Several years earlier, Buck, ironically, had emphasized the value of baseball marketing. "I'm absolutely amazed when I go up to Wrigley Field. The place is packed, and there's nobody over thirty years old," he said. "And the last few years I'm seeing the same thing in St. Louis and other cities. After that long stretch when baseball was being knocked as an old man's game, baseball is really all the way back among the young. And the reason is that it has finally learned how to sell itself." At the ballpark, true. But not on network television and other national electronic and print media—those catalysts of American thought and behavior.

Not all the way back.

Not yet.

Will baseball ever again be "all-meaning . . . the link with the outside," as Willie Morris wrote of his 1940s childhood in Yazoo City, Mississippi? I doubt it. Ours is a more heterogenous, fractured, restless country: At its best, baseball is too—what?—Rockwellian for some. No one game will dwarf America the way baseball once did. But the pastime can be better, do more, shed—as it has over the last decade—the marketing sleepwalk silhouette it cast over the mid-'60s to mid-'70s. It can again, in sum, be *primus inter pares.*

In 1977, for instance, the pastime's first syndicated television series, "This Week in Baseball," took to the airwaves. Narrated, baroquely, by The Voice—"Mel *is* 'This Week,' " Merle Harmon said. "I've never seen a show like it so closely synonymous with one person"—the program was a half-hour potpourri of major-league highlights, lowlights, features, and comic miscellany, and became sport's highest-rated TV serial, a fetching and inspired display. Seen, today, in nearly 80 percent of the country, "The show's got a waiting list of sponsors," said Joe Reichler, its patriarch and director, who was as responsible as anyone for weaving Allen, after a decade's hiatus, back into baseball's cloth. "I knew Mel hadn't done anything on a national scale for a long time—in a way, he was like a golden flash from the past. But quality is quality, I knew the voice, and I figured, 'Hell, if he was great in the forties and fifties, the early sixties, why wouldn't it work again? Why couldn't fans love him now?' "

It had; they did; as an ancillary dividend, the series revitalized Mel's career (by the eighties, Allen was handling Yankees' SportsChannel cablecasts, highlight films and other sports voice-overs, and commercials for such entities as General Mills and Eastman Kodak. "It's not wrong to call him 'Mr. Baseball,' " Joe Falls said in 1984. "Allen has been at it for over six decades, and that's a tremendous accomplishment"; noted Dick Young, "He's the Comeback Kid. His voice—that wonderful, unmistakable voice—is all over the place"); and one felt almost irrational pleasure at *Sports Illustrated*'s profile of The Voice as "back where he belongs, an old campaigner, a keeper of tradition. If baseball is back, Mel Allen must be too," it read. "Salaries and cities and even grass may change, but Allen, the venerable Voice of Summer, remains forever the same. 'Hello, everybody, this is Mel Allen!' he says at the start of every Yankee game on cable TV. The voice is rich, thick, and southern, to many the most recognizable in baseball. When you hear it, it's summer again, a lazy July or August afternoon with sunlight creeping across the infield. For years he was a forgotten man, but it has all come back to him in abundance. The taste must be sweet. Like the game itself, Allen is timeless." Said Reichler: "Everywhere I go, ballplayers tell me they watch 'This Week.' It's like a status symbol—you see a good play made during the week and somebody'll say, 'Jesus, just wait until Mel gets a hold of *that* one.' " Added *TV Guide*: "Allen's smooth delivery with a trademark 'How 'bout that?' is central to the show's appeal."

In 1981, baseball's appeal was buoyed by "The Baseball Bunch," an Emmy Award–winning program hosted by Johnny Bench, designed, primarily, for children, and debuting over 118 stations—"We brought in the San Diego Chicken for a light touch, Tom Lasorda to play a character called 'The Wizard,' and child actors to play the Bunch," said Reichler. "Our whole aim was to make the show entertaining enough so that kids would pay attention to the lessons it taught"—and in the mid-1980s, by two more successful offshoots of Major League Baseball Productions (MLBP): "The Greats of the Game," a Tim McCarver–hosted retrospective on yesterday's heroes, and the made-for-and with-ESPN series, "Baseball's Greatest Hits." "Sure, we got started late," avowed Joe Podesta, former president of MLBP's umbrella group, the Major League Baseball Promotion Corporation. "When I first came to baseball in 1973, the only films we did were the highlights of the World Series and All-Star Game. That was the only historic record of the game. Now we've got our syndicated series—and we aim not just at hard-core but also borderline fans." Said Bryan Burns, in a rare bow to fact, "Nineteen eighty-five was our first year for an effort I'm very proud of—the Baseball Newsatellite facility in Stamford, Connecticut, which downlinks the signals of all local TV baseball games—that is, keeps track of practically every play in the baseball season. [In 1986, the bigs also bore a *radio* news-satellite programming service.] Three times a day we send a thirty-minute feed of the best highlights of every game, interviews and features, to those television stations around the country who've signed up for the service. It can be used on evening sportscasts, sports briefs, morning reports, whatever. What it means is that we've taken control of our own product—we compile baseball's most exciting moments, and almost as soon as they happen, ship them to viewers at home."

Creatively, it became apparent, baseball was coming in from the cold. But as "Game"'s disaster shows, not all the way in.

Not yet.

Even after "This Week" and "The Greats" and "The Baseball Bunch," the major leagues have not flung off, entirely, their erratic recent past.

But they can and, moreover, through television and print marketing, *should*—for they sit in a big washtub full of chances to evoke again—not exactly as in the Eisenhower years but close; as close as this multifarious age allows—every American emotion from laughter to love to eternal newness: eternal as in athletic rivalry, newness as in spring.

To renew baseball as a network TV sport is the bigs' first priority. Above all, that means the Saturday "Game." It dictates, too, that because, like Saigon in April 1975, Sunday afternoon lies unoccupied, the major leagues should plant their each-weekly flag atop a *Sabbath* network series. They should also embrace cable, for by tapping and generating interest in the Braves, Cubs, or Yankees, its influx has stirred and often *created* fans formerly un-moved, for whatever reason, to turn to network telecasts. "Our research shows that there are three national teams—the Yankees, Dodgers, and Braves," NBC's Rich Hussey said in 1989. "I ask taxi drivers in every city

I'm in, and I am constantly amazed at the response the Atlanta Braves have. Many people follow them because they're on the cable all the time. I was in New Orleans one week, and the taxi driver said he didn't follow LSU, but, of course, he was a Braves' fan. And the reason is cable: Its effect is tremendous." Added Scotty Connal, "Baseball's beauty is that it doesn't have to choose *between* different types of exposure. Sure, it needs free coverage on an NBC, but don't forget: Baseball can also benefit more than any sport from cable coverage on networks like ours. We're on every day; basically, all we show are sports; and baseball is really the only daily game. Its highlights, interviews, scores — it fills our void like nothing else. For baseball, in terms of cable v. conventional, an NBC v. ESPN, it's not a case of either/ or." Theoretically and, I think, in fact, each should profit from its opposite's appeal. "A strong argument can be made," Frank Dolson has written, "that widespread cable telecasts of baseball games have done much to increase the popularity of the sport." Or, to the Michelob Generation, why not say it? Baseball can have it all.

Increasingly, baseball is, and should, breed weekly and special programs for cable networks, not merely local stations — ESPN's "Major League Baseball Magazine," for example, a reply to the multiplicity of Rozellian programming that pimples USA, HBO, and ESPN. Baseball can, and should, produce syndicated shows to fill the game's November–March cable and conventional network void — a tour of the Hall of Fame with Vin Scully, a derivative of football's "The Men Who Played the Game," an analogue to the NFL's "Great Teams/Great Years." It should publish an official monthly magazine, as the NBA and National Hockey League have in *hoop* and *GOAL!*; produce such softcover books as *NFL Report* and the *NFL Media Guide* of interest and affordability to young and middle-income fans; and counter the Rozelles' blizzard of coffee table-type books (since 1980, their Creative Services Division has released more than fifteen works to baseball's none) by hatching hardcover volumes that enhance, promotionally, The Game. "I can't understand why baseball hasn't emulated the National Football League in establishing a Properties office," columnist Ross Newhan wrote in the mid-1970s (a decade later, it did), "the successful vehicle which handles advertising, commercials, products, and the NFL Library." In 1979, *The Wall Street Journal* estimated the revenue of NFL Properties at *ten times* higher than baseball's; Ueberroth himself, upon becoming commissioner in October 1984, scored "the lack of importance baseball has heretofore placed on national promotional marketing and ideas." Six years later, merchandising helped baseball's properties' receipts to actually *pass* the NFL's.

Today, more than ever, baseball is licensing, *nationally,* aggressively, programs, posters, and pennants, T-shirts, bedspreads, and records; broadcasting, *nationally,* numerous five-minute preseason spots (e.g., the pastime's greatest moments, featuring actual play-by-play) over CBS Radio the first weekend in April; airing, *nationally,* the largest network radio schedule since Mutual's "Game of the Day." Now, let it go further: televising, *nationally,* the bigs' traditional Opening Day match from Cincinnati (or Washington, should its team revive); airing, *nationally,* a Monday–Friday afternoon radio "Game of the Day" and a Sunday early-evening CBS Radio baseball call-in and talk show; arranging, *nationally,* to show *more* baseball to the 40 percent of America *sans* cable—while *reducing* ESPN's coverage for the six in ten households *with* it. These ideas would equalize the baseball available to all viewers—and warrant action or, at the very least, debate. They would be as easy to implement—most of them, anyway—as the 1972 Nixon landslide over McGovern—and invest the major leagues with a renascent appeal.

"I think baseball should take great comfort in what lies ahead—that is, if baseball controls its *future,* not the other way around," Ernie Harwell told me. "The overwhelming edge pro football has had—really, its only edge over baseball—was network television. Its fortunes have been totally tied to national TV, and when the networks were striding like Olympians in the sixties and seventies, it was a terrific advantage baseball couldn't match."

"And network television is still a factor," I said.

"Yes, but what more can football do with it? How many more games a year can you show?" Harwell said. "Baseball, on the other hand, *can* do more—much more. And it's got other advantages that football can't equal. It's central to the folklore and history of this country. It's part of Americana in an age—ours—more receptive to traditional values than a decade or two ago. It's a daily game that soaks up radio and newspaper coverage—the greatest talking and reading game there is. Its highlights are shown every night on newscasts across America—that never used to be the case. It's benefiting from SuperStations that didn't exist in the past. All of this means a different bottom line. Especially with network audiences being chipped away by cable, football's one *asset* doesn't necessarily mean as much as it once did; at the other end, baseball's *assets* can mean a whole lot more. What baseball has to do now is utilize those strengths—play them for all they're worth. What baseball has to do is bring the game to every American."

At *that* time, baseball *will* be back.

All the way.

Even when, of a summer day in 1862, during the bleakest epoch of the Civil War, Abraham Lincoln broke free of the White House long enough to take his son, Tad, to a baseball game; even when the Gas House Gang became a Depression rallying point for a people besieged by fear that the future was over; even when Dwight Eisenhower, forsaking one Opening Day as president to play golf at his Augusta, Georgia, retreat, was scorched by editorialists for his audacity (how *dare* he?) in slighting The American Game—even then, baseball was not, as some have reminisced, a spiritual crucible, America's good tidings to Zion.

It is not—never has been—as winsome as Lassie, as resplendent as the College of Cardinals, as pervasive (God save us) as Lucille Ball reruns. But it is, I think, in an almost mystical and cherished way, this nation's richest cultural inheritance—older than the Broadway musical; less brooding and convoluted than Faulkner; less regional than the Grand Ole Opry; more populist, even, than the grand Walt Disney.

"It is the chosen sport of the American people," James Michener has written, "the one game that most faithfully adheres to the great traditions of the people." When baseball stumbled in the 1960s, mocked as somehow the most trivial of pursuits, it mirrored a broader national sickness; a sense of moorings being ripped away, of social leprosy loose in the land. It is intriguing, I believe, that as America later reclaimed its sanity, its people have rediscovered baseball.

Shortly after the end of World War II, Pope Pius XII spoke of how "the American people have a genius for splendid and unselfish actions." To enlarge the major leagues' contemporary following, to penetrate the marketplace of imagery and stereotypes with newfound commitment to promote— yes, to value ideas, borrow from the competition, live in the present, and *sell*—baseball's unbroken poetry and strengths, to make this simple, complex, and innately American enterprise The Game not simply of Our Fathers but also Our Sons—to do this, as baseball, by itself, *can,* would be a splendid and unselfish act.

14
So Long, Farewell

"And I would have an end to all, an end."
— Arthur Symons

RED STARS

Quinones hits a very high fly ball to right field. That will end the inning! . . . But one to be remembered! . . . And they give the Reds — the folks here at the stadium — a standing O. At the end of one — I said one — the Reds 14, the Astros 0.

— MARTY BRENNAMAN, August 3, 1989.

Riverfront Stadium, Cincinnati, OH. A 1950s song said, "The music goes round and round." Three decades later, the Redlegs embraced its lyrics. In one-third of an amazing first inning, Cincinnati collected fourteen runs and sixteen hits, and moved Houston manager Art Howe to mutter, "Now I know what blitzkrieg is about." Length of the Reds' turn at bat: thirty-eight minutes. Records: Most hits, singles (twelve), and batters collecting two hits in an inning (seven). Final score: 18-2. For the Astros, it could have been worse. The Reds left the bases loaded while Houston got the last two first-inning outs.

NOBLE NOLAN

The crowd is on its feet again. The count is full — here's the payoff pitch. He struck him out swinging! Strikeout number five thousand is history for Nolan Ryan! . . . And the Rangers converge from all over the field! . . . Ryan has now tipped his cap to the crowd for the second time — as the fans refuse to stop!

— ERIC NADEL, August 22, 1989.

Arlington Stadium, Arlington, TX. Nolan Ryan holds Texas real estate. He must also own a corner of the Fountain of Youth. Before the second-largest home crowd in Rangers history, Ryan fanned Ricky Henderson in the fifth inning (above) to become the first major leaguer to throw five thousand strikeouts. Like other witnesses — among them, Commissioner Bart Giamatti, who died ten days later of a heart attack — Ryan was swayed by the evening's drama. Lost in thought, he drove past Arlington Stadium on the way to the park.

566

A Most (Un)Happy Fella

Robin Ventura will be the batter. . . . Hey, going back — Leyrich — to the wall — oh, he dropped the ball! He juggled all the way, stumbling! Ball goes off his glove! Three runs score. And that will be an error. Can you imagine losing a ball game on a no-hitter!

— Phil Rizzuto, July 1, 1990.

Comiskey Park, Chicago, IL. On the eightieth birthday of baseball's oldest site, Andy Hawkins got a present he would prefer to return. Two days after Dave Stewart and Fernando Valenzuela threw no-hitters — the first pitchers to do so on the same date — the Yankees' righty followed suit. The difference: Hawkins lost, 4–0, sabotaged by three eighth-inning errors (the last, Jim Leyrich's misplay, above) that plated four unearned runs. Said the Bombers' victim/virtuoso: "I guess you could say my dream came true. I just never expected it to hurt this much."

Both a Fielder & Hitter Be

Stewart ready. He pitches. There's a drive to deep left field. That's outa here. Where is it going to land? On the roof! Out of the ballpark! Cecil Fielder has become the third man in the history of Tiger Stadium to hit one out of here in left field. It hit the roof and bounced out of Tiger Stadium! A tremendous homer by Cecil Fielder!

— Paul Carey, August 25, 1990.

Tiger Stadium, Detroit, MI. In four major-league seasons, Cecil Fielder had hit thirty-one home runs. Leap ahead to 1990: Implausibly, in the evening's previous at-bat, Fielder smacked his fortieth homer of the regular season. Now, four innings later, the Japanese League expatriate became the first Tiger to hit a ball over the left-field roof of the Bengals' emporium. Fielder finished with fifty-one home runs, the first American Leaguer to eclipse fifty since the M & M Boys of 1961.

Catch a Falling Crown

Right field . . . Brunansky dives! Did he get it? Yes, the Red Sox win! No, he dropped the ball! He dropped the ball! Wait! He got it! Believe it, New England!

— Gary Thorne, October 3, 1990.

Fenway Park, Boston, MA. "If the gods truly had it in for the Boston Red Sox, as New England has assumed for seven decades, Tom Brunansky would have lost Ozzie Guillen's drive in the full moon that hung over Fenway Park," wrote the *Chicago Tribune*'s Andrew Bagnato. "Or he would have slipped as he stepped on the warning track. Or dropped his glove as the ball hit the webbing." Instead, the Deity summoned the Catch to counter Red Sox ignominies of the past. Brunansky's tumbling, two-on, two-out ninth-inning grab of Guillen's drive gave Boston a 3-1 victory, clinched the A. L. East pennant on the final night of the season, and sent the Sox forth on a Mission Impossible: Winning a playoff against the world champion A's.

The Buccos Walk the Plank

Myers stares in for the sign from Jeff Reed. Here's the pitch. A swing and a drive into center field! That's hit deep! Back to the wall, Hatcher. He leaps. The ball goes over his glove and off the wall! Bonilla has a double — he's going for third! Here comes the throw into third base — and he's out!

— John Rooney, October 9, 1990.

Riverfront Stadium, Cincinnati, OH. In a playoff reminiscent of their 1972 clash, Cincinnati beat Pittsburgh for its first pennant since the '76 Big Red Machine. The six games were riveting; four were decided by one run; in the end, matters turned on the play of Cincinnati's outfield. Eric Davis' eighth-inning *gotcha* of Bobby Bonilla saved Game Four and, ultimately, the Championship Series. Said Reds' manager Lou Piniella of outfielders Davis, Paul O'Neill, and Billy Hatcher: "We've shown America what Cincinnati fans have known all year."

A's'tronomical

Red Sox have a run in, it's 3-1, Oakland. Here's the pitch by Honeycutt. Swing, and a line drive at short. Gallego has it — he fires across! . . . And there it is! A repeat for the Oakland Athletics as Mike Greenwell grounds out to end this series. And for the second time in three years the Oakland Athletics win the American League pennant by sweeping the Boston Red Sox!

— Jim Hunter, October 10, 1990.

Oakland Coliseum, Oakland, CA. The A. L. Championship Series was less collision than farce. Scoring one run in each contest, the Red Sox were out-scored, 20-4, in an *à la 1988* Oakland rout. Leading men: Dave Stewart, going 2-0 with a 1.13 earned run average; the A's' bullpen, yielding no runs in 6.2 innings; and obliging Red Sox batters, plating one of twenty-two runners in scoring position. Next to the guillotine, one presumed: the National League champion Reds.

The Cincinnati Kids

There goes Hatcher! . . . And the pitch is hit in the air to dead center! Back goes McGee. Away back! To the wall! It's gone! . . . They want him to take a curtain call!

— Vin Scully, October 16, 1990.

Riverfront Stadium, Cincinnati, OH. Almost everyone, including the author, said of Cincinnati, *no way:* The defending champion A's were a dynasty in the making. What happens? Eric Davis smacked a gargantuan first-inning, Game-One blast, and the Reds were off and winning — 7-0, then 5-4. Back to Oakland for World Series Games 3-5 — where the A's, we tut-tutted, were sure to make a comeback.

So Jose Canseco taps slowly to third. And the Reds are one out from one of the great and shocking moments in baseball history. It was David and Goliath all over again. And I'll tell you what. The only dynasty I know is a Chinese white wine. . . . Two and one the count to Lansford. And Myers' fastball is popped up! Back of first — Todd Benzinger in fair ground! And the Cincinnati Reds are champions of the baseball world! It is met by shock and silence, disbelief and disappointment here in Oakland! But it is over! It is official! And the Reds have done the unthinkable! They swept the lordly Oakland A's four straight. The final score: The Reds 2, the Athletics 1.

— V.S., 10/20/90.

Oakland Coliseum, Oakland, CA. Stunning America and, perhaps, themselves, the Reds beat Dave Stewart to complete the most improbable Classic since the Mays/Rhodes Giants shocked the '54 Indians. Mixing Jose Rio's two victories, Billy Hatcher's seven straight hits, Chris Sabo's long-ball thundering, and a superb bullpen — the "Nasty Boys" — Cincinnati became the first Autumn Occasion team to sweep the club which swept *its* Series opponent a season earlier. For Oakland, a winter of discontent. For baseball's oldest franchise, a truly indelible feat.

Déjà Vu All Over Again

Here's the windup, and the two-two pitch. He struck him out swinging! It's Nolan's no-hitter number seven! Roberto Alomar has struck out — and Nolan Ryan has done it again!

— Mark Holtz, May 1, 1991.

Arlington Stadium, Arlington, TX. At forty-four, defying the laws of probability, average, and the planet Krypton, Nolan Ryan bested time and the Toronto Blue Jays — leading the majors in team batting — by striking out sixteen, including at least one in every inning, in a record seventh no-hitter of his Brigadoon career. A philosopher once said, "Words have a longer life than deeds." He never met baseball's Superman.

The Sun (Eclipsed) King

Rickey goes. The pitch is taken. He's going to have it — he does! Stealing third base, Rickey Henderson — no contest! Jerks the bag from its moorings — and holds it aloft — representing 939!

— Bill King, May 1, 1991.

Oakland Coliseum, Oakland, CA. While Ryan accepted kudos with Gary Cooper modesty, Rickey Henderson celebrated his 939th career stolen base the same night—passing Lou Brock—by imitating Muhammad Ali. Less full of good taste than himself, Henderson told the crowd, "Lou Brock was a great base stealer, but today I'm the greatest of all time."

"To My People"

As one they stand and applaud! The batter . . . Chris Gwynn—the top Dodger pinch-hitter . . . Two outs in the bottom of the ninth—twenty-six in a row have been retired by Dennis Martinez. One and two pitch. In the air, center field! El Presidente! El Perfecto!

—Dave Van Horne, July 28, 1991.

Dodger Stadium, Los Angeles, CA. "Only a Nobel Prize in literature could have more importance in this country," a radio caller said after Nicaragua's Dennis Martinez pitched a perfect game—the fifteenth in big-league history—for Montreal over Los Angeles. Martinez became the first opposing pitcher to throw a complete game no-hitter in the thirty-year existence of Dodger Stadium. He also reacted as a home-town hero should. "I had no words to say," he said of the final out. "I could only cry. I dedicate this one to my people."

Where Blue Jays Soar

Roberto Alomar has stolen his fifty-third base. A fly ball will win it now. Joe Carter at the plate. The winning run—the American League championship—ninety feet away. The pitch—a swing—and a base hit! And the Blue Jays are the champs! The Blue Jays are the champs of the American League East!

—Tom Cheek, October 2, 1991.

Skydome, Toronto, ON. On an evening where the Blue Jays defied the impossible—drawing more than four million spectators at home in a single season—they also defied history. In 1985-87-89, the Jays had crumbled in the stretch—becoming Canada's answer to the Red Sox. Tonight, Joe Carter's single capped a two-run ninth-inning rally to give Toronto a 6–5 victory, the American League East, and, possibly, entrée to redemption—the League Championship Series.

Worst to First

Three and two the count to Roberto Alomar. Aguilera on the mound. Has the sign. He winds, and delivers. Swing, and a fly ball to deep left field! Gladden going back, he's at the wall, and makes the catch! And the Minnesota Twins are the champions of the American League!

— JIM HUNTER, October 13, 1991.

Skydome, Toronto, ON. In 1990, the Twins placed last in the American League West. A year later, they rose like Lazarus to win the division and beat Toronto in the playoff. In the category of who-would-have-thunk-it: Minnesota swept Games 3–5 at Skydome; Chuck Knoblauch had seven hits, most by a rookie in LCS play; and Twins' relievers yielded no earned runs in 18⅓ innings. Less surprising: the brilliance (two home runs, six RBIs, .429 average) of series' MVP Kirby Puckett.

COME WITH THE WIND

Stretch by Smoltz. The pitch to Cedeno. A high fly ball to right field! It's fairly deep! Back goes Justice! He's got it! And the magic number for Atlanta is down to one! The Braves have clinched a tie for first!

— PETE VAN WIEREN, October 5, 1991.

Atlanta-Fulton County Stadium, Atlanta, GA. Like the Minnesota Twins, the Braves were perpetual losers; they finished last in 1990; at best, they might win — what? — the International League. What happened next would amaze playwright Arthur Miller. The '91 Braves drew a record 2.1 million fans; inspired a hand movement that became a national craze — the Tomahawk Chop, done to an Indian war chant; and overcame a two-game Dodgers' lead in the last eight games. On the next-to-last day, the Braves beat Houston. Moments later, the Giants blanked L.A. Result: Atlanta, N.L. West champion, the least likely titlist since the '69 Mets.

A check on second — here's the pitch. Olson swings, and rips it far down the left-field line! The ball goes to the corner — Ronnie Gant scores! And Olson has an RBI double! One-nothing, Atlanta!

— JOHN ROONEY, October 16, 1991.

Three Rivers Stadium, Pittsburgh, PA. America knew certain Braves' heirlooms — Terry Pendleton, the N.L.'s Most Valuable Player, fleet outfielder Ron Gant, and David Justice, he of the Will Clark/Stan Musial swing. If Atlanta was to win the LCS, one presumed, such Gullivers would dominate. Yet as Greg Olson drove in Gant to win Game Six (Atlanta took the final set, 4–0), it finalized a Lilliputian triumph. Who *were* these guys, anyway — infielders Mark Lempke and Rafael Belliard and pitchers like John Smoltz, Steve Avery, and Tom Glavine? Players — unsung no more — who brought the Braves their first pennant since 1958.

A CLASSIC CLASSIC

Aguilera delivers. Fastball — slapped to left field. Base hit! Here comes Gladden's throw!
Here comes Justice! He scores! And the Braves win it — their first victory of the World
Series!

— VIN SCULLY, October 22, 1991.

Atlanta-Fulton County Stadium, Atlanta, GA. After winning the World
Series' first two games, Minnesota seemed bent to sweep. Enter the Classic's
most improbable hero since 1960's Bobby Richardson. When Mark Lempke
singled home David Justice in the twelfth inning to win Game Three, 5–4, it
marked the first of three straight nights he drove a stake into the hearts of the
Twins. The next day, he tripled in the ninth inning and scored the winning
run; an evening later, Lempke hit two more triples and dazzled in the field.
After Game Five, he was hitting .439 and the Braves led, three sets to two. As
scriptwriters shook their heads, the Series moved back to Minnesota.

The two-one pitch to the Minnesota center fielder. It's driven to deep left-center field! Back
goes Keith Mitchell! It is gone — home run, Puckett!

— V.S., 10/26/91.

The Metrodome, Minneapolis, MN. In 1987, the Twins took Games Six and
Seven at home to win the World Series. Now, Kirby Puckett applied traces of
instant replay. In another night of wondrous theater — four of the Classic's first
six games were decided by a run; two went extra innings — Mr. Twin had three
hits, knocked in three runs, and made a circus catch at the left-center field wall.
Puckett's *touché* came in the eleventh inning — only the fourth game-winning,
extra-inning home run in Series history. As K. C. and the Sunshine Band sang,
"Oh, what a night."

So Larkin, the left-hand hitter, up there. Bases loaded, one out, and the game on the line.
Pena, right foot on the rubber. You can taste the pressure here in the Dome as Alejandro
straightens up. And the pitch to Larkin. Swung on — a high fly ball into left-center! The
run will score! The ball will bounce for a single! And the Minnesota Twins are
champions of the world!

— V.S., 10/27/91.

The Metrodome. "It breaks your heart," Bart Giamatti wrote of baseball. "It is
designed to break your heart." It also lifts them like no sport can. Which terms
define the 1991 Fall Classic? Start with delightful, delicious, delovely — and stop
at the Twelfth of Never. In a Game Seven for the ages — in a series where five
sets were decided in the last inning, and four the last at-bat — in a match of
indescribable tension, ending an Oktoberfest for all time — Gene Larkin's one-
out, bases-loaded, tenth-inning pinch-single scored Dan Gladden to beat At-

lanta, 1–0, and take the World Series. Heroes included Jack Morris, who threw the final-game shutout, an Iron Curtain bullpen, infielder Chuck Knoblauch and catcher Brian Harper, and baseball's most eardrum-popping fans. Perhaps Morris, who joined the Twins as a free agent and was the Series MVP, best caught the storybook: "It's unfortunate that anyone had to lose this Series because this was a true classic in every sense of the word."

15
Finale

"So it's the laughter, we will remember—
whenever we remember, the way we
were."
—Alan and Marilyn Bergman

WHEN I WAS WRITING *LONG TIME GONE*, MY VALENTINE TO A TIME MARKED BY insurrection, endless love, and talk of "impudent snobs," when date lines veered from Kent State to Attica, *estrangement* meant both fact and shibboleth, Viet Nam polarized the nation, and thoroughly modern Milhous led it—the bittersweet and unforgettable early 1970s—I would turn on a record player and listen to their literate, often brooding, and frequently quite wonderful songs. They reflected, brilliantly, I found—these melodies of Chicago, Led Zeppelin, and Three Dog Night—the age's beauty and belligerence, its truth intuitively *felt*, not arrived at by logic. Listening, I was catapulted by their exaggerated energy—back to Cambodia and the Silent Majority; to Peace With Honor and *The Greening of America*; back to "Stairway to Heaven" and "Suite: Judy Blue Eyes" and "Let me make this perfectly clear." The music made reminiscences animate and spoke of sadness, empathy, and evenings in the rain. It was real, familiar, passionate. Its temper, almost subliminally, evoked a state of mind.

There were few landmarks—a rare recording here; a play-by-play transcript there; photos, magazine stories, and yellowy cartoons; mostly, interviews with the principals—to transport me, in a similar fashion, to the broadcasters of my youth.

I could still hear, it was true, Vin Scully on network radio; there were Martin, Thompson, and Harwell yet beguiling the American League, and Jack Buck, investing the Midwest Swifties with his fourth decade of fancy footwork, and Phil Rizzuto, less provincial than unusual, and Allen, the opiate of baseball Voices, dancing deftly across the cable and syndicated stage. And what of the timeless Caray? My certainty denied a soupçon of doubt: At seventy-plus going on forever, Holy Cow! would outlast us all.

As 1980s and nineties baseball announcers, they were prominent, ongoing; my mind's eye could actually *see* them perform. But the others, now gone or semi-retired: To recall the Jimmy Dudley of 1961, or Earl Gillespie, whose Wisconsin dream turned to nightmare, or the Gunner, his life as much a folk tale as travelogue, or Waite Hoyt, whose stories were limitless and exquisite, or Byrum Saam and Ray Scott in their prime—one must, in a pinch, retrieving the virtues of the past, fall back on memory itself.

574

However vague and selective memory may be, there is no trick, in trying to recapture that time, to observe that I was extraordinarily lucky, as were millions of my generation, through sheer accident of birth.

At the very age in life when one is most impressionable, at the very point of radio and television coverage unrivaled in baseball chronicles, in an era when baseball, more than any sport, quickened the American throb, it was my fortune to encounter—often, within a few hours of any late-fifties- and early-sixties weekend—a broadcast world of such variety and skill that today, from a distance of more than two decades, I wonder at its amplitude.

Ol' Diz and Pee Wee, Bob Wolff and Bud Blattner, Curt Gowdy and Lindsey Nelson. The two Jacks, Brickhouse and Quinlan. The Voice. The Possum. The Old Commander. The Ol' Redhead. They were proud, on occasions humane, more often simply human, capable of envy and egomania, also capable of kindness, but as a group—here, consensus and, I think it fair to say, the simple facts uphold me—more magnificent at what they did than any broadcast camarilla in baseball history: depict The Game not in black and white, even when the picture was, but with muted tints and bold pastels, a Rubik's Cube of color.

They were all announcing, *at the same time*, near or atop the peak of their careers—future Hall of Famers, institutions, and household words; propped up by a thin underlay of journeymen—and they sketched every game through paint-by-number. Were you a thousand miles from the monuments at Yankee Stadium, or the ivy at Wrigley Field, more fragrant and spectacular each year, or the lovely green-on-green milieu of Tiger (née Briggs) Stadium, or the lush stretch of Forbes Field acreage grown heavy with base hits? No, you weren't; you were *there*. Your radio and television became the brush; even on TV, your imagination supplied the shadings; and using prose, cat-calls, and baseball intellection to fill in the hues, the Voices constructed scenes and *Märchen* with a wondrously wide range of strokes.

In the broadest terms, they shadowed the baseball proletariat to a collective degree that succeeding playactors would never equal, and that their predecessors had not approached. Their identities were discriminate, their talents eclectic and profound, and they remind me, even now, of Joseph Alsop's lyric paean to Franklin Roosevelt a century after his birth—"Maybe I have become a sorry praiser of the past; but this is a personal memoir," he said, "and if I truly feel that there were giants in the land in the Roosevelt years, I claim the right to say so"—except that, to the baseball fans of my generation, these announcers were not giants, exactly or even only, but as friends are around the dinner table, almost family.

"I hear America singing," wrote the poet Walt Whitman, "the varied carols I hear."

I hear the Voices lingering. *Selah* and *Amen*.

Alexandria, Virginia,
Blue Hill, Maine, and
Caledonia, New York

Sources

Portions of this book have appeared in slightly different form in *America's Dizzy Dean*, *Baseball Bulletin*, *Baseball Digest*, and *Baseball* magazine.

Grateful acknowledgment is made for permission to reprint excerpts from the following:

Beyond the Sixth Game, by Peter Gammons, reprinted by permission of Houghton Mifflin Company, 1985.

FDR: A Centenary Remembrance, by Joseph Alsop, copyright The Viking Press, 1982. Reprinted by permission of Thames and Hudson Limited.

Inside Sports, May 1984. Reprinted by permission of Century Publishing Company.

North Toward Home, by Willie Morris, reprinted by permission of Houghton Mifflin Company, 1967.

Rhubarb In the Catbird Seat, by Red Barber with Robert Creamer, reprinted by permission of Doubleday and Company, 1968.

Supertube, by Ron Powers, reprinted by permission of Coward-McCann Company, 1984.

The Broadcasters, by Red Barber, reprinted by permission of Paul Reynolds Agency. Published by the Dial Press, 1970.

The Detroit Tigers, by Joe Falls, reprinted by permission of Macmillan Publishing Company, 1975.

The Dodgers, by Tommy Holmes, reprinted by permission of Macmillan Publishing Company, 1975.

The Gas House Gang, by J. Roy Stockton, reprinted by permission of A.S. Barnes and Company, 1945.

The Summer Game, by Roger Angell, reprinted by permission of Simon and Schuster, Inc., 1973.

The Way It Was, edited by George Vecsey, reprinted by permission of Mobil Oil Company, 1974.

All of the play-by-play commentaries in *Voices of The Game* are reprinted with the expressed permission of the Commissioner of Baseball's Office. Grateful acknowledgment is also made to: ABC Television, Baseball Hall of Fame, Bob Wolff, CBS Radio, Fleetwood Recording Co., KABC— Los Angeles, KCMO—Kansas City, KDKA—Pittsburgh, KFMB—San Diego, KMPC—Los Angeles, KNBR—San Francisco, KYW—Philadelphia, Major League Baseball, Mel Allen, Mutual Radio, NBC Radio, NBC Television, SportsChannel—New York, the twenty-six major-league clubs, WABC—New York, WBAL—Baltimore, WCBS—New York, WCCO—Minneapolis, WTMJ—Milwaukee, WERE—Cleveland, WFBR—Baltimore, WFLD—Chicago, WGN—Chicago, WHDH—Boston, WHN—New York, WINS—New York, WJR—Detroit, WLW—Cincinnati, WLWT—Cincinnati, WSB—Atlanta.

Bibliography

Allen, Mel and Fitzgerald, Ed, *You Can't Beat the Hours*. New York: Harper and Row, 1965.

Alsop, Joseph, *FDR: A Centenary Remembrance*. New York: The Viking Press, 1982.

Angell, Roger, *Five Seasons*. New York: Simon and Schuster, 1978.

_____, *Late Innings*. New York: Ballantine Books, 1982.

_____, *The Summer Game*. New York: Popular Library, 1978.

Armbruster, Frank, *The Forgotten Americans*. New Rochelle, New York: Arlington House, 1972.

Barber, Walter (Red), *The Broadcasters*. New York: Dial Press, 1970.

_____, *Rhubarb In the Catbird Seat*, with Robert Creamer. Garden City, New York: Doubleday, 1968.

Berry, Henry, *Boston Red Sox*. New York: Rutledge Books, 1975.

Broeg, Bob, *Super Stars of Baseball*. St. Louis: The Sporting News Publishing Company, 1971.

Chester, Giraud and Garrison, Garnet and Willis, Edgar, *Television and Radio*. New York: Meredith Corporation, 1971.

Coleman, Ken, *So You Want to be a Sportscaster*. New York: Hawthorn Books, 1973.

Cosell, Howard, *Cosell*. New York: Playboy Press, 1973.

_____, *Like It Is*. New York: Playboy Press, 1974.

Durso, Joseph, *Yankee Stadium*. Boston: Houghton Mifflin, 1972.

Enright, Jim, *Chicago Cubs*. New York: Rutledge Books, 1975.

Falls, Joe, *Detroit Tigers*. New York: Rutledge Books, 1975.

Gammons, Peter, *Beyond the Sixth Game*. Boston: Houghton Mifflin, 1985.

Golenbock, Peter, *Dynasty*. Englewood Cliffs, New Jersey: Prentice-Hall, 1975.

Gowdy, Curt with Hirshberg, Al, *Cowboy at the Mike*. Garden City, New York: Doubleday, 1966.

Harris, Jay S., *TV Guide: The First 25 Years*. New York: Simon and Schuster, 1978.

Hodges, Russ, *Baseball Complete*. New York: Grosset and Dunlap, 1952.

_____, *My Giants*. Garden City, New York: Doubleday, 1963.

Holmes, Tommy, *The Dodgers*. New York: Rutledge Books, 1975.

Honig, Donald, *Baseball's 10 Greatest Teams*. New York: Macmillan, 1982.

_____, *The American League*. New York: Crown, 1983.

Hutchens, John K. and Oppenheimer, George (edited by), *The Best in The World*. New York: The Viking Press, 1973.

Jennison, Christopher, *Wait 'Til Next Year*. New York: W.W. Norton & Company, 1974.

Kahn, Roger, *The Boys of Summer*. New York: Harper and Row, 1971.

Kalinsky, George and Shannon, Bill, *The Ballparks*. New York: Hawthorn Books, 1975.

Koppett, Leonard, *The New York Mets*. New York: Macmillan, 1970.

Leuchtenburg, William E., *The LIFE History of the United States*. New York: TIME-LIFE Books, 1976.

Lewine, Harris and Okrent, Daniel, *The Ultimate Baseball Book*. Boston: Houghton Mifflin, 1979.

Lindberg, Richard, *Who's On 3rd? The Chicago White Sox Story*. South Bend, Indiana: Icarus Press, 1983.

Lipsyte, Robert. *SportsWorld*, New York: Quadrangle, 1975.

Major League Baseball Promotion Corporation, *Baseball: The First 100 Years*. New York: Poretz-Ross Publishers, 1969.

_____, *The Game and the Glory*. Englewood Cliffs, New Jersey: Prentice-Hall, 1976.

_____, *The World Series: A 75th Anniversary*. New York: Simon and Schuster, 1978.

_____, *This Great Game*. New York: Rutledge Books, 1971.

Manchester, William, *One Brief Shining Moment*. Boston: Little, Brown and Company, 1983.

McNeil, Alex, *Total Television*. New York: Penguin Books, 1980.

Metz, Robert, *CBS: Reflections In a Bloodshot Eye*. New York: Playboy Press, 1975.

Michener, James A., *Sports In America*. New York: Random House, 1976.

Morris, Willie, *North Toward Home*. Boston: Houghton Mifflin, 1967.

National Football League Properties, *The First 50 Years*. New York: Simon and Schuster, 1969.

National League, *A Baseball Century*. New York: Rutledge Books, 1976.

The New York Times Company, *The Sixties*. New York: Arno Press, 1980.

Powers, Ron, *Supertube*. New York: Coward-McCann, 1984.

Reichler, Joseph, *Baseball's Great Moments*. New York: Bonanza Books, 1983.

Reidenbaugh, Lowell, *Take Me Out to the Ball Park*. St. Louis: The Sporting News Publishing Company, 1983.

Rosenthal, Harold, *The 10 Best Years of Baseball*. New York: Van Nostrand Reinhold Company, 1979.

Schlossberg, Dan, *The Baseball Catalog*. Middle Village, New York: Jonathan David Publishers, 1980.

Schulman, Arthur and Youngman, Roger, *How Sweet It Was*. New York: Bonanza Books, 1976.

Smith, Richard Norton, *Thomas E. Dewey and His Times*. New York: Simon and Schuster, 1982.

Smith, Robert, *Illustrated History of Baseball*. New York: Grosset and Dunlap, 1973.

Smithsonian Exposition Books, *Every Four Years*. New York: W.W. Norton and Company, 1980.

Stockton, J. Roy, *The Gas House Gang*. New York: A.S. Barnes and Company, 1945.

Vecsey, George (edited by), *The Way It Was*. Mobil Oil and McGraw-Hill Book Company, 1974.

White, Theodore H., *In Search of History*. New York: Harper and Row, 1978.

————, *The Making of the President 1960*. New York: Atheneum, 1961.

————, *The Making of the President 1964*. New York: Atheneum, 1965.

Index

ABOUT THE AUTHOR

Voices of The Game is Curt Smith's third book.

Prior to its release, Mr. Smith authored two highly acclaimed books. The first, *America's Dizzy Dean*, was a *Sports Illustrated* Major Book of the Month Club selection, and was called "a masterpiece" by the *Christian Science Monitor* and "remarkably eloquent" by the NBC Radio Network; the second, *Long Time Gone*, focused on America in the early 1970s and was styled "cultural history, passionately felt and lyrically expressed" by syndicated columnist Jeffrey Hart and "entrancing, a splendid insight into a turbulent decade" by Hugh Sidey of *TIME* magazine.

A writer who works in Washington, D.C., Mr. Smith previously served as a Senior Speechwriter in the Reagan Administration and as Senior Editor and National Affairs Editor of *The Saturday Evening Post* magazine. He has also served as feature writer for the Gannett Company, public relations spokesman for Hamilton College, and Chief Speechwriter for John B. Connally's 1980 Presidential campaign.

Mr. Smith grew up in Caledonia, New York, was educated at Allegheny College and Geneseo State University, and now lives in Alexandria, Virginia. He is the author of award-winning stories on subjects as varied as Floyd Patterson, Roberto Clemente, and Richard M. Nixon, and has written articles for such publications as *The Washington Post, The New York Times, Newsweek,* and *Sports Illustrated*.

Mr. Smith lists among his interests music, military history, and rooting — "usually in vain" — for the Boston Red Sox. Of *Voices of The Game*, he notes: "The Roman philosopher Seneca said, 'He who receives a benefit with gratitude repays the first installment on his debt.' Millions of Americans have benefited from baseball broadcasting. This is one installment on their debt."